Rhetorical Criticism

Communication, Media, and Politics
Series Editor: Robert E. Denton, Jr., Virginia Tech

This series features a range of work dealing with the role and function of communication in the realm of politics, broadly defined. Including general academic books and texts for use in graduate and advanced undergraduate courses, the series encompasses humanistic, critical, historical, and empirical studies in political communication in the United States. Primary subject areas include campaigns and elections, media, and political institutions. *Communication, Media, and Politics* books will be of interest to students, teachers, and scholars of political communication from the disciplines of communication, rhetorical studies, political science, journalism, and political sociology.

Rhetorical Criticism

Perspectives in Action

Third Edition

Edited by
Jim A. Kuypers

ROWMAN & LITTLEFIELD
Lanham • Boulder • New York • London

Acquisitions Editor: Natalie Mandziuk
Acquisitions Assistant: Sylvia Landis
Sales and Marketing Inquiries: textbooks@rowman.com

Credits and acknowledgments for material borrowed from other sources, and reproduced with permission, appear on the appropriate pages within the text.

Published by Rowman & Littlefield
An imprint of The Rowman & Littlefield Publishing Group, Inc.
4501 Forbes Boulevard, Suite 200, Lanham, Maryland 20706
www.rowman.com

6 Tinworth Street, London SE11 5AL, United Kingdom

British Library Cataloguing in Publication Information Available

Library of Congress Cataloging-in-Publication Data

Names: Kuypers, Jim A., editor.
Title: Rhetorical criticism : perspectives in action / edited by Jim A. Kuypers.
Description: Third edition. | Lanham : Rowman & Littlefield, [2021] | Series: Communication, media, and politics | Includes bibliographical references and index.
Identifiers: LCCN 2021009830 (print) | LCCN 2021009831 (ebook) | ISBN 9781538138137 (cloth ; alk. paper) | ISBN 9781538138144 (paperback ; alk. paper) | ISBN 9781538138151 (epub)
Subjects: LCSH: Rhetorical criticism.
Classification: LCC PN4096 .R52 2021 (print) | LCC PN4096 (ebook) | DDC 809.5/1—dc23
LC record available at https://lccn.loc.gov/2021009830
LC ebook record available at https://lccn.loc.gov/2021009831

∞™ The paper used in this publication meets the minimum requirements of American National Standard for Information Sciences—Permanence of Paper for Printed Library Materials, ANSI/NISO Z39.48-1992.

Brief Contents

Contents

Preface

Rhetorical Criticism: Perspectives in Action—now in its third edition—is designed to introduce students to the exciting art of rhetorical criticism.

It is no secret that the criticism of rhetoric can be a challenging topic to grasp. So much of criticism, although of a high quality, is difficult for "the uninitiated" to comprehend, which makes initially learning how to *produce* criticism that much more difficult. This book came about because I wanted to offer both upper-division undergraduates and beginning graduate students an assessible resource when first encountering rhetorical criticism. The latest edition stresses this accessibility even more strongly.

Fostering creativity was another concern. I am not the only teacher whose students desire a "template" or a "rubric" from which to work, some "formula" to use when writing criticism. Giving them just that when first teaching about rhetorical criticism is difficult to avoid. After all, we do have to initially teach from *some* starting point, and the initial steps we take can be very much the same in most classrooms. And yet, from my conversations with others who teach criticism, it seemed I was not alone in wanting to stress the very personal nature of criticism, to expose students to both the freedoms and constraints involved. Thus, throughout this text, the chapter authors and I stress both the objective and subjective nature of rhetorical criticism and its artistic nature.

These two concerns—accessibility and creativity—led to the creation of the book you now hold in your hands. Several additional features are designed to facilitate the effective teaching of rhetorical criticism.

First, well-known perspectives and modes of rhetorical criticism are covered, but other less known yet important perspectives are also presented. The chapters introduce students to important rhetorical principles, terminology, and theorists, using a wide variety of perspectives and orientations toward performing criticism. In addition to finding chapters on traditional criticism and dramatism, you will also find chapters on ideographical criticism, criticism of metaphor, and more. New to the third edition is a chapter on visual rhetoric and another on digital rhetoric.

Second, each chapter detailing a perspective is written by an expert scholar (or scholars) in that area; instead of one person writing a short synopsis of numerous perspectives, a noted expert with experience using a particular perspective has written about it. This approach allows students to discover quickly how personalities influence the practice of criticism and even the teaching of criticism. Because critics with well-developed voices wrote the chapters contained in this book, students will benefit from exposure to these voices, hopefully beginning the process of developing their own critical voice.

Third, each chapter in parts II and III features a "critical essay" or "extended examples" section, showcasing the perspective in action. In some cases, then, these are brief original essays written by the chapter author(s) and composed specifically for this textbook. In other instances, the chapter author(s) opted instead to focus on the interpretive dynamics that their perspective encourages and so provide several extended examples of criticism using that perspective. Reading through various other textbooks on criticism, I have found that they sometimes include high-quality works of criticism for students to read—often reprinted from scholarly journals. The drawback here, though, is that these articles were originally written for the readers of a particular scholarly journal; they are not easily accessible to beginning students, many of whom will have had little, if any, previous exposure to criticism. Such scholarly essays may actually defeat their purpose of providing useful examples of criticism for new critics to emulate. On the other hand, the critical essays and extended examples contained in this new edition of *Rhetorical Criticism: Perspectives in Action* were written specifically with *student accessibility* in mind. Each essay and extended example provides a touchstone for students to use when crafting their own essays, as well as facilitating effective, ethical argument development and good writing skills.

The potential danger with touchstones is that they can be so good that they trample over, rather than encourage, novice critics. The chapters in this book seek to avoid this. Criticism is an artistic process, yet far too often this personal nature of criticism remains a mystery to students. There are rules, but there are also instances when if followed they would stifle the critical process and produce sterile criticism. I believe strongly, though, that students benefit from knowing a basic structure around which to organize their initial efforts at writing criticism. To this end, I asked the contributing authors, when they chose to write an original essay, to loosely follow the DAE organizational model for criticism (description, analysis/interpretation, and evaluation). Some authors did just that, and some did not follow that pattern so closely. Since not all perspectives or rhetorical artifacts lend themselves equally well to the DAE model, students are presented with instances that deviate from this model and are given reasons why this deviation is desirable—thereby empowering them to consider similar decisions for themselves as they move from introductory to more advanced levels of critical understanding.

Fourth, and stressing further the artistic and individual nature of criticism, chapters discussing a perspective contain the author's "Personal Reflections" on the decisions made while writing the essay or extended examples. Any writing project involves decisions about what to include or exclude, what to stress, and what to ignore. These personal comments allow students to see what questions and concerns guided the author as he or she wrote.

Fifth, each chapter provides a "Potentials and Pitfalls" section that calls attention to the particular strengths and weaknesses the given rhetorical perspective possesses. Authors expose those aspects of the rhetorical artifact that their particular perspective highlights, thus stressing the artistic and insight-producing aspects of the critical process. These comments shed light on how different perspectives both enable and discourage particular readings of texts.

Sixth, and new to this edition, each chapter (beginning with chapter 2) provides "Discussion Questions" and "Activities" to allow greater interaction with the rhetorical perspective under consideration.

Finally, authors provide an annotated recommended reading list, a "Top Picks" list, for students who wish to study a particular perspective or mode of criticism in greater detail. Some authors prioritize the readings, thus helping students read, in order, those articles and books most helpful when beginning the process of writing criticism using a particular perspective.

It is my sincere hope that this book will encourage students to ask new questions about the rhetoric around them and that, in doing so, they will fulfill the critic's quest to produce both insight and understanding about the world in which we live.

Jim A. Kuypers
Virginia Tech
Blacksburg, VA

Acknowledgments

I wish to give special acknowledgment for their helpful comments to the anonymous reviewers of this book. A special thank you of appreciation is extended to those who have adopted this textbook; I value your support and feedback. All of the authors with whom I worked on this project were a joy. I learned much from them and thank them for their participation. It is with gratitude that I mention Virginia Tech, which paid my salary and also funded library services such as interlibrary loan and EBSCOhost which were absolutely necessary to the completion of this project. The value Virginia Tech places on scholarship allows projects such as this book to be undertaken and completed.

1

Essential Elements of Rhetorical Criticism

The Big Picture

Jim A. Kuypers

Do you believe in knowledge for knowledge's sake, that learning is of value in and of itself? I do. Certainly the exercising of our minds is as important, and often as enjoyable, as is the exercising of our bodies. That said, sometimes is it not simply refreshing to see the immediate, practical benefits that follow the investment of our intellectual time? Think about whatever it is that you wish to do once you graduate. Then ask yourself if the ability to

- create new knowledge instead of simply echoing what others say;
- discover aspects of our world, our society, and our culture that others do not see;
- generate greater insights into human communication and civic participation;
- communicate effectively to impart greater understanding of issues, concepts, and events;
- possess a greater understanding of how and why humans communicate; and
- develop your thinking processes toward a razor-like effectiveness

will help you achieve your life goals. I suspect that in most cases the answer is yes. Importantly for us here, these are also some (yes, only some!) of the more obvious benefits derived from learning rhetorical criticism.

Aside from the above-listed benefits, there is a creative, imaginative aspect to rhetorical criticism that is both exciting and enriching, having the potential to tap into the very core of our personalities. We will go into a more comprehensive definition of **rhetoric** in the next chapter, but for now, think of rhetoric as strategic, intentional communication designed to persuade or to achieve some identifiable objective. **Criticism**, whose definition we will also later expand, is a method particularly well suited to analyzing and interpreting how rhetorical communication works. Taken together, then, **rhetorical criticism** is the analysis, interpretation, and evaluation of the persuasive elements of communication. At least, that is the place from which we begin in this book, although later we will see just how expansive and rich this definition can be. Rhetorical criticism is a humanizing activity. By that I mean it produces knowledge that helps us to better understand who we are as human beings. Additionally, it is a form of activity that engages and enriches human insight, imagination, creativity, and intellect. It allows for the creation of new knowledge about who we were, who we are, and who we might become.

When first learning about rhetorical criticism, just as in many new endeavors, the essential basics can seem overwhelming: new ideas, new words, new associations, new conditions, and so on. There are new concepts with which to wrestle; moreover, the application of those concepts will probably be unlike anything to which you will have previously been exposed. Keep pressing on; over time the new words will no longer seem so new, and eventually you will experience the opening of an entirely new intellectual world. By the end of this book, you will see human communication in an entirely new light and possess understandings and insights into how we communicate that you could not even have imagined before.

Just as engaging in criticism is a type of exploration, *learning* about criticism is exploration as well. Sometimes when we explore we do not know our final destination, and that is part of the allure of the journey. This book is your guide to "the big picture" while exploring the topic of criticism. To get the most out of this experience, there are a few items I encourage you to keep in mind while working your way through the various ideas to which you will be exposed.

To help you with the discovery process, this book is divided into three main sections and four appendixes. In the first section, "Overview of Rhetorical Criticism," you will be introduced to the concepts of rhetoric, criticism, and two other important considerations. In chapter 2 you will discover rhetoric's powerful history and also be provided with a foundational definition of rhetoric. This definition, rhetoric as *the strategic use of communication, oral or written, to achieve specifiable goals*, is our starting point, and as the book progresses you will see how different critics and theorists have expanded or modified this definition. In short, chapter 2 will help you to develop a firm understanding of what rhetoric is, and also help you to understand the power of symbols and how they are used in human communication. As you read through this chapter, it will help to consider rhetoric as something you use every day; think of actual examples from your own life, whether personal experience or something you have seen in the news, on an entertainment show, social media, or what have you.

Chapter 3 introduces the concept of criticism. Keep in mind when reading this chapter that criticism involves much more than offering an opinion; it is a way of generating new knowledge and insights about how communication works to persuade and how symbols interact to form meaning. Criticism is also a way to develop critical-thinking abilities, something that will enhance your quality of life, be it in personal or professional ways. I know, it is almost certain that you have previously been promised exposure to ways of thinking critically and have walked away disappointed. Here, though, you will be introduced to **rhetorical perspectives**, which are different ways of viewing how we communicate (or theoretical orientations a critic uses to help guide the criticism of rhetoric). The idea is that by using different perspectives to view instances of communication, we can learn more about how communication works. In this chapter we explore the nature of criticism, examine how criticism is performed, and also discover how criticism differs from other ways of producing knowledge, such as the scientific method. You will come away from this chapter better able to think insightfully about the communication around you, and with a good understanding of how to actually begin writing criticism.

The next two chapters expose you to two key concepts in rhetorical criticism. The first is the rhetorical situation, which is a theoretical explanation for what makes certain types of communication rhetorical. Although infrequently used as a stand-alone perspective for engaging in criticism, the concept of the rhetorical situation is quite important for understanding how persuasive communication operates. The next concept is that of genre. In some senses, every example of discourse contains elements of other examples of discourse, and as situations repeat themselves, so too do the elements speakers use when addressing these situations.

For example, if you have been to more than one commencement or convocation, you will have noticed that all of the main speeches sounded familiar in some ways; perhaps you even experienced a moment of déjà vu. Sure, there were differences linked to the particular graduating class and probably to the person giving the main speech. But there were also repeating elements that were expected in terms of what you would consider appropriate remarks for a speech concerning graduating students. This works for other types of communication as well: keynote addresses, eulogies, wedding toasts, apologies, and so on. The chapter on genre explores the importance of these repeating forms.

The second section, "Perspectives on Criticism," contains seven chapters introducing different perspectives that you can use when performing criticism: "The Traditional Perspective," "Close Textual Analysis," "Criticism of Metaphor," "The Narrative Perspective," "Dramatism and Kenneth Burke's Pentadic Criticism," "Feminist Analysis," and "Ideographic Criticism." These represent important perspectives in criticism in use now or in the past. There is not just one way of performing criticism but many. Each perspective offers new and exciting ways to view communication, thus allowing you to better unleash *your* imagination and powers of observation. The essential idea to keep in mind with each chapter is that you will be learning a distinct and insightful way of analyzing instances of rhetoric. As you learn about different perspectives, you will most likely discover that you like some better than others, that one or two "speak to you" in a way that the others do not. This is as it should be. Not every perspective will hold the same appeal for everyone, which is one of the reasons there are so many. Criticism is not a one-size-fits-all endeavor. Another reason that there are so many perspectives is that not all instances of communication are the same, nor do they yield insights in the same manner. Some perspectives are better suited to understanding a particular instance of communication than are others.

The third section, "Expanding Our Critical Horizons," contains five chapters, each of which covers an orientation toward viewing rhetoric and criticism that broadens their scope beyond the more traditional or established perspectives covered in the earlier section. In a sense, they push the boundaries we have thus far created for our definitions of *rhetoric*, *criticism*, and *theory*. In "Eclectic Rhetorical Criticism," you will discover ways to blend aspects of different perspectives in order to invent new and insightful ways to analyze instances of rhetoric. In "Criticism of Visual Rhetoric" you will learn different ways to critique visual images to better explore their rhetorical nature. In "Criticism of Popular Culture and Social Media," you will be given the means to better examine contemporary and popular uses of communication, much of which you might experience every day. In "Criticism of Digital Rhetoric," you will become familiar with the differences between traditionally conceived rhetoric and rhetoric as expressed in a digital format, including social media. In "Critical Rhetoric," you will be exposed to what is called the *critical turn* in rhetorical studies, and also to new purposes for criticism. In each of these chapters, ask yourself how the concepts being shared modify or enlarge the definitions of rhetoric and criticism that came before. Again, you may find that you gravitate toward some of these approaches more so than others, and that is a sign (as with the other perspectives) that you may have discovered a perspective "speaking your language."

Finally, in the appendixes, you will find helpful information as you move through this book and beyond. In the "Writing Criticism: Getting Started" entry, you will discover a brief introduction to a way of initially thinking about writing criticism. It contains straightforward advice about the important elements in any piece of criticism and can act as a guide when you first begin writing your own criticism. In the "Additional Rhetorical Perspectives and Genres" entry, you will find brief overviews of other perspectives and approaches used by rhetorical critics. These are designed to give you a taste of the broader picture that is rhetorical criticism.

In the "Glossary of Terms," you will find key terms used in the various chapters of this book. Some are common throughout all the chapters, and others will be specific to a particular perspective covered in one chapter. You will know when a term is in the glossary because it will be in **bold** when you first encounter it in this book. So, for instance, you will find the terms *rhetoric* and *criticism* mentioned above (in bold) in the glossary. Finally, in appendix D, there is an important essay by noted rhetorical critic Edwin Black on the concepts of objectivity and politics in criticism. Should a critic be objective? If so, to what degree? And what is objectivity in criticism, anyway? These questions elicit different answers from critics, and this essay provides an excellent starting point for discussion of these crucial issues.

I (and the individuals who have contributed chapters to this book) invite you to engage with the ideas in the following pages; I hope you find them as exciting as we do, and that they will enrich your understanding of human communication.

I

OVERVIEW OF RHETORICAL CRITICISM

2

What Is Rhetoric?

Jim A. Kuypers and Andrew King

Rhetoric has been around for millennia; it has many meanings, some old, some new. To get at the heart of its definition, let us first consider how the term *rhetoric* is most commonly used today. When a politician calls for "action, not rhetoric," the meaning seems clear; rhetoric denotes hollow words and flashy language, as exemplified in these contrasting headlines: "Obama Should 'Reconcile the *Rhetoric* with *Action*' to End Religious Intolerance, Says Rev. Samuel Rodriguez"[1] versus "On Energy and Climate, Obama *Action* Makes Up for Lack of *Rhetoric*."[2] Contemporary usage also connotes associations with deceit and tricks that mask truth and forthrightness. For example, former President Richard M. Nixon used the term *rhetoric* in this way in his 1969 inaugural address: "The simple things are the ones most needed today if we are to surmount what divides us and cement what unites us. To lower our voices would be a simple thing. In these difficult years, America has suffered from a fever of words; from inflated rhetoric that promises more than it can deliver; from angry rhetoric that fans discontents into hatreds; from bombastic rhetoric that postures instead of persuading." Although the type of rhetoric of which Nixon speaks is often worthy of study, it also leaves one thinking that it is certainly not the kind of language that an intelligent and civil person would willingly wish to use. Finally, sometimes rhetoric is simply used synonymously with communication, as exemplified in these two headlines about President Trump's public discourse: "Trump Rhetoric Freshly Condemned After Mass Shootings"[3] and "President Donald Trump's Rhetoric Not to Blame for Mass Shootings: Mick Mulvaney."[4] Same "rhetoric," different interpretations.

Rhetoric is also used to describe what some today consider fancy, embellished, or over-ornamental language. This contemporary perception of excess has its roots in eighteenth- and nineteenth-century American oratorical practice. During these centuries before radio, television, and the internet, public speeches were opportunities for audiences to be both informed and entertained; a certain lushness of language was both expected and desired. It was not at all uncommon for speeches to last several hours and for speakers to use no notes. This style of American speaking was most evident in patriotic orations and is well represented in George Caleb Bingham's painting, *Stump Speaking*. Albert Beveridge, in his 1898 speech "The March of the Flag," provides a common example of what we might consider embellished speech today:

It is a noble land that God has given us; a land that can feed and clothe the world; a land whose coastlines would enclose half the countries in Europe; a land set like a sentinel between the two imperial oceans of the globe, a greater England with a nobler destiny.

It is a mighty people that he has planted on this soil; a people sprung from the most masterful blood of history; a people perpetually revitalized by the virile, man-producing working-folk of all the earth; a people imperial by virtue of their power, by right of their institutions, by authority of their heaven-directed purposes—the propagandists and not the misers of liberty.[5]

Although the above examples are certainly forms of rhetoric, they but scratch the surface of rhetoric's deeply rich meaning, leaving out those meanings representing rhetoric's most powerful and important qualities. The study of rhetoric is an invention of early Western civilization, and we can trace its roots back over 2,600 years to the fledgling democracies of ancient Greece.

A CONCISE SKETCH OF THE RHETORICAL TRADITION

The Greeks developed the original model of rhetoric, which for them was a systematic body of knowledge about the theory and practice of public speaking in the law courts, in the governing assemblies, and on ceremonial occasions. Rhetoric was codified by Aristotle in his famous treatise, *The Rhetoric*, written somewhere around 335 BC. He defined rhetoric as the "power of discovering the means of persuasion in any given situation," a much more comprehensive and intellectually respectable meaning than today's common attributions of empty words and deception. Rhetoric was viewed as a practical art and was studied, discussed, and debated by educated Greeks, who expected each other to speak well, eloquently, and persuasively. Citizens were even expected to defend themselves in court by their personal rhetorical prowess, thus making the study of rhetoric even more important. The sophists, wandering teachers in the ancient world, often taught rhetoric as popular courses designed to prepare ambitious youths for fame and success. The Greeks believed in the power of the spoken word and delighted in hotly contested debate; they even held oratorical contests as part of the Olympics. On the other hand, and exemplifying the Greek love of debate, philosophers such as Plato condemned rhetoric, finding it a serious rival to philosophy in the ancient educational system.

Later, the Roman republican government provided many opportunities for the practice of rhetoric in their popular assemblies, in provincial governing bodies, in their law courts, and in their huge civil service and military. The best-known Roman orator was Marcus Tullius Cicero (106–43 BC), who took over the Greek ideas of rhetoric and adapted them to the needs of a far-flung world empire. From modest origins he rose to the highest office in Rome, the consulship, and was considered by many to be the greatest lawyer, speaker, and writer of his day. Fifty-eight speeches and nine hundred letters have come down to us; they still read well today and stand as models of powerfully persuasive oratory, biting wit, and incredible verbal skill. Cicero argued for an ideal **rhetorician**, an orator-statesman who would use rhetoric as a means of serving the people. A century later, Cicero's rhetorical teaching was codified by the first imperial professor of rhetoric in Rome, Quintilian (AD 35–96), who was Rome's greatest teacher and codifier of rhetorical knowledge. Thus, the Greco-Roman world established a tradition of discourse that has been taught throughout Western history and continues to grow and to develop down to our own time in the early twenty-first century.

Saint Augustine (AD 354–430) was largely responsible for early Christian uses of rhetoric, and his writings were used extensively by churchmen and intellectuals throughout the Middle

Ages. Augustine reasoned that since the Devil had full access to all of the available resources of rhetoric, others ought to study it if only for their own protection. The Church eventually agreed, declaring that knowledge of rhetoric's great power was essential for everyone, and both "in theory and practice the Christians forever influenced the development of rhetorical thought."[6] Likewise, the influence of rhetoric on the spread of Christianity should not be underestimated. During the Middle Ages, rhetoric was at the heart of education. It was taught in the cathedral schools. It inspired the great university debates and disputations, and it set rules for the composition of sermons and royal proclamations. It even extended its domain over poetry and letter writing, and rhetorical modes of expression guided government bureaucracies and discourses between kingdoms.

In the Renaissance, rhetoric became even more important, recapturing the high status it had enjoyed at the time of Cicero. Renaissance leaders revered Cicero as the ideal of the practicing rhetorician, the active agent in the service of the state and the people. Jean Dietz Moss notes that "a widening wave of literacy extended beyond the church and the court to include a secular public, merchants, bankers, lawyers, artisans and others of the middle class."[7] In the fifteenth and sixteenth centuries, rhetoric dominated philosophy, literature, and politics. Early in the seventeenth century, the great Italian rhetorician Giambattista Vico took René Descartes head-on, writing that truth is discovered through the rhetorical process of invention (discussed in chapter 6), not only through scientific observation, as Descartes maintained.[8] Vico's work extended the intellectual scope of rhetoric to include the study of language and the evolution of society, and it fit in well with other works of the period that were pushing back against a growing **scientism** that was advancing into all aspects of life at that time.[9]

During the late eighteenth century there was a vast expansion of the middle class in Britain and North America. The tremendous growth of literacy was aligned with the growth of the press and the publishing industry. Similar to the advent of the internet, the printing press was a dynamo for the circulation and expansion of knowledge. As a result, rhetoric expanded beyond matters of political and legal conflict to areas of reading, criticism, and judgment. Vast fortunes were being made via the Industrial Revolution, and upwardly mobile and newly rich individuals were eager to assimilate the speech, ideas, and manners of their higher-status counterparts in the aristocracy. The three greatest rhetorical theorists of the period were Hugh Blair, Richard Whately, and George Campbell. Each was a Christian minister, and each emphasized matters of ethics and of individual accountability in their rhetorical theory.

The nineteenth century was a time of huge industrial, political, and educational expansion in Europe and the United States. Parliamentary democracy penetrated to many points of the globe. Nineteenth-century practitioners of rhetoric cultivated the discipline as a form of individual intellectual training. They believed that knowledge of rhetoric would prepare any speaker or writer from age fifteen to age ninety to inform, persuade, or entertain any audience at any time on any occasion. The numerous and optimistic how-to-do-it rhetorical manuals of that day were an invitation to train in the privacy of one's own home for both self-improvement and social power. One example was the young Frederick Douglass studying his rhetoric book in secret in order to prepare for a career in public life that would lift him out of both slavery and poverty. Rhetorically based eloquence was seen as a means of gaining entry to the corridors of power. Books provided strategies for persuading others and provided models of great speeches for readers to imitate. A pantheon of great orators and their greatest speeches was established through books such as Chauncey A. Goodrich's *Select British Eloquence* in 1852. The book contained the speeches of the greatest British orators together with critical guides for study and tips on rhetorical emulation. Collections of great American orators soon followed, and these became style models for ambitious youth who saw the acquisition of rhetorical skill as a path to influence and wealth.

Although rhetorical treatises had been written since before Aristotle's day, academic departments focusing on rhetoric did not come into being until the early twentieth century; beginning in America, many evolved into what we today call departments of communication.[10] In these early departments, often known as departments of speech, scholars recovered the full range of the classical tradition and greatly expanded the study of rhetoric.[11] Rhetorical criticism became the major thrust of study, and theory was developed to explain the vast changes wrought by mass media, modern propaganda, and the immense social movements and revolutions of the first half of the century. In the latter half of the century and into the early twenty-first century, students of rhetoric moved far beyond the classical tradition. Traditionally scholars focused on how exemplar speakers—gifted and influential individuals—used rhetorical arts to shape their world and affect social change. More recently scholars have inverted this relationship and have begun to study the ways in which history and culture have shaped the practice of rhetoric itself. The very conditions in which rhetoric takes place are objects of study, and they include who is allowed to speak in a public place, whose speech will be taken seriously, and the range of ideas that are considered debatable at any given time. Scholars have also emphasized the role of language and symbols in the process by which social influence occurs, and they have broken down the walls between visual, verbal, and acoustic messages. Our understanding of rhetoric now includes far more than public speaking, as indispensable as that is; focusing on understanding symbolic action in many different forms and settings, it embraces discourse in print, radio, television, social media, and even our smartphones. Small wonder, then, that rhetoric is now being studied across a whole spectrum of academic subjects and is among the central disciplines of our time.[12]

THE MANY MEANINGS OF RHETORIC TODAY

Accordingly, approaching the quarter mark of the twenty-first century, we find a greatly expanded study of rhetoric, along with an ever-growing litany of definitions. We now move to sharing a pragmatic introduction to some of those meanings.

Rhetoric not only has a persuasive element; it has an informative one as well. For example, you might want to persuade someone to buy an Apple iPhone instead of a Google Pixel 4, or you might want to persuade your friends to have dinner with you at your favorite restaurant. Both instances would use rhetoric. However, in order to effectively persuade, you must first provide information in the form of supporting materials such as testimony, examples, stories, definitions, and the like. In short, you must use more than mere assertions as your arguments. In this sense, rhetoric involves the proper interpretation, construction, and use of supporting materials to back up assertions and gain audience acceptance.

With this in mind, let us begin with a working definition of *rhetoric*. When we use the term **rhetoric** in this chapter we mean *the strategic use of communication, oral or written, to achieve specifiable goals*. There are two main ideas expressed by this definition. One involves the strategic, or intentional, nature of the language we use; the second involves knowing what goals we wish to reach through the language we use. This is an intentionally narrow definition of *rhetoric*, but we think using such is justified for now. After all, we need someplace to begin the inquiry, and it seems to us that a definition rooted in the most practical examples of intentional persuasion is a good place from which to launch our discussion.

The Strategic Nature of Rhetoric

We use symbols to communicate. These symbols essentially are something we use to represent something else. Words, whether spoken or written, are such symbols. Musical notes are such symbols as well. Certain gestures are symbolic representations of meaning, too. Of importance to us here is that words, spoken or written, are symbols whose meanings are more readily agreed upon than the meanings of other symbols used in communication. That is to say, the lion's share of those hearing or reading a particular word can come to some consensus concerning its meaning, whereas this does not hold true with other types of symbols. For example, the symbols used in art, architecture, dance, and clothing are all vague in their meanings; thus a communicator would have less control over their precise interpretation by a given audience. Unfortunately, the further we travel from the *intentions* of the communicator, the closer to the *inferences* of the audience we find ourselves. Since rhetoric works using symbols, the more variation in the symbolic meaning (the meaning of a series of *words* versus the architectural meaning of a doorway, for example), the less precision in the communication in general.

Nonetheless, rhetoric viewed from this broader aspect should be considered. For example, Sonja K. Foss wrote that "*rhetoric* means the use of symbols to influence thought and action. Rhetoric is communication; it is simply an old term for what is now called *communication*."[13] In a later work she refines this definition of rhetoric as "the human use of symbols to communicate."[14] Rhetoric, from Foss's view, does involve action on the part of a communicator; it involves making conscious decisions about what to do. However, it also involves a larger conception in that it takes into consideration the impact symbols have on receivers, even if unintended. The range of potential rhetorical symbols according to Foss is vast: "Speeches, essays, conversations, poetry, novels, stories, comic books, websites, television programs, films, art, architecture, plays, music, dance, advertisements, furniture, automobiles, and dress are all forms of rhetoric."[15]

Foss presents an extremely broad definition, one that both includes and clashes with a more pragmatic conception of rhetoric. One could even argue that her definition is so broad as to claim that any form of human action or creation, when perceived by another, is a form of rhetoric. One can certainly argue what should or should not be considered as rhetoric, and Foss's conception does have merit. For the present, though, let us content ourselves with considering a narrower and pragmatic definition. As Marie Hochmuth Nichols wrote, "Rhetoric is an act of adapting discourse to an end outside itself. It serves many ends, from promoting decision to giving pleasure. It does not include ships, guns, an alluring sun, the dance, or the Cathedral of Chartres. It does not include rolling drums or the sound of marching feet; it does not include extralinguistic symbols of peace or the clenched fist of power. It does not deny that there are other symbolic forms for altering behavior, which often accompany or reinforce it."[16] Conceptions of rhetoric similar to that given by Foss minimize the important fact that as one moves further away from the use of symbols with generally agreed-upon meanings (words) to the use of symbols with imprecise meanings (furniture, dance), one finds that the *intentions* of the **rhetor**, or communicator, play less a part in the rhetorical exchange and that the *impressions* of the receiver play a greater role.[17] In this sense the meaning behind the rhetoric moves from the person crafting the message to the impressions of those receiving the message, irrespective of the intentions of the original communicator.

The concern with intentions was not lost on Hoyt Hopewell Hudson, an early twentieth-century rhetorical theorist, critic, and poet.[18] In his landmark essay, "Rhetoric and Poetry,"

Hudson highlighted the differences between efforts aimed at rhetorical influence (rhetoric) and efforts aimed at symbolic expression (poetry). He began his comparison by citing numerous great poets in order to demonstrate the general focus of a poet: "The Poet . . . keeps his eye not on the audience or the occasion, but on his subject; his subject fills his mind and engrosses his imagination, so that he is compelled, by excess of admiration or other emotion, to tell of it; compelled, though no one hear or read his utterance."[19] Hudson clearly marked where rhetoric begins and poetry ends to better discuss their differences: "For the moment, then, we shall say that poetry is for the sake of expression; the impression on others is incidental. Rhetoric is for the sake of impression; the expression is secondary—an indispensable means."[20]

This distinction is subject to exceptions, and here Hudson showed a graceful and discerning grasp of the differences between rhetoric and poetry, providing examples of how a poet might stray into the field of rhetoric. For example, a poet envisioning a speaker attempting to persuade listeners must use rhetoric—Mark Antony in Shakespeare's *Julius Caesar* and the speeches of the fallen angels in the first and second books of *Paradise Lost* are two such examples (as are the courtroom scenes in the various iterations of the hit TV series *Law & Order*). Hudson calls this imitative rhetoric, which may be studied for its own sake. A poet may at times consider the audience (a drama, for example), but there exist differences in the conception of the audience: "The poet thinks of a more general and more vaguely defined audience than the orator. The poet may even think of all mankind of the present and future as his audience."[21] Hudson even provided a loose scale to depict the range from the most purely poetical—personal lyrics and rhapsodic poems; then idylls and pastoral poetry; then narrative poetry, romance, and the epic—to the more purely rhetorical, such as tragedy and comedy, and finally didactic poetry, satire, odes, and epigrams. Hudson also demonstrated how an orator might cross over into the field of poetry: "Though the orator's end is persuasion, it is not hard to believe that there are moments in his discourse when this end is forgotten in his delight or wonder before some image which fills his inner eye. In such moments he has his eye on the subject, not the audience."[22]

Considering all of the above, we can clearly see the differences between the more personally *expressive* use of ambiguous symbols—poetry, painting, dance, and architecture—and the more publicly *impressive* use of symbols with generally agreed-upon meanings: words spoken and written for the sake of persuasion. It is the latter that is the focus of this chapter and many of the chapters beyond. This is not to say that other forms of more ambiguous rhetoric cannot be studied but rather that we will take our first step on the firmer soil of rhetoric understood as strategic and intentional. Later chapters in this book will expand this definition of rhetoric.

Rhetoric as Goal-Oriented Communication

Coming back to the definition of rhetoric we gave above, we find that rhetoric is strategic because it is intentional. Communicators who wish to control the manner in which their messages are understood plan ahead. They think about what they are going to say and what impact their words are likely to have on those listening to them. When they use rhetoric in this way, they provide reasons for their listeners to agree with them. Just as importantly, rhetoric is intentional in the sense that it is employed only when words can make a difference. That is to say, rhetoric is *persuasive*. It seeks to influence our personal and collective behaviors through having us voluntarily agree with the speaker that a certain action or policy is better than another action or policy. Rhetors often think about their goals so that they are better able to plan what to say for a desired effect. Since there is no scientific certainty to human affairs—

that is, we do not know with complete certainty which policy will produce the absolute best results—rhetoric attempts to persuade listeners that one policy will *probably* be better than another. It is in this sense, then, that rhetoric is based on probability—communicators try to convince us not so much that their proposed course of action is the only correct one, or that it will work with guaranteed certainty, but rather that it *probably* will reap greater success than competing solutions. The trick for the person trying to persuade is to make certain that the level of probability is high enough to convince the particular audience being addressed that a certain course of action will be the best course of action for them.

Rhetoric works toward a goal, then. It may involve simply trying to have your audience believe a certain way, or it could work toward the enacting of one course of action or policy over another. In suggesting that rhetoric is policy oriented, we mean to say that it seeks to influence how those receiving the rhetoric act at either a personal or a public level. Policy at the personal level involves decisions about our beliefs or actions completely within our control. For instance, almost twenty million college students found themselves asking in early spring 2020: "With the ongoing COVID-19 virus situation, should I return to campus after spring break or stay at home?" Beyond this, all of us also use rhetoric to influence those around us. For example, think of the last time you were together with a group of friends and you were trying to decide where to go for dinner. You most likely had several competing options and had to advance good reasons for choosing one venue over another. The policy option resulting in action is simple: where to go eat. Your attempt at persuasion here involves more than just your actions; it involves deciding what to do for a group: the outcome is not solely under your control. At a more public level, consider the November 20, 2014, words of President Barack Obama concerning his executive order on immigration. He asserted that it would fix the system "while giving undocumented immigrants a pathway to citizenship if they paid a fine, started paying their taxes, and went to the back of the line."[23] The public policy here involves allowing up to ten million illegal immigrants to stay in the country with federal assistance should they meet certain requirements. Senator Jeff Sessions of Alabama offered a competing policy option, one that would deny funding to the president's executive order and add "enforcement-only measures like universal E-Verify, ending catch-and-release, mandatory repatriation for unaccompanied alien minors, ending asylum loopholes, and closing off welfare for illegal immigrants."[24] The public policy here involves ending the president's plan to provide the means of citizenship for illegal immigrants and tightening border security. Which option one prefers depends on many factors, including the evidence each politician presents to show how his plan would produce the best results for the greatest number of citizens, as well as the personal values of each citizen. And just because there are policy options available does not mean they will work or be acted upon. The public discussion about the policies both Obama and Sessions advanced are ongoing even today.

A more detailed yet quite common example of how rhetoric works shows that the good reasons rhetoric uses to persuade us very often incorporate the human qualities we use every day when communicating with a goal in mind. A friend of ours was president of her neighborhood's homeowners' association for several years. At one point during her tenure her neighborhood experienced a rash of mail thefts. The postal inspector and sheriff's department could do little; this was a rural setting, wooded, with little likelihood of catching whoever was stealing unless someone was willing to keep watch twenty-four hours a day. Our friend decided that the post office could be prevailed upon to install lockboxes in place of the old stand-alone mailboxes. The post office agreed but decided to place the new boxes near the entrance to the neighborhood, in a wooded area alongside the road where there was no light during the evening hours. Our friend asked that they be placed in a more central, lighted area, but the postal worker said no. Not to be swayed, our friend continued her use of rhetoric.

She used common examples in her efforts: Many of those who would be getting the mail would be women, driving alone or with their children. With daylight savings time soon to end, they would be driving home at night after a day at work. Where the postal service wanted to place the mailboxes would necessitate the women getting out of their cars and walking away from them in order to get the mail. Our friend pointed out that if even one woman were attacked, then that particular postal worker would feel terrible. She also pointed out the very real possibility of the postal service being held legally responsible for any attacks that were facilitated by poorly placed boxes. The next day she had a phone conversation with the regional director of the postal service, and by the next week the new boxes were in, and in a better location so that nobody driving at night would have to get out of his or her car in order to collect the mail.

The persuasive effort used by our friend tells us a great deal about the nature of rhetoric. She used no extravagant arguments; rather, she used everyday logic and reasoning (the community's common sense), evoked a little emotion within her listeners (feelings about someone getting hurt), and ended up getting what was best for those in her neighborhood. It was not that her arguments had no weakness or that they were scientifically reasoned out. Rather the arguments she used were constructed in order to convince the postal authorities that there was a high possibility that what she said would happen would indeed happen. And that possibility was just high enough to persuade them to agree with her. So, this example shows how rhetoric is used every day. Importantly, though, it also points out that rhetoric is concerned with *contingent* matters. Simply put, rhetoric addresses those problems that can be changed through the use of words. Stated another way, the outcome of the situation is contingent upon what is said. So, for example, it was only because the possibility existed for having the location of the mailboxes moved that rhetoric was able to effect a change.

As the above example shows, rhetoric is goal directed. Our friend knew she wanted those mailboxes in a different location. She then thought of ways of constructing her arguments so that they would work with her particular audience—in this case, the postal workers who could change the location of the boxes. As you think about the goals communicators have in mind, it is important to remember another important aspect of rhetoric. When rhetoric is used, it is concerned with *informed opinions*. Most of us are not a mathematician trying to prove an equation or a chemist following a formula. Instead we deal with human beings thinking on uncertain matters; we deal with their facts and their opinions. Humans act based on what appears probable to them, not always on what they know for certain.

When we deal with policy-oriented questions of what we should do in a particular situation, there is no way to demonstrate using the scientific method that a certain course of action will be the best. Although *we* might know with certainty, those with whom we communicate may feel just as certain about a different course of action—think of the Obama and Sessions examples above. What rhetors do, then, is try to persuade their listeners that their proposed course of action has the maximum probability of succeeding. Successful rhetors attempt to narrow the choices from which their audiences can choose. These audiences may have many choices for action; rhetoric helps them to decide which course is the best to take. Summing up such a position, Gerard Hauser wrote, "Rhetoric, as an area of study, is concerned with how humans use symbols, especially language, to reach agreement that permits coordinated effort of some sort. In its most basic form, rhetorical communication occurs whenever one person engages another in an exchange of symbols to accomplish some goal. It is not communication for communication's sake; rhetorical communication, at least implicitly and often explicitly, attempts to coordinate social action."[25] As Donald C. Bryant so succinctly put it, rhetoric is not a body of knowledge but a means of applying knowledge: "It does rather than is."[26]

The Moral Dimensions of Rhetoric

The foregoing example has illustrated the strategic and goal-oriented nature of rhetoric. Rhetoric always presupposes the existence of an audience. A person addresses a particular audience anchored in time, space, culture, and circumstance. Intellectuals who dismiss rhetoric and wish to present unvarnished truth are often people who do not understand the power of audiences. Like Plato, they believe that what they see as clear ideas, strong evidence, and a rational plan of reform are enough. They underestimate the influence of emotion, self-interest, fear of change, and the ways in which unequal power distorts communication.

The very practice of rhetoric has an impact on the practitioners. But persuading others is always a matter of negotiating between ever-changing local conditions and the enduring principles of political judgment. Deliberation helps nurture audiences by strengthening the norms of fairness. Consider for a moment that communities do not exist prior to talk. Neither do they exist simply because someone says that this or that grouping of people is a community. They are built over time through communal understanding, argument, negotiation, and common action. Rhetorical practice is ethical in nature because it is advisory, and this advice has consequences for which the advice giver is held accountable. As Richard Weaver wrote, "it has the office of advising men with reference to an independent order of goods and with reference to their particular situation as it relates to these. The honest rhetorician therefore has two things in mind: a vision of how things should go ideally and ethically and a consideration of the special circumstances of his auditors. Toward both of these he has a responsibility."[27] Rhetoric is not an ethically neutral act such as target shooting or throwing clay pots on a wheel. Participation in rhetorical discourse involves people in building citizenship and constructing community. And the decisions they make or the ideas they embrace can ruin or enrich their lives. Thus, rhetoric is an ethically significant practice that seeks to engage audiences in sound judgment; those judgments have consequences that we can judge to be good or bad.[28]

Finally rhetoric sustains democratic culture. Rhetoric uses accepted beliefs to produce new beliefs and in so doing builds the stock of communal wisdom. It safeguards the stable beliefs that provide communal identity yet allows the community to manage change in ways that do not rend it apart and leave its people adrift.

A LARGER CONCEPTION OF RHETORIC

We mentioned earlier that the concept of rhetoric is expansive. In our discussion above we intentionally focus on a pragmatic and utilitarian conception of rhetoric. As will be reflected by some of the chapters in this book, rhetoric can be conceived in slightly larger ways. For instance, Charles Bazerman wrote that

> [rhetoric is the study] of how people use language and other symbols to realize human goals and carry out human activities. Rhetoric is ultimately a practical study offering people greater control over their symbolic activity. Rhetoric has at times been associated with limited techniques appropriate to specific tasks of political and forensic persuasion. . . . Consequently, people concerned

with other tasks have considered rhetoric to offer inappropriate analyses and techniques. These people have then tended to believe mistakenly that their rejection of political and forensic rhetoric has removed their own activity from the larger realm of situated, purposeful, strategic symbolic activity. I make no such narrowing and use rhetoric (for want of a more comprehensive term) to refer to the study of all areas of symbolic activity.[29]

"All areas of symbolic activity" certainly widens the scope of rhetoric's influence. Some have enlarged our understanding of rhetoric further by making the argument that it can also have unintentional, even unconscious elements in its persuasive effect. As Kenneth Burke noted in the mid-twentieth century, rhetoric can work toward the promotion of **identification**, "which can include a partially unconscious factor in appeal."[30] Burke explained his concept of identification this way: "A is not identical with his colleague, B. But insofar as their interests are joined, A is identified with B. Or he may identify himself with B even when their interests are not joined, if he assumes that they are, or is persuaded to believe so. You persuade a man only insofar as you can talk his language by speech, gesture, tonality, order, image, attitude, idea, identifying your way with his."[31] For example, a person might use symbols associated with wealth or class when writing a news story. Upon exposure to these symbols, a reader might identify with the nuances of wealth or class without being fully aware of doing so.[32] Brooke Quigley explained that "the need to identify arises out of division; humans are born and exist as biologically separate beings and therefore seek to identify, through communication, in order to overcome separateness. We are aware of this biological separation, and we recognize additional types of separation based on social class or position. We experience the ambiguity of being separate yet being identified with others at the same time."[33] As Burke wrote, humans are "both joined and separate, at once a distinct substance and consubstantial with another."[34] Burke was interested in the "processes by which we build social cohesion through our use of language. His goal [was] that we learn to perceive at what points we are using and abusing language to cloud our vision, create confusion, or justify various and ever present inclinations toward conflict, war and destruction—or our equally-present inclinations toward cooperation, peace and survival."[35]

Other ways that critics examine this notion of the unintentional aspects of rhetoric involve the study of **ideology** in the language we use. Ideology in this context is any system of ideas that directs our collective social and political action. We cannot escape some form of ideology since we are raised and educated within a society that is organized around a particular ideology. A more specific definition suggests that an "ideology is a set of opinions or beliefs of a group or an individual. Very often ideology refers to a set of political beliefs or a set of ideas that characterize a particular culture. Capitalism, communism, socialism, [fascism,] and Marxism are ideologies."[36] Thus a speaker using rhetoric would, intentionally or not, be grounding the ideas in his or her speech in a particular ideology. Critics looking at ideology generally do so from two broad perspectives. One involves looking at how ideology exists in society as systems of belief. Critics here simply want to know how ideology works in our society. In our speaker case above, how did ideology manifest itself in the speech? Most critics who study ideology go beyond this, however, and ground their understanding of ideology in the works of Marx, Engels, and Lenin. According to Jim A. Kuypers,

> One views ideology in this tradition as a false consciousness; it is a negative influence that distorts one's ability to think and perceive the world. In this perspective, ideologies contribute to the domination of the masses because they present a distorted picture of the world, thus debilitating one's ability to reason (think of an infection of the mind). For instance, consider religious and nationalist components to American ideology (America: land of the free, home of the brave; the American

dream). Following the ideology as distortion metaphor, these components act to dominate members of the working class because the ideology has these workers believing that they actually are working for God and country, when in reality, according to Marxists, they are working for the dominant power elite (and the Capitalist system that steals their labor from them).[37]

In this case, then, a critic looking at our same speech mentioned above would be looking for how that speaker possessed a false consciousness imposed by a particular ideology, many times looking in particular at how it impacts race, gender, or class, and then make suggestions about how to break free from the constraints imposed by that ideology. James Jasinski offers insight into these two broad ideological trends of criticism, stating that "the difference between the traditions is primarily one of emphasis; the Marxist tradition considers ideology as an object of critique or something that needs to be overcome, whereas the belief system tradition views ideology as an object of disinterested analysis or something that needs to be studied."[38]

WHAT FUTURE FOR RHETORIC?

But despite our friend's success in the matter of the postboxes, is there still an important future for rhetoric? Some persons worry that the places for public deliberation are becoming smaller and fewer. They remind us that beyond the scope of the town meeting and neighborhood conclave, significant issues are selected and framed by the mass media, not local citizens. These issues are debated by so-called experts while the citizenry watches, sometimes enjoying the "illusion" of participation, but often feeling like powerless spectators, even in this internet age of social media feedback. Scholars such as Jürgen Habermas argue that such civic voyeurism could undermine the legitimacy of our institutions. After all, most Americans have never discussed beyond the comfort of their own homes public education, free enterprise, the income tax, gun control, or our immigration laws, yet they are imposed upon us by the dead hand of the past. These systems were largely developed before we were born and are imposed upon us without our consent. Their direction is mostly in the hands of unaccountable public officials who enjoy lifetime tenure as unelected public servants. Policy details are complex, often known only to special-interest groups.

Since many of our problems of race, ethnicity, poverty, health, and aging have been placed in the hands of government and state bureaucracy, they are in many ways removed from the arena of public discussion. Further, the sheer number of issues and the volume of information concerning them are mind numbing and intimidating. Matters that were once seen to be the province of ordinary citizens are now the property of specialized technical elites. We may fear that although these "intellectuals" can organize data and design complex "solutions," they may understand very little about the fears, prejudices, and aspirations of ordinary people. Denied participation in civic debate, we become less skilled in managing discourse. Increasingly, we may view ourselves as mere masses manipulated by experts, not active citizens who are in charge of their own fate.

Finally, it can be argued that the ever-increasing elite focus on diversity and multiculturalism has destroyed the basic consensus that the practice of rhetoric requires. Rhetoric was born in the Greek polis, a small face-to-face homogenous community in which civic identity was girded by the premise that everyone shared a common destiny. Our society is becoming vast congeries of warring interest groups characterized by unbridgeable controversies and sedimented suspicion. Thus some critics argue that rhetoric is a method that only worked in the past and that it no longer has a place in twenty-first-century life.

We argue that these criticisms are nothing new and actually predate the rise of a multicultural, technologically advanced mega-state. In one form or another they have been made for the past century. Despite numerous pronouncements about the death of rhetoric and civil culture, persuasive discourse persists. The practice of rhetoric is alive and well. Audiences and speakers are still engaged in building practical wisdom. Common dilemmas are still being attacked and resolved. Can rhetoric still be powerful, useful, and moral? Roderick P. Hart and Courtney Dillard think so, writing in 2001:

> Is deliberation still possible? Some say no, others find the question fatuous. In defense of deliberation they point to democracies in which women were given the vote by men and in which blacks were enfranchised by whites. They find wars being stopped by college students, environmental laws being passed by the children of corporation executives, and Nelson Mandela's cause assisted by a distant band of college professors. They point to an American president being driven out of office by free press, a Russian president honored for dismantling a mighty Communist machine, and an Iraqi dictator stopped in his tracks.[39]

But what of today, approximately twenty years later? Is public deliberation still possible? One need only look at the rapid rise of the Second Amendment sanctuary movement across the nation or at public (and Congressional) discussions about social media giants such as Facebook and Twitter acting as a new, technological public sphere.

Circumstances may change, but as long as we live in a republic operating with democratic ideals, we simply cannot do without rhetoric. In fact, knowledge about the wise use of discourse has never been more necessary than it is today. Just as we begin to think that people are not communicating in the public sphere as much as they did in the past, we discover that social media such as Twitter, Pinterest, Tumblr, Instagram, VK, Vine, and Meetup are bringing them together in new and creative ways.[40] We also discover that blockbuster console video games such as *Grand Theft Auto*, *Call of Duty*, and *Halo* are dynamic productions using rhetoric to enhance game play, while others use rhetoric to make moral assertions.[41] Little wonder the study of rhetoric is enjoying a vast revival throughout our system of higher education. And after a one-hundred-year hiatus, the study of rhetoric is also seeing a resurgence in Europe.[42] The chapters that follow will give you a sense of the variety and artistry of rhetorical discourse and of the cultural and historical faces that have shaped it. As you move through each chapter, you will find that the conception of rhetoric it advances modifies or moves beyond the working definition we provided above. This is as it should be. Take note of *how* the conception changes. Rhetoric is nuanced and may be understood on many different levels. Each chapter that follows underscores this idea and will present a point of view that will add rich variety to the definition given above.

SUGGESTED READINGS

Bryant, Donald Cross. "Rhetoric: Its Function and Its Scope." *Quarterly Journal of Speech* 39 (1953): 401–424.

Hauser, Gerard A. *Introduction to Rhetorical Theory*. 2nd ed. Prospect Heights, IL: Waveland Press, 2002.

Hudson, Hoyt Hopewell. "Rhetoric and Poetry." *Quarterly Journal of Speech Education* 10, no. 2 (1924): 143–154.

Nichols, Marie Hochmuth. "Rhetoric and the Humane Tradition." In *Rhetoric: A Tradition in Transition*, edited by Walter R. Fisher, 178–191. Lansing: Michigan State University Press, 1974.

Smith, Craig R. *Rhetoric and Human Consciousness: A History*. 5th ed. Prospect Heights, IL: Waveland Press, 2017.

DISCUSSION QUESTIONS

1. With which definition of rhetoric do you feel most comfortable? Why?
2. How is rhetorical reasoning different than scientific reasoning?
3. What is the moral dimension of rhetoric?
4. As rhetoric's definition is enlarged, does it become of more or less practical use to us?

ACTIVITIES

1. Share an example of when you used rhetoric to obtain a specific goal. Explain.
2. Either singly or in small groups, choose an opinion piece from a news source. Argue why or why not it is a successful use of rhetoric.
3. In a small group, envision what America would look like if rhetoric was not practiced? How would government, schools, and other institutions operate?

NOTES

1. Michael Gryboski, "Obama Should 'Reconcile the Rhetoric with Action' to End Religious Intolerance, Says Rev. Samuel Rodriguez," *Christian Post*, February 5, 2015, emphasis ours, http://www.christianpost.com/news/obama-should-reconcile-the-rhetoric-with-action-to-end-religious-intolerance-says-rev-samuel-rodriguez-133642.

2. Amy Harder, "On Energy and Climate, Obama Action Makes Up for Lack of Rhetoric," *Wall Street Journal: Washington Wire*, January 20, 2015, emphasis ours, http://blogs.wsj.com/washwire/2015/01/20/on-energy-and-climate-obama-action-makes-up-for-lack-of-rhetoric.

3. Caitlin Oprysko, "Trump Rhetoric Freshly Condemned After Mass Shootings," *Politico*, August 4, 2019, https://www.politico.com/story/2019/08/04/beto-orourke-trump-el-paso-white-nationalist-1445700.

4. Ben Gittleson and Justin Doom, "President Donald Trump's Rhetoric Not to Blame for Mass Shootings: Mick Mulvaney," ABC News, August 5, 2019, https://abcnews.go.com/Politics/crazy-people-carry-shootings-guns-mulvaney/story?id=64744298.

5. Speech contained in Ronald F. Reid, *American Rhetorical Discourse*, 2nd ed. (Prospect Heights, IL: Waveland Press, 1995), 657.

6. James L. Golden, Goodwin F. Berquist, and William E. Coleman, *The Rhetoric of Western Thought*, 4th ed. (Dubuque, IA: Kendall/Hunt, 1989), 128–129.

7. Jean Dietz Moss, "Renaissance Rhetoric: An Overview," in *Encyclopedia of Rhetoric* (Oxford University Press, 2001), 681.

8. Giambattista Vico, *De Italorum Sapientia*, 1710.

9. For a more detailed explanation of this growing scientism, see Craig R. Smith, *Rhetoric and Human Consciousness: A History*, 5th ed. (Prospect Heights, IL: Waveland Press, 2017), 235–264.

10. Andrew King and Jim A. Kuypers, "Our Roots Are Strong and Deep," in *Twentieth-Century Roots of Rhetorical Studies*, ed. Jim A. Kuypers and Andrew King (Westport, CT: Praeger, 2001).

11. For examples of such growth, see Theodore Otto Windt Jr., "Hoyt H. Hudson: Spokesman for the Cornell School of Rhetoric," *Quarterly Journal of Speech* 68, no. 2 (1982): 186–200; and Edward P. J. Corbett, "The Cornell School of Rhetoric," *Rhetoric Review* 4, no. 1 (September 1985): 4–14.

12. For overviews of the development of rhetorical theory, see the following: Hoyt Hopewell Hudson, "The Tradition of Our Subject," *Quarterly Journal of Speech* 17, no. 3 (1931): 320–329; Smith, *Rhetoric and Human Consciousness*.

13. Sonja K. Foss, "The Nature of Rhetorical Criticism," in *Rhetorical Criticism: Exploration and Practice* (Prospect Heights, IL: Waveland Press, 1989), 4.

14. Sonja K. Foss, "The Nature of Rhetorical Criticism," in *Rhetorical Criticism: Exploration and Practice*, 5th ed. (Prospect Heights, IL: Waveland Press, 2017), 3.

15. This and the immediately preceding quote, Foss, *Rhetorical Criticism*, 4th ed., 5.

16. Marie Hochmuth Nichols, "Rhetoric and the Humane Tradition," in *Rhetoric: A Tradition in Transition*, ed. Walter R. Fisher (Lansing: Michigan State University Press, 1974), 180.

17. As will be seen in chapter 3, "What Is Rhetorical Criticism?," one "receiver" of the rhetoric is the critic who examines the instance of rhetorical discourse. The further removed from agreed-upon meaning the symbols under consideration are, the more power the critic has over deciding what they mean (over and above what the author of the rhetorical discourse intended them to mean). This can, and sometimes does, lead to abuses by the critic. For more on this see Jim A. Kuypers, "*Doxa* and a Critical Rhetoric: Accounting for the Rhetorical Agent through Prudence," *Communication Quarterly* 44, no. 4 (1996): 452–462.

18. For the contributions of Hoyt Hopewell Hudson, see Jim A. Kuypers, "Hoyt Hopewell Hudson's Nuclear Rhetoric," in *Twentieth-Century Roots of Rhetorical Criticism*, ed. Jim A. Kuypers and Andrew King (Westport, CT: Praeger, 2001); Windt, "Hoyt H. Hudson."

19. Hoyt Hopewell Hudson, "Rhetoric and Poetry," *Quarterly Journal of Speech Education* 10, no. 2 (1924): 145.

20. Ibid., 146.

21. Ibid., 148.

22. Ibid., 153.

23. Barack H. Obama, "Remarks by the President in Address to the Nation on Immigration" (White House, Office of the Press Secretary, November 20, 2014), http://www.whitehouse.gov/the-press-office/2014/11/20/remarks-president-address-nation-immigration.

24. Jeff Sessions, "Immigration Handbook for the New Republican Majority," Office of Senator Jeff Sessions, January 20, 2015, http://www.sessions.senate.gov/public/_cache/files/67ae7163-6616-4023-a5c4-534c53e6fc26/immigration-primer-for-the-114th-congress.pdf.

25. Gerard A. Hauser, *Introduction to Rhetorical Theory*, 2nd ed. (Prospect Heights, IL: Waveland Press, 2002), 2–3.

26. Donald C. Bryant, "Rhetoric: Its Function and Its Scope," *Quarterly Journal of Speech* 39 (1953): 401–424. In honor of the fiftieth anniversary of this landmark essay, *Advances in the History of Rhetoric* published a special collection of essays from noted rhetorical critics (see vol. 7, no. 1, 2004). See, too, Bryant's "Rhetoric: Its Function and Its Scope: *Rediviva*," in *Rhetorical Dimensions in Criticism* (Baton Rouge: Louisiana State University Press, 1973), 3–23.

27. Richard M. Weaver, "Language Is Sermonic," in *Dimensions of Rhetorical Scholarship*, ed. Roger I. Nebergall (Norman: Department of Speech, University of Oklahoma, 1963), 54. This essay is conveniently found in Richard L. Johannesen, Rennard Strickland, and Ralph T. Eubanks, eds., *Language Is Sermonic: Richard M. Weaver on the Nature of Rhetoric* (Baton Rouge: Louisiana State University Press, 1970), 201–225.

28. For more on the relationship of rhetoric, ethics, and the communication discipline, see Pat J. Gehrke, *The Ethics and Politics of Speech: Communication and Rhetoric in the Twentieth Century* (Carbondale: Southern Illinois University Press, 2009).

29. Charles Bazerman, *Shaping Written Knowledge: The Genre and Activity of the Experimental Article in Science* (Madison: University of Wisconsin Press, 1988), 6.

30. Kenneth Burke, "Rhetoric—Old and New," *Journal of General Education* 5 (1951): 203.

31. Kenneth Burke, *A Rhetoric of Motives* (Berkeley: University of California Press, 1969), 20, 55.

32. Burke, *A Rhetoric of Motives.*

33. Brooke L. Quigley, "'Identification' as a Key Term in Kenneth Burke's Rhetorical Theory," *American Communication Journal* 1, no. 3 (1998), http://ac-journal.org/journal/vol1/iss3/burke/quigley.html.

34. Burke, *A Rhetoric of Motives*, 21.

35. Quigley, "'Identification' as a Key Term."

36. Vocabulary.com, s.v. "Ideology," http://www.vocabulary.com/dictionary/ideology. The *Oxford English Dictionary* defines ideology as "A systematic scheme of ideas, usually relating to politics, economics, or society and forming the basis of action or policy; a set of beliefs governing conduct," http://www.oed.com.ezproxy.lib.vt.edu/view/Entry/91016?redirectedFrom=ideology&.

37. Jim A. Kuypers, "The Rhetorical River," *Southern Communication Journal* 73, no. 4 (2008): 353.

38. James Jasinski, *Sourcebook on Rhetoric: Key Concepts in Contemporary Rhetorical Studies* (Thousand Oaks, CA: Sage, 2001), 313.

39. Roderick P. Hart and Courtney L. Dillard, "Deliberative Genre," in *Encyclopedia of Rhetoric*, ed. Thomas O. Sloane (New York: Oxford University Press, 2001), 213.

40. Irene Tamí-Maury, Louis Brown, Hillary Lapham, and Shine Chang, "Community-based Participatory Research through Virtual Communities," *Journal of Communication in Healthcare* 10, no. 3 (2017), 188–194; Joel Penney and Caroline Dada, "(Re)Tweeting in the Service of Protest: Digital Composition and Circulation in the Occupy Wall Street Movement," *New Media & Society* 16, no. 1 (2014): 74–90; Jeffrey T. Grabill and Stacey Pigg, "Messy Rhetoric: Identity Performance as Rhetorical Agency in Online Public Forums," *RSQ: Rhetoric Society Quarterly* 42, no. 2 (2012): 99–119.

41. Rasmus Karkov, "GTA Is the Great Contemporary Novel," *Scientific Nordic*, April 1, 2012, http://sciencenordic.com/gta-great-contemporary-novel; Gerald Voorhees, "Play and Possibility in the Rhetoric of the War on Terror: The Structure of Agency in Halo 2," *Game Studies* 14, no. 1 (2014), http://gamestudies.org/1401/articles/gvoorhees; Shaun Cashman, "The Rhetoric of Immersion in Video Game Technologies" (PhD diss., North Carolina State University, 2010), http://repository.lib.ncsu.edu/ir/bitstream/1840.16/6105/1/etd.pdf; Heather M Crandall and Carolyn M. Cunningham, "Playing for Change: Rhetorical Strategies in Human Rights Video Games," *Relevant Rhetoric: A New Journal of Rhetorical Studies* 9, (2018), 1–26.

42. For example, see the Rhetoric Society of Europe, http://eusorhet.eu.

3

What Is Rhetorical Criticism?

Jim A. Kuypers

The previous chapter provided a working definition of *rhetoric*. This chapter introduces you to another concept: *criticism*. The purpose of this chapter is to show you how you can be a critic of rhetoric, and why this is an important, enriching activity. **Criticism** is "the systematic process of illuminating and evaluating products of human activity. [C]riticism presents and supports one possible interpretation and judgment. This interpretation, in turn, may become the basis for other interpretations and judgments."[1] When we critique instances of rhetoric, we are allowing ourselves to take, through careful analysis and judgment, a closer, critical look at how rhetoric operates to persuade and influence us. Specific acts of rhetoric that critics single out to analyze are called **rhetorical artifacts**. Criticism has many broad applications, but in general it is a *humanizing* activity. That is to say, it explores and highlights qualities that make us human—the good and the bad, the sublime and the droll, the beautiful and the ugly. It is not about being negative or finding fault in everything. For Donald C. Bryant, "common notions of criticism seem to involve or to imply some analytical examination of an artifact or artifacts, of some human transaction or transactions, toward the end of comprehension and realization of the potential of the object or event. Most notions of criticism extend also to appreciation and on to appraisal or judgment."[2] For our purposes, we are interested specifically in **rhetorical criticism**: the analysis and evaluation of rhetorical acts. We are looking at the many ways that humans use rhetoric to bring about changes in the world around them.

T. S. Eliot is reputed to have said, "We do criticism to open the work to others." This is exactly what we are about when we perform rhetorical criticism. On this point Wayne Brockriede wrote, "By 'criticism' I mean the act of evaluating or analyzing experience. A person can function as critic either by passing judgment on the experience or by analyzing it for the sake of a better understanding of that experience or of some more general concept or theory about such experiences."[3] Even more to the point concerning rhetorical criticism, Bryant wrote that it is "systematically getting inside transactions of communication to discover and describe their elements, their form, and their dynamics and to explore the situations, past or present, which generate them and in which they are essential constituents to be comprehended and judged."[4] Rhetorical critics have varied reasons and purposes for producing criticism, but for those viewing it as a form of art, we engage in criticism for two broad reasons: *appreciation* and *understanding*. Simply put, we wish to enhance both our own and others' understanding of the rhetorical act; we wish to share our insights with others and to enhance their appreciation of the rhetorical act. These are not vague goals but quality-of-life issues. By improving understanding and appreciation, critics offer new and potentially exciting ways for others to see the world. Through understanding we also produce knowledge about human communication; in theory this should help us to better govern our interactions with others.

CRITICISM AS A METHOD

In its most basic form, a method is a particular manner or process for accomplishing a task. The researcher's task—humanist, social scientist, or scientist—is to generate knowledge. The methods researchers use to accomplish this task vary greatly, however. The use of rhetoric is an art; as such, it does not lend itself well to scientific methods of analysis. Criticism is an art as well; as such, it is particularly well suited for examining rhetorical creations. Numerous critics have commented upon the humanistic, personal nature of the study of rhetoric. Marie Hochmuth Nichols, for instance, wrote that humane studies, of which the study of rhetoric is a prominent example, are "concerned with the formation of judgment and choice." Such studies teach us that "technical efficiency is not enough, that somewhere beyond that lies an area in which answers are not formulary and methods not routine." Beyond "the area of the formula lies an area where understanding, imagination, knowledge of alternatives, and a sense of purpose operate."[5] That area of which she writes is, of course, criticism.

The ways that the sciences and the humanities study the phenomena that surround us differ greatly in the amount of the researcher's personality allowed to influence the results of the study. For example, in the sciences, researchers purposefully adhere to a *strict* method (the scientific method). All scientific researchers are to use this same basic method, and successful experiments must be 100 percent replicable by others, else they fail. An experiment performed at Virginia Tech must be replicable under the same constraints at the University of Tokyo, or anywhere else in the world. The application of the scientific method may take numerous forms, but the overall method remains the same—and the personality of the researcher is excised from the actual study. Generally speaking, the researcher's likes and dislikes, and his or her religious and political preferences, are supposed to be as far removed as possible from the actual study and its reported findings. Even the language scientists use to describe the results of their studies distances them from those very results. For example, in scientific (as well as social scientific) essays, one normally finds a detached use of language, with researchers forcing themselves into the background by highlighting the study itself: "This study found that . . ." or "The conclusions of this study suggest that . . ."

In sharp contrast, criticism (one of many humanistic methods of generating knowledge) actively involves the personality of the researcher. The very choices of what to study, and how and why to study a rhetorical artifact, are heavily influenced by the personal qualities of the researcher. In criticism this is especially important since the personality of the critic is considered an integral component of the study. Further personalizing criticism, we find that rhetorical critics use a variety of means when examining a particular rhetorical artifact, with some critics even developing their own unique perspective to better examine a rhetorical artifact.[6] Even the manner in which many critics express themselves in their writing brings the personal to the fore. Many use the first-person singular in their writing: "I found . . ." instead of "This study found . . ." These distinctions were apparent to Edwin Black, who forcefully wrote,

Methods, then, admit of varying degrees of personality. And criticism, on the whole, is near the indeterminate, contingent, personal end of the methodological scale. In consequence of this placement, it is neither possible nor desirable for criticism to be fixed into a system, for critical techniques to be objectified, for critics to be interchangeable for purposes of [scientific] replication, or for rhetorical criticism to serve as the handmaiden of quasi-scientific theory. [The] idea is that critical method is too personally expressive to be systematized.[7]

In short, criticism is an art, not a science. It is not a scientific method; it uses probability-based methods of argument; it exists on its own, not in conjunction with other methods of generating knowledge (i.e., social scientific or scientific). As Hochmuth Nichols articulated so well, "It is reason and judgment, not a [computer], that makes a man a critic."[8] Put another way, insight and imagination top statistical applications when studying rhetorical action.

THE CRITICAL ACT

At this point you should have a general idea of what rhetorical criticism is. Yet a question remains: How is it performed? In short, how does one actually "do" criticism? Where does one begin? And how does one ensure that criticism is more than mere opinion? Superior criticism is not performed mechanically, similar to following a recipe or a set of instructions to build something; neither is it scientific in the sense of following a strict experimental protocol. It is, however, quite rigorous and well thought out, with critics following certain norms when producing criticism. After all, good critics are trying to generate understanding and insight; they are not supposed to be simply flashing their opinions about. In general, there are three stages involved in the **critical act**, in producing criticism: conceptual, communication, and counter-communication.

The Conceptual Stage

The conceptual stage takes place in the mind of the critic; it is an act of cerebration. It is a private act, and its purpose is to generate some type of insight concerning the rhetorical artifact. Since this is a very personal act—that is, not mechanistic—there is no standardized way critics go about flexing their cerebral muscles. What works for one critic might not work for another. Often, though, insight is generated in one of two very broad ways. The first is a type of spontaneous inception. Think of the *Eureka!* of Archimedes, or of the proverbial lightbulb popping on inside your head. Critics often generate involuntary, almost instinctive reactions to rhetorical artifacts. This involves more than a simple reaction to the artifact, however, because critics are trained to observe, and their training has a bearing on what they see in an artifact. In a sense, the experienced critic has assimilated particular ways of viewing rhetoric; these modes of seeing are part and parcel of the critic's personality. Some critics may even come to see rhetorical artifacts in such a way that others recognize it as characteristic of that particular critic. The more a critic learns about rhetoric, the more that critic sees the world with a rhetorical understanding, and the more likely that critic will be to generate spontaneous insights.

The other broad way a critic might generate insight is through a somewhat systematic examination of a rhetorical artifact. With this approach the critic uses some type of guide, formal or informal, that allows for an orderly progression through the rhetorical artifact. A more formal guide might take the form of a theoretical perspective on rhetoric, which we will discuss below. A more personal and informal guide could be a question the critic has about the workings of the world (often called a research question). Simply put, the critic starts with a question or two in mind and then examines various rhetorical artifacts looking for answers to that question. For example, Stephen Howard Browne, the author of the chapter on "Close Textual Analysis," asks in his critical essay questions such as, "what is the primary theme in the rhetorical artifact?" and wishes to discover "how it superintends the symbolic action of the text as it unfolds." He continues, writing that he wants "to ask further about the internal structure of this movement and how this structure assists in the production of the speaker's message." He also asks, "Similarly, what kinds of images, metaphors, and other dimensions of style animate Obama's arguments and give them conspicuous form?" With those questions in mind, Browne decided that using a type of criticism called close textual analysis would be a fruitful perspective to use when looking at different rhetorical artifacts. In this way some authors are guided by their initial research questions in both the decision about what perspective to use and also in what to look for in the rhetorical artifacts they examined.

Whether a critic spontaneously generates an insight or searches a rhetorical artifact for information, it should be the critic, not the method or perspective, that is in control of the insights and knowledge generated. As Black wrote, "The critic's procedures are, when at their best, original; they grow ad hoc from the critic's engagement with the [rhetorical] artifact."[9] Of course, not all insights generated prove sound, and some ideas are never meant to move beyond mere personal musing. In my experience, it is only a small minority of ideas that create roots and actually grow. These ideas move to the next stage of the critical act: communication.

The Communication Stage

The second stage of the critical act is a quasi-public act of writing[10] out the criticism in preparation for sharing it with others. This stage of the critical act encompasses the private act of writing, sharing initial ideas with trusted friends and colleagues, and ultimately sharing with a wider audience. Your reasons for writing criticism will help to determine the particular audience for whom you write. For example, you could be writing a letter to the editor of your local paper concerning the rhetorical efforts of a politician running for office, you could be writing an entry for readers of your blog, you could be writing a term paper for your professor, or you could be writing with a specific scholarly journal in mind. When writing you must always keep in mind the audience with whom you intend to share your criticism. Recall that part of the purpose of criticism is to enhance the understanding and appreciation of others concerning the rhetorical artifact. On this point Black wrote, "The critic proceeds in part by translating the object of his criticism into the terms of his audience and in part by educating his audience to the terms of the object. This dual task is not an ancillary function of criticism; it is an essential part of criticism."[11]

When sharing your criticism with others, it is not simply a matter of providing a detailed picture of your opinions. You are instead sharing *propositions* with those who will be reading your work. Propositions are only naked assertions, however, until you provide a very basic step: giving supporting evidence with which to back up those assertions. Craig R. Smith wrote that critics must hold themselves to high "standards of argumentation" when writing criticism. Specifically, he suggested that, "when we write criticism . . . we ought to confine ourselves to solid argumentation inclusive of valid arguments built on sufficient and high quality evidence produced from close textual readings and masterings of context."[12] In short, critics must *invite* their audiences to agree with them. This is accomplished through stating their case and then providing evidence for their audience to accept or reject.

For example, consider the short speech given by Baltimore Ravens running back Ray Rice on May 23, 2014, following the February 19, 2014, release of a video showing him dragging his unconscious wife (then fiancée Janay Palmer) from an Atlantic City casino elevator.[13] Police said the part of the tape not released showed that Rice struck his wife "with his hand, rendering her unconscious," before dragging her out of the elevator.[14] After over a month of negative publicity for Rice, the Ravens, and the NFL in general, including charges of chauvinism and turning a blind eye toward domestic violence, the situation was only getting worse.[15] On March 27, 2014, Rice was indicted on aggravated assault charges, eventuating in a plea deal that involved counseling. The next day he and Janay Palmer were married. As the NFL continued to stand up for Rice, the negative publicity continued to grow. Finally, on May 23, 2014, Rice held a press conference along with his wife, during which time he addressed the situation.

After watching the video and reading the transcript of his apology, I can honestly say that it was not only a rhetorical dud but a failed speech as well.[16] Yet so far we have only my opinion, undifferentiated among so many others. I might go further, however, and make specific assertions concerning the speech. I could say that Rice's speech did not work well in that it simply failed on several levels. For instance, it showed a lack of preparation; it lacked true elements of an apology; it demonstrated a lack of logical consistency; he potentially insulted his wife during the speech; and, ultimately, it failed as an apology.

At this point you would find yourself with additional information, but still I have only provided you with *unsupported assertions*. I have merely given you additional, although better focused, opinions about the speech. I move into the realm of criticism when I provide support for these assertions of mine, when I provide you with evidence that asks you to agree with me or that makes you aware of some aspect of the speech that you had previously overlooked (the sharing of insights). For example, I could provide specific sentences from Rice's speech that I feel support my assertions. On the matter of lack of preparation, I could quote Rice: "I usually prepare my speeches just coming off the top [of my head], but during the time I had, I had a chance to jot a lot of things down."[17] Yet the speech was full of awkward grammatical structures and lacked any real sense of organization. For instance, Rice said although we know no "relationship is perfect, but me and Janay together, what counseling has done for us . . ."[18] Concerning lacking true elements of an apology, I could mention that he failed to actually apologize to his wife Janay for knocking her unconscious, and she was sitting right next to him. Additionally, he never said exactly what he was apologizing for; instead, he used the vague "this situation that me and my wife were in" or "this thing [that] happened with me and my wife."[19] In a sense, he was shifting the blame onto a situation instead of onto his own shoulders.[20] In terms of logical consistency I could point out this passage: "Throughout this time, we really had the time to reflect on each other . . . but me and Janay together, what counseling has done for us—we want the world to see that it definitely did help us out."[21] He adds that he is working to change and become a better husband, father, and role model. Yet Rice then turns around and tells the listening press, "I want you to know that I'm still the Ray Rice that you know or used to know or grown to love. I'm still the same guy." And later, "We're still the same people, and I'm still the same person."[22] One does not logically say, "I have done all this self-help work that has been effective" and then go and say, but "I'm still the same old guy." In terms of insulting his wife, recall that the tape showed him dragging his unconscious wife out of the elevator, and that police said the full tape showed him striking her with his hand prior to that. Speaking of avoiding failure, of bouncing back from this legal and moral quagmire in which he found himself, Rice said, "Failure is . . . It's not getting knocked down, it's not getting back up."[23] Who knocked down whom, and who did not get back up and was dragged unconscious from an elevator? Finally, evidence of the speech's failure comes when the criticism persists and even grows following his speech, and Rice is compelled to re-apologize months later on July 31, 2014. At this press conference, Rice actually stated, "Last time [in the May press conference], I didn't publicly apologize to my wife. I realize that hit home with a lot of people."[24] Even had the second apology been stellar (for instance, without more "hit" references) it was too late, and ultimately, Rice was cut by the Ravens in September, 2014. He has not played professional football since.

The main point to remember from this example is that critics are trying to argue for a certain understanding of the rhetorical artifact. In this sense they are actually using rhetoric to try to gain acceptance of their ideas. The best critics simply do not make a judgment without supplying good reasons for others to agree with them. On this point, Bernard L. Brock et al. wrote, "Statements of tastes and preference do not qualify as criticism. [Criticism is] an art of evaluating with knowledge and propriety. Criticism is a reason-giving activity; it not only posits a judgment, the judgment is explained, reasons are given for the judgment, and known information is marshaled to support the reasons for the judgment."[25]

The idea of rhetorical criticism being a form of argument is not new. For example, Wayne Brockriede wrote in 1974 that useful rhetorical criticism must function as an argument to be effective criticism.[26] In his landmark essay, Brockriede advanced five interanimated characteristics of how rhetorical critics could construct a strong argument:

> (1) an inferential leap from existing beliefs to the adoption of a new belief or the reinforcement of an old one; (2) a perceived rationale to justify that leap; (3) a choice among two or more competing claims; (4) a regulation of uncertainty in relation to the selected claim—since someone has made an inferential leap, certainty can be neither zero nor total; and (5) a willingness to risk a confrontation of that claim with one's peers.[27]

More significant arguments will have a greater number and strength of the five above characteristics than less significant arguments. This is to say, the five qualities of arguments given above are on a sliding scale of sorts. The fewer of the five, or the weaker in form, the less the criticism is an effective argument. The greater the number of the five, or the stronger in form, the greater the likelihood that the criticism is an effective argument. As Brockriede wrote, "When a critic only appreciates the rhetoric or objects to it, without reporting any reason for his like or dislike, he puts his criticism near the nonargument end of the continuum. On the other hand, when an evaluating critic states clearly the criteria he has used in arriving at his judgment, together with the philosophic or theoretic foundations on which they rest, and when he has offered some data to show that the rhetorical experience meets or fails to meet those criteria, then he has argued."[28]

Rhetorical Perspectives

The propositions and claims used by a critic are generally contextualized through the use of different perspectives used in criticism. A **rhetorical perspective** is a theory-centered point of view a critic uses to help guide the criticism of a rhetorical artifact. As pointed out by Raymie E. McKerrow, "There is no single approach or perspective that stands above all others as the preferred means of enacting a critical perspective on any [rhetorical] artifact. That said, it is equally the case that some approaches are better suited to analyze specific artifacts or events."[29] Because a rhetorical artifact is a multidimensional, complex, and nuanced event, there is not one best way of viewing it (although some ways can be better for certain artifacts than others). Moreover, no one effort to describe or evaluate the artifact will yield all the knowledge that there is to know about that artifact. Rhetorical perspectives allow critics to view a rhetorical artifact from different angles, with the vast majority of academic criticism, since its inception, taking its structure from a particular perspective. Since the 1960s there has been an incredible expansion of perspectives critics have used to better understand the rhetoric that surrounds us. By one count, over sixty formally recognized perspectives have been cataloged,[30] with many more being used and with some critics even blending perspectives (thus, today we see more examples of multi-perspectival or eclectic criticism). Later in this book you will be exposed to many popular perspectives designed for generating insight and understanding about rhetorical artifacts, and even more are mentioned in the appendixes.

Using an established perspective to produce criticism has both strengths and weaknesses. One particular strength is that adopting a perspective allows you to see an artifact differently than if no perspective had been adopted. In a sense, using a perspective allows you to see the world in a particular way. Adopting a rhetorical perspective also allows you to stay focused because, when properly used, the perspective *guides* (rather than dictates) your analysis. It provides a road map of sorts, and if you stay on a particular perspective's road you will see parts of the countryside (of the rhetorical artifact) differently than if you had taken another road. This can be particularly useful for novice critics who are often bewildered by the enormous range of options any one rhetorical artifact offers for analysis. On the flip side of that coin, adopting a particular perspective will introduce certain biases into the criticism, because any given perspective can only provide an incomplete picture and also encourages you to view the world in a certain manner. The downside to using a road map is that even as you see certain parts of the countryside, you miss the other sights that taking a different road would have allowed you to see. The potential problem with this in terms of criticism, as Lawrence Rosenfield wrote, is that a "critic who comes upon a critical object [rhetorical artifact] in a state of mind such that he has a 'set of values' handy (or, indeed, any other system of categories) does not engage in a critical encounter so much as he processes perceptual data."[31] Put another way, what Rosenfield points out to us is that a critic who follows too closely the dictates of a particular perspective runs the risk of producing stale and lifeless criticism. Such a critic is simply looking for what the perspective suggests should be identified. In short, improperly used, a perspective would be allowed to *dictate* rather than guide what a critic does in the analysis.

The perspectives presented in this book represent a wide array of critical possibilities. Some are well known and widely practiced; others are less known but extremely powerful in their potential. As you become familiar with these perspectives, you will see how they differ in the type of material they allow a critic to focus on, as well as the type of material they exclude. A central question remains, however: *How does a critic choose which perspective to use?* The choice is guided by several factors. First, the critic's personal interest will play a crucial role in determining which perspective to adopt. As you study the perspectives shared in this book, you will find that some appeal to you, whereas others do not. This attraction or aversion is natural, so your first clue to which perspective to use should be your personal interest in that perspective. Second, and just as important, a critic must consider the unique characteristics of the rhetorical artifact being examined. As already mentioned, perspectives focus a critic's attention on certain aspects of a rhetorical artifact. A critic should take this into consideration when choosing a particular perspective to use, since any given perspective will not fit every rhetorical artifact. Some, even when there is a sound fit, might need modification. More experienced critics may choose to combine perspectives, modify perspectives, or develop a completely novel perspective, and this is something we will look at in the chapter on "Eclectic Rhetorical Criticism: Combining Perspectives for Insights"—the choice is the critic's to make. Of course, the greater your understanding of rhetoric and of the nuances of different perspectives, the greater your ability to discern the intricacies of individual rhetorical texts, and thus the greater the likelihood of producing vibrant criticism.

A note on theory as a goal of criticism   Although the promotion of understanding and appreciation are generally accepted goals in criticism, in academic criticism one finds a strong interest in the development of theory about rhetoric through the practice of criticism. Put another way, advancing your propositions (discussed above) through different rhetorical perspectives has potential to make an important contribution to the development of a critical vocabulary for both you and other critics to use. The greater our vocabulary, the greater the precision with which we can discuss rhetorical phenomena. The importance some scholars place on this was not lost on Mike Allen, who asked numerous rhetorical critics what made for publishable academic criticism; most "persons said that the scholarship had to contain an argument that related to theory and extended our understanding of theory."[32] James Darsey pointed out in 1994 that "the presumption in favor of [criticism] in the service of theory is so well established at this time that, in my experience, the failure to conform has been used as the primary reason to recommend against publication." And in response to this situation he asked, "Must we all be rhetorical theorists?" essentially arguing in his essay that, No, we should not.[33] The tension between these two positions exists still today. Arguments for greater or lesser inclusion in criticism of the development of theory[34] aside, almost all academic criticism—at least that which sees publication—contributes in some way to both the understanding of human communication and the development, or at least the understanding of, rhetorical theory. Regardless of which emphasis is greater, significance is important. Irrespective of how much or little theory is explored in one's criticism, I agree with Stephen E. Lucas, who wrote, "In the last analysis, our scholarship will be judged, not by the perspectives from which it proceeds, but by the quality of the insight it produces."[35]

The Counter-Communication Stage

Once the criticism is actually performed, the final stage of the critical act, counter-communication, is entered. This is a public act, and at this stage the critic shares openly with others. For instance, you might have a blog, vlog, or YouTube page and publish your criticism there. Your criticism could take the form of a submission to venues such as the *American Thinker, Huffington Post, or Quilette.* If published, it will allow others (possibly hundreds of thousands) the opportunity to share your thoughts and perhaps to respond. In more academic settings, students will submit their essays and receive feedback from their professors and possibly their classmates; or perhaps professors and some students will have written their essays for a conference presentation or for submission to a scholarly journal. The idea is to share your criticism with some segment of the public with the hope that it will provoke some type of feedback; the best criticism attempts just this.

Feedback can take many forms, as can public exchanges about the critic's ideas. Students will receive comments from their professors, and professors receive comments from their reviewers. If published, an essay then receives wider responses. The point is, once released to this public realm, a critic's work takes on a life of its own, whatever the venue of publication. Feedback, positive or negative, should be viewed as what it is: evidence of the critic entering into a larger conversation. A response that critics often encounter, though, is a reply indicating *de gustibus non est disputandum*, "there is no disputing taste." In other words, you might hear from others that your point of view is simply a subjective opinion and that their point of view is equally valid. Yet we have already seen that criticism is far more than mere opinion. So, if you made certain to provide the good reasons mentioned earlier, then the exchange does not boil down to "I'm right, you're wrong," but to arguing who can see the fullness of the rhetorical artifact better, or who has an actual insight. As Brockriede wrote, "Critics who argue are more *useful* than critics who do not."[36] Along these same lines, Black wrote, "The critic can only induce us, and therefore it is we, the readers of criticism, who demand the critic's compliance with certain of our expectations. We expect the critic to see things for us that we are unlikely to see for ourselves until the critic has called them to our attention."[37]

What we are about during this stage of the critical act is none other than entering into dialogue about matters of importance. The exchange and discussion of ideas is crucial to criticism; only the best criticism provokes this. Actually, the cry of many critics might well be, "Love me, hate me, but don't ignore me." Remember that good criticism *is* an act of rhetoric.

KEY ISSUES IN CRITICISM

When you begin to write your criticism, it will be helpful to know about five key issues with which all critics wrestle at some time or another. These issues are long-standing and have various "resolutions," with different critics taking different approaches to the same issue. For now it is enough to know the important questions these issues invite you to ask, not that you have the answers. By conscientiously thinking about these issues, you will be in a better position to produce deliberate, thoughtful, and well-informed criticism.

What to Include

One important issue involves the most basic element in criticism: *what to include in your writing*. Of course, there are many ways one could write criticism, but generally speaking your essay should contain three components: a description, an analysis, and an evaluation. Every critical essay should have these components in some form, but each essay will present them in a slightly different manner (and this will be seen in examples contained in the chapters that follow).

Description

Description refers to both a description of the rhetorical artifact and, particularly in more academic settings, a description of the theoretical background or perspective used in the essay.

Description of artifact　A description of the artifact is crucial if your readers are to be able to follow you. The way you describe the artifact may well be the only exposure they have to it, so you must take great care in presenting as accurate a picture as possible. This accuracy is facilitated by approaching the artifact with a fair and open mind. By setting aside personal politics or ideological "truths," and approaching the artifact with a sense of curiosity, the critic allows the artifact, in a sense, to speak initially on its own terms. Judgments may certainly be made, and appreciation or disdain expressed, but they must be made after two conditions are met: one, the fair-minded description of the inner workings of the artifact have been presented for the world to see; and two, the standards of judgments used by the critic are provided for all to see. These ideas are also discussed in appendix D, "On Objectivity and Politics in Criticism."

Description of theoretical perspective   Although the promotion of understanding and appreciation are generally accepted goals for all criticism, more formal criticism (e.g., term papers, conference presentations, etc.) is grounded in a theoretical perspective where some level of discussion centered on the theory being used to perform the criticism is expected as part of the description section. So the issue becomes how much or how little theory development there should be in formal criticism, and this is a long-standing point of contention among scholars. Some, such as McKerrow, believe that although "there are numerous approaches to criticism . . . each is worthy of being considered in relation to the question or problem being addressed [by the critic]. That means, in practice, that whether or not the essay contributes to theory development will depend on the purpose underlying the critical act."[38] Thus, whether or not a critical essay contributes to theory development instead of to some other goal will depend upon the types of questions the critic is asking at the start of the criticism. Not all agree with McKerrow, however, and many researchers possess a strong interest in the development of theory about rhetoric through the practice of criticism,[39] as discussed earlier in this chapter ("The Communication Stage").

Since the 1980s some have pushed this theory-centered view further, though, advancing the opinion that this is the primary end of criticism. On this point, William L. Nosthstine et al. wrote, "'Theory' has become virtually the singular objective of criticism. . . . [C]ontributing to theory *is* regarded as the fundamental goal of [rhetorical] criticism."[40] Although perhaps true of many academic journals, there are numerous exceptions. As noted by James Jasinski, the "two most common patterns in the [communication] literature are (a) theory provides a [perspective] that is utilized in critical practice (theory serves criticism) or (b) criticism contributes to theorization through its heuristic capacity, through illustration and hypotheses testing, and through the reflexive implementation of theoretically-derived [perspectives] (criticism serves theory)."[41] Most readers want to know in which rhetorical theories your perspective is grounded and exactly how you are using the theory to guide your analysis (theory serves criticism); the more academic the essay, the more detailed this description will be, as will be the strength of the call to see your analysis adding to the pool of theoretical knowledge. This drive toward generation of theory is so strong for some academic critics that the very quality of criticism is judged by the contributions made to the growing body of rhetorical theory. Sonja Foss represented this point of view when she wrote that the "purpose of rhetorical criticism is to explain how some aspect of rhetoric operates and thus to make a contribution to rhetorical theory. The critic who is attempting to contribute to rhetorical theory does not view an artifact for its own qualities alone but instead moves beyond the particularities . . . to discover what that artifact suggests about symbolic processes in general."[42]

For others, though, theory is a means to an end: the generation of insights into a rhetorical artifact with the ultimate goals of producing understanding and appreciation of that artifact and of our common humanity. From this point of view, the artifact comes first, then theory development only if convenient or advantageous; critics are seen here as artists, not builders of theory. In a summary of the tension between criticism for insight and criticism for theory, Richard B. Gregg pointed out that "critics need not consciously set out to contribute to theory; it is often enough to gain a thorough understanding of a rhetorical event for its own sake. On the other hand . . . critical interpretations always imply theoretical positions, whether consciously articulated or not."[43] I have written elsewhere that mandating that critics produce theory forces them into a mode of production that diminishes the personal and artistic qualities of criticism. As the role of theory lessens, with theory as an "increasingly gentle influence rather than prescription, the greater role the critic's personality assumes and the humanistic aspects of rhetorical criticism come to the fore. Of course, this later form of criticism is difficult to publish today given the theory-centric nature of our discipline."[44] For now, though, at least among academic-oriented journals, theory building is an important consideration; there are numerous exceptions, however, especially with eclectic criticism and conceptually oriented criticism on the rise.[45]

Description of "importance" When you describe the artifact and the theoretical perspective used to examine it, you will also want to relay the importance of the artifact, the study, or both. In short, at some point you will want to justify what you are doing. Given the countless appeals for our attention each day, readers may well ask, "Why is this important for me to know?" Although *you* might think what you are doing is important, not everyone else will think the same way. It is up to you to share with others the reasons why they should invest their time and energy to read what you have written. Another way of looking at this is highlighted by John W. Jordan, Kathryn M. Olson, and Steven R. Goldzwig:

> in building the case for rhetorical criticism one desires to publish in a scholarly journal, both the newness and significance of the critical claim (not the object of criticism) count, but significance counts more heavily. The critical essay that contains within itself a developed statement of its value to rhetorically trained readers beyond its author and a statement of the larger implications triggered when readers agree or disagree with the essay's point matters more . . . than one whose justification rests on the fact that no one else has used that combination of rhetorical concepts and texts—yet.[46]

Analysis/Interpretation

After you share with your readers what you will be examining (the rhetorical artifact), how you will be going about that examination (rhetorical theory), and the importance of what you are doing, you move on to the actual analysis of the rhetorical artifact. This section of your essay will generally consume the most space. When I say *analysis*, I mean both analysis *and* interpretation. They are not the same, but neither are they completely separate. In one sense, **analysis** is discovering *what is in* a rhetorical artifact, and **interpretation** is determining *what a rhetorical artifact means*. Analysis asks us to explain how the rhetorical artifact works; it provides a sketch of sorts, showing how the artifact is put together: what its parts are, how they go together, and what the whole looks like. The type of analysis depends on the temperament of the critic, but also on the theoretical perspective guiding the criticism.

Interpretation was once a strongly contested term in criticism. Some critics held that rhetorical criticism should involve a minimum of interpretation. For example, Barnett Baskerville, writing at a time (1953) when critics looked primarily at speeches, suggested that they were fairly straightforward in their meaning. They are "seldom abstruse or esoteric. . . . A speech, by its nature, is or should be immediately comprehensible, hence the interpretive function of the critics is seldom paramount."[47] Not all critics agreed with Baskerville on the nature of interpretation. Thomas R. Nilsen, for example, wrote a few years later that "if within the meaning of the speech are included the many attendant responses, the more subtle understanding and conceptions evoked by the speech and their possible consequences, then interpretation is a much needed function of the critic."[48] By the late 1970s some degree of interpretation had become an accepted part of criticism. Critic Michael Leff pointed out that it is with "the act of interpretation by which the critic attempts to account for and assign meaning to the rhetorical dimensions of a given phenomenon."[49] Such interpretations can focus on the external or internal dynamics of a rhetorical artifact. External interpretations focus on how the rhetorical artifact interacts with the situation that surrounds it, and internal interpretations focus on how different parts of the rhetorical artifact act together in forming a whole.

On January 8, 2020, President Donald J. Trump delivered an important speech in response to a tense international situation with Iran. In addition to addressing the nascent crisis, the speech also allows us to explore the dual critical functions of analysis and interpretation. Prior to this speech, on December 27, 2019, Iranian proxies launched rockets at an Iraqi air base that killed an Iraqi American civilian contractor and injured several American soldiers,[50] and on December 31, 2019, Iran-backed supporters of an Iraqi Shia militia attacked the American embassy in Baghdad. In partial response to these and other Iranian-backed actions, on January 3, 2020, President Trump ordered the drone attack near Baghdad International Airport that killed Major General Qassem Soleimani, head of Iran's Qud Force, and a known terrorist leader responsible for over six hundred American deaths and thousands of Muslim deaths.[51] In response to this strike, on January 7, Iran launched more than a dozen ballistic missiles at two U.S. air bases in Iraq which, although destroying some infrastructure, claimed no lives. According to American news media, these "recent developments were expected to spark global fear of a US war in the Middle East."[52] On January 8, 2020, President Trump delivered his speech in response to this situation with Iran.

An *analysis* could discover many things about this speech, including basic facts or President Trump's characterization of Iran. It is important to focus on what is actually in a speech (or other rhetorical artifact) before moving on to interpretation. Some media outlets failed to do this, making embarrassing mistakes in the process of analysis. For instance *Rolling Stone* magazine said it was a fifteen-minute speech when it was only slightly longer than nine minutes,[53] and the *Palmer Report* stressed that a general standing behind the president gave a "horrified look" when Trump mentioned hypersonic missiles, implying that the president had leaked that "which appeared to have been classified information."[54] Yet video shows that there was no such horrified look from either general in attendance,[55] and even a cursory glance at the topic shows that it is no secret America possesses hypersonic missile technology.[56] In terms of President Trump's characterization of Iran in the speech, consider these passages:

> As long as I am President of the United States, Iran will never be allowed to have a nuclear weapon.
> For far too long—all the way back to 1979, to be exact—nations have tolerated Iran's destructive and destabilizing behavior in the Middle East and beyond. Those days are over. Iran has been the leading sponsor of terrorism, and their pursuit of nuclear weapons threatens the civilized world. We will never let that happen.
> Peace and stability cannot prevail in the Middle East as long as Iran continues to foment violence, unrest, hatred, and war. The civilized world must send a clear and unified message to the Iranian regime: Your campaign of terror, murder, mayhem will not be tolerated any longer. It will not be allowed to go forward.[57]

Analysis allows us to see these statements as characterizations of Iran; beyond this, analysis ends and interpretation begins. Just what do these characterizations mean? In criticism, one usually finds interpretation of content linked with the theoretical perspective used, or to an individual critic's personal point of view. For instance, the *Washington Post* published this interpretation of the speech:

Trump's Iran policy has been a catastrophic failure. "The civilized world must send a clear and unified message to the Iranian regime: Your campaign of terror, murder, mayhem will not be tolerated any longer," Trump said. But that in itself is an acknowledgment of his own failure.

When the president came into office, we had a painstakingly negotiated agreement that by the consensus of the entire international community was successfully restraining Iran's nuclear program. Trump not only abandoned that deal, he instituted a "maximum pressure" campaign against Iran, arguing that if we crippled their economy, they'd become less aggressive in the region and crawl back to the negotiating table, whereupon they'd give us whatever concessions we asked for.

The very fact that we're in the position we are now demonstrates that this policy has failed.[58]

Of course, such assertions are a form of argument and thus would necessitate that the author provide evidence that other nations felt the nonproliferation deal was working, and also an explanation as to why, after the signing of the deal, Iran's military and terrorist-related provocations were increasing, not decreasing. In criticism, interpretations are more than opinion and need evidence as well.

Importantly, there are often alternate interpretations. Take, for instance, this interpretation of Trump's speech published by CNN:

What was clear throughout Trump's speech . . . was that he did not want to be perceived as backing down from an enemy. The first words he uttered were: "As long as I am president, Iran will never have a nuclear weapon." And within minutes, he echoed his initial statement: "Iran has been the leading sponsor of terrorism and their pursuit of nuclear weapons threatens the civilized world. We will never let that happen."

Trump also repeatedly noted that he was doing things that should have been done by past presidents. "Soleimani's hands were drenched in both American and Iranian blood," said Trump at one point. "He should have been terminated long ago."

This isn't your father's (or Obama's or Bush's) United States, Trump seemed to be saying. *We are de-escalating for the moment. But don't assume that we won't re-escalate if you, Iran, keep poking at us.*[59] [italics in original]

In the end, these examples might make it seem as if analysis and interpretation are two separate steps. That is not the case at all. The very first step a critic takes, deciding what the rhetorical artifact actually is, is itself an interpretive act. For instance, is President Trump's speech an attempt to stand strong against Iran, an attempt to save face, or a statement of policy? We separate out these steps (analysis-interpretation) for the sake of discussion. As you write criticism, become aware of how analysis and interpretation comingle and energize each other. On this point, Michael Leff cogently wrote,

The act of interpretation mediates between the experiences of the critic and the forms of experience expressed in the [rhetorical artifact]. To perform this act successfully, critics must vibrate what they see in the [rhetorical artifact] against their own expectations and predilections. What critics are trained to look for and what they see interact in creative tension; the two elements blend and separate, progressively changing as altered conceptions of the one reshape the configuration of the other.[60]

Through the analysis and interpretation section of your essay, you share your insight and understanding of the artifact, and you actively make a case for your conclusions, which leads to the final component of a criticism essay: evaluation.

Evaluation

Evaluation of the rhetorical artifact boils down to the judgments you make about it. However, judgment is more than an expression of like or dislike. It necessitates first that you know the thing that you are studying; it also necessitates that your judgments are shared with the goal of enriching both understanding and appreciation. Judgments may certainly be made, and appreciation or disdain expressed, but they must be made after two conditions are met: one, the fair-minded description of the inner workings of the rhetorical artifact have been presented for the world to see, and two, the standards of judgment used by the critic are provided for all to see. In short, the expression of judgment is conjoined with the reasons you think the way you do. The standards of judgments used will differ depending on the type of rhetorical perspective used and also on the critic's personality. As you acquire information on the different theoretical perspectives contained in this textbook, notice what type of information they allow you to gather about the rhetorical artifacts. This is a clue about the types of value judgments a particular perspective allows. Usually these will revolve around differing combinations of the ethics, effects, truth, and aesthetics involved in the rhetorical transaction.[61] The standards of judgment on which you rely should flow from the perspective you use to examine the rhetorical artifact; thus, how the concepts above will be understood is directly related to the perspective you use.

Choice of Theoretical Perspective

Another important issue facing critics is the seemingly easy decision concerning *which perspective to use in their critical endeavor*. Simply put, how will a critic go about producing criticism? As you read additional chapters in this book, you will most likely find that a certain perspective appeals to you. You may not know why, but you seem to gravitate toward it; you just like it for some reason. It seems natural for you to use, and as you use it, you become increasingly familiar with its nuances and potentials. Some critics are well known for producing insightful and nuanced work using a particular perspective. For example, Andrew King is well known for using Burkean theory in his work; Marilyn Young's work using the situational perspective is another such example; critical rhetoric and the name Raymie McKerrow are no strangers; and so on with many of the chapter authors in this textbook.

Perspectives are not to be used as templates or rubrics, however. Although they do suggest a particular way of viewing the world, as the critic you must direct the criticism. When novice critics first begin to use a perspective, they often do apply it *rigidly* to the rhetorical artifact. Yet criticism, like any activity worthy of learning well, benefits from practice. As critics become more knowledgeable about the perspective they use, they often become more *flexible* in its application, allowing for personal insight and interests to guide the criticism. The personality of the critic begins to blend with the perspective used. The best criticism involves this. As Michael Leff has written, "Interpretation is not a scientific endeavor. Systematic principles are useful in attempting to validate interpretations, but the actual process of interpretation depends on conjectures and insights particular to the object [rhetorical artifact] at hand."[62]

Regardless of the perspective chosen, a critic must be cautious in its application. Perspectives are to help a critic, not control the criticism; a successful critic's ideas blend in with those of the perspective. Perspectives are not molds into which rhetorical artifacts are to be poured—eventuating in mechanistic and rigid criticism—what some call *cookie-cutter criticism*. Black puts this idea, and the consequences, in proper perspective:

Because only the critic is the instrument of criticism, the critic's relationship to other instruments will profoundly affect the value of critical inquiry. And in criticism, every instrument has to be assimilated to the critic, to have become an integral part of the critic's mode of perception. A critic who is influenced by, for example, [Burkean dramatism] and who, in consequence of that influence, comes to see some things in a characteristically dramatistic way—that critic is still able to function in his own person as the critical instrument, and so the possibility of significant disclosure remains open to him. But the would-be critic who has not internalized [Burkean dramatism], who undertakes to "use" it as a mathematician would use a formula—such a critic is certain (yes, *certain*!) to produce work that is sterile. An act of criticism conducted on mechanistic assumptions will, not surprisingly, yield mechanistic criticism.[63]

Some critics, myself included, take the process of assimilation one step further by blending and developing their own framework from which to proceed with criticism. This type of criticism is often called *eclectic* criticism, and is discussed in chapter 13; it involves "the selection of the best standards and principles from various systems of ideas."[64]

Initial Approach

Yet another issue involves *how one should approach a rhetorical artifact* (what Ed Black below calls rhetorical "transactions"). Should one begin with a theoretical orientation or should one begin with the artifact itself?[65] Black described this distinction as *etic* and *emic* orientations. One using an etic orientation "approaches a rhetorical transaction from outside of that transaction and interprets the transaction in terms of pre-existing theory"; in contrast, one using an emic orientation "approaches a rhetorical transaction in what is hoped to be its own terms, without conscious expectations drawn from any sources other than the rhetorical transaction itself."[66] These orientations are quite distinct, and although there are instances in which they might blend, such are infrequently encountered.

Both orientations have strengths and weaknesses. An etic orientation allows for a fuller development of rhetorical theory. The major end of criticism would be to develop and advance rhetorical theory, thus adding to our overall knowledge concerning human communication. A potential weakness with the etic orientation is that critics may very well find exactly what they expect to find, even if it is not really there in the rhetorical artifact; in short, the rhetorical artifact is sometimes forced into a mold. An emic orientation allows for a more nuanced description of the rhetorical artifact and also provides more room for the critic's personality and intuition to play a part in the criticism. A weakness with the emic orientation can arise because critics may "aspire to so sympathetic an account [during the descriptive and analysis/ interpretive phases of criticism] that the critic's audience will understand that object as, in some sense, *inevitable*."[67] This is to say that the rhetorical artifact might be viewed as never having experienced the possibility of being in any other form, that those who created it had no choice but to create it in the form they did. On this point Leff wrote, "The critic at some point . . . in the interpretive process comes to form a conception of the object as a whole. . . . This conception . . . is something other than the actual expression in the text; otherwise, there would be no interpretation. Consequently, while still engaged in the interpretive act, the critic constructs a meaning for the object, an hypothesis or model that explains what it is."[68] The difficulty in this process lies with the "good faith" of the critic. After such a sympathetic account of the rhetorical artifact, the critic might find it challenging to return to a more objective role during the evaluative phase of criticism.[69]

Objectivity or Subjectivity?

Yet another concern involves *the notion of criticism as an objective or a subjective (even political) endeavor*. It is clear that criticism is not a scientific act; the very best criticism involves the personality, insights, and imagination of a critic. Yet for all that, there are critics—I among them—who maintain that a certain degree of objectivity is necessary for honest, productive criticism. I do not mean that critics ought to possess or are capable of possessing a computer-like detachment from the object of criticism. This would surely produce a sterile criticism devoid of its lifeblood: the critic's intermingled intuition, insight, and personality. What I am suggesting with the term *objective criticism* is that the critic approach the artifact under consideration with a fair and open mind, with a *detached curiosity*. In this sense the critic sets aside personal politics or ideological "truths" and approaches the artifact with a sense of curiosity. The artifact under consideration should not be altered to fit the prejudgments of the critic but allowed to voice its inner workings to the world. The work of the critic is to make certain that this voice is intelligible to and approachable by the public.

This in no way detracts from the critic's bringing to bear an individual stamp upon the criticism produced; nor is it the antiseptic application of theory upon an unsuspecting rhetorical artifact. It suggests instead that the critic must learn how to appreciate the inner workings of a text, even if, personally, the critic abhors the artifact or wishes it to be other than it is. In this sense, the critic is being "objective," or disinterested, when approaching and describing a text.[70] My notion of objectivity is somewhat similar to the notion of "appreciation" put forth by Lawrence W. Rosenfield. I position my notion of objective criticism between a politically partisan criticism and detached scientific objectivity; Rosenfield positions "appreciation" between ideologically driven criticism and scientific objectivity. For Rosenfield, appreciation is "founded on an inherent love of the world, while [scientific] objectivity, the effort to establish distance on the world (for whatever laudable ends) sometimes betrays an essential distrust of the world, a fear that one will be contaminated in some manner if one is open to its unconcealment."[71]

Although I agree heartily with Rosenfield that "partisan involvement may be a civic virtue, but insight derived therefrom must be continually suspect,"[72] other critics disagree with us, as you will discover while reading some of the chapters that follow. For these critics, the act of criticism involves a more active attempt at persuasion of their audience in all three phases of criticism—description, analysis/interpretation, and evaluation. Very often the direction of this persuasion takes its cue from the political ideology of the critic. For example, Robert L. Ivie defined productive criticism as "a detailed and *partisan* critique."[73] According to Ivie, a critic "intentionally produces a strategic interpretation, or structure of meaning, that privileges selective interests . . . in specific circumstances."[74] The purpose of criticism is made clear: those who engage in rhetorical criticism are, or should be, advocates. Viewed in this manner, "criticism, as a specific performance of general rhetorical knowledge, yields a form of scholarship that obtains social relevance by strategically reconstructing the interpretive design of civic discourse in order to diminish, bolster, or redirect its significance. [Criticism] is a form of advocacy."[75]

Often some attempt at political fairness is made, although the result is still the politicization of the critical act. For example, Michael Calvin McGee wrote, when relating oneself to criticism, "the first thing a rhetorician should do is to identify her political orientation. Her syllabus should contain a paragraph describing the trajectory of her course. Her book should have a Chapter that aligns her politics with that politics practiced in the workaday world by political parties competing for control of the State. She must be fair, describing the politics of those who disagree with her in a light that leans more toward portraiture than caricature."[76]

However, regardless of such an attempt, I agree with Rosenfield when he asserts that a difficulty with ideological criticism is that the "very notion of commitment to an ideology, no matter what its value system, implies a kind of immunity to those experiences of the world which in any way contradict the ideology."[77] Further clarifying this politicization of criticism, McGee expressed, "That which [ideologically driven] critics do today is proactive, openly political in its acknowledgment of its bias and its agenda to produce practical theories of culture and of social relations (including political relations)," and thus appears to embrace the very situation Rosenfield described above.[78]

Although summarizing a much larger conversation on this topic, the positions advanced are clear. On the one hand we have critics striving to keep personal politics from the initial stages of the criticism—most notably, during the description and analysis phases of the critical act. This position presupposes that part of the purpose of criticism is to produce knowledge that disputants can draw upon when making decisions about how to live—academic critics should not be partisan agents of social change. On the other hand we have academic critics allowing their personal politics to guide them during all three stages of criticism. This position presupposes that critics begin by seeing the world differently than the public they seek to persuade and that the job of the critic is to produce partisan social change in the direction of that critic's choosing.[79] A good example of this contrast is found when looking at the chapters on traditional criticism and feminist criticism.[80] For an outstanding examination of this tension, see the cogent essay by Edwin Black, "On Objectivity and Politics in Criticism" in appendix D.

WRAPPING UP

We have covered a great deal of ground in this chapter. Most notably we have explored the definition and nature of criticism, particularly rhetorical criticism. We specifically looked at how criticism is a method of generating new knowledge just as the scientific method is a method of generating new knowledge. The three stages of the critical act (conceptual, communication, and counter-communication) alerted us to basic elements involved in producing good criticism, and also to rhetorical perspectives. Finally, we looked at four key concerns in criticism today: what to include in our criticism (description, analysis/interpretation, and evaluation), the choice of a theoretical perspective, how to initially approach a rhetorical artifact, and objectivity and subjectivity in criticism.

The chapters that follow will give you a sense of the variety and artistry of rhetorical criticism. As you move through each chapter, you will find that the way the author(s) practice criticism both modifies and moves beyond the definition I shared with you in this chapter. Take note of *how* the nature and scope of criticism changes in each chapter. Criticism is not a sterile endeavor, and you will find that some of the chapters resonate more strongly with you than do others. Just like rhetoric, criticism is nuanced and may be understood on many different levels. Each chapter that follows underscores this idea and presents a point of view that will add rich variety to your overall understanding of the critical act.

SUGGESTED READINGS

Black, Edwin. *Rhetorical Criticism: A Study in Method*, ix–xv, 1–9. Madison: University of Wisconsin Press, 1978.

Brockriede, Wayne. "Rhetorical Criticism as Argument." *Quarterly Journal of Speech* 60 (April 1974): 165–174.

Jasinski, James. "Criticism in Contemporary Rhetorical Studies." In *Sourcebook on Rhetoric*, 125–144. Thousand Oaks, CA: Sage Publications, 2001.

Kuypers, Jim A., ed. *Purpose, Practice, and Pedagogy in Rhetorical Criticism.* Lanham, MD: Lexington Books, 2014.

Rosenfield, Lawrence W. "The Experience of Criticism." *Quarterly Journal of Speech* 60, no. 4 (1974): 489–496.

DISCUSSION QUESTIONS

1. How is criticism a "humanizing" activity?
2. Where would you draw the line between analysis and interpretation? Where does one end and the other begin?
3. Review the definition of objective criticism. Can criticism be objective? Should it be objective?
4. Should theory building be a part of the critical process? If so, explain how.

ACTIVITIES

1. Think of a time when a friend or family member talked to you at length. Describe what was said. Taking the definition of rhetoric provided in the previous chapter, analyze and then interpret what was said.
2. In a small group, discuss your preference for either the emic or etic approach toward criticism.
3. In a small group, discuss which interpretation of President Trump's speech about Iran makes more sense to you. Go to the original sources and then make your case.

NOTES

1. James Andrews, Michael C. Leff, and Robert Terrill, "The Nature of Criticism: An Overview," in *Reading Rhetorical Texts: An Introduction to Criticism* (Boston: Houghton Mifflin, 1998), 6.

2. Donald C. Bryant, *Rhetorical Dimensions in Criticism* (Baton Rouge: Louisiana State University Press, 1973), 25.

3. Wayne Brockriede, "Rhetorical Criticism as Argument," *Quarterly Journal of Speech* 60 (April 1974): 165.

4. Bryant, *Rhetorical Dimensions*, 35. These characteristics might well appear in other forms of criticism, and Bryant points out that in "rhetorical criticism . . . the essential *external* reference of discourse, the context both immediate and antecedent, the suasory potential in the situation, plays an organic part different from the part it plays in other criticism" (35).

5. Marie Hochmuth Nichols, *Rhetoric and Criticism* (Baton Rouge: Louisiana State University Press, 1963), 7.

6. See "The Experiential Perspective," in *Methods of Rhetorical Criticism: A Twentieth-Century Perspective*, 3rd ed., ed. Bernard L. Brock, Robert L. Scott, and James W. Chesebro, 85–95 (Detroit, MI: Wayne State University Press, 1989).

7. Edwin Black, *Rhetorical Criticism: A Study in Method* (Madison: University of Wisconsin Press, 1978), x–xi.

8. Marie Kathryn Hochmuth, "The Criticism of Rhetoric," in *A History and Criticism of American Public Address*, vol. 3, ed. Marie Kathryn Hochmuth (New York: Russell and Russell, 1954), 13. Hochmuth later changed her name to Marie Hochmuth Nichols.

9. Edwin Black, "On Objectivity and Politics in Criticism," *American Communication Journal* 4, no. 1 (2000), http://ac-journal.org/journal/vol4/iss1/special/black.htm.

10. This is not to say that one could not orally deliver criticism. Certainly a critic could prepare a response as a speech or public presentation. One could even prepare criticism for a podcast or YouTube video. Since the majority of academic criticism is written, my primary focus is on that form in this chapter.

11. Black, *Rhetorical Criticism*, 6.

12. Craig R. Smith, "Criticism of Political Rhetoric and Disciplinary Integrity," *American Communication Journal* 4, no. 1 (2000), http://ac-journal.org/journal/vol4/iss1/special/smith.htm.

13. For a complete time line of the situation, see Louis Bien, "A Complete Timeline of the Ray Rice Assault Case," *SB Nation*, November 28, 2014, http://www.sbnation.com/nfl/2014/5/23/5744964/rayrice-arrest-assault-statement-apology-ravens.

14. The State of New Jersey vs. Raymell White, Complaint Number 0102-S-2014-000728, February 15, 2014, http://gamedayrcom.c.presscdn.com/wp-content/uploads/2014/02/ray-rice-police-report-arrest-hit-girlfriend.jpg.

15. For a different perspective on this incident, see: William L. Benoit, "Roger Goodell's Image Repair on the Ray Rice Suspension," *Relevant Rhetoric* 9 (2018), http://www.relevantrhetoric.com/Roger%20Goodell's%20Image%20Repair.pdf.

16. Video of the speech can be viewed here: https://www.youtube.com/watch?v=WJBkG_kyqxI.

17. "Full Transcript from Ray Rice News Conference," *Baltimore Sun*, May 23, 2014, http://www.baltimoresun.com/sports/ravens/ravens-insider/bal-full-transcript-from-ray-rice-news-conference-20140523-story.html.

18. Ibid.

19. Ibid.

20. This is where using rhetorical theory and previous examples of criticism could come in. For instance, I could use Bruce E. Gronbeck, "Underestimating Generic Expectations: Clinton's Apologies of August 17, 1998," *American Communication Journal* 2, no. 2 (February 1999), http://ac-journal.org/journal/vol2/Iss2/editorials/gronbeck/index.html. Or perhaps look at the classic study by B. L. Ware and Wil A. Linkugel, "They Spoke in Defense of Themselves: On the Generic Criticism of Apologia," *Quarterly Journal of Speech* 59 (1973): 273–283. The insights these critics share concerning how apologia works could then influence how I see Rice's speech and what insights I might have.

21. "Full Transcript from Ray Rice News Conference."

22. Ibid.

23. Ibid.

24. Cindy Boren, "Ray Rice Apologizes for Domestic Violence Incident, Calls It 'Biggest Mistake of My Life,'" *Washington Post* (*The Early Lead* blog), July 31, 2014, http://www.washingtonpost.com/blogs/early-lead/wp/2014/07/31/ray-rice-apologizes-for-domestic-violence-incident-calls-it-biggest-mistake-of-my-life.

25. Brock, Scott, and Chesebro, *Methods of Rhetorical Criticism*, 13.

26. Brockriede, "Rhetorical Criticism as Argument," 165–174.

27. Ibid., 166.

28. Ibid., 167.

29. Raymie E. McKerrow, "Criticism Is as Criticism Does," *Western Journal of Communication* 77, no. 5 (2013): 547.

30. For instance, see Ronald Matlon and Sylvia Ortiz, *Index to Journals in Communication Studies through 1995* (Annandale, VA: National Communication Association, 1997).

31. Lawrence W. Rosenfield, "The Experience of Criticism," *Quarterly Journal of Speech* 60, no. 4 (1974): 491.

32. Mike Allen, "Special Section: What Constitutes Publishable Rhetorical Scholarship: Heavy Lies the Editor's Fingers on the Keyboard," *Communication Studies* 54, no. 3 (2003): 355.

33. James Darsey, "Must We All Be Rhetorical Theorists? An Anti-Democratic Inquiry," *Western Journal of Communication* 58 (1994): 173.

34. See also the discussions about the purpose of criticism in Jim A. Kuypers, ed., *Purpose, Practice, and Pedagogy in Rhetorical Criticism* (Lanham, MD: Lexington Press, 2014).

35. Stephen E. Lucas, "Renaissance of American Public Address: Text and Context in Rhetorical Criticism," in *Landmark Essays on American Public Address*, ed. Martin J. Medhurst (Davis, CA: Hermagoras Press, 1993), 199.

36. Brockriede, "Rhetorical Criticism as Argument," 173.

37. Black, "On Objectivity."

38. McKerrow, "Criticism Is as Criticism Does," 546.

39. For an example of this discussion, see the special issue on the subject of theory in academic criticism titled, "The Role of Theory in Critical Rhetoric," in *Western Journal of Communication* 77, no. 5 (2013). See also Allen, "Special Section: What Constitutes Publishable Rhetorical Scholarship: Heavy Lies the Editor's Fingers."

40. William L. Nosthstine, Carole Blair, and Gary A. Copeland, *Critical Questions: Invention, Creativity, and the Criticism of Discourse and Media* (New York: St. Martin's, 1994), 34. See also Darsey, "Must We All Be Rhetorical Theorists?"

41. James Jasinski, "The Status of Theory and Method in Rhetorical Criticism," *Western Journal of Communication* 65, no. 3 (2001): 252.

42. Sonja K. Foss, "Constituted by Agency: The Discourse and Practice of Rhetorical Criticism," in *Speech Communication: Essays to Commemorate the 75th Anniversary of the Speech Communication Association*, ed. Gerald M. Phillips and Julia T. Wood (Carbondale: Southern Illinois University Press, 1990), 34–35. This view is in keeping with that expressed by Roderick Hart, "Contemporary Scholarship in Public Address: A Research Editorial," *Western Journal of Speech Communication* 50 (1986): 283–295. See, too, the collection of essays in the *Western Journal of Communication* 77, no. 5 (2013), which, in summary, essentially state that, *at the very least*, "editors, reviewers, and authors should give priority to explicit contributions to theory" (558).

43. Richard B. Gregg, "The Criticism of Symbolic Inducement: A Critical-Theoretical Connection," in *Speech Communication in the Twentieth Century*, ed. Thomas W. Benson (Carbondale: Southern Illinois University Press, 1985), 60.

44. Jim A. Kuypers, "Artistry, Purpose, and Academic Constraints in Rhetorical Criticism," in *Purpose, Practice, and Pedagogy in Rhetorical Criticism*, ed. Jim A. Kuypers (Lanham, MD: Lexington Books, 2014), 87.

45. Additional signs of the potential turn toward appreciation of unique insight over theory generation or extension can be found in several of the chapters in Jim A. Kuypers, ed., *Purpose, Practice, and Pedagogy in Rhetorical Criticism* (Lanham, MD: Lexington Books, 2014).

46. John W. Jordan, Kathryn M. Olson, and Steven R. Goldzwig, "Continuing the Conversation on 'What Constitutes Publishable Rhetorical Criticism?': A Response," *Communication Studies* 54, no. 3 (2003): 401–402.

47. Barnett Baskerville, "The Critical Method in Speech," *Central States Speech Journal* 4, no. 1 (1953): 2.

48. Thomas R. Nilsen, "Interpretive Function of the Critic," *Western Speech* 21, no. 2 (1957): 70. Essay reprinted in Thomas R. Nilsen, ed., *Essays on Rhetorical Criticism* (New York: Random House, 1968), 86 97.

49. Michael Leff, "Interpretation and the Art of the Rhetorical Critic," *Western Journal of Speech Communication* 44 (1980): 342.

50. Elizabeth McLaughlin and Luis Martinez, "US Civilian Contractor Killed, Several Troops Injured in Rocket Attack on Iraqi Military Base," ABC News, December 27, 2019, https://abcnews.go.com/Politics/us-civilian-contractor-killed-troops-injured-rocket-attack/story?id=67949811.

51. For an example of this, see: Monica Showalter, "Photos: Top 10 Atrocities from the Now-Vaunted Soleimani," *American Thinker*, January 5, 2020, https://www.americanthinker.com/blog/2020/01/photos_top_10_atrocities_from_the_lefts_vaunted_soleimani.html#.XhI_gkZ_Vrk.twitter; Chris Pleasance, "Terrorist General with the Blood of THOUSANDS on His Hands: Qassem Soleimani Masterminded the Killing of Hundreds of US Troops in IED Attacks, Helped Assad Slaughter His People in Syria, Was an Ally of Hezbollah and 'More Powerful than Iran's President,'" *DailyMail*, January 3, 2020, https://www.dailymail.co.uk/news/article-7847905/Qassem-Soleimani-terrorist-general-blood-THOUSANDS-hands.html.

52. Luis Martinez and Elizabeth McLaughlin, "Iran Launches Missiles at US Military Facilities in Iraq, Pentagon Confirms," ABC News, January 7, 2020, https://abcnews.go.com/International/iran-launches-missiles-us-air-bases-iraq-us/story?id=68130625.

53. Andy Kroll, "None of Trump's Iran Policy Makes Sense. All of It Is Dangerous," *Rolling Stone*, January 8, 2020, https://www.rollingstone.com/politics/politics-news/trump-iran-speech-madman-theory-935117/.

54. Bill Palmer, "Donald Trump Sniffs and Slurs His Way through Lifeless, Confused, Incoherent Iran Speech," *Palmer Report*, January 8, 2020, https://www.palmerreport.com/analysis/sniffs-slurs-confused-speech-donald-trump/24254/.

55. Video can be viewed here: "Watch President Trump's Speech after Iran's Strike," CNN, January 8, 2020, https://www.youtube.com/watch?v=5PEyPez-5H8.

56. See https://www.lockheedmartin.com/en-us/capabilities/hypersonics.html, and Amanda M. Macias, "US Successfully Flies Its Newest Hypersonic Missile on B-52 Bomber, Lockheed-Martin says," CNBC, June 17, 2019, https://www.cnbc.com/2019/06/17/us-air-force-successfully-flies-its-newest-hypersonic-missile-on-its-mighty-b-52-bomber.html.

57. Donald J. Trump, "Remarks by President Trump on Iran," White House, January 8, 2020, https://ee.usembassy.gov/remarks-by-president-trump-on-iran/.

58. Paul Waldman, "Opinion: Five Takeaways from Trump's Garbled Speech on Iran," *Washington Post*, January 8, 2020, https://www.washingtonpost.com/opinions/2020/01/08/five-takeaways-trumps-deranged-speech-iran/.

59. Chris Cillizza, "Donald Trump Takes the Off-Ramp in Iran Confrontation (for Now)," CNN, January 8, 2020, https://www.cnn.com/2020/01/08/politics/trump-iran-speech/index.html.

60. Leff, "Interpretation," 345.

61. For detailed examples of these, see Karlyn Kohrs Campbell and Thomas R. Burkholder, *Critiques of Contemporary Rhetoric*, 2nd ed. (Belmont, CA: Wadsworth, 1997), 109–127.

62. Leff, "Interpretation," 343–344.

63. Black, *Rhetorical Criticism*, xii. The pentad is explained in chapter 10.

64. Pauline Kael, *I Lost It at the Movies* (Boston, MA: Little, Brown, 1964), 309.

65. This is not a new problem in rhetorical theory. See Leff, "Interpretation."

66. Edwin Black, "A Note on Theory and Practice in Rhetorical Criticism," *Western Journal of Speech Communication* 44 (1980): 331–332.

67. Black, "A Note on Theory and Practice," 334.

68. Leff, "Interpretation," 345.

69. For a different take on the etic/emic orientation that includes a methodological suggestion for emic criticism, see W. Charles Redding, "Extrinsic and Intrinsic Criticism," in *Essays on Rhetorical Criticism*, ed. Thomas R. Nilsen (New York: Random House, 1968), 98–125.

70. This section based on Jim A. Kuypers, "Must We All Be Political Activists?," *American Communication Journal* 4, no. 1 (2000), http://ac-journal.org/journal/vol4/iss1/special/kuypers.htm.

71. Rosenfield, "The Experience of Criticism," 495.

72. Ibid., 492.

73. Robert L. Ivie, "A Question of Significance," *Quarterly Journal of Speech* 80, no. 4 (1994), emphasis mine.

74. Robert L. Ivie, "Productive Criticism," *Quarterly Journal of Speech* 81, no. 1 (1995).

75. Robert L. Ivie, "The Social Relevance of Rhetorical Scholarship," *Quarterly Journal of Speech* 81, no. 2 (1994).

76. Michael Calvin McGee, "On Objectivity and Politics in Rhetoric," *American Communication Journal* 4, no. 3 (2001), http://ac-journal.org/journal/vol4/iss3/special/mcgee.htm.

77. Rosenfield, "The Experience of Criticism," 494.

78. McGee, "On Objectivity."

79. How and why we practice rhetorical criticism is an ongoing conversation. Those seeking to better understand the changing nature of our critical practices have a wonderful resource in the following special collections of essays published in 1957, 1980, 1990, 2000, and 2001. Taken together they present a wonderful opportunity for students of rhetoric to better understand criticism's changing nature. See "Symposium: Criticism and Public Address," ed. Ernest Wrage, in *Western Speech* 21 (1957). These essays were later reprinted along with five others in Thomas R. Nilsen, ed., *Essays on Rhetorical Criticism* (New York: Random House, 1968). See also, "Special Report: Rhetorical Criticism; The State of the Art," ed. Michael C. Leff, *Western Journal of Speech Communication* 44, no. 4 (1980); "Special Issue on Rhetorical Criticism," ed. John Angus Campbell, *Western Journal of Speech Communication* 54, no. 3 (1990); and "Special Issue: Rhetorical Criticism; The State of the Art Revisited," *Western Journal of Speech Communication* 65, no. 3 (2001). One might also consider Kuypers, ed., *Purpose, Practice, and Pedagogy in Rhetorical Criticism.*

A critical exchange focusing on the purposes of rhetorical criticism is found in "Criticism, Politics, and Objectivity," ed. Jim A. Kuypers, *American Communication Journal* 4, no. 1 (2000), http://ac-journal.org/journal/vol4/iss1/index.htm; "Rhetoric, Politics, and Critique," ed. Mark Huglen, *American Communication Journal* 4, no. 3 (2001), http://ac-journal.org/journal/vol4/iss3/index.htm; and the final essay in the exchange, Jim A. Kuypers, "Criticism, Politics, and Objectivity: *Redivivus*," *American Communication Journal* 5, no. 1 (2001), http://ac-journal.org/journal/vol5/iss1/special/kuypersresponse.htm.

Another resource on the historical changes in rhetorical criticism is the special issue of *Rhetoric Review* dedicated to Ed Black. See "Interdisciplinary Perspectives on Rhetorical Criticism," *Rhetoric Review* 25, no. 4 (2006).

80. For an overview of this tension between criticism geared toward an end goal of understanding and appreciation and criticism as ideologically motivated, see Jim A. Kuypers, "The Rhetorical River," *Southern Communication Journal* 73, no. 4 (2008): 350–358. For an excellent essay that explores a method of criticism that mixes elements of both types of criticism, see Jason Edward Black, "Paddling the Rhetorical River, Revisiting the Social Actor: Rhetorical Criticism as Both Appreciation and Intervention," in *Purpose, Practice, and Pedagogy in Rhetorical Criticism*, ed. Jim A. Kuypers, 7–22 (Lanham, MD: Lexington Books, 2014).

4

Understanding Rhetorical Situations

Marilyn J. Young and Kathleen Farrell

Lloyd F. Bitzer defines a **rhetorical situation** as "a complex of persons, events, objects, and relations presenting an actual or potential exigence which can be completely or partially removed if discourse introduced into the situation can so constrain human decision or action as to bring about the significant modification of the exigence."[1] Further, he writes, in "any rhetorical situation there will be at least one controlling exigence which functions as the organizing principle: it specifies the audience to be addressed and the change to be effected."[2] The rhetorical audience, then, is that which can alleviate the exigence. There are three main parts to the rhetorical situation: the **exigence** is "an imperfection marked by urgency; it is a defect, an obstacle, something waiting to be done, a thing which is other than it should be";[3] the **audience**, which is the group of persons who have the power to modify the exigence, is the second component. Bitzer also wrote of **constraints**, which are an important consideration in that they influence both what can be said and what should not be said:

> [Constraints are] made up of persons, events, objects, and relations which are parts of the situation because they have the power to constrain decision and action needed to modify the exigence. Standard sources of constraint include beliefs, attitudes, documents, facts, traditions, images, interests, motives and the like; and when the orator enters the situation, his discourse not only harnesses constraints given by the situation but provides additional important constraints—for example his personal character, his logical proofs, and his style.[4]

USING THE RHETORICAL SITUATION

Although the rhetorical situation's utility can be applied to contemporary events such as the use of Twitter in presidential campaigns[5] or the use of internet-based résumés,[6] looking back at historical events can be particularly helpful in illustrating how the above concepts work.[7] Thus, as an example, when President Franklin Roosevelt addressed Congress following the Japanese attack on Pearl Harbor, he was responding to that attack as the controlling exigence. The attack would seem to require a response in kind—a declaration of war. Yet Roosevelt was constrained by the Constitution, which grants Congress the responsibility for declarations of war. The attack, then, required Roosevelt to ask Congress to declare war on Japan; in that way, the controlling exigence (the attack) entailed the necessary audience (Congress) and the action to be taken (the declaration of war).

Yet it was not enough for Roosevelt to merely address Congress, for even with a declaration of war, Roosevelt needed the support of the American people. It is also true that the public needed to hear from the president in this time of crisis. In light of this, his speech was designed to respond to two exigencies: the need for a declaration of war and the need of the people to hear from their leader.[8]

Compare this rhetorical situation to that which confronted President George W. Bush following the 9/11 attacks on the World Trade Center and the Pentagon in 2001, some sixty years later. How were these situations different? In this case it was not immediately obvious who was responsible for the attacks; yet even when the instigators had been identified, Bush did not seek a declaration of war. When he spoke to the American people, Bush announced the military action he had ordered against Afghanistan; he did not ask either Congress or the people for permission. In the years since Pearl Harbor, presidents have found ways around the requirement to seek a declaration from Congress, relying instead on their authority as commander in chief of the armed forces; in fact, no president has asked for a declaration of war since Roosevelt in 1941, even though the United States has been involved in hostilities in several countries. So we must ask ourselves, "What is the exigence, who is the audience, and what are the constraints?" What has changed since 1941 and the attack on Pearl Harbor?

Public Knowledge and Rhetorical Situations

Bitzer's ideas about the rhetorical situation are best understood when considered in relation to his notions of **public knowledge**, where he articulates his understanding of the role of the public in rhetorical practice.[9] When he refers to the "public," Bitzer is not referring to the audience, although these concepts may overlap. Bitzer's construction of the public is a community of persons who share values, interests, and outlook. Publics form around specific values, ideas, policies, and proposals. Yet Bitzer recognizes that these publics are fluid, that specific publics can form, disband, and re-form in a different configuration. Further, there can be "sub-publics" within a larger public, such as ethnic coalitions or some political groups within a particular community, or factions within a political party, such as the Tea Party subset of the Republican Party. These persons are interdependent and possess the power to validate community truths and values. It is groups like these that have the power to "authorize" decisions and actions—not in any formal way as with Congress but in the sense that some decisions become part of the public sense of truth and value.[10]

Part of the function of the public in a situation such as December 7, 1941, is to authorize the president to seek declarations of war in times of attack. In a way this is the actualization of the notion embedded in the US Constitution: "with the consent of the governed." That consent is offered formally through Congress, but it is also granted informally through the notion of public assent, a concept that is most successful when public knowledge is informed and has coalesced. For instance, it is obvious that President Bush felt public support for the military action he took against Afghanistan, even in the absence of a declaration of war.

American democracy works because we believe it will—and we therefore defer to its precepts. In that sense, democracy is a process of communication, and it is the role of the public through discourse to communicate—formally and informally—its assent to the actions of our leaders. For example, at the conclusion of World War II, in the face of strong public sentiment to "bring the troops home," Roosevelt could not guarantee our allies the presence of an American occupying force in Europe; Churchill's proposal for an alliance of the "English-speaking peoples" fell on deaf ears, and American women, who had been the backbone of the workforce during the war, were expecting to return home to make room for returning soldiers. The public authorization for the war effort and its exigences no longer existed; decisions had to reflect that new truth. Similarly, President Obama felt that public authorization for the war in Afghanistan had waned to the point where it was time to conclude American involvement and bring the troops home. How had the exigence changed between 2001 and 2011?

In the case of the Japanese attack on Pearl Harbor, the situation—and the exigence—was relatively clear, as was the fitting response. When things are not so clear, the development of public knowledge becomes critical; before assent can be communicated, the public must accumulate enough knowledge to

1. agree on the situation itself,
2. understand the options open for a fitting response, and
3. debate the costs and benefits of those options.

If these elements do not materialize, the notion of public assent cannot entail the notion of consent but rests instead on ignorance. In today's fast-paced world of social media, public assent or dissent is communicated instantaneously through platforms such as Twitter, as well as email, and more traditional forms of communication (mail, phone calls, and polls, for example). How has the change in communication media changed Bitzer's concept of "public knowledge" and the ability to coalesce public opinion?

RHETORIC AS SITUATED

Bitzer's ideas are grounded in the notion that all rhetoric is "situated." That is to say, rhetorical discourse derives its meaning from the situation in which it is created. Absent that situation, meaning is often lost. Think about the "great speeches" in American history; how many of them make real sense outside the time in which they were spoken? Certainly, there are speeches that may come alive while one is studying the era in which they were salient, and many "great" speeches have passages that ring through the ages. Usually, though, these are passages that can be given new life by applying them to a current situation; you see a lot of this sort of application on social media sites such as Facebook. Nevertheless, by far the majority of speeches given in this country during its existence have fallen into obscurity, not because they were not good examples of the art and craft of speech making but because they no longer speak to us.

Even those speeches that carry powerful impact over time derive much of that strength from the situation they address. For example, Roosevelt's Pearl Harbor Address to the Nation, judged the fourth most influential speech of the twentieth century, draws its power from the situation we described above.[11] Ronald Reagan's 1987 Brandenburg Gate Address is remembered today not so much for commemorating the 750th anniversary of the founding of Berlin as it is for its confrontation with then Communist Party secretary Mikhail Gorbachev over the Berlin Wall. In front of the iconic Brandenburg Gate, near the Berlin Wall, Reagan challenged the Soviet leader to advance the cause of "freedom and peace" when he uttered the now-famous line, "Mr. Gorbachev, tear down this wall." The speech drew its power from the situation of continuing confrontation between the Soviet Union and the United States and Gorbachev's attempt at political reform within the Soviet Union. Martin Luther King Jr.'s "I Have a Dream" speech was named the "most influential speech of the twentieth century" not only because of its eloquence and the power of its metaphor but because of its enduring salience amid ongoing racial friction. Abraham Lincoln's Gettysburg Address, full of imagery and poetry, nonetheless is memorable at least in part because of the situation in which it was conceived: a commemoration of the deadliest battle in American history, a great civil war testing the strength of the union, and a challenge that tried the principles of equality and liberty on which that union was founded, as well as the fact that we need to continuously renew our commitment to those ideals. On the other hand, Lincoln's second inaugural, considered one of the best inaugural addresses ever given, is nonetheless remembered only in part, through elegant and eloquent passages that remain salient today. Like most great addresses, those passages are the ones the public has "authorized" by moving them into public knowledge.

In Bitzer's view, the situation in which rhetoric is called forth encompasses more than the context of the speech or the events that gave rise to the occasion for the speech. It includes all of the elements that influenced the moment: the events, the individuals involved, the circumstances, and the relationships among these factors. Thus, returning to Roosevelt's request for a Declaration of War, the situation would consist of Roosevelt himself and the attack on Pearl Harbor; but it would also include the Congress and the Constitution, the negotiations that had been going on between the United States and Japan, the ongoing war in Europe, the widespread isolationism of most Americans prior to the attack, and so on.

We have drawn primarily on military policy examples (Pearl Harbor in 1941 and 9/11 in 2001) to illustrate the situational method because those events present pretty clear-cut cases of exigence. But it is equally valuable to use this approach to examine the rhetoric emanating from a wide range of issues such as immigration, calls for a ban on assault-style weapons, the use of deadly force in confrontations between police and racial minorities, voting rights, calls to break up Google, any number of US Supreme Court decisions, and many more. Even non-US examples are amenable to situational analysis.[12]

In analyzing a speech using the situational perspective, the critic must take into account the totality of the situation and must consider the role or roles played by each element. For sake of discussion, we offer these suggestions as guiding questions in a situational analysis:

- What are the elements that constitute the particular situation? Initially, this list should be inclusive, even exhaustive; elements can be omitted later if analysis demonstrates their role to be negligible.
- What role or roles did each listed element play?
- What is the dominant element, or exigence, that will govern the response?
- In terms of the response to the situation, was the exigence modified and the response "fitting"?

These questions are not all-inclusive steps in a method to be applied as a sort of "cookie cutter." They do, however, provide a beginning point for analysis that focuses on the significance of the situation. As with any critical effort, it is the rhetorical artifact that will determine how the critical narrative develops. Situational analysis is seldom used as a stand-alone tool to evaluate a rhetorical artifact; more typically, it enriches other analytical methods by providing a deeper understanding of context in all its dimensions.[13] Only by understanding the full context of a rhetorical event can the critic comprehend and evaluate the artifact itself.

POTENTIALS AND PITFALLS

The beauty of situational analysis is that it allows the critic to account for outside forces that impact a rhetorical event in ways that other methods do not. If we recognize that all rhetoric is situated—that it is dependent for meaning on the time, place, and circumstances in which it occurs—then situational analysis allows us to perceive rhetoric as an organic phenomenon. We are then able to view differently those rare instances of discourse that transcend the situation and live on in national memory. Situational analysis also allows us to examine the choices a rhetorician makes in constructing a particular discourse. Those choices are ultimately influenced by the situation in which the discourse arises—whether ceremonial or as a result of crisis. It also combines naturally with a number of other critical perspectives, allowing the critic to construct a richer, more robust analysis.

There are criticisms of the situational perspective; it is seen by some as mechanistic. Additionally, the idea of the exigence is viewed by some theorists as robbing the rhetor of invention,[14] because, in Bitzer's view, the exigence calls forth rhetoric to craft a fitting response, and if the response is not deemed fitting, the response is not rhetorical. While this is a pretty shallow view of situational analysis, it does cause some to reject its utility as a critical tool.

There is also the possibility that the critic might overlook elements that are not part of the situation but that would illuminate the rhetorical artifact, such as logical elements, rhetorical or stylistic devices, and fallacies. Finally, the critic must not lose sight of the fact that rhetors are responsible for what is said, regardless of the forces that impinge on their rhetorical choices.

SITUATIONAL PERSPECTIVE TOP PICKS

Bitzer, Lloyd F. "Functional Communication: A Situational Perspective." In *Rhetoric in Transition: Studies in the Nature and Uses of Rhetoric*, edited by Eugene E. White, 21–38. University Park: Pennsylvania State University Press, 1980. Bitzer responds to his critics and offers some modifications of his theory.

———. "Rhetoric and Public Knowledge." In *Rhetoric, Philosophy, and Literature: An Exploration*, edited by Don Burks, 67–94. West Lafayette, IN: Purdue University Press, 1978. In this essay Bitzer discusses his theory of public knowledge: how cultural truths are absorbed by groups and used to acknowledge new information and authorize action in response to rhetorical situations.

———. "Rhetorical Public Communication." *Critical Studies in Mass Communication* 4, no. 4 (1987): 425–428. Bitzer discusses public communication, focusing on "journalists as a new and important class of rhetors."

———. "The Rhetorical Situation." *Philosophy and Rhetoric* 1 (1968): 1–14. This is the essay where Bitzer first explains situational analysis.

Brown, Jonathan David. "Understanding Bitzer's Rhetorical Situation." *Journal of Tourism Studies* 14 (2015): 99–104. Brown discusses Bitzer's theory of the rhetorical situation. This is a very good explanation of the concept for nonacademic audiences.

Grant-Davie, Keith. "Rhetorical Situations and Their Constituents." *Rhetoric Review* 15 (1997): 264–279. Grant-Davie argues that the roles of rhetor and audience are dynamic and interdependent. Audience as a rhetorical concept has transcended the idea of a homogenous body of people who have stable characteristics and are assembled in the rhetor's presence.

Kuypers, Jim A., Marilyn J. Young, and Michael K. Launer. "Of Mighty Mice and Meek Men: Contextual Reconstruction of the Iranian Airbus Shootdown." *Southern Communication Journal* 59, no. 4 (1994): 294–306. The authors use criticism informed by a situational perspective to examine the rhetoric surrounding the incident in 1988 when US forces shot down an Iranian passenger airliner in the Persian Gulf.

Patton, John H. "Causation and Creativity in Rhetorical Situations: Distinctions and Implications." *Quarterly Journal of Speech* 65 (1979): 36–55. Patton notes that exigences, although necessary conditions for rhetorical discourse, are not, in themselves, sufficient conditions. Underlying this argument is the assumption that "rhetoric is essentially historical" and that it is through invention and creativity that the rhetorical situation is appropriately addressed, producing the "fitting response" that every rhetor seeks.

Smith, Craig R., and Scott Lybarger. "Bitzer's Model Revisited." *Communication Quarterly* 44, no. 2 (1996): 197–213. The authors discuss responses to Bitzer's theory and describe Bitzer's own attempts to refine it. What is most significant to Smith and Lybarger, however, is that Bitzer, in his refinements, opens the door to a more complex view of perception and situation.

Turnbull, Nick. "Political Rhetoric and its Relationship to Context: A New Theory of the Rhetorical Situation, the Rhetorical and the Political." *Critical Discourse Studies* 14, no. 2 (2017): 115–131. Turnbull posits an alternate way to understand Bitzer's situational theory and apply it to rhetoric and politics.

Young, Marilyn J. "Lloyd F. Bitzer: Rhetorical Situation, Public Knowledge, and Audience Dynamics." In *Twentieth Century Roots of Rhetorical Criticism*, edited by Jim A. Kuypers and Andrew King, 275–301. Westport, CT: Praeger, 2001. Young reviews the criticism of Bitzer's work and argues that most of his critics have underestimated the power of the theory of the situation. Bitzer's theory gains power and becomes more complete when considered in conjunction with his ideas about public knowledge.

DISCUSSION QUESTIONS

1. What is the difference between Bitzer's notion of the rhetorical situation and the context of a rhetorical artifact?
2. How is the setting of a rhetorical act different than the rhetorical situation?
3. What is Bitzer's concept of the audience in the rhetorical situation?
4. How does an exigence function in the matrix of situation: exigence, audience, constraints?
5. What is Bitzer's definition of rhetoric? How is it different from the definitions offered by other rhetorical theorists, such as Edwin Black?

ACTIVITIES

1. Take a rhetorical analysis you have already completed using a different rhetorical perspective and reanalyze it using Bitzer's situational approach. What differences do you find? Similarities? What do you learn about the rhetorical artifact that you did not know before?
2. Divide into groups and conduct a scavenger hunt in your classroom building. Look for five rhetorical artifacts; determine the exigence that each artifact addresses, who the intended audience appears to be, and what constraints exist or are assumed in the presentation of the artifact. The artifacts you find can be textual or visual. Select one of the artifacts to use for a short presentation to the class in which you describe and analyze the artifact through the lens of the rhetorical situation.
3. Consider a common, recurring rhetorical situation, such as the President's State of the Union Address, and examine it from the perspective of the rhetorical situation. How might the situation (exigences, constraints, even audience) differ from year to year and president to president?

NOTES

1. Lloyd F. Bitzer, "The Rhetorical Situation," *Philosophy and Rhetoric* 1 (1968): 6. According to the Webster Dictionary online, http://www.merriam-webster.com, *exigence* [*exigency*] is "that which is required in a particular situation."

2. Ibid., 7.

3. Ibid., 6.

4. Ibid., 8.

5. Janet Johnson, "Twitter Bites and Romney: Examining the Rhetorical Situation of the 2012 Presidential Election in 140 Characters," *Journal of Contemporary Rhetoric* 2, nos. 3/4 (2012): 54–64.

6. John B. Killoran, "The Rhetorical Situations of Web Résumés," *Journal of Technical Writing & Communication* 39, no. 3 (2009): 263–284.

7. It is also taught extensively in communication and English courses. See Troy B. Cooper, "The Impromptu Rhetorical Situation," *Communication Teacher* 33, no. 4 (2019): 262–265.

8. See, Franklin Delano Roosevelt, "A Day That Will Live in Infamy," at http://www.american rhetoric.com.

9. Lloyd F. Bitzer, "Rhetoric and Public Knowledge," in *Rhetoric, Philosophy, and Literature: An Exploration*, ed. Don M. Burks, 67–94 (West Lafayette, IN: Purdue University Press, 1978).

10. For an example of how situation and public knowledge interact, see Marilyn J. Young and Michael K. Launer, "KAL 007 and the Superpowers: An International Argument," *Quarterly Journal of Speech* 74, no. 3 (1988): 271–295. This essay also introduces the concept of "pre-knowledge."

11. See http://americanrhetoric.com/newtop100speeches.htm.

12. As just three examples, see Cheri Hampton-Farmer, "Slippery Dilemma: Tony Blair's Rhetorical Response to Fuel Tax Protesters," *American Communication Journal* 16, no. 1 (2014): 52–61, http://ac-journal.org/journal/2014-2015/Vol16/Iss1/ACJ_2014-018_Cheri4.pdf; Bruce Dadey, "Identity, Narrative, and the Construction of the Rhetorical Situation in Euro-American and Aboriginal Cultures," *Journal of the Canadian Society for the Study of Rhetoric* 4 (2011): 1–21; and Yao Huimin and Wang Ximing, "On Bitzer's Situational View of Rhetoric," *Journal of Xi'an International Studies University* 2 (2009): 29–33.

13. As an example of just such an analysis, see Jim A. Kuypers, Marilyn J. Young, and Michael K. Launer, "Of Mighty Mice and Meek Men: Contextual Reconstruction of the Iranian Airbus Shootdown," *Southern Communication Journal* 59, no. 4 (1994): 294–306; and Jim A. Kuypers, "The Press and James Dobson: Contextual Reconstruction after the Ted Bundy Interview," *Florida Communication Journal* 18, no. 2 (1990): 1–8.

14. For instance, Richard Vatz argues that, in explicating his theory of situation, Bitzer fails to account for the creativity of the rhetor. In making his argument, Vatz provides some of the grounding for the role of perception within a rhetorical situation. See Richard E. Vatz, "The Myth of the Rhetorical Situation," *Philosophy and Rhetoric* 6 (1973): 154–161; and Richard E. Vatz, "The Mythical Status of Situational Rhetoric: Implications for Rhetorical Critics' Relevance in the Public Arena," *Review of Communication* 9, no. 1 (2009): 1–9. Of note is that in his 2009 article, Vatz fails to mention Bitzer's 1980 "Functional Communication: A Situational Perspective," where Bitzer addresses concerns raised by his critics.

5

Generic Elements in Rhetoric

William Benoit and Mark Glantz

To help understand a complex and variegated world, we frequently make use of generalizations that are often referred to as stereotypes. We can use a generalization such as "Ashley's a conservative" to draw reasonable, but not certain, conclusions about Ashley. If we want to know whether Ashley supports private-school tuition vouchers, the best way to find out the answer to this question is to ask Ashley, or to locate a statement by Ashley about her position on vouchers. These kinds of direct options, however, are not always available. In the absence of better ways to answer our question, we can use Ashley's political leanings to make an educated guess about her position: Because many conservatives support vouchers, Ashley, who we happen to know is a conservative, probably supports vouchers, too. Knowing something (support for private-school vouchers) about most members of a group (conservatives) allows us to make educated guesses about other members of that group (Ashley). Similar generalizations about groups of discourse or "genres" can also be helpful.

Generic rhetorical criticism is based on the idea that observable, explicable, and predictable rhetorical commonalities occur in groups of related discourses as well as in groups of people. Austermühl, for instance, demonstrated that presidential speechwriters who were developing inaugural addresses for incoming presidents looked at inaugurals given by earlier presidents. He offered examples of such consultations by the speechwriters for John F. Kennedy, George H. W. Bush, and George W. Bush.[1] It is clear that rhetors (and their writers) believe that discourse produced in situations similar to the current context is relevant to the creation of new rhetorical messages.

A critic using the generic approach would first identify a distinctive group or category of discourse, a genre: for example, presidential nominating convention keynote speeches, graduation commencement speeches, presidential inaugural speeches, speeches of apology, or eulogies. Then, the critic utilizing the generic method adopts an *inductive* approach, examining numerous past instances of this genre to develop a description or generalization of its common characteristics. It is also important for the critic to explain *why* speeches of this kind ought to have the commonalities found in the analysis. As an example of this approach, let us take a look at presidential nominating convention keynote speeches as an extended example.[2] These speeches are designed to sound a "key" note or set the tone for the convention. The keynote is designed to celebrate the ideals of the party and the fitness of the nominee to represent the party in the general election campaign and, ultimately, to win the office of the presidency for the nominee. All such keynote speeches are given in a similar situation: the Republican or Democratic presidential nomination convention. The result of this process, the description of the rhetorical characteristics of a genre (keynotes, for instance), can be used in at least three important ways.

First, **generic descriptions** can be used as part of a rhetorical theory that describes rhetorical practices according to genre. Rhetorical theory can describe the practice of rhetoric, as well as offering prescriptions about how it ought to be conducted. Inductive generic descriptions can provide an empirical foundation for descriptive rhetorical theory. For example, we might want to describe the practice of campaign rhetoric (keynote speeches), political rhetoric (state of the union addresses), or ceremonial rhetoric (commencement addresses, eulogies). If so, the generalizations discovered through a generic analysis could be very useful to theory building.

Second, generic descriptions can be used by practitioners, by rhetors who seek advice about how to develop a speech that falls into that genre. Those who are confronted with a need to invent a particular kind of discourse can be guided by systematic descriptions of past instances of that kind of discourse. For instance, Kyle R. King's scholarship on the narratives of gay male athletes who publicly self-disclose their sexuality could serve as an instructive resource to individuals who find themselves in similar situations to Michael Sam and Jason Collins.[3] To cite another example, if someone needs to write a eulogy, it could be very useful to know what other eulogists have said in the past. A description of the practice of past eulogies could give you ideas, a starting point, and perhaps even "model eulogies" to imitate.

Third, rhetorical critics can apply what we have learned about a genre to help understand and evaluate other, as yet unexamined, instances of that genre. That is, we can compare a new instance of a genre to past practices. For example, on March 20, 2003, President Bush announced the beginning of Operation Iraqi Freedom, the war in Iraq. We can learn something about this speech by comparing it with other presidential speeches announcing military action. We could compare the 2003 speech with an earlier speech of this kind, but it would be more efficient to compare it with the results of a generic rhetorical criticism that describes a group of similar speeches.[4] Examining more past instances could make the generic description more accurate than looking at one or two (although rhetors can choose to stray from convention, so no generic description guarantees similar discourse from other rhetors). As another example, although not quite a declaration of war, we could do the same with President Obama's September 10, 2014, "Statement by the President on ISIL," in which he outlined America's course of military action against that terrorist group.[5] We can ask how this announcement, on the surface similar with declarations of war, matched up with actual declarations of war. Presidential candidate announcement speeches are almost certain to occur every four years, and we can use our understanding of past announcements to understand and evaluate current practice.[6]

It should be obvious that the fundamental assumption of genre criticism is that rhetorical artifacts examined by a critic to establish a genre, or to develop the inductively derived generic description, will resemble in important ways other rhetorical artifacts that fall into that genre. The power of generic criticism is that, if this assumption is reasonable, critics, practitioners, and theorists can learn something about some rhetorical artifacts by examining other similar rhetorical artifacts. Rhetorical critics, schooled in the humanistic tradition, do not ordinarily make this idea explicit, but the basic argument is that the texts studied in a generic rhetorical criticism are a sample of a larger population of texts and that the results of generic rhetorical criticism can be generalized to other similar discourses. Of course, the generalizations derived from the discourses that are being studied to identify and define the genre must be applied cautiously to other discourses. Discourses that belong to the same class or genre and therefore have *some* similarities could also be different in other important ways. For instance, Ashley may be one of the few conservatives who do not favor school vouchers as suggested earlier.

Furthermore, the generic description is inherently limited by the characteristics of the artifacts examined to develop the description. The process of genre criticism can only describe—not improve on—the actual practice of discourse. This means that if rhetors who have created discourse in a genre have not yet discovered the best or most effective approach for that kind of rhetoric, the generic description developed using existing messages cannot possibly include the optimum approach.[7] It also means that as our culture changes through time, discourses that were effective or appropriate in the past—the discourses studied to describe the genre—may be ill-suited to understanding future discourses given in different times. The remainder of this chapter covers three broad areas: the theory and practice of generic rhetorical criticism, the idea of generic description, and the idea of generic application.

THE THEORY AND PRACTICE OF GENERIC RHETORICAL CRITICISM

A common thread in this literature is that genres are a class, set, or group of related discourses. For example, Walter R. Fisher argues that "a genre is a category" and "genres are generalizations."[8] Similarly, Jackson Harrell and Wil A. Linkugel explain that, "at base, genre means class. A genus is a class or group of things. The decision to classify a particular group of things as a genus rests on recorded observations which indicate that one group of entities shares some important characteristic which differentiates it from all other entities."[9] This statement contains an important implicit claim: a genre, or each member of a genre, is distinct from other genres.[10] A convention keynote is one kind of campaign speech, and these speeches are different in some ways from nominating convention acceptance addresses,[11] presidential television spots,[12] or presidential debates.[13] Because these messages are all forms of presidential campaign discourse, they probably share some features in common, but if they are distinct genres they must have distinguishing differences. Political campaign messages should be different in some ways from other kinds of discourses, such as eulogies or commencement addresses.

Generic criticism generally falls into one of four broad areas. Some genre studies seem to adopt a *situational* base, identifying a genre based on the situation in which the discourses arise, such as examination of gallows speeches or inaugural addresses.[14] Other instances of generic criticism seem to focus on *purpose*, including life termination justifications, investigations of agitation and control, redemption, and polarization.[15] Still other genre studies focus on the rhetorical characteristics of groups of *rhetors*, including studies of scientists;[16] early African American feminists;[17] radical-revolutionary speakers;[18] radical, liberal, and conservative rhetors;[19] the religious right;[20] or the radical right.[21] Finally, some genre studies focus on characteristics of the *medium* of discourse, such as analysis of political blogs,[22] political pamphlets,[23] or songs.[24] There can be no question that a great deal of interesting and useful scholarship of an extremely diverse nature has been conducted under the rubric of generic rhetorical criticism. It can be difficult to explore this literature, because critics do not always label their work "generic criticism" even though we might consider it as such. In reviewing this body of literature, however, three areas seem to stand out: the relationship between situation and genre, the relationship between purpose and genre, and the relationship of genre to other elements. To each of these ideas we now turn.

Situation and Genre

Rhetorical scholars have described recurrent forms of discourse since at least as early as Aristotle's *Rhetoric*, which identified three broad genres of rhetoric: forensic (legal), deliberative (legislative), and epideictic (ceremonial).[25] Edwin Black offered one of the earliest, if not the earliest, conceptual discussions of the assumptions of the rhetorical genre:

> First, we must assume that there is a limited number of situations in which a rhetor can find himself. . . . To be sure, there may be accidental factors peculiar to a given situation; but our assumption is that there will be a limited number of ways in which rhetorical situations can be characterized, and that the recurrent characteristics of rhetorical situations will make it possible for us—if we know enough—to construct an accurate and exhaustive typology of rhetorical situations.[26]

Black explicitly assumes that the number of rhetorical situations—and therefore, the number of potential genres—is limited. This makes the task of identifying genres and locating a sufficient number of texts to study more practical than if there were an infinite number of rhetorical situations. Black continues his description:

> Second, we must assume that there is a limited number of ways in which a rhetor can and will respond rhetorically to any given situational type. Again, there may be accidents of a given response that will prove singular, but on the whole—we assume—there will be only a finite number of rhetorical strategies available to a rhetor in any given situation, and his playing his own variations on these strategies will not prevent the critic from identifying the strategies as characteristic of the situation.[27]

This assumption that there are a limited number of potential responses means that the texts of a genre are likely to share common features (which the critic can identify and describe). The alternative, an unlimited number of responses, could mean that every member of a genre could be completely different. Finally, Black discusses the possible uses of generic rhetorical criticism:

> Third, we must assume that the recurrence of a given situational type through history will provide the critic with information on the rhetorical responses available in that situation, and with this information the critic can better understand and evaluate any specific rhetorical discourse in which he may be interested.[28]

So, understanding past instances of a genre may provide insight into other examples of that kind of rhetorical message. Of course, the artifacts that participate in or belong to a genre will not be identical in all regards, but for generic criticism to be a useful method of criticism, the similarities must be important ones.

The emphasis on understanding genre as rooted in a particular situation is popular in the literature.[29] Harrell and Linkugel assert that genres are situationally based: "We think that rhetorical genres stem from organizing principles found in recurring situations that generate discourse characterized by a family of common factors."[30] Similarly, Karlyn K. Campbell and Kathleen Hall Jamieson's oft-quoted definition stipulates a situational base for rhetorical genres:

> Genres are groups of discourses which share substantive, stylistic, and situational characteristics. Or, put differently, in the discourses that form a genre, similar substantive and stylistic strategies are used to encompass situations perceived as similar by the responding rhetors. A genre is a group

of acts unified by a constellation of forms that recurs in each of its members. These forms, in isola-
tion, appear in other discourses. What is distinctive about the acts in a genre is the recurrence of
the forms together in constellation.[31]

The term *constellation* is especially well chosen, suggesting that the recurrent elements appear
in a recognizable configuration or pattern. The point that rhetors work from their perception
of a situation is also important.

Purpose and Genre

A second thread in the literature grounds genres in the rhetor's purpose.[32] Carolyn Miller
points out that "genres have been defined by similarities in strategies or forms in the discourse,
by similarities in audience, by similarities in modes of thinking, by similarities in rhetorical
situations." Her recommendation is that "a rhetorically sound definition of genre must be centered not on the substance or form of a discourse but on the action it is used to accomplish."[33]
In our opinion, there is overlap between situational and purposive approaches to genre, but
they are not entirely identical.

Certainly we must keep in mind that the rhetor's purpose and the rhetorical situation frequently coincide. For example, eulogists face a situation in which a person has died. When
a person dies, the survivors will never again be able to see or talk with the deceased, a cause
for sadness. A death also reminds everyone concerned in a very direct fashion that they are
mortal. Hence it is appropriate for a eulogist to praise the departed, to ease the transition, and
to try to help auditors deal with their grief and heightened sense of mortality. As Jamieson
and Campbell explain it, "In Western culture, at least, a eulogy will acknowledge the death,
transform the relationship between the living and the dead from present to past tense, ease
the mourners' terror at confronting their own mortality, console them by arguing that the
deceased lives on, and reknit the community."[34] Here, the situation and the rhetor's purpose
are completely compatible, and it is difficult to see or draw a distinction between the situation
and the rhetor's purpose.

However, it is not always the case that a rhetor's purpose is completely consistent with
the situation. For instance, consider a eulogy for someone killed by a gunshot wound. If the
eulogist felt strongly about gun control, he or she might choose to include such an appeal
in the eulogy; if the eulogist did not feel strongly about gun control, he or she would likely
not discuss gun control. An appeal for gun control is not a necessary part of such a eulogy.
If a eulogist failed to praise the deceased, the eulogy would seem odd and incomplete if not
wrong, but if a eulogist failed to include a plea for gun control, the omission would not make
the speech seem incomplete. Although the particular situation may be seen to authorize such
an appeal for gun control (unless the deceased was a staunch Second Amendment supporter),
it does not require it; rather, the rhetor's purpose (advocating gun control) would determine
whether to include this idea in the eulogy.

To extend this analogy one step further, consider Rick Kahn's plea at Minnesota Democratic
senator Paul Wellstone's memorial service: "We are begging you to help us win this Senate
election for Paul Wellstone." In these cases, the rhetor's personal purpose produced discourse
that was in part irrelevant to if not incongruent with the immediate situation. Nothing in this
eulogy's situation authorized this topic. Although a listener might happen to agree in principle
with the appeal to vote for a Democrat to replace Wellstone, such an appeal has nothing to do
with the deceased or the eulogy itself. It seems inappropriate; a plea to vote for a Democrat

probably detracted from the ceremony for many in the audience, particularly the Republican friends and colleagues of Wellstone who attended the service.

As a final argument for the importance of distinguishing between situation and purpose, consider any rhetorical discourse that occurs in a controversy. Those rhetors who supported and opposed Prohibition spoke and wrote in essentially the same situation. Similarly, the situation confronting pro-choice and pro-life advocates is exactly the same. These groups of rhetors—and it would be easy to add additional groups to this list—produce noticeably different rhetorical artifacts, and the primary reason for those differences was their purpose, not differences in the situation. Of course, one could argue that opponents' perceptions of the situation are different, but Lloyd Bitzer at least argues that the situation consists of "objective and publicly observable historic facts in the world we experience."[35] In principle, one could say that everyone lives in a unique situation, but enough shared perceptions exist to allow genre criticism to be useful. Thus, the rhetors' purpose can be a source of generic similarities in rhetorical messages, and while purpose may overlap with situation, conceptually they are distinct concepts.

Genre: "Act" at the Intersection of Scene, Purpose, Agent, and Agency

The third thread in the literature highlights the relationship of situation and purpose with three other considerations. There is no question that situation and purpose do, or should, influence the production of discourse. However, in actuality, five factors jointly influence the production of rhetorical discourse. Kenneth Burke's notion of ratios[36] helps clarify the relationships between these factors,[37] and it will be discussed in greater detail in a later chapter. For now, though, it is enough to know that ratios are found within a rhetorical artifact (actual discourse) and are comprised of two terms from what Burke called a pentad—an act, scene (or situation), agent, agency, and purpose. Ratios essentially describe the influence of one of these elements on a second one. Given that in this chapter we are discussing the production of discourse (our *act*), "act" is the second term in each of the possible combinations of ratios, so we are actually looking at the effect that the first term in the ratio has upon the act. So, when we examine a rhetorical artifact with genre in mind, we find these ratios:

- Scene-act: the situation (scene) in which a discourse (the act) is produced exerts an influence on that discourse.
- Purpose-act: the rhetor's purpose, goal, or intent influences the discourse he or she produces.
- Agent-act: the nature of the rhetor (the agent) influences the discourse he or she produces.
- Agency-act: the means (agency) used to create the discourse, including the communicative medium, influences the discourse.

The scene-act ratio corresponds to situationally based approaches to genre (e.g., gallows speeches, inaugural addresses). The purpose-act ratio relates to genre approaches based on the rhetor's purpose (e.g., polarization, resignation, containment[38]). The agent-act ratio pertains to genres focused on the rhetor (e.g., radical, liberal, or conservative). Finally, the agency-act ratio corresponds to studies of kinds of discourse (e.g., pamphlets, songs). All four of these combinations can influence the production of discourse and can serve as the basis for a genre.

Situations are opportunities for discourse, which rhetors may choose to exploit to further their own purposes. This can help explain why discourse that occurs in similar situations, such as the eulogies discussed above, would share important similarities. However, some rhetors have different purposes, which can also influence the discourse they produce, even when they face similar situations. Think of the gun-control example given above, for example. We believe, however, that critics are certainly capable of identifying or creating groupings of discourses that share a common source (such as situation, purpose, or rhetor) but that ordinary people have not conceptualized at any level. A little imagination can devise diverse categories that could be used to divide discourses into a variety of groupings.

GENERIC DESCRIPTION: AN INDUCTIVE APPROACH

We want to stress that there is no single way to write a genre criticism. It is important for a rhetorical critic who wants to write a generic rhetorical criticism to read a variety of genre studies before attempting the task. Still, some observations are worth making. There are two fundamental approaches to genre criticism: generic description (inductive) and generic application (deductive).[39] **Generic description** must come first; critics cannot apply a genre that has not yet been described. **Generic application** begins with a generalization and applies it to specific members of the genre. Generic application begins with a genre that has already been described; it applies the characteristics of that genre deductively to another instance of that genre in order to explain and/or evaluate it. We discuss generic application in the section that follows.

When critics suspect the existence of a genre, they may use generic description to examine particular instances of a possible genre for common features. There are three fundamental steps in this process: (1) identify the defining characteristic(s) (e.g., the situation, purpose, or kind of rhetor that constitutes the genre); (2) carefully scrutinize examples of the possible genre to identify similarities; (3) explain the observed similarities in terms of identifying characteristics (identifying the "internal dynamic" of the genre). Each of these steps is discussed below.

Identifying the Defining Characteristic(s)

If the critic believes that he or she may have found a useful genre, he or she must identify the defining characteristic(s) of that candidate genre. For example, the defining characteristic could be the situation/scene in which the rhetorical artifacts occur (such as keynote speech or eulogy), the rhetor's purpose that prompts the rhetorical discourses (for example, celebrating the party's presidential nominee or helping the bereaved confront their own mortality), salient characteristics of the rhetor/agent (for example, Republicans or women), or the medium/agency that shapes the artifacts (for instance, a speech, television spot, or political debate). One cannot select artifacts at random to discover genres; the critic must be able to clearly define the candidate genre in order to select appropriate particular rhetorical artifacts, that is, instances of the category, for analysis.

For example, President Bush's speech of March 20, 2003, is an example of a speech announcing a war. However, it may not be clear whether speeches about al-Qaeda and ISIS/ISIL are about *war* (perhaps the struggle against terrorism is not the same as a war against a country). The genre critic needs to make a clear decision about which messages to include in a study. However, given a clear understanding of the defining characteristics of the candidate genre, the critic can select appropriate texts for scrutiny. As another example, consider presidential speeches announcing American involvement in peacekeeping missions. In one study, Jason A. Edwards, Joseph M. Valenzano III, and Karla Stevenson examined instances of American presidents announcing US involvement in UN peacekeeping missions.[40] They found distinct elements that differentiated those speeches from war announcements as well as crisis speeches.

Having identified the defining characteristics of the candidate genre, the critic must acquire several instances of the discourse in question for analysis. The critic must be prepared to read, watch, and/or listen to the artifacts repeatedly, closely, and carefully in order to determine whether these texts have rhetorical commonalities and what those commonalities are. Two important questions arise in this phase of generic description: what to look for and how many instances to examine.

Unlike most other rhetorical perspectives, generic rhetorical criticism helps the critic decide *which* artifacts to examine but does not prescribe *how* to analyze those artifacts. For example, a critic employing the generic approach could look for metaphors commonly used in war speeches. A genre critic might look to see whether such speeches displayed similar rhetorical visions or fantasy themes or used narrative in similar ways. A genre critic could also look at stylistic elements (e.g., alliterations, personification) in groups of related messages. A potential genre could be analyzed for the arguments it employs. Thus, the method of generic rhetorical criticism helps the critic decide which rhetorical artifacts to examine and it tells the critic to look for commonalities, but the generic method itself does not help the critic know precisely which sorts of rhetorical similarities to look for. The whole idea of genre criticism is that rhetorical artifacts in the past can be studied and that the results of this study will tell us about future artifacts of the same kind (or other past artifacts that were not included in the initial study). Thus, it is very important for the critic to select the appropriate artifacts to study; inclusion of artifacts that do not really belong to the genre will produce a flawed study.

In our opinion, a critic using the generic approach should be familiar with numerous ways of performing rhetorical criticism and with rhetorical theory generally. It is useful to know what features might be important in a genre. When the critic utilizing the generic approach is repeatedly reading the artifacts of the candidate genre, he or she may notice that certain kinds of metaphors are used frequently. Or the critic could notice that the rhetors seem to be engaging in a certain narrative form frequently. Critics using the generic approach who are generally familiar with numerous rhetorical perspectives are probably more likely to notice important rhetorical similarities than critics who are not widely read.

Generic description, as noted above, is an inductive approach. This means that it is subject to the tests of inductive argument. The most important test is whether a sufficient number of instances—in this case, enough rhetorical artifacts—have been examined.[41] There is no simple answer to this question: The number of instances a critic should examine to establish the nature of a genre depends in part on the complexity and variety of the artifacts examined. The greater the complexity of the artifacts in the possible genre, and the more variety in the artifacts, the greater the number of instances that ought to be studied to have confidence in the study's conclusions. The number of artifacts needed also depends on how prominently the common rhetorical features appear in the artifacts. The more obvious and important the rhetorical similarities, the fewer artifacts may be needed to persuasively establish the genre. If few artifacts are available and they are difficult to acquire, readers may accept a critic's decision to examine fewer of them. If the variety in artifacts examined is extreme, the critic may wish to consider whether multiple genres are at work (see the discussion of hybrid genres below).

Identifying Similarities

Once the texts to be analyzed have been identified and located, the generic rhetorical critic must examine them carefully to identify rhetorical similarities. If the critic discovers seemingly important similarities in the texts under scrutiny, he or she should organize those commonalities and locate clear examples from the discourses that can be used to illustrate the features of the genre. For example, if we were to simply say that war speeches often include metaphors, that would not be as clear as if we gave examples of metaphors from such speeches.

It is possible that any randomly selected group of speeches will show similarities simply through the operation of coincidence. Most speeches are supposed to have introductions, main bodies, and conclusions, but that does not mean they all belong to the same genre. We suspect this may in part account for Campbell and Jamieson's statement that "a genre is composed of a constellation of recognizable forms bound together by an internal dynamic."[42] Harrell and Linkugel write about the "organizing principles found in recurring situations that generate discourse characterized by a family of common factors."[43] The point is that the common rhetorical features that are discovered through generic description must be explained by the genre's identifying feature (or internal dynamic or organizing principle). Consider again keynote speeches. These discourses are designed to encourage viewers to support the nominee; because of this, it makes perfect sense for a keynote to praise the party's nominee. Similarly, the two presidential nominees face off in the general election campaign, so it is reasonable for a keynote speaker to attack his or her nominee's opponent. Thus, the nature of the situation facing the rhetors who deliver keynote addresses can explain the presence of certain rhetorical features in those addresses.[44] This raises the question of subgenres. For example, would it be useful to distinguish between keynote speeches after a seriously contested nomination and keynote speeches to an essentially unified party?

Explaining Observed Similarities

Because coincidental similarities are possible in rhetorical discourse, it is important to explain the similarities found in the rhetorical texts. Those who base genres on rhetors' purposes must be able to link those purposes to the common features of the rhetorical artifacts in those genres. For example, the similarities found in messages of redemption (following Kenneth Burke) should be related to that purpose.[45] We should be able to explain why common features of discourse that is designed to polarize[46] issues and ideas should be expected to occur in artifacts with that purpose. Rhetors who engage in rhetoric designed to agitate or control[47] should produce messages that can be better understood through a consideration of that purpose.

Those who base genres on the nature of groups of rhetors must be able to link the common rhetorical features to the character of those rhetors. For instance, we ought to be able to account for similarities in messages produced by rhetors with similar political beliefs (e.g., radical, liberal, conservative) by considering those beliefs.[48] If those who belong to the religious right[49] produce similar messages, the critic using the generic approach should be able to show how their political/religious beliefs explain the existence of those similarities. We might wonder again about the possibility of subgenres: Are Republican keynote speeches different from Democratic ones? Are eulogies delivered by men different from those given by women? Should the ethnicity of the rhetor be used as the basis for developing subgenres?

GENERIC APPLICATION: A DEDUCTIVE APPROACH

The process of generic application can occur only after someone has already conceptualized a genre. Most commonly, genres would be developed through generic description: inductively describing the nature of a conceptually related group of speeches. However, it is possible that one could generate a generic description theoretically, rather than through an examination of instances of that genre. Regardless of how the genre was conceptualized, generic application includes three basic steps.

First, a genre must have already been described. The critic pursuing generic application must identify the nature of the genre ("keynote speeches") and then describe the salient features of that genre. What would discourses in the genre be likely to look like or to have in common? Second, an artifact that is a member of the genre is identified and shown to participate in, or belong to, the genre described in the first step. For example, one might choose to apply the genre of keynote speeches to Senator Elizabeth Warren's 2016 keynote speech. In this step, the critic refers to the defining features of the genre (in this case, situational) and demonstrates that the new artifact belongs to the genre. This is an important step, because, as Robert C. Rowland correctly observes, "if a work is inappropriately placed in a given category the analysis of it inevitably will be flawed."[50]

Sometimes this step will be quite simple. If "keynote speeches" is considered to be a genre, it should be sufficient to note that the artifact under consideration is identified as one. Similarly, the conditions under which Supreme Court Justice Ruth Bader Ginsburg offered her minority opinion in the case of *Burwell v. Hobby Lobby Stores, Inc.*, ensured her rhetoric would be understood as an instance of judicial dissent.[51] In other cases, an argument might be necessary. If the genre is defined by the rhetors' purposes, the critic may need to provide evidence of the rhetor's likely purpose in the new artifact. If the genre is defined by situation, it is possible that the critic may need to provide a rationale for the claim that the rhetor and/or the salient audience perceived the situation as the critic suggests. It must be clear to the reader of the rhetorical criticism that it is reasonable to view the new artifact as a member of the genre.

Finally, the critic is ready to begin making arguments about the "new" artifact based on the claim that it is a member of the genre. Here, evidence for these arguments can be based on the description of the genre as a standard for evaluation as well as on the message itself. It is possible to draw a variety of conclusions in a generic application. For example, the critic might measure the new artifact against the standards articulated in the genre: based on past examples, is the new artifact well or poorly conceived? Did the rhetor include the proper elements and were they developed effectively?

If the artifact shares the common features that comprise the genre, there is no problem for the critic. The "internal dynamic" explains why these features ought to occur in the kind of genre identified by the defining characteristics. Of course, if the new artifact follows the strictures of the genre but appears to have been a failure, the critic has some explaining to do. Even more complex is when the artifact violates the expectations established during the critic's initial description of the genre. What can the critic utilizing the generic approach conclude if the artifact does not conform to the characteristics of the genre? Although there can be numerous reasons that account for deviations from the genre, there are four that deserve special attention. First, it is possible that the "new" artifact does not really belong in the genre. The critic should make certain that the discourse being examined in fact fits the defining characteristics of the genre. It is conceivable that the critic may decide either that the artifact does not really belong in the genre after all or that the defining characteristics need to be revised.

Second, the artifact could be a **generic hybrid**,[52] which means it "belongs" to two genres at once. If so, it could contain some of the rhetorical features specified in each of the genres that contribute to the rhetorical hybrid. If the critic has reason to believe that this discourse is not unique, that other messages may well resemble this one, the critic may propose the existence of a hybrid.

Third, it is possible that the rhetor who created the artifact under examination made mistakes. Perhaps the rhetor did not understand the implications of the situation. Perhaps the rhetor did not examine previous artifacts or deliberately chose to ignore them. It is possible that the rhetor did not correctly analyze the audience or chose to ignore them. Perhaps the rhetor is creating discourse in order to further a purpose that is not really inherent in the situation. The critic using the generic approach, however, should make arguments about why the differences between the artifact and the common features of the genre were mistakes if that is the claim being advanced.

Fourth, it is also possible that the rhetor is experimenting and improving the genre rather than making errors. Rhetors may not yet have discovered the optimum discourse, and the rhetor being analyzed here may have developed an idea or ideas about how to invent a better discourse. For instance, President Ronald Reagan experimented with his State of the Union (SOTU) Address in 1982 when he directed his audience's attention to Lenny Skutnik, who was seated beside the First Lady. Reagan praised Skutnik for diving into icy water to rescue the survivor of a plane crash. Never before had a president used anything other than language strategies in their SOTU speeches, but ever since, presidents have used ordinary citizens, seated near the First Lady, to emphasize key values and policies in their address.[53] Reagan's addition to the genre was deemed successful by most observers and has since become commonplace. Ironically, when an audience has developed expectations, it is possible that they will not like the changes, even if a more objective analysis concludes that the changes made by the rhetor are improvements. Here again, if the rhetorical critic believes that the differences between the artifact and the common features of the genre are an improvement, the critic must explain why the changes should be considered improvements.

Finally, it is possible that a new genre is emerging and developing. We point to social media as an example of potential sites for new genres to arise. As new media—and as media that contrast sharply with existing media (e.g., a limit on the number of characters in a tweet)—emerge, users must jointly develop conventions for discourse in this medium. Experimentation would probably occur in such media, not to improve the genre but to create it.

POTENTIALS AND PITFALLS

Generic rhetorical criticism has many advantages. First, genre criticism is well designed for attempting to understand the nature of rhetorical practice. What do speeches announcing a war, or inaugural addresses, or diatribes, or resignation speeches look like? What features do they have in common and why should these commonalities exist? Generic description can help rhetorical theorists and practitioners alike. Furthermore, generic application can help rhetorical critics understand and evaluate new examples of speeches that belong to a given genre once generic description has occurred.

The rhetorical critic must keep in mind that the generic method offers advice on which speeches to study, but not on precisely how to study them. As we suggested before, another critic could look at inaugural addresses (or any other genre) looking for metaphors, narratives, or fantasy themes. Any particular method of rhetorical criticism can be used to guide the critic's analysis of the speeches in a genre. The terms substantive and stylistic in Campbell and Jamieson's definition suggest that a genre may contain similarities of different kinds of rhetorical elements.

One limitation of generic analysis is that the method lumps good messages with mediocre and bad ones.[54] The inductive method of generic description suggests that the critic locate a sufficient number of examples of the potential genre. It never suggests that the critic only examine successful messages or place the best texts in one subgrouping and the failures in another. As discussed in the preceding section, it is conceivable that a rhetor creating a keynote speech in the future could try something new, something better than any previous keynote. Unless we believe that the best possible examples of discourse in a genre have already been created, there is always room for improvement.

It can also be argued that generic rhetorical criticism ignores the nuances of individual rhetorical discourses. We feel that this criticism applies more to rhetorical criticism that focuses too heavily on description. By its very nature inductive generic description searches for commonalities among the instances of a genre, ignoring differences between individual discourses in that genre. Because the critic who is conducting generic description is attempting to discover what these texts have in common, the differences can be considered irrelevant. Of course, subsequent generic application should focus on the individual nuances of the specific instance of the genre under examination. For example, keynote speeches from 1960–1996 attacked on average in 48 percent of their utterances. But Barbara Jordan's Democratic keynote in 1976 contained only a single attack.[55] A critic using the deductive generic approach could argue that Jordan failed to include enough attacks on the opposing party. However, understanding the particular nuances of this speech might shed some light on her reluctance to attack. So, while generic description must by nature ignore the nuances of individual members of the genre, generic application can and should take particulars into account.

Generic rhetorical criticism takes advantage of the fact that, while no two discourses are identical, discourses do fall into groups or genres that have important similarities. Knowing the nature of these groups and their common rhetorical characteristics can be useful to rhetors, theorists, and practitioners alike. Of course, critics must never lose sight of the fact that there *are* differences even between members of the same genre, and critics must realize that genres can develop over time and potentially improve over past practice. Still, intelligent use of generic rhetorical criticism can provide powerful insights into the nature of rhetorical discourse.

GENERIC RHETORICAL CRITICISM TOP PICKS

Benoit, William L., Joseph R. Blaney, and P. M. Pier. "Acclaiming, Attacking, and Defending: A Functional Analysis of Nominating Convention Keynote Speeches, 1960–1996." *Political Communication* 17 (2000): 61–84. This essay takes a more explicitly content analytic approach, but it is still concerned with identifying important common features of this message form.

Campbell, Karlyn K., and Kathleen H. Jamieson, eds. *Form and Genre: Shaping Rhetorical Action*. Falls Church, VA: Speech Communication Association, 1978. This volume pulls together essays from a diverse array of scholars addressing the nature of genre.

Clark, Thomas D. "An Analysis of Recurrent Features in Contemporary American Radical, Liberal, and Conservative Political Discourse." *Southern Speech Communication Journal* 44

(1979): 399–422. This essay is interesting because unlike most genre studies, Clark contrasts three different (although related) groups of discourse.

Condit, Celeste M. "The Function of Epideictic: The Boston Massacre Orations as Exemplar." *Communication Quarterly* 33, no. 4 (1985): 284–299. A classic treatment of a genre that is often overlooked.

Jamieson, Kathleen H., and Karlyn K. Campbell. "Rhetorical Hybrids: Fusions of Generic Elements," *Quarterly Journal of Speech* 68 (1982): 146–157. Genres are not always static. This essay discusses the merging of two genres into a single new genre.

Ware, B. L., and Wil A. Linkugel. "They Spoke in Defense of Themselves: On the Generic Criticism of *Apologia*." *Quarterly Journal of Speech* 59 (1973): 273–283. One of the earlier studies of genre and a classic treatment of the important genre of apologia.

DISCUSSION QUESTIONS

1. Do you think any new genres have emerged in social media? If so, what are they?
2. Have you ever been part of the audience for a message that participates in a genre? If so, which genre and which message?
3. Have you ever created a message that is part of a genre? Is so, which genre?
4. Pick a genre and a message from that genre. Identify two distinct audiences that could have seen, heard, or read that message. Discuss whether that message was equally appropriate for these two different audiences.
5. Select a genre. Do you think some media (such as television broadcasts, tweets, face-to-face conversation, internet websites) are better suited for that genre than other media?
6. If a rhetor invented a message that obviously violated the conventions of that genre, how might audiences react?

ACTIVITIES

1. Choose a genre. Develop an outline for a possible message in that genre.
2. Find a message that is part of a genre. Discuss how well (or how poorly) it followed the conventions of that genre.
3. Discuss why two rhetors in similar situations might develop very different messages (if you think this is possible).

NOTES

1. Frank Austermühl, *The Great American Scaffold: Intertextuality and Identity in American Presidential Discourse* (Amsterdam: John Benjamins, 2014), 3–5.

2. William L. Benoit, Joseph R. Blaney, and P. M. Pier, "Acclaiming, Attacking, and Defending: A Functional Analysis of Nominating Convention Keynote Speeches, 1960–1996," *Political Communication* 17 (2000): 61–84. Such knowledge about keynote addresses has even made its way into assignments given in public speaking courses. See, David C. Deifel, "The Keynote Address and Its Occasion," *Communication Teacher* 21, no. 1 (2007): 1–5.

3. Kyle R. King, "Three Waves of Gay Male Athlete Coming Out Narratives," *Quarterly Journal of Speech* 103, no. 4 (2017): 372–394.

4. For rhetorical criticism of justifications of war, see Kathleen M. German, "Invoking the Glorious War: Framing the Persian Gulf Conflict through Directive Language," *Southern Communication Journal* 60 (1995): 292–302; Robert L. Ivie, "Presidential Motives for War," *Quarterly Journal of Speech* 60 (1974): 337–345; and Mary E. Stuckey, "Remembering the Future: Rhetorical Echoes of World War II and Vietnam in George Bush's Public Speech on the Gulf War," *Communication Studies* 42 (1992): 246–256.

5. Barack Obama, "Statement by the President on ISIL" (White House, September 10, 2014), http://www.whitehouse.gov/the-press-office/2014/09/10/statement-president-isil-1.

6. Judith S. Trent, "Presidential Surfacing: The Ritualistic and Crucial First Act," *Communication Monographs* 45 (1978): 281–292; William L. Benoit, Jayne R. Goode, Sheri Whalen, and Penni M. Pier, "'I Am a Candidate for President': A Functional Analysis of Presidential Announcement Speeches, 1960–2004," *Speaker & Gavel* 45, no. 1 (2008): 3–16.

7. William L. Benoit, "In Defense of Generic Rhetorical Criticism: John H. Patton's 'Generic Criticism: Typology at an Inflated Price,'" *Rhetoric Society Quarterly* 10 (1980): 128–135.

8. Walter R. Fisher, "Genre: Concepts and Applications in Rhetorical Criticism," *Western Journal of Speech Communication* 44 (1980): 291.

9. Jackson Harrell and Wil A. Linkugel, "On Rhetorical Genre: An Organizing Perspective," *Philosophy & Rhetoric* 11 (1978): 263.

10. Thomas D. Clark, "An Analysis of Recurrent Features in Contemporary American Radical, Liberal, and Conservative Political Discourse," *Southern Speech Communication Journal* 44 (1979): 400–401.

11. William L. Benoit, William T. Wells, P. M. Pier, and Joseph R. Blaney, "Acclaiming, Attacking, and Defending in Nominating Convention Acceptance Addresses, 1960–96," *Quarterly Journal of Speech* 85 (1999): 247–267.

12. William L. Benoit, "The Functional Approach to Presidential Television Spots: Acclaiming, Attacking, Defending 1952–2000," *Communication Studies* 52 (2001): 109–126.

13. Malin Roitman, "Constructing One's Arguments Based on Refutations of the Other's Discourse. A Study of the Traditional Presidential Debate: Chirac/Jospin (1995) versus Sarkozy/Royal (2007)," *Argumentation* 29, no. 1 (2015): 19–32 (obviously a cross-cultural application); William L. Benoit and Allison Harthcock, "Functions of the Great Debates: Acclaims, Attacks, and Defense in the 1960 Presidential Debates," *Communication Monographs* 66 (1999): 341–357.

14. Bower Aly, "The Gallows Speech: A Lost Genre," *Southern Speech Journal* 34 (1969): 204–213; Karlyn K. Campbell and Kathleen H. Jamieson, "Inaugurating the Presidency," *Presidential Studies Quarterly* 15 (1985): 394–411; Halford R. Ryan, "Roosevelt's Fourth Inaugural Address: A Study of Its Composition," *Quarterly Journal of Speech* 67 (1981): 157–166. Other recent situational examples include Ryan Neville-Shepard, "Triumph in Defeat: The Genre of Third Party Presidential Concessions," *Communication Quarterly* 62, no. 2 (2014): 214–232; Mary Lay Schuster, Ann La Bree Russell, Dianne M Bartels, and Holli Kelly-Trombley, "Standing in Terri Schiavo's Shoes: The Role of Genre in End-of-Life Decision Making," *Technical Communication Quarterly* 22, no. 3 (2013): 195–218; Tess Slavíčková, "The Rhetoric of Remembrance: Presidential Memorial Day Speeches," *Discourse & Society* 24, no. 3 (2013): 361–379; and Tammy R. Vigil, "George W. Bush's First Three Inaugural Addresses: Testing the Utility of the Inaugural Genre," *Southern Communication Journal* 78, no. 5 (2013): 427–446.

15. Mike Duncan and Jillian Hill, "Termination Documentation," *Business Communication Quarterly* 77, no. 3 (2014): 297–311; John W. Bowers, Donovan J. Ochs, Richard J. Jensen, and David P. Schultz, *The Rhetoric of Agitation and Control*, 3rd ed. (Prospect Heights, IL: Waveland Press, 2009); A. Cheree Carlson and John E. Hocking, "Strategies of Redemption at the Vietnam Veterans' Memorial," *Western Journal of Speech Communication* 49 (1988): 14–26; Andrew A. King and Floyd D. Anderson, "Nixon, Agnew, and the 'Silent Majority': A Case Study in the Rhetoric of Polarization," *Western Speech* 35 (1971): 243–255; Richard D. Raum and James S. Measell, "Wallace and His Ways: A Study of the Rhetorical Genre of Polarization," *Central States Speech Journal* 25 (1971): 28–35.

16. Carolyn R. Miller and Jeanne Fahnestock, "Genres in Scientific and Technical Rhetoric," *Poroi: An Interdisciplinary Journal of Rhetorical Analysis & Invention* 9, no. 1 (2013): 2–4.

17. Karlyn K. Campbell, "Style and Content in the Rhetoric of Early Afro-American Feminists," *Quarterly Journal of Speech* 72 (1986): 434–445.

18. James Chesebro, "Rhetorical Strategies of the Radical-Revolutionary," *Today's Speech* 20 (1972): 37–48.

19. Thomas D. Clark, "An Exploration of Generic Aspects of Contemporary American Campaign Orations," *Central States Speech Journal* 30 (1979): 122–133.

20. Bernard K. Duffy, "The Anti-Humanist Rhetoric of the New Religious Right," *Southern Speech Communication Journal* 49 (1984): 339–360.

21. Dale G. Leathers, "Belief-Disbelief Systems: The Communicative Vacuum of the Radical Right," in *Explorations in Rhetorical Criticism*, ed. G. P. Mohrmann, Charles J. Stewart, and Donovan J. Ochs (University Park: Pennsylvania State University Press, 1973), 124–137.

22. Lotta Lehti, "Blogging Politics in Various Ways: A Typology of French Politicians' Blogs," *Journal of Pragmatics* 43, no. 6 (2011): 1610–1627.

23. Carl R. Burgchardt, "Two Faces of American Communism: Pamphlet Rhetoric of the Third Period and the Popular Front," *Quarterly Journal of Speech* 66 (1980): 375–391.

24. David A. Carter, "The Industrial Workers of the World and the Rhetoric of Song," *Quarterly Journal of Speech* 66 (1980): 365–374.

25. Aristotle, *The Rhetoric*, trans. W. Rhys Roberts (New York: Modern Library, 1954).

26. Edwin Black, *Rhetorical Criticism: A Study in Method* (1965; repr., University of Wisconsin Press, 1978), 133.

27. Ibid.

28. Ibid.

29. See Lloyd F. Bitzer, "The Rhetorical Situation," *Philosophy & Rhetoric* 1 (1968): 1–14; cf. William L. Benoit, "The Genesis of Rhetorical Action," *Southern Communication Journal* 59 (1994): 342–355; Lloyd F. Bitzer, "Functional Communication: A Situational Perspective," in *Rhetoric in Transition: Studies in the Nature and Uses of Rhetoric*, ed. Eugene E. White, 21–38 (University Park: Pennsylvania State University Press, 1980). For more on the rhetorical situation, see Marilyn J. Young, "Lloyd F. Bitzer: Rhetorical Situation, Public Knowledge, and Audience Dynamics," in *Twentieth-Century Roots of Rhetorical Studies*, ed. Jim A. Kuypers and Andrew King, 274–301 (Westport, CT: Praeger, 2001).

30. Harrell and Linkugel, "On Rhetorical Genre," 263–264, italics omitted.

31. Karlyn K. Campbell and Kathleen H. Jamieson, *Form and Genre: Shaping Rhetorical Action* (Falls Church, VA: Speech Communication Association, 1978), 20.

32. Situational factors and evidence from the text and rhetor can be used to make an argument about the rhetor's likely purpose.

33. Carolyn R. Miller, "Genre as Social Action," *Quarterly Journal of Speech* 70 (1984): 151.

34. Jamieson and Campbell, "Rhetorical Hybrids: Fusions of Generic Elements," *Quarterly Journal of Speech* 68 (1982): 147.

35. Bitzer, "The Rhetorical Situation."

36. Kenneth Burke, *Counter-Statement* (1931; repr., Berkeley: University of California Press, 1968); Kenneth Burke, "Dramatism," *International Encyclopedia of the Social Sciences* 7 (1968): 445–452; Kenneth Burke, *A Grammar of Motives* (1945; repr., Berkeley: University of California Press, 1969); Kenneth Burke, "Questions and Answers about the Pentad," *College Composition and Communication* 29 (1978): 330–335. See, too, vol. 1, no. 3, of the *American Communication Journal*. There you will find essays on each of the following topics: "motive," "sacrifice and moral hierarchy," "identification," "the pentad," and the cycle of "guilt, purification, and redemption." http://ac-journal.org/journal/vol1/iss3/curtain3.html.

37. William L. Benoit, "Beyond Genre Theory: The Genesis of Rhetorical Action," *Communication Monographs* 67 (2000): 178–192.

38. Howard W. Martin, "A Generic Exploration: Staged Withdrawal, the Rhetoric of Resignation," *Central States Speech Journal* 27 (1976): 247–257; Gerald L. Wilson, "A Strategy of Explanation: Richard M. Nixon's August 8, 1974, Resignation Address," *Communication Quarterly* 24 (1976): 14–20; Ryan

Neville-Shepard, "Containing the Third-Party Voter in the 2016 U.S. Presidential Election," *Journal of Communication Inquiry* 43 (2019): 272–292.

39. Harrell and Linkugel, "On Rhetorical Genre"; Robert C. Rowland "On Generic Categorization," *Communication Theory* 1 (1991): 143.

40. Jason Edwards, Joseph Valenzano, and Karla Stevenson, "The Peacekeeping Mission: Bringing Stability to a Chaotic Scene," *Communication Quarterly* 59, no. 3 (2011): 339–358.

41. Edward Shiappa and John P. Nordin, *Argumentation: Keeping Faith with Reason* (Boston, MA: Pearson, 2014); David L. Vancil, *Rhetoric and Argumentation* (Boston, MA: Allyn and Bacon, 1993).

42. Campbell and Jamieson, *Form and Genre*, 21.

43. Harrell and Linkugel, "On Rhetorical Genre," 263–264, italics omitted.

44. William L. Benoit and J. J. Gustainis, "An Analogic Analysis of the Keynote Addresses at the 1980 Presidential Nominating Conventions," *Speaker and Gavel* 24 (1986): 95–108.

45. Carlson and Hocking, "Strategies of Redemption."

46. King and Anderson, "Nixon, Agnew, and the 'Silent Majority'"; Raum and Measell, "Wallace and His Ways."

47. Bowers, Ochs, Jensen, and Schultz, *The Rhetoric of Agitation and Control*.

48. Chesebro, "Rhetorical Strategies"; Clark, "An Analysis of Recurrent Features"; Leathers, "Belief-Disbelief Systems."

49. Duffy, "The Anti-Humanist Rhetoric."

50. Robert C. Rowland, "On Generic Categorization," *Communication Theory* 1 (1991): 129.

51. "Fear the Frill: Ruth Bader Ginsburg and the Uncertain Futurity of Feminist Judicial Dissent," *Quarterly Journal of Speech* 101 (2015): 72–84.

52. Jamieson and Campbell, "Rhetorical Hybrids." See also, "Rebekah Perkins Crawford, "Infiltrative Rhetoric for LGB Inclusion: The LDS Version of Supportive Families, Healthy Children Pamphlet," *Western Journal of Communication* 82 (2018): 259–275; Jacob W. Justice, "From Communist Nightmare to American Dream: Hybrid Rhetoric in Senator Marco Rubio's 2016 Tribute to José Fernández," *Southern Communication Journal* 83, no. 1 (2018): 28–40.

53. Allison M. Prasch and Julia Scatliff O'Grady, "Saluting the 'Skutnik': Special Guests, the First Lady's Box, and the Generic Evolution of the State of the Union Address," *Rhetoric & Public Affairs* 20, no. 4 (2017): 571–604.

54. Benoit, "In Defense."

55. Benoit, Blaney, and Pier, "Acclaiming, Attacking, and Defending."

II

PERSPECTIVES ON CRITICISM

6

The Traditional Perspective

Forbes I. Hill

Traditional criticism, sometimes referred to as neo-Aristotelian criticism, is usually taken to mean criticism guided by the theory of rhetoric handed down from antiquity. Although this theory takes several different shapes and forms, they are mostly variations on a theme—that while rhetoric describes reality and does not create it, our perceptions of the real world can be changed by persuaders who insist that their own perceptions are more accurate or, at least, more advantageous to themselves or to the public interest. The tools for changing other peoples' understanding of reality are arguments that can be analyzed by a rhetorician; arguments are presented in language, which in most cases is believed to have more impact when it keeps perspicuity but is made attractive with artfully plotted phrasing. Normally the arguments are marshaled in a compelling order and presented to the listeners by speakers who have mastered the art of **paralinguistic features** (varying volume or rate of speaking, for example) and the art of **kinesics** (using the body to convey meanings and emotions). This is a pragmatic, or utilitarian, conception of rhetoric.

Some critics have used traditional theory to explain advertisements, propaganda, docudramas, and even novels and films, especially those with a covert propagandistic purpose. This is, of course, not a new idea. In the early 1920s, Hoyt Hopewell Hudson advocated broadening the paths of rhetorical study to include pamphleteering, newspapers, editorial writing, radio broadcasting, advertising, propaganda, and others.[1] Although usually not practiced in stand-alone form today, the ideas derived from Aristotelian criticism are regularly used and range from analysis of journalist fabrications,[2] to university student requests to faculty,[3] to how corporations attempt to justify genetically altered foods to consumers,[4] to numerous others. In short, whenever there are direct attempts at persuasion, the traditional perspective may prove useful.

TRADITIONAL CRITICISM

The **traditional perspective** assumes that criticism entails both explication of what went on when speakers engaged listeners or readers, and evaluation of how well the speakers performed the task of changing these receivers' understanding of reality. These twin tasks, explication and evaluation, together comprise the rhetorical critique. In its simplest form, it is a critique of the assumed interaction of a speaker with his audience or an author with his readers at a particular point in time. But in their more complex forms, rhetorical critiques may be used to explicate and evaluate the performance of several speakers or writers engaged in a campaign or perhaps a social movement, for example, a study of the changing rhetorical arguments in the campaign for abortion reform during the twentieth and early twenty-first centuries.

Aristotle, often considered the fount of traditional criticism, was no doubt thinking of the interaction of an individual with a particular audience when he set out the elements that we today use for analysis: "A discourse involves three factors: the speaker, the matter about which he speaks, and the persons to whom he is speaking."[5] If we add to this, as most rhetoricians do, the occasion on which the speech is given, it is still a simple plan for a critique. This plan may be made more inclusive by using slightly more complex terms that are near synonyms for the four factors. In place of the term *speaker*, for example, we often use *source*, by which is meant ghostwriter, public-relations agent, campaign committee, advertising team, and so on. In place of the matter about which one speaks, modern writers use the term *message*; that is, whatever matter is formulated for transmission to others. In place of persons who are addressed, we use *audience*. The audience is understood as the group of people who have similar reactions to the message, and in some modern cases these auditors are not even in the same space as the person presenting the message; they may be reading the message in a book or receiving it by television or podcast. For occasion the term *context* is now used. Traditional criticism is highly contextual; it looks at source, message, and audience as they interact within a given span of time.

Ultimately, the traditional perspective's "point of view," Herbert Wichelns wrote, "is patently single. It is not concerned with permanence, nor yet with beauty. It is concerned with effect. It regards a speech as a communication to a specific audience, and holds its business to be the analysis and appreciation of the orator's method of imparting his ideas to his hearers."[6] Even if we expand this notion of audience to include a number of related groups of people, targets of a persuasive campaign for example, we are still dealing with *effect*—that is, analysis and appreciation of the method used by strategists planning the campaign to impart their ideas to these people over this limited period of time.

Wichelns's concern with effect follows Aristotle's statement, "The audience is the end—the reason for making the discourse."[7] Aristotle believed that all natural activities are directed toward some end state: ***telos*** in his language; hence his philosophy is said to be teleological. He thought that the telos of any activity was its purpose for being and defined its essential nature. This orientation is basic to traditional criticism. Some utterances may be entirely self-expressive—crying "Ouch!" when one touches a hot stove, for example. Rhetorical utterances, however, are not primarily expressive; they are made holding in the forefront of one's mind the impact they will have on other people upon whom one seeks to impress one's ideas. They are the product of strategic choices about how the speaker wants auditors to respond.

An account of the audience logically comes first when one is composing a critique of a rhetorical event. Nevertheless, it is in practice difficult to start a highly contextualized critique such as the one a scholar writes without answering the question, When does this audience come into being and under what conditions? Reconstructing the audience is inseparable from determining the context of a rhetorical production.

What follows is an overview of how one might begin a criticism that uses the traditional perspective, although not all critical efforts of this nature follow this exact pattern. The majority of traditional critiques do, however, touch upon the following five areas: recreation of the context, recreation of the audience, description of the source of the message, analysis of the message, and evaluation of the discourse.

Recreating the Context of Rhetorical Events

What is the context in which the speech occurred? Context is often divided into two parts: the physical setting for the event or events, the so-called mise-en-scène, and the social and political context out of which the need for using rhetoric arose. An oft-cited example in traditional criticism is Abraham Lincoln's Gettysburg Address. Why did President Lincoln go to speak at Gettysburg? One reason is that the State of Pennsylvania had planned a ceremony dedicating a cemetery right on the battlefield where many thousands had fallen. Near the field, but somewhat removed from the burial operations, a platform was erected on which sat numerous important political figures. The audience, numbering some twenty thousand, stood near rows of graves in the crisp November sun. Is this mise-en-scène important? Definitely so in this case. The fact that Lincoln was facing the field of battle and the graves is a controlling factor over the speech: "We are met on a great battlefield of that war; we have come to dedicate a portion of that field as a final resting place." Often, however, the setting is not so important. If a contemporary president makes a statement from a news studio in a large city, a description of the scenery may actually get in the way of creating an adequate critique. The studio might be anywhere; the important question, aside from whether or not he's in prime time, is what was the political situation that this administration thought required a presidential speech?

While the actual scene is often described, the social or political context must also be described. For example, Lincoln could have turned down the invitation to appear at Gettysburg. He was not the featured speaker; the ceremony was centered on a great oration to be delivered by another. Lincoln was in a busy period of his presidency, overwhelmed by the various duties of the office and by the cares of his family life. He chose to go to Gettysburg because of the importance of the occasion: it was the celebration of a battle where many lives had been lost. It was also an opportunity to make news in anticipation of the coming presidential campaign. But above all, it was time for him to put his spin on the significance of the war, to prepare for the postwar period of reconciliation. He dropped everything to take an exhausting train journey to the battlefield.[8] This is the political context of his speech.

For the critic, creating the political context is often a difficult task. Out of all the events in the life of the speaker and the history of the times, which are those that determine the rhetorical situation? Answering this question becomes even more difficult the further removed one's rhetorical artifact is from the present day. The critic simply cannot reproduce a complete account of an era as the jumping-off place for his critique. For example, it is obviously important to President Trump's "Remarks by President Trump in Address to the Nation [about the coronavirus]"[9] that COVID-19 had been spreading rapidly across the globe and in parts of the United States and that, despite the federal policies enacted up to that moment, it was being viewed as a continuing threat, with growing concern and even fear in some quarters.[10] However, is it also important to know that there was not consensus across the world about the best way to handle the situation, or that the country was divided over wanting more or less federal government control over American lives during this time? A narrative about all these factors could overwhelm a critic's account of the presidential statement itself. The speechmaker must make these decisions about inclusion; the critic then provides an evaluation. The effect various factors have on the message should usually be the principal criterion for their inclusion in the section of an essay that recreates the context. For example, clearly the growing fear concerning contracting the virus impacted the construction of the speech, and we see that in the speech itself where President Trump offers this: "The vast majority of Americans: The risk is very, very low. Young and healthy people can expect to recover fully and quickly if they should get the virus. The highest risk is for elderly population with underlying health conditions. The elderly population must be very, very careful."

Constructing Audiences for Rhetorical Events

Those receiving a message are collectively known as the audience. Traditional rhetoric re-gards them as free agents who make largely rational choices about the matters at hand. Their choices are influenced by their emotional states but are not infinitely malleable. Traditional rhetoricians divide audiences into three kinds: either they are jurors in a court of law, who decide about a public or private action that took place in the past (**forensic discourse**); they are legislators, or decision makers, who decide about some course of action to be taken in the future (**deliberative discourse**); or they are spectators who come to experience a celebration or commemoration of some person or event—that is, a ceremony in the present (**epideictic discourse**). Aristotle, at least, emphasized the audience's function as decision makers; even the auditors at a ceremonial speech, who primarily serve as spectators at a performance, in the final analysis are judges of the expedience and inexpedience of decisions made by those who are praised or blamed at the occasion.[11]

One must discover, then, which of these kinds of audience a speaker was asking to make a decision. Often this choice is obvious, as in the case of Roosevelt's War Message, which ends, "I ask that the Congress declare that since the unprovoked and dastardly attack by Japan on Sunday, December 7, 1941, a state of war has existed between the United States and the Em-pire of Japan." But what can be said of the Gettysburg Address? What decision did Lincoln expect his audience to make? To care about the honored dead? They already cared—cared enough to have come in most cases from far away. Even those who read his speech in the newspapers undoubtedly cared at a time when everyone had a relative who fought in the war.

Lincoln also recommended a course of action, that we "take increased devotion to the cause for which they gave their last full measure of devotion." Does this phrase's orientation to the future make the speech deliberative? After a careful examination of text and context, Garry Wills judged it to be a speech that changed people's attitude toward the war: no longer were they to be caught up in the blood and guts of the fray, or even the contentiousness that brought on the war. They were to transcend such matters, which go unmentioned in the ad-dress, and to see the war as a necessary phase in the nation's progress toward a more perfect union. If we accept this interpretation, then it is clearly a ceremonial speech. It does not aim at a decision about some imminent course of action. By praising the common sacrifice of all those who struggled in the Battle of Gettysburg, it aims to change people's whole belief system from one that dwells on the strife to one that is oriented to the making of peace. Use of praise and blame to forge the auditors into an audience that agrees on common values, such as peace and progress, is what ceremonial addresses are all about.[12]

The choice of the kind of audience at which the discourse is aimed is in this, as in other cases, not obvious. Making that choice requires careful examination of the text as well as the context. This examination is complicated when rhetorical productions are designed to change the perceptions and beliefs of more than one group of people, as is often the case in modern times. Take Ray Rice's May 23, 2014, speech of apology discussed in an earlier chapter. This speech addresses several distinct groups and is in response to numerous competing moral and social contexts. In antiquity one could conceive of the audience as those citizens in the popular assembly. With the advent of mass media and twenty-four-hour news coverage, however, the concern with audience takes on especial importance for the critic.

Back to Roosevelt's War Message. Ostensibly addressed to Congress, it was heard on the radio by over sixty million people, with even more reading it later (with a total population of 132 million at the time); its brevity and simplicity are a clue that it was intended to be a deliberative speech aimed at a decision by the larger audience of Americans. The War Message, heard in schools and churches and public buildings throughout the country, may have been one of the last speeches where members of the media audience were in contact with each other. However, then as now, an address by a great public figure is heard by an audience totally fragmented—a collection of individuals. Does this make a difference? Traditional criticism seems forced to answer this question in the negative. Here is why this is so.

Any analysis of the audience is a construct. Let us say that a speaker's audience is the US House of Representatives: 435 members from fifty states. That is a diverse group, and even in the age of maximum information, one can hardly know empirically what the range of individual opinions is, especially since there are always some curmudgeons that defy classification. A rhetorical strategist needs to make a profile: most are not young, none are poor (the 2020 rank-and-file congressional salary is $174,000 per year—roughly in the top 10 percent of the total *household* income bracket; beyond salary, they are wealthy, with a net worth estimated at five times the US median), almost all affect some kind of Judeo-Christian religious belief, almost all are committed Democrats or Republicans, most desire to be reelected, and none of them reveal the whole truth about themselves. This profile is based on a minimum of real data. It is what Aristotle would call *probability*, that is, what one would reasonably expect about people elected every two years as representatives. Since some improbable things actually happen, we also expect that several members do not fit the profile, but we ignore them. Given the right subject—for example, the March 2020 CARES (Coronavirus Aid, Relief, and Economic Security) Act—Congress can be forged into something that approaches a unity; they can become a true audience. The House (363–40) and Senate (96–0) willingly voted to authorize the use of over two trillion dollars to support Americans during this time.

Though the media audience is fragmented, can we construct it in the same way we constructed the Congress? We do have data about them: there are polls, both formal and informal, and sometimes focus groups. The polls are often broken down demographically; regions of the country are separated; the young are separated from those in their prime and the elderly, the wealthy from the middle class and the poor, women from men, whites from blacks, and blacks from Americans of Asian descent. Aristotle provides some probable statements characterizing these groups. He states that the young are sanguine and expect life to become better for them; the elderly are more skeptical, having often experienced failure. The wealthy expect to control affairs; the poor tend to expect disappointment.[13] Although Aristotle did not characterize women as distinct from men or take into consideration racial characteristics, modern pollsters do tabulate data for women and contrast it to that for men, and consider how the races differ on issues. Such hints about the ages and fortunes of people provide us with materials to refine polling questions and to better interpret polling data.

From polling data and Aristotle's character sketches, a critic can construct a profile of the fragmented media audience. The profile, if carefully made, will probably be nearly as accurate as one's profile of a divided Congress. The critic operating from a traditional perspective should search biographies and eyewitness accounts to find out how the speaker conceived of the audience so that he can contrast the speaker's construction with potentially more accurate ones.

Describing the Source of the Message

Traditional rhetoricians have historically thought about the source as a singular person—an orator skilled in the art of speaking. The roster of speakers who fulfilled that vision is almost, but not quite, congruent with the list of great statesmen. Most orators wrote their own speeches, perhaps with a little editorial help. From this point of view it makes sense to ask questions such as, What was the nature of the orator's unique personal charm? What was his education? What were the orator's peculiar qualifications as thinker and stylist? What obstacles did the orator overcome on the road to rhetorical celebrity? Such questions are the stuff of rhetorical biography. It is still a pleasure to read a short biographical essay—one that touches the peaks of a man or a woman's speaking career, say a Bernie Sanders or a Sarah Palin. When done well, it makes the reader consider himself a close watcher of a great career.

Historical figures may still be treated this way. Imagine a retrospective of Franklin D. Roosevelt: his homeschooling directed by an imperious mother, his editorship of the *Harvard Crimson*, his mediocre performance in law school, his dashing entrance into politics, his marriage to the woman who became a truly remarkable public figure in her own right, his overcoming a crippling illness to reestablish an impossible political career, his use of that remarkable voice to compensate for an inability to move around the platform, his discovery of radio, his adventurous spirit, and yes, his confidence that bordered on arrogance, making him at times a divisive figure. Such an essay can never go out of date.

As exciting as a rhetorical biography can be, though, it is only a small part of a traditional critique. In recent times a speaker is likely to serve as a spokesman for an organization: he is a cabinet member or public-relations officer of an agency or corporation. The message he delivers is not his own; even if the speaker drafted it, numerous others in the organization have edited it and revised to the point where it has become a car put together by a committee. Take the March 25, 2015, comments made by incoming White House communications director Jen Psaki. She spoke on Fox News's *The Kelly File*. Host Megyn Kelly asked Psaki if trading Sgt. Bowe Bergdahl for five Taliban terrorists last year was "worth it" given the army's recently announced desertion charges against Bergdahl. Psaki replied, "Was it worth it? Absolutely. . . . We have a commitment to our men and women serving in the military, defending our national security every day, that we're going to do everything to bring them home if we can, and that's what we did in this case."[14] Psaki was speaking for President Obama and his administration, not for herself.[15]

Under these circumstances it no longer makes sense to ask about the speaker's education, or his unique language choices. The question is, What kind of a committee of writers put together the message? What interests did they represent? For a president, this often means State versus Defense, for example. How did the writers work together and interface with the spokesman? What does the text show about how they built a favorable public image for the spokesman? How did committee and spokesman construe what would build credibility? Covering factors such as these is what we now mean by describing the source. Additionally, it is still relevant to ask, did the spokesman deliver the message with conviction? With a flair? Did he show great energy? Was he serious or lighthearted? Did he dominate the audience and seem to reach into their hearts? Appropriate delivery is itself a source of credibility.

Analyzing the Message

The traditional perspective begins its consideration of the message by asking about the text—a written document that recreates what a speaker said to that audience on that particular occasion. If one is going to consider questions of proof or of rhetorical style, it is desirable to have an accurate account of the verbal utterance of the moment, or at least of what the author intended a reader to read.

Often a good text is available; some independent agent has made an audio or video recording. We should be alert if the recording or document is available only from the source. Texts are often edited; it is well attested that congressmen may revise the Congressional Record at any time until the printing presses start to move. Often a speaker will be asked to write out his remarks for publication after the presentation. The importance of finding a reliable text is well exemplified by this example: the text published by the *Boston Globe* of Professor George Wald's signature utterance, "A Generation in Search of a Future," furnished to the newspaper by the speaker does not contain the lines italicized here:

> Nobody is the aggressor any more except those on the other side. *And this is why that, that Neanderthal among Secretaries of State—Rusk—went to such [applause]—went to such pains, went to such pains, stuck by his guns, because in him, uhh, stubbornness and density take the place of character, [laughter] uhh, went to such pains to insist as he still insists that in Vietnam we are repelling an aggression. And if you're repelling an aggression, anything goes.*

This characterization of Dean Rusk is grotesquely unfair; he never held that if you are repelling an aggression, anything goes, and he did not resemble Neanderthal man. Professor Wald apparently had second thoughts when he edited this passage out of the version he gave the press. The independent recording put out by Caedmon Records gives what he said unedited.[16] It also shows why the unedited version is important: Wald received by far the most vociferous reaction to these statements of anything else in his speech. They resonated wildly with an audience of 1960s radicals who were united in their hatred of established authority figures such as the secretary of state. What you know from other sources about Wald's audience is amply confirmed.

The further back one goes in history the more difficult the problem. The text of the Attic orations derives from copies made by the orators as examples for use in the schools of rhetoric. Naturally the orators transmitted to the schools only the fairest texts of what they said. Speeches in the eighteenth- and early nineteenth-century House of Commons and House of Lords were mostly recreated by reporters who stood closely packed in the galleries, where they were not supposed to make transcriptions of the proceedings. The Lincoln-Douglas debates were collated from newspaper reports by Lincoln; it is small wonder that his speeches look more finished in the received text than Douglas's. The traditional critic will often need to make a caveat about most speeches: "I don't vouch for every word of the text; I worked with the best text available."

The traditional perspective considers the message itself under the headings (or canons) of *invention, disposition*, and *style*. By **invention** is meant the finding of appropriate materials for the discourse. This is usually done by checking through an inventory of stock materials—**topics** or topoi—looking to see whether the speaker has used all available means of persuasion, as Aristotle put it. Topical thinking is a type of systematic brainstorming using predefined categories. Although developed in ancient times, more recent applications are available. For example, John Wilson and Carroll Arnold developed sixteen topics for the contemporary student. These include the "existence or nonexistence of things"; "degree or quantity of things, forces, etc."; spatial attributes"; "attributes of time"; "motion or activity"; and "form, either physical or abstract."[17] By **disposition** is meant the arranging of these materials in a structure as well plotted as the order of battle when skilled generals make a plan for victory. Structure can be influenced by many factors, although it is generally agreed upon that your audience, topic, and purpose play a deciding role. By **style** is meant the use of the right language to make the materials of exposition and argument clear and convincing. We will now consider each of these in turn.

Invention

When a critic seeks to investigate invention, he is dealing with both artistic and inartistic proofs. **Artistic proofs** are the invented proofs. They are created by the speaker, the arguments that he uses to try to persuade the audience. They are usually, if somewhat inaccurately, grouped under the headings of logos, ethos, and pathos. **Inartistic proofs** are not created by the speaker but instead exist on their own: contracts, wills, our federal and state constitutions, or other documents, for example.

In relation to *logos*, the critic should look to see whether the appropriate commonplace arguments, deduced from the list of topics, have been used. **Logos** refers in general to logic based on reason. This is not a scientific logic but rather a rhetorical logic, one based on probability. Those creating arguments need to construct them based on common notions of what is probable. To prosecute a company for spreading toxic waste, one looks for the green water and brown air in the neighborhood; the prosecutor seeks out people who claim to be sick and compares them to those in comparable areas who are not sick. He points to the prevalence of cost cutting among companies who look at the bottom line, the absence of witnesses and regulators, and the arrogant behavior of company executives. These are the commonplaces of environmental claims, and failure to use them should be construed as not making the most effective speech possible. A critic would look for such commonplaces.

Although there are many ways to examine the logic used in a speech, one particularly important aspect to be examined is the concept of the enthymeme. The essence of the **enthymeme** is that some parts of the logical argument are omitted when the speaker or writer can predict that the auditors will supply them. Take this example from Richard Nixon: "The American people cannot and should not be asked to support a policy which involves the overriding issues of war and peace unless they know the truth about that policy. Tonight I would like to answer some of the questions that I know are on the minds of many of you listening to me."[18]

This is a typical example of an enthymeme that builds the speaker's credibility and that also requires the listener/reader's participation in supplying a crucial missing term. Presented as a traditional **syllogism**, it would look like this:

Premise 1: All policies that the American people should be asked to support are policies about which they will know the truth.

Premise 2: The policies which I reveal when I answer your questions are policies that the American people should be asked to support.

Conclusion: The policies which I reveal when I answer your questions are policies about which you will know the truth.

Nixon's actual statement is making the claim that he will tell the truth about his policies. He says that the American people should not be asked to support his policies unless they know the truth about them. Although I supplied all three parts of the syllogism, Nixon never actually explicitly claims that he is going to tell the truth. The second premise I give is actually not stated by Nixon; rather, *one is tempted to supply it in one's own mind*, and if the listener supplies it, the very activity of completing the logical structure starts the process of the listener assenting to the argument. As Lloyd Bitzer wrote, "Enthymemes occur only when speaker and audience jointly produce them. . . . Because they are jointly produced, enthymemes intimately unite speaker and audience and provide the strongest possible proofs."[19] This process will be completed unless the auditor checks himself and looks at it. He is more likely to yield to the process because the formal logic behind this argument is good enough, though the second premise is unsupported and probably false.

Persuasive discourse is constructed so that there are usually a large number of ethos claims. **Ethos** is basically an interpretation by the audience of qualities possessed by a speaker as the speaker delivers his message. Thus, by the way a speaker argues, an audience makes judgments about his intelligence, character, and goodwill. A speaker becomes unpersuasive if he has to claim directly, "I did not have sexual relations with that woman" (Bill Clinton) or "I'm honest in my dealings with people" (Mitt Romney). If he needs to state it in this bald way, he has already lost credibility. An exposition of how a speaker establishes ethos is a significant part of a traditional critique. Sometimes the discourse will contain a narrative of the discovery of the right course of action. Such a narrative shows the good sense of the spokesman and his advisers, who did not make decisions off the top of their heads but only after consideration and reflection. The way in which a speaker supports his arguments and organizes his materials can impact the assessment of his intelligence. Very often his character—moral qualities—can be assessed by how qualities such as justice, courage, generosity, and so on are exhibited in his arguments.

Finally, a speaker could also show goodwill by finding common ground with the readers/listeners. The speaker who comes to campus tells us, "I remember when I was a student; like so many of you I didn't have enough time in the day to do everything. I worked part time in the dining room and stole away to the quietest corner of the library every night. But hard as that was, it was worth it." Speakers also indulge in a little subtle flattery: "You who have a university education easily recognize that group behavior differs from individual behavior." Commenting on such statements is part of a traditional critique as it relates to ethos.

The first step in dealing with **pathos** in the critique is identifying the emotional states that dominate the discourse. The speaker's words will *invite* us to feel a particular way. Sometimes this is obvious. In the case of Roosevelt's War Message, the emotional states are anger and confidence. The anger springs from our sense of betrayal by an inferior people from whom we are entitled to receive respect. The confidence comes from our feeling of unity and our sense of righteousness. Roosevelt amplified the sneakiness of the attack and the innocent lives lost to bring people into a greater state of anger, and he represented himself as speaking for all our people, who recognize the facts of Japanese aggression, which are so obvious that they speak for themselves. When auditors are angry enough, they minimize feelings of fear; they become ready to accept with confidence hardships and sacrifices: hence the above listed *pathe* are the stuff of war messages.

Another example is seen in the commercials for the Christian Children's Fund,[20] now called ChildFund International. These commercials begin with images of children in truly impoverished conditions. Many of the children are shown playing in what might be raw waste and garbage; many have flies around their eyes and walk with distended bellies. This is quickly contrasted with images of those children helped by this charity: better clothing, healthier looking, and so forth. All this in the background reinforces the same verbal message by the speaker. Your emotional register goes from pity and perhaps guilt to hope. A critic would look for these emotional appeals and determine their effectiveness in moving us along toward doing whatever it is the speaker wishes us to do: in the case of the Christian Children's Fund, sponsor a child.[21] Not all appeals to emotion will be so easy to detect; the critic must step back and carefully look for these.

Disposition

The critic must also ferret out disposition, or the speech's organization *as it relates to persuasion*. In almost no case is a discourse arranged randomly, though occasionally a speechwriter will try to make it appear random. Roosevelt's War Message, Stelzner points out, falls almost into two halves, separated by the sentence, "As Commander in Chief of the Army and Navy I have directed that all measures be taken for our defense." All material prior to that sentence is in the past tense and the Japanese Empire is the actor. What follows that sentence is in the present tense; the president, Congress, and the people become the actors.[22] Such is the disposition of this celebrated speech.

Take Lincoln's address at Cooper Union for another example; it divides into three parts: first a forensic section in which the speaker refutes the belief that Congress could not constitutionally legislate as to slavery in the federal territories; then a shorter constructive section on the idea that Republicans are the ones who perpetuate the constitutional doctrines of the Founding Fathers, and it's the Southerners who have made a radical change; and then the shortest section, a little deliberative speech to Republicans exhorting them to act with restraint while refusing to compromise their basic ideals. From accusation to constructive defense to exhortation (in long, shorter, and shortest sections) is the pattern for disposition in the Cooper Union Address. There ought to be some discernible rationale, as in the cases cited, for the disposition of the materials of the discourse. It is the task of the critic to figure out that rationale.

Style

Traditional criticism treats the style of the discourse as part of the persuasive force of the arguments. Style must be, however, both appropriate to subject and audience. In most cases clarity is assumed as the cardinal virtue of style. Clarity is achieved with factors such as using common words, avoiding jargon, creating metaphors that make matters vivid, using active verbs, and avoiding more than the minimum of adjectives. The speaker who uses such locutions as "the optimum moment of contact" is probably not persuading as well as one who says "timing's important; there's a right moment for everything." That is, of course, unless the audience is composed of those predisposed to accept a specific technical vocabulary. When Thomas Paine refutes the argument that America has flourished under her former connection with Great Britain by writing, "We may as well assert that because a child has thrived upon milk that it is never to have meat," he chooses a metaphor that is both concrete and familiar.[23] Observations of this sort are the meat of traditional criticism in relation to clarity of style.

Yet working against this preference for the unmodified common word is the notion that style should make an impression—that statements should have a certain heft to give an idea presence. That is also a precept of traditional rhetoric; the style of public address is never colloquial, though it may be deliberately kept simple. So the speechwriter is to make a certain admixture of long words and a few unusual ones; he is occasionally to look for a unique way of phrasing something even amid the clichés.

Clarity and impressiveness are also to be gained from figures of syntax: parallel structure of clauses and sentences and the devices that reinforce it. When Lincoln declaimed, "Fondly do we hope, fervently do we pray that this mighty scourge of war may speedily pass away," he created a syntactical structure that speaks seriously; it is hard, however, to sing it to a merry tune. The contrast of hope and pray (antithesis) would be entirely broken up if he had said, "Fondly do we hope and we also pray fervently." *Fondly* and *fervently*, too, must be in the same grammatical position in each clause; then the alliteration works to reinforce the structure. The rhyming of *pray* and *away* (epistrophe) is also important to the structure. Traditional rhetoric views this artistry in structuring prose as a significant part of rhetorical effectiveness. These rhetorical figures of speech are more than window dressing; they are an important part of the persuasive process.

Summary

When looking at the message, a critic will look to see whether the discourse is deliberative, forensic, or epideictic. Deliberative discourse is concerned with the future, and its auditors are asked to make judgments about future courses of action. Forensic discourse is concerned with past acts, and its auditors are asked to make judgments concerning what actually happened in the past. Epideictic discourse is set in the present and concerns speeches of praise or blame. Its auditors are being asked to make judgments concerning how well the speaker accomplishes his goals.

Generally a critic looks for three items in a text: invention, disposition, and style. Under invention, a critic looks to see how well the speaker created his rhetorical appeals: were all the available means of persuasion used? Both artistic—logos, ethos, and pathos—and inartistic proofs will be examined. A critic will also look hard at the disposition or organization of a speech to determine its impact upon persuasive effect. Finally, a critic will look at the style of the speech. How might the language choices made impact the persuasive effort?

Evaluating the Discourse

Aristotle lays down the rule that a discourse should be judged by whether it uses sound method: "it is not the function of rhetoric to persuade but to observe the available means of persuasion for situations like this one, just as in all the other arts. For example, the function of medicine is not to make healthy, but to bring the patient as far toward health as the case permits. For sometimes it is impossible to bring health, but one must give sound treatment."[24]

If he follows this rule, the critic goes through a checklist of the available lines of argument to see if any are omitted that might persuade this audience on this subject; he considers the possible ways of disposing the narrative and arguments to see if the best way has been used; he looks at the stylistic devices that clothe the arguments to see if there are others more appropriate to the situation. If everything is done, he is ready to render a judgment: this must be the best discourse—or possibly it falls short in some of the ways described below. Regardless, there is a certain concern with the aesthetics involved with the speechmaking process: How well were the arguments constructed? Was the message well organized? And was the style used appropriate for the specific audience?

In practice, almost no critic is wholly satisfied with this kind of purely internal critique. Almost invariably critics add some kind of external measure. The legislature did not pass the bill. The jury did not convict. The voters did not elect the candidate. The president gave a speech on the economy, and the stock market rose or fell. These *effects* are the simplest indicators of success, but we know that they are often misleading. Sometimes legislators have commitments that make it impossible for them to respond even to the most finely crafted speech. Some juries will nullify the law because of their sympathy for the defendant even though the presentation of the case has been artistically satisfactory.

We may look to somewhat more indirect measures as well. The legislature took up the bill next session or the one after and, without much additional debate, passed it. The jury did not convict, but all the editorial writers agreed that they should have. The stock market immediately reacted like a bear to the president, but two weeks later the bull market began, and it ran a long course. Take, for example, Susan B. Anthony, who was the center of controversy throughout most of her life but never lived to see woman's suffrage. When the suffrage amendment finally passed, she was honored as the ancestor of all suffragettes. These historical results are, perhaps, more just indications of the success or failure of a persuasive campaign than a decision made in the midst of the struggle. George Orwell's critique of the totalitarian tendencies of the modern state did not result in the overthrow of any totalitarians, but it has become a standard against which states are judged; the use of Orwellian language is almost universally taken as the sign of approaching danger.

Thus a critic using the traditional perspective will discuss the speech's internal dynamics, but also touch upon its impact on its audience. Rhetoric, viewed from a traditional perspective, is used for a purpose, it is intentionally created, and this is taken into consideration when a critic offers an evaluation. A thoughtful discussion of the historical context and some speculation on the influence of the discourse forms the conclusion of a traditional critique.

CRITICAL ESSAY

Much of the writings of those who have used traditional criticism have assumed a general knowledge concerning the classical roots of the rhetorical theory that underpinned the criticism. The essay that follows proceeds along the same path. Instead of a fully developed review of the literature, this essay instead focuses on putting into practice traditional criticism as outlined above. You should be aware, however, that if you are writing for an academic audience you most likely will need to take time to define your terms and outline your theoretical perspective.

When reading this essay, look for the reconstruction of context, the construction of audience, a discussion of the source (speaker), and an analysis of the message (look in particular for a discussion of invention, disposition, and style). Finally, look for an evaluation of the rhetorical artifact.

MR. DOUGLASS'S FIFTH OF JULY

Following the Compromise of 1850 the abolitionist movement, somewhat dispirited by the failure to block the Fugitive Slave Law, renewed its efforts to publicize the evils of slavery. In Rochester, New York, which was a center of antislavery activity, the Rochester Ladies' Anti-

Slavery Society decided to mark Independence Day 1852 with their own celebration featuring an address by their neighbor, the famous abolitionist speaker, Frederick Douglass. The celebration was held on July 5th since the 4th fell on a Sunday, and the custom of that era prohibited secular events on the Sabbath.

The Rochester Ladies rented Corinthian Hall, where five to six hundred people assembled, having paid 12 cents each as entry fee.[25] After the opening prayer and a reading of the Declaration of Independence, Mr. Douglass made his presentation: "What, to the Slave, is the Fourth of July?" His recitation, according to Frederick Douglass's paper, was "eloquent and admirable, eliciting much applause throughout." Before the meeting was adjourned, "A Request was . . . made that the Address be published in pamphlet form, and seven hundred copies were subscribed on the spot." It was also published in Frederick Douglass's paper on July 9 and many times subsequently. Perhaps we should now consider it an American classic. It is especially appropriate to make a critique like this using the standards of traditional rhetoric because Mr. Douglass and many in his audience were familiar with these standards.

The Audience

In constructing Douglass's audience, let us first ask, who is to make a decision about what? Those immediately before the speaker were abolitionists, their sympathizers, and their friends. Many of them were followers of William Lloyd Garrison, with whom Douglass had recently made a rancorous break. Douglass demanded that they condemn slavery—not just in an intellectual way, but with an emotional fierceness that would keep them agitated until it was abolished. What the audience might have expected on the Fourth of July was a speech praising our ancestors, our country, and our people. In an astonishing reversal Douglass gives them a discourse of uninterrupted blame: a true epideictic speech of vituperation.

If the audience before him consisted of antislavery zealots, it was nevertheless not of one mind about how slavery was to be ended. A special group of auditors were strict Garrisonians, who believed that the Constitution supported slavery and, since it did, should be wiped away, and a new Republic without the South should be established to avoid any contact with the evil of slavery. Others present took a more centrist position, and some may have been opponents of slavery only in the sense that they thought it an evil whose spread should be prevented. The auditors were united enough in their antislavery sentiments that Douglass could give a speech so critical of the Republic that no patriot would sit still for it. A different audience, even in the North, might have driven him from the platform.

But what of the reading public, the ones who got the speech from the papers and pamphlets? At first the address was carried only by the abolitionist papers; there Douglass could be assured of a favorable response. Soon it was published as a pamphlet, probably circulated mostly to abolitionists and those to whom they were proselytizing. The pamphlet certainly had no circulation in the South. Three years later an extract containing the most impassioned parts of the Fifth of July oration was made an appendix to Douglass's second autobiography, *My Bondage and My Freedom*. In this form it enjoyed a national circulation. A measure of acceptance by the larger audience was guaranteed by the indubitable fact: the American Revolution did not bring freedom to the slave. On the other hand, there must have been an ample number of readers irritated by the insult to our great national holiday. We can reasonably conclude that the oration aimed at energizing the friendly rather than converting the hostile.

The Spokesman

By 1852 Frederick Douglass was well known as a speaker: he had traveled throughout the Northeast and the middle states as a full-time agitator for the Massachusetts Anti-Slavery Society from 1841 to 1845. Born in 1817, he spent the first twenty-one years of life as a slave.

Nevertheless, he learned to read and write as a child. In his autobiographies he tells the story of getting an important book, *The Columbian Orator*, used in the schools as a source of precepts exemplified by extracts from speeches and dramas. In 1838 he escaped from the plantation, making his way north to Massachusetts. He changed his name from Frederick Augustus Washington Bailey, but after publication of the first autobiography, *Narrative of the Life of Frederick Douglass, an American Slave*, his cover was blown; he could have been arrested as an escaped slave. He fled to England, where he lectured on temperance and abolition until his freedom was bought from his old master in 1847. In England he became the most glamorous spokesman for the antislavery cause; the one who spoke from firsthand experience and with great fervor and eloquence. On his return, "a series of enthusiastic reception meetings was held to honor him; he completely dominated the annual meeting of the American Anti-Slavery Society, held on May 11, 1847; and two weeks later his coworkers installed him into the Garrisonian establishment by electing him president of The New England Anti-Slavery Society."[26]

The sponsors of the Fourth of July celebration in 1852 knew what they were doing when they made Frederick Douglass their main speaker. He was at the height of his oratorical powers in 1852, a physically impressive figure, obviously strong and vital with a large head of hair, not yet gray, and a resonant baritone voice. He could be counted on to give a good show, as he had many times before. It hardly needs to be said that the whole ceremony was built around that good show the orator was expected to give. In the nineteenth century, as Garry Wills has remarked, the orator at a public celebration was intended to be a virtuoso performer who presented a long speech replete with rhetorical flourishes. Anything less would disappoint the people who came to celebrate.[27] Douglass was conscious of his obligation to perform: "I have been engaged in writing a Speech," he wrote Gerrit Smith after the fact, "for the 4th. July, which has taken up much of my extra time for the last two or three weeks. You will readily think that the Speech ought to be good that has required so much time."[28]

Disposition and Summary of the Speech

Douglass's **exordium** is given over to a conventional expression of modesty: "He who could address this audience without a quailing sensation, has stronger nerves than I have. I do not remember ever to have appeared as a speaker before any assembly more shrinkingly, nor with greater distrust of my ability, than I do this day." In this case, as in most such expressions in eighteenth and nineteenth century orations such expressions must be taken ironically. The speaker could not have failed to know that he was among the dozen most-celebrated orators of his time.

Douglass organized the central section of this address on the principle of contrast between *then* and *now*. The first third of this section consists of conventional praise for what happened in the past. He does what any Fourth of July orator would be expected to do: celebrate the birth of the nation. This occasion is to you "what the Passover was to the emancipated people of God." It is "easy now to flippantly descant on how America was right and England wrong, but when your fathers first talked this way, they were accounted plotters of mischief, agitators and rebels, dangerous men." They petitioned the Throne, but the British government kept its course, with "the blindness which seems to be the unvarying characteristic of tyrants since Pharaoh and his hosts were drowned in the Red Sea." One can view this section like a classicist, as an historical narration; or one may see it as the first part of the section that is usually called the proof (which follows naturally assertions). In either case, the reason for praising the courage of the Fathers is to prepare for a contrast with contemporary politicians, and the reference to the Passover and to Pharaoh is meant to cue us to the denunciation of slavery to come. Typically in conventional speeches these historical narrations are used for foreshadowing.

Suddenly Douglass switches gears: he no longer speaks about then but now and announces his subject: "AMERICAN SLAVERY." He identifies himself as a speaker for the bondman, who knows that America is false to the past, false to the present, and solemnly binds herself to be false to the future. "What have I, or those I represent, to do with your independence. . . . The sunlight that brought life and healing to you has brought stripes and death to me. This Fourth is yours not mine. You may rejoice; I must mourn. . . . I do not hesitate to declare, with all my soul, that the character and conduct of this nation never looked blacker to me than on this 4th of July!" The rest of the proof is taken up by a development of the blackness of character and conduct of the nation. The arguments used to justify slavery are mere rationalizations, not even worthy of serious refutation. He makes outstanding use of the stylistic figure *paralepsis*, claiming not to be refuting these arguments, while in fact making a summary refutation of each.

"Must I undertake to prove that the slave is a man? Of course not; it is beyond doubt: you hold him responsible for crimes like other humans. Laws in most Southern states forbid teaching him to read. No one makes such laws about the beasts of the field. When the dogs in your streets, when the fowls of the air, when the cattle on your hills, when the fish of the sea and the reptiles that crawl shall be unable to distinguish the slave from a brute, then will I argue with you that the slave is a man!" He claims not to make the arguments that he has made. Is not man entitled to liberty? That's not a matter to be debated by Republicans, to be settled by logic and argumentation. "How should I look today, in the presence of Americans, dividing and subdividing a discourse, to show that men have a natural right to freedom?" Douglass concludes that he cannot argue this (though he has) because: "There is not a man beneath the canopy of heaven who does not know that slavery is wrong for him."

Is it not wrong "to make men brutes, to rob them of their liberty, to work them without wages, to keep them ignorant of their relations to their fellow men, to beat them with sticks, to flay their flesh with the lash, to load their limbs with irons, to hunt them with dogs, to sell them at auction, to sunder their families, to knock out their teeth, to burn their flesh, to starve them into obedience and submission to their masters?" Such a system is obviously wrong; "I have better employments for my time and strength than such arguments would imply," Douglass avers, but, of course his list of these oppressions of slavery has made the strongest of arguments.

Is slavery sanctioned by God? "There is blasphemy in the thought. That which is inhuman cannot be divine! Who can reason on such a proposition? They that can, may: I cannot." But he *has* reasoned. Thus with repeated paralepsis, Douglass minimizes the justifications for slavery into insignificance. He concludes his refutation, "What to the American slave is your 4th of July?" A day which reveals to him, more than all other days, the gross injustice and cruelty to which he is the constant victim. The extent of the gross injustice and cruelty is now to be exemplified through several examples.

There is the internal slave trade, thought somehow to be more respectable than the African slave trade. Douglass uses his unique ethos; he claims to have been born amid the sights and scenes of the trade. He lived in Baltimore near the market, so he saw the fleshmongers in action, driving their chained victims to the depot, and recalls how the sounds still linger in his memory.

There is the Fugitive Slave Act, through which Mason and Dixon's line has been obliterated; New York has become Virginia, and the power to hold, hunt, and sell men, women, and children remains no longer a mere state institution but is now an institution of the United States. In court two witnesses testify that this individual is the escaped slave; he may not testify on his own behalf or bring witnesses, and at the end of the proceeding he is taken in chains back to slavery. By way of amplification, this law stands alone in the annals of tyrannical legislation.

There is the attitude of the clergy who support the Fugitive Act. Using the traditional topos (topic) of inconsistency between their behavior and their pretensions, Douglass charges: "if the Fugitive Slave Law concerned the right to worship God according to the dictates of their own consciences, a general shout would go up from the church demanding repeal, repeal, instant repeal." But the church of our country does not esteem the law as a declaration of war against religious liberty. In supporting the law the church has made itself the bulwark of American slavery, and the shield of American slave hunters.

In his **peroration** Douglass does find some hope. For the first time he explicitly invokes the Declaration of Independence, "the genius of American Institutions." It is at the head of the obvious tendencies of this age. "No nation can now shut itself up from the surrounding world, and trot round in the same old path of its fathers without interference. The time was when such could be done. . . . But change has now come over the affairs of mankind. Walled cities and empires have become unfashionable. The arm of commerce has borne away the gates of the strong city. Intelligence is penetrating the darkest corners of the globe. God speed the year of jubilee the wide world over."

It is plain that from the disposition of the material in an order where one part follows another that there is a logical structure to Douglass's oration. The arguments are vividly sketched rather than developed, and the figure, paralepsis, is used to justify not giving them a full development. What is more notable is the use of the *pathe*, which are not just sketched but are amply developed.

Douglass's Use of Pathos and Ethos

Fundamental to the effect of this speech is pity: pain at a destructive evil when it comes on those who do not deserve it. We feel this when we think that we could easily suffer in the same way as the objects of our pity. Identification with the sufferer is a necessary condition of pity. The slave in this oration does not deserve to be shut out from the independence ceremony; we are celebrating independence, but he is not independent. He "is engaged in all manner of enterprises common to other men, digging gold in California, capturing the whale in the Pacific, feeding sheep and cattle on the hillside, living, moving, acting, thinking, planning living in families as husbands, wives and children, and, above all, confessing and worshipping the Christian's God, and looking hopefully for life and immortality beyond the grave." We can see ourselves in his position: what would it be like for us to be always subject to sale, instant separation from our families, perhaps never to see them again? The slave dealer socializes with the buyers; he is "ever ready to drink, to treat, and to gamble. The fate of many a slave has depended upon the turn of a single card; and many a child has been snatched from the arms of its mother by bargains arranged in a state of brutal drunkenness."

We who are free and believe in virtue and family are those who can feel the injustice of undeserved disaster, particularly as we are not so close to the disaster ourselves as to be filled with dread (which drives out pity). The black person is the type of those pitiable; he is never at ease; if he has committed no crime, it hardly matters; whether he is honest and industrious or the opposite, it does not make him safe. He is subject to the whim of the master; what happens to him is not tied to merit; it usually comes undeserved. No good thing occurring to a slave is ever sure for more than a minute, so good fortune is hard for him to enjoy. The listeners' pity for the slave becomes a basis for anger, the pain that is felt at an unjustified debasement of ourselves or those near to us. Anger must be directed against persons; in this case, against the slave drovers, the legislators, and the clergy. Douglass visualizes anger against the practicing slave merchants: "I see clouds of dust raised on the highways of the South; I see the bleeding footsteps; I hear the doleful wail of fettered humanity on the way to the slave markets, where the victims are to be sold like horses, sheep, and swine, knocked off to the highest bidder. There I see the tenderest ties ruthlessly broken, to gratify the lust, caprice and rapacity of the buyers and sellers of men." By definition those we get angry with are those who devalue their victims, as when they treat those we identify with as horses or swine. We get especially angry when the signs of victims' suffering are brought before the eyes (and ears) as when the "fettered marchers' footsteps bleed," and we hear them wail.

Legislators became fully complicit in this debasement of the slave with the Fugitive Slave Act. They put the power of the United States behind the right to hold, hunt, and sell men, women, and children as slaves. They made the fugitive a bird for the sportsman's gun and make the "broad republican domain a hunting ground for men. Your lawmakers have commanded all good citizens to engage in this hellish sport." The law makes mercy to the fugitive a crime and pays judges to try them. Again, anger is justified because the legislators have debased those we now identify with, making them animals to be hunted by sportsmen and forbidding making them subject to acts of humanity and mercy. Yet, these legislators have no regrets; while they enforce this law, they celebrate a tyrant-killing, king-hating, people-loving, democratic, Christian America.

The clergy, too, are targets of anger. They are indifferent to what is happening to the slaves, so they also, in effect, debase them. "If the law abridged the right to sing psalms, to partake of the sacrament, or to engage in any of the ceremonies of religion, it would be smitten by the thunder of a thousand pulpits. A general shout would go up from the church demanding repeal, repeal, repeal!" The fact that the church of our country (with fractional exceptions) does not esteem "the Fugitive Slave Law as a declaration of war against religious liberty, implies that the church regards religion simply as a form of worship, an empty ceremony, and not a vital principle, requiring active benevolence, justice, love and good will towards man. It esteems sacrifice above mercy, psalm-singing above right doing." The religious leaders consider what is happening to the slaves insignificant; in their preoccupation with the forms of religion, they belittle real humans.

Lastly there is the role of shame in the address. Shame is a pain that is felt at doing bad things that bring a person into ill repute. It is obviously most felt by people who have pretensions to virtue, like you Americans, who are tyrant-killing, king-hating, people-loving Christians. You are ready to carry democracy to all the countries of the world, so long as it does not imply freedom for the slave. Even your inferiors, like the savages or the subjects of Kings and tyrants, are not guilty of practices more shocking and bloody than are the people of these United States at this very hour. Those who stand outside the system, like God and the crushed and bleeding slave, cannot help but denounce this shamefulness, "in the name of humanity which is outraged, in the name of liberty which is fettered, in the name of the constitution and the Bible, which are disregarded and trampled upon." Acts of cruelty, such as supporting the slave trade, are particularly shameful, taking advantage of weakness, playing the coward in the face of the slave merchant, enacting laws that protect his shameful dealing.

Frederick Douglass's use of pathos is supplemented by his peculiar ethos. He lived through slavery: who is to tell him that his view of suffering by the slaves is not accurate? This is especially true of the section on the slave market:

> To me the American slave trade is a terrible reality. When a child, my soul was often pierced with a sense of its horrors. I lived on Philpot Street, Fell's Point, Baltimore, and have watched from the wharves the slave ships in the Basin, anchored from shore, with their cargoes of human flesh, waiting for favorable winds to waft them down the Chesapeake.
>
> The flesh-mongers gather up their victims by dozens and drive them chained to the general depot in Baltimore. When a sufficient number have been collected here, a ship is chartered for the purpose of conveying the forlorn crew to Mobile or to New Orleans.
>
> In the deep darkness of midnight, I have been often aroused by the dead heavy footsteps and the piteous cries of the chained gangs that passed our door. The anguish of my boyhood heart was intense; and I was often consoled, when speaking to my mistress in the morning, to hear her say that the custom was very wicked; that she hated to hear the rattle of the chains and the heart rending cries. I was glad to find one who sympathized with me in my horror.

This kind of eyewitness account, buttressed by the reluctant testimony of the slave mistress herself, is hard to deny. The emotions of pity, shame, and anger are fully exploited in these ways.

Douglass does not criticize the Revolution; rather, he identifies with the ideals of the founding fathers. Washington could not die until he had broken the chains of his slaves. The fathers in their admiration of liberty lost sight of all other interests. They believed in order, but not the order of tyranny. The Constitution they framed is a "GLORIOUS LIBERTY DOCUMENT." Douglass also picks up considerable credibility from his familiarity with the Bible. Asking him to praise the Fourth of July is like the Hebrews being asked to sing a song of Zion after having been removed to a foreign land (Psalm 137:1–6). The preachers who justify the fugitive slave law are like the scribes and Pharisees "who pay tithe of mint, anise and cumin" while ignoring the weightier matters of the law, judgment, mercy, and faith (Matthew 23:23).

Douglass even identifies his position with the Constitution. It is the fundamental law. It is a slander on the memory of the Fathers to believe that it guarantees slavery. In his peroration Douglass identifies his views with progress: "intelligence is penetrating the darkest corners of the globe . . . oceans no longer divide, but link nations together." All the good things of the Bible and history and those that are coming to us, he identifies with his cause when building ethos.

Rhetorical Style

A traditional rhetorician would describe the language of this address as grand style. The emotional tone is enhanced by a fullness in the development of relatively simple themes. Here is a series of *parallel* phrases in which Douglass develops the statement that the Fourth of July is a day which reveals to the slave, more than all other days, the gross injustice and cruelty to which he is the constant victim.

> To him, your celebration is a sham; your boasted liberty an unholy license; your national greatness swelling vanity; your shouts of liberty and equality hollow mockery; your prayers and hymns, your sermons and thanksgivings, with all your religious parade and solemnity are to him mere bombast, fraud, deception, impiety and hypocrisy—a thin veil to cover up crimes which would disgrace a nation's savages. There is not a nation on the earth guilty of practices more shocking and bloody than are the people of these United States at this very hour.

One can easily point to the rhetorical hyperbole of this series—could even an intelligent slave think that all the celebration is utterly false, that there is no pious feeling to the hymns and sermons nor anything but self-deception to the feeling of national pride? Could the educated black man not have known of the shocking and bloody practices of the French troops in the Napoleonic wars or the Australia of the prison ships? We understand, of course, that this flamboyance is part of the show, and while there's more than a grain of truth to it, there's also a grain of salt.

It is justified because it is told from the point of view of the slave, though certainly not in the language of the slave. There is the exploitation of **anaphora**, the repetition of the same word or phrase at the beginning of each clause, along with the hint of a rhyme in vanity, mockery, hypocrisy, and bloody—just enough there to constitute **epistrophe**, the repetition of the same phrase at the end of each clause. More than that, however, how many words does it take to say that much of the pageantry on the Fourth is hypocritical, something that we all have occasionally felt at the end of an overlong ceremony? The excess of near synonymy is there to build the rhythm into a solemn march, abruptly broken by the conclusion of that last sentence with the finality of "at this very hour."

One of the characteristics of grand style is the freedom in the use of rhetorical figures of speech. These figures, such as anaphora and epistrophe, are useful in lectures and expositions, but figures of thought such as hyperbole and paralepsis are the language of feeling. Rhetorical questions are of this sort, particularly when used in a sequence that builds, like this one:

Would you have me argue that man is entitled to liberty? That he is the rightful owner of his own body? Must I argue the wrongfulness of slavery? Is that a question for Republicans? Is it to be settled by the rules of logic and argumentation, as a matter beset with great difficulty, involving a doubtful application of the principle of justice, hard to be understood?

This sequence in particular is an example of how a series of rhetorical questions gets a listener into the mindset of yea- or nay-saying.

Besides rhetorical questions, there is the use of paralepsis as principle for structuring the section refuting the imagined justifications of slavery. By claiming not to refute these justifications he belittles them almost out of existence. Taken all in all, the style of this speech is exciting, as befits this kind of occasion.

Evaluation

If we take the purpose of this speech to be vituperation, bringing people into a state of wrath and fury at the institution of slavery, a greater success at using the resources of the traditional perspective could hardly be imagined. It is a real case of strategic employment of all the available means of persuasion. As an educational tool, to be sure, it falls short. The view of slavery is without depth or nuance. All that is presented are chains, beatings, and moanings. It is stereotyped; it is the propagandist's-eye view of the institution. Douglass's purpose, however, was *arousal*, not *education*. One would like to think that he could have accomplished both purposes, but that is not what he set out to do.

It seems to have been almost a total failure in convincing the Garrisonians. Though Douglass quoted Garrison favorably three times and closed with a complete rendition of one of his anti-slavery poems, they were not mollified; they continued to hold the view that the Constitution must be rewritten and the union reestablished without the South. The many reprintings of this famous address indicate the extent to which it has intrigued readers over the years. For us it is a window onto a long lost stage dominated by men whose states of feeling are far different from ours. But it fully exploits the precepts of traditional rhetoric.

PERSONAL REFLECTIONS

This essay could have taken forms different from that written above. For example, I decided to make the essay more of a journey through the stages of traditional criticism than a regular-style academic paper. I did this because I thought it would make traditional criticism more accessible for those new to criticism. I wanted a bit more of a conversation and less of the usual academic paper. Traditional-style criticism is not lacking in sophistication, so a more accessible journey through the stages seemed better than putting up a bunch of lists for you to follow.

It is not unusual for those drawn to traditional criticism to also be drawn to history. I am very certain this shows in many of the examples I have used in this essay. This reflects my personal interests in American political history, as does my choice for a rhetorical artifact to analyze for my essay. Frederick Douglass's Fifth of July oration was one of hundreds of such orations I could have chosen to study. I decided on this one since it is the most famous and is most likely to be familiar to you; moreover, I simply like this speech. My decision to use this particular speech was also influenced by my liking for Douglass's orations in general. The efforts of almost any speaker could have been analyzed, however.

POTENTIALS AND PITFALLS

I am certain that you noticed that in the above examples for speakers I used many contemporary speakers. This represents both a potential and a pitfall of traditional-style criticism. Far too often those teaching traditional-style criticism give the impression that it is only useful for explicating historical texts. Nothing could be further from the truth. Traditional criticism will serve you well even if you decide to look at a contemporary speaker such as President Trump, Bernie Sanders, Zig Ziglar, Malala Yousafzai, or even a corporate campaign or how universities look at student complaints.[29] The choice of rhetorical artifact is up to you. What differentiates traditional-style criticism from the other critical perspectives to which you will be exposed has to do with the type of information that is generated.

Another potential pitfall involves formulaic criticism—also known as cookie-cutter criticism. This is often the result if one simply uses theory as a checklist, looking for instances of each and every concept covered and then writing it down to share. This is simply not criticism. Yes, there is some of this type of criticism written by those using a traditional perspective; it has been, after all, practiced longer than any other perspective covered in this book. Be that as it may, it is also a common pitfall associated with numerous critical perspectives. The possibility for formulaic criticism rests more with the critic than with the perspective used. To avoid formulaic criticism, you need to learn as much about the perspective you intend to use as possible. A good place to start is with the top picks I list below. There you will find excellent examples of criticism that is reflexive, not stale.

TRADITIONAL CRITICISM TOP PICKS

Cooper, Lane. *The Rhetoric of Aristotle, an Expanded Translation with Supplementary Examples for Students of Composition and Public Speaking.* New York, London: D. Appleton and Company, 1932. The gold standard translation for this text. It went unchallenged for decades until Kennedy's book was published in 1991. Either one will work well. See George A. Kennedy, *Aristotle on Rhetoric: A Theory of Civic Discourse* (New York: Oxford University Press, 1991).

Hitchcock, Orville A. "Jonathan Edwards." In *A History and Criticism of American Public Address*, ed. William Norwood Brigance, 213–237. New York: McGraw-Hill, 1943. This essay represents a classical application of traditional criticism.

Hochmuth [Nichols], Marie Kathryn. "The Criticism of Rhetoric." In *A History and Criticism of American Public Address*, vol. 3, ed. Marie Kathryn Hochmuth. New York: Russell and Russell, 1954. A solid definition of rhetoric as conceived during the reputed heyday of traditional criticism. The essay complements well a functional approach to communication studies and rhetorical criticism.

Howell, Wilbur Samuel, and Hoyt Hopewell Hudson. "Daniel Webster." In *History and Criticism of American Public Address*, vol. 2, ed. William Norwood Brigance. New York: McGraw-Hill, 1943. An excellent essay that shows the possibilities of traditional criticism when it moves beyond analysis of a single speech and occasion. Debunks the common understanding that traditional criticism is only concerned with single speeches and immediate effects.

Thonssen, Lester, A. Craig Baird, and Waldo W. Braden. *Speech Criticism.* 2nd ed. New York: Ronald Press, 1970. You may well find a copy of this once-common text in your school's library. In it you will find detailed explanations of the concepts outlined in this chapter.

The following is a short selection of more contemporary essays that draw on the traditional perspective in greater or lesser degrees. They show the dynamic possibilities for using the perspective today.

Gross, Alan G. "Renewing Aristotelian Theory: The Cold Fusion Controversy as a Test Case." *Quarterly Journal of Speech* 81 (1995): 48–62.

Henry, David. "The Rhetorical Dynamics of Mario Cuomo's 1984 Keynote Address: Situation, Speaker, Metaphor." *Southern Speech Communication Journal* 53 (1988): 105–120.

Hogan, J. Michael, and L. Glen Williams. "Defining 'the Enemy' in Revolutionary American: From the Rhetoric of Protest to the Rhetoric of War." *Southern Communication Journal* 61, no. 4 (Summer 1996): 277–289.

Holcomb, Chris. "'Anyone Can Be President': Figures of Speech, Cultural Forms, and Performance." *Rhetoric Society Quarterly* 37, no. 1 (2007): 71–96.

Ritter, Kurt, and David Henry. *Ronald Reagan, the Great Communicator*. Westport, CT: Greenwood Press, 1992.

Schrader, Valerie Lynn, Lauren J. Joseph, and Barbara Wade. "A Question of 'Rights' vs. 'What is Right': A Textual Analysis of the Anti-Defamation League's and President Barack Obama's Statements Regarding the Proposed Islamic Center Near Ground Zero." *Ohio Communication Journal* 50 (2012): 49–71.

Zagacki, Kenneth. "Eisenhower and the Rhetoric of Postwar Korea." *Southern Communication Journal* 60, no. 3 (Spring 1995): 233–246.

DISCUSSION QUESTIONS

1. Do you think traditional criticism is relevant today? Why or why not?
2. In what ways can traditional criticism move beyond analyzing single speakers?
3. With what other types of discourse, beyond the political examples given here, would traditional criticism be fruitful to use?

ACTIVITIES

1. Go to a social media source with which you are familiar (it can be your own). Examine a post and the responses using the traditional perspective.
2. Go to a news source and look for an editorial or opinion piece. Subject that to a traditional analysis. What is the perspective helpful in discovering? What might be a weakness?
3. Get in a small group. Have one person tell a story about what he or she did the previous weekend. Now have the group evaluate that story for elements of logos, pathos, and ethos. Change the story to make each artistic proof stronger.

NOTES

Changes to the original essay since the first edition of *Rhetorical Criticism: Perspectives in Action* were made by the editor, Jim A. Kuypers.

1. See Hoyt Hopewell Hudson, "De Quincy on Rhetoric and Public Speaking," in *Studies in Rhetoric and Public Speaking in Honor of James Albert Winans by Pupils and Colleagues*, ed. A. M. Drummond (New York: Century, 1925), 133–152; and Hoyt Hopewell Hudson, "The Field of Rhetoric," *Quarterly Journal of Speech Education* 9, no. 2 (1923): 167–180.

2. Steve Urbanski, "A Neo-Aristotelian Critique of 'Jimmy's World': New Ideas in a Long-Debated Journalism Fabrication," *American Communication Journal* 18, no. 1 (2016): 1–14.

3. Su-Hie Ting, "Ethos, Logos and Pathos in University Students' Informal Requests," *GEMA Online Journal of Language Studies* 18, no. 1 (2018): 234–251.

4. Jeffrey Gauthier and Jeffrey A. Kappen, "Corporate Rhetorical Strategies in the Legitimation of Genetically Modified Foods," *Journal of Communication Management* 21, no. 3 (2017): 218–235.

5. *Rhetoric*, I 3, 1358a 37–1358b 1.

6. Herbert Wichelns is routinely given credit for broadening the communication discipline's rhetorical horizons to include written as well as oral discourse in his 1925 essay, "Literary Criticism of Oratory." However, in "Hoyt Hopewell Hudson's Nuclear Rhetoric," Jim A. Kuypers convincingly argues that Hudson is deserving of this credit. Kuypers cites Hudson's 1921 essay, "Can We Modernize the Study of Invention?" where Hudson implied the use of topics for "speech or argument." The "Field of Rhetoric" contains more explicit definitions. In this essay, Hudson fully defined the term *rhetoric*, which included the study of written as well as oral discourse. Because rhetoric is the "faculty of finding, in any subject, all the available means of persuasion," the rhetorician is "a sort of diagnostician and leaves it to others to be the practitioners; the rhetorician is the strategist of persuasion, and other men execute his plans and do the fighting. In practice, however, and in any study of the subject, this distinction can hardly be maintained, since the person who determines the available means of persuasion . . . must also be, in most cases, the one to apply those means in persuasive speech and writing." See Herbert A. Wichelns, "The Literary Criticism of Oratory," in *Studies in Rhetoric and Public Speaking in Honor of James Albert Winans by Pupils and Colleagues*, ed. A. M. Drummond (New York: Century, 1925), 209; Hoyt Hopewell Hudson, "Can We Modernize the Theory of Invention?," *Quarterly Journal of Speech Education* 7, no. 4 (1921): 326; Hoyt Hopewell Hudson, "The Field of Rhetoric," *Quarterly Journal of Speech Education* 9, no. 2 (1923): 169–170; and Jim A. Kuypers, "Hoyt Hopewell Hudson's Nuclear Rhetoric," in *Twentieth-Century Roots of Rhetorical Criticism*, ed. Jim A. Kuypers and Andrew King (Westport, CT: Praeger, 2001).

7. *Rhetoric*, I iii, 1358a 3–4.

8. Garry Wills, *Lincoln at Gettysburg: The Words That Remade America* (New York: Touchstone Books, 1993).

9. Donald J. Trump, "Remarks by President Trump in Address to the Nation [about the coronavirus]," White House, March 11, 2020, https://ge.usembassy.gov/remarks-by-president-trump-in-address-to-the-nation-march-11/.

10. Steven Hayward, "A Partisan Virus," *Powerline*, March 31, 2020, https://www.powerlineblog.com/archives/2020/03/a-partisan-virus.php.

11. *Rhetoric*, II 18, 15–17.

12. H. L. Mencken disagrees with Lincoln's assessment: "The Gettysburg speech was at once the shortest and the most famous oration in American history. Put beside it, all the whoopings of the Websters, Sumners and Everetts seem gaudy and silly. It is eloquence brought to a pellucid and almost gem-like perfection, the highest emotion reduced to a few poetical phrases. Lincoln himself never even remotely approached it. It is genuinely stupendous. But let us not forget that it is poetry, not logic; beauty, not sense. Think of the argument in it. Put it into the cold words of everyday. The doctrine is simply this: that the Union soldiers who died at Gettysburg sacrificed their lives to the cause of self determination that government of the people, by the people, for the people, should not perish from the earth. It is difficult to imagine anything more untrue. The Union soldiers in the battle actually fought against self-determination; it was the Confederates who fought for the right of their people to govern themselves." H. L. Mencken, *A Mencken Chrestomathy* (New York: Vintage, 1949), 222–223.

13. *Rhetoric*, II 2–12.

14. "Obama Administration Official Defends Bergdahl Trade Despite Charges," FoxNews.com, March 26, 2015, http://www.foxnews.com/politics/2015/03/26/bergdahl-to-be-charged-with-desertion-official-says.

15. Some have called such utterances part of an "administrative text." For a fuller explanation, see Jim A. Kuypers, Marilyn J. Young, and Michael K. Launer, "Of Mighty Mice and Meek Men: Contextual Reconstruction of the Shootdown of Iran Air 655," *Southern Communication Journal* 59, no. 4 (1994): 294–306; and Jim A. Kuypers, *Presidential Crisis Rhetoric and the Press in a Post Cold War World* (Westport, CT: Praeger, 1997), 3–8.

16. Caedmon Records, TC 1264.

17. John F. Wilson and Carroll C. Arnold, *Public Speaking as a Liberal Art*, 5th ed. (Boston: Allyn and Bacon, 1983), 83–88.

18. Nixon, "The Great Silent Majority," November 3, 1969, http://www.americanrhetoric.com/speeches/richardnixongreatsilentmajority.html.

19. Lloyd L. Bitzer, "Aristotle's Enthymeme Revisited," *Quarterly Journal of Speech* 45 (1959): 408.

20. For an example commercial see, "Christian's Children Fund (Train Spot)," YouTube.com, accessed April, 8, 2020, https://www.youtube.com/watch?v=D6PBiDNroQQ

21. Editor's note: I wish in no way to minimize the work of the Christian Children's Fund, which at the time was an outstanding charity. For current information on ChildFund International see: https://www.charitynavigator.org/index.cfm?bay=search.summary&orgid=3499.

22. Jane Blankenship and Hermann G. Stelzner, eds., *Rhetoric and Communication: Studies in the University of Illinois Tradition* (Urbana: University of Illinois Press, 1976).

23. Thomas Paine, *Common Sense*, 1776.

24. *Rhetoric*, I 1, 1355b 10–16.

25. In 2021 dollars, that is somewhere between $3.00 and $5.00.

26. Gerald Fulkerson, "Exile as Emergence: Frederick Douglass in Great Britain, 1845–1847," *Quarterly Journal of Speech* 60 (February 1974): 69–82.

27. Wills, *Lincoln at Gettysburg*.

28. Douglass to Gerrit Smith, July 7, 1852. Copy of original letter in possession of author. Original located in the Gerrit Smith Papers Collection at Syracuse University Libraries.

29. Gauthier and Kappen; Ting.

7

Close Textual Analysis

Approaches and Applications

Stephen Howard Browne

Close textual analysis (CTA) refers to an interpretive practice, the aim of which is to explain how texts operate to produce meaning, effect persuasion, and activate convictions in public contexts. To this end CTA attends in detail to the interplay of ideas, images, and arguments as they unfold within the spatial and temporal economy of the **text**. The rewards of such an approach may be glimpsed, for example, if we think of Martin Luther King Jr.'s masterful "I Have a Dream" speech of 1963. Here, we would follow the address from its first words, deliberate and restrained; note the mounting intensity, the shape and direction of its metaphors; and follow the movement of the text to its thunderous conclusion. The general conviction underlying such an approach is that rhetorical texts are active, dynamic, and complex; explaining how they work therefore requires a keen sensitivity to the play of language itself.

Practitioners of CTA generally view their art less as a method per se than as a disciplined search for the linguistic particulars that eventually comprise the whole of a given rhetorical performance.[1] Students and scholars working in this vein are thus particularly attuned to the nuances, echoes, and subtle gestures that exist in the object of their study. It thus requires a sensibility cultivated by broad reading across the humanities and asks that we bring to the task a literary critic's sharp eye for textual detail. A cultivated and disciplined engagement with history, literature, and philosophy will go a long way toward preparing the rhetorical critic for such work. Above all, however, a basic love of the human language, in all its glories and all its messiness, is requisite.

Although CTA may be put to work across a broad range of genres—critics have used it to better understand orations, films, visual rhetoric, pamphlets, and poetry—one key premise drives virtually all such analysis. This premise holds that the rhetorical force of a text can never be presumed as given or fixed; rather, its rhetorical force is the result of a complex set of symbolic forces set into play at the moment of utterance. The critic working from this perspective accordingly seeks to identify and account for this process. In the following pages, we will explore the main principles guiding the practice of CTA, we will place this approach within certain historical and disciplinary contexts, we will consider a brief case study, and we will note several lines of argument raised by critics of CTA. We turn first to four principles upon which the practice of CTA rests.

CTA GUIDING PRINCIPLES

Principle 1: Rhetorical Texts Are Sites of Symbolic Action

What does this "mean"? By way of an answer, it will help here and throughout this chapter to have beside you a copy of Barack Obama's Philadelphia speech of March 2008.[2] As you look it over and perhaps recall reading or viewing it previously, you might ask one of two questions: either "What does this speech mean?" or "What is it doing?" The first question encourages us to think of texts as containers of ready-made semantic units that may be extracted from the text as needed. Put another way, the speech itself may be said to offer a guide for answering the question "What is this text about?" "Well," you might reply, scanning through the paragraphs, "it means just what it says; let me quote a few lines and you'll get the gist of the matter." In one sense, of course, this is a perfectly reasonable response. It does not, however, offer a very close look at how the speech functions as a text, or, more specifically, as a rhetorical text. Why? Because the response fails to take into account the **symbolic action**, or the language-in-motion that defines the dynamics of the rhetorical performance. Close textual critics thus tend to view such texts as verbs, so to speak, *and to ask not what a text means but what it does*. If you happened to see the speech on television or YouTube, or if you have now read it for the first time, pause for a moment and ask yourself, "What does this text do?"

Once this question is posed at the outset, a world of interpretive possibilities opens into view. Imagine for a moment the nearly infinite ways in which a text may be said to act. It may disclose or camouflage, seduce, exalt, debase, deface, deflect, direct, invite, distance, defer, deny, destroy, create, recreate, form, deform, reform, silence, provoke, tickle, numb, transcend, descend, portend, threaten, demur, announce, renounce, or pronounce. Texts may inaugurate, promise, plead, deny, decry, dissemble, lie, waffle, tempt, dissuade, disabuse, or deter. They may call out, call for, call on, call in, call to, or call a cab. The point is surely evident by now, but however basic the insight, such a view of textual action attunes us to the manifold ways in which we can understand what, precisely, is rhetorical about a given text: the decisive and distinctive manner in which it acts in the world.

Principle 2: Form and Content Cannot Be Divorced

If CTA is particularly alive to the active nature of rhetorical texts, it is similarly sensitive to the interplay of form and content shaping that action. Close textual critics accordingly seek to correct a lingering tendency, dating well back into antiquity, to view properties of **form**—that is, images, tropes, the "style" of a given rhetorical production—as somehow distinct from the essential content of its message. In its most reductive expression, this tendency suggests that we invent something to say—what it is we really want to get across to our auditors or readers—and then trick out the message with appealing drapery, the better to arrest attention or gratify the aesthetic appetite of our audience. This view of style is not uncontested, however, and theorists of language since the early twentieth century have taught us that such a view is illusory and that if we are to make plausible sense of how rhetoric works, we need to reunite what has been put asunder. Form and content belong together. To invoke King's address again, consider how integral his use of figures and other imagery is to the meaning of his message. At a minimum, they may be said to arrest attention, establish pace and meter, and make concrete otherwise abstract principles of justice and redemption.

Our second principle seems to be mere common sense, but in fact it presents us with difficult issues from the outset. For example, while it is the case that form and content cannot be separated, they are not the same thing. And if form and content are not the same, then how are they different from one another? In order to answer that question, we need a working definition of each. Here, too, we need to acknowledge that both terms are notoriously slippery and the objects of considerable academic debate. For the purposes of this chapter, let us take *form* to refer to those linguistic resources that give conspicuous structure to otherwise abstract formulations. To play with this definition for a moment, note how abstract it is. It needs form! So let's put it another way, with apologies to William Butler Yeats: "form is to content as the dancer is to the dance." Here the abstract is given heightened intelligibility by embodying itself in a concrete and dynamic image. Form and content need each other. By extension, we may take **content** to refer to that dimension of a message reducible to the level of a proposition. Let us turn to the Obama text again for an example of how this principle plays out in practice:

> I can no more disown him [Wright] than I can disown the black community. I can no more disown him than I can disown my white grandmother—a woman who helped raise me, a woman who sacrificed again and again for me, a woman who loves me as much as she loves anything in this world, but a woman who once confessed her fear of black men who passed by her on the street, and who on more than one occasion has uttered racial or ethnic stereotypes that made me cringe.

Now, what can we say about the interplay of form and content in this passage? With respect to its content, we can ask, "What is the basic proposition here?" We might answer, "The fact that Reverend Wright has his faults, like all of us, is insufficient grounds for disowning him." To leave it at this, however, is to miss the rhetorical force imported to the proposition by virtue of the form in which it is expressed. We would want also to note, for example, the parallel constructions initiating the first several lines: "I can no more disown him. . . . I can no more disown him." Not only do they establish the metrical cadence of the passage, but they rather ingeniously invoke the Obama campaign's mantra of personal empowerment. We observe, too, how the proposition is inscribed into a narrative account of the candidate's grandmother, who comes to represent a kind of universal type—human, warts and all—with whom we can identify and whose image is thereby made to soften the specter of Reverend Wright. Form and content in this way are seen to sponsor each other.

Principle 3: Text Informs Context, and Vice Versa

The emphatic emphasis CTA places on the text as such invites the suspicion that we may have here too much of a good thing. That is, does it not stand to reason that the more closely we look at an "object," the further we remove ourselves from the **context** in which that object appears? And does this not bracket out information essential for understanding such texts, especially in their rhetorical aspect? We will attend to this question in greater detail later; here it is sufficient to stress that if indeed contextual considerations are made to drop by the wayside, then of course we have a real problem. The good news is that nothing of the kind is entailed by the practice of CTA. On the contrary, it is inconceivable that a satisfactory interpretation of rhetorical texts is possible without taking all relevant features of the context into consideration.

Still, we are left with the question as to how a given text is best attuned to its context. Once again, the answer is contingent upon a matter of definition: what, after all, is a "context"? Is it the immediate exigence to which the text responds? Certainly that plays a part, but what about those rhetorical performances that seem less beholden to such pressing forces—meditations, say, in the manner of Ralph Waldo Emerson or Elizabeth Cady Stanton? And in what sense can we say that contexts are bound by fixed conceptions of space and time? The Declaration of Independence, for example, continues to be expropriated for all manner of rhetorical purposes, not only in the United States but in revolutionary Vietnam, Poland, and the nations of South America. At a minimum, then, we need to adapt a very elastic sense of what qualifies as relevant context, make a sound case for stipulating one rather than another, and set about the task of informing our textual analysis with systematic reference to its contextual environment.

One particularly useful approach to this interpretive work is to acknowledge that while each text is distinctive on its own terms, it yet partakes in and deploys an indefinite range of other texts and discursive modalities. Another way of thinking about this phenomenon is to view contexts as themselves texts of a kind, from which a speaker or writer borrows on an as-needed basis. For a brief example of how this works rhetorically, let us turn again to the Philadelphia speech. Clearly we have an immediate exigence: popular disapproval of comments made by Obama's minister, thought to have been racially charged and in violation of basic norms of civil and political discourse. The speech is self-evidently an effort to allay such anxieties as those Reverend Wright stirred up. But there is more to the matter than that, because part of the text's rhetorical achievement is to resituate, or recreate, another and more compelling context in which the speech itself hopes to be understood. For evidence of this process, we turn, as always, to the text itself. What other texts or discursive modes does the speaker import into his own speech? A quick glance gives us the answer:

US Constitution
Declaration of Independence
Hebrew Bible/Old Testament/New Testament
Personal narrative
Sermon
Testimony
Memoir
Novel
Supreme Court decision
Anecdote

The point is clear: texts work rhetorically by responding to exigencies, yes, but they work as well by reconstituting their own interpretive contexts. On reflection, we can see how this process moves both ways: contexts inform texts, and texts inform contexts. Thus it is not unrealistic to predict that Obama's speech will itself enter into the vast storehouse of rhetorical resources and become available to ensuing speakers as they seek to effect change in the world. The speech, that is, emerges from one context, realigns itself, and eventually becomes part of an even greater context.

Principle 4: Rhetorical Texts Exhibit Artistic Density

Our fourth principle may best be considered an extension and summary of the foregoing discussion. Like the others, it seems perhaps uncontroversial, even obvious. In fact, however, the principle of artistic density cuts to the heart of CTA. How does it do this, and why does it matter? To get at these questions we need to step back for a moment and see where CTA came from, the company it keeps, and how it distinguishes itself from other reading practices.

The discipline we now associate with communication departments in the United States originated in large measure by breaking away from the academic study of English. The major argument justifying this new development was that "speech communication" attended to related but significantly different phenomena: not literature as such, but the products of human beings moved to express themselves to persuasive ends in largely oral and public contexts. This interest could of course claim a heritage dating well into Western antiquity, but it had gradually been subsumed under the auspices of literary study. Early twentieth-century champions of the revitalized discipline thus sought to distinguish their work from that of literary critics, who were concerned to explain aesthetic properties of poems, novels, plays, and the like. Rhetorical critics, on the other hand, laid claim to those speech activities that were self-evidently more instrumental, time bound, and broadly political in character: orations, parliamentary debates, and sermons, for example. As the discipline grew and flourished throughout the century, this emphasis on the pragmatics of human communication tended to bracket out, and sometimes repudiate altogether, the aesthetic dimensions of rhetorical practice.[3]

Why this apparent indifference or even hostility to the aesthetic? For many, the answer was programmatic: the very identity of our discipline required that we sustain the differences separating rhetorical studies from literary criticism. For others, it had to do with certain political investments in situating rhetorical acts within their material and ideological milieu. To preoccupy oneself with aesthetic concerns was to forget or elide the dynamics of power (the political aspects) that superintend all rhetorical productions.

Now, there are legitimate reasons for such anxieties, but students of CTA tend to reject the premises upon which they are based. Above all, such reasoning presupposes that we cannot in principle have it both ways, that a zero-sum game seems to be in play when we consider either the rhetorical or the aesthetic. That is, to engage the one is to discount the other. On reflection, however, we must ask, is this really the case? Can we not ask after the ways in which the aesthetic can be put to rhetorical purposes? Indeed we can, if only by simply reminding ourselves that rhetoric is, after all, an art and that such an art may be glimpsed by attending to techniques of production. Surely it causes no damage to King's "I Have a Dream" oration to acknowledge its artistic achievement; more positively, a full accounting of that achievement goes a long way toward explaining its enduring rhetorical legacy. And this, in the end, may be taken as the basic rationale for CTA: by submitting texts to close inspection, we are able to see better the ways in which rhetoric works at its most fundamental levels of operation. Put another way, it is difficult to see how we can understand the whole of King's speech or any other text without attending to its parts. Ultimately, we arrive at the technical process through which that whole is rendered coherent and compelling.

Taken together, our four principles should prepare us for a sensitive and instructive reading of Obama's Philadelphia speech. We will turn to the text shortly, but here might be a place to indicate what CTA is not. This will help clear further misconceptions from our path and free us from the weight of unwanted and unwarranted concerns. We have already alluded to several of these: skilled textual critics do not turn a blind eye to context, they do not reduce the "meaning" of texts to the propositions advanced by the texts' authors, and they do not entertain the aesthetics of the text in the manner of "art for art's sake." In addition, it is worth stressing that CTA, for all its attention to the "how" of textual production, does not satisfy itself with a mere naming and listing of such techniques. The aim, rather, is to provide a comprehensive account of how the parts cohere into a whole greater than the sum of those parts. Further, CTA is clearly more than an advanced version of textual appreciation; on the contrary, it arms the critic with material with which to render judgment as to efficacy, ethics, success, and failure. Important also is the position that CTA is not a "method" as such, if we mean by that term a specific how-to program for textual analysis. This is not to imply that it is simply impressionistic. It is rather to insist on a rigorous and evidence-bound explication that nevertheless leaves ample room for the play of critical insight and authorial voice. Finally, it is useful to remind ourselves again that CTA involves a great deal more than paraphrasing what is expressed in the text; it seeks rather to ask, as we did with reference to our first principle, "What is this text doing?"

CRITICAL ESSAY

Now let us turn to our case in point. In the following, I offer one interpretation of Barack Obama's March 18, 2008, speech in Philadelphia. The analysis is designed as an exercise in CTA and aims to illustrate several—certainly not all—features of this approach. Among the questions I ask of this text is, from what family of rhetorical acts does it take inspiration? That is, can we identify one or more **generic antecedents** that seem to guide the speaker's treatment of his theme? We are then led to ask what this theme is and how it superintends the symbolic action of the text as it unfolds. We want to ask further about the internal structure of this movement and how this structure assists in the production of the speaker's message. Similarly, what kinds of images, metaphors, and other dimensions of style animate Obama's arguments and give them conspicuous form? Mindful, too, of contextual forces at play in the text, we will need to identify both the immediate exigence to which the speech responds and the ways in which it seeks to transform the contexts in which it asks to be interpreted. A number of other questions germane to the text may be asked and answered, of course, and no pretense is made here to a final or even authoritative exposition of the text. Far from it, I encourage the reader to contest, elaborate, or otherwise engage this particular rendering. The presumptive payoff is a deeper understanding of how texts work to induce conviction and impel audiences to action.

CLOSE TEXTUAL ANALYSIS OF BARACK OBAMA'S MARCH 18, 2008, SPEECH IN PHILADELPHIA

The unprecedented nature of Obama's campaign for the Oval Office all but ensured the most intense kind of public and media scrutiny. The first African American making a serious bid for the office, running against the female with realistic chances for nomination, taking place in a time of war on two fronts, a faltering economy, and widespread concern over the nation's capacity to deliver healthcare to its own citizens. Within such a heated environment, partisan supporters can be almost as dangerous as the official opposition, as Obama, Clinton, and McCain were each to discover from their respective camps. No supporter raised as great a firestorm, however, as the Reverend Jeremiah Wright, pastor of Chicago's Trinity United Church of Christ and longtime spiritual guide to the Illinois senator. The reverend was known for addressing his congregation in language of exceptional intensity, color, and, sometimes, provocation. One such sermon, in which he expressed his disappointment with US race relations with the recurrent phrase "Goddamn America," was captured on video, was frequently replayed across a variety of media, and was very soon the object of widespread condemnation.

All campaigns run into stumbling blocks, of course, and although some are undone by such episodes, most manage to survive and push on to their fated ends. But for many this was a different matter. At stake was not just the candidate's affiliation with the intemperate pastor but the persistent questions haunting the nation's past and present race relations. Senator Obama had offered the prospect—however idealized—of a "post-race" America, in which an African American might run for the highest office in the land and be judged, in the words of Martin Luther King Jr., "not by the color of his skin but by the content of his character." Now this promise appeared to be on the verge of collapse. Obama and Clinton were still neck and neck in the polls, conservative talk show hosts were banging their drums of disapproval, and it soon became obvious that the candidate had to say something. On the morning of March 18, before a nationally televised audience, Senator Barack Obama stepped to the podium across the street from Philadelphia's famed Independence Hall and delivered, to that point, the most important speech of his life.

The situation was thus novel in many respects, but that does not mean that the speaker was bereft of resources. On close reading, we discover that, consciously or not, he drew on a rich and enduring rhetorical genre known as the "jeremiad."[4] The term takes as its referent the imposing figure of the prophet Jeremiah in the Torah and Christian New Testament. For thousands of years, the prophet has served as a model for a particular type of rhetoric, marked by lamentation over the fallen state of a chosen people, the dangers of failing the terms of a sacred covenant, and the urgent need to restore oneself and one's community into a proper relationship with God and the world. It is not a rigid model, and had been put to different uses in different ways throughout the history of the genre. But its key components—(a) covenant, (b) violation, and (c) atonement—have remained relatively stable over time. On review of Obama's text we see that there is no need to impose this model; the speech rather gives evidence of this tradition at every step. We may then allow the text to teach us, so to speak, how to understand its rhetorical task by taking up its own cues. To this end, the following analysis is organized according to each of the three functions noted above.

The very first words out of the speaker's mouth alert us to the centrality of promise to American collective identity: "We the people, in order to form a more perfect union." By thus invoking the inaugural lines of the US Constitution, Obama reminds his audience that they, like their forebears, are bound together in a civically sacred trust. That document announced to the world the arrival of a unique moment in the world, when plain white men—not yet blacks, Native Americans, or women—entered into an "improbable experiment in democracy." We are hence called to be mindful that the ideal of perfection is just that—an ideal—and moreover an ideal which remains to be fully met. But the very notion that a nation could be founded under the promise to nevertheless keep striving toward such a goal remains a fact of striking historical significance, and it gives shape and direction to all that follows.

One of the hallmarks of early colonial jeremiads was their belief that the new immigrants were a select people who had endured great hardship to enter upon a "journey into the wilderness." The scriptural resonance to the Israelite exodus from slavery into freedom is unmistakable and underscores the sense that Americans were embarked upon a journey of their own. John Winthrop's sermon on board the *Arbella* perfectly captures this sense of simultaneous righteousness and anxiety that was to mark American exceptionalism for centuries to come: "For we must consider that we shall be as a city upon a hill. The eyes of all people are upon us, so that if we shall deal falsely with our God in his work we have undertaken, and so cause him to withdraw his present help from us, we shall be made a story and a by-word through the world."[5] Winthrop understood that the success of that journey was very much a matter of literally keeping the faith, of staying on the right path. In context, of course, Obama's appeal to this imagery is secular and civic, but the rhetorical work it effects is analogous. And where the Pilgrims were severely reminded of their departures from the path, their failure to keep the covenant, so America needs its own reminder. Here was a nation blessed by freedom, bounty, and democratic government, but whose promise to form a more perfect union was stained by the "original sin of slavery, a question that divided the colonies and brought the convention to a stalemate until the founders chose to allow the slave trade to continue for at least twenty more years, and to leave any final resolution to future generations."

Now we see the first instance of a structural dynamic that will direct the course of the speech generally. Put simply, it works by first introducing a positive—in this case, America's promise to work toward an ideal. Here we see the concept of *covenant* at work. Obama then asserts a negative example (slavery) of how that promise has been broken—hence the *violation* of that covenant. The former assumes expression in the celebratory or affirmative mode—hence the location of Obama's address beside Constitution Hall in Philadelphia's historic section. The latter gets articulated in the form of accusation or lament—hence the speaker's insistence on acknowledging those moments when American's have failed their own aspirations.

On the path, off the path; but now what? In keeping with the jeremiad's purposes, the speaker is obliged not to leave matters there, but to alert his audience that a choice now presents itself: either the people can opt to remain off the path, or choose to return and keep struggling toward their professed ideal. The people, in short, have the means to redeem themselves if only they would, and it is the work of the speaker to animate them toward acting on that choice alone. Here then we see the third function of the jeremiad—the means to *atonement*. The Constitution itself contained the language upon which such action could be authorized, but ultimately, he stresses, "What would be needed were Americans in successive generations who were willing to do their part—through protest and struggle, on the streets and in the courts, through a civil war and civil disobedience and always at great risk—to narrow the gap between the promise of our ideals and the reality of their time." This commitment acting upon choice is the key to redemption itself, but it presupposes yet another promise, and that is to act together as a community or a people collectively striving toward that more perfect union. In the speaker's words, "we cannot solve the challenges of our time unless we solve them together—unless we perfect our union by understanding that we may have different stories, but we hold common hopes; that we may not look the same and we may not have come from the same place, but we all want to move in the same direction—towards a better future for our children and our grandchildren."

We are now only five paragraphs into the text, but already the basic coordinates have been set. Its overarching theme—the need to act together to form a better version of America—is activated within a given genre, the jeremiad, and unfolds through successive stages of covenant, violation, and atonement. Thus form, content, and purpose collaborate to produce an artistic whole in a process that will be recapitulated throughout the performance, in a manner suggesting variations on an orchestral motif. We now consider this dynamic at work in the second and central phase of the speech.

Barack Obama was not born in Chicago, but even as a young man he made the city his political home. Shortly after earning his law degree from Harvard University, he took up residence in Hyde Park, whence he launched a systematic and very successful campaign to insinuate himself into the complex network of Chicago politics. If every step was not calculated, most were, and before long this son of a white American mother and Kenyan father had moved to the forefront of that city's center of power. Along the way, Obama encountered and fell under the spiritual tutelage of the Reverend Jeremiah Wright, a prominent leader in the black community and, by all accounts, a spellbinding speaker. As we noted above, he could on occasion cross a line thought by many to be taboo by vehemently denouncing America and its benighted record on race relations. When one such performance hit the airwaves, Obama was severely criticized for associating with the pastor and was called upon to address the issue. He did so briefly by denouncing Wright's more excessive language, but made clear that he continued to hold his mentor in high regard. This effort did little to allay the controversy, and at length Obama undertook to settle the matter once and for all—hence the Philadelphia speech.

How the speaker manages the Jeremiah Wright issue is perforce key to the address as a whole. To better understand it, let us return to our Pilgrims for a moment. One of the striking characteristics of their sermons is the way in which seemingly all events of note are relegated to the status of an example or manifestation of God's disposition. Are crops bountiful and children healthy? Evidence of divine pleasure. Are famine and sickness in the village? Evidence of divine wrath. Was a two-headed calf born on the Dooleys' farm? Divine warning. In short, the latter-day Jeremiahs sought to convince their flocks that virtually everything could be properly understood and acted upon not with reference to the event itself but to an overarching narrative in which any given phenomenon is but an episode. Its meaning was not inherent to the event but in the greater story still unfolding. For Winthrop and his fellow shipmates, for example, the meaning of their journey was not limited to a group of malcontents, or land hunger; it had to be comprehended in terms appropriate to the age-old narrative of slavery, exodus, freedom, and redemption.

Now, what does all this have to do with Obama's response to the Wright matter? On closer inspection, we see that the jeremiad provides the speaker with a means to render the controversy into a minor but noteworthy episode in America's own story and its march toward a more perfect union. By transforming the "meaning" of Reverend Wright from a media-generated bogeyman into an allegory of America writ large, Obama strips him out of the hands of his critics and reinscribes Wright into a more meaningful and instructive lesson than could otherwise have been the case. Taking up our organizing principles, we can plot the process by which this transformation is effected:

Covenant (affirmation of the positive)
The man I met more than twenty years ago is a man who helped introduce me to my Christian faith, a man who spoke to me our obligation to love one another; to care for the sick and lift up the poor. He is a man who served his country as a US Marine; who has studied and lectured at some of the finest universities and seminaries in the country, and who for over thirty years led a church that serves the community by doing God's work here on Earth—by housing the homeless, ministering to the needy, providing day care services and scholarships and prison ministries, and reaching out to those suffering from HIV/AIDS.

Violation (exposing and condemning the negative)
But the remarks that have caused this recent firestorm weren't simply controversial. . . . Instead, they expressed a profoundly distorted view of this country—a view that sees white racism as endemic, and elevates what is wrong with America above all that we know is right with America. . . . As such, Reverend Wright's comments were not only wrong but divisive, divisive at a time when we need unity; racially charged at a time when we need to come together to solve a set of monumental problems.

Atonement (restoration and redemption)
But I have a firm conviction—a conviction rooted in my faith in God and my faith in the American people—that working together we can move beyond some of our old racial wounds, and that in fact we have no choice if we are to continue on the path of a more perfect union.

Close textual analysis takes as a given that texts have direction, that they unfold within a temporal economy established by the text itself. Obama's oration is doubly interesting because it not only has direction but is also about direction. We have charted this fact above by observing how the speaker avails himself of certain features native to the jeremiad. It will come as no surprise, then, that this ancient rhetorical genre is activated and sustained through conspicuous word choice, which is to say its "style" collaborates in effecting the intended message. Again, this sense of style in no way views such word choice as ornamentation or afterthought. On the contrary, it is constitutive of the message itself, which may be grasped

by attending to the Judeo-Christian imagery at work throughout the text and its appeal to the
path as its leading trope.

We have already made reference to a number of scriptural allusions. It may be useful at this
point to pause and consider them in the aggregate. A quick list of resonant terms and phrases
is suggestive:

Original sin
Promise
Bondage
Faith (repeatedly)
Love one another
God's work
Foot of the cross
David and Goliath
Moses and Pharaoh
Christians in the lion's den
Ezekiel's field of dry bones
Vessel of hope
Do unto others as we would have them do unto us
Let us be our brother's/sister's keeper

Mindful that such usage is meaningful only within the contours of the text itself, we
nevertheless glimpse the point. Obama's appeal to scriptural imagery functions not only to
underscore his own ethos as a man of faith but to enrich the rhetorical force of the message itself. Taken together, we may observe that each allusion invokes different facets of
the covenant binding the nation to its historical mission. Broken or repaired, forgotten or
remembered, this covenant weaves through the speech as it presumably weaves through
America's own journey toward the full realization of its promise. Hence the Hebrew Bible/
Christian Old Testament imagery of original sin, bondage, and faltering faith is transformed
within the text into the New Testament emphasis on love, charity, and redemption. This
sense of forward movement is punctuated further by recurrent appeals to the image of the
path and its clustered associations. Thus:

Travel across the ocean
The long march of those who came before us
Path to understanding
Path of a more perfect union
That path means embracing the burden of our past

However briefly, the above rendering suggests how the formal and ideational content of
the text work together to create an artistically coherent message. The overall argument—that
America has within itself the moral capacity to renew its commitment to form a more perfect
union—is mobilized through a series of structural and stylistic resources, which together offer
the speaker's audience a reason to believe and to act on such belief.

We are now in a position to revisit the four principles of CTA inaugurating this essay. Each
asks a certain kind of question the critic needs to grapple with in coming to terms with his or
her particular text. Let us take them up individually in the order presented.

1. **The text is a site of symbolic action**. Such a principle prompts us to then ask: "What does a text
   do?" By way of an answer, and with reference to Obama's speech, we can now say that *texts act
   by summoning rhetorical resources (i.e., the jeremiad) to impose meaningful order on the world
   and, if successful, to make that order a compelling basis for conviction.*

2. **Form and content cannot be divorced**. Here we must ask: "How do they collaborate to create meaning and effect persuasion?" Obama's address teaches us that *form (i.e., metaphors, allegories, etc.) imparts to content conspicuous intelligibility, and content (i.e., reasons for forgiving Reverend Wright) imparts to form propositional argument.*

3. **Texts inform contexts, and vice versa**. If this is the case, then we need to ask: "How do texts recreate or restructure context?" On reflection, we are led to see that *texts borrow from other texts and discursive traditions to reorder the terms in which they hope to be interpreted.* Thus Obama, for example, invoked founding state papers, the Bible, and sermons to reorient his critics from one view toward another.

4. **Rhetorical texts exhibit artistic density**. That said, we may well ask: "How is such artistic density manifested, and to what end?" The Obama speech illustrates that *texts reveal their own techniques of production, and to the extent that these techniques yield a coherent and compelling product, they invite attention and assent.*

PERSONAL REFLECTIONS

I first came to the study of close textual analysis as a graduate student at the University of Wisconsin. There I encountered a small but remarkable group of critics who combined deep historical and philosophical learning with a keen interest in discovering how texts manage to do what they do. Then as now, such close attention to texts seemed the ideal means to open windows to other vistas and distant horizons. By peering intently at Booker T. Washington's Atlanta Exposition Address, for example, I learned not only how metaphors operate to invite interpretation but about race relations in the New South, the importance of pageantry to regional identification, and styles of African American leadership. For this reason, CTA offered a venue for bringing into focus wide-ranging interests—indeed, kept me from ranging *too* widely and without direction.

After more than two decades in the field of rhetorical criticism, one's interests are bound to grow and change. And while I now pursue other avenues of inquiry, including rhetoric and public memory, social movements, and rhetoric in the early republic, one constant has remained firmly in place: the conviction that rhetorical texts are just as worthy as any other genre of close, patient, and imaginative interpretation.

POTENTIALS AND PITFALLS

No interpretive practice can presume to be complete or satisfactory on every count, and CTA is no exception. Through the years, it has both attracted and provoked some of the discipline's most able critics. This essay has sought to demonstrate the gains to be had from this approach, but it would be incomplete without some attention to its limits. Several of these have been mentioned, notably, the alleged tendency to bracket out contextual dynamics. Still, at least two persistent concerns remain about the assumptions upon which CTA is built and the tendencies it encourages in practice: its reliance on an ideal critic/audience construct and its privileging of canonical texts. In the following, I briefly develop each critique but leave counterarguments to the reader's discretion.

The first criticism of CTA takes us to near ground zero in the work of interpretation. In effect, it asks, what are we really saying when we claim that a unit of language means this or that? We have already discarded the notion that meaning resides objectively and inherently in the unit itself, and we have stressed that, for rhetorical criticism at least, it is best to attend to what language does in a given context. But we are not out of the woods yet and need to press further on the question. When, as the author of this essay, I claim that such and such a passage in Obama's speech means or does something, what am I really saying? Am I making a claim about what the audience supposedly thinks? Inasmuch as I have no access to its mental activity at the moment of performance, I can make no such claim. Nor am I attributing certain intentions to the speaker, as in, "This is what Obama really means here." Again, I have no grounds for arguing along these lines: who knows what his (or his speechwriters') intentions were? And even if we did know, what would it have to do with the ways in which his listeners and readers made their own sense of the oration?

In the face of such questions, CTA (but not CTA alone) finds itself exposed to the criticism that it posits an ideal reader and an ideal audience. That is, the critic implicitly operates from a privileged position, as if to say, "I offer to you the reader the preferred interpretation of this text." True, the critic is obliged to argue for his or her rendering and be otherwise held to the highest standards of scholarship. But if we cannot plausibly ascribe intention to the speaker, or reception to the audience, then is not the critic in effect saying, "This is how I think the text works"? And if that is the case, on what basis can we generalize beyond the critic's self-reporting?

The second line of criticism advanced against CTA is more politically charged but no less insistent. It holds that practitioners of the art tend almost invariably to seize upon texts of unquestioned cultural significance and artistic achievement. There are exceptions to this argument, but then there can be no mistaking the fact that CTA in general concerns itself with canonical texts. In rhetorical studies, for example, critics associated with the practice have featured the Declaration of Independence, Jefferson's first inaugural address, Lincoln's major addresses, Elizabeth Cady Stanton's "Solitude of Self," FDR's first inaugural address, and King's "I Have a Dream" speech.[6] These are, of course, perfectly understandable as fit objects of interpretation. So what is the problem? In the view of some critics, lavishing such attention on the masterpieces of American discourse unwittingly reproduces a suspect standard of what gets to count as a masterpiece, or, more pointedly, privileges the very concept of masterpiece—itself, these critics argue, a gendered and presumably outdated category. Why not use CTA to study vernacular expressions, forgotten texts, those without the cultural cachet of a Jefferson or Lincoln? One might respond that in principle nothing is stopping critics from looking at quotidian texts; but in practice, the lion's share of attention is directed at the presumptively "great" rhetorical productions of American history. In doing so, is not CTA complicit in silencing or otherwise bracketing out the many marginal voices of our cultural heritage?

Close textual analysis came of age in the field of communication studies during the 1980s and was closely associated with the work of several rhetoricians at the University of Wisconsin. The discipline, like many in the humanities, was undergoing significant transformations, especially with respect to what was called the politics of interpretation. Critics and theorists were increasingly concerned to expose the epistemological and methodological assumptions underlying their scholarly work. Operating within this climate, CTA came under considerable scrutiny for reproducing certain habits that were thought to be suspect; we have noted above two such lines of critique. A third, and for our purposes final, such argument continues to challenge its practitioners and is in fact an extension of the concern over idealizing and canonizing the text as an object of inquiry. Put simply, this critique asks us to reconsider what it is that texts—much less textual criticism—can really tell us about the power of language and the language of power.

So what is the explanatory force of a given text? One way to get at this question is to ask another: is a text a cause or an effect? For those skeptical of CTA, the answer tends to focus on the latter. That is, the text is an effect. The line of argument runs something like this: humans are decisively shaped by the material, social, and ideological forces within which they act. Consequently, what they produce—including texts—are themselves the result or effect of these forces. To claim that a text is unique, or the hallmark of individual genius, or otherwise independent of the political milieu in which it is produced is to remain trapped in an idealized and delusory model of interpretation. Here the claim is not that texts are incapable of instigating action in the world; it is rather that texts alone can never be accorded such a primary role. They can only be, again, the effects of power relations already extant and operating in a given historical moment. Close textual critics will want to ask themselves whether such reasoning makes sense and, if so, how their own practice systematically acknowledges the point. Is CTA politically naive? Does it tend to extract the text from the very interstices of power that gives rise to texts in the first place? Or can we have it both ways, that is, justify the focus on a single text even as we place it in situ and within the material conditions of its own making?

These are all legitimate questions, but again they are perhaps best addressed by those now considering the possibilities and limits of CTA for the first time. At a minimum, we may conclude that we have in CTA a robust and systematic resource for the interpretation of rhetorical texts, that it offers a means of understanding how texts work by engaging them carefully and with great detail, and that it sets on display the very human drama of language in action.

CTA TOP PICKS

Benson, Thomas W. "The Rhetorical Structure of Frederick Wiseman's *High School.*" *Communication Monographs* 47 (1980): 233–261. Benson presents a fine-grained analysis of the famed documentary filmmaker's masterpiece, with special emphasis on the play of form and content.

Black, Edwin. "Gettysburg and Silence." *Quarterly Journal of Speech* 80 (1994): 21–36. A subtle but provocative analysis of Lincoln's address, Black's essay is sharply attuned as much to what Lincoln did not say as what he did say.

Browne, Stephen H. "Encountering Angelina Grimke: Violence, Identity, and the Creation of Radical Community." *Quarterly Journal of Speech* 82 (1996): 55–73. Browne examines the first public statement by the early abolitionist and finds evidence of a radical consciousness coming into being.

Campbell, Karlyn Kohrs. "Stanton's 'Solitude of Self': A Rationale for Feminism." *Quarterly Journal of Speech* 66 (1980): 304–312. Campbell explores Stanton's speech as a statement on the human condition, which in turn operates as a summons to enlightened political action.

Hariman, Robert, and John Louis Lucaites. *No Caption Needed: Iconic Photographs, Public Culture, and Liberal Democracy.* Chicago: University of Chicago Press, 2011. The authors make a compelling case for the power of photographs to reflect, organize, and reconstitute ideological investments.

Kennerly, Michele. "The Mock Rock Topos." *Rhetoric Society Quarterly* 43, no. 1 (2013): 46–70. An original and striking approach to the work of texts, especially as they collaborate and compete with rival forms of representation.

Lucas, Stephen E. "Justifying America: The Declaration of Independence as a Rhetorical Document." In *American Rhetoric: Contexts and Criticism*, ed. Thomas W. Benson, 67–131. Car-

bondale: Southern Illinois University Press, 1989. A tour de force essay combining close tex‑
tual analysis, deep historical learning, and sharply observed insights into the founding text.

Lyon, Janet. *Manifestoes: Provocations of the Modern.* Ithaca, NY: Cornell University Press, 1999.
Lyon provides a rich and sophisticated analysis of how texts perform ideological work.

Middleton, Richard, ed. *Reading Pop: Approaches to Textual Analysis in Popular Music.* Oxford:
Oxford University Press, 2003. A wide‑ranging but rigorous collection of essays in the tex‑
tual analysis of contemporary musical forms.

Wilson, Kirt H. "Political Paradoxes and the Black Jeremiad: Frederick Douglass's Immanent
Theory of Rhetorical Protest." *Howard Journal of Communication* 29, no. 3 (2018): 243–
257. Wilson provides an expert account of how genre and textual action work to compel
social action.

DISCUSSION QUESTIONS

1. Ghostwriters have played a significant role in public affairs since antiquity. Does the fact that a given text has been composed by someone other than the speaker pose any problems for CTA? What kind of claims, if any, need to be qualified? Disallowed?

2. Many critics associated with CTA are drawn to texts of unusual complexity, nuance, and aesthetic achievement. This is understandable, but challenging: in what sense, if any, can we account for the rhetorical power of a text with reference to its artistic properties?

3. You will have observed that students of CTA frequently operate at the level of word choice and syntax. Can they do so in the same manner with texts that have been trans‑ lated? What specific challenges does translation pose to the close analysis of texts?

4. CTA tends to assume that what is there, in the text, is of primary importance. At the same time, we may note that on occasion what is NOT in the text may be of genuine interest. How does one account for textual absence?

5. CTA is traditionally associated with the interpretation of written texts. Do the reading practices suggested in this essay apply equally to other symbolic forms, say the photo‑ graph, or symphonic performance, or monuments?

ACTIVITIES

1. As mentioned above, many critics associated with CTA are drawn to texts of unusual complexity, nuance, and aesthetic achievement. But what about more common or simple texts? In a small group, decide on a common or simple text and then agree on a way that CTA could enhance our appreciation for how the text functions.

2. In a small group, look through the news headlines of the day from at least two different news sources. Pick a story on the same subject provided by two of the news sources. Use CTA to examine both stories. What does CTA tell us about the differences/similarities of the stories?

NOTES

1. In addition to essays noted in the "CTA Tops Picks" section, the following articles are representa‑ tive of some of the notable works of close textual analysis: Michael C. Leff and Gerald P. Mohrmann,

"Lincoln at Cooper Union: A Rhetorical Analysis of the Text," *Quarterly Journal of Speech* 60 (1974): 346–358; Kenneth Burke, "The Rhetoric of Hitler's Battle," in *The Philosophy of Literary Form*, 191–220 (Berkeley: University of California Press, 1971); Amy R. Slagell, "Anatomy of a Masterpiece: A Close Textual Analysis of Abraham Lincoln's Second Inaugural Address," *Communication Studies* 42 (1991): 155–171; Michael C. Leff, "Things Made by Words: Reflections on Textual Criticism," *Quarterly Journal of Speech* 78 (1992): 223–231; and Martin J. Medhurst, "Reconceptualizing Rhetorical History: Eisenhower's Farewell Address," *Quarterly Journal of Speech* 80 (1994).

2. Transcripts are readily available online. One such transcript can be found at the National Public Radio website: http://www.npr.org/templates/story/story.php?storyId=88478467.

3. For summaries of the early twentieth-century growth of the communication discipline, see Thomas W. Benson, "The Cornell School of Rhetoric: Idiom and Institution," *Communication Quarterly* 51 (2003): 1–56; Jim A. Kuypers and Andrew King, eds., *Twentieth-Century Roots of Rhetorical Studies* (Westport, CT: Praeger, 2001); and Theodore Otto Windt Jr., *Rhetoric as a Human Adventure: A Short Biography of Everett Lee Hunt* (Annandale, VA: Speech Communication Association, 1990).

4. See especially Sacvan Bercovitch, *The American Jeremiad* (Madison: University of Wisconsin Press, 1978); and James R. Darsey, *The Prophetic Tradition and Radical Rhetoric in America* (New York: New York University Press, 1999).

5. For an examination of Winthrop's sermon, see Stephen Howard Browne, "Errand into Mercy: Rhetoric, Identity, and Community in John Winthrop's 'Modell of Christian Charity,'" in *Rhetoric, Religion, and the Roots of Identity in British Colonial America*, ed. James R. Andrews (East Lansing: Michigan State University Press, 2007), 1–36.

6. Representative essays treating these texts include Stephen E. Lucas, "Justifying America: The Declaration of Independence as a Rhetorical Document," in *American Rhetoric: Contexts and Criticism*, ed. Thomas W. Benson (Carbondale: Southern Illinois University Press, 1989), 67–131; Stephen Howard Browne, *Jefferson's Call for Nationhood: The First Inaugural Address* (College Station: Texas A&M University Press, 2003); Garry Wills, *Lincoln at Gettysburg: The Words That Remade America* (New York: Simon and Schuster, 2005); Suzanne Daughton, "Metaphorical Transcendence: Images of the Holy War in Franklin Roosevelt's First Inaugural," *Quarterly Journal of Speech* 79 (1993): 227–246; and Drew Hansen, *The Dream: Martin Luther King and the Speech that Inspired a Nation* (New York: Ecco, 2003).

8

Criticism of Metaphor

John W. Jordan

The movie *Moneyball*, based on the real-life story of an unconventional baseball executive who revolutionized the sport, has a scene that provides a useful starting point for what will be discussed in this chapter.[1] The scene begins with Oakland Athletics' General Manager Billy Beane, played by Brad Pitt, feeling conflicted about what may be the most important decision of his life. He has been offered the job to manage the Boston Red Sox, but at the cost of leaving behind his current team and their unmet goals. Billy confides in his assistant, Peter Brand, played by Jonah Hill. Peter is not a "baseball guy" but a numbers man, calm and analytical, a pure logic engine juxtaposed against Billy's emotional passion for the game. For Peter, it's an easy decision—take the Red Sox's offer—and he can't understand Billy's hesitation. Thinking he may have something to help Billy see the situation more clearly, Peter asks his boss to watch some game footage with him.

The video is of a minor league ballplayer who has a paralyzing fear of rounding first base after a hit. During the particular at-bat in the video, the hitter's worst fear comes true. He gets a hard smack on the pitch and sends the ball flying, but as he touches first base he trips over himself and tumbles to the dirt. Billy winces in embarrassment for the hitter, and notes sadly that he can hear the other players laughing at the fallen runner. But Peter tells Billy that everyone is laughing because, unbeknownst to the hitter, he actually hit a home run. The other players were laughing in encouragement, urging the hitter to get up and round the bases. Billy smiles as the realization crosses his mind. The player was so fixated on his fear that he failed to notice the better option in front of him. Unsure whether Billy gets the point, Peter matter-of-factly tells him, "It's a metaphor." Billy kindly replies, "I know it's a metaphor." And the scene ends with the two friends understanding one another.

Like Billy, most of us can recognize a **metaphor** when we meet one. Metaphors are not meant to be obscure. Even so, recognizing a metaphor and knowing how and why they work—or fail to—are very different skills. And knowing further how to think critically about metaphors is an even rarer. After all, Billy understood Peter's metaphor, but he still turned down the Red Sox and stayed with Oakland. Just because a metaphor is used does not guarantee the desired outcome. At the same time, we should not base our entire judgment of a metaphor on whether it achieves its desired outcome alone. Peter did not persuade Billy, but he helped Billy settle his mind. In that regard, the metaphor served a useful purpose. We need

111

to consider not just the metaphor itself but the broader circumstances surrounding it. We need to understand what metaphors are and what they do, how they are folded into and joined with other rhetorical devices, and how we might approach them critically and analytically to best articulate our conclusions to others.

Metaphor, and its companion figure, **simile**, often are discussed as means of working with comparisons in rhetorical texts. David Zarefsky points out that "a comparison can help people to accommodate a new idea or new information by deciding that it is similar to what they already know or believe. Comparisons can be made vivid by using similes and metaphors."[2] Zarefsky's comment suggests how metaphor and simile are alike: both are comparisons of one thing to another; one is familiar, the other less so. Technically, the difference between metaphor and simile is that similes always include either *like* or *as*, while metaphors do not. Thus, saying that "posting your home address on social media is *like* opening your front door to burglars" is a simile, while "posting your home address on social media opens your front door to burglars" is a metaphor. Regardless of whether the figure is technically a metaphor or a simile, it functions to make the idea more understandable and purposeful. In that sense, distinctions between metaphors and similes matter little. Therefore, for the remainder of this chapter, we will refer to these figures of speech simply as **metaphors**.

Despite the important stylistic functions metaphors contribute to meaning, critics are most interested in their *rhetorical* functions, their capacity to influence the thoughts and actions of audiences. Kenneth Burke highlighted this importance when he called metaphor one of the four master **tropes**.[3] We need to probe metaphor as a strategic means of expression, the outcome of which is never guaranteed but for which precise criticism can provide an explanation. This chapter explores the rhetorical functions of metaphor, and suggests how conducting a critique of metaphors might proceed. These concepts will be illustrated through a variety of examples drawn from different media.

HOW METAPHORS WORK

A metaphor consists of two terms that draw a comparison between two things—people, places, situations, events—that belong to "different classes of experience."[4] One of these two terms, usually called the **tenor** or focus, is *relevant* to or *continuous* with the topic under discussion. The tenor is the object, concept, or issue that is presumed to be not fully or correctly understood by the audience, according to the rhetor's point of view. The tenor is the "thing" that the rhetor is trying to help the audience understand. The other term, usually called the **vehicle** or frame, is *discontinuous* with, or of a different class of experience from, that topic.[5] The vehicle typically is a more familiar or understood object, concept, or issue that will be used to help form the audience's understanding of the tenor. When the two terms, the tenor (or focus) and the vehicle (or frame), are brought together by the rhetor— be they a speaker, writer, director, programmer, artist, or other kind of content creator—to form a metaphor, audiences are invited to see the comparison between the two and realign their thinking on these concepts.

Metaphors are used because rhetors and their audience start from different places of understanding. Closing this gap is a persuasive act, which Michael Osborn describes as a miniature dialectical process embedded within discourse in which meanings are contested and resolved. Skillful makers of metaphor will guide or control this process so that it becomes a kind of controlled disruption that turns the direction of thought in an intended direction. Interpreters overcome the felt distance or even tension within a metaphor by forming lines of association between tenor and vehicle that make sense of the figure. Therefore, lines of association are justifications or arguments that the interpreter develops to negotiate the differences initially felt between tenor and vehicle.[6]

The purpose of a metaphor is to disrupt the uncertainty that exists between idea and meaning, and between rhetor and audience. The rhetor attempts to shift the audience's thinking more toward their own. It is a promissory rhetoric. When a rhetor uses a metaphor, they ask the audience for a little faith and patience as understanding is built, and thus a good metaphor also entices the audience. Even so, no rhetorical device can satisfy all needs for all audience members, nor can rhetors have a perfect understanding of how their audience will interpret their messages. Thus, for those critiquing metaphors in rhetoric, we must not only seek to understand the "most fitting" interpretation of a metaphor, we must also explore its context and plausible alternative interpretations that may impact the rhetor's ability to connect with their audience through metaphor.

Rhetorical Functions of Metaphor

Metaphors prompt audiences to comprehend one thing, represented by the tenor, "in terms of" another, represented by the vehicle. When that happens, certain characteristics of the vehicle are "carried over" to the tenor, thus providing a new understanding of that term.[7] According to Malcolm O. Sillars and Bruce E. Gronbeck, "metaphor, because it draws an analogy among situations that are unrelated (e.g., 'the war on drugs,' 'a marriage of convenience,' 'loan sharks'), is a way to create new thought through language use. Thus, it is central to making sense through language."[8] That sense making, however, depends on whether the rhetor has clearly established the metaphor to the degree that it is obvious to the audience which of the vehicle's attributes "carry over" to the tenor. If not, the metaphor may fail.

Let us examine Martha Cooper's example of metaphor's rhetorical function. She writes:

> Probably the classic metaphor is, "man is a wolf." This statement encourages the audience to associate the characteristic(s) of a wolf with man. Stated more directly, the pattern is simply "man is like a wolf." The metaphor *works like* an enthymeme[9] in that the audience is asked to participate by supplying the characteristics of a wolf and drawing the comparison between wolves and man. The metaphor, by suggesting an association, triggers a pattern of thinking in which comparisons are chained out.[10]

If the audience makes the *appropriate* association between "man" and "wolf," their understanding of humans changes to what the rhetor needs them to think in order to advance the argument. But this is not automatic. After all, wolves walk on four paws and have tails. Although possible, it is doubtful that when the rhetor says "Man is a wolf," they intend for men to be seen with *those* wolf-like traits. On the other hand, wolves are strong, powerful, and cunning apex predators. It is almost certainly *these* wolf-like characteristics that the rhetor intends the audience to "carry over" in their thinking about humans, primarily males. Thus, audiences must "get it"; they must complete the enthymeme *appropriately* for the metaphor to have its intended effect, which means the rhetor must establish the context for the metaphor such that the audience recognizes which wolfish attributes are pertinent to the argument at hand.

We also should keep in mind that the connection between the tenor and the vehicle is not a one-way street. As the metaphor encourages the audience to think about which aspects of a wolf are most applicable to men, their thoughts about wolves may change, seeing their predatory behavior not as the result of evolutionary adaptation to their environment but as purposefully strategic, ambitious, and perhaps even political. As a metaphor enters into the language of an argument, both the tenor and the vehicle may undergo reconsideration; it is not the tenor alone that transforms. These transformations grow from what anthropologist J. David Sapir calls "the simultaneous likeness and unlikeness of the two terms." According to Sapir, "by replacing a term continuous to a topic with one that is discontinuous or by putting the two in juxtaposition, we are compelled . . . to consider each term in relationship to the other."[11] In the process of associating the tenor and vehicle, their differences and likenesses gain emphasis. Or, in the words of Kenneth Burke, the metaphor "brings out the thisness of that, or the thatness of this."[12] Michael Leff explains that this thought process "works in two stages; the juxtaposition of the two terms first causes the vehicle to assume a pattern of foreground associations, and then this pattern serves to direct our understanding of the tenor." The "mutual attraction of terms belonging to different classes," Leff writes, "causes a response that decomposes the elements associated with these terms and then recombines them into a new structure of meaning."[13] In the case of our example, "man is a wolf," the process is complete when the metaphor has performed its *rhetorical* function of persuading the audience to think of someone in terms of the appropriate characteristics of a wolf.

Cooper's assertion that metaphors function like enthymemes—arguments in which the audience participates in forming the conclusion—is especially important for rhetorical critics. Since the function of metaphor depends on cooperation between the rhetor and the audience to produce meaning, both must be part of the same "speech community." That is, at a minimum, they must share knowledge, experiences, beliefs, attitudes, and values that allow the rhetor to form, and the audience to complete, the enthymeme appropriately.[14] This does not mean they agree on everything, but they must recognize both the content and context of the rhetorical situation. Imagine an audience member with no knowledge whatsoever of wolves. For them, the metaphor "man is a wolf" would do little to alter their understanding of humans, and might give them a very skewed introduction to what wolves are like. Similarly, an expert on wolves may not be able to displace their knowledge in order to appreciate the metaphor, thinking instead only of how unlike wolves are to humans. For them, saying "man is a wolf" might seem particularly ridiculous. These are just a few examples of why we cannot assume that rhetors and audiences will always be able to agree on how to connect the tenor and vehicle. As Leff explains, "metaphor draws its materials from communal knowledge, achieves its effects through the active cooperation of the auditor, and assumes its form in relation to a particular context."[15] If the rhetor and audience are from different speech communities, the metaphor is likely to have little effect. Thus, we cannot conduct our metaphor criticism without also attending to the features that surround and enable a metaphor's interpretation.

Metaphor and Context

Sometimes the associations between the metaphoric tenor and vehicle seem relatively straightforward, and we barely pay them notice. But we should. Consider the sound an iPhone makes when taking a photo—the camera "click." That sound is not organic to the phone, meaning it is not the actual sound coming from the process the iPhone uses to produce an image. It actually is the sound of a Canon analog camera from the 1970s, recorded by an Apple sound engineer and used metaphorically.[16] There is almost nothing similar between how an analog camera from the 1970s and a modern smartphone capture an image. But Apple decided users needed an audio signal to help them understand what the phone is doing. Apple's guidelines for app design highlight a belief in the importance of metaphors, stating, "People learn more quickly when an app's virtual objects and actions are metaphors for familiar experiences—whether rooted in the real or digital world."[17] Even so, the metaphor really only works if the iPhone user is familiar with analog cameras and their sounds, which seems increasingly less likely as analog cameras fade into history. The sound still does its job of letting the iPhone user know a photograph was taken, but it no longer functions practically as a metaphor as the sound has no other context than itself. This is along the lines of what Robert L. Ivie describes as a metaphor becoming "literalized," or when audiences no longer distinguish between the two things being associated but think of them as identical. As he explains, "We are in the presence of a literalized metaphor when we act upon the figurative as if it were real, not recognizing that two domains of meaning have been merged into one despite their differences."[18] Rather than hearing the iPhone's "click" as a metaphor, we simply think of it as the sound the smartphone makes—not a reference to a thing but the thing itself. This indicates why we need to look beyond the metaphor itself to its context and use.

Metaphors have the potential to alter how audiences understand not just the subject under discussion but its situation. According to Leff, "Since metaphoric structure limits and organizes our perception of a situation, it seems to establish the ground for viewing that situation; it creates a perspective and hence defines the space in which we encounter the situation. A metaphoric meaning localizes our attention . . . it produces a frame within which we can synthesize our reactions to the ongoing flow of events in time."[19] Metaphors seek to direct how we think about issues and the actions we take with regard to those issues. Metaphors encourage audiences to focus on those details most relevant to the tenor-vehicle dynamic, perhaps at the expense of other details or ways of interpreting them. Psychologist Jeffrey Scott Mio asserts that "metaphors can act as both filters that screen out much of the available information, leaving only the core ideas consistent with the metaphors, and as devices to collapse disparate information into smaller, more manageable packets."[20] This helps explain why metaphors can be powerful when employed correctly, due to their ability to help rhetors focus their audiences' attention on useful details.

But we want to be wary of ascribing too much power to rhetors who use metaphors. Audiences are not powerless in the face of metaphors. If audience members lack familiarity with the references used by a rhetor, they will not magically understand the metaphor simply because the rhetor wishes it. Similarly, even if a rhetor belongs to the same speech community as his or her audience, if the rhetor is clumsy in his or her choice and/or application of metaphors, the rhetor runs the risk of confusing or putting the audience off. Rhetors must be skilled in reading the situation and anticipating their audience's knowledge in order to construct useful metaphors which employ appropriate vehicles to aid the audience's understanding and appreciation of the tenor.

We can observe the importance of this skill in an example of a metaphor that is technically correct—meaning it has the proper components and form—but potentially fails its own rhetorical context. In this example, the video gaming news hub, FextraLife, posted a very positive review of *Nioh 2*, calling the game "practically perfect."[21] One of the review's primary arguments was that the game provided "amazing value for money and well worth day one pricepoint." To drive home the point that the game "is a day 1 buy," the review concludes with an extended metaphor emphasizing how much the sequel improves upon the original. The review states: "It's not the same game with a new coat of paint. It's a better version of the original game with a full on leather seat rework, new state of the art navigation and audio systems, the best tires you could find, and it gives you a massage as you drive!"[22] This is the only metaphor in the entire review, and its placement at the end punctuates the persuasive appeal to purchase the game.

The metaphor works just fine on a technical level. It takes an unknown element as its tenor—playing *Nioh 2*—and seeks to provide an understanding through the vehicle (rather literally) of a luxury car. The general idea of "similar but better" is conveyed sensibly, but it is also a bit clumsy and introduces unnecessary confusion to a point that should be more straightforward. At no previous point in the review are cars mentioned; the conversation shifts suddenly from a video game rooted in ancient Japanese history to luxury car features. Not only is the shift abrupt, it is not a clear improvement to the audience's understanding. What does it mean for a video game to give the player a massage in the way a luxury car seat can? The car's features become the focus of the metaphor, when the focus should be on the game. The metaphor also seems out-of-place contextually. The review's multiple references to the game's value-for-price do not imply an audience unconcerned with money nor experienced with luxury cars. Thus, the metaphor seems inconsistent with the overall rhetorical sensibilities of the review and distracts from the larger message.

The appropriateness of a metaphor must be judged not solely on its technical merits but on how the metaphor fits the context of its larger argument, as well as with the audience for whom it is intended. In this instance, the inconsistency is not so much between the tenor and vehicle but between the metaphor and its rhetorical context. This is not to say that audiences would fail to get FextraLife's general point. Metaphors seldom are binary propositions of either total enlightenment or complete confusion. Metaphors are always about an approximation of meaning, but that does not mean that there are not better and lesser metaphors. FextraLife's metaphor works, just perhaps not as well as a different choice, given the framework of the larger argument and the implied audience. A rhetor can never control how an audience will interpret their message, but they can control which metaphors they use, and that choice obviously greatly influences the sensibility of a metaphor in its rhetorical context.

Metaphors can be a double-edged sword for rhetors. Metaphors may produce a desired rhetorical effect, but they also can trap rhetors. Because we are desperate to understand something new, we may be hasty in our metaphor selection, grasping at anything that seems familiar. This may be why Alissa Wilkinson describes metaphors as "inescapable, no matter how apt, misleading, or simply inadequate they may be. They're key to how humans wrap their minds around phenomena they don't totally understand."[23] Metaphors always involve compromise between the helpfulness of their framework for understanding and the potential skewing of that understanding by the inevitable misalignment between the tenor and the vehicle.

"Anything mysterious, frightening, or unknowable," Wilkinson goes on to explain, "will inevitably get stuffed into a framework drawn from something we do understand."[24] To illustrate, Wilkinson examines war metaphors' frequent use during virus outbreaks—in particular, how war metaphors dominated the rhetoric of the COVID-19 pandemic that began in late 2019. As the virus spread across the globe, citizens and leaders alike searched for meaningful ways to explain what was happening. Although chart-based metaphors such as "flattening the curve" were popular initially, "war" soon became the primary trope for discussing the "threat" of the virus and our "fight" against it. Microbiology is difficult to understand, but we are much more familiar with war. As Wilkinson puts it, "Humans have understood war for all of human history. So it's no big surprise that the war metaphor keeps cropping up."[25]

Even though we remind ourselves that discussing disease as "war" is not ideal, we keep coming back to the metaphor.[26] Doctors and nurses are "frontline troops," the virus is an "invisible enemy" that is "attacking" people and needs to be "defeated," and those stricken by the illness are "casualties."[27] The war metaphor provides an emotional sensibility for the disease's impact. Obeying safer-at-home instructions could be understood as a citizen contributing to the war effort. Thoroughly washing one's hands and wearing a face mask in public could be understood as ways of ensuring the enemy does not further penetrate our lines of defense and inflict more casualties. The war metaphor even provides a sense of optimism—no matter how hubristic—that one day we will defeat the virus and declare victory. Metaphors are never merely informative; they are also persuasive and result in material action. We shape our behavior according to our understanding of the world, and if a large part of how we understand the world is through the metaphors we use to create that understanding, then our metaphors in turn shape our behavior. Or, as Wilkinson notes, metaphors "are a kind of grammar our brains rely on to operate."[28]

One of the risks presented through metaphors, however, is that they can provide a false sense of security, misleading us into equating familiarity with understanding. In such instances, rather than the metaphor aiding our understanding of the unknown, it may hinder more accurate insights. For example, when President Trump tweeted about COVID-19 that "The Invisible Enemy will soon be in full retreat!," his use of war metaphors seemed intended to encourage Americans that, even though we could not see our enemy, we could imagine that we already were making progress toward its defeat.[29] But others claimed that such metaphors were not helpful and were perhaps even harmful. Dr. Eugene Gu argued that war metaphors misdirected attention away from the scientific reality of the virus and its impact. "The coronavirus is not an invisible enemy," Gu stated. "Thanks to modern technology and science, we can see every intricate detail of the coronavirus. . . . which are key to understanding and finding a safe and effective vaccine."[30] Gu and others who disagreed with COVID-19 war metaphors were not bickering over ornamental language but about the best way to approach a global pandemic. Action follows understanding, and understanding is born from language. According to Gu, scientific inquiry, not military maneuvering, was the more effective means for addressing COVID-19, whose neutralization would come not with a "retreat" but a "safe and effective vaccine." The difference is not inconsequential. War metaphors lead us in one direction, scientific metaphors in another. It matters in terms of who people listen to, which entities receive funding and support, and what we consider to be the desired outcome for the pandemic. As such, debates over metaphor selection and usage are critical to examine, as their impact can be extensive.

In her analysis of the impact of war metaphors on COVID-19's public rhetoric, Wilkinson highlighted the importance of thinking through the implications of metaphorical language. She and others suggested alternative metaphors that might be of more use in helping the public understand and cope with a pandemic, such as presenting "healing as a journey or a river, which can remind us of the passage of time and the connectedness of everyone who embarks on the same trek or follows the same path."[31] Nobel laureate economist Paul Krugman used medicinal metaphors to defend the wisdom of safer-at-home orders, stating, "we're going into the economic equivalent of a medically induced coma, in which some brain functions are temporarily shut down to give the patient a chance to heal."[32] While acknowledging that no metaphor can ever be perfect, Wilkinson's analysis asks us to think about how metaphors both constrain and enable pathways of thinking about complex ideas. We should not think only of the one-to-one comparison between the unknown and familiar but also analyze how the use of any metaphor necessarily impacts future decisions and, in many instances, entire social patterns.

In sum, metaphors work by forging comparisons between two otherwise unrelated things. More importantly, they have the capacity to perform powerful rhetorical functions, altering the thoughts and actions of audiences. Even so, although metaphors are potentially powerful fig-ures of speech, their use also entails potential risk, and we must never forget that they are strate-gies with the potential to go wrong. Finally, metaphors must be situated within contexts, which also must be analyzed and critiqued as part of the overall argumentative frame. With this in mind, we turn now to how we might make use of this knowledge when critiquing metaphors.

CRITIQUING METAPHORS

Metaphors thus far have been discussed primarily through their technical workings—how the tenor and vehicle fit together, and the role context plays in the cognitive, linguistic, and audience suitability of a metaphor. It is rare for a metaphor to be the sole persuasive device in a rhetorical text. The more common situation is that one or more metaphors are folded into the overall appeal, and are used creatively to support and amplify key concepts as the rhetor feels necessary. A critique which focuses exclusively on a metaphor is rarely sufficient to satisfy the curiosity of those seeking to understand the entire argument. This is not to diminish the importance of metaphors or the need to think about them critically but instead to properly contextualize metaphors within the text.

CRITICAL ESSAYS

In what follows, we will consider examples of rhetors using metaphors to help their audiences understand unfamiliar concepts. The first examples are drawn from the vivid world of food and restaurant criticism, and the second focuses on a specific metaphor sustained throughout the 2019 film *Parasite*.

EXAMPLE 1: METAPHORS AND RESTAURANT REVIEWS

Food and restaurant critics have the difficult task of helping their audience decide whether spending time and money at a certain restaurant will be worthwhile. Anyone can list the ingredients in a dish, but to convey the idiosyncrasy of how the meal tastes in a way that an audience will find useful requires skill and creativity. This task is complicated by the fact that tastes and preferences are highly subjective. A good restaurant review seeks to help the prospective diner imagine what the experience of eating at that place will be like. It therefore should not surprise us that food critics employ a variety of rhetorical strategies to communi-cate their ideas, and one of their most relied-upon devices is the metaphor.

Let us look at a few examples from the iconic Jonathan Gold, who, before his passing in 2018, was a renowned restaurant critic for various publications, chiefly the *Los Angeles Times* and *LA Weekly*, where he became the first-ever food writer awarded the Pulitzer Prize for his "zestful, wide ranging restaurant reviews, expressing the delight of an erudite eater."[33] Among the reasons his reviews were so popular and praised was that Gold made Los Angeles's "food understandable and approachable to legions of fans."[34] Gold did not simply document what a restaurant had to offer; he wrote about the experience of having a meal there as a full human, not just a stomach, and connected to curious readers through writing about food. He sought to persuade his audience to try new experiences, not just new or trendy dishes, and to see a restaurant as a gateway to culture. Like all critics, Gold had rhetorical obstacles in his way that he needed to overcome through the skilled use of language, especially metaphor.

Gold's metaphors for the food he ate often did not try to pinpoint the food's flavor profile. Rather, his metaphors tended to be more experiential, asking the reader to think not just about flavor but about sensation and even memory. Gold was known for incorporating a broad array of metaphors into his writing. "Writers and editors," wrote one of his contemporaries, "were touched by Gold's empathetic, excitable reviews, all of which contained references that reached far beyond food."[35] We may use his writing to demonstrate the wide range of metaphors that can be incorporated into a rhetorical text. The two examples we will examine highlight this range. The first will be a very straightforward metaphor, presented in an obvious form and immediately identifiable as a specific metaphor. The second will be a more abstract metaphor in both form and function, requiring a more contextualized and nuanced reading in order to digest the point Gold seemed to be making. Comparing and contrasting how the metaphor works in each instance provides us with a better understanding of the breadth of possibility in metaphor.

As our first example from Gold, consider his review of one restaurant's Oaxacan *mole negro*, in which he described the sauce as "so dark that it seems to suck the light out of the airspace around it, spicy as a *novela* and bitter as tears."[36] Although it is clear that Gold is using metaphors to describe the food, at first brush, it may seem unconventional to use the vehicle of a *novela* or tears to help a would-be diner understand the tenor of what the sauce on a plate of food looks and tastes like. Nevertheless, Gold makes the metaphor itself noticeable, and thus the task becomes to try and figure out what the connection between the tenor and vehicle are, and what to pay attention to as we consider it further.

When critiquing a metaphor, it is important to assess what the rhetor's purpose is and the audience toward whom that purpose is directed. We know Gold sought to inform his readers about the restaurant he visited and the experience of dining there. Additionally, his language suggests characteristics of the audience he hoped to persuade—not the actual readers, because no one can predict who will or will not read a food review—but the ideal or anticipated reader he imagined would be persuaded by his words. This imagined "reader" is what Edwin Black termed the "second persona" or the "implied auditor," a useful fiction created by rhetors to give them a direction to steer their message. A careful reading of the rhetorical language in a text "extracts from it the audience it implies," enabling critics to "observe the sort of audience that would be appropriate" to the rhetoric.[37] Using the contextual and symbolic clues within the text—what Black called "tokens"—we can make a reasonable guess as to the "implied auditor" Gold's metaphors likely would attract. From the nonfood but experiential metaphors he employed, the implied auditor begins to take shape. Gold was not writing for "foodies" but for those eager to learn something about themselves and their community through excellent dining. One need not be an experienced foodie in order to read Gold, but one must be open to thinking of food as an experience.

Gold explained that he meant for his metaphors to convey "a sense of wonder" about "the greatest Los Angeles cooking."[38] He argued that each restaurant reviewed offered a unique experience that should be met on its own terms. Gold never promised that the diner would have the same experience as he did, only that the diner would find the outing worthwhile on some level. If we keep these ideas in mind as we revisit his metaphor of the *mole* that was "so dark that it seems to suck the light out of the airspace around it, spicy as a *novela* and bitter as tears," his rhetorical purpose comes into clearer focus. The restaurant offers a dish that is delicious, but the taste of the sauce is neither the beginning nor end of its pleasures. This food is worth seeking out because it delights the eyes, mouth, and mind. This certainly is an elaborate way of basically saying, "I think people will like this restaurant," but this is why metaphors are so attractive—they help us feel something beyond the ordinary, beyond just a sauce on a plate of food. Gold's use of a noticeable yet intriguing metaphor seeks to persuade readers that they are not just paying for calories but creating a memory.

Our second example from Gold is less direct and perhaps even more puzzling at first glance. Indicative of his style, some of Gold's metaphors run the risk of being too abstract, but that is the risk a rhetor sometimes must take to have his or her words stick in the audience's mind. Common metaphors that have become literalized do not spark our imaginations. To make an impact, metaphors must be understandable but not overly familiar, and the rhetor's skill is demonstrated in how he or she negotiates between those two goals. Thus, in our second example, we find Gold reviewing a Beverly Hills restaurant frequented by Hollywood stars, which serves his "favorite corned-beef hash in the world." That statement is the only time dining food is mentioned in the entire review. The review immediately becomes quite abstract as a restaurant review, reading more like an anecdote than a dining guide. Much of the review is not even about the restaurant's food but who eats there and why, with Gold name-dropping several Hollywood celebrities, but without a sense of being starstruck. Most of Gold's review is spent recounting an occasion when he dined there with a friend, "an editor who knows Hollywood the way Julia Child knows a rump roast."[39] While his very starstruck friend is concerned only with spotting all the famous people in the room, Gold's attention is held tight by his corned-beef hash and martini, which he does not comment on further.

To be sure, a restaurant review that all-but-fails to mention, let alone focus on, the actual food being served may seem to have missed its purpose. This is where we as critics need to place some faith in the rhetor, or at least be humble enough to doubt our first reactions and stick with the text. Someone as accomplished as Gold is unlikely to have made such an egregious error, or to have gotten it past his editor. But from a more rhetorical point of view, we should question first if we need to reorient our own thinking about where to look for a metaphor. In order to identify Gold's trope, we need to take a step back from looking for direct and obvious metaphors to find the abstract metaphor he creates through this review. The metaphor at work in this review is not as obvious as the metaphors he used to describe the *mole*. Recalling that Gold's primary purpose in his reviews was to describe not the food *but the experience of eating at a restaurant*, we can see how the anecdote of the two diners—himself and his friend—is an extended metaphor for the experience he seeks his readers to understand. He is not comparing the food to something else but instead comparing the two dining experiences—his guest's and his own. Gold uses these as metaphors for the two types of diners who might best appreciate what the restaurant can provide. The reader is asked to consider if they are closer in taste to Gold or to his companion. For food fans, the food there is so good a diner may not even care that there are famous people at nearby tables. For those who more closely relate to Gold's stargazing friend, the restaurant is a great place to see famous faces while also getting a fine meal. The metaphor is not as direct or obvious as the first example, but by understanding Gold's purpose and looking again for the rhetorical trope that gives his words sensibility, we can discover the more abstract and extended metaphor in play. Gold's rhetoric suggests an awareness of what interests his readers about this restaurant, and tailors his message to them, even if it requires them to reorient their thinking toward his message. His metaphors are the means by which his readers can understand the opportunity in front of them—not just to walk away with a belly full of delicious food but an entire cultural experience worth telling someone else about.

Whether describing the sauce on a plate or dining among Hollywood royalty, Jonathan Gold's creative use of metaphors enabled his readers to construct an idea of what they might be in for if they visited one of his recommended restaurants. And he was not alone. Gold was neither the first nor last person to use bold metaphors to talk about food as an experience beyond the plate. He happened to achieve a particular level of success and notoriety, but metaphors and food are a standard pairing. Indeed, as we expand our thinking about food and dining through the frequent metaphors we encounter in their descriptions, food itself can be viewed as a metaphor for culture, community, identity, love, and other tenors. "How we communicate through food," explain Ashli Quesinberry Stokes and Wendy Atkins-Sayre in their analysis of Southern food rhetoric, "strengthens our understanding of why food is such a vital part of culture."[40] And part of that vitality is found not just in the sustenance food provides but in how our use of metaphors about food has helped us understand so much more about ourselves than just what's on our plates or in our bellies. In the hands of a skilled rhetor, metaphors of a broad variety can elevate and enhance any subject.

EXAMPLE 2: *PARASITE'S* USE OF ODOR AS A METAPHOR FOR SOCIOECONOMIC INEQUALITY

Metaphors can be a powerful means for conveying complex ideas and emotions in any communication medium and on virtually any topic. Our next example comes from the film *Parasite*, specifically its use of odor to make a point about social prejudice. Films can be a particularly effective medium for metaphors, as audiences look to movies to take them "away from their mundane reality and into a story world."[41] By paying close attention to how a filmmaker uses symbolic language rhetorically—from characters to dialogue to setting and everything else—we gain insight into how metaphors in movies create meaning and enable interpretation. We also should remind ourselves that the inherent inequality—however slight—between the tenor and vehicle means that no metaphor can ever convey *only* what the filmmaker intends, no matter how big a budget or talented a cast; there will always be room for other perspectives. Films often provide a rich text to work with when analyzing metaphors for these reasons, giving critics a good deal to work with.

In what follows, I critique how director and writer Bong Joon Ho's 2019 Oscar-winning film, *Parasite*, develops odor as a metaphor throughout the narrative to guide the audience's understanding of the film's plot, its characters, their motives, and their behavior toward one another. As such, odor can be studied usefully as a rhetorical statement from the director about social justice and the possibility of change. My argument is not that odor is the only element of significance in the film, or even its only metaphor (it is not), nor that the film should be studied only through the lens of metaphor criticism. Rather, my goal is to explain how something useful can be gleaned from an intensive examination of this particular metaphor and its rhetorical deployment throughout the film, and that by understanding the filmmaker's use of this metaphor, other elements of the movie become more accessible for consideration and critique.

On my first viewing of *Parasite*, I only came to suspect that odor was doing something interesting in the film in the very last scene in which it is used as a **trope**. This formed the initial question in my mind: "Is the director using odor metaphorically in order to make a point that advances the narrative?" I rewatched the film and focused on how odor and various characters' reactions to it are presented to the audience as purposeful, not accidental. I questioned why odor was being used as a vehicle, to what tenor it was connected, and how this metaphor helps the story become more accessible. The film is set in South Korea and the dialogue is in Korean, but *Parasite's* depiction of those struggling to rise above their circumstances, of success being represented through material luxury and privilege, of the moral struggle to reconcile who one is with who one wishes to be, are themes shared across many cultures and people. Thus, despite not speaking the language and relying on the subtitles, I still consider myself part of the film's speech community, at least to the extent that I feel able to conduct a reasonable analysis of the film's use of metaphors and other narrative devices.

As mentioned, odor is far from the only metaphor in *Parasite*. Stairways and their up-and-down mobility also suggest which characters have higher status than others, and are seen frequently in the film as people ascend stairways to places of wealth and luxury, or descend into squalor. In fact, writer and director Bong Joon Ho referred to this film as his "stairway movie."[42] But odor—or, more specifically, characters' reactions to particular odors—also features prominently in the film at key moments, including the dramatic climax. I argue that odor is a more intricate and poignant metaphor in the film for social status than stairways, as odor is a less obvious way of identifying class than the familiar tropes of "upper" and "lower." A less common metaphor may be the director's way of bringing surprise and emotion unavailable through a more obvious metaphor. The director indicated he was aiming to jolt the audience's emotional sensibilities with his film, saying that "making the audience feel something naked and raw is one of the greatest powers of cinema."[43] His ability to elicit such feelings relies on his rhetorical skill in using metaphors is unconventional ways.

Parasite focuses primarily on two families: one is working poor, struggling daily just to survive and unable to get ahead; the second family is fabulously wealthy, enjoying every luxury and privilege money can buy. Through a bit of luck and a lot of deception, the poorer family systematically infiltrates the wealthy family's household, scheming their way into staff positions that enable them to live off the wealthy family. Everything seems to be going fine until it is revealed that there is a third family living in hiding in the grand house, who threatens to expose the first family's lies. The tension escalates to the point of calamitous murder and retribution, and all three families suffer immeasurable loss by the end. The movie routinely is praised as a "masterpiece" that moves audiences through its twisted maze of emotion and suspense.[44] Using odor as a starting point, we can better navigate the plot and the larger social message this award-winning film suggests. I will not cover every instance of the film in which odor is used metaphorically (there are many) but rather will focus on those moments which seem most significant to the narrative and the audience's emotions.

Characters' negative reactions to odor and "stink" appear early in the film, but the metaphor's significance takes longer to develop. In the opening scene, we are introduced to the poorer family in their cramped and untidy semibasement apartment. The father of the family, Ki-taek, sits at the small kitchen table, picking moldy bits from his stale bread. The film is quick to establish that the family is suffering financially. But they still have their pride. The father glances down at a large insect and disgustedly flicks it away with his finger, muttering "Damn stink bugs."[45] This first reference to odor as "stink" may seem insignificant, but its importance is revealed through additional negative reactions to odor that demonstrate the metaphor becoming a theme. The richness of a metaphor in a rhetorical text is not always immediately noticeable nor completed in a single reference. We must pay attention over the course of the text to observe how metaphors are built through strategic repetition.

The film is careful not to be too subtle with this odor metaphor, however, lest the audience miss it. Before long, we see that Ki-taek has schemed his way into being the chauffeur for the patriarch of the wealthy family, known as Mr. Park. Sitting in the back seat of his luxurious Mercedes, Mr. Park complains to Ki-taek about his housekeeper quitting unexpectedly. In actuality, she was forced into leaving due to Ki-taek's plotting, clearing the way for Ki-taek's spouse, Chung-sook, to become the new housekeeper. Mr. Park laments to Ki-taek that without a housekeeper, his home will soon fall apart. "We're in trouble now," he sighs. "In a week, our house will be a trash can. My clothes will start to smell." It is worth noting that smelly clothes is how Mr. Park defines "trouble." This is a proudly odorless man—so wealthy that neither he nor his clothes stink. Whereas Ki-taek and his family cannot escape the stench of their subbasement apartment, for Mr. Park, odor is something he feels removed from. The metaphor of odor is used to instruct the audience as to the divides between these two families. The director is building up the audience's familiarity with how he wishes them to perceive odor in the film, so that when he needs it to count the most—during the climax—it will.

Rhetoric is about building sympathy and understanding with an audience, and that takes time and repetition. Movies work rhetorically in how they unfold their plot, allowing the audience to make connections based on previous scenes even if the characters seem oblivious to what is happening. For example, in the first scene in *Parasite* after Chung-sook has joined the Park household in the guise of the replacement housekeeper, we finally see both families under the Parks' roof. The poorer family have completely infiltrated the wealthy family's house and lives. But cracks already start to form. In this scene, Mr. Park returns from a shopping spree for his son. He glides up his staircase with Ki-taek trailing behind, barely visible behind all the goods he carries for his boss. Ki-taek and Chung-sook, pretending they do not know each other while masquerading as driver and housekeeper, arrange the boxes on the table so that Mr. Park's son can open them. Ki-taek leans past the boy, who seems to notice something odd, and sniffs Ki-taek's jacket repeatedly. He then runs over to the new housekeeper, Chung-sook, and sniffs her clothing. Turning toward his parents, he exclaims, "It's the same! They smell the same!" Embarrassed, the boy's mother tells him to go to his room to work with "Jessica," who is actually, Ki-jung, the daughter from the poorer family, pretending to be the boy's therapist. The child replies as he walks away, "Jessica smells like that, too." In terms of the movie's plot, this scene is important in a "from the mouths of babes" revelation that at least one member of the Park family sees through the disguises of the poorer family, putting them at risk just when they thought everything was going so well. But in terms of how odor is used metaphorically, the scene takes on additional significance. By this point in the film, the audience has been taught through repetition to pay close attention to odor, and that it has a significance beyond its surface meaning. What is an embarrassingly rude moment for the Park family is a blaring alarm for the audience, all because the boy sniffed out the deception. Ki-taek's family have successfully entered the Park home, but they cannot leave behind their true identities, the stench of which clings to and betrays them. The ethical valuation of the metaphor at this point remains ambiguous, however. Should the audience feel good that this family of liars cannot escape the truth? Or should they feel sad that a down-on-their-luck family, who simply are taking advantage of the opportunities afforded to them, cannot ever leave their past lives behind? The film allows the tension to hang in the air a bit longer.

Given the attention already placed on odor, it unsurprisingly factors significantly in *Parasite*'s major plot twist. At roughly the midpoint of the film, the poorer family discovers that someone has been living in a secret underground shelter beneath the Parks's huge house. The shelter's occupant is the husband of the previously dismissed housekeeper, whom she moved into the shelter to avoid the loan sharks threatening his life. Of importance to our metaphor criticism at this point is how the shelter dweller is marked by his smell. As the semibasement family descends into the hidden shelter, the son quickly covers his nose with his shirt, signaling the overwhelming stench in the dweller's lair. The shelter family and the semibasement family both are poor and living off the oblivious Parks, but the son's reaction to the shelter's smell clearly establishes which family is "lower" than the other. Throughout the remainder of the film, these two "low" families battle each other to keep their collective secrets away from the Parks. The semibasement family are momentarily lifted by the fact that, however much they differ from the wealthy Parks, they at least are not down at the level of the shelter family. The film's metaphorical hierarchy of odor is now complete, with each family positioned on the social ladder according to how they are reacted to by their scent. The Parks have no stink at all, the semibasement family smells mildly unpleasant, and the shelter family reeks. And while it may at this point seem redundant for the film to use metaphors of both odor and elevation to signify differences in social status, the film soon places more prominence on odor as the means for understanding the characters' relationships.

Soon after the subbasement family temporarily halts the threat posed by the shelter dwellers, they are reminded by the Park family that they do not truly belong among the elite. The Parks unexpectedly return home from a trip, during which Ki-taek's family had been making liberal use of the Parks' home as though it was their own. Following a series of comical close calls with nearly being caught by the Parks, Ki-taek and his two children are forced to hide under the large coffee table in the Parks' enormous living room until they can slip away undetected. In the meantime, they are trapped as Mr. and Mrs. Park snuggle on the living room sofa, unaware that they are not alone.

Mr. Park detects something as he settles himself. "Wait a minute," he says. "Where's that smell coming from?" When his wife asks what he means, he replies, "Mr. Kim's smell." ("Mr. Kim" is the alias Ki-taek uses as Mr. Park's driver.) "You must have smelled it," Mr. Park continues, not knowing he is very much in earshot of Ki-taek. "That smell that wafts through the car, how to describe it?"

"An old man's smell?" Mrs. Park suggests.

"No, no, it's not that," he replies. "What is it? Like an old radish. No." The camera at this moment cuts to Ki-taek, hiding beneath the table, disappointment registering across his face as he hears how the employer he admires thinks of him. "You know when you boil a rag?" Mr. Park continues. "It smells like that." But Mr. Park is not yet finished:

> Anyway, even though he always seems about to cross the line, he never does cross it. That's good. I'll give him credit. But that smell crosses the line. It powers through right into the back seat.

Ki-taek can only lay still, unable to defend himself from Mr. Park's maligning. To Mr. Park, Ki-taek is a competent driver, but his most memorable quality is that he stinks.

This scene is an excellent example of how a rhetor—in this case, the filmmaker Bong Joon Ho—may use the symbolic resources of their medium—dialogue, cinematography, audio, editing—to develop a metaphor in a meaningful and compelling manner for the audience. During this scene, Ki-taek and the audience learn much about Mr. Park and his view of the world through his exposition on odor and status, but we also learn of his arrogance. Mr. Park never once questions why that odor is present on his sofa. He simply accepts it with a weary sigh, never imagining that Ki-taek and his family truly crossed a line by partying in his house while he was away. This arrogance also is why he fails to recognize that the smell is coming directly from Ki-taek, "Mr. Kim," who is literally underneath Mr. Park's nose at that moment, but Mr. Park does not even bother to investigate. Ki-taek and his family are trapped by their odor, reminded that no matter how well they hide their true appearance, there is something about them that will always be distasteful to people like the Parks. The metaphor of odor as inescapable socioeconomic inequity plays beautifully and achingly in these moments.

We jump ahead now to the film's dramatic climax, in which odor again serves as the audience's guide to the plot and characters. The Parks decide to throw an impromptu birthday party for their spoiled son and enlist Ki-taek's family—still in their roles as household staff—to help. Ki-taek is tasked with driving Mrs. Park to several high-end boutiques to pick up expensive party supplies. She is on her phone the entire time, chatting joyfully with her other wealthy friends whom she invites to the party. As she does this she hands off her selections to Ki-taek, barely glancing at him as he labors behind her, a human shopping cart.

On the return drive to the house, Mrs. Park sits in the back of the Mercedes with her bare feet casually resting on the passenger-side headrest. Continuing to laugh with her phone friend, Mrs. Park catches her breath as something hits her nostrils. She glances at Ki-taek, and places a finger under her nose to block the odor. She is no longer laughing. She sniffs again, coughing a little as the smell reaches her throat, and fixes her eyes on Ki-taek. Whatever she is smelling is quite unpleasant to her, and she seems to know the source of the odor that has invaded her space. When she lowers her window to let in some fresh air, Ki-taek notices but says nothing. Her bare feet are still on the headrest, inches from his face, but it is *his* scent that offends. His odor is the metaphor that enables the audience to comprehend how trapped he feels in his unchangeable life. Perhaps this is righteous. After all, he and his family achieved their positions through fraud and even killing. Why shouldn't they suffer some consequences? We know that Ki-taek increasingly feels unable to rid himself of his stench and the lower-class life it symbolizes, but we do not yet know how much further he will go to do so. At this point, the metaphor seemingly does not favor a clear moral outcome, keeping several options in play as the movie accelerates toward its conclusion.

Back at the Park house, the birthday party is in full swing, but the celebrations will be short-lived. In parallel with the overall arc of the movie itself, the birthday scene starts with joyful whimsy but ends in tragedy. Ki-jung, still pretending to be the Park son's therapist, "Jessica," brings the birthday cake out to the party guests in the backyard. Unbeknownst to them, but quite obvious to the audience, the shelter dweller has escaped his confinement. Driven insane by months of solitude and Ki-taek's family's abuse and killing of his wife, he seeks vengeance. Armed with a kitchen knife, he stumbles out into the birthday party, pushing through the crowd in a frenzy, and plunges his knife into Ki-jung's chest. He calls out for Chung-sook, his wife's nemesis, whom he holds responsible for his wife's death and for taking her place as housekeeper. She begins fighting the dweller, with each being wounded during their battle. Ki-taek is in a daze as he kneels at his mortally wounded daughter's side, unable to comfort her. As he watches the party guests scramble in terror, he sees that his own son also has been attacked by the dweller. In a matter of seconds, Ki-taek's family has been shattered.

Unaware and unconcerned with Ki-taek's tragedy, Mr. Park shouts at him to "Get the car!" to drive the Parks's son, who has fainted from the chaos, to the hospital. Mr. Park shouts for Ki-taek to toss him the car keys, and he obliges, but they do not make it. In true cinematic fashion, the keys are landed on mid-flight by the shelter dweller and Chung-sook, locked in fierce battle. The dweller and the housekeeper wrestle atop of the keys until Chung-sook strikes a killing blow, piercing the dweller's side with a grill skewer. Mr. Park scrambles to push the dweller off the car keys. But as he rolls the dweller aside, he is overcome by the dying man's stench. The movie enters slow motion as Mr. Park's entire body winces from the smell, physically recoiling. The camera cuts to show Ki-taek watching Mr. Park's revulsion, not at the blood or violence but at the odor. In the moment when his own son's life is most in danger, Mr. Park stops to pinch his nostrils shut before reaching for the keys. Not even his own son's life can cause Mr. Park to overcome his disdain for the stench of the lower classes. This finally is too much for Ki-taek. He snaps. He picks up the dweller's knife and follows after his employer. Catching him, he plunges the knife into Mr. Park's chest, killing him. Regaining his senses, Ki-taek takes advantage of the chaos and slips away into hiding, ironically secluding himself in the now-vacant shelter the dweller previously occupied.

Now that we know the narrative context, let us focus more specifically on that climactic scene and its use of metaphor. The turning point is Mr. Park recoiling at the dweller's stench, as it is Ki-taek's witnessing of this repulsion that pushes him to kill, which is the movie's most significant action. But why would the sight of Mr. Park pinching his nose warrant such violence from Ki-taek? Here we see most clearly how odor as a metaphor brings the story to its dramatic heights. From the initial flicking of a stink bug to the final knife plunge, we can analyze how bad odors function rhetorically in *Parasite* to depict Ki-taek's tragic descent into violence. Odor in *Parasite* is not just a scent given off by things but the representation of human purpose and immutable fate. Stated differently, in following odor as a metaphor throughout the film, we are able to observe how, as George Lakoff and Mark Johnson theorize, metaphor is "primarily a matter of thought and action and only derivatively a matter of language."[46] Metaphors are not merely figures of speech but a means by which human thoughts and deeds may be put into action and understood.

I do not suggest that *Parasite*'s odor metaphor is the *only* way to understand the film. Rather, I argue that it provides a useful means for considering the film and its implications for how we are asked to think about class and society, who bears responsibility for whom, and why the current state of class affairs seems unchangeable. It is not surprising that social and economic differences are represented through several metaphors in this film, including not just odor and staircases but through the contrasting families themselves. As Sara Hayden observes, "The nation-as-family metaphor has a long history,"[47] and *Parasite*'s family metaphors enable society-wide ideas about class and status to play out dramatically in a way that allows audiences to interpret the characters and react to the narrative consequences.

Nevertheless, odor is the metaphor that most signifies the status of the families in *Parasite*, from those who believe they have none (the Parks), to those who cannot escape their stink no matter what they try (the semibasement family), to those whose stench places them at the absolute margins of civilized society (the shelter dweller). In many ways, odor is used as a counter-metaphor to the more familiar trope of elevation to signify social status. The characters in the film ascend and descend staircases frequently and with ease, and thus the illusion of social mobility is presented metaphorically, and even sustains Ki-taek's misguided optimism throughout the film. Getting access to a better job, a better home, and a better life seemingly is just a matter of "moving up." Every evening Ki-taek's family descends, going back down to their semibasement apartment, and every morning they ascend once again toward their idea of heaven, the Park house. But that ease of movement is revealed as a false promise of being able to work one's way out of one's circumstances. No matter how high Ki-taek ascends, he discovers he will never be allowed to belong—the odor of his working class-ness clings to him and finds its way to the noses of people like the Parks. Ki-taek realizes he will never be free of his stench, at least not as long as it is people like the Parks whose nostrils matter most. If he cannot change who he is—how he smells—then his only option is to get rid of those who think he stinks. But Ki-taek's blow against his perceived oppressor solves nothing and helps no one.

Parasite director Bong Joon Ho sought to depict the despair of the working poor and the dream-crushing narcissism of the wealthy in a dramatic yet purposeful way, and he chose odor as the metaphor. For those who lack the means, a better life is only a fantasy. Those who have the means will find reasons to sniff out and reject those they feel do not belong in their realm. In the end, optimism and whimsy yield only tragedy and despair. The movie is quite a grim commentary on the problems of social hierarchies, offering no optimism for the audience to cling to. The metaphor of odor thus may be too heavy-handed, categorizing an entire class of people as cemented in misery with no hope of change but through criminal violence, which itself does not produce meaningful change for the characters.

Thus we might conclude that the metaphor is too stifling, offering the audience nothing to build an idea of change around, just a different means for depicting despair. Or we may conclude it is spot on, able to make sensible through a few choice sniffs what sociologists and economists have struggled for decades to explain. The inescapability of odor may be a way of helping some understand why class upward-mobility is so difficult to achieve; it is not merely a matter of individual will or talent but a deeply rooted societal prejudice. Equally possible is that the film's metaphors may be viewed as a cautionary tale for those with wealth, urging them to remain vigilant in their affairs lest the lower classes infiltrate and destroy them. Like all rhetorical texts, *Parasite* offers much for the audience to consider, and the audience must make their own determination. Our task is to help them by demonstrating a method for reading some of the key rhetorical strategies involved in the text, which in this instance means critiquing the significance of odor as a significant metaphor in the film's rhetoric.

PERSONAL REFLECTIONS

The person who looks for metaphors in public discourse will never have to look long. When I was deciding the examples I wanted to use in this chapter, I had nothing but options in front of me. In fact, earlier drafts of this chapter included even more examples. I settled on the included metaphors because I wanted to showcase metaphor's variety and creative capacity. I decided not to analyze metaphors in a more formal text, like a public speech, for two specific reasons. The first is that my colleagues and predecessors in the communication discipline have already created outstanding analyses of metaphors found in more traditional rhetorical texts (some of which are mentioned below), and those should be read and appreciated in full. The second reason was to demonstrate that metaphors turn up virtually anywhere, so much so that we often encounter them without realizing that we are dealing with a metaphor, or that it might be more meaningful than we assume. The question is not, "Where do we look for metaphors?"—because they surround us. The question I believe is more important is, "What happens when we really start to pay attention to them?"

For me, the process of trying to answer that second question has always put me someplace interesting, and reminds me not to make easy assumptions about language. For example, I do not regularly read restaurant reviews and am not a "foodie." But when I heard about Jonathan Gold's reputation for writing abstract reviews that also garnered him a large following and critical acclaim, I wanted to learn why that might be. Diving into his reviews led to me discover both how often he used metaphors and how broadly. I appreciated his creativity and began to understand why he had earned so much praise. I do not know if he had an amazing palate or not, but his writings prove his talents in working with language. By following his metaphors and thinking through them, many new insights became available to me. Metaphors have much to teach us, not just about the tenor + vehicle of that moment but about how we connect to the world through language.

Applying that same interest to movies, video games, pandemic rhetoric, and anywhere else, I find that metaphors stimulate me intellectually and help me to feel that I am more able to make sense of the world around me. Not all metaphors are great and not all metaphors deserve equal attention, but knowing how metaphors work and how to analyze them means that I never have to worry about feeling lost in a world filled with them.

POTENTIALS AND PITFALLS

When analyzing a rhetorical artifact through its metaphors, it is important to keep two items in mind: First, paying close attention to metaphors is one, but not the only, way to highlight meaningful language in a text. Metaphors are often powerful and useful, but they are not the only items of note in a text. Second, even if a powerful and useful metaphor dominates a text, good critics must always justify their approach to the analysis and explain why their readers may learn something useful by following along. The contents of an artifact do not automatically justify its analysis. Good rhetorical criticism takes the time to justify its claims. And good rhetorical criticism also recognizes its limits. A single analysis cannot—nor should it attempt to—cover everything in a rhetorical artifact. A critic should never feel the obligation to explain everything—but what one decides to explain must be explained well.

METAPHOR CRITICISM TOP PICKS

The following scholarly works are suggested as exemplars of metaphor criticism that are well worth the attention of beginning rhetorical critics:

Black, Edwin. "The Second Persona." *Quarterly Journal of Speech* 56 (1970): 109–119. Black's groundbreaking essay argues that rhetorical texts create an imaginary role, or "persona," which the audience is persuaded to adopt. This persona is revealed through stylistic and ideological "tokens" found within the text that suggest the persuasive mindset of this ideal audience member and the author's ambitions.

Cisneros, J. David. "Contaminated Communities: The Metaphor of 'Immigrant as Pollutant' in Media Representations of Immigration." *Rhetoric & Public Affairs* 11 (2008): 569–601. Popular rhetoric about immigration often seeks to establish images of "problem-solution" relationships. Cisneros advances an alternative view, maintaining that the "immigrant as pollutant" metaphor depicted in mediated messages can have serious consequences for the public's perception and treatment of immigrants.

Condit, Celeste M., Benjamin R. Bates, Ryan Galloway, Sonja Brown Givens, Caroline K. Haynie, John W. Jordan, Gordon Stables, and Hollis Marshall West. "Recipes or Blueprints for Our Genes? How Contexts Selectively Activate the Multiple Meanings of Metaphor." *Quarterly Journal of Speech* 88 (2002): 303–325. The authors evaluate why "recipe" did not successfully replace "blueprint" as the dominant metaphor in 1990s public discourse about genetic research, despite calls from experts that it should. They assess context as a central variable in the construction of multiple meanings in rhetorical transactions, and how audiences do not act strictly in accordance with what a rhetor may desire.

Foley, Megan. "From Infantile Citizens to Infantile Institutions: The Metaphoric Transformation of Political Economy in the 2008 Housing Market Crisis." *Quarterly Journal of Speech* 98 (2012): 386–410. Historically state-citizen relationships feature government metaphorically as parent and the people as children. Foley argues that the response to the housing crisis reversed this relationship, with citizens as parents to "infantile institutions."

Jensen, Robin E. "From Barren to Sterile: The Evolution of a Mixed Metaphor." *Rhetoric Society Quarterly* 45 (2015): 25–46. Jensen examines the evolution of reproductive metaphors in seventeenth- to nineteenth-century discourses and how they apply to early twentieth-century metaphors. Her findings suggest implications that enabled women to be positioned "more or less at fault for their lack of children," based on the bias in reproductive metaphors.

Leff, Michael. "Topical Invention and Metaphoric Interaction." *Southern Speech Communication Journal* 48 (1983): 214–229. Leff takes issue with conventional treatments of rhetorical precepts, in which argument falls discretely within the province of invention and metaphor within the rubric of style. Grounding his analysis in the teachings of interaction theory, he explores metaphor's inventional potential through a close reading of Loren Eisley's essay, "The Bird and the Machine."

Osborn, Michael. *Michael Osborn on Metaphor and Style.* East Lansing: Michigan State University Press, 2018. A collection of some of Osborn's most significant essays, updated and revised, with his scholarly reflections on critiquing metaphors. For students serious about understanding metaphors in rhetoric, Osborn's work cannot be overlooked.

Tuck, Eve, and K. Wayne Yang. "Decolonization Is Not a Metaphor." *Decolonization: Indigeneity, Education & Society* 1, no. 1 (2012): 1–40. The authors warn against the negative consequences to a cause if it is employed uncritically as a metaphor. Specifically, the authors argue that when "decolonization" is employed as a metaphor to discuss contemporary trends in education, it harms efforts to address and understand the actual effects of settler colonialism on Indigenous lives and lands. Their analysis is a call for mindfulness when employing metaphors.

Metaphor: Additional Readings

Ceccarelli, Leah. "CRISPR as Agent: A Metaphor That Rhetorically Inhibits the Prospects for Responsible Research." *Life Sciences, Society and Policy* 14, no. 24 (2018). https://doi.org/10.1186/s40504-018-0088-8.

Condit, Celeste M. "Pathos in Criticism: Edwin Black's Communism-as-Cancer Metaphor." *Quarterly Journal of Speech* 99 (2013): 1–26.

Daughton, Suzanne M. "Metaphorical Transcendence: Images of the Holy War in Franklin Roosevelt's First Inaugural." *Quarterly Journal of Speech* 79 (1993): 427–446.

McCue-Enser, Margret. "Genocide in the Sculpture Garden and Talking Back to Settler Colonialism." *Quarterly Journal of Speech* 106, no. 2 (2020): 179–204.

Owen, A. Susan. "Memory, War and American Identity: *Saving Private Ryan* as Cinematic Jeremiad." *Critical Studies in Media Communication* 19, no. 3 (2002): 249–282.

DISCUSSION QUESTIONS

1. Identify three key considerations rhetors should take into account when using a metaphor to communicate their idea. Why are these important items to consider?

2. What are the three key factors audiences should use to judge the appropriateness of a metaphor when they encounter one in a rhetorical message, and why?

3. Suppose you are part of a three-person communication team for a local business soon after the COVID-19 shutdown period began in March 2020. You are tasked with creating a message to your customers explaining why your business is temporarily closed, while also sounding optimistic. One of your colleagues suggests using war metaphors to demonstrate fighting spirit. Your other colleague argues for environmental metaphors to communicate the need for calm yet courageous leadership. Yours is the tie-breaking vote. Which will you pick, or what will you offer as an alternative? Remember that you need to be able to explain your decision reasonably and sensibly.

ACTIVITIES

1. Advertisers favor metaphors because of their wide applicability. In a group or individually, construct an advertisement relying primarily on metaphor. Identify what the tenor and vehicle of the metaphor are, and explain how your ad seeks to bring them together in the audience's mind. Explain why the tenor and vehicle are appropriately related. To what type of audience would the metaphor be most appealing, and why?

2. Find an example of a metaphor that you understand and connect with. Instead of looking just at the tenor and vehicle, focus on the contextual knowledge needed to understand the metaphor. What cultural references does the metaphor draw from? What personal experiences would someone need to understand the metaphor? What do these suggest about the target audience's age, income, education, background, and other biographical markers?

3. In this activity you will construct a metaphor to introduce a smartphone to someone who has never used one before. Merely listing the smartphone's features will not be sufficient. You need to help them achieve a more significant sense of what the device is and how it might improve their lives. Construct a rhetorically rich metaphor for the smartphone. To do this, you first will need to answer contextual questions. With whom are you conversing? What cultural knowledge do you share with them? When you have decided upon your answers to those questions, write out your metaphor. Then, explain the decisions that informed how you constructed your metaphor. Why do you believe your metaphor would work for your implied auditor?

NOTES

The first and second editions of this chapter were authored by David Henry and Thomas R. Burkholder, both of whom have allowed John Jordan to assume the role of chapter author. Changes since the second edition are those of Jordan.

1. *Moneyball*, directed by Bennett Miller (Culver City, CA: Columbia Pictures, 2011).

2. David Zarefsky, *Public Speaking: Strategies for Success*, 7th ed. (Boston: Pearson, 2014), 301. For more on metaphor as argument, see Steve Oswald and Alain Rihs, "Metaphor as Argument: Rhetorical and Epistemic Advantages of Extended Metaphors," *Argumentation* 28, no. 2 (2014): 133–159.

3. Kenneth Burke, *A Grammar of Motives* (Berkeley: University of California Press, 1969), 503.

4. Michael Leff, "Topical Invention and Metaphoric Interaction," *Southern Speech Communication Journal* 48 (1983): 217.

5. Leff, "Topical Invention," 216–217; J. David Sapir, "The Anatomy of Metaphor," *The Social Uses of Metaphor: Essays on the Anthropology of Rhetoric*, ed. J. David Sapir and J. Christopher Crocker (Philadelphia: University of Pennsylvania Press, 1977), 7.

6. Michael Osborn, *Michael Osborn on Metaphor and Style* (East Lansing: Michigan State University Press, 2018), 11.

7. Burke, *A Grammar of Motives*, 503–504.

8. Malcolm O. Sillars and Bruce E. Gronbeck, *Communication Criticism*, 2nd ed. (Prospect Heights, IL: Waveland Press, 2001), 102.

9. For a review of enthymeme, see the chapter on "Traditional Criticism" in this book. See, too, Lloyd L. Bitzer, "Aristotle's Enthymeme Revisited," *Quarterly Journal of Speech* 45 (1959): 399–408.

10. Martha Cooper, *Analyzing Public Discourse* (Prospect Heights, IL: Waveland Press, 1989), 111, emphasis mine.

11. Sapir, "The Anatomy of Metaphor," 9.

12. Burke, *A Grammar of Motives*, 503.

13. Leff, "Topical Invention," 217.

14. On this point, see Todd Vernon Lewis, "Religious Rhetoric in Southern College Football: New Uses for Religious Metaphors," *Southern Communication Journal* 78 (2013): 202–214.

15. Leff, "Topical Invention," 219.

16. Jeniece Pettitt, "Meet the Man Who Created Apple's Most Iconic Sounds—Sosumi, the Camera Click and the Start-up Chord," CNBC.com, March 24, 2018. https://www.cnbc.com/2018/03/24/jim-reekes-the-apple-sound-designer-who-created-sosumi.html.

17. "Human Interface Guidelines: iOS Design Themes," Apple Developer, accessed April 21, 2020. https://developer.apple.com/design/human-interface-guidelines/ios/overview/themes/.

18. Robert L. Ivie, "Cold War Motives and the Rhetorical Metaphor: A Framework of Criticism," in *Cold War Rhetoric: Strategy, Metaphor, and Ideology*, ed. Martin J. Medhurst, Robert L. Ivie, Philip Wander, and Robert L. Scott (East Lansing: Michigan State University Press, 1997), 72.

19. Leff, "Topical Invention," 219.

20. Jeffery Scott Mio, "Metaphor, Politics, and Persuasion," in *Metaphor: Implications and Applications*, ed. Jeffery Scott Mio and Albert N. Katz (Mahwah, NJ: Lawrence Erlbaum, 1996), 130.

21. Fexelea, "*Nioh 2* Review: Practically Perfect," FextraLife.com, March 10, 2020, https://fextralife.com/nioh-2-review-practically-perfect/.

22. Ibid.

23. Alissa Wilkinson, "Pandemics Are Not Wars," Vox.com, April 15, 2020, https://www.vox.com/culture/2020/4/15/21193679/coronavirus-pandemic-war-metaphor-ecology-microbiome.

24. Ibid.

25. Ibid.

26. See Jing-Bao Nie, Adam Lloyd Gilbertson, Malcolm de Roubaix, Ciara Staunton, Anton van Niekerk, Joseph D. Tucker, and Stuart Rennie, "Healing Without Waging War: Beyond Military Meta-

phors in Medicine and HIV Cure Research," *American Journal of Bioethics* 16, no. 10 (2016): 3–11; and Dhruv Khullar, "The Trouble with Medicine's Metaphors," *Atlantic*, August 7, 2014. https://www .theatlantic.com/health/archive/2014/08/the-trouble-with-medicines-metaphors/374982/.

27. Wilkinson, "Pandemics."

28. Wilkinson, "Pandemics."

29. https://twitter.com/realDonaldTrump/status/1248630671754563585.

30. https://twitter.com/eugenegu/status/1248631683659644928.

31. Wilkinson, "Pandemics."

32. Paul Krugman, "The Covid-19 Slump Has Arrived," *New York Times*, April 2, 2020, https:// www.nytimes.com/2020/04/02/opinion/coronavirus-economy-stimulus.html.

33. "The 2007 Pulitzer Prize Winner in Criticism," The Pulitzer Prizes (n.d.), https://www.pulitzer .org/winners/jonathan-gold.

34. Andrea Chang, "Los Angeles Times Restaurant Critic Jonathan Gold Dies at 57," *Los Angeles Times*, July 21, 2018. https://www.latimes.com/local/obituaries/la-fo-jonathan-gold-obit -20180721-story.html.

35. Daniela Galarza, "The Very Best of Jonathan Gold," *Eater*, July 23, 2018, https://www.eater .com/2018/7/23/17600982/jonathan-gold-best-work-reviews-writing.

36. Jonathan Gold, "Moles La Tia: Beyond the Magnificent Seven," *LA Weekly*, January 21, 2009. https://www.laweekly.com/moles-la-tia-beyond-the-magnificent-seven/

37. Edwin Black, "The Second Persona," *Quarterly Journal of Speech* 56 (1970): 111–112. It is important to emphasize that the second persona is a rhetorical invention of the rhetor. Therefore, the second persona also is a product of how the rhetor reads culture, including his or her assumptions and biases, which may or may not be shared by the actual audience who eventually engages with the text. A helpful discussion of the assumptions made by rhetors about audiences and their implications can be found in Sara C. VanderHaagen, *Children's Biographies of African American Women: Rhetoric, Public Memory, and Agency* (Columbia: University of South Carolina Press, 2018): 109–116.

38. Jonathan Gold, *Counter Intelligence: Where to Eat in the Real Los Angeles* (New York: LA Weekly Books, 2000): vi–vii.

39. Gold, *Counter Intelligence,* 119–121.

40. Ashli Quesinberry Stokes and Wendy Atkins-Sayre, *Consuming Identity: The Role of Food in Redefining the South* (Jackson: University of Mississippi Press, 2016): 4.

41. Melanie C. Green, Timothy C. Brock, and Geoff F. Kaufman, "Understanding Media Enjoyment: The Role of Transportation Into Narrative Worlds," *Communication Theory* 14, no. 4 (2004), 311.

42. E. Alex Jung, "Bong Joon Ho on Why He Wanted *Parasite* to End With a 'Surefire Kill,'" *Vulture*, January 14, 2020, https://www.vulture.com/2020/01/parasite-ending-explained-by-bong-joon-ho.html.

43. Jung, "Bong Joon Ho."

44. Leah Greenblatt, "Korean Export *Parasite* May Be the Class-Conscious Thriller of the Year," *Entertainment*, October 9, 2019, https://ew.com/movies/movie-reviews/hope-movie-review-stellan -skarsgard/.

45. *Parasite*, directed by Bong Joon-ho (Seoul, South Korea: CJ Entertainment, 2019). The film's dialogue is spoken in Korean. My transcription of the dialogue comes from the film's English subtitles.

46. George Lakoff and Mark Johnson, *Metaphors We Live By* (Chicago: University of Chicago Press, 1980), 153, 156, and 157.

47. Sara Hayden, "Family Metaphors and the Nation: Promoting a Politics of Care through the Million Mom March," *Quarterly Journal of Speech* 89, no. 3 (2003): 198.

9

The Narrative Perspective

Robert C. Rowland

In January 2020, the American public was, according to the *New York Times*, "enthralled" by the announcement that Prince Harry and his wife Meghan Markle, the Duchess of Sussex, planned to live in North America for part of the year and pull back from some aspects of their royal duties. The *Times* added that "As the Harry-and-Meghan drama unfolds in breathless headlines and acres of news commentary," it raised questions such as "What kind of society do the British want: open or closed, cosmopolitan or nationalist, progressive or traditional?"[1] While the public was fascinated with the royal couple, there was vastly less press or public attention on issues of much greater direct impact on the lives of ordinary people in either Britain or the United States, including failing infrastructure, major instability in the Middle East, and a global warming crisis that was reflected in the finding that 2019 was the second hottest year on record and the decade of the 2010s the hottest ever.[2]

What explains public fascination with the decision of Prince Harry and Duchess Markle to live part of the year away from Britain and try to develop a somewhat independent life apart from their role as members of the royal family? The answer is that events that are easily understood as stories with compelling characters and an interesting plot draw more attention than reporting on complex issues, such as America's needed infrastructure renewal, Middle East diplomacy, or the nuances associated with climate change arguments and predictions.

It is more than that people love stories. More broadly, researchers have demonstrated that narrative is a human universal found in all cultures and throughout human history.[3] There is strong evidence in cave paintings and other artifacts that humans have told stories for tens of thousands of years. Although ancient humans told stories around the fire and in caves, modern humans use all forms of human communication to tell stories. The popularity of narrative easily can be demonstrated by looking at the daily television guide, a listing of movies at the local theater, or a glance at the best-seller list. Television is dominated by shows that tell stories, from *Game of Thrones* to *NCIS*. Fifty years ago the shows might have been *Gunsmoke*, *Leave It to Beaver*, and *I Love Lucy*, but narrative always has dominated the medium. And even on programs that at first glance seem to be news or issue oriented, narrative is very common. *60 Minutes* is a news show, but the focus of each episode is on using narratives about real people to explore an issue or other topic. Films and books are also dominated by narrative, both fictional and in the form of biography.

133

Narrative is not just a form of entertainment but also a means for understanding the world. From the law to economics, and even to the hard sciences, scholars have recognized the importance of narrative.[4] In the remainder of this chapter, I lay out in more detail why we like stories and how they work to explain our world. I begin by describing **narrative form** and explaining the functions that narrative fulfills. I also describe a number of approaches that have been taken to analyzing narratives in rhetoric and describe in some detail Fisher's "narrative paradigm." After enumerating current perspectives on narrative, I present a critical essay in which I develop a system for interpreting narratives and analyze a story concerning American children abducted to Saudi Arabia to illustrate how a rhetorical critic can break down the form and function of a social narrative. I conclude this chapter by evaluating the strengths and weaknesses of the narrative approach and citing recommended essays for further reading.

DESCRIBING NARRATIVE FORM AND FUNCTION

What is a narrative and how is it different from other rhetoric? The answer is that **narratives** are stories, and stories function differently than descriptive or argumentative rhetoric. It is one thing to make a strong argument for fighting terrorism in the Middle East, but quite another to tell a story about how terrorists are oppressing ordinary people in the region in order to support an implicit claim that the United States should attack the bases of terrorists.

Narrative Form

What are the component parts of any story? Any story contains characters, a setting, a plot, and a theme. Stories are not about statistics. They are about the actions of **characters** (mostly people, but sometimes animals and other beings) in relation to other characters and the environment. The main action of a story centers on one or more protagonists. We sometimes call the protagonist the hero or heroine. If there is a protagonist, there must also be an antagonist (or villain), whose narrative function is to create conflict in order to carry the story forward. Oftentimes the antagonist will be a person who fights against the protagonist, although in some cases the antagonist may be the natural environment or even some weakness inside the hero. From Old Testament narratives such as the story of David and Goliath to the present day in great popular film series such as *Star Wars*, the focus is on the conflict between the protagonist and the antagonist.

The most fundamental principle concerning the relationship between the protagonist and antagonist is that they must be of approximately equal power for the story to be compelling. *Star Wars* would not have been a good film if Darth Vader had been opposed by one of the robots. The point is that if the difference in power between the protagonist and the antagonist is too great, the plot of the narrative will not be interesting because the ultimate outcome will be a foregone conclusion. *Jaws* would have been a much less successful film and novel if the killer fish had been a crazed catfish rather than a giant shark.

The point that in effective stories the relationship between the protagonist and antagonist must be based on near parity also illustrates the difference between effective and true stories. In the real world, people often fight against insurmountable odds and have essentially no chance of success. Or a person may face an antagonist so weak that there is no question about his or her ultimate success. The point is that what makes a story true and what makes it compelling are related but different concepts.

There are a number of types of protagonists. Sometimes the protagonist will be a great hero, even an angel or god. In others cases, the protagonist will be an ordinary person who does great deeds. In still other narratives, the protagonist may be one of us or even inferior to us in ability or intellect.[5] In some stories there may be multiple protagonists and antagonists. It would seem that anyone, even a college professor, can be a protagonist in a given narrative. Although there are many possible types of protagonists, from a rhetorical perspective they fall into two basic types. The protagonist can be one of us and serve the rhetorical function of creating a sense of commonality with the audience, or the protagonist can be greater than us and serve as a model for action. When the hero is one of us, his or her rhetorical function is to create what the great critic and theorist Kenneth Burke called a sense of identification or consubstantiality.[6] This type of protagonist is a regular person who shows us what it is like to live his or her life. In other stories, the protagonist is not one of us but instead a hero who serves as a model for action. Throughout American history, the Founding Fathers have served this kind of rhetorical function. We continue to tell stories about them in a radically different time (Madison didn't have much to say about global warming) because they serve as heroic models, and we still need such models.

Stories rarely involve just a hero and a villain. Often there are a host of other characters, including friends, acquaintances, bystanders, and so forth. These supporting characters assist the protagonist or serve as obstacles to be overcome, thereby supporting the primary conflict between the protagonist and antagonist. Supporting characters also may be used to illustrate narrative themes or create sympathy in the audience. In a film about World War II, a supporting character may be killed or wounded early in the narrative to demonstrate the inhumanity of war. Finally, supporting characters may comment on the action, either to create comic relief or to critique the actions of the protagonist or the antagonist.

The second basic component that defines any story is **setting**, where and when the story takes place. Stories can take place literally anywhere and anytime. In fact, there are science fiction and fantasy stories that take place in a different universe. The important point about setting is that stories can transport us out of our here and now to places very different from our own world. For example, although it is difficult for early twenty-first-century Americans to understand the horrors of the Holocaust, through narrative Elie Wiesel and others have taken us to Auschwitz and made us see the horrors of the death camps. Through the power of setting, narrative can be used to break down barriers to human understanding.[7]

The third component of narrative form is **plot**, the action of the story. Although literary theorists have built theories about plot types, and historians have developed approaches for explaining historical narrative, from a rhetorical perspective there are two important points to be made about plot. First, the function of the plot is to keep the attention of the audience and reinforce the message in the story. Therefore, the plot generally builds to a climax that resolves the conflict between hero and villain because the story would not be very interesting if the biggest obstacle were overcome at the beginning of the story. Similarly, the plot must be varied enough and include enough action to keep the audience's interest. The second point about plot is, as Lewis O. Mink notes, what makes a good plot and what makes a true story are sometimes different things.[8] In a gripping mystery, for instance, it may be crucial that a trash truck arrived in the first scene on Wednesday morning. In real life, however, the only meaning may be that Wednesday is trash day. Nor do real-life stories always move in a gradual pattern of escalating conflict to a final climax that resolves the conflict.

The final component of narrative form is **theme**—the message of the narrative. In some narratives, the theme may be quite explicit. In other instances, the theme may be implied but not explicitly stated. On the surface, George Orwell's classic novel *Animal Farm* is a fantasy story about animals taking over an English farm. Underneath the surface, the novel is usually treated as an allegorical attack on communism and the Soviet Union. The larger point is that some narratives require more understanding of context and rhetorical type in order to identify the theme than do other narratives. The rhetorical critic also needs to keep in mind that in stories where the theme is not explicitly stated there may be considerable variation in audience interpretation. This points to an important difference between narrative in literature and narrative in rhetoric. Although much literature is rhetorical in that it supports a persuasive message and some narrative rhetoric is also literature in the sense that it possesses great aesthetic power, what makes a good theme in the two related contexts is somewhat different. In great literature, the theme may be quite complex and very subtle. In contrast, rhetorical critics are primarily interested in narratives that attempt to persuade an audience. This persuasive function of rhetorical narrative usually requires a theme that is either explicit or clearly implied. If the theme is subtle or overly complex, the audience may miss it. Consequently, great literature often fails as rhetoric because the theme is too complex for the mass audience. On the other hand, great rhetorical narratives often are inferior literature. Harriet Beecher Stowe's novel about the horrors of slavery, *Uncle Tom's Cabin,* is generally not considered to be great literature. The characters are based on simple stereotypes and show little subtlety. But there is no question that Stowe's novel had an immense rhetorical impact on popular attitudes about slavery in the North in the years leading up to the Civil War.

In summary, the four primary components of narrative form are characters, setting, plot, and theme. The first three components define what narrative form is, and together they create the theme, which is what the narrative means. To this point, I have focused on narrative rhetoric that tells a complete story in order to make a point. In some cases, however, the rhetor may not retell a complete narrative but only give the audience a scene from that narrative or tap into a narrative that is well known to the audience. In these variants of narrative form, the rhetor relies on the capacity of the audience to fill in the meaning of the narrative from the scene that is presented or to pull out of the well-known narrative the appropriate meaning.

After considering the formal components that define narrative rhetoric, it is appropriate to consider the rhetorical functions that narrative fulfills. If the components of narrative *form* describe what narrative is, the components of **narrative function** describe what rhetorical narrative does to an audience.

Narrative Function

There are two related but somewhat different sets of functions fulfilled by narrative form: epistemic and persuasive. Epistemology is the study of how we come to know. We often use narrative, as Mink suggests, as a "primary cognitive instrument" for comprehending the world.[9] Thus, we make sense of the impact of global warming by considering stories of how it is affecting real people around the globe. Al Gore powerfully used narrative in his award-winning book, *An Inconvenient Truth*, to achieve this function, thereby providing the audience with a means of understanding the problem and what to do about it.[10]

While people use narrative to understand the world, they also sometimes create narratives to persuade others. This rhetorical function is fulfilled by stories in four ways. The first function of narrative is to keep the *attention* of the audience. I made the point earlier that popular culture is chock full of narrative, because people like stories. You would have to look long and hard in the television guide to find a show on a topic such as "Dartmouth College experts talk statistics." But virtually every channel runs fictional or nonfictional stories about people and their lives.

Popular reaction to the events of 9/11 illustrates the power of narrative to energize an audience. Prior to September 2001, experts on terrorism were well aware that there was a serious risk that terrorists might use weapons of mass destruction. Although the risk was known, there was little public attention to it because it did not fit into what the public found to be a credible narrative. Airplanes flying into tall buildings was perceived to be the stuff of summer adventure movies, not real life. After September 11, however, there was a powerful narrative to go with the warnings of the experts. That narrative energized the audience to support action dealing with terrorism.

It is important to note that the key issue in terms of persuasiveness is not the truth of the narrative, but its credibility. Prior to September 11, a narrative about terrorists using weapons of mass destruction against the United States was not perceived to be credible, no matter how many experts suggested that such an attack could occur. On the other hand, a narrative may be perceived to be credible when there is little support for it. It is widely believed, for instance, that the nuclear power accident at Three Mile Island was a major disaster. In fact, the best data suggests that there was very little radiation released and that many of the safety systems worked effectively.[11] However, the strong data I have mentioned in no way undercuts the powerful social narrative describing Three Mile Island as a nuclear disaster.

The second rhetorical function of narrative is to create a sense of *identification* between the audience and the narrator or characters in the narrative. Great novels such as Harper Lee's *To Kill a Mockingbird* played a role in the civil rights movement because they helped create a sense of identification between white and black Americans. Lee's novel and many other stories showed the white audience that the black characters in the books were people just like them. The publication of Lee's novel, *Go Set a Watchman*, with its depiction of Atticus Finch not as a saintly protector of the innocent but as a segregationist, may undercut the capacity of *Mockingbird* to produce that same sense of identification in the future.[12] Even so, one of the most powerful functions of narrative is to generate in the reader/viewer/listener the understanding that "I'm like him or her."

The third rhetorical function of narrative is to *break down barriers* to understanding by transporting us to another place or time. This function is similar to the identity-related function, but it deals with place, time, and culture rather than personal identity. People view the world based on their own experiences and culture, meaning that they often find it difficult to understand a radically different culture or time. Narratives work better than other forms of rhetoric for ripping us out of our time and culture and placing us in another place/time. For example, contemporary Americans may have great difficulty understanding the strict social regulation of women's role in the mid-nineteenth century. While works of history can describe women's roles in that period, narrative is a more powerful vehicle for bringing home the restrictions women faced.

The final persuasive function of narrative is to *tap into values and needs* in order to create a strong emotional reaction. A story about the death of an innocent child, the horrors of the Holocaust, or life in a Syrian refugee camp can link to emotions in a way that statistical data and other forms of argument cannot do. A study proving that several hundred children die a year because of improperly installed car seats, for example, lacks the emotional punch of a narrative about the death of a single baby. The narrative produces this emotional reaction because the story links directly to basic values and needs such as life and security.

After identifying the form and function of narrative rhetoric, it is important to consider approaches that rhetorical critics have taken to the study of narrative. In the next section, I summarize various approaches to narrative, paying special attention to Walter Fisher's seminal analysis of the "narrative paradigm."

APPROACHES TO NARRATIVE RHETORICAL CRITICISM

With the rebirth of the study of rhetoric early in the twentieth century, rhetorical critics tended to follow the example of Aristotle in building theories of rhetoric and methods for analyzing it. As mentioned in chapter 6, critics who were influenced by Aristotle, often called neo-Aristotelian or traditional critics, usually focused on the three modes of proof identified by Aristotle (logos, ethos, and pathos), which broadly speaking defined rational argument, appeals to credibility, and rhetoric that produced an emotional reaction. In this system, there was little room for the analysis of narrative. As recently as forty years ago, there was not a sizable literature identifying narrative approaches to rhetorical analysis. Walter R. Fisher and Richard A. Filloy got at this point in a 1982 essay on "Argument in Drama and Literature: An Exploration," where they noted that "argument has been conceived traditionally in terms of clear-cut inferential structures, a judgment that limited the study of narrative forms of persuasion."[13] They went on to argue that many narratives, including novels such as *The Great Gatsby* and plays such as *Death of a Salesman*, make arguments. Although Fisher and Filloy cited a number of modern critics, including Kenneth Burke and Wayne Booth, who had focused on narrative forms of rhetoric, their main point was that critics had not recognized the importance of narrative. In retrospect, the failure to focus on narrative is astonishing.

In this crucial essay, Fisher and Filloy saw a need for a method to test "one's interpretation of a dramatic or literary work."[14] They outlined a four-step process in which the critic first determines "the message, the overall conclusions fostered by the work." At a second step, the critic tests the message by evaluating the "reliability" of the narrator, the words and actions of the other characters, and the descriptions of the scenes in the story. At a third step, the analyst considers the outcomes of the story as a means of asking "whether the story rings true as a story in itself." Finally, the critic should test "(a) whether the message accurately portrays the world we live in and (b) whether it provides a reliable guide to our beliefs, attitudes, values, and/or actions."[15]

The Narrative Paradigm and Rhetorical Criticism

Although Fisher and Filloy provided a method for analyzing argument in narrative, their approach remained quite close to traditions emphasizing rational communication. The final step in their narrative methodology essentially called on the critic to do an argumentative analysis of the claim in a given story. Fisher, however, had realized that narrative was more than just a type of argument. It also was a basic form of human communication, what he would call a "paradigm" for understanding all communication.

In a series of essays and an important book, Fisher laid out the characteristics of the **narrative paradigm** and claimed that it functioned as an alternative to traditional rationality, which he believed provided little guidance for citizens concerned with issues of public moral conflict. He argued that traditional rationality privileged the perspectives of experts and created a situation in which ordinary citizens felt disempowered.[16] His solution was to claim that human beings were essentially storytellers, what he called "homo narrans."[17] He based this judgment on the fact that narrative is a human universal found in all cultures, concluding that all communication, "whether social, political, legal or otherwise, involves narrative."[18] In his book he reemphasized that all communication is narrative, stating, "All forms of human communication need to be seen fundamentally as stories."[19]

Instead of traditional rationality, Fisher argued for the value of narrative rationality. He argued that narrative rationality is a human universal since everyone knows what makes a good story and that, as a consequence, standards of narrative rationality provided a way around the elitism inherent in what he called the "rational world paradigm."[20] Fisher embraced two principles for testing narrative reason: *narrative probability* and *narrative fidelity*. He defined **narrative probability** as a standard for testing "what constitutes a coherent story."[21] He later explained that narrative probability involved three related tests of coherence: structural coherence, which involves testing the internal consistency of the narrative; material coherence, which involves "comparing and contrasting stories told in other discourses"; and characterological coherence, which tests the consistency of action by the characters.[22] In addition to narrative probability, Fisher argued that the critic should apply the standard of **narrative fidelity**, in which an audience considers "whether the stories they experience ring true with the stories they know to be true in their lives."[23] He later added that standards of formal and informal logic also could be applied at this point "*when relevant.*"[24]

According to Fisher, the narrative paradigm was superior to other approaches to understanding human communication because narrative is a universal form of communication. He also argued that the standards of narrative rationality provided a way around expert domination and a means of identifying stories that recognize "the truths humanity shares in regard to reason, justice, veracity, and peaceful ways to resolve social-political differences." He cited stories by Lao-tse, Buddha, Zoroaster, Jesus Christ, and Mohammed, as well as works by political leaders such as Lincoln, Gandhi, and Churchill, as meeting these standards.[25]

The narrative paradigm drew a great deal of critical attention. Many critics praised Fisher and the paradigm for illuminating the way that narrative functions in human communication. Others argued that the narrative paradigm was unclear or overly broad. Barbara Warnick and Robert Rowland both argued that the parameters of the paradigm were unclear, that the standards of narrative rationality were not adequately specified, and that there was a difference between a credible and a true story.[26] Rowland also claimed that narrative was better understood as a mode of discourse as opposed to a paradigm and that it was important to distinguish between works that actually told stories and works that described a topic or made arguments.[27] He also argued that Fisher's criticism of traditional rationality was overstated and that the standards of narrative rationality could not be applied to works of fantasy or science fiction, because those genres were judged by criteria different from realistic fiction.[28] Although there was considerable debate about the value of the narrative paradigm, there was no disagreement about the importance of studying narrative. Fisher deserved praise for highlighting the importance of narrative as a form of human communication.

APPLICATIONS OF THE NARRATIVE PARADIGM

Fisher's work awakened rhetorical critics to the importance of narrative. The result was a huge increase in narrative criticism. The narrative criticism that was produced fell into two main categories. A number of critics borrowed from Fisher's terminology, especially the standards of narrative rationality, as the primary method of their critique. Others used an inductive approach to narrative analysis to discover the specific narrative pattern at the heart of a given story.

An example of the first category of narrative criticism is Ronald H. Carpenter's analysis of "Admiral Mahan, 'Narrative Fidelity,' and the Japanese Attack on Pearl Harbor."[29] Carpenter uses Fisher's terminology to critique the narrative power of works by Alfred Thayer Mahan on naval power. Mahan was a US Navy officer who wrote extensively on naval history and strategy. According to Carpenter, the Japanese government was influenced by Mahan's work because it possessed strong narrative fidelity that made his story "'ring true' for the Japanese prior to the attack on Pearl Harbor."[30] Another example of a critique that drew heavily on Fisher's terminology was Thomas A. Hollihan and Patricia Riley's "The Rhetorical Power of a Compelling Story: A Critique of a 'Toughlove' Parental Support Group."[31] In this essay, Hollihan and Riley analyzed the narratives found in a "toughlove" support group that advocated parents taking extremely strong stands against adolescent children who behaved badly. They concluded that the "toughlove" narrative "met the needs" of group members and "fulfilled the requirements for a good story," including both narrative fidelity and probability. Hollihan and Riley went on to argue that the "toughlove" story was a dangerous one because it could encourage parents "to get a quick-fix to their problems by ejecting their children from the house when far less drastic actions would be more appropriate."[32]

Numerous works utilizing terminology drawn from Fisher's analysis of the narrative paradigm could be cited. In general, these essays used a two-step critical process, first breaking down the narrative into coherent themes and then applying the standards of narrative rationality to assess those themes. It is important to recognize that these critics tended to use Fisher's terminology for a purpose quite different than that originally proposed by Fisher. Fisher touted the narrative paradigm as an alternative to traditional rationality. In contrast, critics used the standards of narrative rationality to explain why a particular audience found a given story to be persuasive. It also should be apparent that the narrative paradigm did not provide critics with a complete road map for how to identify the themes and strategies in a given narrative. This led critics to develop inductive approaches to narrative analysis.

Under the inductive approach, the critic does not apply a preexisting theory of narrative but instead discovers the implicit narrative pattern in a given story. Many examples of scholars taking this approach could be cited. Thomas Rosteck analyzed narrative form in Martin Luther King Jr.'s final speech. Martha Solomon and Wayne J. McMullen argued that the film *Places in the Heart* was an "open text" that possessed a number of conflicting ideological themes. Sally J. Perkins discovered the narrative structure found in two feminist plays about the sixteenth-century feminist Queen Christina of Sweden. Robert Rowland and Robert Strain argued that Spike Lee's film *Do the Right Thing* possessed an underlying narrative form similar to Greek tragedy.[33] Stephanie Kelley-Romano uncovered the structure of conspiracy narratives, and Mike Milford and Robert Rowland identified allegorical form in the contemporary science fiction series *Battlestar Galactica*.[34] Many other examples could be cited.

William F. Lewis's essay "Telling America's Story: Narrative Form and the Reagan Presidency"[35] is a typical example of the inductive approach. Lewis argues that much of Reagan's persuasiveness can be traced to his success as a storyteller. He identifies two different kinds of stories in Reagan's rhetoric: anecdotes and myths. Anecdotes are small stories that Reagan used to keep the interest of his audience. In contrast, myth "informs all of Reagan's rhetoric."[36] Lewis shows how Reagan used both kinds of stories to generate support for his program and explains why the American people found Reagan's narratives to be so compelling, even though according to Lewis they often were inaccurate.

Lewis brilliantly illuminated much of the reason for Reagan's popularity; at the same time, Lewis's analysis also illustrated the difficulty with the inductive approach to narrative analysis. Inductive critics do a detailed analysis of the narrative and pull out of that analysis the narrative theory that applies to the particular work of rhetoric. In effect, they build a new theory of how to approach narrative in every essay. This doesn't provide much guidance for future criticism. Thus, there is need for a general approach to narrative analysis that provides the critic with tools for discovering the narrative pattern in any given story. In the following section, I develop such an approach.

NARRATIVE ANALYSIS: A SYSTEMATIC PERSPECTIVE

The narrative critic needs a perspective that is clear and provides a means to explore the complexity present in any given narrative. The best means of achieving both of these ends is to apply a critical approach that moves in a three-step process from the *form* of the narrative to the *functions* fulfilled by the story, and finally to an *evaluation* of how effectively the narrative functions persuasively with a given audience.

The first step in this process is to identify the four formal elements that define all stories: characters, setting, plot, and theme. In relation to characters, it is important to think not only about who the characters are but what they represent and their function in the story. It is especially important to consider whether the protagonist is an "everyman" or "everywoman" or whether he or she is a hero to be followed. After identifying the protagonist(s), it is important to identify the antagonist and supporting players and consider their role in the story. Discovering the fundamental conflict between the protagonist and the antagonist will provide the critic with a major clue concerning the plot structure and also the theme of the narrative. Similarly, it is important to consider the roles played by supporting characters and how they are depicted.

After identifying the characters, the critic should focus on the setting. In many cases the setting will be both a particular place and also by implication other places of relevance to the audience. So, a film such as *Selma* clearly is set in the American South during the civil rights movement, but more broadly it can be seen as a story about human empowerment that has relevance for anyone fighting against oppression in any culture. The next step is to identify the plot. The primary function of the plot is to keep the attention of the audience, but careful analysis may reveal the underlying message of the narrative. The plot often moves in a pattern of rising action in which more and more difficult problems occur, leading to the final crisis in which the issue is resolved. The critic should list the main events in the story and consider what those events reveal about the message of the story.

Finally, based on the analysis of characters, setting, and plot, the critic should be able to identify the theme or themes in the story. Here, it is important to recognize that narratives often work by implication and that explicit calls for specific action are rare. In fact, there are many stories in which the underlying narrative form supports a different theme than that enunciated by the narrator. Even so, careful consideration of the interaction of the characters, setting, and plot should reveal the theme or themes in the story.

In summary, the first step in narrative analysis is to identify the characters and the roles they play, the setting in which the action occurs and any more general implied setting, and the plot pattern present in the narrative and what that plot pattern implies about how the audience should react. From this information, the critic should be able to identify the themes in the story and the actions requested of the audience.

In the second step, the critic tests the degree to which the narrative fulfills the four rhetorical functions identified earlier. Initially, this means considering whether the story is compelling for the audience. The critic also should consider whether the narrative is designed to create a sense of identification between the audience and characters (or the narrator) in the story. Questions to consider include, Who does the author want us to like or admire? Does the author create a sense of identity between the reader/viewer/listener and the protagonist or other characters? Third, the critic should consider whether the story is designed to bring the message home by placing the audience in a setting very different from their own lives. If the story is set in Des Moines, the answer is probably no. But if the story is set in a sweatshop in China, the story may well be designed to show ordinary Americans what life is like in a superpower that is still in some ways a developing nation. Finally, the critic should consider whether the narrative taps into basic values or needs in order to produce an emotional reaction in the audience. In testing this rhetorical function, it is important to remember that the story does not directly tug on the heartstrings of the audience. Instead, it uses the incidents in the story to tap into values and needs shared by audience members in order to produce the emotional response.

The last step in narrative analysis is to take the findings of the first two steps and make a coherent argument about the functioning of the particular story. Here, the critic links together the formal and the functional analyses to make an argument about how the story functions (or why it fails to function) for a given audience. Public opinion data or reports of public response to a given narrative may be cited as additional evidence to support an overall claim. At this stage, the critic should ask three final questions. First, the critic should consider whether the formal elements of the narrative are compelling. For example, Is the plot interesting? Are the characters appealing (and in the case of the antagonist, revolting)? Does the author transport us to the setting of the story? Second, the critic should summarize the degree to which the story fulfills the four rhetorical functions of narrative. If the story fulfills all four, that is a sign that it is a powerful and coherent narrative. If it fails to fulfill any of the functions, that suggests strongly that it failed as a story. If, on the other hand, it fulfills some of the functions, but not all, the critic must consider the importance in the particular context of the functions that were fulfilled.

Finally, the critic should consider the credibility of the story for the audience. I mentioned earlier that the truth and credibility of a story are very different things. In the run-up to the Iraq War, the story that Iraq was quite close to developing nuclear weapons clearly resonated with the audience. While it was a powerfully resonant narrative, it also was not true. As this example illustrates, it is important to consider whether the narrative is a credible one for a given audience and to recognize the risk that some false stories may resonate strongly.

Earlier, I noted problems with the standards of narrative rationality (narrative probability and narrative fidelity) developed by Walter Fisher in his discussion of the narrative paradigm. Although those standards may have limited value for evaluating the accuracy or truth of a narrative, they are immensely useful for making judgments about the credibility or believability of a narrative. Narrative probability and fidelity get at two aspects of narrative credibility. Humans tend to believe stories that are coherent and stories that are consistent with personal experience. Thus, we expect people to behave in a consistent fashion, and we interpret events through the lens of our own experience in society. Therefore, the critic can use standards of narrative fidelity and probability to assess whether a story had credibility for a given audience.

At the end of the third step, the critic should be able to make a coherent argument about the rhetorical effectiveness of the narrative for a given audience. It is important to note that this judgment is always in relation to a particular audience. What seems coherent to an early twenty-first-century American audience might seem ludicrous to an audience in fifteenth-century Japan or elsewhere or in another time/place. An example may make this point clear. It has widely been reported that many in the Arab world believe that Israel organized the 9/11 attacks and that several thousand American Jews did not show up for work at the World Trade Center on September 11. In fact, there is exactly no data supporting this story, because it is false. However, a significant portion of the Arab world apparently finds it to be credible. This audience has been exposed to extremely harsh anti-Israeli rhetoric for many years in the context of the Israeli-Palestinian conflict. In this context, what would seem obviously absurd to almost any American apparently seems quite credible to some Arabs.

Summary of a Systematic Perspective on Narrative Analysis

Step 1—Form Identification

    A. Identify characters, character types, and what they represent.
    B. Identify the place in which the narrative is set and what it represents.
    C. Sketch the plot pattern and identify points of conflict.
    D. Reason from the characters, setting, and plot to the stated or implied theme.

Step 2—Functional Analysis

    A. Does the narrative energize the audience?
    B. Does the narrative create a sense of identification between characters or the narrator and the audience?
    C. Does the narrative transport the audience to a place or time different from contemporary life?
    D. Does the narrative tap into basic values or needs of the audience?

Step 3—Linking Formal and Functional Analyses: An Evaluation

    A. Are the formal elements and the plot compelling?
    B. Does the narrative effectively fulfill narrative functions?
    C. Is the narrative credible for a particular audience?

In the last few pages, I have explained an approach to narrative analysis that can be applied systematically to any narrative. It also can be used to critique speeches and essays that tap into societal narratives. However, I have not provided an approach to testing the epistemic function of narrative. How can the critic apply rhetorical standards in order to test the accuracy of a given narrative? The short answer is that rhetorical standards are of very limited value in making such a judgment. The stories told to justify going to war in Iraq illustrate this point. The American people found those stories to be quite coherent, but coherent and true are not the same thing. A story about a popular president risking his presidency and his legacy by having sex with a young White House intern would have to be viewed as incoherent. So would a story about hanging chads and butterfly ballots deciding a presidential election. But these incoherent stories did occur. The point is that rhetorical critics are in a good position to judge the persuasiveness and credibility of a narrative, but the tools of the critic are not nearly as useful for judging the accuracy of the story.

CRITICAL ESSAY

In this section, I illustrate the systematic perspective on narrative criticism by analyzing a narrative concerning children abducted to and held in Saudi Arabia. In a number of instances,

Saudi men have married American women and, after the marriage failed, abducted their children to Saudi Arabia, where the children have been held against their will. A congressional hearing told the stories of several mothers who had their children taken from them and their efforts to get them back.

A NARRATIVE ANALYSIS OF STORIES ABOUT CHILDREN ABDUCTED TO SAUDI ARABIA

On June 12, 2002, Representative Dan Burton, then chairman of the House Government Reform Committee, held a hearing on "U.S. Citizens Held in Saudi Arabia."[37] In the introduction of that hearing Representative Burton made the following statement:

> Today we're going to hear the stories of three mothers who had their children snatched away from them. Three things stand out in each of these stories: One, the brutal treatment of women in Saudi Arabia; the incredible courage of these women who did everything they could to rescue their children; and finally, the total lack of effort by our State Department to challenge the Saudi government.
>
> These stories are all so powerful that I'd like to talk about each one of them in detail. But I'm not going to do that, because I can't tell their stories nearly as well as they can. But I do want to mention a few key facts.
>
> Pat Roush has been living this nightmare for 16 years. In those 16 years, she has seen her two daughters one time for two hours. Her ex-husband came to the United States in 1986, kidnapped their two young daughters in violation of a court custody order, and took them to Saudi Arabia. An arrest warrant was issued here in the U.S., but the Saudi government did absolutely nothing.
>
> The year before that, when Pat went to Saudi Arabia to try to salvage their marriage, her husband beat her so badly that two of her ribs were broken and the Saudi police didn't do anything then either.
>
> Over the last 16 years, U.S. ambassadors have come and gone in Riyadh. Some have tried to help and some have not. But it's clear that the Saudis were never told by senior officials that this was a problem that was going to affect the relationship between our two countries.
>
> In 1986, the U.S. ambassador was told by his boss that he had to maintain impartiality in the Roush case. Why? Pat Roush's husband broke the law. An arrest warrant was issued. Why should we maintain impartiality? To me, that attitude goes right to the heart of this problem. Ambassador Ray Mabus deserves special credit in this case. In 1996, he started a new policy: No one from this man's family was allowed to get a visa to come to the United States, it caused a big problem for them.
>
> Unfortunately, after a year, Ambassador Mabus returned to the United States and his policy was discontinued. If this policy had been kept in place, it might very well have put the pressure on them to return these children to their mother. I'm very disappointed that that didn't happen.
>
> We were told just this week that Pat's youngest daughter, Aisha, who is now 19, was recently forced into a marriage with a Saudi man. Pat's older daughter, Alia, was forced to marry one of her cousins a year ago.
>
> Now let me say a few words about Monica Stowers. In 1985, she went to Saudi Arabia with her husband and two young children. When she arrived, she realized for the first time that her husband had a second wife and another child. She didn't know about that. Their marriage fell apart after six months. Her husband divorced her and had her deported without her children.
>
> In 1990, Monica heard that her ex-husband was abusing her children. She went back to Saudi Arabia. She took her children and went to the U.S. embassy to ask for help. Did they put her on the next plane to America? No. At the end of the day, they told Monica that she had to leave the embassy. She pleaded with them not to kick her out. She told them that she would be arrested for overstaying her visa. But the consul general had the Marine guards carry them out. Sure enough, she was arrested. That actually happened.
>
> Can you imagine that? An American citizen is in a crisis, a mother and her young children, and the embassy staff tell the Marines to drag them out of the embassy so they could be arrested. That actually happened.

Monica is not here today. For most of the last 12 years she has stayed in Saudi Arabia to protect her children. She can leave any time she wants, but her husband refuses to allow their daughters to go. Her ex-husband tried to force her daughter into a marriage when she was only 12 years old. And Monica will not abandon her. While Monica can't be here to testify, her mother, Ethyl Stowers, is here to speak on her behalf, and we're very glad to have her here.

The third story we're going to hear about today is about Miriam Hernandez-Davis and her daughter Dria. They're both here to testify today. The reason they can both be here today is not because anybody in the United States government came to their rescue. The reason that Miriam's daughter is here today is that Miriam was able to scrape together $180,000 to pay two men to smuggle Dria out of Saudi Arabia.

Even though Miriam's husband kidnapped their daughter in 1997, and even though the FBI issued an international warrant for his arrest, she got almost no help from the State Department or our embassy.

The courage of these women, Pat Roush, Monica Stowers and Miriam Hernandez, and their kids, is just incredible to me. You've all endured terrible pain as a result of what's happened, and it's a real honor to have all of you here today.

These are not isolated incidents. These are three examples of a much bigger problem. The State Department has a list of 46 recent cases involving as many as 92 U.S. citizens who have been held against their will in Saudi Arabia.

The root cause of this problem is the Saudi government. They have refused to respect U.S. law and U.S. arrest warrants. The law in Saudi Arabia lets Saudi men keep American women and children in Saudi Arabia even when they're in violation of court orders, even when arrest warrants have been issued, and even when they've abused their wives and their children. And that's just wrong.

We can't let this go on. Our relationship with Saudi Arabia is important, but this just can't be allowed to continue. The only way we're going to resolve this problem and get these kids home again is by elevating this issue, letting the American people and the people throughout the world know about it. This has to be raised with the Saudis at the highest levels. The Saudis have to be made to understand that if they let this go on, their relationship with us is going to suffer. And I don't think that's happened yet.

Approaching Burton's Statement from a Narrative Perspective

At first glance, Representative Burton's statement does not look much like the narratives that dominate popular culture in film, fiction, and television. He seems to be making an argument to change US policy toward Saudi Arabia. Underneath the surface, however, Burton skillfully uses narrative to support his political agenda. The stories that he tells reflect his anger at both the Saudis and US officials who fail to confront them. My starting point for approaching Burton's story is a comment by Walter Fisher: "what makes one story better than another" can be explained based on two "features" of the story—"formal and substantive."[38] Fisher is getting at two fundamental goals of narrative analysis, to identify how the story works on an audience and the characteristics of narrative form and content that allow it to produce that impact.

Before the critic can discover the functions served by Burton's narrative, he or she must first uncover the defining characteristics of the story itself. Just as a cook begins with a list of ingredients, the analyst must pull out of the story the ingredients making up the narrative. Since Fisher and Filloy focused on how drama and literature often serve an argumentative function, critics have recognized that narrative themes come out of the interaction of characters (including the narrator), the setting, and the plot.[39] Thus, the narrative analyst should begin by identifying the rhetorical forms (characters, setting, plot, and theme) that define the story and move from there to a consideration of rhetorical function.

After the linkage between narrative form and function has been identified, the rhetorical critic can assess the persuasive value of the narrative. Here, the key goal is to consider whether the narrative will be perceived as a "coherent story" that will "ring true" for the audience.[40] Three rules of thumb are particularly useful in that regard. In general, persuasive narratives

will contain formal characteristics (plot, setting, characters, and theme) that the particular audience will find interesting. (This is the principle that explains why so many television shows
focus on emergency room doctors, homicide cops, or high-profile prosecutors and so few on
college professors.) A second rule of thumb is that narratives which effectively fulfill the four
functions I have described are more likely to influence an audience than narratives that do not
fulfill those functions. Finally, narratives that possess "formal coherence,"[41] or credibility for a
particular audience because they draw on aspects of that audience's world, are more likely to
have persuasive impact than those that do not. Thus, by moving from form, to function, and
then to how the form influenced the function, the critic can explain what was in the narrative,
how it worked (or failed to work) on an audience, and draw an overall conclusion about the
impact of the story. In the following section, I apply this approach to narrative criticism to the
statement of Representative Burton.

Narrative Form and Function in Burton's Statement

Representative Burton's statement combines narrative with appeals to basic American values and rational argument. In the conclusion, he builds the argument that "The root cause of
this problem is the Saudi government." He also appeals to values of justice and concern for
the innocent when he attacks the Saudi government for failing to "respect U.S. law." Burton's
ultimate claim is that the president should pressure the Saudi government to release the abducted children. Implicitly, Burton assumes that a threat from the president to Saudi leaders
that failure to release the children could cause "their relationship with us . . . to suffer" would
be sufficient to motivate the Saudis to act.

Although Burton relies upon an appeal to basic values and rational argument in the conclusion of his statement, the dominant strategy is narrative. Burton uses the stories of three
American women—Pat Roush, Monica Stowers, and Miriam Hernandez-Davis—to build the
case that the US government has failed its citizens and must take remedial action. In Burton's
three related mini-narratives, the protagonist is the American mother. All three women are
depicted as strong and loving mothers who have sacrificed mightily for their children and
suffered greatly. Pat Roush tried to salvage her marriage and suffered broken ribs as a consequence. She worked for sixteen years to protect her children. Monica Stowers stayed in Saudi
Arabia for "most of the last 12 years . . . to protect her children." And Miriam Hernandez-
Davis "scrape[d] together" $180,000 of her own money in order to save her daughter Dria.
These three women are in a sense everywoman. In a desperate situation, they refused to give
in and instead fought for their children.

There are three different but related antagonists in Burton's narrative. At one level, the
role of antagonist is played by the husbands who took the children, abused them by forcing
them into marriage or other acts, and prevented them from leaving Saudi Arabia. In Burton's narrative, the husbands and their abuse are not described in any detail. They figure far
more prominently in the testimony of the women later in the hearing. At a second level, the
antagonist is the Saudi government. In his brief retelling of Roush's story, Burton states that
in response to both the kidnapping of Roush's children and physical abuse that broke "two
of her ribs" "the Saudi police didn't do anything." Although Burton clearly views the Saudi
government as tyrannical and Saudi society as uncivilized, the focus of his fury is on the US
government, which in his telling was more concerned with trouble-free relations than with
the rights of American citizens. In relating Roush's story, Burton cites an American ambassador
who "was told by his boss that he had to maintain impartiality in the Roush case." Burton then
asks "Why? Pat Roush's husband broke the law. An arrest warrant was issued. Why should
we maintain impartiality?" Later, he tells about how when Monica Stowers and her children
sought help in the American embassy, "the consul general had the Marine guards carry them
out." In Burton's narrative, the government has become utterly spineless. The one government

official who wasn't gutless was Ambassador Ray Mabus, who tried to pressure the Saudis into releasing Pat Roush's children. In Burton's narrative, Mabus plays a heroic role, but in another sense his personal story supports the larger point that American policy has been quite weak. While Mabus's policy "might very well have put the pressure on" the Saudis, after he returned to the United States, "his policy was discontinued."

The only other characters in Burton's narrative are the children who are not discussed in any detail. Their role is that of innocent victim. These innocent children have suffered not only from being taken from their mothers but also from being abused by their fathers. Both daughters of Pat Roush were forced into arranged marriages. The children of Monica Stowers also were abused. The only child who has been saved is Dria, the daughter of Hernandez-Davis. And Dria is safe not because of the action of the United States, which provided Ms. Hernandez-Davis with "almost no help," but because Hernandez-Davis spent her own money to get her child back.

The primary setting of Burton's narrative is in Saudi Arabia. Saudi government and society are described as uncivilized. They do not respect law. Worse, they do not protect innocent women and children from abusive husbands. It is a society in which the child of Monica Stowers can be forced into a marriage at the age of twelve. While the primary setting of the story is in Saudi Arabia, there is a sense in which the story is set in a soulless bureaucracy that no longer understands the difference between policy and principle. In Burton's narrative only the mothers and Mabus understand that the lives of innocent children must be protected at all cost.

The primary plot devices in Burton's narrative are betrayal and commitment. The women and their children are betrayed first by their husbands, but in a more fundamental sense by their own country. In Burton's narrative the husbands are almost faceless. He describes their actions as terrible, but as typical of their society. His real fury is reserved for the US government, which has failed its citizens by kowtowing to the Saudis. In sharp contrast to the government, the three mothers acted with great courage. Burton's feeling about them comes through quite clearly: "The courage of these women . . . and their kids, is just incredible to me. You've all endured terrible pain as a result of what's happened, and it's a real honor to have all of you here today." There clearly is a relationship between the two plot devices. Burton's narrative is based on the premise that if the government had not betrayed the women and their children, but had acted with the commitment shown by the mothers, the kids would have been saved.

There are two primary themes in Burton's narrative. One theme simply concerns the women and their children. In Burton's narrative these innocent people have been abused because of their betrayal by their husbands (and fathers). The other theme is implicit. While Burton explicitly attacks the State Department for failing to fight for the abducted children, by implication he argues that if we just had the courage to stick by our principles as the mothers and Ray Mabus did we would have been able to force the Saudis to release the kids.

The analysis of Burton's narrative makes it quite clear that the story fulfills all four functions of narrative. First, the narrative is well designed to grab the attention of the audience. At the end of the statement, Burton notes that the three stories "are not isolated incidents." He adds that "The State Department has a list of 46 recent cases involving as many as 92 U.S. citizens who have been held against their will in Saudi Arabia." The statistic that Burton cites is not nearly as compelling as the three narratives. Later in the hearing, Deputy Assistant Secretary of State for Near Eastern Affairs Ryan C. Crocker testified that "we [the State Department] have no higher priority than the safety and security of our citizens. I believe our record shows a consistent and sustained engagement on child custody cases in line with this priority. But as noted above, we operate in accordance with the laws of our two governments, laws that do not mesh well on civil and social issues."[42] After hearing the stories of Roush, Stowers, and Hernandez-Davis, Crocker's statement comes across as mere rationalization. The stories of the three women send the message that when the welfare of small children who are American citizens is at stake, the government of the United States of America, the strongest nation by far on the planet, should have acted far more strongly.

Burton's story also fulfills the second and third functions of narrative rhetoric. Burton uses the three stories to create identification between the audience and the three mothers. Implicitly, he tells us that this could happen to your sister or your daughter or your grand-daughter. He also draws on the power of narrative to transport us to a different place or time. This function is most clearly fulfilled in his description of how Monica Stowers fled with her children to the American embassy and then was kicked out by American marines on the order of the consul general. Although Burton's description is brief, one image comes through quite strongly—an American bureaucrat ordering marine guards to escort a mother and small children out of the embassy to be arrested by the Saudi police. Here, Burton takes us to two uncivilized places—Saudi Arabia that does not respect the law or the rights of women and children and an American embassy that no longer fights for American citizens.

Burton's narrative also clearly taps into basic American values such as justice, freedom, and honor and also basic human needs concerning family and children. The narrative produces two strong emotional reactions, anger and guilt. It produces anger at the government for selling out our own citizens and guilt that we haven't done more to help the women and their families.

Although Burton's retelling of the three stories is brief, it is also quite powerful. His narrative brings life to what otherwise might seem a complex foreign policy dispute. The setting, characters, and plot produce a powerful theme that transforms the arcane diplomatic fight into a call for justice. Burton also effectively fulfills the functions of narrative, especially in relation to shared identity. Clearly, he creates a sense of identification between the women and their children on the one hand and other Americans on the other. He also uses the power of narrative scene to take us out of our here and now to force us to see that similar actions could happen to members of each of our families.

Burton's story also has great narrative credibility. The story possesses internal coherence and also rings true with what we know about treatment of women and children by some Islamic fundamentalists. The story is coherent in two senses. First, the Saudi husbands and their government consistently act to deny the women and their children any rights. Second, the story is coherent in its depiction of an American State Department more interested in geopolitics than protecting the rights of American citizens. Finally, the story clearly rings true with what people know about Saudi society, a culture so traditionalist that until very recently women were not allowed to drive, and which still places dramatic limits on how women can live, limits not found in the United States or Western Europe for centuries. In summary, Burton's narrative powerfully sets forth the case that the United States should use all of our power and moral authority to pressure the Saudi government to release children of American mothers and Saudi fathers to the custody of the American mothers and allow them to leave the country.

The previous analysis does not, however, tell us if such a policy in fact would be a good idea. Burton's narrative is by its very nature one-sided, favoring the rights of the mothers over the fathers. We have no rhetorical means of testing whether the stories he tells are accurate. Nor do we know whether US pressure would be effective in gaining release of the children. Citizens of the United States would be outraged if a foreign government pressured this nation to act because it perceived our culture to be immoral. Surely the Saudis are no different. It is quite possible that pressuring the Saudis might be counterproductive.

There is also the possibility that larger issues involving oil supplies and stability in the Persian Gulf simply require that the United States look the other way on this issue. I find that position distasteful and immoral, but the effect of US pressure on the stability of the Saudi regime is certainly a relevant question. The key point is while the standards of narrative criticism are quite useful in revealing how Burton's narrative effectively presents a particular perspective, they do not provide much guidance in determining whether that narrative is either factual or would be the basis of good public policy. Those questions are at their base not rhetorical in nature.

PERSONAL REFLECTIONS

The key decision that I made in approaching the Burton story was to let the rhetorical analysis emerge from the form and function of the narrative. One of the perils of rhetorical analysis is the danger that the critic will use a method as a set of blinders rather than as a powerful lens to explain how the rhetoric functions. Thus, an argumentation critic might always find rhetoric to be dominated by argument or a critic focused on metaphor always finds that metaphors dominate the rhetoric. Any rhetorical theory and the terminology associated with it can be turned into a similar set of blinders that essentially shapes the critical process.

To avoid the danger of a terminology becoming a set of blinders, while still producing theory-based criticism, my approach is always to begin by identifying the defining formal characteristics of the rhetoric in question, to move from that analysis of form to a consideration of rhetorical function, and then to consider how rhetorical theory illuminates the linkage between rhetorical form and function. The three-step approach developed in the essay is designed to achieve that aim.

In sum, rhetorical critics need a wide-ranging knowledge of rhetorical theory and methodology, but along with that knowledge, they need a healthy skepticism about those theories as well. That skepticism helps critics avoid a situation in which a theory no longer illuminates rhetorical action but becomes a set of blinders.

POTENTIALS AND PITFALLS

The discussion of a variety of approaches to narrative analysis and the presentation of a systematic approach to narrative criticism suggests several potential benefits and pitfalls associated with the rhetorical analysis of narrative. The most significant potential benefit is to reveal the power of narrative in our society. There is no question that narrative is an extremely powerful rhetorical form. If the battle is between strong statistics on one side and a compelling narrative on the other, there is little doubt that at least in the short run, the narrative will be more influential. People love stories, and stories are powerful means of making connections with others and tapping into basic values and needs. The immense power of narrative makes it especially important that critics uncover how narratives function. Although a number of theorists (myself included) have critiqued the narrative paradigm, the field of rhetorical criticism owes an enormous debt to Walter Fisher for pointing out so forcefully the importance of narrative.

Although narrative criticism can be quite useful, it is not without pitfalls, three of which are particularly important. First, narrative criticism is most easily and appropriately applied to rhetoric that is clearly a story. However, much rhetoric draws on stories that are in some sense out there in the society. A speaker or writer might refer to a story about the Founding Fathers or a story about Lady Gaga or Monica Lewinsky and assume that the audience would fill in the details. The problem is that it is difficult for the critic to know how the audience fills in those details or exactly what gets filled in. There is also a fine line between an example included as support material in a speech or essay and a developed narrative. While the line between these two types of rhetoric is a fine one, the line is also important. There is a difference between a member of Congress citing the example of Pat Roush and the more developed story told by Burton. Narrative criticism is much more applicable to the developed story as opposed to the implied reference or short example. The critic can distinguish between these two rhetorical types by considering whether the story in any rhetoric is developed in such a way that it fulfills any or all of the persuasive functions of narrative that I identified earlier. If it does fulfill those functions, the story usefully can be treated as narrative. If it fails to fulfill those functions, it may be more appropriate to consider it an extended example.

A second pitfall of narrative criticism relates to the variability in how human beings interpret stories. Narrative critics need to recognize that not all people prefer the same kinds of stories. A glance at the best-seller list for fiction supports this judgment. Some of us love fantastic novels about space or romantic stories about dashing men and ravishing women; others like murder mysteries or historical novels. My point is that human beings like very different types of stories. If that is true in relation to fiction, it probably is true about other types of narratives as well. While Fisher is right that narrative is a human universal, it seems clear that the standards by which people evaluate stories are culturally based, rather than universal. I made this point earlier when I noted that many in the Arab world found the story that Israeli intelligence had orchestrated the September 11 attacks to be quite credible, when nearly all Americans found that story to be absurd. Consequently, rhetorical critics need to ground their analysis of a narrative in the attitudes of a given audience and recognize that stories that they find to be credible may not be credible to others.

The final pitfall of narrative analysis relates to variation in narrative type. Narrative criticism works best on stories that support a clear theme and that are grounded in the real world as we know it. Narrative analysis of works of fantasy, science fiction, or allegory is more difficult because the critic must not only discover the underlying narrative pattern but also translate the message out of the category of science fiction or fantasy into the category of realistic narrative.[43] An example may make this point clear. Janice Hocker Rushing has interpreted the first two *Alien* films from a psychological perspective, concluding that in the films "the patriarchy has induced the feminine to fight itself," creating a situation in which "the feminine is actually subverted."[44] My own reading of the films would focus on how the protagonist (Ripley) is both feminine and powerful, thereby sending a message of feminist empowerment, and also on how the films strongly suggest that power and money often produce corrupt decision making.

However, I think it would be very difficult to determine one "correct" interpretation of these films because they are works of science fiction set in a time and place quite far from our reality. There inevitably will be much more variation in the interpretation of works of science fiction, fantasy, and allegory than of realistic narratives, such as that of Burton. This point is easily illustrated in relation to allegory, a type of narrative in which the author uses a story set in a place very different from the contemporary world to imply a judgment about our world. Even when a work of allegory has a very clear theme, such as Orwell's attack on communism in *Animal Farm*, interpretation is more difficult than in realistic narratives. Allegorical interpretation requires the critic to translate the allegory into a realistic narrative prior to analyzing it. This translation stage adds complexity to the interpretive process. Thus, the third pitfall of narrative criticism is that the perspective works most effectively on realistic narratives that lay out a clear conclusion.

Storytelling is one of the hallmarks of human culture. From the time that humans developed the capacity to use symbols, we have told stories. And stories are among the most powerful forms of persuasion. Yet, until relatively recently, rhetorical critics shied away from analyzing narratives and focused almost exclusively on rational argumentation and other rhetorical forms. While argument is clearly important, narrative plays a crucial role in every human culture. Rhetorical critics need a systematic way of explaining how narratives work to persuade audiences. The approach developed in this chapter is a starting point that the critic can use to break down both the forms present in a given narrative and how those forms function in relation to an audience.

NARRATIVE ANALYSIS TOP PICKS

Fisher, Walter R. *Human Communication as Narration.* Columbia: University of South Carolina Press, 1987. In his book, Fisher fleshes out all aspects of the narrative paradigm.

————. "Narration as a Human Communication Paradigm: The Case of Public Moral Argument." *Communication Monographs* 51 (1984): 1–22. This essay is the original statement of the narrative paradigm and the most influential article about narrative published to date in a communication journal.

Hollihan, Thomas A., and Patricia Riley. "The Rhetorical Power of a Compelling Story: A Critique of a 'Toughlove' Parental Support Group." *Communication Quarterly* 35 (1987): 13–25. Hollihan and Riley provide one of the clearest applications of principles of narrative rationality to a real-world story.

Lewis, William F. "Telling America's Story: Narrative Form and the Reagan Presidency." *Quarterly Journal of Speech* 73 (1987): 280–302. Lewis's essay is among the best examples of the inductive approach to narrative analysis. It is accessible and clearly argued.

Milford, Michael, and Robert C. Rowland. "Situated Ideological Allegory and *Battlestar Galactica.*" *Western Journal of Communication* 75 (2012): 536–551. Milford and Rowland show the importance of finding the particular nature of the story in rhetorical analysis, in this case identifying an ideological allegory.

Rowland, Robert C., and Robert Strain. "Social Function, Polysemy and Narrative-Dramatic Form: A Case Study of *Do the Right Thing.*" *Communication Quarterly* 42 (1994): 213–228. Rowland and Strain illustrate the advantages of the inductive approach, but also the difficulty with the approach as a method of criticism.

DISCUSSION QUESTIONS

1. What makes narratives so much more compelling for many audiences than an argument developing the same theme?
2. How does narrative break down barriers and take us out of our "here and now" to another place and time?
3. What makes some stories so compelling that they retain power over generations? *Star Trek* is more than fifty years old and *Star Wars* over forty, but they remain powerful narratives while much has changed in society and culture. What makes such stories so powerful?
4. Millions of Americans believe in conspiratorial narratives that are both incoherent and false. Why do they accept such odd stories?

ACTIVITIES

1. President Donald Trump ran for the presidency arguing that the "American Dream" had become what he labeled American carnage. As president, he has claimed to have

revitalized the American Dream. As a group, please identify the formal characteristics of his two narratives about the American Dream and explain why the narratives have been persuasive for many Americans and have seemed repellent for others.

2. Narrative is among the most powerful forms of political rhetoric. Imagine that your group has been asked to craft a narrative for a pragmatic liberal or pragmatic conservative (someone like former Ohio Governor and Republican John Kasich or Minnesota Senator and Democrat Amy Klobuchar). What kind of story would you advise the candidate to tell?

3. Corporations and other organizations often face crises when they are accused of producing a dangerous product or otherwise harming the public. Using a recent case of such an organizational crisis, identify the characteristics of the most effective narrative that you believe the organization could produce to convince the public to forgive the organization for past wrongdoing or persuade the public that no such wrongdoing had occurred.

NOTES

1. Mark Landler, "'Megxit' Is the New Brexit in a Britain Split by Age and Politics," *New York Times*, January 16, 2020, A7.

2. Henry Fountain and Nadja Popovich, "2019 Was the Second-Hottest Year Ever, Closing Out the Warmest Decade," *New York Times*, January 15, 2020, https://www.nytimes.com/interactive/2020/01/15/climate/hottest-year-2019.html.

3. See Hayden White, "The Value of Narrativity in the Representation of Reality," *Critical Inquiry* 7 (1980): 6.

4. For example, Wallace Martin, *Recent Theories of Narrative* (Ithaca, NY: Cornell University Press, 1986), 7. The most important scholar in rhetoric to focus on its importance is Walter R. Fisher. See "Narration as a Human Communication Paradigm: The Case of Public Moral Argument," *Communication Monographs* 51 (1984): 1–22; Walter R. Fisher, *Human Communication as Narration* (Columbia: University of South Carolina Press, 1987).

5. Northrop Frye has built an entire theory of narrative around the level of heroic power present in the protagonist. See Northrop Frye, *Anatomy of Criticism: Four Essays* (Princeton, NJ: Princeton University Press, 1957).

6. See Kenneth Burke, *A Rhetoric of Motives* (Berkeley: University of California Press, 1969).

7. See Elie Wiesel, *Night*, trans. Stella Rodway (New York: Avon, 1958).

8. Lewis O. Mink, "Narrative Form as a Cognitive Instrument," in *The Writing of History: Literary Form and Historical Understanding*, ed. Robert H. Canary and Henry Kozuchi (Madison: University of Wisconsin Press, 1978), 129–130.

9. Ibid., 131.

10. Al Gore, *An Inconvenient Truth: The Planetary Emergency of Global Warming and What We Can Do about It* (Emmaus, PA: Rodale, 2006).

11. See *Report of the President's Commission on the Accident at Three Mile Island: The Need For Change: The Legacy of TMI* (Washington: Government Printing Office, 1979); Robert C. Rowland, "A Reanalysis of the Argumentation at Three Mile Island," in *Argument in Controversy: Proceedings of the 7th SCA-AFA Conference on Argumentation*, ed. Donn Parson (Annandale, VA: SCA, 1991): 277–283.

12. Michiko Kakutani, "Kind Hero of 'Mockingbird' Returns as Racist in Sequel," *New York Times*, July 11, 2015, A1, A3.

13. Walter R. Fisher and Richard A Filloy, "Argument in Drama and Literature: An Exploration," in *Advances in Argumentation Theory and Research*, ed. J. Robert Cox and Charles A. Willard (Carbondale: Southern Illinois University Press, 1982), 343.

14. Ibid., 360.

15. Ibid.

16. Fisher, "Narration as a Human Communication Paradigm," 4–9; Fisher, *Human Communication as Narration*, 67.

17. Fisher, "Narration as a Human Communication Paradigm," 6.

18. Fisher, "Narration as a Human Communication Paradigm," 7.

19. Fisher, *Human Communication as Narration*, xi.

20. Fisher, *Human Communication as Narration*, 75; Fisher, "Narrative as a Human Communication Paradigm," 8–9.

21. Fisher, "Narration as a Human Communication Paradigm," 8.

22. Fisher, *Human Communication as Narration*, 47.

23. Fisher, "Narration as a Human Communication Paradigm," 8.

24. Fisher, "The Narrative Paradigm: An Elaboration," *Communication Monographs* 52 (1985), 350.

25. Fisher, "Narration as a Human Communication Paradigm," 16.

26. See Barbara Warnick, "The Narrative Paradigm: Another Story," *Quarterly Journal of Speech* 73 (1987): 172–182; Robert C. Rowland, "Narrative: Mode of Discourse or Paradigm," *Communication Monographs* 54 (1987): 264–275.

27. In addition to "Narrative: Mode of Discourse or Paradigm?," see "On Limiting the Narrative Paradigm: Three Case Studies," *Communication Monographs* 56 (1989): 39–53.

28. See "On Limiting the Narrative Paradigm" and Robert C. Rowland, "The Value of the Rational World and Narrative Paradigms," *Central States Speech Journal* 39 (1988): 204–217.

29. Ronald H. Carpenter, "Admiral Mahan, 'Narrative Fidelity,' and the Japanese Attack on Pearl Harbor," *Quarterly Journal of Speech* 72 (1986): 290–305.

30. Carpenter, "Admiral Mahan," 291.

31. Thomas A. Hollihan and Patricia Riley, "The Rhetorical Power of a Compelling Story: A Critique of a 'Toughlove' Parental Support Group," *Communication Quarterly* 35 (1987): 13–25.

32. Hollihan and Riley, "Rhetorical Power," 23, 24.

33. See Thomas Rosteck, "Narrative in Martin Luther King's *I've Been to the Mountaintop*," *Southern Communication Journal* 58 (1992): 22–32; Martha Solomon and Wayne J. McMullen, "*Places in the Heart*: The Rhetorical Force of an Open Text," *Western Journal of Speech Communication* 55 (1991): 339–353; Sally J. Perkins, "The Dilemma of Identity: Theatrical Portrayals of a 16th Century Feminist," *Southern Communication Journal* 59 (1994): 205–214; Robert C. Rowland and Robert Strain, "Social Function, Polysemy and Narrative-Dramatic Form: A Case Study of *Do the Right Thing*," *Communication Quarterly* 42 (1994): 213–228.

34. Stephanie Kelley-Romano, "Trust No One: The Conspiracy Genre on American Television," *Southern Communication Journal* 73 (2008): 105–121; Mike Milford and Robert C. Rowland, "Situated Ideological Allegory and *Battlestar Galactica*," *Western Journal of Communication* 75 (2012): 536–551.

35. William F. Lewis, "Telling America's Story: Narrative Form and the Reagan Presidency," *Quarterly Journal of Speech* 73 (1987): 280–302.

36. Lewis, "Telling America's Story," 282.

37. *U.S. Citizens Held in Saudi Arabia* (hearing of the House Government Reform Committee, June 12, 2002), available online, Congressional Universe, LexisNexis. The passage that is included is a selection from Burton's remarks.

38. Fisher, "Narration as a Human Communication Paradigm," 16.

39. See Fisher and Filloy, "Argument in Drama and Literature," 360.

40. Fisher, "Narration as a Human Communication Paradigm," 8.

41. Ibid., 16.

42. Ryan C. Crocker, "Statement of Ryan C. Crocker Deputy Assistant Secretary for Near Eastern Affairs," *U.S. Citizens Held in Saudi Arabia* (hearing of the House Government Reform Committee, June 12, 2002), available online, Congressional Universe, LexisNexis.

43. See Rowland, "On Limiting the Narrative Paradigm."

44. Janice Hocker Rushing, "Evolution of 'The New Frontier' in *Alien* and *Aliens*: Patriarchal Co-optation of the Feminine Archetype," *Quarterly Journal of Speech* 75 (1989): 10.

10

Dramatism and Kenneth Burke's Pentadic Criticism

Ryan Erik McGeough and Andrew King

Kenneth Burke (1897–1993) was perhaps the most influential rhetorical critic of the twentieth century. A critic, editor, poet, and traveling lecturer, Burke traversed a wide array of intellectual circles. As a result, his unorthodox ideas cut across academic disciplines (in a bookstore, Burke might be found in the communication, literary criticism, sociology, or philosophy sections) in order to explore the role of language in human action. Across his multiple books and essays, Burke developed a theory of language and human action he called **dramatism**. Dramatism contains a number of Burke's central ideas, including terministic screens, identification, and, most famously, the **pentad**.

ORIGINS OF DRAMATISM

Kenneth Burke's unique contributions to rhetorical criticism stem from his distinctive intellectual background. Burke briefly attended the Ohio State University before dropping out and moving to New York City, where he sat in on seminars at Columbia University. During the 1920s, he integrated himself into the artistic and intellectual renaissance in Greenwich Village. During this time and into the 1930s, Burke spent time conversing, and later clashing, with Marxist intellectuals. He edited a literary magazine and engaged in long debates with other critics. All of these perspectives influenced Burke's approach to criticism. Recognizing that "every insight contains its own special kind of blindness," Burke found each perspective simultaneously valuable yet incomplete. An intellectual omnivore and pragmatist, Burke drew on insights from what he found most valuable within numerous schools of thought and combined them in novel ways.

Burke, like most major thinkers, was also profoundly influenced by the world in which he lived. He left home and started college as the First World War raged in Europe. His intellectual debates in the 1920s and 1930s focused on a wide array of topics, including art, politics, communism, fascism, democracy, and the power of language to create social change. Burke observed the power, limits, and consequences of language as the world marched toward catastrophic war for a second time. In 1938, Burke published a deeply insightful analysis of Hitler's *Mein Kampf;* he hoped that carefully analyzing Hitler's rhetoric might help prevent it from working in the United States.[1] He spent the Second World War writing *A Grammar of Motives*, which explores the role of language in how we attribute motives and understand the actions of others. These two works not only reveal the influence of Burke's context on his writings but also demonstrate his belief in the power of language and the power of critics to intervene in the world.

DRAMATISM

Burke labeled himself a "word man" and obsessed over words and their capacity to influence human thought and action.[2] Drawing on Aristotle, who described humans as animals who have words, Burke believed that symbol use is what separates human action from the behavior of other animals, which he called motion. Central to dramatism is Burke's contention that humans do not just use words, but that words use us. By this, Burke meant that choosing to describe the world with one set of words rather than another leads us to understand the world in a particular way, and this understanding of the world shapes how we choose to act in it. A dramatistic perspective recognizes that words are more than just the tools we use to interact with one another; they are also the fundamental building blocks by which we construct our understanding of the world. Through language, we orient ourselves in the world and call others to see the world and act as we do.

Dramatism locates this power in language because of the power of words to act as terministic screens. By **terministic screens**, Burke means the capacity of language (terminology) to encourage us to understand the world in some ways while filtering (screening) other interpretations out. Burke claims that "even if any given terminology is a *reflection* of reality, by its very nature as a terminology, it must be a *selection* of reality; and to this extent it must function also as a *deflection* of reality."[3] Thus, no matter how objective we might try to be, the specific language we use to describe an object or event will draw our attention toward some aspects of the event (selecting), and thus away from other aspects (deflecting). For example, in the rhetoric surrounding abortion, activists on both sides have sought to harness the power of language to act as a terministic screen. Activists opposed to abortion identify themselves as "pro-life," while those who support abortion being legal identify themselves as "pro-choice." The first title attempts to frame the issue as being about protecting human life, the second as being about protecting human freedom. Both labels *reflect* a position on the issue of abortion, but they *select* very different aspects of the controversy to highlight.[4] Understanding terministic screens reveals the ways in which all language can be persuasive: words shape the way we see the world by encouraging us to notice some aspects of the world over others.[5]

The capacity of language to function as a terministic screen is just one of the ways Burke argues that persuasion occurs unconsciously. Another is through what Burke labels **identification**. In fact, Burke argues that contemporary persuasion occurs less through logical weighing of arguments and more through the often unconscious processes by which we align ourselves with others. In a mass-mediated society, Burke recognized that we are awash in persuasive appeals, and we simply cannot take the time to rationally evaluate all of them. Burke felt he needed a stronger term to describe the goals of the mind-changing industries in our society (advertising, sales, politics, etc.). Persuasion in a consumer-orientated mass society involves emotion, lifestyle choices, and systematic appeals to deeply held values. Thus, Burke adopted the term *identification* as more descriptive of the goals of public rhetoric. Identification suggests more than mere like-mindedness; it connotes individuals "acting together" and sharing common feelings, "sensations, concepts, images, ideas and attitudes."[6] Dramatism is designed to give us a deep awareness of the nature and resources of identification and a discerning eye for its costs and consequences.[7]

Of course, Burke also recognized that "identification is compensatory to division."[8] By this he means that any articulation of "us" also implies (either implicitly or explicitly) "them." In recent years, activists protesting with the slogan "Black Lives Matter" have often encountered counter-protests using the slogan "Blue Lives Matter." These clashes, whether in person or on social media, reveal conflicting identifications of who counts as "us" and who counts as "them." Identification occurs when you choose a path of action not simply based on weighing the pros and cons of that action but because you perceive that action as aligning you with other people like you. Whether in aligning yourself with a political party, associating with people who share your values, or buying products designed to project a particular image of yourself, Burke recognized the power of identification in shaping our actions.

THE PENTAD

Burke worried that because so much of persuasion is unconscious, we often embrace appeals uncritically without understanding their implications. Burke understood that our forms of language and experience are interlocked and that spokespersons in advertising, government, public relations, and media know how to use these persuasive forms. After twice watching the nations of the world follow their leaders to war, Burke hoped to provide a method that might help people become more savvy consumers of persuasive messages. He developed pentadic criticism to make visible how persuaders use language to change our beliefs and influence our actions. Burke argued that the master form was the common story, a form that was generated by the structure of our minds. Burke developed his critical method based on that form. The method he invented is simple yet complex, flexible yet straightforward, prosaic yet poetic. Its purpose is to help defend us against the tremendous flood of persuasive messages that assault us every moment of our waking lives.

Burke published this famous method in the last year of World War II in the pages of his 1945 book, *A Grammar of Motives*.[9] Despite its eventual celebrity, the new approach was not an immediate hit; the use of Burke's insights spread slowly at first. His work was first brought into the spotlight by rhetorical critic Marie Hochmuth Nichols,[10] who wrote two very influential articles explaining Burke's methods and theories.[11] Today dramatism is studied by a large and diverse group, including both rhetorical and literary critics, philosophers, social scientists, and even theologians. Once it was only used as a tool for textual analysis, but its uses have grown to include methods of composition and of psychological, sociological, and philosophical analysis. This chapter will confine its attention to the core mission of pentadic criticism: the development of a method that can help people resist the flood tide of persuasive messages that assault them and to develop persuasive messages of their own.[12] What follows is far from exhaustive, but it will give the reader a strong hint of the kinds of help that Burke has to offer.

Where Does It Come From?

Burke did not so much "invent" pentadic criticism as revamp and expand schemes inherited from earlier critics. Like most perspectives, it is a combination of earlier ideas. From Aristotle's *Poetics*, Burke took the ideas of dramatic form and the power of stories in human history.[13]

Aristotle affirmed the centrality of human storytelling to the formation and maintenance of community. Our stories lie at the root of our identity; we can learn a lot about people by the kinds of stories they tell. Aristotle was also a great name giver and classifier; he believed that we need a good set of labels if we are to talk sensibly and at length about anything. Accordingly, he constructed a useful vocabulary, labeling all the parts of narrative structure. With a common set of categories, critics could better decide what made narratives strong or weak, beautiful or ugly, effective or clumsy. He left us names for the central features of the common story, names such as plot, character, spectacle, dialogue, and concept. Burke renamed these parts with the words *act, agent, scene, agency,* and *purpose.*[14]

From the great Roman poet Horace, Burke took the notion of generative categories. Generative categories are the building blocks of creativity. They not only provide the skeleton and structure of a story; they also serve as a stimulus to invent new ideas, to clothe the bones with new nerves, tendons, and sinews. Two thousand years ago in a still-admired essay giving advice to would-be writers, Horace used a series of basic questions as building blocks in playwriting and storytelling. In his famous work *Ars Poetica,* Horace advised his readers on a method of composing stories, a method so universal that it did not matter whether the writers were fifteen or ninety, libertines or monks, intellectuals or merchants.[15] All they had to do was apply his categories to a subject, and they could produce a text. Horace believed that all stories were the product of the answers to a series of basic questions. Who are the main characters? What is the place in which they are set? What is the nature of their conflict or problem? What is the era in which the story is set? What is their purpose? What are the means they use to solve their problems and what obstacles do they face? And what kind of resolution can be made?

Horace argued that if you answered those questions in an imaginative way, you would produce the germ of a story. Modern journalists honor Horace when they tell us that the way to write a complete news story is to answer the basic questions: What happened? Who did it? Where and under what circumstances was the action done? When did it happen? How was the thing done? Why was it done? Burke borrowed these questions and updated them. He maintained that the questions could be used to gain a complete understanding of any human action and how we explain the motives from which it arose. Burke does not use the term *motive* in the legal or formal sense. It is simply a name we give to our acts, a strategic symbolic summing-up of an action.

From the language scholar and coauthor of *The Meaning of Meaning,* Ivor Armstrong Richards, Burke took the idea of the importance of form in art.[16] Burke was interested in the aesthetic appeal of form, particularly narrative form.[17] **Form** is a pattern that invites our participation; it arouses our desires and promises to fulfill them. We see the power of form when we know a pattern and expect it to be repeated. At a wedding, we typically expect someone to officiate and for the couple to exchange vows and/or rings. At a sporting event, we know the event is beginning when we are asked to rise for the singing of the national anthem. At a religious service, we might expect each meeting to begin (or end) with a prayer or a song. Ritual forms give us a sense of order, piety, shared community, and emotional closure. Burke has made us acutely aware of the power of narrative form, a form that dominates our orientation toward the world. In tragic plays, individual conflicts are represented as clashes between good and evil; in order to restore order, evil must be vanquished. In comedies, we recognize that the characters are neither inherently good nor evil but are fools to be laughed at. Burke noted that comedians make use of our socialization to conventional forms. We expect jokes will have a punch line; we expect that football squads will punt on fourth and long, and that heroes will (usually) win out in the end. Form invites our participation; we become caught up in it. Artists and writers use form to draw us into their works; propagandists and advertisers use musical, visual, and verbal forms to gain our compliance. Burke's pentadic criticism helps us recognize the widespread use of dramatic form. Dramatic form is one of the most common ways that we interpret events. It is one of the great human lenses we employ to discover meaning in our environment. Dramatic form, Burke tells us, is much bigger than theatrical performance; it is embedded in the structure of our minds. Thus, *dramatic form exists logically prior to our experience.* It is like an actor waiting in the wings to come on stage and interpret for us what it is that we are seeing and hearing as we move through the world. In this sense, dramatic form is literal, not metaphorical. The scheme of dramatic form is not a metaphor derived from a study of lots of drama or years of going to conventional theater and watching plays. In fact, the contrary is true. The movies, plays, stories, and news events are endless imitations and reincarnations of dramatic form.

Why Is It Important?

Frightened by the growing alliance of big commerce and big media, Burke began to worry about the future of self-government in North America. Despite his associations with leading figures of the Left, Burke was, in many ways, an old-fashioned Jeffersonian who believed that issues and ideas ought to come from the bedrock of the people, not from mandarin intellectuals and technical elites. His little farm in Andover, New Jersey, was close to his ideal, a place where groups of people met for free discussion of just about everything under the sun, but especially the local, state, and federal policies of their government. But how could this model thrive or even survive in an America now dominated by corporations, mass media, and government bureaucracies? How would American citizens maintain autonomy and agency when surrounded by agents and institutions who were trying to manipulate them? Advertising, propaganda, slanted news, and corporate public relations; political action groups, social movements, and cults; together with Hollywood and mass media have saturated the environment with persuasive images and words. During the Great Depression, Burke witnessed the rise of Hitler, Mussolini, Franco, Stalin, and later Mao, demagogues who manipulated millions of followers through messages greatly amplified by nearly absolute control of public media.

But even in the open societies of democratic Britain and the United States, he noted that large masses of Western citizenry suffered from fear, confusion, or deep cynicism as a result of being inundated by messages from every corner. After the great stock market crash of 1929 and the ruin of millions of families, our economic system seemed to have failed. Back-to-the-land agrarians, technocrats, communists, fascists, and other disaffected groups emerged from the wreckage. Spokespersons who had formerly been dismissed as cranks and utopians were getting a hearing. Burke noted that many of his fellow citizens were confused, uprooted, and fearful. He believed that without guidance they would not know how to discover the content and the consequences of these competing ideas. Unlike European thinkers whose answer was guidance by a class of intellectuals, Burke thought that people ought to be able to analyze and understand public questions on their own. In particular they ought to be able to discover the personal agendas and disguised advantages that people often hide beneath idealistic rhetoric. In the old American spirit of self-help and individualism, Burke offered a perspective that would unmask personal motives and separate personal advantage from high-sounding public promises.

By the 1930s, after spending years associating with writers in Greenwich Village, translating the work of Thomas Mann, and reviewing the work of many of the leading writers of the day as editor of the *Dial* (then one of America's foremost literary magazines), Burke had become profoundly convinced of the power of artists to influence people.[18] He believed that the role of the artist was crucial in society and that the artist to a much greater extent than the psychologist and the social worker could perform a therapeutic role in society. Embracing a tradition running back to Aristotle, Burke believed that the writer could be a kind of physician of society. He was a pioneer in raising environmental awareness, an early voice warning about the polarization of class and race and about the unsustainability of our agricultural system and industrial system.[19] For the last five decades of his existence, all of his efforts were dedicated to giving people the analytic tools to resist manipulative persuaders and to seek a more poetic vision of society.

Advertisers, propagandists, and hustlers of all kinds like to have us respond rapidly and un-critically to their messages. They want us to act without stopping to reflect deeply on the full meaning of their message. But a critical perspective means that we stop to do some analysis; and this time of reflection prevents the rapid stimulus-response kind of action so dear to mass-marketing persuasion. Charles King, a former creative director of one of the world's largest ad agencies (and brother of one of the authors), joked that he wanted people who saw the ads to respond like Pavlov's dogs. He wanted them to rush to buy the product, not to engage in an analysis of its claims and benefits. Criticism not only delays our reactions to messages; it may also *modify* our reactions. It can allow us to reframe the message in an alternative way, or adopt other attitudes toward it, or perhaps think about the intentions of the maker of the message, or about the long-term consequences of acting on such a message. In thinking deeply about one's attractions to the language and imagery of various products, one might also discover some useful things about one's mind and heart. Thus the practice of criticism not only helps us make better choices; it may also be transformational.

How Does It Work? Or, The Naming of the Parts

Burke opens *A Grammar of Motives*—the famous book in which he first fully develops the pentad—with a question: "What is involved when we say what people are doing and why they are doing it?"[20] This question is more complex than simply "What do people do and why?" Burke's question also asks us to consider what is involved "when we *say*" what people are doing and why. Thus, Burke is interested not only in what people do, but also in how we choose to describe their actions and attribute the reasons behind those actions. Analyzing the choices a speaker makes when explaining past actions or advocating future actions can help us identify his or her motives. By **motive**, Burke means the underlying worldview and philosophy of the speaker and the worldview the speaker wants us to adopt (in the following sections, we iden-tify a philosophy that corresponds with each part of the pentad).

Any given action might be explained in multiple ways (for example, a professor might condemn a student for cheating by saying the student did so because he or she is dishonest, or excuse the action by saying the student comes from a home that puts immense pressure on him or her to get high grades). Because of this, Burke recognizes that how a speaker chooses to explain another person's action reveals something about the speaker. Thus, the dramatistic pentad is not about finding the underlying and absolute truth of a situation. Rather it is a method of discovering multiple perspectives on why people do what they do. Which perspec-tive a person uses to explain an action helps us to better recognize the motive of the speaker. Burke encourages us to analyze language not for its truth but for its strategic uses. As Clarke Rountree puts it, dramatism is useful for "explaining what he, she or others, say about his, her or their own past present, and future actions or the past, present and future actions of others."[21] According to Burke, language is a mode of symbolic action, most often used as a means of presenting oneself to others. As we noted earlier, Burke does not say that our daily lives resemble a drama. He says life *is* a drama. Thus we perceive the world in dramatic terms with plots, antagonists, protagonists, settings, motives, and so on. We are hardwired for drama. No wonder our news coverage, no matter how chaotic and enigmatic the events being covered, is broken into news *stories* and put into dramatic form. It is our primary way of making sense of the world. Often the dramatic frame features a battle over meanings, perspectives, and values.

The five rhetorical elements of the dramatistic pentad are act, scene, agent, agency, and purpose. Burke praises them for their universal application to discourse. He says their "participation in common ground makes for transformability."[22] The pentad is made up of five parts that are universally found in all narratives. Each of these parts is phrased as a question. What happened? Who did it? Where and when and under what constraints? With what means and modes? Alleging what purpose? The goal of pentadic analysis is not to simply name each of the five parts but rather to identify the relationships between them. Exploring these questions allows the critic to determine which of the five parts dominates the others. This interpretation must be made by the critic, who will do so by answering the basic questions about an action described in the text. According to Burke, the answers to these questions will circumscribe the range and variety of reasonable interpretation.

Act

Act is the term for dramatic action. It answers the question, *what is* the action? What happened? What is being done? What is going on? It is associated with the philosophy of realism. Realists believe that the truthfulness of any belief rests upon the closeness of its correspondence with reality. Discourse that emphasizes the primacy of action has a deep hold on us. We admire devotees of action, and even when doing nothing would be a sensible course, or when there is little agreement about what to do, we still admire the leader who rushes headlong into an act. And we do so even when we suspect it may be a bad thing to do. We have a fear of too much reflection. We hold Hamlet in contempt because it takes him so long to act. But we love action heroes who act without hesitation or reflection. Long ago Edmund Burke noted that a big noisy destructive government policy was more admired than a wise quiet temperate policy. Too much reflection and analysis frightens people. We tend to associate thoughtful decision making with passivity, a state that fills red-blooded Americans with fear. (Burke's most succinct statement of act is found on pages 64–69 of his *Grammar of Motives*.)

Scene

Scene is the dramatistic term for the context of the act. Texts that emphasize the power of the surrounding environment or the coercive power of circumstances feature the philosophical doctrine of determinism. Many adventure stories that show people battling the elements or the power of nature emphasize scene. People who believe in situational ethics argue that circumstances are more important in determining our deeds than are our received moral codes. Those who argue that crime is a result of slum living and can be solved by clearing out such neighborhoods are making an argument that emphasizes scene. During the middle of the last century, some literary editors came to believe that the greatest American literature could only be written in the American South. Thomas Jefferson believed that only farmers tending local, independent farms could maintain sustainable agriculture. Persons have often attributed magical properties to place. Ancient people often believed that special places such as oracles, sacred groves, or aligned hilltops possessed special power. Others attribute power to labyrinths, caves, or even buildings with special atmospherics. Many early religions adopted the idea of a sacred center. In the inner sanctum, only the gods could dwell; in the second circle, high priests; and on the profane margins, the worshippers. In romantic novels, the outer scene seems sympathetic to the inner state of the characters. Duels are fought against the background of a storm, and lovers break up in the dead of winter. (Burke's richest definitions of scene can be found on pages 127–132 of his *Grammar of Motives*.)

Agent

Agent is the term for the person or persons who perform the actions. Not just who, but *what kind* of agent are they? Is the person performing the action a king or a servant, smart or foolish, lazy or ambitious? American folklore has honored people with strongly assertive personalities. We assume that strong leadership is vital for success in business and sports. Those who speak of the indispensable person are emphasizing the importance of the agent in human affairs. Much has been written about the charismatic leader who triumphs in spite of obstacles, setbacks, and enemies. Texts that emphasize the agent feature the philosophical viewpoint of idealism. Ronald Reagan was fond of talking about great American heroes. His celebrations of these people emphasized the power of an individual's inner resources against adverse circumstances. For Reagan the agent was always more powerful than the scene in which he or she was set. Character triumphed over circumstance. Sports analysts comparing LeBron James and Michael Jordan frequently argue for Jordan's superiority not because of his superior skills but because Jordan is a proven winner. (Burke's clearest description of the agent can be found on pages 171–175 of his *Grammar of Motives*.)

Agency

Agency is the dramatistic term for the means the agent uses to do the deed. It is the method, the technique, the apparatus, or the institution we use to get the thing done. Spokesmen for various technologies tend to emphasize a technological fix for all our problems. Bureaucrats tell us that the system is the solution. Arnold Schwarzenegger used to tell people that his method was the one that produced the best results. Those who emphasize agency as the dominant term in their messages tend to espouse a philosophy of pragmatism. Pragmatism is the philosophy that the most important aspect of any idea is its ability to produce good results. In other words, a good idea is one that is useful to the believer in the idea. We are bombarded with courses selling us special methods of building our bodies, transforming our personalities, or becoming immensely wealthy. Self-help books promise us seven strategies to save our marriages, three dynamic verbal techniques for successful negotiation, or a special technique to increase intelligence or expand memory. (Burke's most compelling explanation of agency can be found on pages 275–278 in his *Grammar of Motives*.)

Purpose

Purpose answers the question, why? Moralists often emphasize this question in their messages. Purpose has to do with the justification for the action. Its driving focus is on the value of objectives, goals, and courses of action. Those who strongly emphasize purpose tend toward a philosophy of mysticism. Messages emphasizing purpose feature ends rather than means. Purposive thinkers and writers often speak of acts as small parts of a much larger system. We must protect our family as a part of helping the community. Helping the community furthers the greatness of the nation. The greatness of the nation is necessary to advance civilization. There is a natural tendency for messages centered on purpose to move toward transcendence. Cicero advised Roman youth to study rhetoric in order to enter the Senate. In entering the Senate, they preserved the Republic. In preserving the Republic they carried the Roman message of order and prosperity to the newly conquered peoples of the empire. In embodying the Roman message, they served the gods who had clearly favored the spread of the Roman Way throughout the world. (Burke's most illuminating discussion of purpose occurs on pages 292–297 in his *Grammar of Motives*.)

The Ratios

Because each of these elements is interconnected in a dramatic structure of action, Burke calls them a *grammar of motives*. Thus, what is important is not simply locating and naming each of the five terms in the way a newspaper might answer, Who? What? Where? Why? and How? Rather, the pentad allows us to identify the relationships *between* each of these terms. In any one discourse, one of these elements usually dominates the others, and this ratio allows us to name or characterize the action. The predominance of one term over the others gives each drama a characteristic shape. It makes certain types of actions and reactions seem more sensible than others. Since a text or a speech represents a persuasive act, we will pair each term with act in our examples below: thus, scene-act, agent-act, agency-act, purpose-act, and even act-act. In theory one might use more than twenty ratios by simply pairing each term with every other term in sequence. This level of complexity is seldom necessary for actual critical practice, however.

Scene-Act Ratio

How does the place or the circumstances define the meaning of the act?

Example: In this bad economy, I was unable to find a job.
Example: Attending a good school will help children to succeed later in life.
Example: Given the distractions of Paris, it was hard to get much work done.
Example: A beautiful and revitalized downtown area will attract creative people to settle here from across the nation.

In each of the above examples, the scene dominates our understanding. The scene of an action may radically change how we understand that action. The same act (threatening someone with a weapon) might be read as unjust in one setting (at a bar) and justified in another (if your home is being broken into). The scene is also sometimes used to justify power. Leaders sometimes point to dangerous situations in order to justify expanding their powers. For example, supporters of the Patriot Act argued that surveillance of US citizens was justified in a post-9/11 world. Karl Marx believed that class conflict was a situation (scene) that would gradually ripen into revolution. During the military service of one of your authors, he was told again and again that available forces on the ground and the local terrain determine military tactics. We are often told that a failed plan might have worked in a different place. Soldiers are told that they must fight harder to defend their homeland and that fighting on native soil will bring a special zeal to their efforts.

Philosophical position: Texts that emphasize scene downplay free choice and emphasize situational determinism. They tend to emphasize the power of circumstances over individual decisions. Clarence Darrow excused the behavior of many criminals by arguing that they were victims of bad heredity and merciless environment. Supporters of social welfare programs point to bad schools and failing local economies as reasons that such programs are needed. Speakers who advise accommodating to circumstances emphasize the deterministic power of scene.

Agent-Act Ratio

How important is the nature of the actor in the execution of an act?

Example: Given her natural talent, it is no surprise Rihanna became the wealthiest female musician in the world.
Example: Only Albert Einstein could have made this discovery.
Example: Given how corrupt our politicians are, we should expect them to pass bad laws.
Example: From a proven winner like Arnold Schwarzenegger, you can expect miracles in whatever he tries to do.

An agent-act ratio comes into play whenever we connect character and behavior. This ratio is at work when we understand an action as being a result of the person who performed it. Opponents of social welfare programs (see the scene-act example) may argue that such programs reward people who are lazy and that individuals could overcome growing up in bad schools or a failing local economy if they put their minds to it. American historians often argue that George Washington was a humble homebody. These traits led him to decline becoming king or serving more than two terms as president, which set a precedent that transformed the US presidency. Persons who look for charismatic leaders to solve their problems tend to emphasize the agent over other terms.

Philosophical position: Texts or speeches that emphasize the agent reflect idealism. Idealism emphasizes ambitions, values, and meanings. It asserts that the characteristics of individuals shape their actions. Character is seen as far more important than the force of circumstances or the existence of resources or special techniques.

Agency-Act Ratio

What methods or tools enabled the performance of an act?

Example: Serena Williams's success is a result of her secret training methods.
Example: Only advances in technology can bring economic growth to this region.
Example: Peer-reviewed journals will produce more accurate information than other information sources.
Example: I could not submit my assignment on time because my internet was not working.

As Charles Kneupper observed, "Give a child a hammer and everything will be treated like a nail."[23] An agency-act ratio represents actions as a result of the available means/technologies.

When an act succeeds, it is a result of having adequate means to accomplish the goal. When an act fails, it is a sign that the available means are insufficient. Or as an Indy driver once said, "Victory is 80 percent car, 15 percent team, and 5 percent driver." For those who speak from an agency perspective, the system is always the solution.

Philosophical position: Texts or speeches that emphasize agency demonstrate pragmatism. Pragmatism is the doctrine that the best idea or solution is one that produces the best outcome. Methods are judged by their consequences. The best method is the one that allows us to get things done.

Purpose-Act Ratio

How does a larger goal influence the act?

Example: In order to end World War II, the United States chose to drop atomic bombs.
Example: If capitalism is to function successfully, it must allow people to fail.
Example: If you want to enter the bar, you have to show your ID.
Example: I may have made several mistakes, but I had the very best intentions.

One might describe this ratio in the following manner: in order to get X you have to do Y. Another version of the purpose-act ratio is the generic, "If you want to make an omelet, you have to break a few eggs." Television programs such as *24* and *Homeland* portray federal agents torturing captives for information. The shows portray torture as ethically questionable—but ultimately justified—because the larger goal is to prevent a terrorist attack. In a purpose-act ratio, the ends justify the means. The individual act is simply a necessary step toward the more important end. The danger to such an orientation is that temporary methods often sabotage one's goals. Although torture was portrayed on television as an effective means to prevent terrorism, images of detainees being tortured by Americans in Abu Ghraib prison were used as an effective recruiting tool by terrorist organizations and thus undermined efforts to stop terrorism.

Philosophical position: Since purpose is merely another name for the goal of an act, speeches or texts that emphasize purpose suggest the concerns of mysticism. Such texts tend to move toward the transcendent. Decisions are always seen in terms of a larger program or more important goal. In some examples of this kind of rhetoric, means are entirely subordinated to ends. One might be urged to break local laws for the sake of a higher or divine law. In the American civil rights movement, Martin Luther King Jr. reminded followers that they must act in accordance with God's will—even if that meant acting in ways that would lead them to be arrested. Understood from a purpose-act ratio, such actions were justified because their broader purpose warranted breaking unjust laws.

Act-Act Ratio

Was the action a response to a previous action?

Example: My roommate made dinner, so I washed the dishes.
Example: He made a large donation to her campaign; she will repay him once she is elected.
Example: I hit him because he hit me first.
Example: The governor passed a controversial law, so a group of citizens tried to recall him.

In an act-act ratio, an action is simply explained as a response to a preceding action. An act-act ratio might serve as justification for a series of actions: in response to the British parliament passing the Tea Act, protesters in Boston boarded a British ship and threw all of the tea into the Boston Harbor. In response to the Boston Tea Party, the British parliament passed what were known in the colonies as the Intolerable Acts; in response to the Intolerable Acts, the colonies organized the Continental Congress. Such justifications are common in political situations as well as in everyday life. Perhaps the most striking example of a policy dominated by an act-act ratio was the Cold War's doctrine of mutually assured destruction (MAD): neither the United States nor the Soviet Union wanted to use a nuclear weapon because they knew the other side would respond by using their own nuclear weapons.

Philosophical position: Texts that emphasize act suggest realism. Realism is a philosophy that says that it does not really matter what people *are*. What is important is what they *do*. From this position, broad terms such as "the People" or "the national character" or "the common good" are seen as silly abstractions. From this perspective, there is no such thing as "the public" pursuing the "common good." Instead, presidents or political parties are just empty agents who act on behalf of one interest group or another. Behavior is what counts, and most rhetoric is seen as a mask or a justification for self-interested action.

We could elaborate on more ratios. Any of the terms of the pentad might be seen as dominating the others. For example, how did the situation influence the means we chose (scene-agency)? How did who we are affect our goals (agent-purpose)? But the five above are enough to illustrate the twofold power of the pentad.[24] Suffice it to say that the pentad can provide a lively sense of the limits of any single perspective and the necessity of viewing messages from several points of view. In looking at the feasibility and effectiveness of any public proposal, exploring the pentadic ratios allow us to critique it from a multiplicity of views. For instance, does an agent appear to understand the scene in which he or she operates? Are the agencies or methods selected by the agent appropriate to the scene? Is the agent capable of dealing with the situation? Does he or she have the character, expertise, and support? Is the purpose used in order to justify acts that seem to undermine it in an Orwellian fashion, such as militarizing the state to achieve order, or using censorship to prevent the spread of subversive ideas?

CRITICAL ESSAYS

Given the nuanced complexities offered by the pentad, instead of offering a single essay for you to read to grasp the ways in which such criticism can be applied, we offer instead several examples of this particular perspective, followed by a brief discussion of things to consider when grappling with motives and competing frames, as well as identifying dominant terms.

EXAMPLE 1: PURPOSE AND AGENCY IN OBAMA'S SECOND INAUGURAL ADDRESS

When giving his second inaugural address in 2012, President Barack Obama faced a distinct challenge since his second term began with a Republican-controlled House, many of whose members had run on promises to oppose or limit most government action. As such, Obama's second inaugural responded to public arguments over how much (or little) the federal government should do. Obama opens his address by quoting the Declaration of Independence:

What makes us exceptional—what makes us American—is our allegiance to an idea articulated in a declaration made more than two centuries ago: "We hold these truths to be self-evident, that all men are created equal; that they are endowed by their Creator with certain unalienable rights; that among these are life, liberty, and the pursuit of happiness."

Today we continue a never-ending journey to bridge the meaning of those words with the realities of our time. For history tells us that while these truths may be self-evident, they've never been self-executing; that while freedom is a gift from God, it must be secured by His people here on Earth. The patriots of 1776 did not fight to replace the tyranny of a king with the privileges of a few or the rule of a mob. They gave to us a republic, a government of, and by, and for the people, entrusting each generation to keep safe our founding creed.[25]

A critic using the tools of dramatism will quickly notice a few important things about Obama's message: First, Obama seeks to create identification by articulating commonality around "what makes us American." Second, notice how Obama makes purpose the dominant pentadic term. In the first paragraph, what makes us American (agent) is our allegiance to a common creed (purpose). In the second paragraph, Obama states that when "entrusting each generation to keep safe our founding creed" (purpose), the founders of the nation "gave to us a republic, a government of, and by, and for the people" (agency). In other words, Obama portrays a world in which our common purpose is what makes us American and government is the agency by which the creed may be protected. He then claims that, "fidelity to our founding principles requires new responses to new challenges; that preserving our individual freedoms ultimately requires collective action." Again, fulfilling of purpose requires not just action but collective action—the sort of action made possible through the agency of government. Many media pundits saw Obama's second inaugural address as a somewhat generic encomium to America. A quick application of the pentad reveals how Obama sought to undermine his political opponents by unifying Americans behind a common purpose that would justify governmental action.

EXAMPLE 2: STRESSING THE AGENT

Republicans frequently emphasize the role of the agent in discussing political issues. This is particularly true of Donald Trump, whose 2016 presidential campaign focused extensively on trying to convince voters that he was a unique agent capable of accomplishing things other candidates could not. Early in his campaign, he sought to distinguish himself from his primary competitors; in his second campaign advertisement, he claimed, "politicians are all talk, no action. . . . My opponents have no experience in creating jobs or making deals. The fact is, I'm going to make the greatest trade deals we've ever made in our country."[26] Trump often describes himself as the most knowledgeable person on any given topic, famously making claims such as "I know more about ISIS than the generals do," "I think nobody knows more about taxes than I do, maybe in the history of the world," and "nobody knows more about technology than me." This approach reached its peak in his nomination acceptance speech at the 2016 Republican National Convention, in which Trump stated "Nobody knows the system better than me, which is why I alone can fix it."[27]

Political pundits were quick to treat such statements as arrogance or bombast. Dramatism, however, can help a savvy rhetorical critic look deeper to recognize an underlying rhetorical strategy at work. Throughout the 2016 campaign Trump also frequently offered a vision of the scene of the election and country that portrayed it as particularly unjust for Republicans. In his articulation of scene, news media were going to treat Republicans unfairly, and government bureaucrats were going to "rig the system" to make it difficult to accomplish anything. This description of scene works in two ways: First, it creates identification by echoing beliefs about media-bias that are likely to resonate with Republicans and many Independents. By describing the world in ways that align with the preexisting beliefs of his target audience,

Trump shows them that he sees things the way they do, and thus begins creating identification. Second, he describes a situation so challenging that any regular politician would fail. This description of scene sets up Trump's repeated emphasis on how he is a unique agent. A pentadic analysis helps us to see Trump's statements about himself not merely as bombast but as part of a broader rhetorical strategy of positioning himself as an agent whose unusual background in business/media and lack of political experience were actually strengths that would allow him to navigate the scene and succeed where other candidates would fail.

EXAMPLE 3: AGRARIAN CONCERNS

The Slow Food Movement, the Farmers' Market Movement, and the Neo-Agrarians are all social movements touting the need for sustainable agriculture and an organically produced food supply. Their rhetoric has a heavy scenic component. Like Thomas Jefferson and Wendell Berry, they argue that we must encourage local small individual farmers over corporate agriculture.[28] They argue that individual owners act responsibly while corporate farms overproduce, exhaust the soil, cut down tree breaks and let the precious topsoil blow away. While they destroy rural communities by displacing individual owners, they are also quick to abandon the countryside once they have exhausted the soil and the water supply. These people use many scenic words such as community, local, American earth, husbandry, organic, and home place. Like Wes Jackson they speak of the magic of "becoming native to the place" in their quest for a responsible and sustainable agriculture.[29] These repetitive patterns of good words Burke called "clusters" and therefore we should expect to find some opposite words, bad words that he called "agons." In the rhetoric of the Neo-Agrarian we find that opponents have a different group of scenic terms routinely applied to them: inorganic, rootless, unsustainable, wasteful, global, etc.

This strategic emphasis on scene has great strengths. Environmental movements have encouraged us to be more familiar and mindful of our natural surroundings. They emphasize the ways in which our environments have tremendous effects on our individual and social well-being. On the other hand, an extreme form of this emphasis might degenerate into determinism. We might be told that the scene has already determined the results and we are helpless to try to change an outcome. Opponents of scenic rhetoric might argue that in its strongest forms it reflects a philosophy of naïve materialism and determinism.

MOTIVES AND COMPETING FRAMES

Burke taught us that motives are not fixed things but "a term of interpretation, and being such it will naturally take its place within the framework of our Weltanschauung as a whole."[30] According to Burke, "motives" are the names we give to our actions. We may use a weighted vocabulary to talk about our building of a suburban development as our contribution to the American Dream of owning one's own home, or we may call it a great opportunity for personal profit. In each case our discourse would reflect a purpose-act ratio. One can envisage a developer using both vocabularies of motive to different audiences on different occasions.

The important point here is that our orientation determines how we characterize events and therefore our motives toward events. Charles Kneupper notes how rival orientations can be at war in our discourse:

For example, if two persons were to observe the actual event in which lumberjacks cut down trees in a forest and one describes the event as "progress" while the other describes it as "the destruction of natural resources," then significant differences of orientation and motives are implied. Both descriptions are strategic interpretations of reality. As Burke notes, "strategies size up situations, name their structure and outstanding ingredients and name them in a way that contains our attitude toward them." The "progress" observer has a favorable/supportive attitude toward the cutting witnessed. . . . [T]he "destruction of natural resources" observer has an unfavorable attitude.[31]

This example notes that people act in different ways toward the same events. And when we want to influence people's responses we will pick out certain factors that appeal to an audience and minimize or obscure factors that may not be received well. As Burke has noted, this is really a power play, a way to define or redefine a particular event. Whoever is able to define the event wins the day in most situations.

Much is at stake in rival dramatic schemes. Many people routinely define the world through the frame of stories. Two of the most common story types we use are tragedy and comedy. Burke tells us tragedy often ends in victimage, death, sacrifice, and grief. Others view events through a comic frame. In a comedy, there is always room for another alternative or point of view, as we recognize that each perspective is limited. Burke wrote of a comic worldview that

the progress of humane enlightenment can go no further than in picturing people not as vicious, but as mistaken. When you add that people are necessarily mistaken, that all people are exposed to situations in which they must act as fools, that every insight contains its own special kind of blindness, you complete the comic circle, returning again to the lesson of humility that underlies great tragedy.[32]

Such an orientation asks us to remember that we could always be the ones who are mistaken, and that—even if we are right and our opponents wrong—being mistaken is an inevitable part of the human condition. Burke was an enemy of polarization. He often noted that polarized alternatives generally ended badly, often in violence and death. Pentadic criticism was his way of breaking the gridlock. The pentad suggests a variety of perspectives, standing places, and attitudes. It is generative, heuristic, creative, and frame breaking. It can help us to see the limitations of our own perspectives, enable us to better understand the perspectives of others, and equip us to more skillfully analyze the messages we encounter in the world.

FINDING THE DOMINANT TERM, GRAPPLING WITH THE TEXT

When analyzing messages, how does one search and find the most important pentadic term? This is done during a close reading of the text. Like an accountant doing an audit, one looks for patterns. Patterns are determined by frequency of repetition. To discover the pattern is to locate the speaker's perspective. Which words are repeated more than others? How do they help explain other aspects of the text? Some texts are heavy on description or scene; others seem to focus more on the methods (agency) by which things are done, and some concentrate on the character of the person or people in the text. Yet others may deal with the justification of the actions described in the text (purpose). David Ling studied Senator Ted Kennedy's Chappaquiddick speech and discovered that most of the words used by Kennedy to characterize his actions related to the scene. Describing the car accident in which Mary Jo Kopechne died, Kennedy blamed the lack of lighting, the narrowness of the bridge, and the darkness of the road without guardrails. He noted that the car filled with water rapidly and that he was disoriented by the murky water, the cold, and the suddenness of events. In other words, the accident was produced by the scene, and Ted Kennedy and Mary Jo Kopechne were both victims of the situation; they were overpowered by circumstances.[33] And when circumstances (scene) produce an accident, it really is nobody's fault. Listeners who expect a leader to be conspicuously active might forgive one who is a victim of circumstances, but they may be disappointed with a leader who was unable to triumph over a bad situation. In Reagan's famous *Challenger* disaster speech in which he memorialized the astronauts killed when the ship exploded, he characterized them as pioneers who had sacrificed themselves so that the world might move forward to the conquest of space. All of his imagery favored the character of the agents, rather than the agency (technology) or the scene (outer space).[34] The speeches of bureaucrats typically emphasize agency (procedures) over the other pentadic terms. An audience of reformers who are enamored of purpose (moral objectives) might find this kind of speech extremely boring. An audience of bureaucrats, however, might find speeches emphasizing procedure and ritual deeply satisfying, if not inspiring.

Ultimately, texts (the speeches, the stories, the descriptions of things) represent what Burke called "multiple versions of reality." We see things in different ways, and these different ways are reflected in our choice of words. Audiences and readers respond to these different ways of seeing, these different perspectives, and they may embrace or reject them. They may find these perspectives good or bad, useful or useless, beautiful or ugly, noble or despicable. Making the perspective visible through the application of the pentad to the text allows us to see why the discourse affects us in a particular way and provides insights into how others see the world. It also helps us to evaluate a text in terms of its power to move an audience and to talk intelligently and at length about that power.

PERSONAL REFLECTIONS

In short, perspective matters. Burke notes that a patient might report a dream to a Freudian analyst or a Jungian or an Adlerian, or to a practitioner of some other school. In each case the "same dream will be subjected to a different color filter, with corresponding differences, in the nature of the event as perceived, recorded and interpreted."[35] Burke's point is that we can identify competing perspectives in a critical self-conscious way and come to some understanding of both their power and their limits. By imagining the same matter from perspectives other than our own, we can come to a more rounded and objective understanding of matters. In short, gaining perspective is at the heart of the pentadic critical method. Perspective shows that provisional truth lies on several sides, but that some perspectives have serious limitations.

The Roman Emperor Marcus Aurelius used a similar method to make important decisions. Withdrawing temporarily from the scene of action, he would visualize the execution and outcome of several possible courses of action. Comparing these outcomes gave him a sense of distance and humility and made him consider the larger community and the long-term consequences of history. He believed that by using this method he became wiser, kinder, and more humane.

In a similar way, dramatistic analysis produces a confrontation of several perspectives, or what Burke often referred to as a perspective of perspectives.[36] While we remain living human beings, we can never transcend the limits of our bodies or our language. We can never get outside or above a message and examine its truth or falsity, its goodness or badness, in a godlike way, or after the manner of a disembodied sage. However, the pentadic method offers us the ability to at least consider a message from multiple angles. By identifying the perspective of a piece of discourse and then looking at it from several other perspectives, we can go far in discovering whether it is wise or foolish, moderate or extreme, helpful or destructive, self-interested or altruistic. In a world in which we are constantly assaulted by calls to action from media mountebanks and political demagogues, this can help us to live more sanely, humanely, and wisely.

POTENTIALS AND PITFALLS

Clarke Rountree and others have cautioned critics against the temptation to use the pentad as a cookie cutter by unimaginatively applying the elements of the pentad to a text.[37] One of the weaknesses of Burke's method is that it could be used almost mindlessly. That is, if applied to any speech, story, or even joke, its categories will yield results. As critics we need to remind ourselves that Burke's goal was to bring deeper understanding, to shake us out of our usual ways of looking at things, and to shake us up by giving us a set of fresh categories. Burke spent much of his life as an outsider, an attacker of established formulas. Thus it would be ironic to treat his pentad as a static, orthodox, tried-and-true method. Despite the formulaic nature of his five-pointed system, one needs to understand that the parts of the pentad are simply tools for analysis, aids to understanding the power and appeal of messages. For Burke, the point of the pentad was not simply to stop after identifying the parts of the pentad, or even after determining pentadic ratios. Instead, Burke hoped the tools of dramatism might help us to consider messages from multiple angles, recognize our own biases, and develop a more complete, complex, and humane perspective.

Despite its seemingly tidy structure, the pentad is a heuristic device that offers critics the ability to recognize—and analyze—change. Also, the same situation might be understood differently from different perspectives. Scenes, for example, can shrink or grow. In his famous speech on the Grenada invasion, President Reagan began talking about the difficulties on the island as an immediate threat to the safety of Americans, but he gradually expanded the scene to include meddling by Cuba and finally a larger plot by the Soviet Union. Burke himself spoke of the plasticity of terms; technology, formerly classified as agency in our culture, had (in his judgment) become an agent, a self-sustaining interest group with an agenda of accelerated technological change.[38] A leader like Castro may be presented as a forceful agent in his youth but as an icon (scene) in his dotage. Ultimately, though the assigning of ratios is an imaginative exercise, not a stodgy formula.

BURKEAN TOP PICKS

Bello, Richard. "A Burkean Analysis of the 'Political Correctness' in Confrontation in Higher Education." *Southern Communication Journal* 61 (1996): 243–252. One of the very best studies of how political correctness went from a god term to a devil term for many embattled academics.

Blankenship, Jane, Marlene G. Fine, and Leslie K. Davis, "The Republican Primary Debates: The Transformation of Actor to Scene." *Quarterly Journal of Speech* 69 (1983):

25–36. A very imaginative treatment of the pentad and how one term can merge with another is seen in this essay.

Brummett, Barry. "A Pentadic Analysis of Ideologies in Two Gay Rights Controversies." *Central States Speech Journal* 30 (1979): 250–261. Burke treats ideology as a vocabulary that justifies the possession of power. Brummett performs a brilliant analysis of rival claims to power in this essay.

Burke, Kenneth. "Dramatism." In *Drama in Life: The Uses of Communication in Society*, edited by James E. Combs and Michael Mansfield, 7–17. New York: Hastings House, 1976. Burke himself has written a street-level, worm's-eye view of dramatism that provides a concrete set of examples. His exposition will satisfy the advanced critic as well as the neophyte.

Burke, Kenneth. "The Rhetoric of Hitler's Battle." In *The Philosophy of Literary Form*, 191–222. Baton Rouge: Louisiana State University Press, 1941. In 1938, Burke wrote a prophetic analysis of Hitler's *Mein Kampf.* This is perhaps the most lucid and penetrating article Burke ever produced.

Ling, David. "A Pentadic Analysis of Senator Edward Kennedy's Address to the People of Massachusetts." *Central States Journal* 21 (1970): 81–86. Presidential candidates are supposed to appear as active agents for us, but Ted Kennedy presented himself as a tragic victim. Ling shows that Kennedy's pentadic choice was a fateful one.

Rountree, Clarke J., III. "Charles Haddon Spurgeon's Calvinistic Rhetoric of Election: Constituting an Elect." *Journal of Communication and Religion* 17 (1994): 33–48. There is much misunderstanding of the idea of predestination in intellectual circles. Rountree uses Burke's ideas about hierarchy and the pentad to explore the confusion over some of the most basic religious concepts in Western civilization.

One of the very best sources for practical applications of Burke's basic critical vocabulary can be found in the *Encyclopedia of Rhetoric and Composition*, edited by Theresa Enos (New York: Routledge, 1996). See Tilly Warnock, "Kenneth Burke," 90–92; Bill Bridges, "Terministic Screens," 722–723, and "Pentad," 499–501; James W. Chesebro, "Dramatism," 200–201; Pat Youngdahl and Tilly Warnock, "Identification," 337–340; and H. L. Ewbank, "Symbolic Action," 710–711.

DISCUSSION QUESTIONS

1. Imagine you have graduated and are in your chosen career. You are asked to give a presentation to a group of clients or coworkers. How might you try to create identification with your audience? How could you use that to help you be more effective in persuading that audience?

2. The two most common ways of explaining an act are through agent-act and scene-act ratios—in other words, saying a person did something because a) they are the kind of person who would do that thing, or b) the situation led them to act in that way. Think about how you explain the actions of others. Do you tend to use agent or scene explanations more? Why? Imagine a coworker fails to show up to work. If that coworker is your friend, how would you explain his or her action? If that coworker is someone you do not know, would you explain it differently? How might those different explanations change how you respond to the same action?

3. Think of a group of people with whom you share a sense of identification. How does that identification shape your interactions with other members of the group? With someone who is not a member of that group?

ACTIVITIES

1. Burke describes "form" as a pattern that creates expectations and then satisfies them. One of the reasons TED Talks have been so successful is that, regardless of topic, they typically follow the same general form. Find and watch three to four TED Talks, and try to identify the elements of the form. How do the introductions work? How do the presenters describe their relationship to the ideas? How do they discuss complex data? How do they use visual aids? How do they conclude?

2. Select a story from a news website and perform a brief pentadic analysis. Begin by identifying each of the elements (act, agent, scene, agency, purpose). Then identify the ratios to see which seems to be the dominant term in that telling of the story. Now try to retell the story in a way that makes a different term dominant. How does that change the story?

3. Locate an advertisement or series of advertisements for a product you own. Look at the language in the advertisements. What do these language choices draw your attention toward? What do they make you think of? What do they draw your attention away from? Consider the images in the advertisements. How have they chosen to represent the product visually? What parts are not being shown? What might a more honest advertisement look like?

NOTES

1. Kenneth Burke, "The Rhetoric of Hitler's Battle," in *The Philosophy of Literary Form* (Berkeley: University of California Press, 1971), 191–220.

2. For an excellent analysis of the origins of dramatism and Burke's focus on words, see M. Elizabeth Weiser, *Burke, War, Words* (Columbia: University of South Carolina Press, 2008).

3. Kenneth Burke, *Language as Symbolic Action* (Berkeley: University of California Press, 1966), 45.

4. Celeste Condit, *Decoding Abortion Rhetoric* (Champaign: University of Illinois, 1994).

5. Burke's clearest explanation of terministic screens can be found in *Language as Symbolic Action*, 44–55.

6. Kenneth Burke, *A Rhetoric of Motives* (New York: Prentice Hall, 1950).

7. Burke's best explanation of identification occurs in *A Rhetoric of Motives*, 19–46.

8. Burke, *A Rhetoric of Motives*, 22.

9. Kenneth Burke, *A Grammar of Motives* (New York: Prentice Hall, 1945).

10. For a full discussion of Nichols's contributions, see John H. Patton, "Marie Hochmuth Nichols's Voice of Rationality in the Humane Tradition of Rhetoric and Criticism," in *Twentieth Century Roots of Rhetorical Studies*, ed. Jim A. Kuypers and Andrew King (Westport, CT: Praeger, 2001), 123–142.

11. Marie Hochmuth, "Kenneth Burke and the 'New Rhetoric,'" *Quarterly Journal of Speech* 38 (1952): 133–144. See also Marie Hochmuth, "Burkean Criticism," *Western Speech* 21 (1957): 89–95.

12. For the clearest statement of Burke's foundational theory of dramatism, see Kenneth Burke, "Dramatism," in *International Encyclopedia of the Social Sciences*, vol. 3, ed. David L. Sills (New York: Macmillan and the Free Press, 1968), 445–452.

13. Aristotle's belief in the centrality of the polis to civilized conduct and culture is well known. For a brilliant discussion of the Aristotelian relationship between narrative culture and community, see Gabriel Lear, *Happy Lives and the Highest Good: An Essay on Aristotle's Nichomachean Ethics* (Princeton, NJ: Princeton University Press, 2004).

14. Burke, *A Grammar of Motives*, xv.

15. See Helena Detmer, *Horace: A Study in Structure* (New York: Olms-Weidmann, 1983); and also R. K. Hack, "The Doctrine of Literary Forms," *Harvard Studies in Classical Philology* 27 (1916): 1–65.

16. On this subject, I. A. Richards wrote three deeply influential books: *The Meaning of Meaning: A Study of the Influence of Language upon Thought and the Science of Symbolism*, with C. K. Ogden (1923), *Principles of Literary Criticism* (1924), and *Practical Criticism* (1929). His studies in psychology and semantics laid the foundation for the close readings of texts that dominated literary criticism for decades after.

17. Burke discusses the power of form in many places. See, for instance, the sections on "Formal Appeal" and "Rhetorical Form in the Large" in *A Rhetoric of Motives*. Also see "Literature as Equipment for Living" in *The Philosophy of Literary Form*, 2nd ed. (Baton Rouge: Louisiana State University Press), 293–313.

18. For a full discussion of Burke's association with literary figures and his editorship of *The Dial*, see Jack Selzer, *Kenneth Burke in Greenwich Village: 1915–1931* (Madison: University of Wisconsin Press, 1996); and Jack Selzer and Anne George, *Kenneth Burke in the 1930s* (Columbia: University of South Carolina Press, 2007).

19. In 1937 Burke speculated about the future importance of "one little fellow named Ecology." For a full statement of Burke's long association with the movement, see "Kenneth Burke on Ecology," in *A Synthesis: Extensions of the Burkean System*, ed. James Chesebro (Tuscaloosa: University of Alabama Press, 1993), 251–268.

20. Burke, *Grammar of Motives*, xv.

21. Clarke J. Rountree III, "Coming to Terms with Kenneth Burke's Pentad," *American Communication Journal* 1, no. 3 (May 1998), accessed July 27, 2015, http://ac-journal.org/journal/vol1/iss3/burke/rountree.html.

22. Burke, *Grammar of Motives*, xix.

23. Charles Kneupper, "Dramatistic Invention: The Pentad as Heuristic Procedure," *Rhetoric Quarterly* (Spring 1977): 129–135.

24. Sonja Foss presents many rich examples of pentadic criticism in the chapter 11 of her *Rhetorical Criticism: Exploration and Practice*, 5th ed. (Long Grove, IL: Waveland Press, 2018).

25. Barack Obama, "Inaugural Address by President Barack Obama," found at https://www.whitehouse.gov/the-press-office/2013/01/21/inaugural-address-president-barack-obama.

26. Nick Gass, "Trump in New Ad: 'Politicians Are All Talk, No Action'," *Politico*, November 5, 2015, https://www.politico.com/story/2015/11/donald-trump-new-ads-215546.

27. Donald J. Trump. "Full Text: Donald Trump 2016 RNC Draft Speech Transcript," Convention speech, Republican National Convention, Cleveland, OH, July 21, 2016. *Politico*, https://www.politico.com/story/2016/07/full-transcript-donald-trump-nomination-acceptance-speech-at-rnc-225974. For a dramatistical analysis of this speech see: Jim A. Kuypers, "The Presidential Nomination Acceptance Speeches of Donald Trump and Hillary Clinton: Terministic Screens and Antagonistic Worldviews," in *Political Campaign Communication: Theory, Method and Practice*, ed. Robert E. Denton Jr. (Lanham, MD: Lexington Books, 2017), 141–168.

28. Berry has authored one of the most enduring books in American eco-criticism. See Wendell Berry, *The Unsettling of America* (San Francisco: Sierra Club Books, 1977). For a sense of Burke's contributions to ecology, see Tarla Rai Peterson, "The Will to Conservation: A Burkean Analysis of Dust Bowl Rhetoric and American Farming Motives," *Southern Communication Journal* 52 (1986): 1–21.

29. Wes Jackson, *Becoming Native to This Place* (Lexington: University of Kentucky Press, 1994).

30. Burke, *Grammar of Motives*, 130.

31. Kneupper, "Dramatistic Invention," 131.

32. Kenneth Burke, *Attitudes Toward History* (New York: New Republic, 1937), 51–52.

33. All materials quoted from David A. Ling, "A Pentadic Analysis of Senator Edward Kennedy's Address to the People of Massachusetts, July 25, 1969," *Central States Journal* 21 (1970): 84.

34. Ronald Reagan, "Address to the American People on the Challenger Disaster," found at www .AmericanRhetoric.com.

35. Burke, *Language as Symbolic Action*, 45.

36. This is Burke's ultimate vantage point. It has roots in the ancient practice of rhetorical exercises that one reads about in Seneca, Marcus Aurelius, and in the spiritual exercises of Pierre Hadot. In preparing to argue a position or make an important decision, the ancients were wont to visualize the matter from several different points of view (from the victim's point of view, from that of the accused, from the vantage of the judge, from that of the victim's family, the accuser's family, the verdict of history, etc.).

37. Rountree, "Coming to Terms."

38. Personal conversation with Kenneth Burke at New Harmony, Indiana Convention, July 10, 1990.

11

Feminist Analysis

Donna Marie Nudd and Kristina Schriver Whalen

WHY FEMINISM?

Susan Faludi once said, "all women are born feminists, but most get it knocked out of them."[1] After the 2016 presidential election spurred Women's Marches and #MeToo hashtags, one might conclude that women reclaimed their birthright. However, the common phenomenon of women declaring a belief in equality but voicing little connection with the term feminism shows more signs of constant fluctuation than consistent gain. For example, an in-depth poll after the 2012 presidential election found that 55 percent of women voters and even 30 percent of men voters consider themselves feminists—a nine-point increase from the last poll conducted in 2008.[2] However, a more recent and general poll, not limited to voters, found that only about a third of women found affinity and identification with feminism. If those polled were young, the number grew to 39 percent, and if the women held a bachelor's degree or higher, the number reached 48 percent.[3] While attempting to understand these fluctuations, National Geographic/Ipsos wrote, "Part of the problem might be that the word feminism has different connotations for different people." They add, "For some American women, it means believing in equal rights for women, regardless of their gender. For others, it might mean privileging women over men. In other words, American women not identifying as feminists is perhaps more indicative of a lack of common agreement or understanding about what the word means, and less of a referendum on their thoughts on discrimination protections for women."[4]

Trying to reach a common definition of feminism, or even describing feminism, remains a daunting and complex task, with theories guiding feminism as diverse as women themselves. With so many veins of thought and varying perspectives, communication scholars Cheris Kramarae and Paula Treichler noted that at its core feminism is, "the radical notion that women are people."[5] Although Kramarae and Treichler's definition does not capture the theoretical disagreements that exist in feminism, it does express the common spirit of most strands of feminism. *Feminism is a pluralistic movement interested in altering the political and social landscape so that all people, regardless of their identity categories, can experience freedom and safety, complexity and subjectivity, and economic and political parity—experiences associated with*

definition

177

being fully human.) It is this definition (or a close approximation) that a growing segment of the population is embracing.

Feminist advocates argue for the necessity and profitability of their activism and critical inquiry by evidencing the patriarchal systems most civilizations have been operating under for several thousand years and the way it limits human potential. Allan G. Johnson writes that three principles encompass the still-present patriarchal system: male domination, male identification, and male centeredness. According to Johnson, **male domination** refers to the simple fact that men have populated most positions of authority in major societies. Men head large corporations, nation-states, churches, colleges and universities, and most other positions of social and economic importance in numbers that far exceed women. Our production of knowledge, in which men are disproportionately the producers of YouTube videos and editors of Wikipedia, form the cultural landscape that reflects male experiences, tastes, and histories. The same is true in the business world. A recent comprehensive study about the world of work shifts the narrative away from the "glass ceiling" and instead focuses on the "broken rung," the first step into leadership that is disproportionately foreclosed to women.[7] A few women have temporarily taken seats of prestige and notable female leaders encourage women to "*lean in*" but it is clear, given how infrequently women succeed, that a patriarchal system prevents movement.[8] Once dominance is established, it's seemingly intractable. As Johnson explains "men can claim larger shares of income and wealth. It means they can shape culture in ways that reflect and serve men's collective interest by, for example, controlling the content of films and television shows, or handling rape and sexual harassment cases in ways that put the victim on trial rather than the defendant."[9]

Johnson believes that a critique of patriarchy is incomplete if it simply notes degrees of male domination. He argues that we must also note instances of **male identification**. Male identification locates our cultural values in maleness and masculinity. According to Johnson, in a male-identified society the activities of men underscore what is preferred, normal, and desirable. The qualities commonly associated with masculinity, such as competition, individualism, invulnerability, rationality, and physical strength, are honored. The qualities commonly associated with femininity, such as cooperation, nurturing, emotionality, and care, are undervalued or trivialized.[10]

Finally, Johnson advocates a focus on our society's **male centeredness**, meaning that our cultural attention is mainly focused on males: "Pick up any newspaper or go to any movie theater and you'll find stories primarily about men and what they've done or haven't done or what they have to say about either."[11] Along these lines, consider that it has become common to apply the *Bechdel-Wallace test* to films, but it is still surprising how many films do not pass its simple three prongs: that two women must be in the film, talk to one another, and talk about something other than their relationships with men.[12] Sporting activities too represent one of many culturally significant areas where men seek and receive acclaim. Large populations of men and women watch men's sporting events. Millions watch the Super Bowl, Monday Night football, the World Series, and the NBA Championship series.[13]

However important it is to point out the features of patriarchy, sexist oppression is not the only oppression of interest to feminism. Late twentieth-century feminism concerned itself with interlocking systems of oppression, noting that most systems of discrimination share common characteristics and must be seen together if liberation struggles are to gain ground. For these reasons, feminist scholars such as bell hooks (who chooses not to capitalize her name) reference the dominant framework as a **white supremacist capitalist patriarchy**.[14] This term underscores that we not only live in a sexist society but a society that discriminates based on economic circumstances and race. In the last decade a profitable discussion on "privilege" has taken root, sown by many feminist and race scholars and further fostered by the deeply personal interrogation of "white privilege" by scholar Tim Wise, whose tome *White Like Me: Reflections on Race from a Privileged Son* is taught in hundreds of colleges and even some high schools.[15] A thorough feminist critique will not fail to interrogate how all these systems of privilege work together to marginalize discrete groups of people and curry favor for others.

So, we will summarize by answering the question that heads this section: Why feminism? Most feminists believe that we live in a complex social structure guided by patriarchy. They believe this patriarchal system must change, and that criticism may be used as a tool to help foster change. Moreover, the understanding of patriarchy cannot be a simple calculation. Engaged human beings are likely to identify egregious cases of sexism; however, most feminists believe that much of the sexism of the patriarchal framework remains unchallenged. Feminists therefore are motivated to expose the fundamental ways, the often subtle, taken-for-granted ways, in which societal members undervalue and diminish women. That done, feminists propose new ideas, assumptions, and viewpoints allowing for humans to realize a wide range of possibilities and promise. In the next section, we will explore these differences and their relationship to rhetorical criticism.

AN INTRODUCTION TO FEMINIST RHETORICAL CRITICISM

Feminist thought has always been quite diverse in its theories and practices. One of the main theoretical differences among various feminists surrounds disagreements over gender differences. This disagreement is referred to in feminist writings as the "minimalist/maximalist debate."[16] A feminist *minimalist* believes that men and women are more alike than different; therefore, the policies and social organizations privileging men can easily adapt to women if they are just granted access. *Maximalists* believe that women and men are more different than alike. With that premise in mind, feminist maximalists argue that women will never achieve success and comfort in social institutions created by men for men, and thus our social and political landscape must be altered or transformed to accommodate the distinctions between men and women.

From this theoretical debate, many categories of feminism have emerged. Jill Dolan notes that we can generally see American feminism separated into liberal, cultural, and materialist segments.[17] **Liberal feminist** approaches locate the oppression of women in the systematic failure to include women in dominant structures and cultural production. A liberal feminist rhetorical critique would be interested in the exclusion of women from systems of representation. Are women given a voice in the political system? Can you find women in recent films you've seen, stories you've read? Did the stories showcase the women as competent, able to solve problems, lead others, and champion a cause? Liberal rhetorical feminist critics are diligently employing language strategies within the current structures to increase the stature and number of women in places of political and social power. Sheryl Sandberg's popular book *Lean In* is a feminist voice from the liberal feminist perspective. As one scholar noted, "Sandberg's definition of feminism begins and ends with the notion that it's all about gender equality within the existing social system."[18] She advocates for personal strategies (like carefully choosing a partner who co-parents equally) for more women to participate in corporate power positions but she does not argue for changes to those structures. Liberal feminists are typically minimalists.

Cultural feminists, on the other hand, are maximalists. They argue that women's nature, primarily shaped by the ability to give birth, is decidedly different from men's. "Because they can give birth, women are viewed as instinctually more natural, more closely related to life cycles mirrored in nature."[19] Cultural feminists argue that women have a unique and valuable perspective that is not adequately reflected in today's society. This deficit of perspective creates a world of domination and violence. Moreover, some cultural feminists have situated themselves within another subcategory of feminist thought, ecofeminism. Ecofeminists believe nature is culturally constructed as feminine and thus subjugated; however, if society actually adopted the nondominating feminine perspective, the likelihood of continuing ecological devastation would diminish. This is just one of many cultural feminist perspectives. A rhetorical critic adopting a cultural feminist perspective is likely to critique current rhetorical practices for their sexist domination as well as suggest ways in which a feminine perspective could rehabilitate the rhetorical situation. In the world of politics, the 2020 Democratic candidate for president, Amy Klobuchar, repeatedly called for a presidency that embraces empathy as a path to end divisiveness of American politics.[20] Does a given communication artifact convey the largely feminine characteristics of caring, nurturing, cooperation, and intuition? Does it glorify aggression, competition, and individualism to the exclusion of other perspectives? How do the messages around us "normalize" a distinctly masculine perspective? How could we infuse and balance our public discourse by including a feminine perspective? These are some of the many questions guiding the explorations of a rhetorical critic who is also a cultural feminist.

Finally, **materialist feminists** believe that symbol-using humans are historical subjects that are largely socially constructed, not biologically driven. A materialist feminist is interested in analyzing social conditions—such as the influence of ethnicity, sexual orientation, and class— that work together to define women and men as categories and seemingly erase the possibility of other categories being established, such as intersex and transgender. As such, this strand of feminism is also interested in unearthing the symbolic systems of gender that oppress all people, not just women. Materialist feminists may study the way masculinity has been constructed in such a way that men, too, have little freedom and dimension in society. So, while liberal feminists are primarily interested in social representation, materialist feminists reveal how people "have been oppressed by gender categories."[21] A materialist feminist might approach a rhetorical artifact by noting the ways in which it situates masculinity and femininity as stale categories, instead of giving the concept room for growth and movement. Do movies, or other culturally significant discourse, outfit men and women with retrograde notions of masculinity and femininity? How so? Can we point to messages around us that transform the somewhat rigid categories of gender in positive ways? These and similar questions would be of interest to the rhetorical critic with a materialist feminist perspective.

Positioning materialist feminism along the minimalist/maximalist continuum demands some attention. Since materialists stress the social construction of gender, they very rarely look for "real" differences and similarities. Instead, materialists question the constructed categories of gender and offer the concepts dimension and redefinition if it aids the attainment of freedom, safety, complexity, subjectivity, and equality—the goals of feminism.

Closely aligned with materialist feminism is the concept of **intersectionality**, a term that gained prominence from the writings of legal scholar Kimberlé Crenshaw. She notes, "Intersectionality is just a metaphor for understanding the ways that multiple forms of inequality or disadvantage sometimes compound themselves. And they create obstacles that are often not understood in conventional ways of thinking."[22] In her seminal legal work, she sought to explain how her client, an African American woman, was not discriminated against because she was a minoritized person, nor did she face discrimination for being female. She suffered injustice because she was both—a woman and an African American. Intersectional analysis is a welcome challenge to established feminist thought. For example, ecofeminism, discussed earlier, lacks an analysis on how race, ethnicity, and ableism complicate environmental harms; hence, it has never gained intellectual traction as originally argued. The environmental justice movement, on the other hand, offers a critique of climate and environmental policies steeped in an understanding of how race, class, and gender form a constellation by which environmental harms are visited on communities of color in very gender-specific ways. Intersectionality acts as a prism through which to approach the study of rhetoric. A feminist scholar applying this prism might note sexism and ask, "where is the racism in this?" Or, upon seeing racism, might ask, "how is the patriarchy also functioning here?"[23]

Although these categories and lenses represent large sects of feminist thought, other feminist strands not covered in this chapter apply a feminist lens to a Marxist perspective, psychoanalytical thought, and global issues; there are even feminists operating from libertarian and conservative political perspectives.[24] Feminists in different academic fields have established a literature base specific to their field of inquiry. Therefore, one is likely to see feminist legal studies, feminist international relations, and feminist medicine as well as feminist literary criticism. Women of color, who have traditionally had a complicated relationship with feminism, are interested in the way their ethnic and racial identities intersect with feminism. If one delves into the literature about feminism, one is likely to see discussions about Chicana feminism, Black feminism, Asian feminism, and Native American feminism to name a few.[25] When engaging in feminist rhetorical criticism, consideration should be given to how the critic positions an argument on the map of feminism so that those reading the criticism know the assumptions about gender infused in the analysis.

In this next section we first briefly outline the history of feminist criticism within the rhetorical tradition. Next, an explanation of the approaches feminist rhetorical critics utilize to analyze our symbolic systems will follow. Alongside these general explanations, numerous specific examples from feminist rhetorical critics are provided.

FEMINIST CRITICISM AND THE CHALLENGE TO RHETORIC

The rhetorical tradition tethers itself to a long history of oral argument and public oratory. This tradition also has an equally long history of excluding female rhetors or feminine ways of speaking.[26] Sometimes this was done either by making public address unavailable to women through systematic discrimination or by refusing to recognize the many women who did take the podium. Today, finding women at the podium is certainly more frequent but still meets disparity. For example, the wildly popular speaking venue, TED Talks, has seen an increase in the number of female speakers (up to a third), but not from women of color (80 percent of speakers are white).[27] Organizers have been unpacking the systematic ways men are privileged by the practices surrounding TED Talks as well as barriers to women accepting an invitation to the stage.[28] An interrogation of silenced or absent voices is one challenge feminist criticism has brought to the rhetorical tradition. Another challenge is an attempt to foreground how gender is operating or being sculpted in particular ways by language choices or the positioning of rhetorical artifacts in our social and political world. By highlighting the intended and unintended meanings created about gender, feminist rhetorical scholars invite critical thinking about our gendered assumptions. When Jean Kilbourne, in her acclaimed series *Killing Us*

Softly, looks at advertisements for the way women's bodies are positioned visually (passively), the way objects for sale are positioned in relation to women's bodies (sexually), and the way claims about "liberation" are used alongside these images (consumedly), she is using this approach. Moreover, feminists are also interested in discovering new symbolic strategies, or making visible little-known language systems, in an effort to dismantle current gender hierarchies. Another important part of feminist rhetorical criticism is suggesting that alternative, yet equally valid forms of producing symbolic meaning exist—historically this has taken form in letter writing or newspapers, or more recently podcasts or vlogs.[29] Although we do know that many women enlisted public address as a vehicle for their ideas, we also know that women's position in society relegated message making to other terrain. Feminist rhetorical criticism reclaims this forgotten rhetorical past. All of these concerns have meant that feminist rhetorical scholars have developed somewhat unique approaches to analyzing rhetorical artifacts.

Having been introduced broadly to some examples of ways feminist rhetorical criticism is attempting to alter the patriarchal past of the rhetorical tradition, the next section concretely outlines some of the more common methods of feminist criticism used by rhetorical scholars. It is not meant to be an exhaustive list, but you should be able to see that many of the approaches discussed in the following section were used in the examples of feminist rhetorical criticism described above.

APPROACHES TO USING FEMINIST CRITICISM

Feminist rhetorical scholars are important to feminism because they see patriarchy as being maintained by a symbolic system and language that defines gender in narrow and specific ways. Through our communication practices and language choices we have both a poverty and power when it comes to gender. The poverty comes when our language use sculpts masculinity and femininity in ways that are not complex, resulting in disparity and domination. Another poverty of thinking occurs when language and communication practices are used so that masculinity and femininity are seen as the only two gendered choices. Many feminists are interested in opening up our symbolic system so that many genders flourish and those wanting to express themselves outside our current binary gender codes of male and female feel the freedom to do so. Herein lays the power of language. By systematically analyzing our language choices and communication practices, one can in part effectively undermine the patriarchal logic of gender. This is the work of feminist rhetorical critics.

There are perhaps countless ways one could go about analyzing rhetorical artifacts for the meaning produced about gender. However, if one looks over the history of feminist rhetorical criticism, four prominent critical techniques emerge.[30]

1. Feminists are interested in *redefining* (or defining) gendered ideals and gendered behavior.
2. Feminist rhetorical scholars are *recovering* communication practices that have been forgotten or considered unimportant.
3. Feminist rhetorical criticism is interested in *recording* the cultural production of the rhetorical artifacts we consume so as to uncover the ways in which gender is created (as well as arguing that gender is created, not natural).
4. Feminist rhetorical theorists engage in a *revisioning* of rhetorical theory; they create new theories of rhetoric that champion feminist ideals.

Redefining (or Defining)

While attempting to redefine what it means to be a gendered human being, feminist rhetorical critics generally undertake one of several tasks. First, feminist rhetorical critics note the way language and other meaning-making activities contribute to stereotypical gendered ideals. Second, feminist critics reclaim words or communication practices used to straightjacket masculinity and femininity and infuse them with new meaning. Third, they try to create new communication strategies that will give nonpatriarchal dimension to people's lives or a language to effectively demystify patriarchy.

Feminist scholars have long held the premise that patriarchy is largely maintained by language—both symbolic and visual. Put differently, male domination, male identification, and male centeredness are stable ideas because the meanings created by our everyday speech acts—in films, media, social media, advertisements, and other artifacts of popular culture—function to keep them anchored. Thus, it is important to note the way in which all the things that convey meaning around us are often used to paint a biased picture of gender. The words we choose, the visuals we find appealing, and the monuments we create, etc., often unknowingly privilege a patriarchal perspective. As such, feminists are interested in making visible the current, and inadequate, rhetorical practices in our culture. Examples are plentiful. To wit, the existence of only two widely used pronouns is argued to be a language system creating a reality in which only two genders are recognized, referred to as the gender binary. In response, feminist and gender scholars have successfully advocated for circumventing grammar rules and allowing *they* to stand in for singular *he* or *she* in our language. Two major style manuals now accept its use. A third, the style manual of the Modern Language Association (MLA), has instead suggested use of sentence structures that avoid pronouns. The MLA aside, it is becoming increasingly common in higher education for people to include their preferred gender pronouns in an email signature line—for example, "pronouns: he/him/his"—thereby underscoring that gender is chosen and not ordained.

Moreover, the term **cisgender** has come into common use. The term is used to describe someone whose outward appearance conforms to societal expectations about their sexed body. The proliferation of its use steers thinking away from the naturalization of gender choices. In other words, before the word was adopted, cisgender people did not have to comment on their gender performance. It was deemed "natural." When everyone is compelled to comment on or mark their own gender performance, it is argued that this creates a "commonality among transgender and nontransgender people."[31] Just as use of the term *sexual harassment*—which did not exist until the second wave of feminism took root in the 1970s[32]—allows women to combat a too-frequent phenomenon, so too does "cisgender" provide a vehicle for marking different places on the gender continuum, without labeling one place as "natural" and another "deviant."

The second definitional technique used by feminists involves taking words that were once used to diminish femininity and reclaiming them for feminist purposes. Slut Walks and "slut shaming" are examples of potent rhetorical tools used by women (and male allies) to critique cultural narratives that suggest female sexuality is deviant. Ringrose and Renold note the goal of Slut Walks, which started in Toronto, "is to push the gaze off the dress and behavior of the victim of sexual violence back upon the perpetrator, questioning the normalization and legitimization of male sexual aggression."[33]

Many feminist critics have taken to writing their own dictionary definitions or altogether rewriting the dictionary.[34] While inventing new language is often considered "against the rules," many feminists argue the language rules are rigged and need to be reorganized and re-invigorated. In a meme-driven society, inventive feminist language is now transmitted quickly, almost in viral fashion. If a rhetor referred to *mansplaining* or *manspreading*, they would likely find an audience already familiar with these descriptive terms created to connote and encode specific gendered experiences and deride the way they diminish women.

Feminist rhetorical criticism utilizing redefinition (1) explains and names how language functions to regulate femininity and masculinity and/or (2) creates or reinvents language that expands the possibilities of gender or turns on its head language used to subdue liberation.

Recovering

Throughout this chapter, you will hear that women and feminine ways of speaking have been systematically excluded from the public realm for much of the rhetorical tradition. However, this exclusion was not complete. For periods of time, generally around social reform platforms such as suffrage and abolition, women produced rhetorical texts. However, in most compilations of public speeches, women account for a small percentage of speakers. Although the historical exclusion of female rhetors is partly responsible for the disparity, it does not always explain their absence. Regardless of the dearth, the notable absence of women "confirms that men continue to serve as standard for communication performance and that women are peripheral in terms of significant discourse."[35]

Karlyn Kohrs Campbell's anthology *Man Cannot Speak for Her* uses the approach of recovering rhetors lost in a male-centered society. Also, Kohrs Campbell's work recovers the rhetorical options surreptitiously proposed by women facing enormous prohibitions. Despite being discouraged from taking the podium, women such as Christine de Pizan, a fourteenth-century French feminist, wrote books for women that clearly serve as rhetorical theory. Christine de Pizan's books, *The Book of the City of Ladies* and *The Treasure of the City of Ladies*, provide discursive theory that differs from the dominant traditions of time, but is no less valuable.

Not all feminist recovering involves archival investigations of classical texts. In contemporary artifacts, our patriarchal society often pushes women to the margins but feminist rhetors foreground their worth. Amy Poehler and Meredith Walker's Smart Girls social media campaign, in which girls are invited to "change the world by being yourself," could be understood as a critical act of recovery. Although Smart Girls began as a Web series in 2007, it now reaches millions of followers across social media by "giving a platform to real women tackling important issues like the 'smart girls' they are."[36] Similarly, the project *Overlooked* by the *New York Times* recognizes that "Since 1851, obituaries in the New York Times have been dominated by white men. Now, we are adding the stories of other remarkable people."[37] They add, "Charlotte Bronte wrote 'Jane Eyre'; Emily Warren Roebling oversaw the construction of the Brooklyn Bridge when her husband fell ill; Madhubala transfixed Bollywood; Ida B. Wells campaigned against lynching. Yet all their deaths went unremarked in our pages until now." Feminist rhetorical critics approaching a rhetorical artifact by recovering are (1) acknowledging rhetors that patriarchy has erased and/or (2) recovering the lost or never seen significance of a visible female rhetor.

Recording

Another analytical approach used by feminists is to record cultural production. This means that the techniques used to create an artifact are scrutinized. An important part of this approach is the understanding that an artifact does not stand apart from the processes that make it. By analyzing these *systems of production*, one can understand quite thoroughly how messages about gender are created and sometimes understand why a message is packaged a particular way. As Douglas Kellner notes, such an approach "can help elucidate features and effects of texts that textual analysis alone might miss or downplay."[38] In sum, this approach analyzes how the rhetorical artifact was put together, not just the end result.

If you have been following Anita Sarkeesian's work on women's representations in video game development on *Feminist Frequency*, you should understand her work both as an example of feminist rhetorical criticism and the kind of criticism that delves into the historical production of representations in the lucrative video game industry. Sarkeesian's "Damsel in Distress" Web video series charts the use of the distressed damsel trope from Greek mythology, through early films such as *King Kong*, to its firm entrenchment in early video games such as *Donkey Kong*. Her criticism records and categorizes the placement of Princess Peach throughout the various incarnations of the popular Mario Brothers games and how game developer icon Shiguro Miyamoto was pressured by industry moguls to turn strong playable females into passive damsels in need of rescue.[39]

A feminist approach to analyzing cultural production (1) uncovers who is behind the rhetorical artifact and (2) closely analyzes how the rhetorical artifact is put together.

Revisioning

Finally, an important part of feminist criticism is creating new theories about rhetoric. This approach analyzes a specific rhetorical artifact or artifacts as part of a larger project that revisions what it means to engage in rhetoric. As mentioned before, the definition of rhetoric was once solely used to describe the written and spoken word used to persuade. Feminist theoretical thought worked hard to expand that definition. This was important feminist work since women, as historical subjects, would be significantly excluded from the rhetorical history if defined so narrowly. The work of Karen Foss and Sonja Foss in this area extrapolates new theories about what constitutes *significant* rhetoric. In their book *Women Speak*, significant rhetoric emanates from ordinary individuals not noted for their historical accomplishments. Females or even groups of females in private as well as public domains create significant rhetoric; significant rhetorical works include ongoing rhetorical dialogues that are dramatically different from speechmaking. This is an important theoretical departure because, as Deirdre Johnson notes, much of the work women do is ritualistic and impermanent;[40] hence, feminist rhetoric should include symbolic activities that are less concrete and finished. Revisioning these theoretical ideas, then, it is possible to see much of what women do as historically significant rhetoric. These activities include baking, children's parties, gardening, letter writing, herbalism, and needlework, among others. These activities produce meaning but have had their significance diminished in the patriarchal world.

Likewise, rhetorical theorists such as Sally Miller Gearhart theoretically question some of the fundamental ideas about the way we disseminate ideas. As a society we have for years believed that trying to persuade somebody through discourse was a rational alternative to violence. However, Gearhart argues that common rhetorical techniques have an ability to produce a personal violation as "real" as violence. Instead of trying to change someone through rhetorical message-making, a feminist rhetorician opposing domination would create a rhetorical situation that makes change possible, but does not insist on change. Using both the feminist rhetorical approach of revisioning and redefining, Gearhart brings new language into the realm of rhetoric. For example, she uses the word *enfoldment* to describe a rhetorical process whereby you offer, make yourself available, surround, listen, and create an opening with your rhetoric, rather than "penetrating the mind" of those you engage.[41] Influenced by Gearhart, other theorists have built on this premise. Foss and Griffin, for example, have outlined a theory of *invitational rhetoric*. This theory suggests a rubric for actualizing rhetoric of nondomination that invites participants to a point of view, but does not create a rhetorical imposition.[42]

These above examples are rhetorical work in which theoretical concepts revision practice; other scholars closely analyze texts and "reread" the text for its feminist possibilities. For example, Suzan Brydon looks at yet another Disney film in which the mother is killed off in the beginning, *Finding Nemo*, and analyzes the rhetorical choices made by the filmmakers about the parenting approach of Marlin, Nemo's father. She concludes that Marlin's character should be understood as performing "mothering" and that "[. . .] Marlin's performance of 'mothering' in *Finding Nemo* (2003) has the potential to make a positive impact on parenting parity and freedom to pursue mothering in new ways."[43]

A feminist rhetorical criticism using the approach of revisioning (1) questions the assumptions underlying desirable rhetoric and (2) offers new rhetorical insights and possibilities as well as liberating frameworks to analyze such rhetoric.

CRITICAL ESSAY

In our careers, we have practiced feminist analysis in each of the four modes outlined above; sometimes as scholars, other times as artists and/or activists. For our essay we have chosen a very different kind of rhetor for critical analysis than others featured in this textbook—an irreverent speaker who has both animal and human characteristics. You may be familiar with other cartoonish human creatures who have an edge—Oscar the Grouch on *Sesame Street*, Ted in the feature-length movie *Ted*, Triumph (the Insult Comic Dog) from late-night television. But our speaker is neither a puppet nor computer-generated. It is Mickee Faust, aka Terry Galloway, who leads the Mickee Faust Club in Tallahassee, Florida. As scholars, we have published other essays related to the queer underpinnings of the Mickee Faust Club,[44] as well as particular community activists' events produced by the company,[45] but in this essay, we focus more on the ceremonial figurehead of the company, Mickee Faust, in order to illustrate the kinds of critical questions and insights a feminist analysis can illuminate.

The essay will begin by briefly describing the company's origins and its mission. And then, we will use the approaches of "redefining" and "recovering" to shed light on the iconic figurehead, Mickee Faust, who presides over the company's seasonal cabarets.

THE MICKEE FAUST CLUB

The Company's Origin and Mission

The Mickee Faust Club, which bills itself as "community theatre for the weird community," is an all-volunteer troupe whose home is in a somewhat dilapidated warehouse, named the Mickee Faust Academy for the *Really* Dramatic Arts, in the heart of an Art Park in Tallahassee, Florida.[46] Founded in 1987 by Terry Galloway (performance artist and author of *Mean Little deaf Queer: A Memoir*) and Donna Marie Nudd (performance scholar and professor of communication at Florida State University), the company is primarily committed to mentoring and producing original, alternative, community-based art with diverse performers, both novice and professional.[47]

The company's mission underscores an Ethic of Accommodation, "an ethic that allows a diverse community—those who are not just underserved but overlooked—to develop its own artistic voice.[48] Although the Mickee Faust Club works in a variety of artistic mediums, the company is most well-known for its seasonal cabarets. The cabarets feature a raucous and wily kind of theater, including political and cultural satires, literary and cinematic parodies, vaudeville sketches, original and adapted songs, and fully staged bad jokes.

Redefining and Recovering

Earlier in this essay, we noted that "Feminist rhetorical critics approaching a rhetorical artifact by *recovering* are (1) acknowledging rhetors that patriarchy has erased and/or (2) recovering the lost or never seen significance of a visible female rhetor." And we noted that "Feminist rhetorical criticism utilizing *redefinition* (1) explains and names how language functions to regulate femininity and masculinity and/or (2) creates or reinvents language that expands the possibility of gender or turns on its head language used to subdue liberation."

In zeroing in on the rhetor in our study, we assume that readers are familiar with Mickey Mouse but not with the titular leader of the Mickee Faust Club—Mickee Faust. Mickee is the foulmouthed, illegitimate, sewer rat brother of that better-known, better-groomed cartoon creation. While Mickee is Tallahassee's tongue-in-cheek answer to a certain unctuous rodent living in Orlando, Mickee's surname, Faust, also pays homage to Göethe's good German doctor whose struggles with the Devil mirror the group's own. Legend has it that illegitimate Mickee grew embittered thinking about the more privileged side of his clan living in splendor—their parade of lights, castles, sleeping beauties, and endless serenades of sappy songs. The dispossessed Mickee satirically lives in exile in Tallahassee where he oversees a subversive brand of theater.[49] Rallying around the rat bastard are seventy or more active members of the Club who call themselves the Faustkateers.

In investigating this cartoonish Mickee Faust, a feminist rhetorical critic, approaching this artifact by *recovering*, might ask—Who is the invisible female rhetor who created this subversive figurehead, Mickee Faust? While the feminist rhetorical critic, approaching Mickee Faust, by *redefining*, might ask—In what ways does Mickee Faust's existence critique society's feminine/masculine binary and/or expand the possibility of gender? To answer those questions, we are going focus on the figurehead, Mickee Faust, as conceived and performed by the performance artist, Terry Galloway. And our analysis will be on Mickee Faust as he functions primarily as an emcee, or a stand-up comedic figure, who opens and closes the seasonal cabarets.

Unlike previous speakers analyzed in this book, this speaker is a hybrid; there is of course the fictional animal, the huge rat, Mickee Faust, described above, but inside that costume is deaf female performance artist Terry Galloway. The challenge for the feminist rhetorical critic initially is to deconstruct that hybrid. Perhaps the best way to do that would be to explore some of the questions we might ask of the character, Mickee Faust, who anchors the Club's cabarets; those we might ask about the writer/actor/creator of Mickee Faust, Terry Galloway; and then begin to explore some of the ways the two might be working rhetorically to complicate gender.

Mickee Faust, the rat

Mickee Faust is a gigantic rat with huge hairy ears, whiskers, and a long skinny black tail on which a rat trap has been permanently snapped. For over three decades, Faustkateers have most often referenced Mickee as a "he," likely because Mickee often wears an oversized

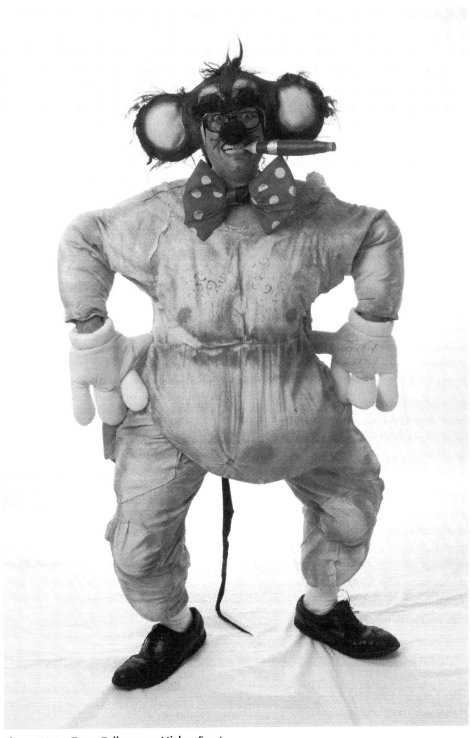

Figure 11.1. Terry Galloway as Mickee Faust

Source: Donna Marie Nudd

man's jacket, with a white shirt topped by a huge colorful polka-dot bow tie, black pants, and extra-large sneakers on the wrong feet; moreover, Mickee is also often seen smoking a cigar and on occasion wielding a club. One could argue that the more accurate pronoun for Mickee in 2020 is "they," because Mickee's gender is fluid. Mickee defies the binary, sometimes seen sporting a queer rainbow jacket, or dancing in a pink tutu, or donning a Carmen Miranda hat. For the purpose of this essay, we'll use Mickee's chosen pronoun "he," but in doing so we ask the reader to keep in mind that Mickee Faust is a rat/person who moves in and out and through gender.

As the Club's leader, Mickee Faust has opened every Mickee Faust cabaret for over thirty years with a monologue and closed each one by leading the Faustkateers in a ritual song, a parody of the songs that framed *The Mickey Mouse Club*, a children's television show in the 1950s. The company produces all original work, written and performed by Faustkateers. A non-thematic cabaret occurs every spring, a "Queer as Faust" cabaret every summer, and a once-every-four-years politically themed cabaret in the fall.[50] The fall cabaret that occurs only in presidential election years is followed with a short cabaret on January 20th that is part of a larger community event, billed as either the Inaugural Bawl or the Inaugural Ball, depending on who was just elected President of the United States.

Feminist rhetorical scholars interested in analyzing the cartoonish rhetor, Mickee Faust, could take several approaches to analyzing how he works rhetorically in the seasonal cabarets.[51] As scholars studying the rhetorical figure who opens the cabarets, we began with archival research, tracking down as many of the original typed scripts of Mickee's opening monologues as possible. Our primary research revealed that, unlike Walt Disney's Mickey Mouse, who seeks to be universally loved, Tallahassee's rather tyrannical Mickee Faust's loosely structured monologues have a type of humor that many would probably find objectionable in any other context. Mickee opens most cabarets with a monologue, typically filled with a series of very bad jokes—sometimes sexist, sometimes feminist, sometimes androcentric, sometimes ableist, sometimes homophobic, sometimes queerly affirmative. Mickee's jokes also include many timely political punches, mostly stabs at conservatives; cumulatively, audiences easily discern Mickee's overall political positioning as radically progressive or subversive.[52]

Mickee Faust, the writer/performer

Inside the rat costume, as noted earlier, is performance artist Terry Galloway. The initial, broader question—who is Terry Galloway—is easily researched because Galloway has been extensively interviewed, has published essays and a memoir, and continues to tour two full-length autobiographically based solo shows.[53] As feminist rhetorical scholars interested in understanding the artifact of Mickee Faust, perhaps the most focused question—what led Terry Galloway to create and perform this character, Mickee Faust?—is the more useful one. From Galloway's publications, we can discern a number of possible answers to that question. Below, we'll highlight two of them.

Galloway's intersectional positioning is quickly transparent in the title of her memoir, *Mean Little deaf Queer*.[54] Galloway's memoir perhaps proves Kimberlé Crenshaw's point that "intersectionality was a lived reality before it was a term."[55] As a child, Galloway was medically deaf, but not culturally Deaf, which meant that she ended up being mainstreamed and never seriously taught sign language. As an expert lip-reader with severe hearing loss who didn't know sign, Galloway wasn't really part of the hearing world or the Deaf world.[56] Her memoir further reveals that she deemed herself to be a "deafie" intent on "passing" in a hearing world; a young girl lusting for power in a patriarchal world; a coming-of-age queer in a heteronormative world; and a very bright, talented theater student who, because of her deafness, was advised to pursue "factory work" by her high school guidance counselor. The strain of this existence resulted in some nervous breakdowns for Galloway; but the intersectional positioning also allowed her to develop an acerbic critique of the institutions—medical, educational, religious, and artistic—that exclude and privilege.

One possible reading of Galloway's creation is that Mickee Faust does appear to be rather literally an alter ego; after all, Mickee is not deaf, and he is a gender fluid, sexually ambiguous, and subversive dictatorial leader of his own theater company.

But that is one of many readings. An equally viable reading might involve tracing Galloway's theatrical education. In one published work, called "Tough," Galloway traces her inability to identify with media representations of disabled children.[57] She notes that with the exception of wild Helen Keller, disabled children in film were almost always victims, helpless saps who needed to be rescued. Roles such as Bess in *Little Women*, the orphan Heidi, and Tiny Tim in *A Christmas Carol* did not interest Galloway, nor did many of the insipid, passive roles available to females. So in part, we are led to believe that it was the paucity of complex roles for disabled children and women that is somewhat responsible for Galloway refocusing her attention on performing comic male roles.

Galloway traces that particular history, from her grammar school performance playing Wilbur in *Wilbur's First Shave*; to playing Falstaff, as well as Bottom, in the University of Texas's experimental Shakespeare at Winedale program; to her signature gumshoe character in the serial, "Jake Ratchett, Short Detective," in Esther's Follies cabarets in Austin, Texas.[58] "Framing the tough male role comically" made Galloway realize that if, she, "the inappropriate, the imperfect, undervalued female—can embody the male (that perfect and valued essence) so absolutely, if so amusingly, then some joke has been turned upon itself."[59]

Thus, a second reading of Galloway's creation of the Mickee Faust character is that he is a culmination of what Galloway learned through the decades theatrically—that creating and/or performing a comic male was more satisfying and engaging to her than any other options.

Mickee Faust, the combination

As academics interested in understanding the rhetorical significance of Mickee Faust, we would like to offer some preliminary thoughts about how this character might be working for audiences at the cabarets. Imagine a couple of tourists wandering through the Art Park who happen to see a couple of actors in bizarre costumes on the sidewalk in front of the Mickee Faust Clubhouse; they realize a show is happening and buy tickets. While those audience members may not know in advance that the show has been created by a left-wing, subversive theater company and might be puzzled initially when they are greeted at the show's opening by an oversize rat figure, they are not entirely "uninformed" either, primarily because of the ubiquitous presence of Mickey Mouse in American culture. A minute into Mickee Faust's monologue, they are likely to "read" Mickee as some type of parody of Mickey Mouse. And by the closing number, in which the entire cast and crew storm the stage wearing multicolored mouse-like balloon ears for the closing song, they know they are right. So even new audience members feel "in" on the joke.[60]

Although new audience members "get" that Mickee Faust is some type of satirical take on Mickey Mouse, that is not all they see and hear. In processing Mickee's monologue, they find themselves laughing at the questionable jokes of a five-foot-two, cartoonish, talking rat. We theorize that new audience members (who would not personally know Galloway) assimilate Mickee Faust as a triad—the huge hairy ears, the whiskers, and rat tail evoke a *creature*; the hyperbolic attire (e.g, oversize jacket, big polka-dot bow tie, sneakers on the wrong feet) suggest comic *male*; while the timbre of the voice (Galloway's) sounds decidedly *female*. We believe Mickee Faust's triad positioning somehow works to give the audience permission to laugh at jokes that they may not necessarily laugh at in other contexts. Consider this opening of Mickee's monologue for spring 2018 cabaret:

Hey, ho, Faustkateers! It's me! Mickee Faust! And this is the Mickee Faust Spring Cabaret—*Make America Faust Again*!

I'd run for President on that slogan but nobody would take me seriously because I'm a cartoon which is not to say our present President isn't a joke. Even a cartoon like me is better informed about the state of the world then our shithole of a President.[61] It's not hard. He didn't even know the difference between Dubai and Abu Dhabi. It's simple. The people from Dubai don't like the old Flintstone cartoons and the people from Abu Dhabi do.

I keep up with the news.

And what is it with all these damn men, whipping out their dicks all the time. They're like a bunch of perverted frogs, going "rub-it, rub-it!"

Let me tell you something, guys. Men making jokes about menstruation—even cartoon men like me—making jokes about menstruation?

Just. Not. Funny.

Period![62]

We argue that Mickee's triad positioning as a male/female/creature grants audience members the right to laugh at a range of jokes dealing with gender and sexuality.

Perhaps predictably, sexuality jokes are very prominent in Mickee Faust's queer-themed cabarets that take place in Gay Pride month, typically held at the Mickee Faust Clubhouse the last two weekends of every June. An excerpt from the Mickee's opening monologue for the Tenth Annual "Queer as Faust," while not *as* raunchy as others we could quote, is still somewhat representative.

I think Faust has some of the toughest gays on the planet. I know we have tough dykes. We have a dyke who kickstarts her vibrator and rolls her own tampons. Whoa!

We have a really kind of dense lesbian in the company as well. She dates men.

And our gay Faustkateers love their lesbian counterparts, especially love the butches. I mean you know, somebody's gotta mow the lawn.

Yeah, yeah, yeah, stereotypes. But see me—I'm like Bugs Bunny. I change my sex as the occasion demands and whenever the hell I want. As a lesbian, I was with a woman who had ESP and PMS at the same time. Yea, a know-it-all bitch. As a gay male I dated a man who was an absolute treasure. Meaning you'll need a map and a shovel to find him. See, I asked him, "whaddya like about me the most—my pretty face or my sexy body?" He said "Your sense of humor." But really I like to be bisexual! How many bisexuals does it take to change a light bulb? However many turns you on.[63]

While this excerpt underscores Mickee's human sexuality, in other monologues, Mickee might be testifying to dating a gerbil or Olive Oil or Amy Winemouse or Goofy. Mickee Faust's cross species/cross cartoon dating history could easily be construed as a critique of the seemingly heteronormative, monogamous, cartoon-chaste relationship of Mickey Mouse and Minnie Mouse.

Our major argument here is that because Mickee's triad—his ratness, his maleness, his femaleness—is always visually or aurally accessible to audience members, audience members do not take umbrage at Mickee's gendered or sexualized remarks in a way they likely would have if the same remarks had been made by a recognizably gendered human being on the same stage.

Let us turn now to the ways Mickee's jokes relate to other common demographics—race, ethnicity, disability. Because a rubber mask of a rat face covers most of Terry Galloway's head, only a small portion of Galloway's white skin is visible to the audience. Hence, if audience members consciously or subconsciously process Mickee's "race" or "ethnicity," they would read it as "white." As a white writer and performer, with progressive political views, Galloway's jokes relating to race (in comparison to jokes related to gender and sexuality) are much more selectively used in Mickee Faust's monologues.

When race is referenced in Mickee's jokes, Mickee's purpose is to critique white oppressors and/or Mickee's own tyrannical nature. In another opening monologue of Mickee's, Louise, a sixty-ish, black performer in our company wanders on stage during Mickee's monologue. Mickee yells, "What the hell are you doing here? Get off my stage! Beat it! Go!"[64] After being threatened by Mickee's club, and then tasered in the back by Mickee, Louise convulses on stage and Mickee gloats: "Ain't that fun! I took a free workshop from the Tallahassee Police Department."[65] This scene occurred on the Mickee Faust stage two months after two Tallahassee police officers were suspended without pay, one for having tased an unarmed African American great-grandmother in the back as she walked away from him.

As a white feminist, Galloway is aware of her own privileged racial positioning in our racist society and she is equally aware that Mickee Faust, who if read racially or ethnically, would be perceived as "white." Because of that, when Mickee's jokes do allude to race, they are used to critique the behavior of white oppressors and/or Mickee Faust's own despotic nature.

Another complex example of Mickee Faust's humor in this regard occurred at the end of one of our recent seasonal cabarets. It is standard procedure for Mickee to summon all the Faustkateers to the stage for the company's closing song, but in this particular show, Mickee's summons appeared particularly mean-spirited, not just to the Faust actors onstage but also to the audience. But first it is important to describe what immediately preceded Mickee's harsh summons.

The last full skit in the cabaret was a madcap parody called "The Tea Party." The skit expertly blended characters from *Alice in Wonderland*'s classic tea party scene with some of the crazed politics of the Tea Party movement. In Faust's 2018 reprisal of the skit, members of The Tea Party (Mad Hatter, March Hare, and Dormouse) are sitting around a long table where there are oversize tea props including a big pink plastic teapot filled with water and large trays of cookies. Alice, played by a short, young-looking, Hispanic woman, interrupts the Tea Party gathering to ask a simple question in which she is unable to get a logical reply. Virtually every time Alice speaks she is cut off by one of more of the Tea Partiers. An excerpt from the middle of the skit:

ALICE. Look, I came here to suggest a way we might . . .

MAD HATTER. Wait! Answer me this riddle: "Why is an albatross like the Constitution?"

MARCH HARE. Ooo . . . riddles!!

DORMOUSE. I bet I know!

(The three Tea Partiers whisper amongst themselves while ALICE sighs heavily and ponders the riddle.)

ALICE. Excuse me?

MAD HATTER. Do you have an answer to the riddle?

ALICE. No, I don't! So what does it mean?

MAD HATTER. I haven't a clue!

(The three Tea Partiers laugh and toast each other.)

DORMOUSE. (yawning) I'm bored. I want to change the topic. Immigration!

ALL THREE TEA PARTIERS. Ooo . . . yes. Immigration!

MARCH HARE. We had such a catchy tune during our campaign. Do you remember it?

(sings) "Twinkle, twinkle migrant brat / Wonder where your papers at?"

ALL THREE TEA PARTIERS. (continuing the song) "Arizona led the way / Private prison's where you'll stay . . ."

(ALICE looks at them in horror, but tries to compose herself.)

MAD HATTER. More tea?[66]

Figure 11.2.   Show Poster: "A Mickee Faust Free-for-All"
Source: Donna Marie Nudd

The Mad Hatter pours water from the huge pink teapot, overflowing the teacups on the table and dousing Dormouse, who had fallen asleep. The skit escalates with the Tea Partiers getting more and more nonsensical, both verbally and nonverbally. Finally, Alice, after listening to the ridiculous Tea Partiers' muttering denials about climate change and witnessing snickerdoodles being tossed every which way, yells, "This is the stupidest tea party I've ever been to in my life!"[67] and marches off.

Stage lights go to black and the audience applauds. Then the house lights go up, first revealing the disheveled Tea Party actors surrounded by the mess they've just made. Mickee Faust enters from the back of the auditorium. As he comes down the center aisle approaching the stage, Mickee yells first to audience members, and then to the actors who just played the Tea Partiers, "Clean this mess up!"[68] And as he yells, he vehemently pitches rolls of paper towels to audience members and actors on stage. Susan Gage, the author of "The Tea Party" script and also one of the actors on stage (she played March Hare), aptly recalls: "That was one of those moments where the audience did an intake of breath, and then laughed at the reference."[69] The reference? A month earlier, Donald Trump had responded to the devastation of Hurricane Maria by visiting a relief station in Puerto Rico and tossing rolls of paper towels into the crowd. In this short bit, Mickee Faust's tyrannical nature is once again underscored, but after the "intake of breath" the audience members simultaneously process the visual rhetoric the way Terry Galloway intended it—as a critique of Donald Trump's lack of compassion for the suffering of Puerto Ricans.

As we continue to think about how audience members make sense of this complex figure-head, Mickee Faust, we turn to one additional index of identity to analyze—disability.

Terry Galloway was profoundly deaf for over fifty years of her life. She is still medically deaf, but now, with two cochlear implants, the technology has given her a much greater range of "hearing." Audience members who know Galloway personally (or know of her deafness from other sources) and who *also* know that Galloway is the performer wearing the rat costume would likely have a unique take on Mickee Faust telling jokes in which the disabled are the target. Why? Because those audience members, the ones familiar with Galloway's biological deafness and her lifelong disability activism, would likely judge Galloway as having the "dis-ability creds" that grant her the right to tell jokes about the disabled because, quite simply, she is perceived as one of them.

But there are also other audience members who are *not* privy to Terry Galloway's autobiography and they too process Mickee Faust; and in doing so they see a character, who is *not* disabled—he is physically able-bodied, and there is nothing about Mickee's voice that would directly signal disability. So for them, Mickee's rat-ish/male/female/white/able-bodied self doesn't have societal permission to tell jokes about the disabled.

Hence the conundrum for Galloway. As a deaf woman, Galloway *loves* the very dark humor shared by her and many of her disabled friends. And yet, she is also aware that her Deaf friends do not view their Deafness as a disability but as a culture; and she also knows that, even though she herself self-identifies as having a disability, she can't speak on behalf of all people with disabilities, because the world of the disabled is tremendously varied. Consider, for example, people who have visual impairments, or Parkinson's disease, or learning disabilities, or PTSD. Finally, Galloway knows that for audience members who do not know her personal history, Mickee Faust, has *no* discernable disability.

Galloway typically solves the conundrum in one of two ways. Sometimes, before telling a disability-themed joke in the opening monologue, Mickee Faust will orally reference, by name, as well as visually gesturing toward, company members who have visible disabilities, such as our open-captioning operators K.C. and Zan in their mobility scooters, thus suggesting we are *all* in on the joke. Other times, Mickee directly shares the stage with company members who would be perceived by most audience members as having the right to use disablist language, the right to mock themselves. Consider Mickee's "monologue" that started the spring cabaret in 2014, where Sam, a longtime member of the company who is visually impaired, has a number of lines:

MICKEE. Hey, hey, hey Faustkateers! Tonight we're going to get down and dirty about all those things we shouldn't—sex, race, religion, politics, with a few blind jokes tossed in just to irritate Sam. We've had some run-ins of late. Hey, Sam!

(Sam enters.)

Here's a joke for you. A blind man walks into a bar . . . and a table. . . and a chair! That'll teach you to defy me. Hey Sam, I heard you and your girlfriend tried to join one of those weird churches and they turned you down.

SAM. Yeah, they said if we wanted to join we had to abstain from sex for three weeks.

MICKEE. And?

SAM. We couldn't do it. Sometime during that second week she dropped a can of paint and I took her then and there.

MICKEE. I take it you're not welcome at that church.

SAM. Yep. We're not welcome at Home Depot either.[70]

These examples are meant to illustrate the ways that Mickee Faust's disability-themed jokes are rather consistently framed: Mickee Faust either alludes to company members with visible disabilities and/or he cocreates the jokes with company members with visible disabilities. This framing signals to the audience that the "disabled community" is in on the joke.

It is important to underscore a yet-uncommented-on reality; Mickee's clubhouse is well-populated with people with disabilities. We can at this time think of no other satirical theater company in the nation in which a third to half of its membership—that includes performers, writers, directors, administrators, technical crew, house management—self-identify as having a disability. As feminist rhetorical scholars, we cannot help but note that while Mickee's disability (i.e., Terry Galloway's deafness) may be invisible to audience members, the disabilities of many of Mickee's minions are very visible.

When asked about the monologue that she shared with Sam, Terry explained:

Within our disability subset in Faust we often mock ableist behavior—we all know it all too well. We consider ourselves "crips with an attitude," and we remain appalled by the fact that people without disabilities can't believe we have sex lives, or tempers or peeves! And they are really surprised when they find out we can have a wicked sense of humor about our own disabilities.

When Sam and I decided to do that opening back-and-forth we chose the Home Depot joke because well, what does it tell you? A person with a disability can have a sex life—and in this case a REALLY active one. The jokes might be groaners but you put them in the context we often put them in and you get the joke plus.[71]

So far, this essay has focused on how the audience might be processing the Mickee Faust figurehead by analyzing his appearance, his jokes in the opening "monologues," and one key transitional "bit"; we now turn to analyze the ritualistic closing of every Mickee Faust cabaret.

As noted earlier, after the last sketch or musical number, Mickee Faust takes over the stage and summons the Faustkateers. From every possible entrance way, every person who was involved in the show makes their way on to the stage, performers typically wearing the last costume they wore, crew members (who are not still operating tech) typically wearing a "Queer as Faust" or "ShakesParody" tee shirt or a Mickee Faust sweatshirt. The only unifying factor that visually links the motley crew assembled on stage as well as the crew members still dutifully at their stations (e.g., members of the band who are still playing the music) is their ears. For this last number, every Faustkateer who has worked in any capacity on this show has donned a cheap Dollar Store headband with two balloons attached (both mismatched in color and size). When everyone is finally assembled on the stage, Mickee leads his Faustkateers in a ritual closing song, a parody of an amalgam of the opening song and reprise from the 1950s era children's television show, *The Mickey Mouse Club*.[72] Here are the lyrics to the Mickee Faust Club Song.

> FAUSTKATEERS. Who's the leader of the cult / slave driving you and me?
>
> MICKEE. Me!
>
> FAUSTKATEERS. M-I-C-K-E-E / F-A-U-S-T.
>
> MICKEE. Mickee Faust.
>
> FAUSTKATEERS. Göethe! [pronounced "Gerrr-Ta"]
>
> MICKEE. Mickee Faust.
>
> FAUSTKATEERS. Göethe! Forever shall we scheme and scheme and scheme . . .
>
> MICKEE. Now it's time to say so long
>
> FAUSTKATEERS. Go home and eat our cheese.
>
> (*softly*) M-I-C.
>
> MICKEE. See you in the sewer!
>
> FAUSTKATEERS. (*softly*) K-E-E.
>
> MICKEE. (*spoken*) Why e-e? Because we don't want to get sued by Disney. That's why!
>
> MICKEE AND FAUSTKATEERS: F-A-U-S-T.[73]

In this closing number, Mickee Faust is again established as the leader of the song and the leader of the company, the one who has been "slave-driving" the Faustkateers to create this cabaret. But there's rebellion in the ranks, so when Mickee insists twice he is the leader, his rat minions twice counter "Göethe" thus implying that their leader has sold his soul to the Devil. Mickee Faust senses a possible rebellion stewing, so when he overhears the Faustkateers' intent to "scheme and scheme and scheme," he typically responds by choosing whomever appears to be the most vulnerable on stage (usually a small child who was in the show or a Faustkateer in a wheelchair) and he pops one or two of their balloon ears. With the sounds of the ears deflating, the Faustkateers then fall in line and finish singing the song. And Mickee, of course, gets the song's punch line.

Although there is this mini-tension at work mid song, ultimately, the song comes across as celebratory. The audience senses the cast and crew's joy in wrapping up another show and once again having provided homegrown, original satire to our Tallahassee audience. It's relevant that the final letters of the song "F-A-U-S-T" are sung by both Mickee *and* the Faust-kateers. It is a unifying, if not corny, moment, where all of us on stage, as well as the techies in the wings, all of us who are wearing balloon ears are, with Mickee himself, collectively, "Mickee Faust." Rhetorically, the closing song reinforces some of the troupe's mythical tropes (Mickee as a rat, Mickee as a tyrannical leader) while also celebrating Mickee Faust as both an unusual figurehead *and* an unusual theater company.

Further Feminist Analysis

Galloway's Mickee Faust artistically demonstrates and reinforces many of the theories of one of the major feminist queer theorists of our time—Judith Butler. A British scholar, David Gauntlett, explains Judith Butler's major idea in a very accessible way.[74] David Gauntlett first presents a diagram that shows the "heterosexual matrix" at work in our society that Butler critiques. In the diagram below, "sex" appears as a binary given (you are born male or female) and then "gender" becomes "the cultural component which is socialized into the person on that basis" which then leads to heterosexuality.

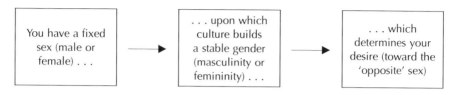

Gauntlett goes on to explain, "Butler's overall argument is that we should not accept that any of these follow from each other—we should shatter the imagined connections. The above model would have to be replaced with something like this:

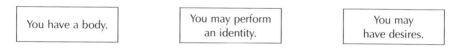

Gauntlett underscores that in the above model "not only have the words become very undeterministic—they assume very little—but also the arrows have gone," so according to Butler, "your body does not determine your gender or identity, and this will not help predict your desires."[75]

For us, Terry Galloway and her Mickee Faust identity (as demonstrated in the opening and closing of the seasonal cabarets) artistically demonstrates Butler's radical second model.

Consider the following.

Galloway has a body.

Terry Galloway's body has been defined in this essay in terms of standard demographics: disability (deaf), race (white), biology (female). But for Butler, the body itself is not fixed; none of these three categories are deterministic. To demonstrate Butler's idea, let's take a closer look at one element of Galloway's body—her deafness. When Terry Galloway first performed Mickee Faust in 1987 in Tallahassee, medical professionals would then, as they still do now, characterize her as profoundly deaf. But because Galloway was trained in speech and theater in her youth and because she had a talent for lip reading, as an adult, Galloway could "pass" in most social situations. In reviewing the three decades that Galloway has been performing Mickee Faust, Galloway went from wearing analog hearing aids to digital ones, and then from having one cochlear implant device to two; in this way, Galloway's body became a bit of a cyborg. This advancement in technology also affected the way Galloway's body, as an actor, could work on the stage. In early Faust cabarets, Galloway's somewhat growly, somewhat muffled voice had a slight lateral lisp and when she was in ensemble numbers, Galloway would typically memorize *everyone's* lines so she could reasonably guess where her line should come in and/or her accommodating fellow actors would give her visual or tactile prompts as cues. Galloway's body in early Faust is not the same body as today. With two cochlear implants, Galloway's body now defaults to look at people's eyes (rather than their lips); her speech is much clearer and crisper; and if an audience member heckles, there's a 50 percent chance she'll "hear" it. In sum, the body is not static.

Galloway may perform an identity.

In her memoir, *Mean Little deaf Queer*, Galloway discusses at length her different performances of identity as she grew up. Again, let us momentarily zero in on one of the many indices of her identity—her deafness. In the memoir, Galloway writes about the various ways she tried to pass as a hearing person, for example, growing her hair long to cover her hearing aids, or playing the class clown (i.e., choosing to be the one *telling* the jokes and monopolizing the conversation, rather than risking the humiliation of looking stupid because, as a lip-reader, she could never completely follow others in group conversations). So in certain contexts, Galloway consciously or unconsciously performed "able-bodied." In other contexts, however, she surmised that it would be better to milk her disability, to play "the gimp" card. For example, she admits:

> Usually when I went to social services hat in hand I felt the need to perform disability—dress disabled—I didn't think they'd give me new hearing aids unless I presented my circumstances as far more desperate than they were.
>
> [. . .]
>
> So the morning of my appointment I put on my usual black. I didn't bother to gel my hair and let it stay flattened to my skull. I skipped the contacts and dug up an old pair of glasses from a hundred prescriptions past. I practiced many expressions of need and settled on one that looked vaguely baby seal–like. I swayed from side to side and adopted some really bad posture. I was just channeling my old deaf childhood self with some touches of Stevie Wonder and *Rain Man*.[76]

So, like all of us, Galloway, performs an identity which is never stable. In some contexts, she will perform "able-bodied," in other contexts she's "disabled." Identity is always a performance, whether unconscious or conscious.

Galloway causes trouble.

In her writings, the theorist Judith Butler advocates that we challenge the traditional views of masculinity and femininity and sexuality by causing "gender trouble." As feminist rhetorical scholars, we studied Mickee Faust's opening monologues and closing presence in the seasonal cabarets in order to analyze how Mickee Faust's character and jokes are likely processed by audience members. The character, Mickee Faust, is one identity that Galloway creates and recreates. In the Clubhouse setting, audience members, see a *body* (a pale-skinned, oversized cartoonish rat, clothed typically in comic male attire with a discernable female voice) *performing an identity* (primarily that of a dictatorial leader of a subversive theater company) who *has desires* (which are as fluid as fluid can be). We found that Galloway successfully "troubles" not just gender and sexuality but also disability and, in a more restricted way, race and ethnicity.

PERSONAL REFLECTIONS

Why did we choose this speaker to analyze for this essay? First, we both found Terry Galloway's character, Mickee Faust, funny. And often in our lives we've heard that feminists are humorless, so focusing on the character created by Terry Galloway was one minor attempt to counter society's oft-repeated, inaccurate claim.[77] Second, we both had years of experience of listening to Galloway's monologues, and witnessing the audience both heartily laughing and also delightfully groaning at the very bad jokes, so there was some feminist part of us that always wondered, *how the hell does Galloway get away with telling disablist and sexist jokes on stage* and *why, as able-bodied feminists, do we find them funny?* So the academic part of us sought to answer those questions.

Galloway has performed the Mickee Faust character for over three decades in a number of different settings. In choosing to focus on the Mickee Faust who opened and closed our seasonal cabarets, we consciously eliminated analyzing Mickee Faust's rhetorical work in other settings: the Mickee who is a character in ensemble numbers within the cabarets, the Mickee who is a community activist, the Mickee who emcees our ShakesParody cabarets, the Mickee who presides over the company's touring shows, the Mickee who has accepted a number of awards, and the Mickee Faust who seeks "World Media Domination."[78]

Nonetheless, we still value our limited feminist rhetorical analysis focused on the Mickee Faust figurehead who opens and closes the seasonal cabarets. Why? Because in the end, we could not think of any other feminist with Galloway's intellectual and artistic credentials who transforms herself into a live, gender-fluid, buffoonish, cartoon figure in the service of feminist ideals that radicalize community theater; she was a lost female rhetor worth analyzing.

POTENTIALS AND PITFALLS

The potential of feminist rhetorical criticism is abundantly clear. By critiquing our assumptions about the way the world symbolically positions gender, feminist rhetorical critics have the ability to invite concrete change to the gendered experience. We return to our definition of feminism: all people, regardless of their identity categories, can experience freedom and safety, complexity and subjectivity, and economic and political parity—experiences associated with being fully human. Feminist analysis invites habits of mind, attitudes, beliefs, and actions that move closer to these liberation goals.

Although we have attempted to explore how the plurality of approaches, strands of thought, and tensions within feminist thought give way to rich, varied, and inclusive critique, some may find the differing perspectives tedious and self-defeating. In fact, it may be argued that feminists spend so much time differentiating the various perspectives and kinds of feminism that it draws focus from the central aim—to critique and dismantle patriarchy. In Adam Grant's *New York Times* bestseller *The Originals: How Non-Conformists Move the World*, he chronicles the many social movements that labored over differences of approach and principle and failed to harness the power of the much greater overlapping agreement. In fact, Grant uses the historical example of Elizabeth Cady Stanton and Susan B. Anthony's rift with fellow feminist Lucy Stone as a prime example of "horizontal hostility," whereby differences of opinion on how to approach a shared goal, in this case women's suffrage, produced intense acrimony. Stanton and Anthony felt that voting rights for other disenfranchised groups could not be supported if the rights did not include women. When Stone supported the Fifteenth Amendment, granting once-enslaved African American men (but not women) the right to vote, the women's suffrage movement splintered. Each leader formed alliances, created competing publications, and ultimately, some historians argue, watered down their combined political might.[79] So, although feminists may ask different questions, their work in feminist rhetorical criticism must balance the discussion of distinction and not lose sight of the object of central critique—patriarchal domination.

Another aspect of rhetorical criticism that requires careful consideration is the selection of the communication artifact. In the critical essay above, the object of study chosen was Mickee

Faust. Although Mickee Faust, as a satirical figurehead, is well-known in the community in which the cabaret resides, every chosen artifact needs to be richly described and made relevant and knowable to those who may have never seen the performance. This is especially true in feminist rhetorical criticism where approaches like recovery and revisioning call upon the reader to interact with the unknown and unfamiliar. The above essay asked the reader to remember other fictional nonhuman characters, from beloved *Sesame Street* creatures to raunchy late-night puppets, as a way to spur recognition of the comic form even if one was unfamiliar with the specific theatrical forum. Rhetorical scholars must take care to make those connections so the critique is transferable to a range of other rhetorical circumstances.

Along the same lines, our critical essay looks at a humorous figurehead that satirizes a treasured cultural icon, Mickey Mouse. As with all comedic artifacts, humor is subjective. Satire and irony can be particularly tricky. Helene Shugart notes some of these pitfalls when analyzing a feminist reimagining of Leonard da Vinci's *The Last Supper*, called *The First Supper*. In her analysis of Susan Dorothea White's painting, she notes that such subversive irony was understood richly and radically by some audiences, but the point was lost entirely by others. In some instances, the "read" of the painting further entrenched the harmful narratives it sought to dismantle.[80]

In all, the artifact chosen must have complexity that makes analysis necessary—a relevant artifact, when richly understood, is able to propel emancipatory promise and practice.

FEMINIST ANALYSIS TOP PICKS

Campbell, Karlyn Kohrs. *Man Cannot Speak for Her: A Critical Study of Early Feminist Rhetoric*. Vol. 1. New York: Greenwood Press, 1989. This book simultaneously investigates feminist rhetoric and offers news ways of thinking about the rhetorical process. One of the most important works in feminist rhetorical scholarship.

———. "Rhetorical Feminism." *Rhetoric Review* 20 (2001): 9–12. A concise essay that provides a survey of the work done by feminist scholars in the field of communication. Beginning critics will find this history very helpful.

Condit, Celeste M. "In Praise of Eloquent Diversity: Gender and Rhetoric as Public Persuasion." *Women's Studies in Communication* 20, no. 2 (1997): 91–116. Condit's article is an excellent example of feminist revisioning. She provides a through rationale for new ways of communicating gender. The article also will further a student's understanding of the different positions on gender that rhetorical scholars take.

Crenshaw, Kimberlé W. *On Intersectionality: Essential Writings*. New York: New Press, 2017. Through a variety of disciplines and perspectives, Crenshaw presents a comprehensive, compelling, and accessible collection of important writings foundational to formation of a theory of intersectionality.

Donofrio, Theresa A., and Alyssa A. Samek. "Jeopardized Bodies: Representations of Race, Gender, and Mortality in the Notorious R.B.G." *Women's Studies in Communication* 42, no. 2 (2019), 140–160. This essay explores some problematic tensions. During a time of call to action against the brutalization of black bodies, the authors examine how the humorous grafting of a rapper personae onto the frail body of Supreme Court Justice Ruth Bader Ginsburg masks racist violence.

Foss, Sonja J., and Cindy L Griffin, eds. *Inviting Understanding: A Portrait of Invitational Rhetoric*. Lanham, MD: Rowman & Littlefield, 2020. Renowned scholars in feminist rhetorical theory provide a multifaceted and revolutionary exploration of the revisioning of persuasion through a feminist lens.

Hamlet, Janice D. "Assessing Womanist Thought: The Rhetoric of Susan L. Taylor." *Communication Quarterly* 48, no. 4 (2000): 420–437. This essay provides an interesting rhetorical analysis of the former editor of *Essence* magazine. The study is an excellent example of feminist scholarship and furthers understanding of womanist scholarship.

Lotz, Amanda D. "Communicating Third Wave Feminism and New Social Movements: Challenges for the Next Century of Feminist Endeavor." *Women and Language* 26 (2003): 1–9. This essay provides students with an overview of feminist thought from the perspective of the communication field. This article is helpful for students seeking to understand the complex and contradictory messages about feminism in the media and elsewhere.

Shugart, Helene. "She Shoots, She Scores: Mediated Constructions of Contemporary Female Athletes in Coverage of the 1999 US Women's Soccer Team." *Western Journal of Communication* 67, no. 1 (Winter 2003), 1–31. Shugart's analysis of famous female athletes unearths the patriarchal strategies used to subordinate these successful and empowered women. Shugart provides theoretical language for understanding these strategies.

DISCUSSION QUESTIONS

1. Are feminist viewpoints generational? In other words, is there a particular strand of feminism that is more likely to be adopted by Generation Z, Millennials, Generation X, or Baby Boomers?
2. Feminist rhetorical analysis is offered not just to promote understanding but also to bring change. Some would argue that teaching these approaches is a form of indoctrination. Do you agree or disagree?
3. Where would you place your own views of gender on the minimalist-maximalist continuum?

ACTIVITIES

1. In 2020, Congresswoman Alexandria Ocasio-Cortez (D-NY) insisted on respect and civility from her Republican colleague, Ted Yoho, during a speech on the House floor. First, use a search engine to locate and watch Ocasio-Cortez's speech or follow the link in the article cited below. Next, read *New York Times* columnist Rebecca Traistser's account of how newspapers positioned Ocasio-Cortez's rhetorical act. See "The Poison of Male Incivility" at https://www.thecut.com/2020/07/aoc-speech-ted-yoho-new-york-times.html. After watching the speech and reading the column, write a descriptive account of the speech that accurately reports Ocasio-Cortez's tenor and tone but revisions her words as something other than "disruptive."
2. Popular culture has assigned the name "Karen" to white women with a demanding demeanor. In this assignment you will both record the elements of this trope and revision "Karen" as "Karla"—a white women who uses her privilege to ally with people of color. To do this form groups of three or four people. Take a sheet of paper and fold it in half. On one side describe at least three to four behaviors and/or characteristics of a "Karen." On the other side, design a new trope that situates white women as allies for people of color. How does Karla talk back or act differently from Karen?

3. Think of a holiday that you celebrate and the rituals of those events performed with family and friends. In three paragraphs, write the following: a) Describe the rituals as they are currently celebrated; b) Describe any gendered elements of those celebrations. For example, do all the men play golf the morning of the Fourth of July? Do all the women do the dishes after the Thanksgiving dinner?; c) Describe how these celebrations might be reimagined to create a celebration steeped in gender parity.

4. Deidre Johnston notes that monuments and memorials often have gendered patterns of representation. For example, monuments are often of specific men (William McKinley) but nonspecific women (Lady Liberty, Madonna of the Trail). By yourself or in groups walk around your college campus or town and record the details of any statues, plaques, fountains, or named buildings. Who is represented? Who is not represented? If you could design and erect a tribute to important but forgotten persons or histories, richly describe your act of recovery and representation.

NOTES

1. Susan Faludi, "Whose Backlash Is It Anyway?: The Women's Movement and Angry White Men," FSU Student Government Summer Lecture Series, Florida State University, Tallahassee, June 25, 1997.

2. "The Feminist Factor: More than Half of 2012 Women Voters Identify as Feminist," *Ms. Magazine*, March 18, 2013.

3. Catherine Morris, "Less than a Third of American Women Identify as Feminists," National Geographic/Ipsos, November 25, 2019.

4. Ibid.

5. This definition appears in Kramarae and Treichler's *A Feminist Dictionary* (Illinois: University of Illinois Press, 1996).

6. Allan G. Johnson, *The Gender Knot: Unraveling Our Patriarchal Legacy* (Philadelphia: Temple University Press, 2014).

7. Rachel Thomas et al., "Women in the Workplace 2019," study by McKinsey & Company and LeanIn.org, https://wiw-report.s3.amazonaws.com/Women_in_the_Workplace_2019.pdf.

8. "Lean in" is a reference to the best-selling book *Lean In: Women, Work and the Will to Lead* (New York: Alfred A. Knopf, 2013), written by Facebook Chief Operating Officer Sheryl Sandberg.

9. Johnson, *Gender Knot*, 6.

10. Johnson, *Gender Knot*, 7–8.

11. Johnson, *Gender Knot*, 9.

12. Rising awareness about the lack of complex female characters ushered in improvements in women's representation in films, resulting in some feminist critics to push for analysis beyond the very basic baseline of the Bechdel test.

13. For example, it is estimated that 102 million viewers watched Super Bowl LIV in 2020 and marketing departments spent up to $5.6 million for each 30-second advertising spot. See Brian Steinberg, "Super Bowl Ads Sell Out Early for First Time in Five Years," *Variety*, November 25, 2019, https://variety.com/2019/tv/news/super-bowl-commercials-2020-fox-sell-out-1203415238/.

14. For a more thorough explanation of the use of this term view *bell hooks: Cultural Criticism and Transformation*, dir. Sut Jhally, Media Education Foundation, 1997.

15. Tim Wise, *White Like Me: Reflections on Race from a Privileged Son*, remixed and revised edition (Berkeley, CA: Soft Skull Press, 2011).

16. For a more thorough treatment of this debate, see Carol Tavris's *The Mismeasure of Woman: Why Women Are Not the Better Sex, the Inferior Sex, or the Opposite Sex* (New York: Touchstone, 1992).

17. Jill Dolan, *Feminist Spectator as Critic* (Ann Arbor, MI: University of Michigan Press, 1988) 3–16.

18. bell hooks, "Dig Deep: Beyond Lean In," *Feminist Wire*, October 28, 2013, https://thefeminist wire.com/2013/10/17973/.

19. Dolan, Feminist Spectator, 7.

20. Susan Lanzoni, "The Politics of Empathy and Race," *Psychology Today*, February 12, 2020, https://www.psychologytoday.com/intl/blog/empathy-emotion-and-experience/202002/the-politics -empathy-and-race.

21. Dolan, Feminist Spectator, 10.

22. Kimberlé Crenshaw, "Kimberlé Crenshaw: What is Intersectionality?," National Association of Independent Schools (NAIS), June 22, 2018, https://www.youtube.com/watch?v=ViDtnfQ9FHc.

23. Mari J. Matsuda, "Beside My Sister, Facing the Enemy: Legal Theory Out of Coalition," *Stanford Law Review* 43, no. 6 (1991): 1183–1192.

24. For an example of a groups that falls into this category, visit the Independent Women's Forum at http://www.iwf.org.

25. For a more thorough listing of the categories of feminism, see chapter 2 in Natalie Fixmer-Oraiz and Julia T. Wood's *Gendered Lives: Communication, Gender, & Culture*, 13th ed. (Stamford, CN: Cengage, 2019).

26. Karlyn Kohrs Campbell, *Man Cannot Speak for Her*, vol. 1 (New York: Greenwood Press, 1989).

27. Carsten Schwemmer and Sebastian Jungkunz, "Whose Ideas are Worth Spreading? The Representation of Women and Ethnic Groups in TED Talks," *Political Research Exchange* 1, no. 1 (2019); and Pamela Fayerman, "TED Talks Presenters: Will Male Domination Continue in Vancouver Videos and Conference?," *Vancouver Sun*, August 1, 2013.

28. Alison Taylor, "TED Talks Rising to the Challenge of Gender Imbalance," *Pique News*, August 8, 2013.

29. For example, see Karlyn Kohrs Campbell, *Three Tall Women: Radical Challenges to Criticism, Pedagogy, and Theory*, Carroll C. Arnold distinguished lecture (Boston, MA: Allyn and Bacon, 2003), 4.

30. See Krista Ratcliffe, *Anglo-American Challenges to the Rhetorical Tradition* (Carbondale: Southern Illinois University Press, 1995). Ratcliffe's work on feminist rhetorical strategies has been adapted for this section. We have expanded her analysis beyond the Anglo-American tradition and added the examination of cultural production as an option in lieu of rereading traditional rhetorical texts.

31. Paula Blank, "Will Cisgender Survive?," *Atlantic*, September 24, 2014.

32. Sue Wise and Liz Stanley, *Georgie Porgie: Sexual Harassment in Everyday Life* (New York: Pandora, 1987).

33. Jessica Ringose and Emma Renold, "Slut-Shaming, Girl Power and 'Sexualisation': Thinking through the Politics of the International SlutWalks with Teen Girls," *Gender and Education* 24, no. 3 (2012): 334.

34. Kramarae and Treichler, Feminist Dictionary. See also Mary Daly's Websters' First New Intergalactic Wickedary of the English Language (Boston: Beacon, 1987).

35. Karen A. Foss and Sonja K. Foss, *Women Speak: The Eloquence of Women's Lives* (Prospect Heights, IL: Waveland Press, 1991), 10.

36. Marianne Schnall, "SNL Star Amy Poehler on Her New Online Show 'Smart Girls,'" *Huffington Post*, January 2, 2009.

37. "Overlooked," *New York Times*, March 18, 2018, https://www.nytimes.com/interactive/2018/ obituaries/overlooked.html?mtrref=undefined&gwh=A8D698872F04B2B41AB689AC1BBDB580& gwt=regi&assetType=REGIWALL.

38. Douglas Kellner, "Cultural Studies, Multiculturalism, and Media Culture," *Gender, Race, and Class in Media: A Critical Reader*, ed. Gail Dines & Jean M. Humez (Los Angeles: Sage, 2015) 10.

39. Anita Sarkeesian, "Damsel in Distress: Part 1—Tropes vs. Women in Video Games," Feminist Frequency series, YouTube, March 17, 2013, https://www.youtube.com/watch?v=X6p5AZp7r_Q.

40. *Monuments are for Men, Waffles are for Women: Exploring Gender Permanence & Impermanence*, video recording, University of California Extension Center for Media and Independent Learning, 2000.

41. Sally Miller Gearhart, "Womanpower: Energy Re-Sourcement," *The Politics of Women's Spirituality: Essays on the Rise of Spiritual Power within the Feminist Movement*, ed. Charlene Spretnak (Garden City, NY: Doubleday, 1982), 143.

42. Sonja K. Foss and Cindy Griffin, "Exploring Rhetoric Beyond Persuasion: A Proposal for an Invitational Rhetoric," *Communication Monographs* 62 (1995): 6.

43. Suzan G. Brydon, "Men at the Heart of Mothering: Finding Mother in *Finding Nemo*," *Journal of Gender Studies* 18, no. 2 (2009): 142.

44. Donna Marie Nudd, Kristina Schriver, and Terry Galloway, "Is This Theatre Queer: Mickee Faust and the Performance of Community," in *Performing Community, Performing Democracy: International Perspectives on Urban Community-Based Performance*, ed. by Susan C. Haedicke and Tobin Nellhaus (Ann Arbor: University of Michigan Press, 2001), 104–116.

45. Kristina Schriver and Donna Marie Nudd, "Mickee Faust Club's Performative Protest Events," *Text and Performance Quarterly* 22, no. 3 (2002): 196–216; and Donna Marie Nudd, "The Left Rewriting America's Best Historical Fiction Finalist: The January 20, 2001 'Inaugural BAWL' in Tallahassee, Florida," *Text and Performance Quarterly* 24, no. 1 (2004): 74–88.

46. The company is all-volunteer, save for occasional funding of company members from arts-related grants.

47. Terry Galloway is the artistic director and Donna Marie Nudd the executive director of the company. The coauthor of this essay, Kristina Schriver Whalen, was an active member of the company (writer, performer, producer, scholar) from 1992 until 1998. The coauthors are grateful for Galloway's feedback on this essay.

48. "The Faust Manifesto," Mickee Faust: Academy for the *Really* Dramatic Arts, https://www.mickee faust.com/, https://twitter.com/mickeefaust, https://www.instagram.com/mickee_minion/.

49. This is the most common version of Mickee Faust's origin; through the years, in interviews, monologues and skits, other versions surface.

50. In years when there isn't a presidential election, Mickee Faust typically produces a Shakespeare production or an original work. For example, in 2018, Mickee Faust produced an immersive theatre event—*A Moveable Murderous Macbeth*, https://www.tallahasseearts.org/event/the-mickee-faust-club -a-moveable-murderous-macbeth/, and in 2019 a tragic-comic musical about rape—*The Mystery of the Violated Vagina*, https://www.tallahasseearts.org/event/mystery-of-the-violated-vagina/.

51. For the purpose of this essay, we want to focus on the figurehead in connection with the seasonal cabarets, but it's important to note that Mickee is visible elsewhere. Mickee Faust is, on occasion, active politically outside the context of the Mickee Faust Clubhouse; for example, Mickee Faust ran for governor of the State of Florida in 2002 and received twenty-three votes statewide, he and his rat minions appeared in a subversive float in the Springtime Tallahassee Parade in 1999, and performed for Occupy Wallstreet protestors in 2011. Mickee Faust also appears at selective celebratory community events; he has, for example, led the annual neighborhood parade around the Art Park. Like his doppelgänger in Orlando, Mickee Faust seeks "World Media Domination," and to that end, he has a radio hour every fifth Friday on FSU's campus radio station, V89, and he put together a collection of video shorts, *Mickee Faust's Gimp Parade* with the expressed desire to cash in on "the lucrative disability-themed video market" (https://www.youtube.com/watch?v=av9qh6alsuI).

52. While most of Mickee's monologues are loosely structured, on occasion, some are much more formally structured, for example, one is a biting parodic rewrite of General Patton's speech, another is Mickee's impassioned political rant after mass shooting at the gay nightclub, Pulse, in Orlando in 2016. Aaron Ellis expertly analyzed the latter: "Disidentification and Queer Worldmaking in Faust's Queer Theatre for the Weird Community," Association for Theatre in Higher Education Conference, August 6, 2017, Las Vegas, Nevada.

53. See Terry Galloway's website: http://www.theterrygalloway.com/sunshine.html

54. Terry Galloway, *Mean Little deaf Queer* (Boston: Beacon Press, 2010).

55. Kimberlé Crenshaw, "Opinion: Why Intersectionality Can't Wait," *Washington Post*, September 24, 2015, https://www.washingtonpost.com/news/in-theory/wp/2015/09/24/why-intersectionality-cant -wait/, accessed February 17, 2020.

56. Donna Marie Nudd, "Mean Little deaf Queer," in *Disability Experiences: Memoirs, Autobiographies, and Other Personal Narratives*, vol. 2, ed. Susannah B. Mintz and G. Thomas Couser (St. James Press, 2019), 470–473.

57. In *Gay Shame*, ed. David M. Halperin and Valerie Traub (Chicago and London: University of Chicago Press, 2009).

58. Terry Galloway, "Taken: The Philosophically Sexy Transformations Engendered in a Woman by Playing Male Roles in Shakespeare," *Text and Performance Quarterly* 17, no. 1 (1997): 94–100.

59. Halperin and Traub, *Gay Shame*, 199.

60. More literary-attuned audience members are also likely to be processing Mickee's surname "Faust" as an allusion to the protagonist is the tragic play by Johann Wolfgang von Göethe, where the Faust character makes a pact with the Devil, and exchanges his soul for unlimited knowledge and sensual pleasures.

61. Galloway's invective alludes to the way that President Donald Trump expressed frustration behind closed doors with people coming to the United States from "shithole countries." See Eli Watkins and Abby Phillip, "Trump Decries Immigrants from 'Shithole Counties' Coming to the US," CNN Politics, January 12, 2018, https://www.cnn.com/2018/01/11/politics/immigrants-shithole-countries-trump/ index.html accessed February 16, 2020.

62. Terry Galloway, "Mickee's Spring 2018 Monologue," in Mickee's Monologues, Mickee Faust Club Office Archives: Scripts, Tallahassee, FL, accessed January 15, 2020. Throughout this essay, we'll be quoting from typed scripts or electronic ones. The coauthors of this essay have corrected misspellings and sometimes reformatted the excerpts from the scripts. For example, some original monologues were only in open-captioning format, which meant there were no more than six words on a line and no speakers' names were listed because these actors' lines were projected, via Powerpoint, onto a screen at the back wall of the theater. Our intention in reformatting these open-captioning scripts, and sometimes adding minimal stage directions, is simply to make them more readable.

63. Faust Backup Disk Drive 2020-01-12: Scripts and Show Files: 2017 QAF X: 2017, "QAF X Caption Ready Scripts," "Mickee QAF X."

64. Faust Backup Disk Drive 2020-01-12: Scripts and Show Files: Z-2014, "Faust Ratro (Fall Retro Cabaret)," Captioned Scripts: Mickee's rato-mono.

65. Ibid.

66. "The Tea Party," Mickee Faust Club Office Archives: Scripts, Tallahassee, FL, accessed January 15, 2020.

67. Ibid.

68. Mickee's lines are quoted here from memory, since script of Mickee's transitional dialogue from last show number into closing song was not in the archives.

69. Susan Gage, "Re: Another Chance to Help a Faust Scholar . . . ," received by Donna Marie Nudd, January 12, 2020.

70. "2014 Spring Cabaret Mickee Monologue," in Mickee's Monologues, Mickee Faust Club Office Archives, Tallahassee, FL, accessed January 15, 2020.

71. Terry Galloway, interview conducted by Donna Marie Nudd, January 30, 2020.

72. The "Mickey Mouse March," was the opening theme song and "Alma Mater" was the reprise song for ABC's *Mickey Mouse Club* which debuted on ABC on October 3, 1955. *Mickey Mouse Club* was as an hour-long show featuring a cast of wholesome children (called Mouseketeers) "presenting skits and musical numbers, as well as introducing special guest stars, serials, Disney Newsreel segments from around the world, and plenty of Disney cartoons," https://d23.com/brief-history-of-disneys-mickey-mouse-club/.

73. Scott Campbell, "Mickee Faust Club Song Lyrics," received by Faust Cast, March 14, 2019.

74. David Gauntlett, *Media, Gender and Identity: An Introduction*, 2nd ed. (New York: Routledge, 2008), 148–149.

75. David Gauntlett, "Queer Theory and Fluid Identitites," in *Media, Gender and Identity: An Introduction*, 2nd ed. (New York: Routledge, 2008), 149.

76. Terry Galloway, *You Are My Sunshine: A Kind of a Love Story*, Donna Marie Nudd's personal collection, Tallahassee, FL.

77. Full disclosure: Terry Galloway is Donna Marie Nudd's wife and Kristina Schriver Whalen's lifelong friend.

78. Mickeefaust.com/vita, accessed September 13, 2020.

79. Adam Grant, *Originals: How Non-Conformists Move the World* (New York: Penguin Books, 2017) 115–122.

80. Helene A. Shugart, "Postmodern Irony as Subversive Rhetorical Strategy," *Western Journal of Communication* 63, no. 4 (1999), 433–455.

12

Ideographic Criticism

Ronald Lee and Adam Blood

For most students, communication is a pragmatic discipline. It provides methods of analysis, a storehouse of strategies, and tried-and-true techniques for aiding an advocate in advancing a cause. Whether in public speaking, argumentation, or persuasion, the paradigm of an advocate moving a specific audience toward a predetermined end dominates undergraduate communication pedagogy. When students approach rhetorical criticism, they typically bring this orientation with them. Understanding the commitments of the pragmatic model, along with its limitations, provides concepts that other approaches radically recharacterize. Of particular note is the so-called **ideological turn**. Although the phrase captures a particular attitude toward criticism, it includes under its umbrella a constellation of different perspectives and methods.

This chapter focuses on Michael McGee's *rhetorical materialism* (theoretical perspective) and *ideographic criticism* (how that perspective is used in criticism). Beginning in the 1970s, McGee wrote a series of essays that changed the way a generation of critics think about, talk about, and do criticism. Even those who reject his program have been obliged to enter an ongoing conversation with his vision of rhetoric and the critical perspective he promulgated: McGee taught at the University of Memphis, at the University of Wisconsin–Madison, and for the twenty years before his death at the University of Iowa. Beyond his own writing, he influenced a generation of Iowa graduate students, a number of whom now rank among the most influential rhetorical theorists and critics in the field. In what follows, we outline a pragmatic approach to criticism. Second, we explain the ideological turn in criticism by contrasting it with the pragmatic approach. Third, we detail the particular commitments of McGee's rhetorical materialism. Fourth, we explain how rhetorical materialism is expressed in the doing of ideographic criticism. Finally, we illustrate the use of ideographic criticism in an analysis of the discourses of loyalty swirling around basketball star LeBron James's decision to leave the Cleveland Cavaliers to play for the Miami Heat and then return four years later.

POINT OF DEPARTURE

In 1968, Lloyd Bitzer wrote a widely read essay entitled "The Rhetorical Situation." It is the classic presentation of an approach that focuses on understanding the strategic way an advocate may overcome obstacles to success and points the critic toward an understanding of the persuasive influence that messages, deliberately employed, have on a targeted audience. Bitzer views a rhetorical work as "pragmatic" because it "functions ultimately to produce action or change in the world." "The rhetor," he writes, "alters reality by bringing into existence a discourse of such a character that the audience, in thought and action, is so engaged that it becomes a mediator of change."[1]

Bitzer's view presupposes that objective conditions in the external world call forth discourses. There is a brute presence to situations; these situations present exigencies (problematic circumstances); and these exigencies can be "completely or partially removed if discourse, introduced into the situation, can so constrain human decision or action as to bring about the significant modification of the exigence."[2]

Assume for a moment that you are taking a class in corporate advocacy. The instructor presents you with a series of case studies along with materials that describe the public-relations response to corporate difficulties. You follow Bitzer's approach to criticism. First, you identify the exigencies (loss of business and profit, civil and criminal prosecution, and so on). Second, you locate the audiences that can be mediators of change and thus ameliorate the exigencies (customers, investors, regulators, and so on). Third, you examine the constraints that limit the range of possible rhetorical responses (economic, legal, ethical, and so on). Finally, you evaluate the rhetorical strategies that these corporations enacted and make judgments about their effectiveness.

IDEOLOGICAL TURN IN CRITICISM

Notice how narrow the range of judgment is in this pragmatic model of criticism. The critic is limited to assessing the skill of advocates in meeting their predetermined ends.[3] Other questions, especially those concerning competing values or the veracity of the discourse, are set aside. The danger is that conventional wisdom and tradition, typically determined in concert with entrenched interests and institutions, become equated with truth. Our student critics may feel restricted to looking at the world through the eyes of corporate officials. "We can clarify this issue," Philip Wander, himself an important figure in the ideological turn, has remarked, "by asking ourselves what in everyday language we would call the person . . . who examines or rewrites drafts of . . . statements so that their impact on specific audiences can be ascertained or improved; for whom policy, audience, and situation are a given and the overriding question is how to assess the effectiveness of the speech?" His answer is "not . . . a critic." "We would," he concludes, "be more inclined to call him or her a 'public relations consultant.'"[4] Once critics begin to ask, "Whose interests are served by these messages that construct this particular version of the truth?" they are dealing with ideology.

Ideology in the most general sense is "any system of ideas . . . directing political and social action."[5] The questions swirling around ideology ask, To what extent are these ideas true or false? What forces perpetuate these particular ideas? What groups benefit from and what groups are disadvantaged by these ideas?

The underlying assumption is that ideology "usually does not mirror the social world . . . but exhibits some transformation of it."[6] We generate concepts, images, and stories about the nature of our world, and these ideas are used to interpret social reality. These interpretations may create falsehood and distortion. Importantly, these distortions are not neutral in their effect, for they work to the advantage of some groups and to the disadvantage of others.

At root, ideology concerns the relationship among discourse, power, and truth. If we spend a few moments with each term, we should arrive at a workable understanding of ideology.

Discourse

The term ***discourse*** refers to "language in use, or more broadly, the interactive production of meaning."[7] This definition highlights a distinction between contextual and abstract uses of language. For the sake of illustration, consider the phrases "moral language" and "moral discourse." As we look at our bookshelves, we see several works of moral philosophy. These authors focus on "language" because they are interested in the linguistic properties of ethical propositions. These scholars provide an account of the meaning of the word *good* in the statement "X is good." Their treatment of this statement is apart from consideration of actual utterances of the word *good*. They do not examine any particular speakers, audiences, or contexts. They are not interested in whether any specific object, person, or state of affairs is in fact good. Instead, their interest is wholly theoretical.

We also have books and journals that contain treatments of "moral discourse." The authors of these works explore the moral utterances of actual speakers—Milton Friedman, Barack Obama, Pope Francis, and many others—in order to understand the meaning of their moral talk in historical context. These scholars do examine particular speakers, audiences, and contexts. Although their interest is in part theoretical, it is a theoretical interest grounded in a concern for the influence of specific moral messages in the world of practical affairs.

Power

Once the term *discourse* is substituted for *language*, the relevance of **power** becomes more obvious. Actual advocates are trying to influence the course of events in a manner that promotes their interests. Some advocates have more resources (money, access, technology, networks of influential friends) than others. Some advocates are pressing a case on behalf of established institutions and traditional ways of doing things, while others are working for groups with little social or economic standing and who find their interests at odds with the status quo. These disparities in position and resources make a huge difference in the ability to influence audiences.

Let us work from the most everyday of examples to grander illustrations of national political life. There is an old saying, "It is a poor scorekeeper who cannot win for his or her team." This aphorism captures one face of power—the illicit power exercised by those in positions of authority. So, in place of the game scorekeeper, we might just as well speak about Jeffrey Skilling, the former president of Enron, and David Duncan, the Arthur Andersen partner who oversaw the auditing of the Enron Corporation books. They are accused of profiting mightily from the creation of false reports documenting Enron's profitability. They had the power to manufacture a misleading discourse that persuaded thousands of investors to put money into their enterprise.[8]

Power is often exercised without any tinge of corruption. The president describes the crisis of terrorism, uses his authority as commander in chief to mobilize the armed forces, and urges the nation's citizens to sacrifice for the common good. Like the previous cases, this is an example of a powerful individual making an explicit decision that alters some state of affairs. And also like the other cases, it is done largely through the use of discourse. The president characterizes a situation as a "crisis," calls forth the historic precedents for the use of military force, and exhorts the citizenry to unite behind the cause.

In the examples we have used thus far, a person or group with power makes an explicit decision to exercise that power to bring about a particular result. Yet many of the most interesting discursive expressions of power are far more subtle and commonplace. Such cases are not the result of a single decision but rather the product of power that is exercised by a way of talking that constitutes social and political culture. These forms of power go under a number of different names depending on the particular theorist and circumstance, including socialization, legitimation, domination, and hegemony. Each term suggests that powerful political, social, and economic interests perpetuate belief systems. Yet, it would be impossible to locate a set of decision makers who consciously decide on such matters. In advanced industrial societies, the apparatus of indoctrination is hidden and often denies its own existence.

Americans do not think of their children's education as an exercise in political propaganda. The schools are viewed as democratic institutions governed by local communities. Education is seen as the objective study of the world. Yet stable societies must have an efficient way to pass on values and customs to each new generation. There are some obvious patriotic lessons taught in the early years of elementary schooling, such as reciting the Pledge of Allegiance and singing "My County 'Tis of Thee," but there are also subtle, supposedly nonpolitical, and yet important beliefs inculcated in children during these formative years. Children learn that they are required to go to school and that school officials have power over them. This power appears sweetly benign as personified by kindergarten teachers. This benevolent image of power is reinforced in the stories of the Founding Fathers, children's paternal conception of the president, and classroom visits by Officer Friendly. Students also learn the importance of order, the value placed on finishing work in a timely matter, and the rewards that come to the best and most obedient students. These are beginning lessons about the merit system in a capitalist economy.[9] As these pupils continue on in their education, they come to understand the country through the positive meanings associated with liberty, freedom, equality, tolerance, and democracy. These concepts are then organized into larger stories such as the American Dream.

The school is not the only institution socializing the citizenry. Advertising, for example, bombards viewers with the values of consumerism. Industrialization and urbanization weakened the traditional sources of socialization—church, family, and ethnic community. Commercial messages filled this void by selling consumers lifestyles, which they may purchase by selecting particular products.[10] Advertising, rather than religion and tradition, has become the dominant source of individual identity. Commercial messages construct for us a particular view of the country, where men and women are beautiful, everyone is affluent, and consumption makes people happy.

To put this point about power in yet another way, those who have the power to define the terms of the controversy have a tremendous rhetorical advantage. This is what examining the relationship between discourse and power makes evident. Powerful interests, through the communication apparatuses of an advanced society, define the very terms of discussion. The United States is a democratic republic; it has an advanced capitalist economy; and it is a predominantly Judeo-Christian nation. These traditions and institutions together create a set of belief systems that shape our view of the world. Their domination of our thinking is virtually invisible because they merely appear as the American way of life.

Truth

From what we have already said about power, we suspect that it is obvious that "truth" is dependent upon standpoint or perspective. There are often various versions of the truth, with each sponsored by a different set of interests. This subjective or contextual conception of truth (small *t*) stands in contrast with notions of universal Truth (big *T*).

If you decide to attend law school, you will be introduced to this sense of the truth. The lawyer's job is to *characterize* the facts and the law in ways that are to the advantage of the client. The law is a rhetorical enterprise, which pits opposing interpretations of the facts and the law against one another. The more persuasive version of the "truth" wins the verdict. Neither the law nor the facts are settled matters but rather objects that may be differently constructed in discourse.

What we have said about the law is equally true of nearly any enterprise concerned with the construction of social reality. For example, many histories are written of the same event. Even when the relevant facts are generally agreed upon, the placement and characterization of those facts within a larger narrative may radically change the meaning of events.[11] So, taken together, discourse and power may create persuasive versions of the truth. These versions may be widely accepted and serve as the basis for decisions in the world of practical affairs.

We fear that the work we have done so far creates too inclusive a domain for ideology. If we define ideology as "any discourse bound up with specific social interests," then it becomes hard to think of any discourse, at least in some remote sense, which does not fall under its umbrella.[12] There is no simple way out of this problem. All we might say is that as social interests are better organized, more powerful, and their relationship to dominant cultural discourses more obvious, we can be more confident in calling such affected discourses ideological. Conversely, as social interests appear disorganized, lacking in influence, and their relationship to dominant cultural discourses are unclear or weak, we may view these discourses as relatively nonideological.

Remember that discourses that meet these criteria may resist the label "ideology." Americans do not typically refer to school curricula, advertising, or the law as examples of ideological discourse. Yet these discourses are paradigm cases of ideology. This quality of ideology denying itself is a central characteristic of the concept. In summary, ideological discourse is a "discourse bound up with specific social interests." It produces a version of the truth and perpetuates belief systems on behalf of powerful interests. This account has set aside many thorny theoretical issues, but for our purposes it is enough to recognize that discourse, power, and truth are bound up in the concept of ideology.

RHETORICAL MATERIALISM

Michael McGee's participation in the ideological turn is based on a particular theoretical perspective on rhetoric, which underwrites a method of critical analysis. We begin with an explanation of McGee's theory, rhetorical materialism, and then proceed to his method, ideographic criticism.

McGee identified himself as a "rhetorical materialist" to distinguish his program from traditional critical-theoretical approaches that had largely dominated the field into the 1970s. This is an important point to grasp. McGee was not theorizing in a vacuum; he was instead providing a perspective that stood in opposition to what was then the prevailing disciplinary paradigm. He was reacting against a regime of rhetorical theory built on the authority of revered figures and texts. At that time, communication scholars largely thought about rhetoric through the ideas and theoretical prescriptions of such great thinkers as Aristotle, Isocrates, Cicero, Quintilian, St. Augustine, Francis Bacon, George Campbell, and Richard Whately. The result of this approach was "a 'rhetoric' which is on its face uninformed by historical or immediate contact with actual practice." "The theory and technique of rhetoric," McGee writes, "come less from human experience than from the metaphysical creativity and inspiration of particular writers." "What has been called 'rhetorical theory,'" McGee contends, "through much of our tradition is not theory at all, but a set of technical, prescriptive principles which inform the practitioner while, paradoxically, remaining largely innocent of practice."[13]

Under this old regime, a speech was determined as eloquent and effective based on the application of classical theories. So, if the speaker was found to follow the advice of Aristotle, then the speech must have been both worthy and successful. Not surprisingly, the discourse surrounding twentieth-century social upheavals, especially the antiwar, civil rights, and women's movements, did not resemble the speeches given by the ancients. The mediated age of celebrity and fifteen-second ads operates on different principles than addresses to the Athenian Assembly, the Roman Senate, or the British Parliament.

By contrast, McGee explored actual rhetorical encounters. His sense of materialism is captured in his definition of *rhetoric*: "Rhetoric is a natural social phenomenon in the context of which symbolic claims are made on the behavior and/or belief of one or more persons, allegedly in the interest of such individuals, and with the strong presumption that such claims will cause meaningful change."[14] Note how this definition expands upon that given in chapter 2; from this definition, we may proceed to unpack the dimensions of rhetorical materialism.

First, the "natural social phenomenon" is the recurring human experience of the relationships among "speaker/speech/audience/occasion/change." You cannot live in the social world without being impacted by these relationships. Each time you are addressed as an audience—for instance, as the reader of this chapter, as a student in a class, or as a citizen of the American Republic—you enter into this confluence of relationships. This is not simply an idea but an unavoidable part of living in the social world.

Second, the phrase "in the context of which" features for McGee the problematic relationship between "discourse" and "rhetoric." Rhetoric represents the entire experience of the complex social relationships among speaker/speech/audience/occasion/change. Discourse is residue that is left behind. It is the copy of the "speech" that has been saved. McGee uses an analogy to explain the rhetoric-discourse distinction. "We can construct," he writes, "the nature, scope, and consequence of a nuclear explosion by analyzing its residue when the raw matter and even the energy inherent in its occurrence have dissipated. Thus it is possible to reconstruct the nature, scope, and consequence of rhetoric by analyzing 'speech' even when 'speaker,' 'audience,' 'occasion,' and 'change' dissipate into half-remembered history." So, from a particular discourse we have the tracings that will permit a "reconstruction *of the whole phenomenon* . . . for it is the *whole* of 'speaker/speech/audience/occasion/change' which impinges on us."[15]

Third, the phrase "symbolic claims" suggests that "*every* interactivity of society contains or comprises a claim on some human being's belief and/or behavior."[16] Unlike conventional accounts of rhetoric, McGee does not distinguish rhetoric from coercion; rather, he understands rhetoric as a species of coercion. It is, he writes, a "coercive agency," but certainly one that is preferable to other physical forms of coercion. It is preferable in two different senses. First, when an audience acquiesces to rhetoric, it does so feeling that some more personal account was given for imposing the speaker's will. Second, the symbolic is preferable because it sublimates the "pain" of more violent forms of coercion. So, rhetoric may be thought of as a more ethical form of coercion, but a form of coercion nonetheless.

Fourth, the phrase "behavior and/or belief" draws the reader's attention to the complexities of moving from a change in belief to altering behavior. Scholars have filled the persuasion and social psychology literature with explanations of the difficulties inherent in the process of changing beliefs to influence attitudes in order to ultimately create new behaviors. This process is complex even in the simplest of direct transactions (speaker–message–target audience), but considerably more difficult to account for in the intricate communication environment of contemporary society. Beliefs and attitudes are shaped by ideology and other diffuse discourses that influence the tenor of an entire society.

Fifth, the phrase "allegedly in the interest of the audience," McGee explains, "calls to attention the relationship between 'speaker' and 'audience' as 'leader' to 'follower.'"[17] The relationship between leader/follower and speaker/audience is a continuing theme in McGee's work. "Every 'audience,'" he writes, "comes together with an interest and the expectation that the 'speaker' will aid in procuring that interest. And every 'speaker' comes to 'audience' with the desire to accomplish an otherwise impossible task by mobilizing a collective force."[18] The tension between the interests of leader and follower, speaker and audience, is at the center of any ideological criticism. The rhetorical creation of a sense of collectivity among audience members requires the invention of messages that harmonize often divergent interests.

Finally, the phrase "the strong presumption that such claims will result in meaningful change" draws our attention to the issue of rhetorical effects. Few social science models of any stripe have much success at predicting cause-and-effect relationships. Certainly, any retrospective claim of a direct effect between a particular feature of a message and a specific historical outcome is foolhardy. The message variable is at best one among a bundle of other forces (economic, demographic, political, cultural, and so forth), and to try to draw specific causal connections is nearly impossible. Yet, in the everyday world, we "conduct a continual deliberation based on our ability to model the environment and to predict the consequences of changing it."[19] Even though we can neither explain nor control all the factors that influence change, we talk as if speech is a powerful agency that can control the environment. This talk creates a sense of the collective and then speaks as if the collective will can shape meaningful social change. In these rhetorical transactions, we construct a discourse that reveals the world in which we live. It is powerfully shaped by the ideological commitments that we share. As these commitments are modified, the messages reflect these changes. We can map the ideological shifts in society by paying attention to these messages.

Given the commitments of rhetorical materialism, how does McGee proceed as a rhetorical critic? What critical apparatus does he mobilize to glean the ideological commitments that are present in a text? The answers to these questions revolve around the concept of the "ideograph."

IDEOGRAPHIC CRITICISM

Critics need a way to move between discourse and ideology; they need a rhetorical window on the exercise of power and the accompanying promulgation of truth. In Dana Cloud's words, they require "an analytical link between rhetoric—understood as situated, pragmatic, instrumental, and strategic discourse—on one hand, and ideology—the structures or systems of ideas within which individual pragmatic speech acts take place and by which they are constrained—on the other."[20]

McGee's concept of the **ideograph** provides just this link between rhetoric and ideology. The definition of *ideograph* is surprisingly complex, given its very ordinary and everyday nature. So, let us begin with a limited list of ideographs and then move to their formal characteristics. In the American context, the following words and slogans are examples of ideographs:

<equality>, <freedom>, <freedom of speech>, <law and order>, <liberty>, <national security>, <privacy>, <property>, <rule of law>, and <separation of church and state>.[21]

McGee lists the "characteristics" that would constitute a "formal definition of 'ideograph.'"[22] We have commented on each of these seven characteristics:

1. *"An ideograph is an ordinary language term found in political discourse."*[23] Ideographs are not technical terms, words used by experts or privileged insiders; rather they are terms that appear regularly in ordinary public talk. These are words that you will encounter on the news, on talk radio programs, in the texts of political speeches, in grade-school classrooms, and in everyday conversation.

2. *"It is a high-order abstraction representing collective commitment to a particular but equivocal and ill-defined normative goal."*[24] On the highest level of abstraction, ideographs are ambiguous, although they have a high emotional affect. For instance, the words <liberty>, <freedom>, and <equality> are emotionally evocative, but they have little cognitive meaning unless tied to specific situations. Either side in the abortion debate might employ the ideograph <liberty>, or either side in the controversy over the meaning of <separation of church and state> may invoke it. Ideographs are "normative" because they are value terms that are used to make judgments. Ideographs are "goals" because they represent something to be obtained or a path to follow. So, political candidates might urge their audiences to pursue the path of <freedom>.

3. *"It warrants the use of power, excuses behavior and belief which might otherwise be perceived as eccentric or antisocial, and guides behavior and belief into channels easily recognized as acceptable and laudable. Ideographs such as 'slavery' and 'tyranny,' however, may guide behavior and belief negatively by branding unacceptable behavior."*[25] The essential function of an ideograph is to warrant the exercise of power. Taking or not taking action is justified in the name of ideographs. Some ideographs are positive (<liberty>, <freedom>, <equality>), and behaviors that can be justified by positive ideographs are regarded as socially acceptable. Some ideographs are negative (<tyranny>, <socialism>, <censorship>), and behaviors that further these values are branded as unacceptable.

4. *"And many ideographs ('liberty,' for example) have a non-ideographic usage, as in the sentence, 'Since I resigned my position, I am at liberty to accept your offer.'"*[26] Ideographs "signify and 'contain' a unique ideological commitment."[27] They are the public vocabulary of ideology. So, when terms such as "liberty" and "freedom" are used in nonideological contexts, they do not function as ideographs.

5. *"Ideographs are culture-bound, though some terms are used in different signification across cultures."*[28] Ideographs are universal because they exist in all societies. Specific ideographs are culture bound. The Anglo-American liberal tradition[29] features a defining set of ideographs—the focus on <liberty>, for instance—that would not appear, or at least not appear with the same significance, in other cultures.

6. *"Each member of the community is socialized, conditioned, to the vocabulary of ideographs as a prerequisite for 'belonging' to the society."*[30] Becoming a member of a culture requires understanding the society's ideographs. As part of being socialized as an American, every schoolchild learns to respect <property>, to love <liberty>, and to guard <freedom>.

7. *"A degree of tolerance is usual, but people are expected to understand ideographs within a range of usage thought to be acceptable: The society will inflict penalties on those who use ideographs in heretical ways and on those who refuse to respond appropriately to claims on their behavior warranted through the agency of ideographs."*[31] These penalties may range

in severity. Speaking in ways that use ideographs inappropriately may result in political marginalization. Absent the appropriate language, advocates will simply fail to find an audience. Rhetorical sanctions may be imposed as deviant rhetors are labeled "traitors," "demagogues," or "extremists." This may result in public scorn and rhetorical exile. Finally, legal and economic sanctions may be inflicted on those who are determined to be guilty of "subversion" or "treason."

Ideographs are especially important for understanding the relationship between leaders and citizens. They are the storehouse of words and phrases from which leaders select appeals to warrant exercises of power. These are the terms that are used when leaders claim to be acting in the name of <the people>.[32] "Ideographs represent in condensed form," Condit and Lucaites explain, "the normative, collective commitments of the members of a public, and they typically appear in public argumentation as the necessary motivations or justifications for action performed in the name of the public."[33]

Like other terms of value, ideographs are often in tension with one another. As McGee writes, "An ideograph is always understood in its relation to another."[34] So <freedom> is understood in relationship to <order>, <responsibility>, and the <rule of law>. In any given circumstance, advocates may argue that one ideological commitment is more important than another. For instance, in the civil rights struggles of the 1950s and 1960s, segregationists and integrationists battled over the preeminence of particular sets of ideographs. Segregationists held that <property> rights permitted proprietors of restaurants, motels, retail stores, and other <private> businesses to decide whom they would serve. If owners of apartment buildings did not want to rent to black families, they should have that prerogative as controllers of private property. Integrationists held that the ideological commitment to <equality> demanded that businesses, which served the <public>, had an obligation to treat each customer alike. The resulting public accommodation and open housing legislation put into law regulations that elevated, in this context, <equality> over <property>.

In brief, this example depicts the synchronic and diachronic dimensions of ideographic analysis. The **synchronic** dimension explores the tension among ideographs at a particular time. In the civil rights illustration, there were advocates positing differing ideological constructions of segregation in an effort to influence passage of specific legislation. The **diachronic** dimension explores a society's changing ideological commitments through time. In America, <equality> has become an ever-more-important ideological commitment, and its prominence has come at the expense of other ideographs, including <property>,[35] and is even now clashing with <freedom of religion>.

We want to return for a few moments to the "point of departure" at the beginning of the chapter. Recall that we contrasted a pragmatic model of criticism (Bitzer's rhetorical situation) with ideological criticism. With the introduction to McGee's ideographic criticism, we want to spend a little time contrasting the two approaches. We draw your attention to three specific differences which we simplify for ease of comparison: the nature of effects, the concept of audience, and assumptions about reality.

Effects. In the pragmatic model, which few working scholars actually employ but is the focus of a great deal of undergraduate pedagogy, the critic is interested in evaluating the impact of a speaker's message on a target audience. The effects are often quite narrow in conception. Did the message have the particular effect that the speaker desired? For instance, did the corporations' public-relations campaigns retain customers and investors? In ideographic analysis, the critic is interested in examining the discourse as a symptom of changes in ideology and, thus, public consciousness. Put differently, the discourse itself is understood as the effect rather than the cause. When ideographs change—for instance, when <equality> displaces <property>—this reflects a change in ideology. The society has begun to justify political actions in new ways and warrant the exercise of power in different terms.

What caused these changes in ideology? This is a very difficult question and is beyond the scope of rhetorical analysis. Typically, such changes are the result of economics, demographics, conflict, or some other social malady. The result of such forces is a change in social reality—the way Americans think about race has changed dramatically over the last century—and these changes are then reflected in the society's rhetoric. These rhetorical changes are marked by new relationships among the culture's ideographs.

Audience. In the pragmatic model, the audience is often assumed to be a fixed target. The audience preexists the message. Thus, the advocate adapts the message to a set of audience predispositions and behaviors. The critic's work is to assess the choices that the rhetor made. In ideographic analysis, the audience itself is taken to be rhetorically constructed. Power is exercised and political actions are justified in the name of <the people>.[36] The audience does not preexist the message but is actually constituted by it. Adolf Hitler constructed the German people as a superior Aryan race. Martin Luther King Jr. constructed a people who were judged by the "content of their character" rather than the "color of their skin." In each case, these definitions of <the people> become ideological premises upon which to justify taking particular forms of political action. Understanding the changing ideological construction of <the people> is at the center of doing ideographic criticism.

Reality. In the pragmatic model of criticism, there is an implicit assumption that an objective situation (circumstances, audiences, constraints) is present that may be altered by the strategic use of discourse. The situation preexists the discourse. In ideological criticism, there is an explicit assumption that rhetoric constitutes reality. As we mentioned earlier, ideological criticism concerns the relationship among discourse, power, and truth. The constellation and relationship among ideographs maps the shape of this rhetorically constituted reality.

FINAL THOUGHTS

All criticism involves making arguments on behalf of judgments. For example, Wayne Brockriede writes that when a critic "states clearly the criteria he has used in arriving at his judgment, together with the philosophic or theoretic foundations on which they rest, and when he has offered some data to show that the rhetorical experience meets or fails to meet these criteria, then he has argued." Confronted with this form of critical argument "a reader has several kinds of choices: he can accept or reject the data, accept or reject the criteria, accept or reject the philosophic or theoretic basis for the criteria, and accept or reject the inferential leap that joins data and criteria."[37]

Using Brockriede's notion of criticism as a template, let us think through how a critic may use ideographic criticism to form an argument on behalf of a judgment. First, ideographs are a kind of *data.* They direct the critic to look for the presence of ideographs in a text. The critic looks both for the tension among ideographs at a single point in time and for the changing patterns of ideographic tensions over time. These patterns are the critic's data.

Second, the *theoretical foundation* of ideographic analysis is rhetorical materialism. It is the commitments of rhetorical materialism that underwrite the relationship among rhetoric, discourse, and ideology. It is only when rhetoric and ideology are understood in particular ways that ideographic criticism becomes compelling. The data provided by ideographs represent patterns of public consciousness. These patterns are maps of changing ideological commitments. As a result, the critic reveals the changing patterns by which power is justified.

Third, ideographic criticism does not present any single set of *criteria for evaluation*. The results of ideographic criticism provide data that underwrite several different forms of evaluation.

(A) An ideographic criticism documents progressive or regressive ideological-rhetorical trends. Celeste Condit and John Lucaites, in their book *Crafting Equality*, have documented the increasingly important role <equality> has played in American public consciousness. By and large, they tell an affirming story of an improving and more just America. The ascendancy of <equality>, they argue, has had positive consequences on the moral quality of our national discourse. Used in this way, the reader is asked to judge the positive and negative quality of the ideographic trend.

(B) Ideographic criticism believes ideology is false consciousness. For these critics, public rhetoric often rationalizes political acts that help the powerful and disadvantage the powerless. Dana Cloud, in her ideographic analysis of family-values discourse, draws precisely this type of conclusion. "<Family values> talk," she writes, "functioned during the [1992 presidential election campaign] to scapegoat Black men and poor Americans for social problems." She continues, "Ultimately, in constructing the family as the site of all responsibility and change, the rhetoric of <family values> privatizes social responsibility for ending poverty and racism."[38] Employed in this matter, readers are asked to accept or reject the discourse as a distortion promulgated for the purpose of established interests.

(C) Ideographic criticism reveals political irony. Irony lies in the incongruity between the actual result and the normal or expected result. By exposing inconsistencies among ideological warrants, it opens up semantic space for resistance. These terms begin to lose some of their positive emotive force, and ultimately these justifications for the exercise of power become less compelling. For example, Celeste Condit and Ann Selzer explored the newspaper coverage of a Kansas murder trial. They found, ironically, that the journalistic standards of <objectivity> led "to a prosecution bias in the reporting of criminal trials."[39] Ironically, objectivity led to bias. This form of ideographic criticism suggests lines of counterargument and alternative political narratives. The reader is left to judge the merits of these new ways of looking at the world.

CRITICAL ESSAY

We have written an analysis of the discourses accompanying the departure of LeBron James from Cleveland in 2010 to play for the Miami Heat and his subsequent return to the Cavaliers in 2014. This sports transaction illustrates the ideographic tension between the <market> and <loyalty>.

THE CONUNDRUM OF <LOYALTY> AND THE <MARKET>: THE DISCOURSES SURROUNDING LEBRON JAMES'S LEAVING AND RETURNING HOME

Living in the shadow of the marketplace, we plant roots in shallow ground. Market theory "teaches that leaving is a virtue" because it fosters "competition."[40] In our work lives, we can expect resources to flow across borders, and capital, labor, and materials to seek the most efficient and profitable location for production. The deindustrialized upper Midwest, now sadly called the rust belt, is a testament to this new condition. Only downsized remnants remain of the steel industry in Youngstown, Gary, and Pittsburgh, tire production in Akron, glass manufacturing in Toledo, or automobile assembly in the Michigan cities of Flint, Hamtramck, and River Rouge. Consequently, US workers can expect to move more often, change jobs more frequently, and make a living under conditions of increasing economic uncertainty.

Likewise, the marketplace weakens our attachment to goods and services. With new search engines, we shop across the range of providers to find what is cheapest and most convenient. According to philosopher George Fletcher, "The values of the marketplace apply today not only in the choice of material products like toothpaste and automobiles but in our relationships with people." "Shifting loyalties," he continues, "is an increasingly common way of coping with a weak friendship, a shaky marriage, a religious community that takes the wrong stand on an important issue, or a nation that has come into the hands of the wrong political party." "Those who exit," he observes, "cannot be faulted for assuming that newly planted roots will yield greener grass."[41]

Despite the dominance of the market, appeals to loyalty are no less prominent. Sellers invest vast sums to create bonds between the public and their wares. What changed during the last century are the rhetorical materials with which these bonds are manufactured. Commercial advertising has turned away from product-based marketing; religious evangelizing has turned away from arguments about theology; and political campaigning has increasingly turned away from issue appeals.[42] Contemporary constructions of loyalty are cobbled together from disconnected images, decontextualized historical references, and mythic fragments. They are, to borrow the language of Alasdair MacIntyre, largely incoherent as a reasoned justification for belief and action.[43]

We may not notice this incoherence because discussions of loyalty are now so frequently comingled with the vocabulary of branding. Yet, this marketing terminology is a species of loyalty with newer, less auspicious, objects of attachment. The appeals by which we claim people have obligations, duties, or owe their faithful allegiance are no small matter. When these appeals rest on shifting sands, commitment becomes hard to secure and misplaced loyalties become difficult to refute.

In this essay, we turn our attention to a case study of disputed loyalty, which garnered a great deal of national attention because it set in sharp relief the tension between the logic of the market and the loyal obligation to community. In the resulting rhetorical fireworks, the act was characterized as "desert[ion]" and "betrayal" and the actor as "narcissistic," "cowardly," "heartless," "callous," and "selfish." Fortunately, in the larger scheme of things, a basketball player exercising his prerogative to change teams in the free-agent market is hardly all that important, though the national clamor around LeBron James's decision to leave Cleveland for Miami rivaled the hand-wringing over Edward Snowden's supposed traitorous NSA revelations.[44]

We do believe, however, that the discourses surrounding professional sports are a useful entry point into the study of loyalty and the marketplace. Sports fandom is built on bonds of attachment among teams, communities, and athletes.[45] These bonds are stressed by the economics of free agency, which encourages players to make decisions that weigh their individual interests against considerations of loyalty.

In what follows, we describe the circumstances and characterize the discourses that swirled around James's decision to leave the Cleveland in 2010 and return in 2014. Second, we unpack the rhetorical complications in the ideographic tension between the <market> and <loyalty>. Finally, we draw conclusions about the rhetorical nature of <loyalty> in the postmodern world.

Leave and Return

Despite being raised by a single mother in the housing projects of Akron, Ohio, LeBron James's athletic talent made him a national celebrity by his late teens. When he bypassed college, a bounce of the NBA lottery ball permitted his hometown team to select him with the first pick in the draft.[46] Cleveland had not enjoyed a championship of any kind for nearly fifty years, but now a native son of Ohio seemed destined to alter its fate.

During his first seven seasons, the league twice named James MVP and he led the Cavaliers to the 2007 NBA Finals. He was regarded as the "best player on the planet," and, befitting his iconic status, was known simply as "King James."[47] But beyond delivering on his athletic promise, James cemented his regional identity. His partner, the mother of his children (and now his wife, Savannah Brinson), had been his girlfriend since the time they were high-school classmates. He built a large home in Akron. He was a generous benefactor to his alma mater, St. Vincent–St. Mary School, and his foundation provided support to schoolchildren in North-east Ohio. He often spoke about where he came from and how it contributed to who he was. He constructed a persona not of a person changed by good fortune but rather as an authentic man who reflected the character of home.

Since the time of Curt Flood and the challenge to baseball's reserve clause, the free-agent market has permitted professional athletes to choose the places they work.[48] So, on July 8, 2010, on the nationally televised special, "Decision," LeBron James announced that he was going to exercise his collectively bargained right to change teams and take his "talents to South Beach." During the next four years in Miami, he played in four NBA Finals and brought two championships to the Heat. Four years later, on June 25, 2014, James decided to return to Cleveland, where he signed a two-year $42.1 million contract and transformed the Cavaliers from one of the worst teams in the league to a favorite to win the 2015 championship.[49]

We focus on two texts produced by the chief protagonists in the drama: Dan Gilbert's public letter to the Cleveland fan base released on the eve of the "Decision," and LeBron James's first-person essay announcing his return to Cleveland. In exploring these discourses, we find a window through which to examine the ideographic tension between the <market> and <loyalty>.

Gilbert's Public Letter

Dan Gilbert was born, raised, and centers his core businesses in Detroit. His company, Quicken Loans, is the second largest retail lender in the United States with 10,000 employees who issued $70 billion in home loans in 2012. He has amassed an estimated $4.8 billion fortune transferring money across the local boundaries that used to define old time banking.[50] He bought the Cavaliers in 2005 for $375 million. Upon James's return in 2015, *Bloomberg News* estimates that the franchise was worth a billion dollars.[51] In the 2013–2014 season, Cleveland ranked 16th in NBA attendance, but after James's announced return, the team sold out every regular season game.[52] James's move to Miami cost, by some estimates, the Cleveland market $2.5 billion in economic activity.[53]

Gilbert, the man of the <market>, penned a public letter, addressed to "all of Northeast Ohio and Cleveland Cavaliers supporters," excoriating LeBron James for exercising his free-agent option.[54] The letter has three parts: the portrayal of James as traitor, the promise of the continued commitment of the Cavaliers' franchise to its supporters, and the observation that "bad karma" would "curse" James and Miami. Each part is built on a persuasive characterization of <loyalty>.

Loyalty is a virtue that characterizes a disposition of persons and their motivation toward action, and is invoked toward particular objects of attachment. So, one might be a loyal spouse, employee, or friend. In a political context, <loyalty> is understood as attachment to community, nation, or political ideals. Because dispositions are mental states, they are inferred indirectly through the interpretation of acts. For Gilbert, leaving Cleveland is an act of "desert[ion]" and "betrayal," and such "disloyalty" is associated with a person of "narcissistic," "cowardly," "heartless," "callous," and "selfish" character.

In the letter's second section, Gilbert contrasts the Cavaliers' organization with its departing player. "The good news," Gilbert writes, "is that the ownership team and the rest of the hard-working, loyal, and driven staff over here at your hometown Cavaliers have not betrayed you nor NEVER [all cap in original] will betray you." The organization's commitment will bring the Cleveland "an NBA Championship before the self-titled former 'king' wins one."

Finally, Gilbert's "[personal] guarantee" of an NBA championship is built on an understanding of vice as a harbinger of "bad karma." "This heartless and callous action," Gilbert writes, "can only serve as the antidote to the so-called 'curse' on Cleveland, Ohio. . . . James (and the town where he plays) will unfortunately own this dreaded spell and bad karma."

If the <market> is a rational arbiter of self-interest, what are the grounds for making <loyalty> claims? James neither abandoned his family, the league, nor the game; he merely changed employers in order to improve his prospects. Not surprisingly, Gilbert's scathing criticism of James does not appeal to any utilitarian calculation of interest. James is guilty of severing a mystic bond. Consider these phrases from the letter:

1. "Unlike anything ever 'witnessed' in the history of sports."
2. "This shocking act of disloyalty from our home grown 'chosen one' sends the exact opposite lesson of what we would want our children to learn. And 'who' we want them to grow up to become."
3. "The self-declared former 'King' will be taking the 'curse' [refers to the Cleveland sports curse] with him down south."
4. "DELIVERING YOU [all caps in original] the championship you have long deserved and is long overdue."
5. "Tomorrow is a new and much brighter day."

The Chosen Nation narrative tells the story of God's covenant with the people of Israel. When this story is transferred to American shores, the Puritans adapted the myth to justify their own "errand in the wilderness."[55] The phrases "delivering you" and "new and much brighter day" evoke the Exodus narrative.[56] In the tradition of the Old Testament prophets, Gilbert warns of God's "curse" upon the unfaithful.

The term "witnessed" is a reference to the Nike advertising campaign, launched in 2005, to pay "tribute to James and acknowledges the legions of fans worldwide who are 'witnessing' his greatness, power, athleticism and beautiful style of play."[57] In the accompanying imagery, fans resemble a Black Church congregation and LeBron's pose, with arms splayed, symbolizes the cross. The "witness" language is drawn from the Book of Acts, where St. Luke speaks of those chosen to testify to the resurrection.[58] Gilbert reinforces the Christian motif with the phrases "chosen one" and "self-declared king."

In his condemnatory discourse, Gilbert allegorically compares James to Moses abandoning his quest for the Promised Land and Jesus forsaking the sacrifice of the cross. This hyperbolic criticism, invented from fragments of the most sacred stories in the Judaic-Christian tradition, ought to shock the public's rhetorical sensibility. Yet, as the *Cleveland Plain Dealer* documented in its media roundup article, "In everywhere but Miami, reaction to LeBron James' decision is overwhelmingly negative."[59] Interestingly, the authors of these negative commentaries often acknowledged the good reasons for changing franchises, but yet found in James's move evidence of his weak character.

James's "Coming Home" Essay

On July 11, 2014, LeBron James announced in a first-person essay, published in *Sports Illustrated*, his intention to return home to play basketball in Cleveland.[60] The text mediates <loyalty> with the ideograph <opportunity>. James explains his journey in three parts. First, he was given an opportunity that required leaving home. Second, the time away was an enriching experience. Finally, upon his return, he is better prepared to help those he left.

This is a familiar genre. It resembles the story of anyone who has gone away to school and returned home. This narrative form is a staple of candidate biographies. Jimmy Carter and Bill Clinton, for instance, grew up in the South; both left home to pursue elite educational and professional opportunities (for Carter, Georgia Tech, Annapolis, and the nuclear Navy; for Clinton, Georgetown, Oxford, Yale, and the legal profession); and both returned to engage in public service so they might improve the places they left.[61]

In James's parallel account, "Miami, for me, has been almost like college for other kids. These past four years, helped raise me into who I am. I became a better player and a better man." "I learned," he continues, "from a franchise that had been where I wanted to go." As a consequence, "I see myself as a mentor now and I'm excited to lead some of these talented young guys." Like Carter and Clinton, who had opportunities to pursue a naval career or a legal career in a large urban law firm, James wanted to bring what he had learned to bear on the problems at home:

> Before anyone ever cared where I would play basketball, I was a kid from Northeast Ohio. It's where I walked. It's where I ran. It's where I cried. It's where I bled. It holds a special place in my heart. People there have seen me grow up. I sometimes feel like I'm their son. Their passion can be overwhelming. But it drives me. I want to give them hope when I can. I want to inspire when I can. My relationship with Northeast Ohio is bigger than basketball.

The reasons for returning were largely unrelated to basketball; they were ties to the mythic chords of place. "But I have two boys and my wife, Savannah, is pregnant with a girl," and "I started thinking about what it would be like to raise my family in my hometown." He elaborates, "The more time passed, the more it felt right. This is what makes me happy." In the closing sentences of the essay, James draws explicitly the parallel between his journey and the life cycle of so many others that leave so they may return better able to help improve the quality of the community:

> I want kids in Northeast Ohio, like the hundreds of Akron third-graders I sponsor through my foundation, to realize that there's no better place to grow up. Maybe some of them will come home after college and start a family or open a business. That would make me smile. Our community, which has struggled so much, needs all the talent it can get.

The appeal to <loyalty> is reconfigured, building a sense of connectedness and obligation that is differentiated from those expressed in Gilbert's message. James speaks of a familial bond, not with the Cavaliers' fan base but the one between himself and his childhood home. This move separates James-as-person from James-as-athlete. This appeal connects <loyalty> to place rather than to an organization and its mission. Put another way, James's account moves out of the shadow of the market.

Ideographic Tensions

An ideograph is "an ordinary language term" representing a "collective commitment to particular but equivocal and ill-defined normative goal." Yet, it has serious justificatory consequences since it "warrants the use of power" and "guides behavior and belief into channels easily recognized as acceptable and laudable." As members of a political community, we are all "socialized, conditioned to the vocabulary of ideographs as a prerequisite for 'belonging' to the society."[62] Ideographs are highly evocative but cognitively ambiguous. As ideographic terms move across contexts, they warrant social action on different grounds. As various ideographs arise in any given circumstance, the dialectical tensions among them stress their equivocal status and generate controversy.

In our discussion, we have largely focused on the tension between the <market> and <loyalty>. We have suggested that various other ideographs swirl around these key terms. Although free agency is a market term par excellence, James speaks and writes in the language of <opportunity>. He views free agency as creating a situation in which he may make a rational decision about taking advantage of <opportunity>.

In the US tradition, the <market> is but one term revolving around the ideological cornerstone of liberal-democratic thought, <property>. Broadly understood, <property> ensures a wide sphere of private action and thoughts, conscience, speech, religion, and association remain the <property> of individuals and, therefore, outside public regulation.[63] In this sense of <property>, James had a right to his own labor and could freely pursue <opportunity>. Yet, in US history <property> has had other meanings and has been used as a justification for the denial of <freedom>. Property rights were the rationale for segregation, because owners of restaurants, motels, theaters, and apartment buildings had the right to determine which customers they would serve. Before the Civil War, human bondage defined slaves as <property> and denied them the right to sell their labor.

Gilbert used language that evokes, at least for some listeners, this older, discredited sense of <property>. He "speaks as an owner of LeBron and not the owner of the Cleveland Cavaliers," Rev. Jesse Jackson said in a press release. "His feelings of betrayal personify a slave master mentality. He sees LeBron as a runaway slave. This is an owner employee relationship—between business partners—and LeBron honored his contract."[64] In the context of an African American–dominated NBA, this characterization forced Commissioner David Stern to fine Gilbert $100,000 for "inappropriate" remarks and to rather gently rebuke Jackson. "However well-meaning Jesse may be in the premise of this one, he is, as he rarely is, mistaken," Stern said. "But he is a good friend of the NBA and our players. Has worked arduously on many good causes and we work together in many matters."[65] In our interpretation, we take Stern to be rejecting any characterization of athletes as the owners' property, while simultaneously acknowledging that Gilbert's language inappropriately echoed this older sense of <property>.[66]

We live in a liberal-democratic culture dominated by appeals to rights. These rights limit the range of public obligation and create a correspondingly large domain of privacy in which citizens can pursue their self-interest. In the present case, James secured his rights through a collectively bargained labor agreement, provisions in a binding contract with the Cavaliers, and the general right of citizens to freely offer their labor.

The concept of loyalty, by contrast, is traditionally conceived as a public obligation, a civic virtue with a dispositional attachment to some end apart from self. Definitions of loyalty employ synonyms such as "devotion," "attitude," "sentiment," "emotional attachment," and "identification."[67] In political terms, loyal Americans possess the requisite sentiment toward their country. The presence of this sentiment is important because it motivates acts in support of the government and leads citizens to willingly sacrifice for the common good.

In the present context, Gilbert's discourse is ambiguous about the objects of James's betrayal. Apparently, it is some combination of team, organization, mission, fan base, and home. When citizens are asked to sacrifice for country, we may ask about their reasons for national attachment. They might list a host of ideographs—<freedom>, <equality>, <opportunity>, <rights>, and so forth. In one important sense, Gilbert is asking James to forfeit the exercise of his <rights> in the name of <loyalty>. This is precisely the logic of the Red Scare, when Joseph McCarthy argued that citizens ought to be willing to sacrifice First Amendment protections of freedom of speech and association to ferret out disloyal subversives. Not surprisingly, because scholarly attention to loyalty has so frequently focused on McCarthyism, the resulting analyses have commonly joined appeals to loyalty with demagoguery.[68] Although the squabble over a basketball player's free agency is hardly momentous in comparison, it is worth examining the parallels to understand the rhetorical logic integral to liberal appeals to <loyalty>.

In the Greek, a demagogue is literally a "leader of the people."[69] Thus, with its modern pejorative connotations, the demagogue is a leader of the people who appeals to the basest instincts of the public. Thus, appeals to class, race, anti-intellectualism, and so forth are often labeled demagogic. Most instances of demagoguery have about them some tension between civic obligation and individual rights. When pressed too far, advocates of civic virtue will inevitably begin to look for "traitors." Hitler found the men who stabbed Germany in the back during World War I. The members of ISIS use a logic of loyalty in their adoption of a philosophy that allows them to deem other Muslims outside genuine Islamic faith, and thus worthy of condemnation, torture, or even execution.[70] White supremacists find the turncoats who are "traitors to their race." In one way or another, the demagogue plays on the tension between obligation to a community and individual rights.

We can ask meaningfully if Dan Gilbert's letter is demagogic. Our answer is necessarily equivocal. Certainly, in one sense, Gilbert employs all the incendiary language of treason in response to James's exercise of his rights to operate in a free <market>. Using our formula that an appeal to civic virtue is used to undermine <rights>, the Gilbert discourse has about it a necessary condition of demagoguery. On the other hand, because the legal framework of contract protected James, because fans, despite their often-indecorous displays of emotion, understand the limited nature of the stakes, and because Gilbert's outrage did not lead to a campaign of persecution, the incendiary discourse had few notable demagogic effects. We suspect, too, because this tension was between <loyalty> and <market> as opposed to <loyalty> and <national security> or <loyalty> and <our way of life>, the rhetorical consequences are muted.

Yet, the Gilbert-James exchange remains an interesting case to think with. First, as we have already said, the demagogic potential of the rhetorical logic of loyalty is clearly present in this case. Second, James's 2014 essay announcing his return home offers a productive way to think and talk about loyalty. The use of mediating ideographs, especially <opportunity>, makes clear the contingent claims of <loyalty>. In LeBron's prose, the journey home is a draw, a responsibility, but one that should not become narrow provincialism. In order to grow and mature, the loyalty to community must find new grounds of attachment.

Postmodernity and the Coherence of Loyalty

The mix of the market and, as noted above, the sacred lend credence to our judgment that contemporary loyalty discourses are often incoherent. Was Gilbert's letter an artless aberration composed in a fit of anger and, therefore, meaningless as a cultural maker of loyalty? It may well have been artless and it was most assuredly an angry rant, but words and images expressed so spontaneously reflect patterns of socialization. Because loyalty runs counter to material self-interest, we readily turn to the realm of the sacred.

Scholars have argued that religion is the quintessential domain of loyalty. "In general," Fletcher writes, "it makes good sense to think of one's relationship to God as a commitment to loyalty." After all, "the faith of the believer is constantly subject to temptation by a false power."[71] Adam and Eve's original sin is an act of disloyalty; the Book of Job is a drama of fidelity; and Peter's denying Christ three times is fear overwhelming devotion. "In its biblical foundations," Fletcher observes, "God is king, father, and protector of his people, who in turn owe him a duty of loyalty."[72] The sacred language of faith and covenant, sin and idolatry provide terms for expressing loyalty and betrayal. Marketing specialists have long understood the usefulness of sacred appeals in establishing brand loyalty.[73] As one group of researchers put it, "Consumption has become a vehicle for experiencing the sacred."[74] Remember the original Nike "Witness" campaign connected buying shoes to the Apostles.

The Gilbert letter's intense emphasis on the most vicious kinds of disloyalty—treason, betrayal, and desertion—in the context of a contractually constructed market makes the mythic fragments of the sacred so obviously incongruent. Ads are not written in the argumentative form of premise and conclusion; they are instead composed of emotionally charged words and images, which short-circuit the consumer's critical faculties. Gilbert's use of this postmodern montage as argument rendered his discourse incoherent.

In the four years that followed James' return to Cleveland, the Cavaliers won an NBA title and competed in four straight NBA Finals. During that time, other high-caliber players made the decision to switch teams. What is notable about these subsequent departures is that, generally, the focus of critique has shifted from the virtue of loyalty to the market value of competition. In 2016, Kevin Durant departed from the Oklahoma City Thunder to join the Golden State Warriors. Commentator Stephen A. Smith described the departure as "the weakest move I've ever seen from a superstar."[75] Competition, which many free market advocates venerate as the central virtue of the marketplace,[76] is at the heart of this critique. Durant was condemned not for violating a bond of loyalty but for pursuing an opportunity that was ostensibly antithetical to competition, leaving a viable competitive roster for one with talent so immense that his addition would undermine parity within the league.

Meanwhile, James has been able to solidify the mythic bond of home that he established in his return essay. When he left the Cavaliers in 2018 to join the Los Angeles Lakers, he faced virtually none of the criticisms accompanying his earlier departure. Gilbert penned yet another letter where he wrote, "The entire Cavaliers franchise thanks LeBron for that precious moment (winning a championship) and for all the excitement he delivered as he led our team to four straight NBA Finals appearances."[77] James was able to further cement his legacy in Northeast Ohio, as he established the "I Promise" charter school, which is currently "helping close the achievement gap in Akron."[78] These events demonstrate James's ability to discursively construct an image of home that transcends market-driven departures.

PERSONAL REFLECTIONS

We came to this essay out of a series of conversations about the strong public reaction to LeBron James's "Decision." We discovered shared, though usually unspoken, standpoints. First, we both sympathized with LeBron James and found Gilbert's public letter an unwarranted diatribe. Second, we both remembered the bitter battle that Curt Flood had waged to overturn baseball's reserve clause. We knew that the Flood struggle had been filled with the evocative language of slavery and freedom, and we could hear echoes of this racial rhetoric in the present case. Third, we are both distrustful of the ethos of the <market>. Consumerism is a persuasive ideology that dramatically influences nearly all spheres of American life, and many of its appeals hardly deserve the description "rational."

Yet, we also brought different perspectives to the discourse. Adam was fascinated by the intensity of fan identification with the team and the resulting strong emotional response to the "Decision." Ron was struck by the parallels between Joseph McCarthy's use of loyalty during the Red Scare and the evocative phrases in Dan Gilbert's public letter. Ideographic criticism gave us the vehicle with which to meld these two perspectives.

Like other critics working in the tradition of the "ideological turn," we readily acknowledge that our construction of the truth is a product of our standpoint. We trust we have offered reasonable arguments for the soundness of our conclusions, but we admit that it rests on suspicions about the misuses of <loyalty> to serve establishment interests.

POTENTIALS AND PITFALLS

Ideographic criticism is especially powerful when applied to discourses that celebrate particular values. This is so for three reasons: (1) Ideographic criticism links the celebration of particular values to the justification of power. (2) Ideographic criticism demonstrates the ways in which a particular celebrated value subordinates and organizes competing values. (3) Ideographic analysis can map alterations in value orientation over time and thus show the changes in a society's public discourse, which reflect changes in the citizenry's public consciousness.

The critic must be careful in generalizing from ideographic analysis. A single speech or a small set of messages may not represent anything particularly important about the public. In fact, the citizenry may resist government leaders' official pronouncements. One lesson we should learn from the fall of the Soviet Union and the communist regimes of Eastern Europe is that the populace often does not accept a regime's justifications for power. Kept in line by the brute force of the state, the citizenry apparently never bought into the government's propaganda. When given an opportunity, they quickly seized the chance to topple their countries' leaders.

In our short essay, we tried to illustrate the increasingly problematic grounds for justifying <loyalty>. The James-Gilbert discourses are a symptom of the problems of commitment in a postmodern world.

IDEOGRAPHIC ANALYSIS TOP PICKS

Andrade, Luis M. "CAUTION: On the Many, Unpredictable Iterations of a Yellow Border Sign Ideograph and Migrant/Queer World-Making." *Text and Performance Quarterly* 39, no. 3 (2019): 203–228. This essay marries migrant/queer world-making theories and ideographic analysis to describe how artists imagined new, often contradictory, worlds to resist modernist notions of citizenship, gender, sex, family, and humanity through (re)drawn iterations of the sign.

Cloud, Dana. "The Rhetoric of <Family Values>: Scapegoating, Utopia, and the Privatization of Social Responsibility." *Western Journal of Communication* 62 (1998): 387–419. This essay explores the phrase <family values> as an ideograph. It examines the ideological force of this ideograph and concludes that it works to victimize the poor. It has the force of blaming the poor for their own circumstances and absolving the fortunate of any responsibility for society's disadvantaged.

Condit, Celeste, and John Lucaites. *Crafting Equality: America's Anglo-African Word.* Chicago: University of Chicago Press, 1993. This prize-winning book is an excellent example of a diachronic analysis of ideographs. The authors trace the development of <equality> through American history.

Condit, Celeste, and J. Ann Selzer. "The Rhetoric of Objectivity in the Newspaper Coverage of a Murder Trial." *Critical Studies in Mass Communication* 2 (1985): 197–216. This essay explores the ideological commitment of journalism to the ideograph <objectivity>. In exploring the coverage of a Kansas murder trial, they demonstrate the ironic effect of <objectivity>. The commitment to <objectivity> leads, these authors contend, to reporting that is biased toward the prosecution.

Ewalt, Joshua. "A Colonialist Celebration of National <Heritage>: Verbal, Visual, and Landscape Ideographs at Homestead National Monument of America." *Western Journal of Com-*

munication 75 (2011): 367–385. This essay is one of a growing number of critical analyses that examines the ideograph as a visual image and not just a term in a verbal text.

DISCUSSION QUESTIONS

1. What are some terms that you think function as ideographs? How do these terms justify the use of power?
2. Think of a speech or public statement of any kind you believe was memorable. What were the key ideographs that the speaker used?
3. What ideographs do you find most compelling? For instance, are you persuaded by arguments that center on <freedom>? Do you support candidates that speak to <family values>?

ACTIVITIES

1. Get a group of students together, and write down as many terms as you can think of that function as ideographs. Discuss each term according to McGee's definition of ideographic discourse.
2. Ideographs are, in McGee's terms "high order abstractions." Choose a term such as "freedom," "democracy," or "equality" and ask ten people to define this term. What do these definitions have in common? How are they different?
3. Think of recent policies that have been enacted by your federal or local government, or new rules that govern your college or university. What ideographic terms could be used to describe the rationale for these policies?
4. Choose an ongoing controversy—gun control, national healthcare, abortion, climate change—and consider the discourses on each side of the issue. Do the same ideographs appear in each side's discourses? How are they used differently? Are particular sets of ideographs in tension with one another?

NOTES

1. Lloyd F. Bitzer, "The Rhetorical Situation," *Philosophy and Rhetoric* 1 (1968): 3–4.
2. Ibid., 6.
3. Philip Wander makes this same point in commenting on the alleged sterility of neo-Aristotelian (traditional) criticism, which shares many of the same commitments as Bitzer's situational approach. See Philip P. Wander, "The Ideological Turn in Modern Criticism," *Central States Speech Journal* 34 (1983): 1–18.
4. Ibid., 9.
5. Antony Flew, "Ideology," in *A Dictionary of Philosophy* (New York: St. Martin's, 1979), 150.
6. Edward B. Reeves, "Ideology," in *Encyclopedia of Religion and Society* (Walnut Creek, CA: Altamira Press, 1998), 234.
7. Robert T. Craig, "Communication," in *Encyclopedia of Rhetoric* (New York: Oxford University Press, 2001), 135.
8. "Enron Fast Facts," CNN, April 26, 2015, http://www.cnn.com/2013/07/02/us/enron-fast-facts.
9. See David Easton and Jack Dennis, *Children in the Political System: Origins of Political Legitimacy* (New York: McGraw-Hill, 1969).

10. See Stuart Ewen, *Captains of Consciousness: Advertising and the Social Roots of Consumer Culture*, 25th anniversary ed. (New York: Basic Books, 2001).

11. See Hayden White, *Metahistory: The Historical Imagination in Nineteenth-Century Europe* (Baltimore, MD: Johns Hopkins University Press, 1973), 1–42.

12. Terry Eagleton, *Ideology: An Introduction* (London: Verso, 1991), 9.

13. Michael Calvin McGee, "A Materialist's Conception of Rhetoric," in *Explorations in Rhetoric: Studies in Honor of Douglas Ehninger*, edited by Ray E. McKerrow (Glenview, IL: Scott, Foresman, 1982), 24.

14. Ibid., 38.

15. Ibid., 39.

16. Ibid.

17. Ibid., 41.

18. Ibid.

19. Ibid., 43.

20. Dana L. Cloud, "The Rhetoric of <Family Values>: Scapegoating, Utopia, and the Privatization of Social Responsibility," *Western Journal of Communication* 62 (1998): 389.

21. Placing a term or slogan inside angle brackets, <liberty>, has become the conventional way of identifying an ideograph.

22. Michael Calvin McGee, "The 'Ideograph': A Link between Rhetoric and Ideology," *Quarterly Journal of Speech* 66 (1980): 15.

23. Ibid.

24. Ibid.

25. Ibid.

26. Ibid.

27. Ibid., 7.

28. Ibid, 15.

29. For a definition of the Anglo-American liberal tradition, see Claus Mueller, *The Politics of Communication: A Study in the Political Sociology of Language, Socialization and Legitimation* (New York: Oxford University Press, 1973).

30. McGee, "The 'Ideograph,'" 15.

31. Ibid., 15–16.

32. See Michael Calvin McGee, "In Search of the 'People': A Rhetorical Alternative," *Quarterly Journal of Speech* 61 (1975): 235–249.

33. Celeste M. Condit and John L. Lucaites, *Crafting Equality: America's Anglo-African Word* (Chicago: University of Chicago Press, 1993), xii–xiii.

34. McGee, "The 'Ideograph,'" 14.

35. See Condit and Lucaites, *Crafting Equality*.

36. See Maurice Charland, "Constitutive Rhetoric: The Case of the *Peuple Québécois*," *Quarterly Journal of Speech* 73 (1987): 133–150; and McGee, "In Search of the 'People.'"

37. Wayne Brockriede, "Rhetorical Criticism as Argument," *Quarterly Journal of Speech* 60 (1974): 167.

38. Cloud, "The Rhetoric of <Family Values>," 387.

39. Celeste Condit and J. Ann Selzer, "The Rhetoric of Objectivity in the Newspaper Coverage of a Murder Trial," *Critical Studies in Mass Communication* 2 (1985): 197.

40. George P. Fletcher, *Loyalty: An Essay on the Morality of Relationships* (New York: Oxford University Press, 1993), 3.

41. Ibid., 4, 5.

42. See William Leiss, Stephen Kline, Sut Jhally, and Jacqueline Botterill, *Social Communication in Advertising: Consumption in the Marketplace*, 3rd ed. (New York: Routledge, 2005); Neil Postman, *Amusing Ourselves to Death: Public Discourse in the Age of Show Business* (New York: Penguin, 2005), 114–141; and Kenneth L. Hacker, ed., *Presidential Candidate Images* (Lanham, MD: Rowman & Littlefield, 2004).

43. Alasdair MacIntyre, *After Virtue: A Study in Moral Theory*, 2nd ed. (Notre Dame, IN: University of Notre Dame Press, 1984).

44. "Edward Snowden: Computer Programmer (1983–)," *Bio Newsletter*, http://www.biography .com/people/edward-snowden-21262897.

45. Hans H. Bauer, Nicole E. Stokbuerger-Sauer, and Stefanie Exler, "Brand Image and Fan Loyalty in Professional Team Sport: A Refined Model and Empirical Assessment," *Journal of Sport Management* 22 (2008): 206.

46. Ryan Jones, *King James: Believe the Hype—The LeBron James Story* (New York: St. Martin's Griffin, 2005).

47. Benjamin Hochman, "Five-Man Race for MVP a Tossup," *Denver Post*, March 19, 2008.

48. Free agency came about through the collective bargaining efforts of the Major League Baseball Players Association following the loss of the Curt Flood case before the US Supreme Court in *Flood v. Kuhn* (1972).

49. Brian Windhorst, "LeBron Deal has Eye on Future Cap," ESPN, July 14, 2014, http://espn .go.com/nba/story/_/id/11207703/lebron-james-deal-cleveland-cavaliers-2-years-421-million.

50. "#341: Daniel Gilbert," *Forbes: The World's Billionaires*, June 3, 2015, http://www.forbes.com/ profile/daniel-gilbert.

51. Scott Soshnick, "James Pushes Cavs Valuation Past Billion-Dollar Mark," *Bloomberg Business*, July 11, 2014, http://www.bloomberg.com/news/articles/2014-07-11/james-pushes-cavs-valuation-past -billion-dollar-mark.

52. "NBA Attendance Report—2015," ESPN, http://espn.go.com/nba/attendance; and "With LeBron James Returning to Cleveland, Cavaliers Tickets Could Be Most Expensive in NBA," *Forbes*, July 11, 2014, http://www.forbes.com/sites/jesselawrence/2014/07/11/if-lebron-james-returns-cavaliers -tickets-could-be-most-expesnive-in-nba.

53. Chris Good, "What Cleveland Lost When It Lost LeBron," *Atlantic*, July 9, 2010, http://www .theatlantic.com/national/archive/2010/07/what-cleveland-lost-when-it-lost-lebron/59480.

54. "Dan Gilbert's Open Letter to Fans: James' Decision a 'Cowardly Betrayal' and Owner Promises a Title before Heat," Cleveland.com, July 8, 2010, http://www.cleveland.com/cavs/index.ssf/2010/07/ gilberts_letter_to_fans_james.html.

55. Richard T. Hughes, *Myths Americans Live By* (Urbana: University of Illinois Press, 2003).

56. Gary S. Selby, *Martin Luther King and the Rhetoric of Freedom: The Exodus Narrative in America's Struggle for Civil Rights* (Waco, TX: Baylor University Press, 2008).

57. "Nike Reminds Fans 'We Are All Witnesses,'" NBA.com, June 5, 2007, http://www.nba.com/ cavaliers/news/witnesses_070606.html.

58. See Acts 1:8, 1:22, 1:26, 2:32, 3:15, 4:33, 5:32, 10:39, 10:41, 14:17, 15:8, 20:24, 22:15, 22:20, 23:11, 26:16, 28:23.

59. "In Everywhere but Miami, Reaction to LeBron James' Decision Overwhelmingly Negative: National Media Links," Cleveland.com, July 9, 2010, http://www.cleveland.com/cavs/index.ssf/2010/07/ as_lebron_james_leaves_clevela.html.

60. LeBron James and Lee Jenkins, "LeBron: I'm Coming Back to Cleveland," *Sports Illustrated*, July 11, 2014, http://www.si.com/nba/2014/07/11/lebron-james-cleveland-cavaliers. Unless otherwise noted, all James's quotations in this chapter come from this letter.

61. Ronald Lee, "Electoral Politics and Visions of Community: Jimmy Carter, Virtue, and the Small Town Myth," *Western Journal of Communication* 59 (1995): 39–60.

62. McGee, "The 'Ideograph,'" 15.

63. John Durham Peters, "John Locke, the Individual, and the Origin of Communication," *Quarterly Journal of Speech* 75 (1989): 387–399; Michael Calvin McGee, "The Flip Side of Privacy," in *Argument in Transition*, ed. David Zarefsky, Malcolm O. Sillars, and Jack Rhodes (Annandale, VA: Speech Communication Association, 1983), 105–115.

64. Brian Windhorst, "NBA's David Stern Fines Dan Gilbert $100,000 for Outburst, Criticizes LeBron James' TV 'Decision,'" *Plain Dealer*, July 12, 2010, http://www.cleveland.com/cavs/index .ssf/2010/07/nba_commissioner_david_stern_f_1.html. The imagery of slavery swirled around the original Curt Flood legal battle against professional baseball's reserve clause. The paternalistic terminology

Donald Sterling used in characterizing his management prerogatives was part of the racial scandal that lead to the NBA's termination of his ownership rights to the Los Angeles Clippers. See Ian O'Conner, "Shame on Stern for Sterling Silence," ESPN, April 30, 2014, http://espn.go.com/losangeles/nba/story/_/id/10857899/shame-david-stern-nba-letting-donald-sterling-stick-around.

65. Windhorst, "NBA's David Stern."

66. Ibid.

67. Clarke E. Cochran, *Character, Community, and Politics* (University: University of Alabama Press, 1982), 25–28; Leonard William Doob, *Patriotism and Nationalism: Their Psychological Foundations* (New Haven, CT: Yale University Press, 1964), 4–9; Morton Grodzins, *The Loyal and the Disloyal: Social Boundaries of Patriotism and Treason* (Chicago: University of Chicago Press, 1956), 21; John H. Schaar, "Loyalty," in *International Encyclopedia of the Social Sciences*, vol. 9 (New York: Macmillan, 1968), 484–487.

68. J. Justin Gustainis, "Demagoguery and Political Rhetoric: A Review of the Literature," *Rhetoric Society Quarterly* 20 (1990): 155–161.

69. Mogens Herman Hanson, *The Athenian Assembly: In the Age of Demosthenes* (New York: Blackwell, 1987), 51.

70. Kurt Eichenwald "ISIS's Enemy List: 10 Reasons the Islamic State Is Doomed," *Newsweek*, September 8, 2014.

71. Fletcher, *Loyalty*, 36.

72. Ibid., 37.

73. See, for example, Russell W. Belk and Melanie Wallendorf, "The Sacred Meanings of Money," *Journal of Economic Psychology* 11 (1990): 35–67; and Priscilla A. La Barbera and Zeynep Gürhan, "The Role of Materialism, Religiosity, and Demographics in Subjective Well-Being," *Psychology and Marketing* 14 (1998): 71–97.

74. Russell W. Belk, Melanie Wallendorf, and John F. Sherry Jr., "The Sacred and the Profane in Consumer Behavior: Theodicy on the Odyssey," *Journal of Consumer Research* 16 (1989): 1.

75. Charlotte Wilder, "Stephen A. Smith Rips Kevin Durant Ditching Oklahoma City," *USA Today Sports*, July 4, 2016, https://ftw.usatoday.com/2016/07/stephen-a-smith-rips-kevin-durant-golden-state.

76. Gary L. Reback, *Free the Market!: Why Only Government Can Keep the Marketplace Competitive* (New York: Penguin, 2009), 13.

77. Matt Eppers, "Cavaliers Owner Dan Gilbert Thanks LeBron James in Classy Farewell Letter," *USA Today*, July 2, 2018, https://www.usatoday.com/story/sports/nba/cavaliers/2018/07/01/dan-gilbert-thanks-lebron-james-classy-farewell-leave-cleveland/750178002/.

78. Erica L. Green, "LeBron James Opened a School That Was Considered an Experiment. It's Showing Promise," *New York Times,* April 12, 2019, https://www.nytimes.com/2019/04/12/education/lebron-james-school-ohio.html.

III

EXPANDING OUR
CRITICAL HORIZONS

13

Eclectic Rhetorical Criticism

Combining Perspectives for Insights

Jim A. Kuypers

I have tried to be as eclectic as I possibly can with my professional life, and so far it's been pretty fun.

—Roland Barthes

Eclectic and *eclecticism* are frequently misused terms. They have been used to call attention to differences not easily categorized, and also by persons unable to find a common thread among ideas. For instance, consider this use of *eclectic*: "Typically off-year elections are used for two things: one is a sort of testing ground, as a dry run for the next year. And two: you get a real eclectic mix of issues that don't have an over-arching theme but that's a little different this year."[1] What the author actually describes is not an eclectic mixture but a *hodgepodge*, which is a confusing or heterogeneous mixture. A more accurate use of *eclectic* would be to label as eclectics those who derive their sense of style or taste from a wide variety of sources. Although seemingly diverse, the common link among the eclectic sources is the person who puts them all together. Sometimes this extends to a common purpose, such as in the school of eclectic medicine, which is "eclectic in the sense that they integrated whatever worked, including [Native American] herbal medicine and homeopathy."[2] For an eclectic, there is a theme. The task for the eclectic critic is to make that theme apparent to others.

When I speak of eclectic criticism, I am not speaking of a jumbled mess of viewpoints presented in an unwieldy manner. The best eclectic criticism takes components of various rhetorical theories and blends them together into a comprehensive whole, all to better explain the workings of an intriguing rhetorical artifact. Pauline Kael wrote that "eclecticism is the selection of the best standards and principles from various systems of ideas. It requires more orderliness to be a pluralist than to apply a single theory. . . . Criticism is exciting because you must use everything you are and everything you know that is relevant."[3] Although some, particularly those who use single perspectives to guide their criticism, might take issue with Kael's assertion about "more orderliness," eclectic critics would certainly agree with Kael's depiction of excitement, not to mention Barthes's use of the term *fun*.

Beyond excitement, though, there often lies a broad sense of exploration. Eclectic critics are frequently drawn to extremely diverse rhetorical artifacts, and analysis of these diverse forms of rhetoric necessitates the development of nuanced, flexible, and diverse perspectives of analysis. On this note, theatrical director and producer David Esbjornson wrote,

> I have an eclectic past . . . but I intentionally have pursued that because there are so many interesting points of view that I want to explore. I think I'm not quite as all over the map as maybe people think. There's a certain reason that I have done all those plays. I tend to gravitate to the writers that I think are trying to say something, or who are outside of the center a bit and who are trying to break in and get their point of view expressed.[4]

Eclecticism has a long history. The term is often used to describe ancient philosophers who followed no particular philosophical school, but instead sought to take what was to them the best of established doctrines in order to construct a new system. The original Greek term, *eklektikos*, simply means choosing the best. Diogenes of Appolonia (fifth century BC) was among the earliest eclectics. By the first century BC, the term *eclectic* was in common use. One of the better-known examples of eclectic philosophers was Cicero, who blended the Stoic, Peripatetic, and New Academic doctrines. As an approach to philosophy and to rhetoric, eclecticism eschews single perspectives and draws its power instead from insights gained from combining multiple theories or perspectives into a blend used for a specific purpose.

Writing of the eclectic critic in particular, Bernard L. Brock, Robert L. Scott, and James W. Chesebro remarked that

> the conscientious eclectic is apt to be more interested in the immediacy of experience than the abstract integrity of a system or method. Such a person will argue that [perspectives] are but more-or-less-complete sets of tools with instructions by which to build scaffoldings and frameworks. They will argue that when what is made is made, the tools are laid aside, the scaffolding torn down, and the framework absorbed. When the eclectic critic does use a [perspective], it is an "open-ended" one that does not force or prescribe a specific [plan] and provides the critic with a great deal of creative decision making. The eclectic approach stresses the critic's ability to assemble and absorb ways of working, subordinating these to the task at hand.[5]

The last sentence is especially noteworthy in that it reinforces the critic's dominant role in producing good criticism. Good critics "absorb" or assimilate theory into their personal perceptions and then bring to bear their eclectically enhanced point of view on the rhetorical artifact. Eclecticism stresses the personality and critical capacities of the critic. On this point Ed Black wrote that it

> is inevitable that any expositor will approach a work from a certain point of view. His frame of reference may be subconscious and unsystematized, but it will assuredly be present, shaping the bias of his interpretation by influencing the direction of his attention, selectively sharpening some and dulling others of his sensibilities, and molding the nuances of his judgment in a thousand imperceptible ways.[6]

In some ways, eclecticism turns the tables, allowing first the critic to influence the perspective and then the perspective to influence the critic.

CRITICAL ESSAYS

Eclecticism is not for everyone, and despite its strengths, only a minority of critics blend and develop their own framework from which to proceed with criticism. The rest of this chapter explores the inner workings of four eclectically oriented essays and one book. The first is *Communication Strategies for Engaging Climate Skeptics: Religion and the Environment* by Emma Frances Bloomfield, and published by Routledge in 2019.[7] Bloomfield looks at the intersection of environmental rhetoric and Christian rhetoric emanating from three Christian groups engaged in activism surrounding the environment. In order for her to successfully analyze this complex interaction of discourse she combines Burkean theory dealing with the concept of identification with insights gained from argumentation theory.

The second is "Cowboys, Angels and Demons: American Exceptionalism and the Frontier Myth in the CW's *Supernatural*," by Joseph M. Valenzano III and Erika Engstrom, published in *Communication Quarterly* 62, no. 5 (2014): 552–568. Valenzano and Engstrom blend television criticism with mythic criticism, religious communication with political communication, and incorporate elements of American exceptionalism in order to produce an eclectic and insightful piece of criticism. The combined approach allows the authors to explain how the television show *Supernatural* enacts a particularly potent message that actually serves a larger American political narrative.

The third is "Texas Vernacular Rock House Structure: Defining 'Home' through Rhetorical Depiction," by Mary Evelyn Collins, published in the *American Communication Journal* 9 (2007): n.p. Collins incorporates elements of rhetorical depiction, theoretical elements of the Arts and Crafts movement, architectural theory, and cluster criticism in order to better understand and appreciate how Texas rock house architecture rhetorically acted to create a spirit of family and home and also a sense of place.

The fourth is "Carnivalesque Protest and the Humorless State," by M. Lane Bruner, published in *Text and Performance Quarterly* 25, no. 2 (2005): 136–155. Bruner looks at public protests in two different cultures using elements gleaned from several different theoretical areas that include viewing the "carnivalesque" as a form of public protest and political performance; he also employs theories of democratic citizenship. Through this analysis he provides insight into how Eastern European protests against communist dictatorships prevailed whereas protests against the communist dictatorship in China failed.

The fifth is "From Science, Moral Poetics: Dr. James Dobson's Response to the Fetal Tissue Research Initiative," by Jim A. Kuypers, published in the *Quarterly Journal of Speech* 86, no. 2 (2000): 146–167. Kuypers employs a judgmental analysis combined with Kenneth Burke's distinction between semantic and poetic meaning in order to analyze James Dobson's response to the legalization of fetal tissue research. Ultimately, using dramatistic theory, Kuypers analyzes the motive underpinning Dobson's discourse to understand how Dobson provided a way out of the moral quagmire science has placed humans in by highlighting mankind's ability to morally act.

Since there is no "one way" of performing eclectic criticism, what follows below are the personal comments of the authors of the above-mentioned works. The authors explain how they feel their work is eclectic and highlight the truly creative aspects of an eclectic style of criticism by focusing on describing the action of creating an eclectic approach to the artifact.

PERSONAL REFLECTIONS

Emma Frances Bloomfield on "Communication Strategies . . ."

As a researcher interested in how various ideologies influence environmental attitudes and behaviors, I began exploring the role that religion and Christianity play in the public's understanding of the environment. In researching this intersection, I encountered an intellectual curiosity that I starting referring to as "The Tale of Two Christianities." The first tale spoke of the interconnectedness of fundamental Christianity, conservativism, and climate change denial, where being a Christian denoted climate skepticism and anti-environmentalism. The second tale expressed the alignment of Christian teachings with environmentalism and how Christians were increasingly adopting a pro-environmental identity. Although the first tale was much more prominent, the second tale was still present and offered a foil to a deterministic or monolithic reading of the relationship between Christianity and the environment. With my interest piqued, I wanted to explore how Christian rhetoric was interpreted as an inventional resource[8] for a variety of environmental attitudes. What determined whether Christianity was a source of anti- or pro-environmental beliefs? How were different Christian environmental attitudes expressed rhetorically?

To answer these questions, I first had to locate texts that would work as exemplars of Christian environmental rhetoric. After choosing to use the digital rhetoric and print publications of various Christian organizations, I then had to identify specific groups that would be representative of "Christian rhetoric on the environment." I considered over a dozen groups as potential case studies and selected three for the book project: The Cornwall Alliance, the Acton Institute, and the Evangelical Environmental Network. I chose these groups because they interpret their faith in different ways to express markedly different attitudes toward the environment. In the book, I argue that the three groups represent three categories within my proposed typology of Christian environmental rhetoric: the separators, the bargainers, and the harmonizers. Aiming to compare and contrast their discourses, I needed theoretical tools that were flexible enough to illuminate a variety of different features within the texts and not prevent me from considering any similarities or differences based on a blind spot of any one theoretical perspective.

I was further drawn to choose a variety of different theoretical approaches due to my subject matter. Considering the interdisciplinary, sometimes called "wicked," problem of climate change as one of the most pressing global problems of our time, I knew it would likely require many types of knowledge and various modes of communication to be addressed. Therefore, I knew I would best tackle the environmental discourses of these three groups by bringing to bear a variety of theoretical perspectives.

After spending time gathering and reading through the rhetoric of the Cornwall Alliance, the Acton Institute, and the Evangelical Environmental Network, two primary rhetorical features emerged as ripe for analysis. The first was the functioning of the groups' discourse to solidify their shared values and the integration of their faith with environmentalism. Therefore, I had to consider the concept of "identity"—how are environmental identities constructed in partnership with or opposition to religious ones? In thinking about religion as a core facet of someone's identity that influences the other aspects, I wanted a perspective that captured the role of identity-building and how that identity manifests in and is constructed by the language that we use. How were the identities of religious environmentalists expressed by each group and what rhetorical features were similar or different in constructing that identity?

To address the topic of identity, I turned to the theories of Kenneth Burke, especially his ideas about identification and how people use language and symbols "to make sense of and explain their views" on topics such as the environment.[9] How Christians name and label their relationship to the environment may seem like an "innocuous choice" but, in fact, these choices create and restrict what we view as appropriate attitudes and behaviors.[10] Referring to these linguistic choices as "terministic screens," Burke emphasized their power as selecting and deflecting certain possibilities.[11] In the discourse of the three groups, the terministic screens often manifested as metaphors that informed their understanding of the relationship between their faith and the environment.

Another rhetorical feature that emerged was how the collected discourse not only had an identity-building function but also an argumentative one. In claiming a religious and environmental identity, these groups were also making arguments about the best way to interpret the Bible and to convince others of the proper relationship between Christianity and the environment. I was interested in the arguments in terms of how they were structured, to where they turned for authority and support for their arguments, and persuasive strategies they used to forward their perspective. Although these groups had the same primary text and traditions to turn to as argumentative resources, I was curious about what ways their leveraging of the Bible and Christian teachings would be different and used to support various environmental arguments.

To address this second feature, I turned to argumentation theory and, more specifically, argument models.[12] This approach enabled me to evaluate the various groups' rhetoric as arguments as to the correct biblical interpretations toward the environment. In other words, each group used the same text but different interpretations of it as grounds to support quite different environmental claims. In the book, I present these models in text boxes, which show how the arguments can be broken down into logical parts. These components can then be easily compared to the argument structures used by other groups to locate important similarities and differences.

As illustrative examples of my eclectic pairing of terministic screens and argument models, I have selected an excerpt from the Cornwall Alliance, the exemplar separator, and summarized my analysis from the book. On its website, the Cornwall Alliance describes itself as "up against a well-funded movement, one that receives millions of dollars from foundations whose agendas are diametrically opposed to the fundamental Christian ethic of the sanctity of human life."[13] This description shows their reliance on the metaphor of war, a terministic screen that positions Christianity and environmentalism on opposite sides of a battlefield. They further argue that "Christians" who view themselves as environmentalists act "contrary to [what is] taught in the Bible" and are "overwhelming anti-Christian."[14] The metaphor of war appears in the terms "diametrically opposed," "up against," "contrary, "anti-," and in other terms used throughout the Cornwall Alliance's discourse to indicate their "strict conception of identity . . . where if one is not good, one must be evil."[15] Expressed as an argument model:[16]

Premise 1: True Christians are good, moral, and believe in Christ.
Premise 2: Environmentalists are evil, immoral, and abandon Christ's teachings.
Conclusion: Environmentalists cannot be "true" Christians.

The metaphor of war supplies the justification for categorizing Christians and environmentalists as opposed to one another, thereby creating a sufficient grounds on which to conclude that Christians cannot and should not be environmentalists.

In analyzing the Cornwall Alliance's discourse, using both methods shows how terministic screens guide the group's argumentation practices and its understanding of the relationship between Christianity and the environment. The Cornwall Alliance thus constructs an aggressive polarized identity that necessitates a shutting out of environmental considerations and uses a strict hermeneutic to distinguish the Christian identity from an environmental one.

This practice is not echoed in the rhetoric of the Acton Institute and the Evangelical Environmental Network. The Acton Institute functions under a terministic screen of "revolution," where climate skepticism will eventually overturn scientific knowledge. The group thus argues that some features of climate science should be adopted and others abandoned. Alternatively, the Evangelical Environmental Network operates under a terministic screen of "harmony," where Christianity and environmentalism are united. The group thus argues that all of climate science can be accepted and that faith drives them to be environmentalists. Using both methods illuminates how interpretations of the Bible become inscribed into a religious identity through shared symbols *and* how those vocabularies both offer and restrict argumentative possibilities.

My rhetorical criticism of the three groups would not have been as rich or as informative if I had not engaged both argumentation and the concept of terministic screens. Alone, I would have considered their discourse only as argument strategies or only as identity-building practices. Together, I could understand how their orientations and approaches to the Bible, climate science, and the environment informed the arguments they made about their Christian ecological identities. For two groups, the Cornwall Alliance and the Acton Institute, their terministic screens informed arguments that led to skepticism toward climate science and either rejection of or cherry-picking from it to support their interpretations of the Bible. For the Evangelical Environmental Network, its blending of climate science and Christianity led it to mold its biblical interpretations to find harmony with mainstream environmentalism.

A look at both the importance of terministic screens and argument strategies enabled me to see prominent ways in which the discourses of these groups differed despite sharing the same faith and the same sacred text. An eclectic approach to criticism opened this project up for more nuanced interpretation that was deeply rooted in what the text offered as opposed to categories I had applied rigidly to the text. In listening to the text and letting it first express some of its many meanings, I selected two approaches, rooted in argumentation and Burkean theory, to best capture the variety of iterations and performances of Christian environmentalist rhetoric.

Joseph M. Valenzano III on "Cowboys . . ."[17]

Ever since 1995, eyewitnesses around the globe, but particularly in the Americas, reported seeing a small bearlike creature attacking local livestock. In Latin America the creature was dubbed the *chupacabra*, but to date it has not been found, and no sightings have been independently verified. This contemporary legend has, over the course of the last twenty years, been the subject of books, movies, and television shows. In fact, a popular way of saying you have attained the unattainable or found the unfindable is to say you have "found the Chupacabra." I like to think that in my own work, which explores the intersection of religion, politics, and popular culture, I have found the chupacabra—because I get to watch a lot of television and movies to complete my research!

I have always been interested in politics, and when I was younger one of my favorite television shows was *The West Wing*. I loved how the show seemed to mirror and discuss current issues and events. I also grew up Catholic, exposed to all the ceremonial trappings and extensive theological readings that come with that particular faith. Additionally, I have always had a very wild imagination, with a keen interest in science fiction and the supernatural. When I first began my career studying communication, I focused on politics, but soon my interests became more varied. For instance, I started to notice the same ceremonial dimensions in politics that occurred in my church. I began to see plenty of overlap between religious faith and the modern popular culture I consumed. Thus, my chupacabra emerged—I knew I wanted to explore how the modern penny dreadful[18] popular culture influenced the understanding of religion and politics for its consumers, and so I undertook the arduous mission of watching a lot of television and reading a wide array of communication research.

There are those who study media effects, those who explore popular culture, others who examine rhetorical theory, and a bevy of scholars who focus their attention on political and religious communication; however, very few bring the literature from all of these areas to bear on a text. In my work I begin with a text that "tells me something," and in my case it's usually a television show or movie. That "something" is a subtextual message that connects the imagination of the producers of the media artifact with a commentary on social, political, religious, and economic issues faced in the real world. I am fascinated with how these connections are made in the artifact and how they produce commentaries on contemporary events and issues that viewers often don't overtly recognize. To explain how the text accomplishes the "something," I noticed I needed to draw on literature from a wide range of fields, thus creating an eclectic criticism of the text. Let me share with you an example of this type of work.

A colleague of mine and I had a chance conversation one day regarding a common interest in a show called *Supernatural*, which airs on the CW network. We both were really interested in the story, but also noticed that it brought elements of multiple faiths together in a single show in a way no other program to our knowledge ever did. The result of this conversation was a set of studies regarding the intersection of politics and religion on television. The first study, published in the *Journal of Media and Religion*, used content analysis to find that *Supernatural* actually privileges the Catholic faith over other religious traditions—something that typically fails on television. The second study, which appeared in the *Journal of Communication and Religion*, analyzed the apocalyptic plotline of the show's first five seasons, illustrating how it functioned as a form of homily to a secular audience. The third article, though, serves as a terrific example of the eclectic nature of the criticism I like to conduct.

In "Cowboys, Angels and Demons: American Exceptionalism and the Frontier Myth in the CW's *Supernatural*," we dove even deeper into our analysis of the show. Not only did it have a distinct religious message but that religious content also served a larger political narrative as well. American exceptionalism is the idea that the United States is qualitatively better than Europe, and in some versions of the myth the United States is ordained by God to serve as the beacon of freedom for the rest of the globe.[19] This is a largely political message, but the "chosen by God" portion brings in a uniquely religious perspective that cannot be ignored.

We blended the religious notion of American exceptionalism with elements of the frontier myth. Specifically, the frontier myth has at its core certain elements of the American Wild West and expansion westward. In a wildly interesting essay on the Donner Party, Mary Stuckey identified four elements of the frontier myth that helped explain the plotlines of *Supernatural*. They were (1) an erasure of indigenous people and others who do not fit mainstream notions of the acceptable; (2) the triumph of American civilization over the wilderness; (3) the allowance for individual aggression when it benefits the larger community's survival; and (4) the idea of movement, key to the notion of Manifest Destiny.[20] Additionally, scholars have noted other key elements of the frontier myth, such as the heroic cowboy character.[21] We then used this frame to explore the episodes of the show in the contemporary context in which they appeared in an effort to learn how they reflected and deflected perspectives about current events. What made the case for this type of analysis even clearer were certain statements made by the show's creative team that made it sound as if they wanted to push an image of a rugged American family fighting in a supernatural wilderness.[22]

So the recipe for our approach in this essay began with the premise that media, especially television, function as today's "cultural storyteller,"[23] advancing ideas, values, and beliefs through the depiction of myths central to a community.[24] We then conducted our analysis by taking the core elements of the myth of American exceptionalism, especially the part about the United States being chosen by God, and the central characteristics of the frontier myth and applied them to the episodes of *Supernatural*. The critical frame was one part media, one part political myth, with a dash of religion. We were not really concerned with demonstrating that the show contained these myths (after all, that would simply be a cookie-cutter analysis). Instead our research questions were focused on asking, What was the payoff of that approach? How did it contribute to theory? and What did it do to the messages being sent to the primarily teenage audience?

The fact is, what we did was not simply scholarship about television or religion or politics, but rather all three. We borrowed from media studies, religion, and political rhetoric to help understand the central messages of the show and the influence they have on how viewers might understand the United States and/or religion. Eclectic criticism such as ours requires researchers to fully immerse themselves in the text, current events, and a multitude of different theoretical perspectives. The more perspectives from which you can draw analytical tools, the more enriching the analysis will be.

Mary Evelyn Collins on "Texas . . ."

I have always been intrigued with a particular style of house that is very common in the Southwestern United States, from Missouri to New Mexico, but most especially in Texas. This interest was prompted by the fact that the only house that my parents actually built was a bungalow in the "rock house" style. It was a transitional time in their lives, and this was perceived to be the house that would become their retirement home. I was not quite three when we moved in, but my older brothers were teenagers, the eldest in college. Less than two years later, with a better retirement plan promised, there was a job change and a move to another town. That house still stands, with the pecan trees my parents planted looming high above its roof, a survivor of Texas storms, a flood, and assorted families with active children.

What began to interest me in recent years was that, with the return of the bungalow in popular new home building, there was a return to Arts and Crafts movement elements used in the new "retro"-look homes. So much reminded me of the charming front porches and roof lines of the Texas rock houses.[25] The version of the Arts and Crafts, or Craftsman, bungalow in America emerged in the eastern United States with stucco walls and river stone columns or brick walls with river stone or stacked stone trim elements. In the far west, California particularly, the bungalow had stucco walls and some flat stone trim. Many "California bungalows" had a Spanish look, with tile roofs and side or rear patios rather than front porches. All over America whole neighborhoods of bungalows were built from 1900 to the early 1940s.[26] Their popularity disappeared after World War II when the new ranch-style home came into vogue.

The bungalow style in Texas used local stone, usually gathered from fields, pastures, and riverbanks. The stones are set vertically rather than horizontally, making the outside wall look like freckles, with the various colors shown on the wide, flat side of the rocks in irregular arrangement. This arrangement was economical, since fewer stones were needed for the outside wall construction than would be needed for a wall with stone set horizontally. The style was used in small, humble dwellings and in large, expensive homes, both in the countryside and in the city.

As I continued to explore the history, I was stunned by the loyalty to these rock bungalows and began to notice that elements from the original designs were appearing in new buildings.

There had been many examples of this style elongated to look similar to the ranch-style house, but in recent years porches, arches, and side patios or terraces appeared in new homes. Even some exterior sections are found in the multicolored flat rock arrangement, although the majority of the exterior might be brick, white limestone, or stucco.

Certainly one can see that this form of architecture has become quite influential and has been receiving preservation interest. Here the key word is *influential*. For if influential, then rhetorical (or, paraphrasing Kenneth Burke, any good communication is rhetorical). Any influential architecture is rhetorical in its visual form. From this beginning premise, I began to look for some rhetorical means—a perspective—to help in the analysis process in order to better understand how this type of home is influential and why.

My first thought was of Burke's cluster criticism, because this type of criticism has been used very successfully in analyzing visual elements in art, architecture, and photography.[27] Looking at the history of the Texas rock house led me to believe that the house itself was highly identified with the values and concerns of those trans-South emigrants who made their way to Texas in order to start a new life in a new place. Burke's idea of identification as consubstantiality,[28] when some individual and some property share a substance, seemed very applicable to emigrants' intention to build a home in the new place that was "solid," "permanent," and connected with the very soil that would bring them their livelihood: the rock being the substance and the values the personal intention. However, this identification was only one part of the problem to be addressed in the rhetorical analysis. The question of regionality or the influence of locale and culture on the nature of the house style and the choice of building materials made it necessary for me to look for additional tools with which to analyze the influence of this particular style.

This brought to mind the rhetorical depiction method developed by Michael Osborn in a seminal essay in the collection *Form, Genre, and the Study of Political Discourse*.[29] Rhetorical depiction as explained by Osborn has five functions: presentation, intensification, identification, implementation, and reaffirmation. Each one of these functions must be addressed in the analysis in order to have a successful discussion of rhetorical depiction and the ultimate outcome of the rhetoric. In the case of the Texas rock house there seemed to be some very appropriate questions to pose from each of the five functions.

First, presentation can be repetitive, that is, showing us what we already know, or innovative, which shows us a new way of knowing when the past no longer works for us.[30] Innovative presentation depends on the use of metaphor to connect to the new way of knowing. Intensification is the expression of heightened feeling, that is, how we see the rhetoric as instigating reaction.[31] Identification, as in Burke, is a sharing of characteristics, but with a narrative quality, identification with the community story.[32] Implementation is the "What do we do?" question. How is the message of the rhetoric put into action? Osborn adds, "Implementation includes the classical idea of deliberative rhetoric for it has to do with the designs of the future."[33] Osborn also asserts that "implementation can be defined as applied identification."[34] The last function of rhetorical depiction is reaffirmation, which means that the rhetoric brings the community back to its identity with its values in a common "appreciation." "Reaffirmative depiction guards the sacred fire around which a nation or a subculture gathers periodically to warm itself in recognition of its being."[35]

The Texas rock house is evidence that families, most new to the state and region, had deliberately decided to establish homes in order to make a new start in new communities. Herein began a new subculture with its shared values. By incorporating insights gained from both Burke and Osborn, I was better able to share with others the fascinating rhetorical strength of the Texas rock houses. My approach was eclectic in that I had to blend rhetorical perspectives in order to better appreciate the underlying rhetorical dynamics that were hidden in the architecture of these houses. In the visual form, such as architecture, there are various elements that connect with values and purpose for those who live within the dwelling. This form of eclecticism is not a jumble or hodgepodge but an evolved process that began with the classical scholars who highly influenced Kenneth Burke and then Burke influenced Michael Osborn. A close reading of either Burke or Osborn will reveal a developmental path of true eclecticism: the ability to see the influential elements in all of communication, no matter the form or genre.

M. Lane Bruner on "Carnivalesque . . ."

Revolutionary discourses are interesting things to study. Thomas Jefferson once famously remarked that "a little rebellion" now and then was a good thing, "as necessary in the political world as storms in the physical."[36] Only the people's stormy uprisings, he believed, ensured a continued focus on republican virtue. But what are these storms? Are they all alike? What is their relationship to the virtuous state? How do we know, for example, when rebellions produce more or less freedom? How can we recognize the best kind of rebellions?

An excellent opportunity to study rebellion was provided in the late 1980s as peoples rose up in communist regimes from China to East Germany to demand more political and economic freedoms. As a rhetoric scholar interested in the relationship between discourse and politics, and how different patterns of communication create different types of political communities, I was eager to study how these rebellions worked (or not). I was especially curious to learn why the rebellions against the Soviet Union were generally nonviolent, productive of more freedom, and helped to develop the rule of law, while those against communism in China were violent, did not produce more political freedom, and made no impact on authoritarian rule.

The methods and theories most appropriate for scholars are driven by the questions they pursue, and those who want to study the world-historical relationship between the rhetorical and the political can hardly rely on one theory or method, or even a small combination of theories and methods. Instead, the *eclectic* critic is also required to be well versed in political, economic, cultural, and philosophical matters as well. This is where eclectic critics' strengths come into play: their relatively broad theoretical and historical background enables them to study the broader relationships between the ways people talk and behave and the kinds of communities they create as a result of that talk and behavior.

To be an eclectic critic, in the sense expressed here, one must follow the sage advice of Cicero and Quintilian, two famous rhetoricians concerned with the development of the virtuous orator: they must be *highly eclectic* in their learning.[37] The virtuous rhetor persuades to improve the community, but a person cannot improve the community unless he or she is exceptionally wise. To be truly eloquent, according to Cicero, the virtuous rhetor must be able to distinguish good from evil, the desirable from the undesirable, the profitable from the unprofitable, all the virtues and vices and how they arise and are transformed, the difference between just and unjust states, as well as to understand the common sense of mankind, the laws of nature, moral duties, and more. One can hardly expect to be a good *critic* of persuasive acts if unfamiliar with the learning required of virtuous persuaders themselves. Nor can the eclectic critic risk being a dilettante, knowing just a little bit about everything. As Quintilian noted, "a little learning is a dangerous thing."[38] Instead, the responsible eclectic critic must seriously study the history of ideas, comparative law, aesthetics, and any other number of similarly important subjects. The guiding principle behind all of the work of the eclectic rhetorical critic is this: what theoretical, historical, and methodological tools must be brought to bear to investigate the world-historical question at hand?

To prepare for my study of rebellion, for example, I first had to decide what my objects of study and guiding research question would be. I then had to decide what I needed to know in order to engage in such a study. I decided that, building upon my prior research on Russia (i.e., on public memory and national identity in Russia during the collapse of communism, and on the rhetorical and political dimensions of the subsequent transition to capitalism), I would limit my study to the rebellions against the Soviet Union.[39] My larger research question, however, led me to expand this initial plan: I wanted to know *why* those rebellions were so successful, so I decided to compare them to a failure. Thus, I also studied the tragic 1989 rebellion against communism in China.

I started exploring this question about productive rebellions by obtaining numerous accounts and histories of the political, economic, and cultural histories of the Soviet Union and China, and then of the rebellions in the old Soviet states and the massacre at Tiananmen Square in Beijing in 1989. One thing became immediately clear, other than the obvious fact that the political, economic, and cultural conditions in both countries were quite different: the protests against the Soviets were generally comic, while those against Chinese communists were anything but. I learned that in Poland, East Germany, Ukraine, the former Czechoslovakia, and elsewhere, resistance against the state, when most successful, was "carnivalesque," that the carnivalesque was a public and comic way of reversing "normal" social roles, and that the carnivalesque had a long and interesting history in Europe.

Not yet deeply understanding the carnivalesque, I next had to obtain the very best studies related to that concept. Here I learned that, from at least Ancient Rome up until the nineteenth century, it was a European custom to have official days set aside when community norms would be comically turned upside down. The master would be the servant and the servant the master. Some scholars saw this strange discursive practice as a means for the powerful to strengthen their grip on society by providing well-managed opportunities to release social tensions; others, however, argued that moments of carnival were excellent opportunities for disempowered people to send serious political messages under the protective cover of "just joking!"

As an eclectic critic, I first enjoyed studying the political, economic, and cultural histories of Russia and China, then studying accounts of the protests themselves, then studying the carnivalesque, and then studying performance theory and social movement theory. If I wanted to study these comic and serious public performances and understand how and why they worked (or did not), these were simply parts of the puzzle I sought to solve.

Here is what the picture looked like once the pieces were in place. In the states attempting to separate themselves from a crumbling Soviet Empire, the initially funny thing was the overly serious communist state officials themselves. Here is an illustrative example. In Poland, during the crackdown on the Solidarity movement, which paradoxically was a workers' movement against a communist state that purportedly represented the interests of the working classes, state employees went around the major cities painting big circles over pro-Solidarity graffiti, a practice that seemed especially ridiculous to some Polish dissidents. The dissidents decided, therefore, to go out at night and repaint the circles as elves, with little feet, hands, and a hat. Over the next couple of years, little elves began to appear everywhere, but the significance of the elf was unclear to state officials. Dissidents would do other silly things such as go in groups to the local zoos and demand "freedom for the bears" while singing communist songs and giving out candy to children. When arrested—though the police had no idea what these crazy people were doing—the news images of happy young people ironically singing communist songs and demanding freedom for the bears were clear enough to everyday citizens: the Soviet Union has always been symbolized by the bear.

Months later, on Children's Day, thousands of children came out of their houses dressed like elves! What was the state to do? The people identified themselves as comic characters, like Smurfs, defending the ethical state and protesting for everything from clean air to inexpensive toilet paper. Eventually, and without directly confronting the state but instead using abstract symbols to communicate comically, the revolutions against the Soviet Union were, for the most part, peaceful and successful. This is not to say that they were successful *only* because of this widespread comic tactic. Still, the tactic worked in large part because of the cultural, economic, and political contexts in which it was used.

There was nothing "funny," however, in China, when dissidents gathered on the central public square in Beijing to demand more political liberty. The Chinese situation was quite different from the situation in the former Soviet territories. The Chinese state was economically and politically stronger. The communist leadership was already preparing to turn the country toward capitalism, but certainly not toward greater political liberties. Ultimately the protest was crushed. Tanks and gunmen opened fire on the protesters, killing thousands. Today, the vast majority of people in China have no memory of the massacre, since it has been erased from their public memory (e.g., the event is not taught in schools, memorial images or videos are not shown on television, and references to the massacre are consistently filtered out of Chinese internet search systems).

My initial investigation concluded, therefore, that carnivalesque tactics were best employed under specific political, economic, and cultural conditions, which I outlined in my study. When deployed in most of the former Soviet territories, they helped to transform them into more economically and politically liberal states. Conversely, I concluded that comic tactics were not used in China, and serious strategies did not work at all.

When this study was concluded, I attempted to describe the specific tactics that were most successfully used, and in what specific contexts, in order to apply them to present-day protests against present-day injustices in other political contexts. Today, for example, groups are using carnivalesque tactics against large corporations, against transnational organizations such as the World Bank, and in support of environmental protection and nuclear disarmament. On the whole, however, they have not often been successful. Why? How can we apply the lessons learned by the anticommunist protests to fight for greater social justice today so that these "storms" can indeed lead to more just states?

In sum, to answer my initial research question (i.e., what constitutes a successful rebellion?), as we have seen, I first had to rely on my prior work on political transformation and public memory in the former Soviet Union, as well as histories and personal accounts of the rebellions of the late 1980s, and they, in turn, led me to study the carnivalesque. Then, however, I actually had to closely study the protest tactics themselves, for these were my "texts." Yes, I was also interested in what the protesters would say and what others would say about them, but I was also interested in the way the protesters communicated their messages through embodied performances. This required studying performance theory and social movement theory to better understand how the comic wave gained momentum. This, as if to complete the research circle, required knowing a lot about economic and political policies in the former Soviet Union and China, and how shifting economic and political policies contributed to varied social and political conditions. Only within this larger context was the function of the rhetorical artifact, the variously situated protest tactics, clear.

Of course, not all rhetorical criticism explores world-historical questions, nor does it try to improve the human condition. For scholars seeking to understand, for example, the dominant tropes and figures in a speech, or the principal metaphors in an advertisement, or the generic expectations in an inaugural address, one primary method and a handful of theoretical concepts may suffice. To critique the discursive construction of national, racial, gendered, or class identities, however, the critic must begin to move into a wider range of methods and theories, as well as broader cultural, political, and economic matters. In the same manner, to critique the larger world-historical relationship between identity and statecraft, and to determine the most virtuous forms of rhetoric, requires even more, just as it would were one to wish to become a virtuous orator. One can never feel completely successful in such an endeavor, given the limits of human understanding, but the potential payoff for the attempt can be great.

Jim A. Kuypers on "From Science . . ."

Years ago I came across a letter written by James Dobson, then president of Focus on the Family. The letter was distributed to over two million constituents of Focus on the Family and concerned the 1993 Fetal Tissue Research Initiative, which legalized scientific experimentation on aborted fetuses. Dobson spoke out against this initiative, in particular calling attention to the immoral nature of the practice, making biblical analogies, and making predictions of eventual cloning of humans for spare body parts.[40]

The letter intrigued me on several levels, and I wanted to study it further. First, Dobson had an enormous potential impact. The audience for his monthly letters was then over two million, but his potential radio audience, to which he read the entire letter, approached 200 million in North America and 550 million worldwide. What were these audience members being asked to believe? Dobson's detractors had called him a televangelist and doctrinal speaker in the past, but this seemed simplistic criticism of someone with such a large multinational and diverse audience. I was interested in discovering whether his letters contained elements of indoctrination, or whether he was communicating truly to a worldwide audience, attempting persuasion rather than indoctrination. Dobson's letter was also noteworthy because it successfully brought together the resources of scientific and moral language. The letter seemed to be using science to argue against a scientific practice; moreover, it appeared to be asking for individual moral action in the face of an impersonal science. I was curious to discover how all of this was being accomplished. Just why did this letter have so much power as I read it? Finally, it simply interested me, having elements of science, Jewish history, God's wrath, individual morality, futuristic predictions, and charismatic appeal.

As I pondered how to go about exploring my questions, I soon realized that no single perspective would do the job I wanted it to do. So, to understand the rich moral culture Dobson's letter represents and reaches out to, I examined it in three stages: first, I performed a judgmental analysis of the letter in order to determine what Dobson's potential reading audience was being asked to believe. I sought also to understand how Dobson met the needs of his regular readers and was able to appeal to other than his usual audience, even while eschewing the type of discursive strategies often employed by doctrinal speakers. Second, using Kenneth Burke's distinction between semantic and poetic meaning as a starting point, I examined Dobson's discourse as a moral-poetic response to the amoral stance of scientific discourse. Finally, I undertook an inquiry of the motive underpinning Dobson's discourse that allowed me to better understand the actions of Dobson's envisioned moral agent.

The end result was a *method* of analysis (criticism) that blended *perspectives* (judgmental analysis and Burkean dramatism—namely, moral-poetic language and motivational analysis) into a critical point of view. This flexible combination allowed me to study the letter on three different levels, thereby more fully explaining the inner and outer workings of the letter better than if I had used any one perspective alone.

What I found amazed me. Judgmental analysis allowed me to discover that Dobson based his initial argumentative appeals upon the language of science (factual, secularly authoritative); however, halfway through his letter he resorted to a different strategy and shifted to adjudicative appeals (judgments relying upon some type of code) based upon the factual evidence he had already submitted as true. This new strategy took on a moral-poetic dimension that acted in opposition to the scientific discourse: scientific discourse (that allows for fetal tissue research) gave way to a moral-poetic discourse designed to allow for individual moral action. The moral-poetic and motivational portions allowed me to discover how Dobson pitted medical research (science) against moral action; used what Kenneth Burke called "poor semantics" (scientism: what society believes to be science; science given the status of a public philosophy) as support for his moral interpretation; and then provided a way out of the moral quagmire science has placed humans in by highlighting our ability to morally act, thereby initiating the possibility for an individual to act morally to achieve societal redemption.

POTENTIALS AND PITFALLS

As with the other perspectives covered in this book, an eclectic approach to criticism has both potentials and pitfalls. When it works well, it certainly offers the critic a great deal of flexibility, and its potential to allow for nuanced insights and new theoretical understandings is quite high. The critic has great freedom to explore, and the potential for allowing greater personality into the criticism certainly exists. However, if a critic does not fully develop the new point of view before undertaking the criticism, the results could be scattered and meaningless observations in place of genuine criticism. In short, the effort to produce criticism might devolve into a *hodgepodge* of poorly related theoretical tidbits and unrelated insights instead of constituting an *eclectic* mix representative of the critic's personal approach to the artifact. Another concern is that it is particularly easy for a critic to construct a point of view that will find exactly what that critic wants to find. Then there is the burden of acquiring enough knowledge in order to practice eclectic criticism. By this I mean that if a critic wishes to use parts of several different perspectives, theories, and ideas in order to derive a new point of view, that critic must first obtain a healthy working knowledge of all the perspectives, theories, and ideas that will be used.

Eclectic criticism offers an amazing amount of freedom in crafting an approach to examine a rhetorical artifact. We must remember, though, that imagination and knowledge go hand in hand. In order for you to create imaginative criticism you must have a great deal of knowledge on different subjects, and so eclectic criticism very often necessitates that you spend considerable time exploring new subjects. Although this can be quite exciting (and the rewards of increased knowledge, the exposure to new ideas, only serves to enrich one's criticism and enhance one's quality of life), it is a step that must be taken with deliberateness and care.

So, it is not without caution that one should approach eclectic criticism. Freedom without responsible constraints is quite often harmful. In addition to the demands upon one's time, there does exist a danger in that it can be easy to play fast and loose with the theories one uses. It can be all too easy for a critic to put together a patchwork of theoretical bits without explaining well their interconnected qualities—the unifying element. And that is a key to good eclectic criticism; the critic must present the unifying idea behind using the different theories to explain the rhetorical artifact.

ECLECTIC CRITICISM TOP PICKS

In some ways you have already been exposed to a portion of top picks in eclectic criticism when you read the commentary about the five projects above. There are certainly more fine examples of eclectic criticism from which to choose. Below I list two articles and a book chapter that I feel provide additional grounding in eclectic criticism should you choose to pursue this type of criticism.

Brock, Bernard L., Robert L. Scott, and James W. Chesebro, eds. *Methods of Rhetorical Criticism: A Twentieth-Century Perspective*, 3rd ed., 88–95. Detroit: Wayne State University Press, 1989. The authors provide commentary on eclectic criticism and link it with what they call the experiential perspective. Thoughtful and insightful, this is highly recommended reading if eclectic criticism is of interest to you.

Gunn, Joshua. "The Rhetoric of Exorcism: George W. Bush and the Return of Political Demonology." *Western Journal of Communication* 68, no. 1 (Winter 2004): 1–23. A beautifully written example of eclectic criticism that examines President George W. Bush's speeches following 9/11. Gunn combines a close textual analysis with elements of biblical metaphor, mythic, genre, and psychoanalytic criticism.

Rosenfield, Lawrence W. "The Anatomy of Critical Discourse." *Speech Monographs* 25, no. 1 (1968): 50–69. Rosenfield provides valuable insight into the nature and varieties of critical discourse, as well as the nature of reason giving and logic in criticism. He explains critical discourse in a manner that opens possibilities for textual analysis that benefits an eclectic approach.

DISCUSSION QUESTIONS

1. What do you see as the main benefits for using eclectic criticism? What are the main drawbacks?
2. Which perspectives covered so far seem to lend themselves well to eclectic criticism?
3. Is eclectic criticism something you could see yourself trying at some point? Why or why not?
4. Of the eclectic criticism examples in this chapter, which do you feel was the most eclectic? How did the author(s) make it accessible to you?

ACTIVITIES

1. Get in a small group and allow one member to choose a rhetorical artifact. Using that artifact as a starting point, each member of the group should decide what combination

of two of the perspectives covered in this book would be "best" for looking at that arti-fact. Share with the group and allow time for discussion.

2. Find other examples of eclecticism operating in our society. How are they similar to what you learned in this chapter? How are they different?

NOTES

1. "Kristina Wilfore Quotes," ThinkExist.com, http://en.thinkexist.com/quotation/typically-off-year-elections-are-used-for-two/984893.html.

2. Michael Tierra, introduction, "What is Eclecticism?," *Planet Herbs*, accessed January 23, 2020, https://planetherbs.com/research-center/history-articles/what-is-eclecticism/.

3. Pauline Kael, *I Lost It at the Movies* (Boston: Little, Brown, 1964), 309. I first came across this quotation in Bernard L. Brock, Robert L. Scott, and James W. Chesebro, eds., *Methods of Rhetorical Criticism: A Twentieth-Century Perspective*, 3rd ed. (Detroit: Wayne State University Press, 1989), 89.

4. "David Esbjornson Quotes," ThinkExist.com, http://en.thinkexist.com/quotation/i-have-an-eclectic-past-but-i-intentionally-have/737562.html.

5. Brock, Scott, and Chesebro, *Methods of Rhetorical Criticism*, 89.

6. Edwin Black, "Plato's View of Rhetoric," in *Readings in Rhetoric*, ed. Lionel Crocker and Paul A. Carmack (Springfield, IL: Charles C. Thomas, 1965), 68.

7. Emma Frances Bloomfield, *Communication Strategies for Engaging Climate Skeptics: Religion and the Environment* (New York: Routledge, 2019).

8. See the chapter on "Traditional Criticism" for a full explanation of this concept.

9. Bloomfield, *Communication Strategies*, 6.

10. Bloomfield, *Communication Strategies*, 8.

11. Kenneth Burke, *Language as Symbolic Action: Essays on Life, Literature, and Method* (Berkeley: University of California Press, 1966), 45.

12. Wayne Brockriede and Douglas Ehninger, "Toulmin on Argument: An Interpretation and Application," *Quarterly Journal of Speech* 46, no. 1 (1960): 44–53.

13. E. Calvin Beisner, "World Magazine Exposes Evangelical Environmentalists' Growing Dependence on Green-Left Funding," Cornwall Alliance, May 30, 2015, para. 11, https://cornwallalliance.org/2015/05/world-magazine-exposes-evangelical-environmentalists-growing-dependence-on-green-left-funding/.

14. Cornwall Alliance, "A Renewed Call to Truth, Prudence, and Protection of the Poor: Evangelical Declaration on Global Warming," http://cornwallalliance.org/landmark-documents/evangelical-declaration-on-global-warming-2/; Cornwall Alliance, "What We Do," para. 3, accessed April 24, 2018, https://cornwallalliance.org/about/what-we-do/.

15. Bloomfield, *Communication Strategies*, 36.

16. Bloomfield, *Communication Strategies*, 36.

17. Excerpt written by Joseph M. Valenzano III.

18. A penny dreadful was a form of serial literature in the nineteenth century that sold for one penny. They were released each week and focused on sensational stories about detectives, monsters, and the supernatural. They were printed on cheap pulp paper (and as a result were sometimes called pulp fiction) and targeted a younger working male demographic. For links to several examples, see http://vichist.blogspot.com/2008/11/penny-dreadfuls.html.

19. Trevor B. McCrisken, *American Exceptionalism and the Legacy of Vietnam: U.S. Foreign Policy since 1974* (New York: Palgrave Macmillan, 2003).

20. Mary E. Stuckey, "The Donner Party and the Rhetoric of Westward Expansion," *Rhetoric and Public Affairs* 14, no. 2 (2011): 229–260.

21. Ray Allen Billington, *Land of Savagery, Land of Promise: The European Image of the American Frontier in the Nineteenth Century* (Norman: University of Oklahoma Press, 1981); Richard W. Slatta,

"Making and Unmaking Myths of the American Frontier," *European Journal of American Culture* 29, no. 2 (2010): 81–92.

22. "Ask Eric," *Supernatural Magazine* 1, no. 3 (April/May 2009): 95.

23. Stewart M. Hoover, *Mass Media Religion: The Social Sources of the Electronic Church* (Newbury Park, CA: Sage, 1988), 241.

24. David Thorburn, "Television as an Aesthetic Medium," *Critical Studies in Mass Communication* 4 (1987): 161–173.

25. This particular movement of revived interest is well documented in several publications. The most comprehensive is *American Bungalow Magazine*, published by the John Brinkmann Design Office, Santa Monica, CA.

26. Chicago is known for its bungalow neighborhoods, featuring houses that are narrow to facilitate more house on a narrow lot, with the front door on the side of the house, with the front room window wall nearest the street. Denver features bungalow neighborhoods with brick bungalows, both single story and story and a half, with front porches and garages.

27. See the discussion in Sonja K. Foss, *Rhetorical Criticism: Exploration and Practice*, 4th ed. (Carbondale, IL: Waveland Press, 2009), 63–96.

28. Kenneth Burke, *A Rhetoric of Motives* (1950; Berkeley: University of California Press, 1969), 41.

29. Michael Osborn, "Rhetorical Depiction," in *Form, Genre, and the Study of Political Discourse*, ed. Herbert W. Simons and Aram A. Aghazarian (Columbia: University of South Carolina Press, 1986), 79–107.

30. Ibid., 82–86.

31. Ibid., 86.

32. Ibid., 89–92.

33. Ibid., 93.

34. Ibid., 92.

35. Ibid., 95.

36. Jefferson's opinions, expressed in a letter to Colonel Edward Carrington on January 16, 1787, proved to be controversial in the wake of the French Revolutions and Shays Rebellion, two rebellions against the upper classes. Cited in Gerald Stourz, *Alexander Hamilton and the Idea of Republican Government* (Stanford, CA: Stanford University Press, 1970), 34.

37. See, for example, Cicero's daunting list in *De Oratore*, in *Cicero: On Oratory and Orators*, trans. J. S. Watson (Carbondale: Southern Illinois University Press, 1986), 100. Quintilian wrote that the ideal orator must be a good person whose character is shaped by philosophy, for rhetoric is a *virtue*. See the *Institutio Oratoria*, vol. 1, ed. Charles E. Little (Nashville, TN: George Peabody College for Teachers, 1951).

38. *Institutio Oratoria*, 23.

39. See M. Lane Bruner, *Strategies of Remembrance: The Rhetorical Dimensions of National Identity Construction* (Columbia: South Carolina University Press, 2002); and M. Lane Bruner and Viatcheslav Morozov, eds., *Market Democracy in Post Communist Russia* (Leeds, England: Wisdom House, 2005).

40. A mere five years later, all that Dobson suggested materialized in science circles. For example, see the December 8, 1998, BBC News article, "Human Spare-Part Cloning Set for Approval," http://news.bbc.co.uk/1/hi/sci/tech/230002.stm. By 2004, British scientists were given formal approval to clone human embryos for "therapeutic purposes." Antony Barnett and Robin McKie, "UK to Clone Human Cells," *Observer*, June 13, 2004, http://www.guardian.co.uk/society/2004/jun/13/health.research.

14

Visual Rhetoric

Natalia Mielczarek

The photograph of the lifeless body of three-year-old Alan Kurdi[1] lying facedown on a Turkish beach in 2015 with water lapping at his face became a global news icon in a matter of hours.[2] The boy, together with his mother and a five-year-old brother, drowned during their journey from war-torn Syria to Greece. The father survived. The family, much like more than four million refugees from Syria at the time, attempted to cross the Mediterranean Sea on inflatable rafts.[3] The photograph, shot by Nilüfer Demir with the Turkish Doğan News Agency, became, as one journalist put it, "a defining symbol of the tragedy of Syria's refugees."[4]

As it made its way through social networking sites and mainstream news media around the world, the image was also published in the English-language version of *Dabiq*, the magazine of the Islamic State (ISIS). In that edition, however, the photograph was deployed to tell quite a different story, one that painted Alan—and others who escaped the "Islamic homeland"—as traitors.[5] Framing it as a piece of visual evidence, ISIS editors claimed that Alan received what he deserved: a just punishment for betraying his country and religious system of values by fleeing to the "lands of the war-waging crusaders ruled by laws of atheism and indecency."[6] Unlike in the mainstream press and on social media, the picture functioned in *Dabiq* as a visual cautionary tale that was supposed to warn those who were considering following in Alan's footsteps. Some in the Western press dubbed it ISIS visual propaganda.[7]

How can the same photograph elicit such startlingly different interpretations? Answering this and other questions of what images mean and how they convey those meanings is what this chapter is about. Every image could be analyzed using multiple perspectives. The concept of visual rhetoric, a broad theoretical approach that investigates persuasive work of and responses to images, offers one glimpse of these processes. It pushes us as audience members to go beyond merely identifying the aesthetics of a photograph or a painting—the color, form, and genre. Visual rhetoric also explores ideas, associations, and connections that we make during the interpretation process, influenced not only by what we see but also by what we already know. It prompts us to consider the functions that an image serves for us, the effect it produces, and the symbolic messages it suggests.[8]

The disparate readings of the Kurdi photograph by different groups of people illustrate visual rhetoric at work. The Turkish reporter posted a news image documenting a failed attempt to flee the conflict in Syria, and scores of viewers—from everyday internet users to politicians and human rights activists—interpreted the image as a metonym for humanity in crisis with a hashtag #humanitywashedashore.[9] To ISIS and its sympathizers, however, the same photograph—but with a wholly different caption and contextual narrative—signified a well-deserved punishment for those who were seen as abandoning their homeland and with it, their faith.

Lives of many images, including the now-famous Kurdi photograph, rarely end after their publication; this is especially true in the digital and social media era where sharing, spreading, and remixing content have become a part of our daily cultural practice.[10] As they get posted, recirculated, and often manipulated online by scores of members of the connected publics, images flow through various platforms and channels—a digital cross-pollination of sorts—and gain rhetorical velocity across channels and time.[11] Upon such reconstitution, images produce fresh compositions and meanings as they change hands online. As such, "from an ecological, rhetorical perspective, images need to be studied as divergent, *unfolding becomings* in order to account for an image's distributed ontology."[12]

In other words, images, especially those that land in the public limelight, rarely have only one version and only one meaning.[13] Such plurality of meanings is called polysemy.[14] Our interpretation of images within the visual rhetorical realm, then, does not happen in a cultural, political, or ideological vacuum. We filter meanings through ideas, beliefs, values, stories, myths, and personal experiences that are a part of our cultural, social, and historical upbringing.[15] Captions and contextual information that accompany images, as I already note with the Kurdi example, also influence what and how we think about what we see.[16]

The term visual rhetoric really has two meanings: the rhetorical artifacts (images) and the scholarly perspectives used to study those rhetorical artifacts. Although rhetoric itself has been studied continuously for over 2,500 years, it was not "until 1970 [that] the first formal call [was] made to include visual images in the study of rhetoric, which until then had been conceived exclusively as verbal discourse."[17] The criticism of visual rhetoric can take many forms. One, championed by Sonja Foss, is very interpretive and posits that images are rhetorical in nature.[18] Another, advanced by David L. Birdsell and Leo S. Groarke, is very pragmatic and posits that not all images are rhetorical in nature.[19] In this chapter I discuss these two perspectives and offer a third that falls in between. All are useful in analyzing visual rhetoric: the Interpretive Perspective, the Visual Argument Perspective, and Iconographic Tracking. I follow this theoretical part with four examples of criticism to show each in action.

THE INTERPRETIVE PERSPECTIVE AND VISUAL IMAGES

Those using an interpretive approach to visual rhetorical criticism are interested in dissecting the meaning and functions that images serve by privileging audience members' interpretations over the motivations of their authors. As such, our analysis shifts from what the author intended for an image to what and how the viewer reads and understands it.[20] This is, according to Sonja Foss, because "once an image is created, scholars who adopt a rhetorical perspective on imagery believe, it stands independent of its creator's intentions."[21]

Foss's approach to studying visual artifacts treats photographs, paintings, advertisements, cartoons, memes, and others as communicative tools that provoke and lead to various responses and interpretations in their viewers.[22] But, according to Foss, not every visual text is visual rhetoric.

What turns a visual object into a communicative artifact—a symbol that communicates and can be studied as rhetoric—is the presence of three characteristics. . . . The images must be symbolic, involve human intervention, and be presented to an audience for the purpose of communicating with that audience.[23]

In other words, visual rhetoric operates on more than just a literal level of meaning making as it generates meaning through symbolic action of what it stands for, not only what it manifestly shows. It is also created through the conscious and often deliberate and strategic action of the people who produce and reproduce it. In and of itself, as Foss points out, a tree is not visual rhetoric. It becomes such once it is decorated with lights and ornaments and stands in homes in December; then a tree turns into a symbol of Christmas.[24] Visual rhetoric also needs an audience, whether real or imagined, so that it can, in fact, address someone to communicate.

The focus of visual rhetoric, then, is not merely on the aesthetics of a composition but also on the symbolism—the meanings tied to cultural symbols—that emerge when audience members engage with a particular image.[25] Symbols, which we will explore in more detail later in this chapter, are rhetorical devices that stand in for something they represent. For example, the star spangled banner stands in for the United States, as does the Statue of Liberty. It is no accident that wedding dresses in Western culture have traditionally been white; the color symbolizes purity and innocence ascribed to the bride through the symbolic meaning of the wedding dress. Symbols, then, are figures of speech that are not literally connected to the objects, people, sentiments, and ideas they represent. There is nothing inherently pure or innocent about the color white in and of itself, once we strip it of its culturally generated meanings and connotations. The rhetorical work of symbols is propelled by a variety of rhetorical tools, including myths, topoi, allusions, and ideas, that circulate in our shared culture and shape our interpretations and understanding of the world around us.[26]

Foss's approach, then, pushes us to go beyond the formal elements of a photograph or a meme such as colors, form, medium, and texture—all of which undoubtedly contribute to our feelings about what we see—and engage in interpretation of meanings that also arise through the symbolic action of the studied artifact. More specifically, a visual rhetorical analysis pays attention to at least one of the following three elements: 1) the nature of an image; 2) the function(s) of an image; and 3) the evaluation of the function(s).[27] Let us take a closer look at all three.

The Nature of an Image involves two components, the presented and suggested elements that work in tandem to formulate a complete reading of a visual piece. Presented elements resemble a formal analysis in art history, where we list the physical attributes of an image, including its size, media, colors, materials used to produce it, and shapes visible in an image. They are stripped of any cultural meanings and connotations; what you see is what you get. For example, if we were to describe the presented elements of a postcard with the Statue of Liberty on it, we would not say that it is a Statue of Liberty. We could first describe the materials of the postcard: a piece of cardboard measuring 4.5"×6" that is laminated on the side that displays a statue of a woman. The woman is clad in what looks like a toga that extends to the ground. The woman's right arm is raised and holds what looks like a torch. Her left arm clutches what looks like a book. Her head dons what resembles a crown, with spikes that protrude out horizontally. The monument looks like it is made of metal; its color is green, presumably from a patina or some other tarnishing.

Suggested elements push the analysis forward to symbolic action. At this stage, we ground the image of interest in our cultural knowledge and inheritance and begin to list ideas, themes, allusions, and concepts that get triggered through symbolic associations. The combination of presented and suggested elements allows us to move beyond what we can see and start interpreting the meanings with the cultural and symbolic backdrops in mind. If we continue with the Statue of Liberty example, the suggested elements begin to rattle off fast: this is not just some unknown monument that the postcard displays. It is the Statue of Liberty, which we recognize instantly because of its signature physical attributes. It is an iconic image ingrained in our cultural tapestry of symbols. But our interpretation does not stop there, of course, as the recognition of the monument as Statue of Liberty connotes specific associations that shape our analysis. We most likely think of freedom and the American Dream—the topoi that have been embedded in American mythology for more than two hundred years. The Statue of Liberty has come to stand in for—or symbolize—America; it personifies it. Those meanings have been enveloped in the collective narrative of the nation and what it represents for more than 130 years.[28]

The Function of an Image is not the same as its purpose, a necessary distinction that Foss makes at this juncture. A function of an image tells us how the image operates for the viewers—what functions it serves for them. Some photographs, for example, serve as commemorations to mark an anniversary; others function as satire that pokes fun of a politician, and so forth. A purpose, on the other hand, is the effect or role that is intended for an image by its creator.[29] The case of the 2008 Obama Hope poster illustrates the distinction clearly.[30] That year, when the street artist Shepard Fairey created the now-iconic poster, he based it on a news photograph taken by the Associated Press journalist Mannie Garcia. Garcia's image's purpose was purely informational, but it functioned for Fairey as a canvas for his poster.[31] Once Fairey released the reworked image, his intended purpose for it was mainly informational and persuasive; the poster quickly became one of the symbols of the Obama campaign and had nothing to do with the original news events that produced it.

The Evaluation of an Image's Function(s) assesses whether the visual piece accomplishes the functions that it suggests. This part of the analysis may, for instance, involve discerning the implications and consequences of the functions.[32] If we continue with the Obama Hope poster scenario, the evaluation of the poster's functions could involve looking at how the Hope poster and its internet memes participated in the presidential campaign and related public debates on social media sites.

VISUAL ARGUMENT

Considering visual rhetoric as **visual arguments** changes the way critics look at a visual rhetorical artifact; they treat images as actual arguments and attempt to decipher them with the help of symbols and other rhetorical devices. The idea is that images, similarly to words, can present premises and lead audiences to particular conclusions.[33] They often do so with the assistance of words to "combine the force of two powerful means of conveying arguments,"[34] making their claims less ambiguous, vague, or arbitrary. By blending both verbal (oral and written) and nonverbal elements, visual arguments become **pragma-dialectic**, meaning that they focus on the process of making the argument as well as on the critical evaluation of posited claims.[35] According to David S. Birdsell and Leo Groarke, this view encourages us to "interpret speech acts in a way that renders them comprehensible, sincere, relevant, consistent, and appropriate in the context of the other speech acts that surround them."[36] These principles "play an important role in the interpretation of speech acts that are figurative, implicit, or metaphorical, or in some other way demand something more than a literal interpretation" as well.[37] These principles can be applied successfully to visual rhetoric as well as to words, with emphasis placed on

> three key "principles of visual communication" that must guide our interpretation: (i) such images can be understood in principle; (ii) they should be interpreted in a manner that makes sense of the major (visual and verbal) elements they contain; and (iii) they should be interpreted in a manner that fits the context in which they are situated.[38]

In some cases visual arguments that do not involve a verbal component such as words may be more persuasive or emotional than written language; the adage "a picture is worth a thousand words" comes to mind. For example, written or oral accounts from Holocaust survivors about the magnitude of the atrocities perpetrated by the Nazis during World War II serve as powerful and moving testimonies and reports of the war. But images of piles of naked, emaciated corpses outside bellowing crematoria in Nazi death camps assault us with the visually mediated enormity and depravity of the systematic extermination of Jews and other groups of people.[39] In this case, they function as documents that reflect realities of war with little room left for imagination. They do not need words to help clarify their point.

Keeping in mind the three key principles of visual communication mentioned above, one can see that the construction and interpretation of visual arguments assumes that images actually do produce meaning, that the context in which they reside is important for interpretation, and that they often call for something more than a literal reading. This is in part because visual arguments can be highly figurative, metaphorical, and implicit as they rely on the interplay between resemblance and representation.[40] In other words, visual arguments capitalize on the argumentative aspects of resemblance by showing what something or someone is through the likeness and similarity to the actual object or person, and they also deploy representation by showing what something or someone stands for through the use of symbols, metaphors, and other rhetorical devices.[41] For example, if we wanted to put forth a visual argument that Big Bird from the popular children's television show *Sesame Street* is evil, we could draw a large yellow bird with a fluffy body—a resemblance to the actual character of Big Bird—but we might replace Big Bird's head with that of the devil. The devil symbolizes evil and wickedness in Western culture, thus leading the audience to reasonably conclude that the claim the drawing is forwarding is that Big Bird is a bad, bad Bird.

But how would the audience members unfamiliar with the meaning of the symbol of the devil know that it represents evil? This is where context is critical. When it comes to visual arguments, three sets of contexts are important to the interpretation process: 1) the immediate visual context; 2) the immediate verbal context; and 3) visual culture. Immediate visual context has to do with what we see visually in relation to the image we interpret. It becomes especially relevant in visual sequences such as movies or instructional materials as we deduce meaning by looking at the image in relation to the series of images that precede and follow.[42] Immediate verbal context has to do with any text, including captions, titles, and in-image writing, that guides interpretation. Visual culture refers to cultural conventions, values, and attitudes that impact the process of seeing, and that influence how someone would both produce and interpret images. It also includes the audience's shared cultural knowledge.[43]

FIVE MODES OF VISUAL ARGUMENTS

Birdsell and Groarke provide a fruitful way of looking at visual arguments while taking into account the more pragmatic concerns discussed above.[44] In their work, meanings behind visual arguments combine the interpretative work of the audience and the intentions of their authors. An image puts forth claims to build propositions of a visual argument that induce us to embrace certain conclusions during the process of interpretation. We decipher these propositions and eventual conclusions based on the content of the image, the various contexts mentioned above, and the cultural meanings attached to symbols, metaphors, and other communicative devices used to build the argument. An image deploys the propositions of a visual argument through one or a combination of five main modes of meaning creation: a flag, a demonstration, a metaphor, a symbol, and an archetype.

Visual flags are images that draw the attention of the audience to the message that they attempt to convey, typically through a striking or arresting composition.[45] For example, a poster painted bright red with "Blood is life. Donate" at the bottom is likely to initially catch our eye because of the vibrant color. The full visual argument that the poster makes, however, is through the combination of the color and the slogan, which propose together that donating blood is equivalent to saving lives.

Visual demonstrations are images that convey messages that are best or most easily expressed visually. A chart or a pictorial instruction manual that lays out procedures step by step through reenactments captured in drawings or videos are some of the most common examples. They often include some wording, but the primary emphasis in visual demonstrations is—to no surprise—on the visual. Let us imagine an instruction booklet for an Ikea armchair.[46] Before a slew of steps that direct us to work in a particular order—from 1 to 10—we first see a pictorial depiction of the included hardware—small icons of screws, nails, and other parts. Drawings in this case are much more effective communicative tools than words, given the nuance of each artifact. The visual argument that the instruction manual seems to posit is that if we use the included hardware and follow the outlined steps, we will indeed end up with the armchair whose likeness is pictured in the booklet. But a demonstration may also be an ad that displays a photograph of a posh hotel room to show what the visitors would experience if they stayed there. In this use, the image works as a piece of visual evidence that demonstrates an anticipated outcome.[47]

Visual metaphors make figurative claims by portraying something or someone as something or someone else. In other words, metaphors use words or expressions to describe something to which they are not applicable in a literal sense. When we say that our neighbor is sly as a fox, we do not literally mean that our neighbor is a fox, the four-legged furry creature that lives in the forest. We simply want to say that our neighbor is cunning. Our lexicon is full of metaphors that allow us to depart from the literal language and use examples that often compare or contrast to illustrate our point. In visual terms, if we wanted to frame someone as easily manipulated and controlled, we could draw this person as a marionette with strings attached to their hands and arms. Such depiction puts forth a claim that others control the person's actions by pulling the strings.

Visual symbols, on the other hand, stand in for something they represent within a cultural milieu: an idea, a sentiment, a point of view. In doing so, they replace words and phrases with, in our case, visual objects that stand in for those ideas, sentiments, and points of view. For example, a gold ring worn by a couple on the fourth fingers of their left hands stands for marriage—or, it symbolizes marriage. In Western culture people usually dress in black (or dark colors) following someone's death; they do so to symbolize an expression of their grief; the black attire symbolizes their mourning. Visual symbols are often similar to visual metaphors in that they, too, can make claims figuratively within a particular cultural context understood and often shared by members of a group.

In addition to such uses, visual symbols "are often used either to state a position or to make a case for one,"[48] sometimes delivering their premises in quite literal terms. Let us consider the no-smoking signs on hospital campuses. They typically display a single cigarette with smoke rising above it placed within a red circle with a diagonal line across it. The symbol puts forth a clear position: smoking here is forbidden. We arrive at the meaning by interpreting the picture of the smoking cigarette and the line across it in tandem. We understand culturally that a diagonal line across something stands in for prohibition.

Visual archetypes are types of visual symbols whose meaning are rooted in popular cultural narratives familiar to audiences.[49] A drawing of a country's president attempting to push a huge boulder labeled as healthcare up a steep mountain makes a claim that the president's job to pass a bill on healthcare is similarly arduous and futile as the work of Sisyphus. An iconic Greek mythology hero, Sisyphus, as a way of eternal punishment, was forced to roll a huge boulder up a hill, only for it to roll back down when nearing the top. What visual archetypes have going for them is their almost universal recognition and familiarity among members of a particular culture as they derive from stories that have circulated for generations. They often do not need much, if any, explanation. One of the more popular and handy visual archetypes often deployed in editorial cartoons and political satire is that of Pinocchio. Borrowed from an Italian children's story about a wooden marionette who transforms into a boy, Pinocchio symbolizes lying as his nose grows longer every time he does. A character drawn with an unnaturally elongated nose, thus, symbolizes a liar.

VISUAL ARGUMENT AS ENTHYMEME

Some scholars of visual rhetoric have treated visual arguments as enthymemes, rhetorical arguments created jointly by the author and the audience with the purpose to persuade.[50] The term derives from Aristotle's work but has been adapted over time in various communication fields. An enthymeme is a type of syllogism. In its classic form, a syllogism, or argument, possesses a major premise, a minor premise, and a conclusion (see the chapter on "The Traditional Perspective"). These parts are often called, "proofs." In the visual context, it describes a relationship between the author of a visual argument and the audience as well as a particular setup of the argument itself. The author is the one who sets up the visual argument through any of the five modes mentioned above, but it is "the audience itself [that] helps construct the proofs by which it is persuaded."[51] In other words, in an enthymeme, the author does not give away the conclusion or one of the premises but relies on the audience members to deduce it based on what they see and what they already know. The author merely walks the audience to the edge of a premise or a conclusion by laying out visual claims through the use of flags, demonstrations, metaphors, etc. It is the audience that deduces the meaning in the end.

That is why some scholars call the enthymeme an "incomplete" or "truncated" syllogism, in that it does not spell out everything. However,

> to say that the enthymeme is an "incomplete syllogism"—that is, a syllogism having one or more suppressed premises—means that the speaker does not lay down his premises but lets the audience supply them out of its stock of opinion and knowledge.[52]

In other words, the argument is there; it is simply implied by the author and inferred by the audience.

If the authors of the visual argument are aware of or share the audience's cultural knowledge or opinions, their visual arguments are likely to be persuasive. They will be understandable and understood precisely because of that familiarity with the cultural references, metaphors, and symbols. For example, using our Pinocchio archetype above, consider a political cartoon that portrays a president of some country with an unusually long nose. But if the target audience of the cartoon never read or heard of Pinocchio, would the cartoon deliver its intended visual argument successfully? Probably not, given the audience's unfamiliarity with the reference. As Valerie Smith writes, "their effectiveness depends on the agreement between the messenger and audience, discovered in the common opinions shaped by the contexts and culture of the people addressed."[53]

ICONOGRAPHIC TRACKING, TRANSFIGURATION, AND INTERNET MEMES

We can certainly see Smith's idea in action with the Hope poster during the 2008 US presidential campaign when the illustration became an instant news icon.[54] It "spoke" to Obama's supporters with a simple one-word slogan, his likeness, and a path that was meant to project a hopeful future. The poster, in fact, became so popular and widely shared online that it transformed into an internet meme, a grouping of self-referential and highly intertextual images that multiply, mutate, and spread online.[55] It functioned as a visual shorthand for expressing disappointment, anger, and rage about a variety of political figures, issues, and everyday occurrences often unconnected to the original purpose of the Fairey's creation. Obama's head was replaced with scores of others, as was the central slogan of the illustration. In short, the poster shifted "from an illustration to propaganda to a genre of critique to a touchstone for law and remix."[56]

These content tweaks set in motion significant rhetorical ripple effects. They led to changes in meaning as the different versions of the original poster entered into relationships with members of the public and each other, effectively transfiguring what was originally a campaign flier into a set of fresh visual statements that often had nothing to do with the campaign, politics, or with Obama himself. Their use and circulation over time illustrated that "an image's meaning is determined by the unpredictable consequences that emerge in its various occasions of use."[57] Another lens through which we can discover and analyze such changes is **iconographic tracking**, an approach to visual rhetoric championed by Laurie Gries.[58] It builds on Foss's examination of images' functions as a key factor in understanding meanings images generate as they circulate across platforms and time. Within this context, to be rhetorical, Gries argues, an artifact has to do more than be created for persuasive purposes and delivered to an audience with that intention. An image becomes rhetorical when it has the "ability to induce changes in thought, feeling, and action . . . and generate material consequences, whether those consequences unfold in conceptual or physical realms."[59] If we continue with the Obama Hope poster example, we see both types of consequences: conceptual, as expressed through new meanings, and physical, as expressed through new memes, photographs, illustrations, posters, etc. that chained out of the original graphic since 2008.

Yet, Gries's approach seems to depart from Foss's interpretive perspective in that it centers on the idea of pieces of visual rhetoric such as photographs and internet memes being in process—in motion.[60] In iconographic tracking, images resemble ongoing performances that change form, medium, genre, and function as they circulate over time; they are never static or finished. This is to say that as images change hands, they turn into "open-ended rhetorical becomings"[61] that are the very consequences of their ongoing lives beyond publication. They multiply, get cloned and splintered into visual derivatives, and undergo what Gries calls transfiguration, changes in functions, which, in turn, produce new meanings.

Such ongoing reconstitutions that happen to images as they traverse the off- and online worlds—the Hope poster was an internet meme, but it was also featured on a tote bag, for example—set up a "futurity, the strands of time beyond the initial moment of production when consequences unfold as things circulate, enter into diverse kinds of relations, and transform across form, genre, and media."[62] The story of Pepe the Frog is a case in point. The character of a green frog personifying a relaxed "feels good, man" attitude illustrates futurity in action. What started out as a funny comic book character in 2005 ended up as a hijacked icon marred in white supremacist and racist rhetoric during the 2016 presidential elections, driving its creator Matt Furie to legal action to "reclaim" Pepe from the dark web.[63] The frog, by becoming a meme, transfigured from a light-hearted joke to a political symbol that, when used by some, communicated racist views. As Pepe's functions changed for their users—from silly to serious to hateful—so did the meanings. The physical reconstitutions of the character—Pepe as Hitler, Pepe as a Nazi, Pepe as then-candidate Donald Trump—went hand in hand with the rhetorical and conceptual becomings, demonstrating the close interdependence among form, function, media, and meaning.

CRITICAL ESSAYS

From company logos on clothing and billboards alongside interstates to ads on social media and old-fashioned shopping catalogues in mailboxes, we are inundated by images that speak to us. Many, in fact, are designed to persuade us: to sell us something, to convince us to vote for a particular candidate or issue, to urge us to donate to a cause, and more. Armed with the basic theoretical principles of visual rhetoric in this chapter, let us take a look at how some selected images deliver their messages and claims. Examples 1 and 2 marry iconographic tracking with Foss's approach to visual rhetoric by delivering a detailed interpretation of the potential meanings of both artifacts, focusing in particular on the changes in functions as a result of their circulation, reconstitutions, and popularity online. Examples 3 and 4 treat images as visual arguments that build their claims through the use of various rhetorical devices including symbols and metaphors.

EXAMPLE 1: #UNWANTEDIVANKA AND THE MARCH ON WASHINGTON

Introduction and Context

The nineteen-second video released by the French government in summer 2019 shows Ivanka Trump attempting to join a conversation already in progress among four world leaders at the economic G20 summit in Osaka, Japan, in June 2019.[64] As French President Emmanuel Macron, Canadian Prime Minister Justin Trudeau, the International Monetary Fund Director Christine Lagarde, and British Prime Minister Theresa May are seen chatting, Trump approaches the group and starts interjecting words and half sentences. Her seemingly unexpected and awkward presence in the group does not elicit much of a reaction from the four dignitaries except for a quick glance by Lagarde toward the end of the clip. All four keep talking among themselves without much regard for Trump's occasional interruptions. Trump comes across as unaffected by such a demonstrably cold reception and continues to gesticulate and interject, as if fully embraced during the exchange.

Scores of internet users and a handful of politicians saw Trump's overtures toward the world leaders as failures of a pseudo-diplomat attempting to insert herself where she did not belong, thus humiliating herself and the country on world stage.[65] Within hours of the video's debut online, American journalist Erin Ryan tweeted a response to what some online perceived as an international embarrassment in the form of a call to action. She mobilized internet users in a June 30, 2019, post to "photoshop Ivanka the unwelcomed interloper" into a variety of scenarios. The specific locations the journalist suggested ranged from artist Beyoncé's Coachella performance to the meeting between President Richard Nixon and Elvis Presley. In Ryan's eyes, the president's daughter was "boxing way above her weight"[66] at the G20 meeting—and apparently needed to be reminded of her place through some internet humor, which quickly turned into mockery. Antagonism toward a particular person or a group has been the driving force for a number of memes over the years, all designed to mock, humiliate, publicly shame, or deliver symbolic social justice in the perceived absence of other recourse.[67] In some cases, racism and misogyny have also become motivations to strike against minority groups and women. Ryan's tweet about Ivanka Trump was accompanied by the hashtag #unwantedivanka, which summarized the sentiments behind the meme campaign: Ivanka Trump was seen as persona non grata who had to be ridiculed for her perceived transgression.

The internet obliged with a vengeance. Scores of memes flooded cyberspace in response. Their authors photoshopped Trump into famous moments in popular culture and important events in world history. She walked on Abbey Road with the Beatles, sat with Jesus and his apostles for the last supper in Leonardo da Vinci's famous painting, participated in the March on Washington alongside Martin Luther King Jr., and appeared in a scene from *The Lord of the Rings*. To place her in the variety of locations, some internet users appropriated Trump's likeness from the G20 video—she wore a pink dress and kept her long blond hair down—while others cut her out from other scenarios in the past, transporting her as she was in those moments: with her mouth open, smiling, donning different outfits, and sometimes gesticulating. To no surprise, she almost always failed to blend into the photoshopped scenes—a recycled, decontextualized, visual signifier who remained an unwelcomed intruder. Her forced, unexpected, and awkward presence in these situations signaled to the audience that she was indeed an #unwantedivanka.

The juxtapositions that the memetic iterations of the G20 scene constructed made her out to be someone who had to be everywhere and meet anyone of note, often defying laws of metaphysics to make an appearance. Although she injected herself only once in the G20 summit video, the memes transformed Ivanka into a notorious interloper who was forced to photobomb other significant moments in history at someone else's pleasure as a measure of mockery and, no doubt, public shaming and punishment for her perceived misstep. The collective rhetorical work of the memes manufactured a reason to dislike and punish her even more by intentionally inserting her into a host of new scenarios to repeat the original perceived transgression from Osaka. The memes strategically multiplied and magnified the G20 moment by making Ivanka reoffend over and over again. By forcing her to transgress repeatedly, the memes set up a self-perpetuating mechanism for online mockery and ridicule. The more she re-offended, the more she deserved to be punished through new photoshopped scenarios that triggered a self-feeding loop of memetic production. Taken together, the memes ultimately transfigured Trump from a senior White House adviser to an obnoxious and arrogant caricature—a laughingstock of the internet.

Although, as noted above, the #unwantedivanka campaign's central message seems uniform, the individual memes offer situation-specific meanings that become apparent through a visual rhetorical analysis of each artifact. One of the most prominent #unwantedivanka memes in the days following the summit was one that inserted Ivanka into the March on Washington at the height of the Civil Rights Movement in the 1960s in the United States.

Presented and Suggested Elements

The template for the meme is a black-and-white photograph that we recognize as an image taken by an Agence France-Presse journalist during the March on Washington for Jobs and Freedom, a massive public demonstration that demanded political, economic, and social justice for African Americans (figure 14.1). About 200,000 participants converged on the Lincoln Memorial in the nation's capital on August 28, 1963, to listen to several speakers, including Martin Luther King Jr. deliver his now famous "I Have a Dream" speech.[68] The scene in the photograph takes place at the steps of the Lincoln Memorial but is shot looking outward at the Reflecting Pool, the Washington Monument, and the Capitol in the background.

An African American man, whom we recognize as King, stands on the right in the frame, with the photographer positioned at King's left back side. The civil rights leader's body faces the crowds, but his upper torso and head are slightly turned in the photographer's direction, though King does not look into the camera. His right arm is raised in a gesture of waving. Clad in a white shirt, a tie, and a dark suit, King looks as if he were saying something, his lips slightly parted. What lies before him is a sea of people who gathered at the foot of the memorial and along both sides of the Reflecting Pool, all the way to the Washington Monument. Two male photographers stand to the right of King, taking his picture. A white woman who is Ivanka Trump enters from the right and blocks King's view, replacing him in the frame.

Figure 14.1. Ivanka and MLK: #unwantedivanka Meme at the March on Washington
Source: The Hill via @ParkerMolloy

She is wearing a black blouse with a pin on one of the lapels and a white flowy skirt. Her hair is pulled back into a ponytail, her smile exposing her teeth. Similarly to King, she is also not looking into the camera but past it. Her right leg sticks out forward mid-step, implying movement. She seems to be walking into the picture and going toward or just past King, who is at the microphone fully engaged. Aside from the two journalists on the stage and a couple of people in the crowd, Trump seems to be the only white person immediately visible in the photograph. She is also the only woman visible on the stage.

At first glance, Ivanka blends in the composition of the photograph as if she were a member of the invited party. Her proportions in relation to other people in the frame are correct, and her likeness has presumably been adjusted through a black-and-white filter to match the aesthetics. She looks in the same general direction as King and the journalists.

Ivanka's mid-step pose captures the manufactured interloper moment in progress as she walks into the historical event. The meme mocks her attempt at conversation at the G20 summit in Osaka fifty-six years later as those around her seem unaware of her presence. The act of entering the frame only confirms and perpetuates her interloper narrative even though she obviously did not put herself on stage with King some seventeen years before her birth.

Trump does not stand with the crowd as a fellow protester nor does she take the microphone on stage to speak to the masses, leaving the purpose of her visit ambiguous. Her lack of prior advocacy work around civil rights for African Americans implies that she is at the march for other reasons than to demand equal economic opportunities for black Americans or to push for a federal civil rights bill as did King and others who spoke that day. Her walk-on appearance seems to be more self-serving than altruistic, resulting in an awkward attempt at networking that echoes the G20 meeting caught on video. She casually enters the scene with a smile on her face, as if aware of her impact. Her physical closeness to one of the most influential figures of the twentieth century in the United States grants her a similar status by mere proximity as all eyes in the crowd and all cameras on the stage are fixated on the pair. As in Osaka, here, too, she finds herself among world leaders.

The meeting between Ivanka Trump and Martin Luther King Jr. is not neutral, considering their disparate backgrounds, difference in ascribed powers, stature in society, and the importance of the event in US history. What adds to the complexity of the interaction is Ivanka's familial connection to a president who has been accused by some of deploying racist rhetoric and sued for anti–African American bias in his business dealings, claims he has disputed and denied.[69] Although the daughter is not her father, she is his surrogate who represents his values and policies as the senior White House adviser. As the only visible white figure on the stage, Trump could be seen as a proxy for the very group—the white establishment, including her father—whose racism King and the demonstrators are protesting. Given her allegiance to her father expressed in numerous public appearances, Ivanka's presence on the stage is an unlikely sign of rebellion. She appears oblivious to the fact that the meeting is aimed at people like her and eagerly moves to the center of the frame. She misreads the situation again in the meme, this time replaying the G20 fiasco in Washington, DC.

And yet, the moment is far from a confrontation. King continues to speak to the masses as he seems unaware of Ivanka's presence behind him or resolved to ignore her altogether. One might see the scene as a visual representation of the Civil Rights era: Black people's tolerance of the oppressor, and white establishment's ignorance of the struggles of the oppressed. Trump's privileged position in society defined by her race, social status, and political ties affords her the ability to interrupt—and misread, even if unintentionally—an event designed to end the very attitude of presumed belonging on display. Standing next to King, Ivanka Trump commandeers attention and is able, however symbolically and fleetingly, to usurp some of King's power simply by being who she is. King, on the other hand, continues to speak up for the rights of African Americans, even though his efforts get intercepted by Ivanka's privilege. In an ironic twist, Ivanka seeks notoriety from the very people who have been invalidated and excluded for generations by the group she represents. This is a scene of missed opportunities for both parties. King is so engrossed in his speech that he wastes a chance to address a representative of the system he wants to change. Ivanka, as someone who potentially could help bring about the change, is just passing by—her legs are in motion—and unable, once again, to initiate conversation.

Functions and Their Evaluation

The seemingly benign and funny meme that inserts Ivanka Trump into the Civil Rights Movement is a mere cog in the churning shaming machine. Similarly to other #unwantedivanka memes, it also exposes Trump's alleged arrogance and lack of qualifications as it sets her up to repeat the Osaka embarrassment at another important event, a transgression that transfigures lighthearted humor into internet meanness.

The meme accomplishes these functions through a number of jarring juxtapositions analyzed above, the central one exposing Trump's lack in comparison to King's abundance in the context of the moment. Trump's record on civil rights activism is practically nonexistent, while King's is his entire legacy and the cause of his looming death. This setup automatically disqualifies Trump from taking the stage at the march and labels her an interloper extraordinaire. It also reveals her perceived inability to read social cues and her eagerness to insert herself into situations that, as one journalist put it, result in "seemingly stilted interactions."[70]

EXAMPLE 2: #UNWANTEDIVANKA AND THE LAST SUPPER

Introduction and Context

Another popular Ivanka meme that spoofed her attempts at conversation with world leaders in Osaka uses the iconic Leonardo da Vinci wall painting *The Last Supper* as a canvas. Meme creators produced at least three versions of the photoshopped image, inserting Trump in different spots behind the table. The one analyzed here displays the president's daughter sandwiched between Jesus and the apostle John, who sits on the right side of Christ (figure 14.2). The original painting was completed in 1498 and illustrates the story of the Last Supper told most prominently in the Bible's four Gospels of Matthew, Mark, Luke, and John. The scene takes place shortly before the crucifixion of Jesus, and serves as the basis for the Eucharist (or Holy Communion), which represents the act of Jesus sharing his body and blood—consecrated bread and wine during Christian services—as his sacrifice and expression of love for humanity.[71]

Da Vinci's scene is set in a room filled with a long table that cuts across the frame. The viewer looks directly at it and those gathered behind it: Jesus at the center and six apostles on each side, arranged into four clusters with three in each group. The table is covered with what looks like a white-and-blue tablecloth and set with plates, glasses, and dishes of food. As one quickly notices, however, the moment captures more than a mere meal. Da Vinci's depiction of the biblical story records a dramatic scene, in which the twelve disciples react to what they had just heard from Jesus: one among them will shortly betray their teacher, triggering a cycle of events that would eventually lead to Christ's scourging and crucifixion. Of note in the painting is that Jesus looks calm and unmoved; his right hand reaches for a nearby dish with food. Those familiar with the Bible are bound to work out the meaning of the gesture quickly. As Jesus reveals the looming betrayal, he identifies the one who will give him up as the one at the table whose hand also reaches for the same dish—the second one on his right side, Judas. The disciples, on the other hand, appear far from tranquil. All are visibly affected, some even disturbed, by what they had just heard. Some point their fingers at themselves and others as if asking Jesus whether they are the culprit. Several huddle and seem to whisper to one another,

Ron DOV
@rez512

Replying to @rez512

♡ 3,444   7:19 PM - Jun 30, 2019

💬 633 people are talking about this   boredpanda.com

Figure 14.2.   Ivanka and Jesus: #unwantedivanka Meme at the Last Supper
Source: Twitter via @rez512

one visibly saying something into another's ear. A couple tap their neighbors' shoulders, and three seem to throw their hands up in a gesture of confusion and disbelief. Although the painting is static, the viewer gets a sense of movement and tension that build up behind the table precisely because of the varied hand gestures and changing facial expressions that seem more animated than still. The visible affect in the painting establishes a scene of witnessing, as if the viewer were a part of the unfolding drama.

The gathered men range in age; some look youthful, donning short and long brown hair, while others seem elderly as suggested by their gray and white hair and beards. All wear robes in the shades of blue, red, and green and sandals as indicated by some of their bare feet peering out from underneath the table. The room where they are gathered looks rather sparse, adorned on both sides with large dark panels that resemble tapestries. Three windows frame the back wall with a view of trees and mountains in the distance.

Presented and Suggested Elements

The same scene unfolds in the #unwantedivanka "Last Supper" meme, except for one additional guest who, quite literally, takes the center stage. A woman we recognize as Ivanka Trump joins a man we recognize as Jesus and the twelve disciples and gets inserted as the supposed Osaka interloper between John and Jesus, a coveted spot at the table. The viewer can only see her bust sandwiched between the two men, her blond hair hanging straight, her face expressionless. She seems to be wearing the same pink dress from the G20 summit. She is disproportionately larger in stature than the other guests, making her head, neck, and upper torso some of the most prominent and noticeable features of the composition. Ivanka's face is slightly shaded, her eyes nearly replaced by black circles. Her arms and hands are invisible, rendering her rather expressionless. Her slightly larger likeness immediately flags her presence as someone who clearly does not belong. She is not visibly engaged in any conversations and looks detached from the flurry of chatter and gesticulations around her.

The feeling of disregard is mutual on the apostles' part. Jesus and the disciples do not seem to notice or acknowledge Ivanka's presence as they continue to be engrossed in their exchanges. In fact, the body of Jesus is slightly turned away from Ivanka and the six men who sit next to her to the right of Jesus as he seems to be fielding questions from the trio immediately to his left. Ivanka's placement between Jesus and John, in fact, fills a gap between the two men. The vacant space in the original painting, some have speculated, is not accidental. DaVinci most likely removed everyone from the immediate vicinity of Jesus—or personal space in today's parlance—to distinguish Jesus as the central character in the scene, one who stands alone.[72]

Following the Osaka interloper narrative, we are led to believe that Ivanka Trump has also made her way to one of the most significant events in Christianity and one of the most iconic visual artifacts in Western culture. As the thirteenth disciple seated at the table during the last supper, Trump, a Jew, joins an elite group of men who are considered the closest students, followers, and friends of Christ. Her sheer presence grants her a similar status through proximity. Her particular placement in relation to Jesus adds even more importance to her participation in the meal because of its specific significance in Christianity. To be seated on the right-hand side of God—in this case the son of God in the Christian trinity—is to receive the highest distinction and favor from God, a blessing that borders on exaltation. The Bible makes a handful of references to the significance of this position as reserved only for the chosen few.[73] As the one immediately to the right of Jesus in the meme, Ivanka asserts herself as the new and "beloved disciple" of Jesus, a phrase that some theologians and Bible scholars agree has been used in Christianity's holy book to refer to John, a follower whom Jesus much loved.[74] Ivanka takes his place, suggesting a close friendship with Christ signified by the imposed seating arrangement.

Another look at the scenario, however, disproves Ivanka's supposed closeness to the guest of honor. Jesus turns away from her and the rest of the disciples on his right to devote his attention to the trio on his left, effectively ignoring her presence, a move that mirrors Osaka's awkward interloping moment. The analogies between the "meme-ified" biblical scene and the G20 moment are, in fact, not hard to find. In both scenarios Ivanka misreads the situation by presuming that she is as qualified and capable as the world leaders she approaches to carry on a conversation and that her presence and contributions are welcomed in each circle. In both cases, she is proven wrong as suggested by the leaders' facial expressions and body language, both of which communicate disapproval and dismissal, branding Trump again an interloper.

Ivanka's privileged position to be included—or to include herself, following the G20 meme narrative—has other implications than joining an exclusive group of the chosen dozen. Her presence creates a subversive story about the Last Supper by insisting that at least one woman was indeed present during the occasion, a claim that the Roman Catholic Church, for example, has rebuffed for centuries.[75] Most recently, the best-selling novel *The Da Vinci Code* written by Dan Brown proposed that the person sitting immediately to the right of Jesus in Leonardo's masterpiece was not John, as art historians, Bible scholars, and historians have claimed for generations; it was Mary Magdalene, who, according to the Bible and biblical scholars, was an ardent follower of Jesus. She was also in a small group of women, according to the Bible, who found the body of Jesus missing from the tomb three days after his death.

In the meme version of the Last Supper, it is Ivanka, not Mary Magdalene, who symbolically grants women access to the upper echelons of the Church through her sheer presence, a feat that has eluded women in the Roman Catholic Church for more than two millennia.

Ivanka's interloping, then, might be perceived as a step toward empowerment and inclusion of women in the male-dominated Roman Catholic institution, thus departing from the initial intent of the #unwantedIvanka campaign. In this interpretation, the meme does not make her out to be an interloper but a trailblazer. Perhaps Trump's appearance at the Last Supper is her answer to her own call to action at the G20 summit's corollary event entitled "Special Event on Women's Empowerment." In her speech, Ivanka Trump urged world leaders—of twenty sitting on the stage, only two were women—to pursue gender equality not only as a civil right but also as a factor in economic growth. Women, she said, are "one of the most undervalued resources in the world."[76] Her presence behind the table could be construed as a step in this direction.

And yet, Ivanka Trump does not take full advantage of her imposed interloping. Unlike in her G20 attempt to insert herself into a conversation with world leaders, she does not try it with this distinguished ensemble, which includes a man worshipped by more than a third of world's population.[77] Trump's access to Jesus is unprecedented because she sits next to him, with no one in her way to initiate a conversation. But Trump looks disengaged and almost bored, disinterested in participating in any of the ongoing discussions. She comes across as unmoved by the revelation that Jesus had just shared with the group, news that visibly rattles everyone else. Her lack of affect communicates coldness and indifference to the man who is about to die. She is not at the table to break bread, as it were, with fellow participants, or to engage in diplomacy as she was so eager to do in Japan. Her despondency suggests that her participation in the scene is random and without much of a cause after all, making her out to be more of a fraud and less of a trailblazer.

Functions and Their Evaluation

The #unwantedivanka Last Supper meme also functions as a tool of public shaming that exposes Ivanka Trump's perceived failure at diplomacy. Her eagerness to be included in the company of some of the most influential world leaders in history gets her in the room but not much further. By making her look disconnected and lost through her frozen body position and blank facial expression, the meme, in fact, prevents her from truly interloping. It draws attention to an incongruity that seems to exist between how Ivanka sees herself and how she is seen by those who participate in the #unwantedivanka meme challenge. As a White House senior adviser who represents the United States at public functions, she comes across in the meme as an ill-equipped and unqualified amateur who is out of her depth on the world stage. By casting her as incapable of engaging even in a simple table conversation, the meme triggers a mechanism that turns Ivanka Trump into a social pariah, the ridiculed interloper who is not even good at interloping. The meme magnifies her perceived weaknesses and calls her out on them by making her fail again, this time in the company of Jesus, a figure who, by all accounts in the Bible, was loving to and accepting of everyone, including his killers. Here, even Jesus turns away from her.

EXAMPLE 3: FLAGS, METAPHORS, AND SYMBOLS:
VISUAL ARGUMENT IN ACTION

Let us now move to interpreting an image that serves as a flag, a metaphor, and a symbol: the 1917 poster produced by James Montgomery Flagg (figure 14.3). Let us start with some context of its production and attitudes at the time toward persuasive images to acknowledge the importance of historical and cultural background in correctly interpreting images. As mentioned

Figure 14.3. The 1917 Uncle Sam Poster by James Montgomery Flagg
Source: US Library of Congress

earlier, visual arguments do not get constructed and should not be deconstructed in cultural, social, and historical vacuums. Their meanings derive from shared and often era-specific symbols, metaphors, and other rhetorical devices that tap into prevailing visual conventions.

For example, it is important to understand why Flagg's illustration was made into a World War I poster. At the time, posters served as the primary visual tools of communication because they were not only easy to reproduce but also beautiful and eye-catching. They functioned as instruments of mass communication to disseminate patriotic messages and calls to action across the country in an era before television and the internet. They could be easily displayed in a variety of public locations and inserted into newspapers and magazines; "their brilliant color and urgent demands projected a sense of patriotism."[78]

Flagg's illustration was among scores that were deployed by the US government in 1917 to boost participation in the war effort.[79] Although the war started in 1914, the United States joined it three years later after declaring war on Germany in 1917.[80] After joining Britain, France, and Russia as an ally, the administration needed to gain the American public's support fast. It created the Division of Pictorial Publicity the same year to inspire, persuade, and recruit on a mass scale; posters played a major role as effective visual communication tools. The Division encouraged and even drafted graphic artists and illustrators to contribute their time and talent to the effort. By the end of the war, the Division produced more than seven hundred posters, all of which deployed patriotic symbols and icons, including the American flag, Uncle Sam, and the Statue of Liberty.[81]

In terms of the immediate visual context in Flagg's image, the poster is a single panel illustration in a series of similar posters designed to promote the war effort. It displays a character known as Uncle Sam, accompanied by "I want you for U.S. Army: nearest recruiting station," with a blank space underneath to write in an address. The image is multimodal in that it combines visual and textual elements, both of which are critical to the creation of the argument. The immediate verbal context makes the point of the poster clear: a plea to join the army and fight in The Great War, as it was called at the time.

But the argument is visually enhanced as the poster functions as a flag and deploys metaphors and symbols to persuade its viewers to sign up and serve. Most immediately, the poster is a flag as it grabs the audience's attention through four primary visual elements: the character of Uncle Sam, his pointing finger, the color scheme, and the size of text embedded into the poster. The bust of Uncle Sam is arresting because of its sheer presence, size, and body language. Uncle Sam confronts the viewer eye to eye and with a somewhat harsh facial expression—he is looking directly at "you." His pointing finger only adds to the striking composition designed to personally call "you"—yes, "you"—to action. The large block letters also grab one's attention because they occupy about one-third of the poster at the bottom, becoming a prominent part of its composition. The patriotic color scheme works in conjunction with the representation of Uncle Sam to signify that the message is of national importance.

To build the claim, the poster is showing something (i.e., the United States) as something else (i.e., Uncle Sam), thus engaging a metaphor to portray the United States as a patriotically dressed elderly man known as Uncle Sam, the personification of the country. The metaphor is effective because it taps into a widely recognized symbol of the bearded man who stands in for the idea of "our" beloved country, this time in need of "our" help. Uncle Sam is in trouble; his stern expression and the pointing finger that targets the viewer alert to the seriousness and urgency of the situation: "you" are needed to do your part to help "your" country. Uncle Sam's appeal gets reinforced by the text that accompanies his likeness, leaving little room for misinterpretation of the intentions behind the call. The claim engages pathos, tugging at the emotions and values surrounding patriotism, civic duty, and what it means to be an American.

What is more, Uncle Sam is going to make serving "convenient" for "you" by listing the address of the nearest recruitment office at the bottom of the poster. By doing so, the poster preempts excuses to back out, thus further compelling the viewer to commit. The visual argument is set up to be highly persuasive and interactive as it demands the audience to take two steps: first, to write in the address of where to report for duty, and second, to actually report.

One of the reasons why "you" may feel compelled to answer the call is the cultural meaning of Uncle Sam. The character, in fact, functions here as a visual archetype. The persona derives from a narrative about a New York State businessman, Sam Wilson, who during the War of 1812 supplied the United States troops with meat.[82] The story goes that the barrels with the goods had "U.S." stamped on them to signify the property of the United States. Some, however, came to treat the acronym as the abbreviation for Wilson's nickname Uncle Sam, treating the name and the country as synonymous.[83] Uncle Sam's character was further developed by cartoonists at the British satirical magazine *Punch*, and the famous American cartoonist Thomas Nast polished the persona of Uncle Sam in the 1870s. By the time Flagg portrayed the character in his famous World War I poster, Uncle Sam had become a widely popular and recognizable visual representation for the United States.[84]

Aside from being an interesting history of symbol formation, the tale of Uncle Sam as a visual archetype provides invaluable cultural context for deciphering the visual argument that the poster makes. Uncle Sam was not just some character in the poster who happened to substitute for the United States by chance. He was—and continues to be—a cultural marker who has stood in for everything associated with America. When Uncle Sam calls, "you" answer. When we look at the three modes together, we can conclude with certainty that the argument that the poster puts forth is a direct plea of the personified United States of America to its citizens to help save her. The message gets clearly stated and reinforced through the color scheme and text embedded in the poster. The visual argument leads to the conclusion that if I am a patriot and love my country, I will enlist and join the war effort. I will answer Uncle Sam's call.

EXAMPLE 4: VISUAL DEMONSTRATION: VISUAL ARGUMENT IN ACTION

To see an effective visual demonstration in action, let us look at a poster prepared by the Centers for Disease Control and Prevention (CDC) on staying healthy during the COVID-19 pandemic (figure 14.4). For context, the CDC has been the go-to government agency during

Figure 14.4. A CDC 2020 COVID-19 Safety Poster

Source: Centers for Disease Control and Prevention

the pandemic that has tracked infections and made recommendations on virus-related issues, from testing procedures to safety measures. As part of that work, the agency has produced a number of public service announcements, many in poster format, to help guide people through the pandemic. The posters have been available for a free download on the CDC's website.

The visual argument in the poster of interest is straightforward and clear: if you engage in the following actions—remain six feet apart from others, wear a mask, and wash your hands—you are going to help protect yourself and others form COVID-19. It is expressed through a series of three steps that literally recreate—or demonstrate—social distancing, mask wearing, and hand washing; no metaphor or symbols needed to get the point across.

The images, however, are not the only building blocks of the argument. Similar to the Uncle Sam poster, this one also sets up its claims through a combination of visual elements and words. The visual parts, as mentioned, demonstrate what people must do to stay healthy and safe. The written components reinforce the argument by explicitly stating what the images already show. The first panel serves as a good example to illustrate how the two elements work in tandem. We see a bunch of people in a park, engaging in different activities, from walking, sun bathing, and reading to practicing yoga and typing on a laptop. Each person or group are separated from one another with some distance to indicate the six-feet recommendation. The drawing, of course, does not capture the distance to scale or even label it; it only implies it. What clarifies the claim is the accompanying text that lays out the distance with precision: "stay 6 feet from others." If the viewers did not already know about the recommended distance, they would not have deduced it from the image alone. The short instruction works together with the visual demonstration to make the argument unambiguous. That is why immediate verbal context is critical to the interpretation process of visual arguments.

PERSONAL REFLECTIONS

The artifacts in this chapter, of course, were not chosen at random. In the early stages of writing one part of this chapter, the #unwantedIvanka meme was at the height of its popularity online; I decided to use it because its journey through social media afforded me a front-row seat. I was able to track the #unwantedIvanka iterations online in real time and note their changing functions upon ongoing reconstitution. The different versions of the meme I encountered allowed me to offer side-by-side interpretative analyses of two versions of the same visual concept to demonstrate the interpretive approach to reading visual rhetoric.

When I was thinking about a visual artifact that would serve as a strong example to explain visual argument, I was hoping to pick a piece that has lingered in our collective cultural consciousness for a while—long enough to work as an easily recognized visual symbol, metaphor, and an archetype. The Uncle Sam poster came to mind immediately as an iconic image that has endured for more than a century, still recycled in ads to this day. That it also turned out to function as a flag was a bonus. For the demonstration function of visual argument, I chose a CDC poster about the pandemic because I happened to write that part of the chapter during the spread of COVID-19. I reasoned that because the poster was a part of the CDC's public awareness campaign, it was presumably seen by scores of people and therefore was somewhat familiar.

POTENTIALS AND PITFALLS

Some 3.2 billion images and 720,000 hours of video get shared online every day[85]—we are inundated and surrounded. As we know from this chapter, images carry messages, and they often want something from us and for us. Knowing what, how, and why is part of the basic visual media literacy that we as media producers and consumers ought to command. We ought to know how to interpret a political ad or how to break down an editorial cartoon as a visual argument to fully participate in public life. In a visual world, these skills serve as part of a language that we need to be discerning news consumers, civic leaders, shoppers, and perhaps even social media influencers.

But, as the genie told Aladdin when granting him three wishes, use your gifts wisely. One of the pitfalls that budding visual rhetoric critics may experience is over-reading or misreading of artifacts. Even though, as the chapter highlights, meanings are in the eyes of the beholders, there is a reasonable expectation on the part of the producers and consumers that some readings of images are more common, that is, more dominant, than others.[86] This premise allows ads to be persuasive, memes to be funny, and viral and iconic images to be symbolic of larger sentiments and events. One of the most helpful tools in deciphering meanings is, as Birdsell and Groarke and Gries remind us, context—historical, social, cultural, political, textual, and so on. Without it, our interpretation is likely to be one-dimensional, impoverished, and stripped of the rich cultural meanings attached to symbols, metaphors, and other rhetorical devices that are the building blocks of interpretation. They are the ones that turn a monument of a woman holding a torch to a shorthand for the United States. The German art historian Erwin Panofsky called context broadly conceptualized as "cultural traditions peculiar to a certain civilization" when he devised his interpretive approach called iconography/iconology to studying works of art.[87] It would serve us well to follow Panofsky's advice and ground our readings of visual rhetoric in accurate and appropriate contexts to avoid unnecessary misunderstandings.

VISUAL ANALYSIS TOP PICKS

Birdsell, David S., and Leo Groarke. "Toward a Theory of Visual Argument." *Argumentation and Advocacy* 33 (1996): 1–10. In this seminal piece, the authors lay out the theoretical grounds for why and how images, similarly to words, are capable of making arguments, thus extending the principles of traditional rhetoric to visual artifacts.

———. "Outlines of a Theory of Visual Argument." *Argumentation and Advocacy* 43 (2007). The authors build on the article above by presenting the building blocks of the theory of visual argument with emphasis on the five modes of delivering visual arguments described in this chapter. They supply the reader with plenty of examples to illustrate how and why visual arguments make their claims.

Finnegan, Cara A., and Diane S. Hope, eds. *Visual Rhetoric: A Reader in Communication and American Culture*. Newbury Park, CA: Sage, 2008. The book offers a collection of studies that approach visual rhetoric from a variety of perspectives, often by demonstrating the use of various methods to deconstruct artifacts.

Foss, Sonja. "Theory of Visual Rhetoric." In *Handbook of Visual Communication: Theory, Methods, and Media*, ed. Ken Smith, Sandra Moriarty, Gretchen Barbatsis, and Keith

Kenney, 141–152. Mahwah, NJ: Routledge, 2005. In this foundational chapter, Foss walks the readers through the theoretical underpinnings of her approach to visual rhetoric. She also formulates a method of interpretation that is designed to uncover the symbolic meanings of images.

Gries, Laurie. "Iconographic Tracking: A Digital Research Method for Visual Rhetoric and Circulation Studies." *Computers and Composition* 30, no. 4 (2013): 332–348. In this article, Gries proposes a new approach to visual rhetoric that acknowledges and emphasizes visual artifacts as performances in progress that change meanings and functions as they change hands over time on- and off-line.

———. *Still Life with Rhetoric: A New Materialist Approach to Visual Rhetorics.* Boulder, CO: Utah State University Press, 2015. Gries builds on the article above in this book by providing an extended theoretical grounding for her understanding and treatment of visual rhetoric as an ongoing process that produces various interpretations as visual artifacts change genre, media, and functions over time.

DISCUSSION QUESTIONS

1. Discuss why and how meanings of a single visual artifact such as a photograph, a painting, or a poster, might change across different cultures and audiences. Use the concepts from this chapter to elaborate on your answer.
2. Is there one "correct" interpretation of a visual artifact? If yes, why? If no, why not? When formulating your answer, please rely on the chapter to support your argument.
3. Divide into small groups. If your group were in charge of a visual ad campaign to encourage people to buy your brand of a candy bar, what factors should you pay attention to from the perspective of visual rhetoric? Think about the evaluation of the nature and functions of an image when formulating your answer. What visual arguments would you want to make?

ACTIVITIES

1. Look around the classroom and find some logos that you see on your classmates' clothing. Using the three perspectives in this chapter to study visual rhetoric, describe what the logos are communicating to you. What meanings and associations do they conjure? Where do you think those meanings and associations come from?
2. Start out this activity as a whole class by finding one iconic news image that you know from history books. Once you agree on the artifact, divide the class into three groups. Group one: your task is to follow Foss's model of interpretive analysis described in this chapter and carry out a study of the iconic image that you chose as a whole class, paying special attention to the presented and suggested elements of the image, its meanings and functions. Group two: your task is to follow Birdsell and Groarke's approach and decipher visual arguments that the same iconic news image makes, considering the five modes of visual argument laid out in the chapter. Group three: do some research online to see how people talked about the iconic image at the time of its initial publication. Were their interpretations different from what groups one and two found? If so, why might this be?

3. Look at any of the following news images: the "pepper-spraying cop" photograph from the 2011 Occupy Wall Street protests at the University of California–Davis, the Situation Room photograph from the 2011 Osama bin Laden military mission, the snapshot of Keanu Reeves eating lunch alone on a bus stop bench, or the picture of the Syrian boy Alan Kurdi's body lying on a Turkish beach. Your next task is to look up internet memes of these news photographs. Do the memes invite the same interpretations as the original news photographs? By using Gries's method of iconographic tracking, what can you say about transfigurations of the original image through the internet memes?

NOTES

1. Initial news reports spelled Alan Kurdi's name as Aylan Kurdi. I use the corrected version. Please view the image here: http://100photos.time.com/photos/nilufer-demir-alan-kurdi.

2. Farida Vis and Olga Goriunova, eds., "The Iconic Image on Social Media: A Rapid Research Response to the Death of Aylan Kurdi," in *Picturing the Social: Transforming Our Understanding of Images in Social Media and Big Data Research* (Visual Social Media Lab, 2015).

3. United Nations Refugee Agency, "More Than Four Million Syrians Have Now Fled War and Persecution," July 9, 2015, https://www.unhcr.org/en-us/news/latest/2015/7/559d648a9/four-million-syrians-fled-war-persecution.html.

4. Adnan Khan, "Alan Kurdi's Father and His Family Tragedy: 'I Should Have Died with Them,'" *Guardian*, December 22, 2015, https://www.theguardian.com/world/2015/dec/22/abdullah-kurdi-father-boy-on-beach-alan-refugee-tragedy.

5. Tessa Berenson, "ISIS Using Photo of Drowned Syrian Boy as Propaganda," *Time*, September 10, 2015, http://time.com/4029205/isis-drowned-syrian-boy-photo/.

6. Ibid.

7. Joanna Paraszczuk, "A Drowned Syrian Boy as ISIS Propaganda," *Atlantic*, September 11, 2015, https://www.theatlantic.com/author/joanna-paraszczuk/.

8. Sonja K. Foss, "Theory of Visual Rhetoric," in *Handbook of Visual Communication: Theory, Methods, and Media*, ed. Ken Smith, Sandra Moriarty, Gretchen Barbatsis, and Keith Kenney (Mahwah, NJ: Routledge, 2005), 141–152, https://www.taylorfrancis.com/books/e/9781410611581/chapters/10.4324/9781410611581-18. Keith Kenney, "A Visual Rhetorical Study of a Virtual University's Promotional Efforts," in *Handbook of Visual Communication: Theory, Methods, and Media*, ed. Ken Smith, Sandra Moriarty, Gretchen Barbatsis, and Keith Kenney (Mahwah, NJ: Routledge, 2005), 153–165.

9. Natalia Mielczarek, "The Dead Syrian Refugee Boy goes Viral: Funerary Aylan Kurdi Memes as Tool of Mourning and Visual Reparation in Remix Culture," *Visual Communication* 19, no. 4 (September 2018), doi:10.1177/1470357218797366.

10. Darin Barney, Gabriella Coleman, Christine Ross, Jonathan Sterne, and Tamar Tembeck, eds., "The Participatory Condition in the Digital Age," in *The Participatory Condition in the Digital Age*, ed. Darin Barney and others (Minneapolis: University of Minnesota Press, 2016), vii–xxxix. Laurie Gries, *Still Life with Rhetoric: A New Materialist Approach for Visual Rhetorics* (Boulder, CO: Utah State University Press, 2015). Natalia Mielczarek and David D. Perlmutter, "Big Pictures and Visual Propaganda: The Lessons of Research on the 'Effects' of Photojournalistic Icons," in *Visual Propaganda and Extremism in the Online Environment*, ed. Carol K. Winkler and Cori E. Dauber (Carlisle, PA: United States Army War College Press, 2014). W. J. T. Michell, *Cloning Terror: The War of Images, 9/11 to the Present* (Chicago: University of Chicago Press, 2011).

11. Laurie Gries, "Iconographic Tracking: A Digital Research Method for Visual Rhetoric and Circulation Studies," *Computers and Composition* 30, no. 4 (2013): 332–348.

12. Gries, "Iconographic Tracking," 335. Emphasis mine.

13. Gries, "Iconographic Tracking," 335. Mitchell, *Cloning Terror*.

14. Richard Howell and Joaquim Negreiros, *Visual Culture* (Malden, MA: Polity, 2012).

15. Mielczarek and Perlmutter, "Big Pictures and Visual Propaganda," 215–233.

16. Ibid.

17. Foss, "Theory of Visual Rhetoric."

18. Ibid.

19. David S. Birdsell and Leo Groarke, "Toward a Theory of Visual Argument," *Argumentation and Advocacy* 33 (1996): 1–10. David S. Birdsell and Leo Groarke, "Outlines of a Theory of Visual Argument," *Argumentation and Advocacy* 43 (2007).

20. Foss, "Theory of Visual Rhetoric."

21. Foss, "Theory of Visual Rhetoric," 147.

22. Foss, "Theory of Visual Rhetoric." Lester Olson, Cara Finnegan, and Diane Hope, eds., *Visual Rhetoric: A Reader in Communication and American Culture* (Newbury Park, CA: Sage Publications, 2008).

23. Foss, "Theory of Visual Rhetoric," 144.

24. Foss, "Theory of Visual Rhetoric."

25. Foss, "Theory of Visual Rhetoric." Megan McFarlane, "Visualizing the Rhetorical Presidency: Barack Obama in the Situation Room," *Visual Communication Quarterly* 23 (2016): 3–13.

26. Roland Barthes, *Image Music Text* (New York: Hill and Wang, 1977). Foss, "Theory of Visual Rhetoric."

27. Foss, "Theory of Visual Rhetoric." Sonja Foss, "A Rhetorical Schema for the Evaluation of Visual Imagery," *Communication Studies* 45, nos. 3–4 (1994): 213–224.

28. Leo R. Chavez, *Covering Immigration: Popular Images and the Politics of the Nation* (Los Angeles: University of California Press, 2001). Robert L. Fleegler, *Ellis Island Nation. Immigration Police and American Identity in the Twentieth Century* (Philadelphia: University of Pennsylvania Press, 2013). US National Park Service, "Statue of Liberty National Monument," retrieved from https://www.nps.gov/stli/index.htm.

29. Foss, "Theory of Visual Rhetoric."

30. See the poster here: https://www.artic.edu/artworks/229396/barack-obama-hope-poster.

31. William W. Fisher III et al., "Reflections on the Hope Poster Case," *Harvard Journal of Law & Technology* 25, no. 2 (2012): 244–338.

32. Foss, "Theory of Visual Rhetoric."

33. Birdsell and Groarke, "Toward a Theory of Visual Argument."

34. Birdsell and Groarke, "Outlines of a Theory of Visual Argument," 108.

35. Frans H. Van Eemeren and Peter Houtlosser, "The Case of Pragma-Dialectics," in S. Parsons, N. Maudet, P. Moraitis, and I. Rahwan, eds., *Argumentation in Multi-Agent Systems, Lecture Notes in Computer Science* 4049 (ArgMAS 2005) (Berlin, Heidelberg: Springer, 2005), 1–28.

36. Birdsell and Groarke, 104.

37. Ibid.

38. Ibid.

39. Barbie Zelizer, *Remembering to Forget: Holocaust Memory Through the Camera's Eye* (Chicago: University of Chicago Press, 1998).

40. Birdsell and Groarke, "Toward a Theory of Visual Argument"; Birdsell and Groarke, "Outlines of a Theory of Visual Argument."

41. Birdsell and Groarke, "Toward a Theory of Visual Argument"; Birdsell and Groarke, "Outlines of a Theory of Visual Argument."

42. Birdsell and Groarke, "Toward a Theory of Visual Argument."

43. Birdsell and Groarke, "Outlines of a Theory of Visual Argument"; Leo Groarke and Christopher W. Tindale, *Good Reasoning Matters! A Constructive Approach to Critical Thinking* (Don Mills, Ontario: Oxford University Press, 2013).

44. Birdsell and Groarke, "Toward a Theory of Visual Argument"; Birdsell and Groarke, "Outlines of a Theory of Visual Argument."

45. Birdsell and Groarke, "Outlines of a Theory of Visual Argument"; Groarke and Tindale, *Good Reasoning Matters*.

46. Here's an instruction manual for an Ikea chair: https://ikeabg.azureedge.net/pdf/59829125.pdf.

47. Birdsell and Groarke, "Toward a Theory of Visual Argument"; Birdsell and Groarke, "Outlines of a Theory of Visual Argument."

48. Groarke and Tindale, *Good Reasoning Matters*, 152.

49. Birdsell and Groarke, "Outlines of a Theory of Visual Argument."

50. Lloyd Bitzer, "Aristotle's Enthymeme Revisited," *Quarterly Journal of Speech* 45, no. 4 (1959): 399–408. Groarke and Tindale, *Good Reasoning Matters*. Valerie Smith, "Aristotle's Classical Enthymeme and the Visual Argumentation of the Twenty-First Century," *Argumentation and Advocacy* 43, nos. 3–4 (2007): 114–123.

51. Bitzer, "Aristotle's Enthymeme Revisited," 408.

52. Ibid.

53. Smith, "Aristotle's Classical Enthymeme," 122.

54. Matte Mortensen, "'The Image Speaks for Itself'—or Does It?: Instant News Icons, Impromptu Publics, and the 2015 European 'Refugee Crisis,'" *Communication and the Public* 1, no. 4 (2016): 409–422.

55. Ryan M. Milner, *The World Made Meme: Public Conversations and Participatory Media* (Cambridge, MA: MIT Press, 2016).

56. Gries, "Iconographic Tracking," 338.

57. Ibid.

58. Gries, "Iconographic Tracking"; Gries, *Still Life with Rhetoric*.

59. Gries, *Still Life with Rhetoric*, 11.

60. Gries, *Still Life with Rhetoric*.

61. Gries, "Iconographic Tracking," 338.

62. Gries, "Iconographic Tracking," 337.

63. Natalia Mielczarek, "Iconographic Tracking of Pepe the Frog Meme through the 2016 Presidential Campaign," in *The 2016 American Presidential Campaign and News. Implications for American Democracy and the Republic*, ed. Jim A. Kuypers (New York: Lexington Books, 2018), 155–180.

64. To watch the video, go to https://www.youtube.com/watch?v=073hfPueac0.

65. Martin Pengelly, "Ocasio-Cortez Leads Critics in Video Showing Ivanka Trump G20 Chat," *Guardian*, June 30, 2019, https://www.theguardian.com/world/2019/jun/30/ivanka-trump-g20-leaders-video-alexandria-ocasio-cortez.

66. Tweet by Erin Ryan posted on June 30, 2019.

67. Natalia Mielczarek, "The 'Pepper-Spraying Cop' Icon and Its Internet Memes: Social Justice and Public Shaming Through Rhetorical Transformation in Digital Culture," *Visual Communication Quarterly* 25, no. 2 (2018): 67–81. Milner, *The World Made Meme*.

68. The Martin Luther King Jr. Research and Education Institute, Stanford University, https://kinginstitute.stanford.edu/.

69. Jonathan Mahler and Steve Eder, "'No Vacancies' for Blacks: How Donald Trump Got His Start, and Was First Accused of Bias," *New York Times*, August 27, 2016, https://www.nytimes.com/2016/08/28/us/politics/donald-trump-housing-race.html. Zeke Miller and Hope Yen, "Accused of Racism, Trump Blasts Black Congressman as Racist," Associated Press, July 29, 2019, https://apnews.com/article/4175ea0e61e746cd95d7c684cd6a59f7.

70. Rym Momtaz and Nahal Toosi, "French Say Oops on Viral Ivanka Moment," *Politico*, July 1, 2019, https://www.politico.com/story/2019/07/01/france-ivanka-trump-reaction-1392084.

71. Ross King, *Leonardo and the Last Supper* (New York: Bloomsbury, 2012), 180–199.

72. Ross King, *Leonardo and The Last Supper*. Vito Zani, ed., *Leonardo Da Vinci. The Last Supper* (New York: Rizzoli International Publication, Inc, 1999).

73. Referenced in the Bible in Romans 8:34 and Psalm 110:1. See also the Westminster Standard, "Text and Scripture Proofs," *Larger Catechism*, Q&A 54, https://thewestminsterstandard.org/westminster-larger-catechism/#51.

74. Jimmy Akin, "The Mystery of the Beloved Disciple," *National Catholic Register*, December 22, 2017, https://www.ncregister.com/blog/the-mystery-of-the-beloved-disciple. King, *Leonardo and the Last Supper*, 180–199.

75. King, *Leonardo and the Last Supper*.

76. Ellen Cranley, "Ivanka Trump Urged Countries to Do More on Women's Rights at G20, Despite Administration's Contradicting Records," *Business Insider*, June 29, 2019, https://www.businessinsider.com/ivanka-trump-womens-empowerment-japan-summit-2019-6.

77. Frank Jacobs, "This Is the Best (and Simplest) Map of World Religions," *Big Think*, March 21, 2019, https://bigthink.com/strange-maps/world-map-of-religions.

78. US Army Heritage & Education Center, "Inspiring a Nation," accessed October 16, 2020, at https://ahec.armywarcollege.edu/exhibits/constitution_center.cfm.

79. Library of Congress, "I Want You for U.S. Army: Nearest Recruiting Station," poster, accessed October 14, 2020, at https://www.loc.gov/pictures/item/96507165/. *Britannica*, "Uncle Sam: United States Symbol," accessed October 14, 2020, at https://www.britannica.com/topic/Uncle-Sam.

80. At the time, close to 10 percent of the US population claimed German origin. Irish immigrants also constituted one of the largest immigrant groups in the country, creating what the United States World War One Centennial Commission called "ethnic group complexities" around joining the war effort. German immigrants and their descendants supported President Woodrow Wilson's neutrality stance; Irish immigrants united around their animosity toward the British. Source: David Laskin, "Ethnic Minorities at War (USA)," *International Encyclopedia of the First World War*, accessed October 22, 2020, at https://encyclopedia.1914-1918-online.net/article/ethnic_minorities_at_war_usa.

81. US Army Heritage & Education Center, "Inspiring a Nation."

82. Library of Congress, "I Want You." *Britannica*, "Uncle Sam."

83. *Britannica*, "Uncle Sam."

84. Ibid.

85. T. J. Thomson, Daniel Angus, and Paula Dootson, "3.2 Billion Images and 720,000 Hours of Video Are Shared Online Daily. Can You Sort Real From Fake?," *Conversation*, November 2, 2020, https://theconversation.com/3-2-billion-images-and-720-000-hours-of-video-are-shared-online-daily-can-you-sort-real-from-fake-148630.

86. Stuart Hall, "Encoding/Decoding," in *Media and Cultural Studies: KeyWorks*, rev. ed., ed. Meenakshi Gigi Durham and Douglas M. Kellner (Malden, MA: Blackwell, 2006), 163–173.

87. Erwin Panofsky, "Iconography and Iconology: An Introduction to the Study of the Renaissance Art," in *Meaning in the Visual Arts*, ed. Erwin Panofsky (Garden City, NJ: Doubleday Anchor, 1939), 26–54.

15

Criticism of Popular Culture and Social Media

Kristen Hoerl and Zoe Farquhar

In early 2016, Super Bowl 50 drew an audience of 111.9 million viewers.[1] That September, the first presidential debate between Hillary Clinton and Donald Trump drew 84 million viewers.[2] According to these statistics, far more people are interested in a matchup between NFL teams than between two candidates vying for the United States presidency. This may trouble those of us interested in civic engagement and democracy. However, widespread interest in the Super Bowl highlights the centrality of popular media to collective engagement. It is often easier for people to strike up a conversation with someone they do not know very well by asking them which Super Bowl team they are rooting for than by asking their thoughts about political events.

Rhetorical criticism of popular culture begins with the premise that the study of discourses of everyday life and entertainment can offer insights about social beliefs, attitudes, and power relations. A rhetorical approach to the study of popular culture embraces a broad conception of rhetoric as "the social function that manages meanings."[3] Rather than locating rhetoric within only those texts intentionally created to achieve a specific goal, this expansive view enables critics to explain how symbolic action comprised of a combination of words, images, moving pictures, and sounds across a myriad of cultural artifacts shape our identities and communities. Raymond Williams, a foundational theorist in the field of cultural studies, famously defined culture as "a whole way of life."[4] This definition is purposefully vague, as it enables critics to explore a wide variety of cultural forms that some might consider lowbrow or trivial, including Hollywood films, television programs, popular music, and social media such as Twitter, Instagram, Reddit, and Snapchat. Although this chapter focuses on commercial media, popular culture is broader in scope. Rhetorical critics of popular culture may be interested in other cultural practices including sporting events, tattoo art, and food culture. Why study such practices? Because the most seemingly mundane practices and discourses can shape our assumptions and worldviews. When we engage with popular culture, we inevitably participate in the political and social struggles of our time. Rhetorical criticism starts from the premise that symbolic action invites shared understanding that provides a basis for collective decision making. The study of how meaning is constructed in popular culture explains the processes by which communities share experiences, maintain social stability, and recognize the need for social change.

Although many disciplines within the humanities study films and television programs, rhetorical criticism of popular culture is distinguished by an investment in civic life. Such criticism seeks to explain how popular texts contribute to broader cultural conversations about social life and politics. An implication of this approach is that the messages of popular culture carry meanings that extend beyond the narrative or aesthetic dimensions of the text by referencing and giving meaning to sociopolitical circumstances. Conscientious rhetoric scholars attend to popular texts as products of their time and read them in the historical and political contexts in which they were created and consumed. By interpreting popular culture texts in these contexts, critics have a basis for explaining how popular culture functions to "make some ideas, positions, and alternatives more attractive, accessible, and powerful to audiences than others."[5] Popular media offer discursive resources and interpretive frameworks for audiences to consider and discuss the social and political issues embedded in the texts of popular culture.

This chapter is different from other chapters in this book. Unlike approaches such as close textual analysis, narrative, and metaphoric criticism, the concept of popular culture is not a method per se. Instead, popular culture is an object of analysis for criticism. Hence, there is no one standard approach toward analyzing popular culture from a rhetorical perspective. In the following section, we discuss a variety of theoretical frameworks and practices that critics have applied to analyze the texts of popular culture. First, we provide a brief overview of some of the most frequently referenced theoretical frameworks for interpreting the meaning of popular culture. Then we describe how scholars have made decisions about text selection and analytical approaches. Not all of these theories and strategies will be useful for one project. Critics' uses of concepts and texts depend on what they find to be most important and the central arguments they wish to make.

THEORIZING THE RELATIONSHIP
BETWEEN CULTURE AND POWER

Although rhetorical critics have analyzed popular-culture texts using a variety of approaches, their scholarship often intersects with and draws upon the work of cultural studies. **Cultural studies** is an interdisciplinary field concerned with the relationship between culture and power. It focuses on the ways that symbolic action reproduces, resists, and transforms existing power relations and conditions of inequality. This approach to criticism explains how mass media construct, affirm, and sometimes challenge social hierarchies based on categories of identity such as race, gender, class, sexual orientation, and nationality. One core tenet of cultural studies is that scholarship should be explicitly interventionist. Because all discourse is positioned within and responds to power relations, critics should be self-reflexive about the ways in which their own social locations shape their criticism. For instance, my coauthor and I need to be aware of how the examples we have chosen for this chapter might reflect our own perspectives as white women who teach students at a university in the Midwest. This awareness should remind us to look for examples that are recognizable to a broader group of students beyond those we work with daily. With this interventionist goal in mind, rhetorical criticism of popular culture not only explains how meaning is constructed within a particular text but also evaluates the implications of the text. For many critics, the point of criticism is to promote social change. Of course, many critics prefer to describe and explain popular culture, stopping short of active intervention.

Rhetorical scholars have drawn from a variety of theories to explain the relationship between culture and power. This chapter discusses four of them: ideology, interpellation, hegemony, and power/knowledge. **Ideologies** are systems of ideas that provide the frameworks through which we understand and interpret social experience. Although language and symbolic action are the means by which ideologies are shared, ideologies are not the product of individual intention. Rather, we unconsciously adopt ideological beliefs as part of the environments into which we are born. Popular culture is a central feature of this environment.

Ideologies for humans are akin to water for fish. We take ideologies for granted because they are an intrinsic part of our everyday lives. A fish realizes the importance of water when it finds itself on the other side of the fishbowl. Likewise, it is only when we have a radically different experience such as visiting a new country that we realize how much we depend on our ideological beliefs to make sense of the world. Without that new experience, the ideologies we grow up with seem to be common sense. One important implication of ideological discourse is that it provides a partial view of reality that privileges some perspectives over others. Ideologies that hold sway in current culture are referred to as dominant ideologies.

Critics of ideology typically draw attention to the ways in which particular instances of ideological discourse make the uneven distribution of resources and other conditions of inequality seem natural. These critics explain how the mundane features of everyday life affirm the interests of powerful classes. Although this approach suggests that some ideologies are better than others, it should not imply that one can gain understanding of reality that is complete or "outside" ideology. Indeed, finding a basis for evaluating ideology is a complex issue. The concept of interpellation explains why seeking to identify discourse that is not ideological is a thorny problem.

Interpellation refers to the process by which ideological discourse constructs subject positions for individuals and groups from which they can make sense of their experience. That is, our own identities are the products of ideology.[6] We internalize ideological discourses that offer us a certain image of our place in the world and then use that image to guide our beliefs and behaviors. Renowned cultural studies critic Stuart Hall explains that ideologies construct for their subjects "positions of identification and knowledge which allow them to 'utter' ideological truths as if they were their authentic authors. . . . [W]e find ourselves mirrored in the positions at the centre of the discourses from which the statements we formulate 'make sense.'"[7] The theory of interpellation explains why it is impossible for us to experience the world outside ideology, but it has also been criticized for offering a static worldview. If our internalized worldview is constructed by dominant ideologies, then how does social change happen?

The concept of **hegemony** explains the role of discourse in the process of social change. Attributed to the work of Antonio Gramsci, hegemony refers to the process by which the social order remains stable by generating the voluntary consent of its members.[8] The **social order** refers to a system of social hierarchies, structures, institutions, relations, customs, values, and practices that correspond to specific ideological assumptions. Thus, consent to the social order is achieved through the construction and circulation of ideological texts. For example, capitalism is widely perceived as the only legitimate economic system in the United States because our news coverage, films, and television programs frequently extol the virtues of free enterprise and hard work as values that enable people to achieve their goals. A key to maintaining this consent to capitalism is to understand people's economic distresses as personal failures that could have been avoided if they had worked harder or smarter. If the majority of US citizens believed that economic distress itself was a result of capitalism, the social order would be in jeopardy. You may note that the concept of hegemony is very similar to that of dominant ideology. One way to distinguish between the two is that dominant ideology is a set of beliefs that suggest that the current distribution of power is common sense, and hegemony is the process by which cultural texts convince us to accept these beliefs.

The concept of hegemony recognizes that ideological discourse must convince marginalized groups that the social order exists in their best interests if that order is to remain dominant. When members of these groups conclude that the dominant ideology does not adequately reflect their experiences and values, they may build alternative ideologies that offer contrasting propositions about the nature of reality and one's place within it. Thus, interpellation is never complete. The struggle between dominant and alternative ideologies is often referred to as a struggle for hegemony. Hegemonic systems are an unavoidable aspect of social life, but they do change form through a process of negotiation between social groups.

Popular culture is an interesting site of struggle because media texts must adapt and respond to changing social conventions. Thus, hegemony is always in a process of negotiation. Counterhegemonic messages may express support for an alternative ideology and question the social order. Because ideologies are always contested, dominant ideologies must be able to absorb and reframe challenges. Such ideological adaption should not be conflated with fundamental social change or the redistribution of power. After all, slight changes in ideological discourse might discourage audiences from thinking about the system as a whole. For example, Dana Cloud explains that mediated discourses about Oprah Winfrey have challenged hegemonic whiteness in American culture by celebrating the success of an African American woman, but they also obscured the reality that black Americans are still more likely to live in poverty than white Americans. Consequently, attention to Oprah's success encourages audiences to support the current system despite ongoing racial disparities in employment, healthcare, and law enforcement.[9] One insight that emerges from this approach to criticism is that texts that appear to promote alternative ideologies at first glance may have hegemonic implications nonetheless. Conversely, other critics have noted that popular culture has incorporated progressive and countercultural values into its content.[10]

Another perspective on power draws from the work of Michel Foucault, who emphasizes that knowledge and power mutually inform one another.[11] Rather than think of power as a repressive force used against others, Foucault regards power as a productive force that circulates through all levels of society. **Power/knowledge** creates and sustains social relations in every instance. Critics of rhetoric find Foucault's discussion of power useful because it foregrounds how meaning is achieved through operations of power. Discourse constructs, defines, and produces objects of knowledge in an intelligible way while excluding other forms of reasoning as unintelligible.[12] Our physical bodies are subject to the regulatory power of discourse because it is through discourse that we become subjects for ourselves and others. Thus, the subject, or a sense of one's individual identity, is constituted in discourse through the specific vocabularies of knowledges that circulate in society. So, by studying those discourses, critics explain how power makes particular social identities intelligible. From this view, discourses of popular culture operate as a disciplinary technology that regulates and organizes bodies. Those who resist such regulation do not make sense within the available vocabularies of knowledge; hence, they are positioned as abnormal, or Other. For instance, relative absence of positive depictions of gays and lesbians in US films and television, particularly before the sexual revolution of the late 1960s, illustrates how Hollywood has positioned the gay community as unintelligible. Of course, that does not mean that the gay and lesbian community does not exist. That people do resist lines of intelligibility reminds us that subjectivity is never stable and is open to change.

STRATEGIES FOR INTERPRETING POPULAR CULTURE AND SOCIAL MEDIA

Selecting/Constructing the Text

Many critics find the aforementioned theoretical frameworks useful to explain why a particular text in popular culture is rhetorically meaningful; however, insightful criticism does not simply apply a particular theoretical framework to a text. For instance, explaining that a specific movie expresses a dominant ideology is not all that interesting because all products of commercial media reflect dominant ideological views in some way. Rather than seeking to apply a particular theory to a popular-culture text, we recommend that critics begin by identifying a text that they are curious about because it offers unique, important, or troubling commentary about public life. Critics often pursue their analysis with a hunch that a particular text gives meaning to an ongoing social conflict or political controversy. Other critics are simply interested in a particular text and want to understand its rhetorical significance more fully.

Critics should think carefully about the texts they select for analysis. They cannot assume that the existence of a text alone legitimizes it as an object of study. Since criticism itself is an act of communicating rhetorically to others, the first step is to explain why a particular text merits scholarly attention. Rhetorical critics part ways with some of their counterparts in film studies whose criticism primarily appreciates the aesthetic merits of a film. Remember that rhetorical critics of popular culture are primarily concerned with how a text contributes to shared understanding about a social or political issue, collective decision making, and/or social justice. If few people are familiar with a text, readers may be hard pressed to care about the analysis. Critics might provide a variety of reasons that explain why a text is worthy of rhetorical analysis based on its popularity, critical acclaim, or resonance with other trends in popular culture.

Some texts become interesting candidates for analysis after a public figure or activist group has referenced them to comment on a political or social controversy. For instance, the television series *The Handmaid's Tale* has been widely interpreted as a commentary about reproductive rights and the need for contemporary feminism. After the streaming service Hulu began airing the program, reproductive rights activists in Australia, the United States, and Ireland wore red robes and white hats reminiscent of those worn on the program to protest restrictions to abortion in their countries. In fact, one political action group has renamed itself The Handmaid Coalition to connect the TV show's themes to their own critique of political oppression against marginalized groups.[13] Another example is astrophysicist and science communicator Neil deGrasse Tyson's criticism of the Academy Award–winning film *Gravity*. After the film's release in 2013, Tyson issued a series of tweets about the film's failures to accurately depict astrophysics. These tweets garnered additional news media attention and online debate about the status of science and science literacy. Thus, *Gravity* and social media discussions about the film may tell us something unique about how cinema participates in public controversies about the merits of scientific discovery and space exploration.

The example of *Gravity* and social media attention to the film illustrates the critic's role in defining the scope of the text. A text typically refers to a self-contained media product such as a particular film, television program, or music recording. But it may also include a variety of products that give meaning to an issue when considered collectively.[14] Barry Brummett defines a text as "a set of signs related to each other insofar as their meanings all contribute to the same set of effects or functions."[15] This definition suggests that the scope of the text may be determined according to the patterns across different products in media culture that share similar messages and themes. These patterns may be more interesting than any one individual text because they construct a structured symbolic environment that encourages audiences to share similar interpretations of the world.

For example, consider the emerging practice of Twitter trolling. One particularly pernicious form of trolling involves responding to feminists' tweets with messages that threaten violence or rape. Although individual tweets that threaten violence are troubling, the pattern of threatening responses that feminist advocates have received reveals a culture of misogyny that exists beyond the attitudes of a few individuals.[16] In deciding the scope of the text, critics should consider whether a particular cultural product is interesting on its own and/or to what extent it is intriguing when considered in relationship to other cultural products.

Even if critics choose to focus an analysis on one particular text, they should consider the rhetorical role of paratexts in giving meaning to the text and its surrounding issues. **Paratexts** are the variety of materials that comment on or refer to a text such as a movie or television program. Advertisements, movie trailers, website reviews, interviews with actors and creators, internet discussions, and fan creations inform audiences about movies, films, and celebrities; consequently, they also guide audiences' interpretations. As Herman Gray notes, these paratexts establish frames through which audiences interpret and discuss popular media.[17] The Handmaid Coalition protest is another kind of paratext that gave explicit political and social meaning to the television program.

Celebrity news coverage and fandom offer another form of paratext. For instance, Beyoncé performed at the 2014 Video Music Awards in front of a giant neon sign displaying the word *feminist*. A critical analysis of her performance might analyze how Beyoncé gave meaning to the idea of feminism. In her performance, she references her husband and hip-hop artist Jay Z. Since most of her fans are likely to follow news coverage of her personal life, the critic would need to discuss how Beyoncé's highly publicized relationship with Jay Z contributed to the meaning of her performance. Alternatively, critics might interpret the controversy surrounding her performance in the Twitter posts responding to her act. Many tweets weighed in on a debate about whether Beyoncé fit the definition of a feminist. An analysis of these tweets would illuminate how social media gave meaning to Beyoncé's performance and to contemporary feminism.

The emergence of digital media has shifted how some critics think about the significance and scope of the text. Whereas rhetorical critics have typically analyzed specific texts in particular contexts, it is difficult if not impossible to determine a single text or context in a digital media environment because users of social media platforms such as Pinterest and Instagram continually remake the images as soon as they view them online. Henry Jenkins, Sam Ford, and Joshua Green describe the digital media environment as "spreadable" to illustrate how meaning in a social media environment is created through the circulation and transformation of messages rather than through one discrete text.[18]

Take for instance, the internet meme, which is an image, hyperlink, video, or hashtag that circulates from person to person through social networks, blogs, or direct email. A rhetorical analysis of an internet meme requires a broad construction of a text because a meme takes form not with an individual instance but through the repetition and adaptation of a symbol through digital space. With the proliferation of digital media, the rhetorical criticism of popular culture has paid increased attention to the confluences and contradictions across different texts responding to a particular issue, controversy, or event.

Although the critic plays a role in text construction, the critic's scope of the text should share some semblance to audiences' consumption practices. Since most audiences view films and television programs in their entirety, an essay about a film or television program should not focus exclusively on one scene to form its conclusions. A critic's analysis would be unconvincing if the messages of one part of the film being analyzed were contradicted by another part of the film. After all, it would make no sense to solely analyze a scene of a lovers' spat if the two reconcile during the film's conclusion.

Analyzing the Text

After you have established the scope of your text, you may begin to analyze its meaning. Rhetorical critics of popular culture explain the symbolic construction of meaning through an analysis of signifying practices within a text. **Signification** explains the process in which meaning is constructed through the relationship among signs within a text. This is something most of us understand implicitly. A sign is something that prompts the reader, viewer, or listener to think of something other than itself. For instance, the image of a campfire posted by a friend on social media might tell you that they are enjoying a relaxing weekend. Photos are examples of iconic signs that structurally represent the objects for which they stand. When you see that picture of a fire, you are not seeing the fire itself but only a sign that represents the fire. When you interact with the sign on your computer screen, you do not feel the warmth of the flame or need an extinguisher close by in case it gets out of control. You are only interacting with the iconic sign that represents the actual fire. A different kind of sign, a symbol, refers to other things on the basis of shared agreement or convention. Words are symbols because their meanings are shared culturally. Thus, the English word *fire* and the Spanish word *fuego* are symbols for the same thing. That English readers recognize the meaning of the word *fire* is the result of collective agreement that the object and the word are related. Images and sounds such as the US flag and the tune of the national anthem are also symbols. Importantly, symbolic meaning changes over time.

The concept of connotation helps to explain how symbolic meaning is contextual. Connotative meaning involves the broader and more fluid associations and values attributed to particular signs. For instance, to say that someone is "on fire" commonly refers to someone's excitement or passion for something, but the fire emoji can also convey that someone is intoxicated, or "lit." Connotative meanings are dependent on the historical and cultural contexts in which particular signs are used. Likewise, they are shaped by their relationship with other signs within a particular context. The US flag has traditionally been associated with values such as freedom and patriotism, but when a protester holds a flag upside down at an antiwar rally, the flag symbolizes protest and criticism of US foreign policy. Roland Barthes highlighted the ideological dimensions of signification. Barthes observed that connotations attain mythic status when they are accepted as common sense.[19] To use the flag example again, every time people in the United States are asked to salute the flag, they are encouraged to express support for US institutions and government policies. In this way, the US flag promotes the idea of American exceptionalism. Protesters who refuse to salute the flag reject this idea as myth. In 2016, then NFL quarterback Colin Kaepernick sparked a national controversy after he protested police brutality by kneeling during the national anthem. Some of his critics interpreted his kneeling as disrespect toward the national anthem and the American flag while his supporters interpreted his actions as anti-racist activism. Two years later, a Nike advertisement featured Kaepernick. In response, some people protested by posting videos of themselves on social media burning their Nike products. Others who supported Kaepernick's protests as well as Nike's choice to use his image showed their support by posting images of their Nike products on social media. These different social media posts illustrate how ideological concerns shaped people's interpretations of Kaepernick and Nike. Their meanings depended upon viewers' prior beliefs and attitudes about patriotism and racial injustice.

A rhetorical critic looks at how different signs within a text (and possibly its paratexts) relate to one another to contribute meaning to a social or political issue. Critics have used a variety of approaches to explain the relationship among texts, both broadly and narrowly defined. An analysis of a narrowly defined text involves looking at how symbolic elements with a particular cultural product interact to create meaning. For example, to analyze a particular movie, the critic might focus on how the dialogue explains characters' motivations and facilitates narrative development. To analyze a particular magazine advertisement or web page, a critic could explain how the arrangements of words and images work together to give meaning to the featured product, issue, or topic. In any case, the critic should consider how the different formal elements that structure the text contribute to the text's meaning. An analysis of a film's dialogue might not be adequate because movies tell stories through the combination of moving images, sound, and dialogue. Thus, the connotations of a particular scene may be communicated not only through what characters say to one another but through other signs including camera angles, lighting, props, and actors' movements in front of the camera.[20] Likewise, to study popular music, a critic should pay attention not only to lyrics but to sounds communicated through chords, rhythms, keys, and instrumentation.[21]

An analysis of a more broadly defined text involves looking at how symbolic elements interact across cultural products. In this case, the critic is analyzing the **intertextual** construction of meaning. An analysis of an internet meme would necessarily be intertextual because the critic would need to explain how the meme's connotations shifted as it circulated and evolved with each use. For example, the Distracted Boyfriend meme[22] first presented the image of a man glancing backward toward a blonde woman in the foreground while holding his (visibly upset) girlfriend's hand in the background. The meme became meaningful as different users circulated the image with different labels for each person in the image. One version labeled the boyfriend "youth," the blonde woman "socialism," and the girlfriend "capitalism." Another version labeled the boyfriend "me," the blonde woman, "Instagram," and the girlfriend, "my homework." Nine months later, the image recirculated, but this time the distracted person is a woman looking at a man in the foreground while her boyfriend looks visibly upset. Each new variation of the meme depends upon viewers' familiarity with earlier versions, so critics need to attend to the meme's circulation. Eric Jenkins recommends that critics think about memes in terms of the modes that structure how people interact with them.[23] The Distracted Boyfriend is structured by relationships in tension with one another, whether they are about personal relationships, political ideologies, or personal interests and obligations, so the meaning of the meme is constructed around viewers' ability to play with these relational tensions in different ways.

Another approach to interpreting a text's meaning in relationship to other cultural discourses is through the concept of allegory. An **allegory** is a narrative that implicitly relates to historical or political issues that are not explicitly mentioned in the next. Traditional critics of allegory identify how characters and events within a narrative correspond with persons, events, and issues outside the narrative. Through this correspondence, the narrative conveys a more subtle secondary meaning beyond its surface meaning. Allegories reinforce broader myths or ideologies. One familiar example is George Orwell's novel *Animal Farm*, a story about barn animals that comments allegorically about the Bolshevik revolution and the development of the Soviet state. Recently, rhetorical critic Jordan Johnson and one of this chapter's authors, Kristen Hoerl, interpreted the superhero movie *Black Panther* as an allegory for neocolonialism, which refers to how international capitalism enables Western nations to influence and exploit the resources of the Global South. To demonstrate that the film functioned as allegory, the essay compared the events on screen to real life instances where the US government intervened in the affairs of African nations. In the movie and in reality, the CIA has worked to bring leaders into power who serve US economic interests.[24]

Another approach to interpreting the relationship between texts is through the concept of **homology**. Barry Brummett defines a rhetorical homology as a situation in which two or more kinds of experience appear to be structured according to the same patterns.[25] A homology is different from an allegory because allegories focus on narratives and verbal discourse, and a homology focuses on formal structures. To analyze a rhetorical homology, the critic compares seemingly different formal structures to identify how they reflect shared values and ideas.[26] For instance, Thomas Salek argues that the movie *The Wolf of Wall Street* is a homology for the American public's ambivalent attitudes regarding financial success. Salek observes that Americans tend to both idolize and abhor people who become wealthy by committing fraud. The movie communicates this ambivalence through both dialogue and visual elements. The movie's cinematic style—the narrative, character development, camera angles, etc.—is a homology for this ambivalence because it makes greed and corruption appear beautiful and grotesque at the same time.[27]

Critics of popular culture should also be attuned to the placement of a particular text within its particular genre. If you watch many films, you are probably already familiar with genres of comedy, drama, action/adventure, documentary, and horror. Generally, rhetorical criticism of popular culture does not revolve around how a particular text fits within a particular genre. However, it is important to recognize how a text's membership within a particular genre conditions audiences' expectations and understandings. For instance, consider the television police drama, a genre popularized by programs including *NCIS* and *Law & Order*. One convention of this genre is that law enforcement agents are always the protagonists. Another is that the guilty person is almost always brought to justice. These conventions implicitly teach audiences to trust in the justness and morality of police detectives and prosecuting attorneys and to be suspicious of defense attorneys and critics of the criminal justice system.[28] Critics may interpret a genre itself to explain how that genre functions ideologically, or they might simply recognize that a text is part of a particular genre to contextualize their analysis. However, critics should also observe when a text violates a generic convention. The television series *How to Get Away with Murder* is an interesting crime drama because it turns out that the law students who investigate murders have also committed murder themselves! By paying attention to moments when a text violates expectations, critics can explain what makes that text unique and interesting.

Evaluating the Text

A rhetorical analysis of a particular popular-culture text typically concludes with an assessment and evaluation of the text's contribution to public life. Critics often identity the beliefs and value systems that are elicited within the text and explain how these value systems might shape audiences' responses to related social conflicts or controversies. They also often describe how the text's messages provide implicit lessons that could inform how audience members understand and act as citizens, workers, and/or family members. A key point of this evaluation should be to address the implications of the analysis for communities who have a stake in issues addressed by the text. One strategy for writing the conclusion is to identify a current event that is related to but different from the text being analyzed. Based on the analysis, the critic might then explain how the text might encourage audiences to understand that issue. Then, the critic might conclude with a statement about whether or not this understanding promotes social justice for the people involved. For instance, one episode of the television crime drama *Blue Bloods* recently depicted the exoneration of a police officer who was accused of beating a suspect without just cause. In the context of the recent news media coverage of police brutality and killings of black suspects, this episode primes audiences to presume that police officers are innocent. This is disconcerting given the evidence that many law enforcement officers have seriously injured and killed unarmed black people. The three critical essays in the following section of this chapter provide additional examples of how to evaluate a popular-culture text.

CRITICAL ESSAYS

This section provides three short critical essays that analyze aspects of the *Hunger Games* film franchise. Released in 2012, *The Hunger Games* is a fictional action film that revolves around Katniss Everdeen, a sixteen-year-old girl who inspires political resistance by challenging her repressive government. In the fictional country of Panem, the majority of citizens work within one of twelve districts that are each devoted to providing material resources to furnish the Capitol, a city that houses the nation's wealthy elites. To discourage the districts from rebelling against the Capitol, the government forces its citizens to participate in the "Hunger Games," a televised competition in which children from each district battle to the death until one child remains. To prevent her younger sister from being forced into the game, Katniss volunteers herself. The ensuing narrative depicts Katniss's struggles as she prepares for the games, participates in them, and convinces the government to allow her and the other remaining survivor Peeta Mellark to live.

This movie is the first of four films adapted from the best-selling young adult novels by Suzanne Collins. It had one of the highest-grossing opening weekends in US history.[29] The sequel, *The Hunger Games: Catching Fire*, was the highest-grossing film released in the United States in 2013.[30] Both movies' box-office successes attest to the films' popularity. Clearly, the movies' narratives resonated with young filmgoing audiences. The first analysis is an allegorical reading of the first movie released in 2012. The second essay summarizes Rachel Dubrofsky and Emily Ryall's argument about the same movie's implications for gender and race relations.[31] The third analysis summarizes Joe Tompkins's critique of the paratexts surrounding the third movie in the series: *The Hunger Games: Mockingjay Part 1.*[32] The similarities across these three readings highlight our mutual interest in evaluating the implications of popular culture for ongoing power relations and social hierarchies. The differences between these readings reflect the diversity of ideological investments and interpretative practices within popular-culture criticism.

EXAMPLE 1: *THE HUNGER GAMES* AS ALLEGORY FOR CLASS STRUGGLE

One explanation for *The Hunger Games'* success is that it resonated with ongoing public controversies that generated extensive media attention when Collins's novels and the movies were released. The movie revolved around the injustices of class inequality and political tyranny. This film shares similarities to alternative ideological discourses that proliferated after the economic turmoil and election of Barack Obama in 2008. Themes within *The Hunger Games* have allegorical resonance to public controversies about capitalism and the role of the federal government. In addition to its allegorical dimensions, the film's emphasis on media spectacle offers implicit lessons about how advocates for change might use mainstream media to their advantage.

Stark class difference is one of the movie's central themes. The image of Katniss's District 12 contrasts sharply from images of the Capitol. The majority of District 12's workers labor in mines and live in modestly furnished homes. Many of them struggle to feed their children. By contrast, the Capitol is a technically advanced city comprised of tall, gleaming buildings and luxurious accommodations for its residents. When Katniss visits the Capitol, she is shocked by the residents' opulent displays of wealth and obsession with fashion. The theme of class difference is also presented by the strategies necessary to win the Hunger Games. Children from Districts 1 and 2, the wealthiest districts, are born and bred to compete in the games. Competitors from these districts have a clear advantage because they have developed skills and strategies through years of training that were not available to the other districts' children. In order to survive, contestants must appeal to donors to fund their resources, including food, water, and medicine. Contestants from poorer districts are at a disadvantage here as well; obviously, viewers from poorer districts have less to give their own children in the games.

The theme of wealth inequality in *The Hunger Games* resonates with issues addressed by Occupy Wall Street protesters a year before the film's release. The Occupy Wall Street movement garnered media attention when protesters occupied Zuccotti Park, located in New York City's Wall Street financial district. Activists condemned economic inequality, greed, and corporate influence on government policy. Their political slogan, "We are the 99%," highlighted the statistic that the top 1 percent of the population earns 24 percent of the nation's income and holds 40 percent of its wealth.[33] A Tumblr page that helped to inspire the slogan, "wearethe99percent.tumblr.com," provides numerous examples of individuals who struggle with debt and poverty despite their college degrees and full-time employment. Like the central theme of *The Hunger Games*, the key theme of Occupy Wall Street is that income inequality unfairly advantages a small minority of wealthy citizens.

Government tyranny is another central theme in *The Hunger Games*. The Panem government enforces districts' participation in the Hunger Games through the deployment of heavily armed soldiers. Mediated messages from the Capitol "welcoming" audiences to the Hunger Games are clearly propaganda. The film's portrayal of government tyranny bears traces of the Tea Party's rhetoric that called for a reduction in the size of the federal government. During President Obama's first term in office, the Tea Party movement characterized the president's tax policies and domestic agenda as an attack on personal and economic freedom.[34] In recent years, Tea Party advocates have sponsored billboards above well-trafficked roads that compare Obama to the world's most brutal dictators. One billboard off highway I-70 in Kansas featured a picture of Obama's face partially obscured by shadows next to a large caption that reads, "Wannabe Marxist Dictator." Audiences concerned about the federal government's threat to individual rights and freedom might find some similarities between the billboards' depiction of Obama and *The Hunger Games'* menacing portrayal of President Snow.

By giving cinematic form to the issues of class inequality and government tyranny, *The Hunger Games* promotes alternative ideologies that question the legitimacy of contemporary capitalism and politics. As audiences are encouraged to identify with Katniss Everdeen's struggles, they are invited to question the morality of income inequality and centralized government. Katniss Everdeen dares to challenge the tyranny of President Snow and refuses to embrace the greed inside the Capitol. Thus, she helps to legitimize Occupy Wall Street and Tea Party protesters' concerns and makes them relatable. Katniss's method of resistance might also provide lessons for resistance to real-world political problems. In this sense, *The Hunger Games* has counterhegemonic potential.

The theme of media spectacle in the movie helps to explain its counterhegemonic implications. President Snow controls the media and uses the spectacle of the Hunger Games in order to win the consent of the Capitol and the districts. The Panem government provides universal access to its state-controlled television so that everyone can watch the games. From the moment their names are announced as the participants in the upcoming game, contestants become objects of surveillance. Cameras follow them throughout their preparations and participation in the games. Although the Hunger Games are coercive, the publicity surrounding them dazzles viewers. Contestants parade around in stunning costumes in the days leading up to the games. During the games, each contestant's every movement is displayed on camera. The movie's focus on spectacle resonates with the enjoyment viewers take in watching reality television game shows in which contestants' dramatic wins and losses are sold to audiences as a form of weekly entertainment. Just as the drama of reality programming sells contestants' struggles to entertain audiences, the Hunger Games are offered to Panem citizens as compensation for and distraction from the Capitol's exploitation of them. President Snow's use of media to spread propaganda about the virtues of the Hunger Games resonates with both Tea Party and Occupy Wall Street activists' criticisms of the mainstream press. As media scholars have noted, the mainstream media promotes the hegemonic order by excluding or downplaying perspectives critical of mainstream politics and capitalism.[35]

The movie offers solutions to the problems of exploitative media, political tyranny, and economic inequality by depicting Katniss's survival strategies. Katniss uses the spectacle of the Hunger Games against the government's intended purposes. She appeals to viewers' sentiments by cultivating the impression that she and Peeta are romantically involved. When she and Peeta attempt to commit suicide together rather than be forced to kill one another, the Capitol is forced to allow them both to live. Ostensibly, to do otherwise could turn the majority of Panem's populace against the government. By performing romantic desire and threatening to kill herself for the sake of love, Katniss manipulates the government's efforts to control Panem's populace. By addressing viewers watching the games, she inspires resistance. The implicit lesson of the film is that the spectacle of popular culture may be a resource for challenging dominant hegemony. By working within its forms and manipulating its pleasures, media producers and those represented by the media may integrate new and revolutionary ideas into public life.[36] This lesson attests to the rhetorical potential of popular culture to promote radical social change in the face of a powerful hegemonic order.

EXAMPLE 2: *THE HUNGER GAMES* AS THE PRODUCTION OF AUTHENTIC WHITENESS AND NATURAL FEMININITY

In contrast to the above reading of *The Hunger Games* as a counterhegemonic allegory for class struggle and political critique, Dubrofsky and Ryalls argue that the movie conveys problematic messages about authentic whiteness and natural femininity. These critics explain how Katniss Everdeen is portrayed as more authentic than the other contestants and residents of the Capitol through her ability to "perform not performing."[37] Katniss's image of authenticity is based on her constant surveillance by the producers of the Hunger Games. Katniss appears uncomfortable and unrehearsed when she is asked to perform on camera even though she must make people like her to win the games. Her expressions of discomfort are a sign of her authenticity and trustworthiness. She is the movie's hero because she clearly does not want to play the game. As Dubrofsky and Ryalls point out, authenticity is a kind of performance; we all perform certain behaviors when we interact with others regardless of our intentions to do so. This particular depiction of authenticity is troubling to Dubrofsky and Ryalls because it draws upon the film's portrayal of Katniss as white and stereotypically feminine.

These critics analyze character development and film techniques to make their case. They observe how black characters are relegated to the background in the film. These characters are developed to the extent that they shed light on the motivations and heroic virtues of Katniss. The character of twelve-year-old Rue is important to the narrative because, as the youngest contestant, she is the most vulnerable. After Rue helps Katniss recover from an injury, Katniss is committed to helping Rue survive. On her deathbed, Rue makes Katniss promise that she will win the game. Rue's death helps to frame Katniss's efforts to win as noble. In addition to character construction, the movie's use of lighting presents Katniss as the "embodiment of natural feminine white beauty."[38] In several scenes, Katniss appears bathed in sunlight and her skin glows. By contrast, less noble characters' faces often appear in shadows. These scenes draw upon conventions in film that have associated whiteness with virtue and innocence. Ostensibly, a white character's heroism can be "read off her body."[39] By subordinating black characters and focusing on Katniss's white skin, the movie naturalizes whiteness. By privileging Katniss's whiteness as a sign of her authenticity, the film implicitly privileges white bodies over racialized bodies. In this way, the film subtly reinforces racist assumptions that black bodies are deviant and Other.

Dubrofsky and Ryalls argue that the film's message about "natural femininity" is also problematic.[40] They note that Katniss appears "naturally feminine" because she does not appear interested in performing particular gender rituals such as wearing makeup and dresses. Katniss's disinterest in performing these rituals "naturalizes her femininity."[41] Her femininity is also authenticated because she does not recognize how beautiful she is. Furthermore, many of her character traits are not explicitly feminine. Katniss does not actually seek romantic relationships, rarely expresses emotion, and does not want children. Yet she exhibits several feminine character traits nonetheless. During the games, she tends to contestants who are injured. Dubrofsky and Ryalls conclude that the movie's focus on her maternal traits suggests that "good women are always already mothers, and their value, strength, and heroism stem from their natural instincts and conventional heterosexual femininity."[42] Hence, the film promotes narrowly defined gender identities that position women who do not exhibit these character traits as outside what may be considered normal and desirable.

EXAMPLE 3: THE *HUNGER GAMES* FRANCHISE AS PROMOTIONAL CYNICISM

While focusing on a single film within the political and historical context of its construction may help the critic explain how a popular-culture text contributes to the process of social change, attention to the paratexts surrounding that film may lead to a different set of observations that challenge the conclusions of scholars who have defined the scope of the text more narrowly. A look at the paratexts surrounding the *Hunger Games* franchise illustrates this point. Lionsgate Films, the movie's production company, marketed the third movie in the series, *The Hunger Games: Mockingjay Part 1*, through an interactive transmedia campaign that included billboard advertisements, websites, Tumblr pages, and YouTube videos. The variety of media platforms illustrates how marketers marshaled many different paratexts to shape the meaning and popularity of the franchise. The campaign included fake advertisements for "Hunger Games" fashion on billboards and a cross-promotional campaign with CoverGirl makeup. The cosmetics brand advertised its makeup collection

"Capitol Beauty" by featuring models dressed in the flamboyant costumes of the Panem Capitol residents. The models' large wigs, dark red lips, and sequined eyebrows appear alongside images of cosmetic products and gold emblems that read, "Capitol Collection." The relationship between the bright colors on the models' faces and the text rearticulates the meaning of the film. In the ads, the citizens of the Capitol signify beauty rather than greed. They are objects of desire rather than objects of scorn.

The marketing campaign also included a website featuring news reports, propaganda, and weather forecasts for fictional Panem and a series of YouTube videos called "District Voices."[43] Both the website and the videos mimic the style of nonfiction media. The Capitol website adapts several conventions of websites designed for governments and cities, including the address, "www.thecapitol.pn," that might plausibly exist for a country. "District Voices" appears to have been produced by a television network owned by the fictional government of Panem. The YouTube series mimics the aesthetics of a video news release promoting the services of a political or commercial organization. In the episode titled "A District 9 Paean to Peeta's Bakery," two young adults, Jimmy Wong and Ashley Adams, speak directly to the camera and perform a cooking demonstration similar to those that frequently appear on morning television news programs to promote a celebrity chef or food product. The video elaborates on the character construction of Peeta Mellark as Adams explains that Peeta's family owned a renowned bakery in his home district. Wong and Adams then make an apple and goat cheese tart in his honor. The program is tongue in cheek as it combines elements of the films' narrative with the genre of a cooking demonstration. Props and dialogue reference the film's theme of class inequality. The kitchen is shabby, the oven is wood burning, and the sleeves of Adams's sweater are full of holes. Wong notes that, "depending on the district you're in, it may be difficult to find some of these ingredients, but the good citizens of Panem are endlessly resourceful, so we're sure you'll find a way." Although the video is ostensibly about cooking, it is clearly not designed to teach the audience to prepare a tart. By blurring the conventions of promotional news media with the narrative elements of *The Hunger Games*, "District Voices" simultaneously mocks the public-relations industry and promotes the *Hunger Games* franchise.

Comparing the narrative themes of the movie with its paratexts, Tompkins observes that the *Hunger Games* franchise constructs contradictory messages. On one hand, the film offers a narrative of mass revolt inspired by class injustice; on the other hand, the viral marketing campaign invites audiences to identify with the wealthy Capitol.[44] Tompkins asks, "How do we make sense of th[e] call for revolution in the form of interactive blockbuster promotion?"[45] Tompkins concludes that the franchise fosters an attitude of "promotional cynicism" that reflects contemporary audiences' ambivalent relationship to contemporary brand culture.[46] The marketing campaign provides multiple cues that ironically position the campaign as transparently fake. Thus, these cues enable fans of the film to recognize the campaign as a commercial ploy and consume it anyway. These cues also help to frame the meaning of the film in a way that undermines the film's counterhegemonic potential. Tompkins concludes that the *Hunger Games* franchise invites audiences to "enjoy the act of desiring class revolt while at the same time *not* taking that desire too seriously."[47] The multimedia marketing campaign has rhetorical implications when considered in the context of the film, recent populist movements in the United States, and prodemocracy movements in Hong Kong and Thailand. Tompkins concludes that the campaign ultimately discourages audiences from seeking social change.[48] Even though US publics are aware of economic inequality, and even though our popular entertainment addresses these conditions in fictional form, brand culture encourages us to maintain the status quo.

PERSONAL REFLECTIONS

While the first two critical essays focus on the film itself as the scope of the analysis, they analyze the film through different frames of reference. The first essay argues that the film primarily resonates with problems associated with class difference and economic exploitation, whereas the second is primarily concerned with the film's implications for race and gender. The third essay shares the first's interest in the film's portrayal of class struggle but defines the scope of the text differently. Consequently, the third concludes that the film has less potential to challenge dominant ideologies about class inequality than the first does. The differences between each essay's ideological frameworks and interpretive practices lead to different conclusions about the film's social and political implications. Is one of these interpretations better than another? Perhaps. It is possible that each analysis offers valuable insights. But it could be equally possible that one interpretation is more meaningful than another. It depends on how well the analysis is supported by textual evidence from the film and its paratexts.

As we elaborate in the next section, critics' interpretations are influenced by their own experiences and subject positions. The analysis of the Hunger Games as an allegory for the Occupy Wall Street movement is shaped by the first author's concerns regarding economic inequality, an interest influenced by her family's prior involvement in the labor movement. This analysis was also influenced by the first author's prior research about social movements, which enabled the first author to draw connections between contemporary dissent and themes in the movie. In fact, all of the choices of examples in this chapter are influenced in some way by the authors' knowledge and commitments. Because we are interested in inclusion, we selected examples to illustrate how critics can analyze popular culture from a variety of perspectives. But we are also concerned with racial injustice, so we chose several examples that explored how mediated texts have addressed that issue. Popular culture gives meaning to a variety of social problems. The task for you as a critic is to determine which problems matter to you and to consider how popular media comment on them.

POTENTIALS AND PITFALLS

Although many academics believe that popular culture is an important site of politics and a potential resource for social change, some scholars do not believe that the texts of popular culture are worthy objects of rhetorical criticism. Given the rhetoric discipline's early investments in promoting civic engagement, some scholars are concerned that the focus on popular culture shifts attention away from public speeches, writings, and videos that directly shape democratic political decision making. For these scholars, the texts of popular culture are secondary to the texts that explicitly address audiences as citizens. Controversies regarding rhetorical criticism of popular culture highlight how critics' decisions about the texts they select for analysis are rhetorical acts. Which texts the critic chooses to study will shape how others understand his or her political and intellectual investments.

Rhetoric scholars who agree that popular culture merits serious analysis do not always share the same methodological approach or interpretive practices. Edward Schiappa contends that many academic critics of popular culture engage in what he refers to as "representational correctness," which he describes as an approach that evaluates particular texts on the basis of criteria that are impossible to meet.[49] The first criterion of *accuracy* requires that a representation of a social group should be authentic to the group's experience to avoid stereotyping; the second criterion of *purity* requires that a representation of social struggle must unequivocally advance social change and justice on behalf of marginalized groups and avoid presenting contradictory perspectives; and the third criterion of *innocence* requires that media texts avoid insulting the groups depicted.[50]

Schiappa laments that rhetorical criticism puts popular culture in a no-win situation. Critics tend to point out how popular culture reinforces stereotypes. For instance, one might critique *The Hunger Games* by pointing out that Katniss required the help of men around her to succeed at the game, reinforcing stereotypes that men are more skilled than women. When popular-culture texts do challenge stereotypes, critics often focus on how these texts reinforce normative beliefs. This kind of criticism might reason that Katniss's success at winning the Hunger Games is largely achieved through her skills as an archer, a skill that may be coded as a masculine strength. Schiappa argues that rhetorical interpretations based on criteria of accuracy, purity, and innocence have limited usefulness because all popular media texts are open to multiple interpretations, and some audiences' interpretations contradict the meanings that creators intended.[51] Further, Schiappa observes that such criticism is usually grounded in the questionable assumption that popular culture influences audiences' attitudes and beliefs.[52] Instead, he suggests that scholars need to explore how audiences respond to particular media representations.[53] To gain this information, Schiappa recommends using quantitative survey methods, which takes us far afield from rhetorical criticism.

Schiappa is not alone in faulting popular-culture critics for ignoring the ways in which different audiences may glean different meanings from the same text. Outside the rhetoric discipline, an approach to studying mass media known as reception studies has shifted away from the text and toward the reader as a site of meaning. Some of this scholarship has used ethnographic methods in which researchers observe how people use and talk about media in their everyday lives.[54] A premise of this work is that the needs and subject positions of audiences shape the reading strategies they use to make sense of a text. A prominent proponent of this position, John Fiske, advances the concept of polysemy, or the idea that different audiences may draw different meanings from the same cultural product.[55] Fiske admits that this does not mean that the text has no influence on audience interpretation. We can reasonably assume that most audiences will draw similar meanings from the combinations of signifiers in a text. However, members of different social groups may draw different associational meanings from the text based on their subject positions and experiences. For example, most viewers probably understand that *The Hunger Games* is a narrative about rebellion against an autocratic and unjust political system, but supporters of the Tea Party may read it as an affirmation that the federal government of the United States has overreached its authority, and supporters of Occupy Wall Street may believe that the movie reflects the exploitation of workers by the 1 percent. Further, people concerned by racial injustice may be more likely to critique the film's lack of empowered black characters. Each of these responses does not account for or explain the diversity of interpretations that are available to analyze the film.

One challenge for critics seeking to study the myriad ways in which audiences use popular culture is that audiences' own interpretations become texts for criticism. These critics might prefer to read a critical analysis of how online media blogs described and evaluated the character of Katniss Everdeen to determine whether the film promoted positive attitudes toward assertive and athletic young women. But analyzing paratexts does not avoid the critique that texts are open to multiple meanings. If different audiences can glean different meanings from a film or television program, then different scholars may also interpret a review of a film or television program from different or competing perspectives. Another problem with preferring viewers' interpretations is that it ignores how some interpretations may be better than others. For instance, a critic who tries to argue that *The Hunger Games* is a homology for fears about global warming will be unconvincing unless they explain how signifiers throughout the film map onto discourses about climate change. There are few if any textual cues across the film's text and paratexts that support this thesis.

Rather than abandon rhetorical criticism for quantitative or ethnographic research, we are committed to rhetorical criticism because we believe that important insights about civic life can be made through thoughtful interpretations of popular culture. The approach we have recommended here is to build an analysis by drawing connections across the variety of signifiers that comprise the text. By thinking carefully about the scope of the text, the critic is in a stronger position to explain how meanings that emerge from the confluences across signifiers enable and constrain interpretation. This approach enables the critic to share important insights about a popular-culture text while acknowledging that his or her choices influence interpretation. By analyzing popular culture through this approach, the critic can explain how audiences might share understandings about social life and how those understandings evolve over time as different texts respond to one another and to their historical, social, and political contexts.

RHETORICAL CRITICISM OF POPULAR CULTURE AND SOCIAL MEDIA TOP PICKS

This list provides just a snapshot of the myriad approaches to rhetorical criticism of popular culture and social media. The synopses of the analytical frameworks and thesis statements of each article demonstrate the variety of perspectives and types of mediated texts that are available to critics. Of course, as media culture changes, these perspectives and textual approaches will expand.

Griffin, Rachel A., and Michaela Meyer, eds. *Adventures in Shondaland: Identity Politics and the Power of Representation.* New Brunswick: Rutgers University Press, 2018. The second section of this edited collection provides different perspectives for understanding how television programs featuring diverse casts including *Grey's Anatomy* and *How to Get Away with Murder* have responded to identity politics regarding race, ethnicity, religion, gender, and sexuality.

Huntington, Heidi. "Pepper Spray Cop and the American Dream: Using Synecdoche and Metaphor to Unlock Internet Memes' Visual Political Rhetoric." *Communication Studies* 67, no. 1 (2016): 77–93. Huntington analyzes the intertextual elements of the Pepper Spray Cop meme to explain how it functioned as a form of visual political rhetoric.

Kelly, Casey Ryan. *Abstinence Cinema: Virginity and the Rhetoric of Sexual Purity in Contemporary Film.* New Brunswick, NJ: Rutgers University Press, 2016. This book uses visual and narrative analysis to argue that several movies including *Twilight* and *Taken* have valorized the neoconservative movement for abstinence from sex until marriage.

Kornfield, Sarah. "Televisual Pregnancy Beauty." *Feminist Media Studies* 19, no. 2 (2019): 163–178. This essay explains how motion picture techniques such as costuming and camera work gave meaning to main characters' pregnant bodies in episodes of the television programs *Bones* and *In Plain Sight.*

McCann, Bryan J. *The Mark of Criminality: Rhetoric, Race, and Gansta Rap in the War-On-Crime Era.* Tuscaloosa: University of Alabama Press, 2017. McCann analyzes the rhetoric of gangsta rap between 1988 and 1996 and identifies its ideological aspects during the War-on-Crime era which continues to disproportionately and negatively impact black people.

Meier, Matthew R., and Cristopher A. Medjesky. "*The Office* was Asking for It: 'That's What She Said' as a Joke Cycle that Perpetuates Rape Culture." *Communication and Critical/Cultural Studies* 15, no. 1 (2018): 2–17. This essay explores how the joke cycle of "that's what she said" in popular media such as *The Office* reinscribes rape culture by normalizing discourse that promotes nonconsensual sexual acts against women while disguising itself as a harmless joke.

Milford, Mike. "Veiled Intervention: Anti-Semitism, Allegory, and Captain America." *Rhetoric & Public Affairs* 20, no. 4 (2017): 605–634. Milford explains how the comic book character Captain America was an allegory for arguments favoring United States involvement in World War II during a time in which anti-Semitic groups promoted isolationism.

Na, Ali. "#AzizAnsariToo? Desi Masculinity in America and Performing Funny Cute." *Women's Studies in Communication* 42, no. 3 (2019): 308–326. This essay explores the #MeToo response to concerns about Aziz Ansari with an intertextual analysis of Ansari's acting and comedy career in the context of the history of representations of South Asian masculinity in Hollywood movies and television.

Oates, Thomas P. "The Erotic Gaze in the NFL Draft." *Communication and Critical/Cultural Studies* 4, no. 1 (2007): 74–90. Oates offers a critical reading of the NFL draft and the paratexts that surround the annual media event. He argues that the discourse surrounding the NFL draft constructs draft prospects as hypersexualized bodies to be owned, reminiscent of chattel slavery auctions.

Spencer, Leland G. "Performing Transgender Identity in *The Little Mermaid*: From Andersen to Disney." *Communication Studies* 65, no. 1 (2014): 112–127. This essay analyzes the short story and animated movie versions of *The Little Mermaid* to argue that the narrative parallels the process of transgendered individuals' identity development.

DISCUSSION QUESTIONS

1. Do you believe that popular culture texts such as television programs, movies, sporting events, and social media are worthy objects for rhetorical criticism? How so or why not?

2. Which forms of popular culture (TV shows, movies, memes, sporting events, etc.) would you analyze as a rhetorical critic? Why?

3. Which of the three critical essays about *The Hunger Games* presented at the end of this chapter do you find to be most compelling? What do your answers tell you about your own interests and ideological commitments in the rhetorical criticism of popular culture?

ACTIVITIES

1. Attempt to go without all forms of media for an entire day. This includes movies, TV, books, magazines, social media, music, news, etc. After your full day without media, write down answers to these questions: What surprised you most about this exercise? What was the hardest form of media to give up and why? What was the easiest medium

to give up and why? What did your day consist of? What does this activity tell you about popular media's impact on our daily lives and our society as a whole?

2. Select a popular meme and identify the different elements that work to create its meaning, including visual images and words or labels. What attitudes or beliefs are expressed? Next, find a second iteration of that same meme. Compare and contrast this version with the first iteration that you analyzed. How does the meaning change with this adaptation? How might viewers' understanding of the meme's message be shaped by their familiarity with previous versions of the meme? What does this teach you about how meaning is constructed intertextually in social media?

3. Select a popular movie and conduct a brief internet search about it. Jot down all of the paratexts that comment on the movie and note what you learn about the movie from these paratexts. How might these messages influence how viewers give meaning to the movie? If you were to analyze this movie, would you include information from one or more of these paratexts to explain the rhetorical dimensions of this movie? Why or why not?

4. Select a twenty-minute episode of a television program and watch it with a group of four to five people. Have each person write down what they think one main idea or lesson might be from the episode without putting their names on their papers. Have one person read each response aloud and then discuss these different interpretations as a group. Is any interpretation more compelling than another? Use your discussion to develop criteria for writing a persuasive rhetorical analysis of a popular culture text.

5. Watch the opening credit sequences to two television programs from different genres. For instance, you might select the opening credits to a situation comedy and a murder investigation or horror program. Take notes on the stylistic elements of each credit sequence including the images, camera angles, lighting, editing speed, and sound. What connotations and feelings do these elements evoke? How do the stylistic elements of the opening credits help you to anticipate the program's themes and tone? Compare and contrast your notes about each opening credit sequence. What do the differences tell you about how style gives meaning to a genre?

NOTES

1. "Historical Super Bowl Viewership," Nielsen Press Room, February 3, 2020, https://www.nielsen.com/us/en/press-releases/2020/super-bowl-liv-draws-nearly-100-million-tv-viewers-44-million-social-media-interactions/.

2. "First Presidential Debate of 2016 Draws 84 Million Viewers," Nielsen Press Room, September 27, 2016, https://www.nielsen.com/us/en/insights/article/2016/first-presidential-debate-of-2016-draws-84-million-viewers/.

3. Barry Brummett, *Rhetorical Dimensions of Popular Culture* (Tuscaloosa: University of Alabama Press, 1990), xii.

4. Raymond Williams, *Culture and Society, 1780–1950* (1958; repr., New York: Columbia University Press, 1983), 325.

5. Bonnie J. Dow, *Prime-Time Feminism: Television, Media Culture, and the Women's Movement since 1970* (Philadelphia: University of Pennsylvania Press, 1996), 7.

6. Louis Althusser, *For Marx*, trans. Ben Brewer (1965; repr., London: Penguin, 1969); Louis Althusser, *Lenin and Philosophy and Other Essays*, trans. Ben Brewer (1970; repr., London: New Left Books, 1971).

7. Stuart Hall, "The Whites of Their Eyes: Racist Ideologies and the Media," in *Gender, Race, and Class in Media: A Text-Reader*, ed. Gail Dines and Jean M. Humez, 2nd ed. (Thousand Oaks, CA: Sage, 2003), 90.

8. Antonio Gramsci, *Selections from the Prison Notebooks*, trans. Quintin Hoare and Geoffrey N. Smith (1971; repr., New York: International Publishers, 2012).

9. Dana L. Cloud, "Hegemony or Concordance? The Rhetoric of Tokenism in 'Oprah' Winfrey's Rags-to-Riches Biography," *Critical Studies in Mass Communication* 13 (1996): 115–137.

10. Aniko Bodroghkozy, *Groove Tube: Sixties Television and the Youth Rebellion* (Durham, NC: Duke University Press, 2001); John Fiske, *Television Culture* (1987; repr., London and New York: Routledge, 2011).

11. Michel Foucault, *Power/Knowledge: Selected Interviews and Other Writings, 1972–1977*, ed. Colin Gordon, trans. Colin Gordon, Leo Marshall, John Mepham, and Kate Soper (1971; repr., New York: Pantheon Books, 1977).

12. Raymie McKerrow, "Critical Rhetoric: Theory and Praxis," *Communication Monographs* 56 (1989): 91–111.

13. Amanda Howell, "Breaking Silence, Bearing Witness, and Voicing Defiance: The Resistant Female Voice in the Transmedia Storyworld of *The Handmaid's Tale*," *Continuum: Journal of Media & Cultural Studies* 33, no. 2 (2019): 216–229.

14. McGee argued that the proliferation of a variety of cultural products has created a fractured media environment. What we understand to be a finished discourse, such as a speech or film, is a reconstruction of fragments of other discourses from which it was made. Thus, the critic's role is to "invent a text suitable for criticism." Michael Calvin McGee, "Text, Context and the Fragmentation of Contemporary Culture," *Western Journal of Speech Communication* 54 (1990): 288.

15. Barry Brummett, *Rhetoric in Popular Culture*, 2nd ed. (Thousand Oaks, CA: Sage, 2006), 34.

16. See Kristi K. Cole, "'It's Like She's Eager to be Verbally Abused': Twitter, Trolls, and (En)Gendering Disciplinary Rhetoric," *Feminist Media Studies* 15 (2015): 356–358.

17. Jonathan Gray, *Show Sold Separately: Promos, Spoilers, and Other Media Paratexts* (New York: New York University Press, 2010), 6.

18. Henry Jenkins, Sam Ford, and Joshua Green, *Spreadable Media: Creating Value and Meaning in a Networked Culture* (New York: New York University Press, 2013), 27.

19. Roland Barthes, *Mythologies* (London: Cape, 1972).

20. For a detailed introduction to the aesthetics and grammars of film, see David Bordwell and Kristin Thompson, *Film Art: An Introduction*, 9th ed. (New York: McGraw-Hill, 2009). For a quick reference guide to film vocabulary, see Timothy Corrigan, *A Short Guide to Writing about Film*, 9th ed. (London: Longman, 2014).

21. For an example of rhetorical criticism of popular music that integrates the analysis of lyrics and sound, see Lisa Foster, "Populist Argumentation in Bruce Springsteen's *The Rising*," *Argumentation and Advocacy* 48 (2011): 61–80.

22. See https://knowyourmeme.com/memes/distracted-boyfriend, accessed May 1, 2020.

23. Eric S. Jenkins, "The Modes of Visual Rhetoric: Circulating Memes as Expressions," *Quarterly Journal of Speech* 100. no. 4 (2014): 442-466.

24. Jordan L. Johnson and Kristen Hoerl, "Suppressing Black Power through *Black Panther's* Neocolonial Allegory," *Review of Communication* 20, no. 3 (2020).

25. Barry Brummett, "Social Issues in Disguise: An Introduction to Sneaky Rhetoric," in *Uncovering Hidden Rhetorics: Social Issues in Disguise*, ed. Barry Brummett (Thousand Oaks, CA: Sage, 2004), 9–10.

26. Barry Brummett, *Rhetorical Homologies: Form, Culture, Experience* (Tuscaloosa: University of Alabama Press, 2004).

27. Thomas A. Salek, "Money Doesn't Talk, It Swears: *The Wolf of Wall Street* as Homology for America's Ambivalent Attitude on Financial Excess," *Communication Quarterly* 66, no. 1 (2018): 1–19.

28. For a nuanced analysis of the rhetoric and history of the crime drama genre, see chapter 1 in Elayne Rapping, *Law and Justice as Seen on TV* (New York and London: New York University Press, 2003), 21–47.

29. Pamela McClintock, "Box Office Shocker: 'Hunger Games' Third-Best Opening Weekend of All Time," *Hollywood Reporter*, March 25, 2012, accessed July 16, 2015, LexisNexis Academic.

30. "'The Hunger Games . . .' Highest Grosser of 2013 in US," *Bollywood Country*, February 25, 2014, accessed July 16, 2015, LexisNexis Academic.

31. Rachel E. Dubrofsky and Emily D. Ryalls, "*The Hunger Games*: Performing Not-performing to Authenticate Femininity and Whiteness," *Critical Studies in Media Communication* 31 (2014): 395–409.

32. Joe Tompkins, "The Makings of a Contradictory Franchise: Revolutionary Melodrama and Cynicism in *The Hunger Games*," *JCMS: Journal of Cinema and Media Studies* 58, no. 1 (2018): 70–90.

33. Ezra Klein, "Who Are the 99 Percent?," *Washington Post*, October 4, 2011, accessed July 19, 2015, http://www.washingtonpost.com/blogs/ezra-klein/post/who-are-the-99-percent/2011/08/25/gIQAt87jKL_blog.html.

34. Thomas Basile, "Once Effective, the Tea Party Has Become Toxic," *Forbes*, April 4, 2013, accessed July 19, 2015, http://www.forbes.com/sites/thomasbasile/2013/04/04/once-very-effective-the-tea-party-has-become-toxic.

35. Kevin DeLuca, Sean Lawson, and Ye Sun, "Occupy Wall Street on the Public Screens of Social Media: The Many Framings of the Birth of a Protest Movement," *Communication, Culture, & Critique* 5 (2012): 487; Todd Gitlin, *The Whole World Is Watching: Mass Media in the Making and Unmaking of the New Left* (1980; repr., Berkeley: University of California Press, 2003); Kristen Hoerl, "Mario Van Peebles's 'Panther' and Popular Memories of the Black Panther Party," *Critical Studies in Media Communication* 24 (2007): 206–227; Kristen Hoerl, "Commemorating the Kent State Tragedy through Victims' Trauma in Television News Coverage, 1990–2000," *Communication Review* 12 (2009): 107–131.

36. The potential for commercial media to provide counterhegemonic messages is limited by the ownership and advertising structure of commercial media. Because commercial products must earn products for media owners, they are ultimately oriented around capitalist goals. Further, most commercial media earn profits through corporate sponsorship and cross-promotion with other commercial products. See Edward S. Herman and Noam Chomsky, *Manufacturing Consent: The Political Economy of the Mass Media* (New York: Pantheon Books, 1988).

37. Dubrofsky and Ryalls, "*The Hunger Games*," 396.

38. Ibid., 401.

39. Ibid., 401.

40. Ibid., 404.

41. Ibid., 405.

42. Ibid., 407.

43. The Capitol, accessed July 18, 2015, www.thecapitol.pn; Brooks Barnes, "With 'Hunger Games' Campaigns, Lionsgate Punches above Its Weight," *New York Times*, November 23, 2014, accessed July 10, 2015, http://www.nytimes.com/2014/11/24/business/media/hunger-games-studio-lionsgate-punches-above-its-hollywood-weight.html.

44. Tompkins, "The Makings of a Contradictory Franchise."

45. Ibid., 88.

46. Ibid., 83.

47. Ibid., emphasis in original.

48. Ibid.

49. Edward Schiappa, *Beyond Representational Correctness: Rethinking Criticism of Popular Media* (Albany: State University of New York Press, 2008), 9.

50. Ibid., 9.

51. Ibid., 10.

52. Ibid., 12.

53. Ibid., 23.

54. Two notable examples are David Morley, *The "Nationwide" Audience: Structure and Decoding* (London: BFI, 1980); Janice Radway, *Reading the Romance: Women, Patriarchy, and Popular Literature* (Chapel Hill: University of North Carolina Press, 1984).

55. Fiske, *Television Culture*, 15–16.

16

Criticism of Digital Rhetoric

Michelle G. Gibbons

"Digital" is one of those frequently used but infrequently defined terms. It has become something of a shorthand for "computer-mediated," which is a crude, albeit not unworkable, way of understanding the "digital" in digital rhetoric. Yet it does have a more specific meaning, referring to a particular type of representation—the discrete, binary 1s and 0s that underlie computational technologies but are not exclusive to them.[1] It is also a term of mushrooming scope, given that digital technologies have become the norm in much of contemporary life. Even the water dispenser on my refrigerator is now a "digital" device. For that reason, **digital rhetoric**, as area of inquiry, refers specifically to work that centers the digital as focal concern, treating it as more than merely incidental. Digital rhetoric encompasses both rhetoric manifested via digital media and the analysis of such rhetoric, with attention in each case to how digitization influences how people engage in and with rhetorical discourse. That is to say, digital rhetoric is fundamentally concerned with the affordances and constraints of the digital, with what it both enables and stymies.[2] In what follows, I first address digital rhetoric's disciplinary scope, before turning to a discussion of how to perform criticism of digital texts, both via traditional approaches and newer, emergent ones. After that, I introduce four short examples, each of which illustrates a different approach to analyzing digital rhetoric.

DIGITAL RHETORIC: SCOPE

Digital rhetoric, as a rhetorical subfield, is neither a singular phenomenon nor a neat and tidy area of inquiry; moreover, not everyone even agrees upon the nomenclature. Damien Smith Pfister prefers the term "networked rhetorics," arguing that it better highlights that which is distinctive about communication in the digital era, wherein networks and the human practices around them present the truly transformative challenge to rhetorical study.[3] As Douglas Eyman writes, "digital rhetoric should be viewed as a field that engages multiple theories and methods rather than as a singular theory framework."[4] As discussed in chapter 2 of this book, rhetoric can be defined in many different ways—more narrowly, conceived primarily as pragmatic, as "the strategic use of communication, oral or written, to achieve specifiable goals" or, more broadly, to encompass "all areas of symbolic activity." Digital rhetoric can proceed via any definition of rhetoric, using any given one to ground attention to the digital, as long as one is clear about which framework guides a given analysis.

Like rhetoric more generally, digital rhetoric encompasses both productive and interpretive traditions. On the production side, it is oriented toward digital making, concerned with using digital technologies to craft rhetorical texts, often in new and multimodal formats, such as videos, visual essays, and the like. On the analysis side, it is concerned with using theories and concepts in order to do rhetorical criticism of digital texts, to understand how they function as symbolic constructions. This chapter focuses on the latter and, in subsequent sections, will introduce some strategies that you may use to do just this, drawing both from enduring rhetorical frameworks as well as more recently developed or reoriented ones.

As befits the broader rhetorical tradition out of which it arises, digital rhetoric is oriented toward public discourse. From rhetoric's roots in ancient Greece, when an emergent democracy gave public deliberation about community issues newfound consequence, and Aristotle and others worked to systematize the principles of persuasion, rhetoric has, as a field, been variously defined and constituted by its focus on public speech.[5] Over time, while that scope has broadened to encompass not just speech but other modalities (the printed word; radio; the digital), the emphasis on publicness endures.[6] Digital rhetoric scholarship sometimes conceives of the internet, in one way or another, as giving rise to a digital **public sphere** (or spheres), virtual spaces in which people engage in rhetorical negotiation of matters of shared community interest.[7] The term blogosphere, for example, points toward the interconnected community of blogs as a distinct arena for public deliberation.[8] We can understand social media platforms in the same fashion, as suggested by the parallel term, Twittersphere.[9] Although some work draws directly from Jürgen Habermas—whose germinal formulation of the public sphere specified its ideal parameters, considering, for example, whether one finds much in the way of rational-critical debate on Twitter—most is more generally oriented toward the digital as the site of public deliberation and rhetorical negotiation or even, more broadly, public symbolic action.[10]

At the same time, digital contexts also complicate rhetoric's orientation to public discourse. The distinction between public and private, never quite as stable and clear-cut as it first appears, is perhaps especially blurry in online spaces, and sometimes seems to disappear entirely. Dating apps, for example, involve the interpersonal facilitation of intimate personal connections, but at the same time include profiles that are, in many ways, public. And perhaps there is no better illustration of the tenuous distinction between private and public in digital contexts than social media, where the interpersonal exchange and the public post are often indistinguishable.[11]

Digital rhetoric is also concerned with larger-scale digital ecologies that underlie communication in online, networked spaces, where connections between and movements among distributed texts are as instrumental as the texts themselves.[12] The ways in which texts move around (e.g., retweet) and the means by which we move through them (e.g., hyperlinks) fundamentally underwrite symbolic action in digital contexts. Take, for example, the dating app. The dating app Bumble enables Instagram integration, whereby potential matches can peruse each other's Instagram posts from within the Bumble app itself. Particularly enterprising social media influencers leverage this capacity to gain followers on their social media accounts in order to boost their public profile in those spaces.[13] Doing so harnesses the interconnectedness of the internet to influence flow and channel traffic, using Bumble for a purpose other than its intended matchmaking one . . . much to the chagrin of those just looking for dates (and not another social media influencer to follow).[14] That said, individuals only exert so much control of this sort, and much of the movement online is shaped via largescale **digital infrastructures** that underlie and shape human activity therein.[15]

It deserves note that some work in digital rhetoric aims to employ digital tools to facilitate criticism, in other words, to produce digitally driven analysis of rhetorical texts—for example, discerning genre via a statistical program that tracks regularities across large bodies of text.[16] This work diverges from dominant techniques and methods of much of the rhetorical criticism tradition, for instance, from many of those worked out in the other chapters in this book. Therefore, this chapter does not address them as they bring us into very different territory. Moreover, their fate within the field of rhetoric is not yet known. Could digital methods for rhetorical criticism be a chapter for a future edition of this book? The answer to that question is yet to be determined.

DIGITAL RHETORIC: IN CONTEXT

Digital rhetoric is part of a broader scholarly enterprise. It has, unsurprisingly, arisen in conjunction with the digital era, as computer technologies have become increasingly central to our communicative lives. It is now practically a truism to list ways this is so: printed newspapers yielding to news sites and apps; speeches experienced as remixed sound bites; and "likes," shares, and upvotes taking the place of nodding heads, cheers, and applause. Although it is practically impossible to ignore just how transformative these developments have been for both the communication discipline in general and the rhetoric field in particular, we are also far from alone in grappling with the digital's implications for our scholarly work. Humanities fields at large are engaged in efforts to explore the digital era's implications for their disciplines, giving rise to the umbrella term "digital humanities" to encompass all such work.

Digitization is at the core of the digital humanities. Since so much of what we now encounter in our daily lives is native to digital contexts, created in and for them, it is sometimes easy to forget that our present experience represents a tiny sliver in the historical time line, and that all those thousands of years of history prior have produced mountains of analog texts: letters, books, handwritten speech drafts, etc. Digitization refers to the process of converting such texts into a digital format, where they then join natively digital ones as fodder for online archives and curated collections such as Duke University's archive of American advertising, 1850–1920.[17] Digital archives can facilitate traditional rhetorical criticism, with the digitization regarded as a mere means of access, incidental to the work of criticism itself. But it is also the case that the archives are in themselves rhetorical constructions.[18] Rhetorical critics may attend to digital archives themselves as "texts" which, for example, in their curations selectively present information and construct narratives. At the same time, archives offer also new possibilities for rhetorical criticism, even present-oriented work. Take the archivization of former President Trump's tweets on a dedicated website.[19] Even if these are someday available on Twitter again, the archive affords new possibilities, such as the ability to search through tweets by topic or date, thereby both facilitating criticism and enabling new orientations to it.

With all that in mind, we will now examine how to proceed with an analysis of a digital text, which includes both selecting and delimiting the text as well as deciding upon a theoretical framework to engage as a lens through which to view and understand it.

HOW TO PERFORM CRITICISM OF DIGITAL RHETORIC

Selecting and Delimiting the "Text" for Analysis

Analytic work that falls under the purview of digital rhetoric generally focuses on texts that promise insight into the distinctive affordances and constraints of the digital. However, it is certainly possible to analyze a speech from many decades ago, one delivered in a traditional fashion (a speaker in front of a roomful of flesh-and-blood audience members) and then subsequently posted on YouTube—or made digital—via a digital rhetoric framework. In doing so, one centers its digitization, as in attending to how it influences how people engage with the speech as persuasive discourse. For one, the analysis might consider how reposting the speech on YouTube alters its symbolic meaning making. Does the account from which it is posted matter? Do the number of views it has received influence how credible we find it? Do the "up next" speeches, and the algorithmically associated content that appears alongside it, influence how it operates rhetorically, just as the context of a traditional address matters?

Much work in digital rhetoric is concerned with that which is native to digital environments, created by, for, or within them. The terrain to explore is considerable, from social media posts[20] to hashtags,[21] apps,[22] blogs,[23] memes,[24] YouTube videos,[25] websites,[26] video games,[27] and more. One can variously focus on content that appears on a particular platform or take the platform itself as analytic site. For example, one might consider the YouTube video as text, or take the YouTube platform itself as such. What may be considered a text becomes rather flexible here, as digital spaces have upended traditional expectations while ushering new forms and formats into existence. In many ways, analyzing digitally native texts invites—perhaps maybe even demands—at least some consideration of digital affordances and constraints and the ecologies within which they operate. That is to say, *when analyzing digital content that is inextricable from its format and environs, it is almost inevitable that one engage with some of the questions and frameworks of digital rhetoric.* That said, any given analysis may be more or less attentive to the sort of central concerns that constitute work as digital rhetoric.

Beyond centering of the digital as a matter of critical insight, in selecting a site for analysis, one must also make choices about demarcation. The matter of how to delineate the analytic site is relevant for just about any work of criticism, but sometimes a site is more naturally, more tidily bounded than others—as in a president's inaugural address or a funeral oration (though demarcation questions still arise. Should the analysis encompass consideration of the speakers who came before, how much history is relevant, what about drafts?). Other sites are just fundamentally messier, offering less intuitive parameters, and critics must impose them in order to generate a discernable, analyzable text. In digital spaces, one finds much of the latter since many digital phenomena are fragmented, ephemeral, and dispersed. Take, for example, hashtags (#). Not only do many individuals use a given hashtag but the same ones may appear across multiple platforms (to include Facebook, Twitter, YouTube, and TikTok). When digital rhetoric scholars analyze hashtags, considering how they shape public discourse, they generally cannot possibly look at every single invocation of a popular hashtag. Take, for example, #BlackGirlMagic, a hashtag that arose as part of a movement to celebrate black women. It took off on social media in 2013, accompanying empowering photographs and other representations of black women.[28] Although it may not be feasible to consider every single iteration of #BlackGirlMagic in a given analysis, one can use various strategies to nonetheless analyze the discursive phenomenon.

There are many ways to demarcate digital texts, and the idea is not that you will arrive at the ideal, perfect focal point amid a vast, sprawling mass of interconnected digital discourse, but that you choose a workable, justifiable focal point, one that enables you to illuminate something about your chosen text and one that you can also explain as you craft your analysis. One might, for example, take a notable rhetor (an influencer, a celebrity, etc.) as focal point, considering some of his or her digital output. In this case, the task becomes more similar to what rhetorical analysis has looked like for much of its history—focusing on the output of a certain rhetor, but with concern for digital mediation of his or her discourse. Several scholars, for example, have studied President Trump's tweets or the digital output of other notable figures.[29]

But for a good deal of digital discourse, individual rhetors fade amid the salience of the interactive, nonlinear exchange. That is to say, when it comes to something such as a hashtag, any given iteration of it is a mere drop in the much larger-scale, collective river, a discursive phenomenon that transcends the individual. Just as a drop of water can only tell us so much about the river it in part constitutes, any given person's use of a hashtag can only tell us so much about the phenomenon of a popular, influential hashtag and the rhetorical work it enacts. The meme serves as another, perhaps even more striking, illustration of this point; memes are cultural elements, such as ideas, images, or textual fragments, that circulate among a collective, while often reworked and repurposed in the process.[30] The meme is itself constituted in and through repeated uptake and as such exists beyond the scope and control of the individual. As Eric S. Jenkins describes, they are "emergent phenomena that express the circulating energies of contemporary existence rather than re-presenting the interests of particular rhetors."[31] Therefore, in the fragmented, collective arrays of discourse that emerge online, individual authorship is not always the most salient factor.

A less author-driven strategy for demarcating a text for analysis is to identify representative examples. In doing so, one follows a long-standing approach in the field, doing focused analysis of a representative example or examples into order to illuminate a more wide-scale rhetorical phenomenon. For example, one might focus on a few iterations of a meme, using those to illuminate some of the ways in which the meme does rhetorical work. A related approach is to choose a random sample of examples.[32] An important limitation, of course, is that which applies to any analysis via example: it will inevitably capture some aspects of a phenomenon, but not others. As a result, it is important to both acknowledge such limitations and offer a rationale for given selections.

The last strategy for establishing analytic boundaries I will mention here is a temporally oriented one. That is, you demarcate the text by honing in on a particular moment in a much longer "conversation." If you were to analyze the #BlackGirlMagic hashtag, you might look at the first tweets to deploy it, or select a time frame, such as a particular hour or day, with the parameters, in part, driven by the hashtag's prevalence.[33] For example, for a very popular hashtag, even a single hour can see thousands of iterations. And once again, as demarcation strategy, it is important to offer a justification, one alert both to what one gains and loses by bounding the analytic site in a particular way.

With all this in mind, let us take a look at some of the rhetorical frameworks a critic might engage in order to approach digital texts. We will first consider some long-standing rhetorical theories, those that constitute enduring frameworks for rhetorical analysis; secondly, we will consider some of the newer approaches that have emerged as rhetoric scholars study rhetoric in digital contexts.

ANALYZING THE DIGITAL TEXT VIA
LONG-STANDING RHETORICAL THEORIES

Some work on digital rhetoric proceeds with enduring rhetorical precepts as a starting point, with the goal of applying and adapting those concepts to digital contexts, such as those discussed earlier in this chapter.[34] Many, if not all, of the specific approaches you have read about in this book could serve as an organizing framework for analyzing digital texts. For example, one could look at an app through the lens of "Dramatism," asking whether it positions a user as agent or agency; or one could look at a video game via the lens of "Narrative," considering how digitization enables its narrative form. Given this, what I describe in this section is not comprehensive, nor does it reflect all of the ways of enacting criticism of digital rhetoric; rather, I instead illustrate some possibilities. At the same time, as James Zappen observes, the "concept of a digital rhetoric is at once exciting and troublesome. It is exciting because it holds promise of opening new vistas of opportunity for rhetorical studies and troublesome because it reveals the difficulties and the challenges of adapting a rhetorical tradition more than 2,000 years old to the conditions and constraints of the new digital media."[35] In the remainder of this section, I explore how genre and social knowledge may serve as frameworks for analyzing digital texts and how one may productively adopt a critical orientation to digital discourse, highlighting the way in which power is brokered in online, networked contexts.

Genre, the subject of a previous chapter, is one enduring rhetorical concept that serves as a productive starting point for the analysis of digital rhetoric. To analyze a text via genre generally means to identify the class or category to which it belongs and then consider how it conforms to or deviates from the conventions of its type. In digital rhetoric, genre analysis is oriented toward the sorts of new digital genres that arise via the affordances and constraints of the digital. It asks what new types and categories of discourse have emerged in our digital era? And why and how do they matter for our collective, shared meaning making? In an early and influential piece on digital rhetoric, Elizabeth Losh positioned genre analysis as central to the study of digital rhetoric, going so far as to say, "to have basic competence in digital rhetoric . . . means to understand the conventions of many new digital genres."[36] Given the state of constant flux that characterizes the digital landscape, with existing genres evolving and new ones emerging, that is easier said than done.[37]

To illustrate the variety of digital genres one engages with on an daily basis, Losh gives the following account of a typical week: "I might contest a parking ticket using an online form, email my minister, notify my health club that there is a mistake on their website, check one son's grades electronically, correct spelling on the other son's PowerPoint presentation homework, make retouching suggestions about family photos, or look for a good local coffee shop recommended by a blog or online newspaper."[38] Read today, it also serves as a striking illustration of the fast-changing pace of digital culture, and the rapid shifts around genre. Just over ten years later, Losh's 2009 list already sounds outdated, and does not include some of the most salient genres of today's everyday digital experience, from Facebook and Instagram posts; to tweets and snaps; to YouTube and TikTok videos; to Twitch streams; to VSCO and Pinterest boards; to Zoom videoconferences; to text messages and the many different apps that populate our phones with news, entertainment, and weather info, and even enable us to track the movements of our very own bodies. Each of these, and the many others not mentioned here, represents a site for rhetorical criticism via the lens of genre, with attention to the ways in which digital affordances and constraints matter.

The digital era also highlights another perennial consideration for rhetoric—its relationship to knowledge.[39] Rhetoric is, of course, a vehicle through which knowledge is conveyed; but, even more importantly, rhetoric is **epistemic**, which is to say that it is instrumental not just in communicating knowledge but, in fact, in shaping and even constituting it. As James Herrick wrote on the latter point, "through rhetorical interaction, we come to accept some ideas as true and to reject others as false. Rhetoric's knowledge-building function derives from its tendency to test ideas. Once an idea has been thoroughly tested by a community, it becomes part of what is accepted as known."[40] In other words, through our rhetorical interactions with each other, a kind of consensus-based knowledge arises, one Thomas Farrell terms **social knowledge**.[41]

The extent to which rhetorical interaction now occurs in and via online spaces raises important questions about digital mediation's influence on epistemic practices. Widespread alarm regarding fake news reflects some such concerns.[42] Sophisticated new technologies and technological practices have altered the landscape of rhetorical interaction through which shared knowledge arises. For example, while misinformation has always been around, it can now be readily shared, at global scale, in unprecedented fashion. Social media bots are programmed to interject content into online public sphere discourse, via the guise of a fake human profile, with the aim of shaping consensus in a particular direction. Notably, those from one country can even employ this technique to attempt to influence public discourse in another to their own advantage.[43] At the same time, algorithms filter the content that finds its way to us, often showing us that which reflects our already existing belief structures, arguably resulting in what Eli Pariser has termed a filter bubble, a condition of self-reinforcing intellectual seclusion.[44] All of which is to say, rhetoric-as-epistemic is differently enacted in the digital era and criticism of digital discourse can aim to discern how this occurs in and through particular texts.

One could also adopt a critical orientation to digital discourse, one attuned to power relations and the ways in which technologies underwrite them in digital spaces. In this manner the rhetorical criticism of digital discourse could attend to the enduring matters of race, class, and gender, as digitally inflected. A critic might consider how online platforms amplify some voices and perspectives while sidelining others. For instance, a growing body of research makes the case that technologies from web browsers to search engine algorithms are, despite appearances of neutrality, quite racialized.[45] Some work aims to counter such marginalization. For example, black code studies initiative offers both methodology and praxis to "center black thought and cultural production across a range of digital platforms, but especially social media," as in Tara Conley's research regarding black feminists' reappropriation of capitalistic platforms and hashtags for their own purposes.[46] With this in mind, a critic adopting a critical orientation might ask how any given digital text is implicated in such cultural dynamics.

ANALYZING THE DIGITAL TEXT VIA REORIENTED/ RECONCEPTUALIZED DIGITAL RHETORICAL PERSPECTIVES

The transformations wrought by the networked digital age also invite new orientations to rhetorical study developed specifically to account for rhetoric in digital contexts. In what follows, I will emphasize three fulcrum points around which rhetoric has been thus reoriented and/or reconceptualized: attention, circulation, and agency.

Richard Lanham, who is credited as the first to use the term digital rhetoric introduces attention as a key term.[47] Though Lanham acknowledges that rhetoric has always, in one way or another, been concerned with attention, he argues that our current moment has exacerbated the dynamic. As he describes, we live in a time of digital chaos.[48] He deploys the concept of the **attention economy** to capture the way in which in our contemporary digital age, attention is the resource in short supply, the one everyone is competing for.[49] One way to perform criticism of digital texts, therefore, is to take attention as a focal consideration, attending to the ways in which a text is competitive or not via this metric.[50]

Viral texts, for example, lend themselves to analysis via attention. **Virality**, in a digital context, refers to the sudden, rapid **circulation** of a text in a short amount of time. Barbara Warnick and David S. Heineman explain some of the factors that lend a text to virality. One is novelty; texts that offer something new, present a new idea, a new format, are more likely to capture attention than the already-familiar or overplayed. Another is pathos, or the elicitation of emotion. Warnick and Heineman argue that texts that evoke emotion are more likely to go viral.[51] For example, take the clip of the 2017 BBC news interview, in which a man is interrupted by his young daughter barging into his home office, followed by his infant son, and his wife frantically crawling on the floor, futilely trying to stay out of view as she grabs them and drags them back out the door.[52] That video, which went wildly viral, checks both of the Warnick and Heineman viral video boxes, offering a humorous and infrequently glimpsed look at work-from-home life.

Malcolm Gladwell uses the term **stickiness** to refer to the quality of a text that motivates us to keep looking at it, that which holds our attention and enables us to retain its message(s).[53] He identifies a number of features that can foster stickiness, including comprehensibility, personal relevance, and a participatory element. He gives the example of a 1978 Columbia Records marketing campaign that asked viewers to look out for a gold box in *Parade* and *TV Guide* issues. If they found it, they could write in to Columbia to claim a free record. Not only was the campaign straightforward, with a proffered personal payoff, but, as the marketing executive behind it explained, it "made the reader/viewer part of an interactive advertising system. Viewers were not just an audience but had become participants."[54] People eagerly hunted down gold boxes, leading to a remarkably successful marketing campaign.

The attentional impact of the participatory experience is perhaps even more salient in digital contexts, which have transformed the ways that texts and audiences relate. Web 2.0 ushered into being all manner of **participatory media**, which engage audiences not only as consumers but as content creators: social media platforms serve as a preeminent example, with participants both regularly perusing and producing content, with blurred lines between the two activities. Henry Jenkins argues that digital media have wrought new forms of participatory cultures, which include "relatively low barriers to artistic expression and civic engagement, where there is strong support for creating and sharing what you create with others."[55] In that sense, in contemporary media environments, interactivity is more standard expectation than novel exception.

The participatory turn, in turn, has facilitated the proliferation of the remixed text, or "third party recomposition," generated via reconfigurations or repurposings of existing textual elements.[56] Remixing is not new and can, in fact, be understood as a centuries-old cultural practice.[57] Digital media, however, underwrite ready creation of many types of remixes, including the ubiquitous meme format in which a background template, whether a photograph of a confused Keanu Reeves or a still frame of woman shouting at a salad-eating cat, is remade via captions that transform its meaning. Memes can do significant cultural work, and when a historically significant image becomes meme-ized, for example, its reworkings may offer reinterpretations of that history.[58]

Given the ubiquity of the remix, rhetors may craft texts with **rhetorical velocity** in view.[59] As Jim Ridolfo and Dànielle Nicole DeVoss describe, in doing so, rhetors strategically compose by considering how others might rework or reuse their text. For example, aware that few will watch the event in its entirety, a politician might focus on incorporating some preplanned lines into a debate, ones they imagine the media will want to replay in their coverage of it. But attention to rhetorical velocity is not just the domain of politics. For example, in delivering post-game remarks, an athlete might deliver a funny, controversial line with the pointed hope that it gets picked up and recirculated on social media to bolster their public profile.

Circulation has thus emerged as a key concern for digital rhetorics. Identifying circulation studies as a distinct—and growing—area of rhetorical inquiry, Laurie Gries describes it as centrally concerned with "discourse in motion."[60] Traditionally, rhetorical criticism has tended to focus on a given text in front of a certain audience in a particular context, without necessarily considering how it got there or where it goes next. And as chapters in this book make clear, we can gain a good deal of insight by analyzing texts in this fashion. However, for some texts, such as memes or viral videos, we are missing a good deal if we do not also attend to the ways in which they move around. That movement, and the reworkings and reimaginings concomitant with it, are constitutive of these texts and underwrite much of what is both interesting and significant about them as public discourse. Gries herself completed a large-scale study of the "rhetorical life" of Shepard Fairey's famous Obama Hope poster, mapping it across the digital terrain, as it was appropriated and transformed in various ways: into commodity, via parody, and as impetus to activism, for example.[61]

In their work on circulation, Henry Jenkins, Sam Ford, and Joshua Green take issue with virality as a central metaphor for contemporary content dispersal, arguing that it construes audiences as overly passive. They use the term **spreadability** to capture how content circulates via people—those who do the work of appropriating and transforming, for example. As they explain, spreadability "refers to the potential—both technical and cultural—for audiences to share content for their own purposes."[62] Whereas stickiness has to do with orchestrating attention, spreadability concerns the dynamics that enable and motivate sharing.[63] Social media posts, for example, are often eminently spreadable, which is to say characterized by the propensity to be passed along, via something as simple as the tap of a finger on a touchpad. Moreover, in being shared, content is often sampled, with bits and pieces thrust forward into new contexts.

The digital age has therefore also drawn attention to the fragmentary, patchwork qualities of texts and textual encounters. Neither is new to digital rhetoric, of course, and Michael Calvin McGee, for one, argued not only that repurposed textual fragments are a fundamental feature of discourse but that the twentieth century was characterized by increasing discursive fragmentation.[64] Yet these qualities have become arguably even more salient in the digital age. In her work on sound bites, Megan Foley refers to the "escalating circulation of sound bites, those ever-shorter fragments of political speech."[65] But as she makes clear, fragmentation does not equate to irrelevance, and suggests instead that "rather than diminishing the relevance of public address, sound bites have amplified the popular investment in public speech."[66] Fragments, in order words, do important rhetorical work.

Finally, agency has emerged as another key conceptual axis in work on digital rhetoric. Agency generally refers to "the capacity to act."[67] Throughout the rhetorical tradition, it has often been presumed, sometimes unreflectively, to firmly lie with the rhetor, who plans and strategizes in order to achieve symbolic inducement. In recent years, theoretical developments in the humanities, such as posthumanism and new materialism, have destabilized and problematized this default assumption.[68] In digital rhetoric, reconceptualizations around agency often take shape by figuring technology itself as agential, thereby unsettling straightforwardly humanist accounts of the strategizing rhetor.

One approach is to consider how infrastructures of the digital organize human activity in such a fashion as to exert agency, shaping, even inducing, human behavior in a manner conceived as rhetorical, exerting what is sometimes called "technical agency."[69] For example, YouTube autoplay defaults—whereby the next episode in a series automatically starts, without any action from the viewer—function coercively by defaulting us into a pattern of binge-watching, thus getting us to spend more time on the service. The default fosters and facilitates the binge, and its manipulation via technological default can shape behavior, as does (though quite differently) persuasive discourse that gives reasons why we should watch the next episode.

Another related approach is to focus on human-technology agential "entanglements." In her work on autism apps, Anne Demo explores the agency-technology relationship, arguing that the apps she studies and others like them "distribute agency through a constellation of human and nonhuman actors."[70] In other words, they constitute an **assemblage**, or a collection of entities, both human and nonhuman, among which agency is distributed.[71] For example, in an autism app, design decisions, algorithms, and preprogrammed tasks shape work in concert with human activity.

Ian Bogost introduced the concept of **procedural rhetoric** to address the agential, rhetorical enactments of digital processes. He explains, procedural rhetoric is "a general name for the practice of authoring arguments through processes."[72] As Bogost explains, process pervades the human experience; for example, one follows a certain process when returning items at a store, one that may include time-limits and receipts. Bogost's interest, however, lies not merely with the existence of processes in general, nor even computer processes in particular, but with how the ways in which a system has us interact with it, via its rules, operates persuasively. Bogost focuses on video games. He gives the example of the McDonald's Video Game, an online game that functions as a critique of McDonald's business model. When you play the game, you control different areas of the industry: the pasture, the farmland, the restaurant, and the corporate office. The choices you make affect profits, and can include bulldozing rain forests, using growth hormones, and serving up diseased meat. As Bogost argues, the choices embedded in the game process, the very rules of the game itself, constitute the argument. In this way it is procedural rhetoric, or an argument via computational procedure.

CRITICAL ESSAYS

As a way of exemplifying the approaches outlined in the previous two sections, I offer four brief examples below. The first two draw on enduring rhetorical frameworks to arrive at insights into digital phenomena while the second two analyze digital texts via reoriented or reconceptualized frameworks. Taken together, the examples suggest ways you might approach the analysis of specific digital texts. They are not fully elaborated critical pieces but illustrations of some possibilities for analyzing digital discourse via perspectives introduced in this chapter.

EXTENDED EXAMPLE 1: ONLINE PUBLIC SHAMING AND GENRE

Just before Justine Sacco, a thirty-year-old public-relations specialist from New York City, boarded a flight to Cape Town, South Africa, she tweeted to her approximately two hundred followers "Going to Africa. Hope I don't get AIDS. Just kidding. I'm white!"[73] By the time her eleven-hour flight landed, her tweet had garnered tens of thousands of responses, with comments like "All I want for Christmas is to see @JustineSacco's face when her plane lands and she checks her inbox/voicemail."[74] The hashtag #HasJustineLandedYet was briefly Twitter's #1 worldwide trending topic and gained so much traction that when she finally arrived, someone was waiting at the airport to take her photograph. The very next day, she was fired from her job. Sacco subsequently explained her tweet as a failed attempt at making an ironic joke.[75] The Sacco incident is frequently recounted as both a cautionary tale of the hazards of social media and an example of the now well-known, much-discussed phenomenon of online public shaming, which occurs when large numbers of people target a specific individual or individuals, sanctioning them in some way via a torrent of humiliating commentary.[76]

Genre offers one enduring rhetorical lens through which to analyze both the Sacco case in particular and online public shaming in general. For one, we might ask whether public shaming qualifies as epideictic discourse, with attention to the ways in which the answer to this question is shaped by digital affordances and constraints.[77] In his delineation of the epideictic genre, Aristotle outlined three characteristic features: (1) its focus on topics of praise or blame, (2) its occurrence at ceremonial occasions, and (3) its displays of eloquence.[78] Public shaming, squarely focused on the matter of blame, readily satisfies the first of these, reinforcing cultural norms by sanctioning those who deviate from them in some way. The other two require that we consider the epideictic genre's possible reconfigurations and new instantiations in and via digital contexts.

For one, online public shaming is certainly not ceremonial in a traditional fashion, or in any way that Aristotle might have envisioned when he wrote the *Art of Rhetoric*. Traditional examples of epideictic address include funeral orations and wedding speeches. Arguably, however, the digital has ushered forth new occasions, new public, ritualized events, which are not organized in and around a particular physical gathering space, but are constituted in and by online discourse. The online public shaming is a digitally driven ceremonial form, one that emerges through a temporally delimited swell of public participation, in which a person is ritually sanctioned for a violation of social norms. That is to say the shaming itself constitutes an occasion, with the "speech" collectively enacted via tweet or other online participatory format.

Unlike the traditional epideictic address, spearheaded by an individual orator who exerts his or her will to deliver a speech, no one person is quite so pivotal in the orchestration of a public shaming. Justine Sacco's public shaming, like others, was a collective phenomenon, brought about not by individuals but by the collective, so individual agency only does so much to account for it. As Jodie Nicotra has argued, online public shaming is better accounted for as an assemblage, in which agency is distributed across multiple actors, both human and nonhuman.[79] Those who tweet are instrumental, but so are the enabling digital technologies and infrastructures. Sacco's public shaming, for example, was both enabled and enacted via the hashtag #HasJustineLandedYet.

Finally, Aristotle observed that epideictic address involves a display of eloquence. In traditional speeches, these tend to take the form of grand stylistic flourish, metaphors, and rhythmic repetitions, etc. . . . Tweets are clearly quite different. Yet the wit that can characterize them, especially those that gain social media traction, is a form of eloquence. The Twitter platform, with its strict character limits, invites the short and the pithy. In the Sacco case, the hashtag #HasJustineLandedYet was precisely that, encapsulating exactly what made the incident so captivating: the suspense of the rapidly escalating public sanction all while Sacco was obliviously sitting in her airplane seat.

EXTENDED EXAMPLE 2: WIKIPEDIA AND SOCIAL KNOWLEDGE

Toward the end of 2019, Elon Musk, the billionaire and CEO of both Tesla and SpaceX, publicly took issue with his Wikipedia entry, specifically its description of him as an investor. Via social media, he requested that "someone please delete 'investor.' I do basically zero invest-ing."[80] According to Musk, because he does not hold stakes in companies other than his own, the descriptor does not apply. The fact that one of the richest people in the world, one with a reported net worth of $151 billion,[81] who runs a company that sends spaceships into orbit, cares enough about his Wikipedia entry to publicly request an edit to a particular word in it speaks to Wikipedia's prominent place in the digital-textual milieu.

Wikipedia is one of the ten most frequently accessed sites in the United States, logging about twenty billion page views a month.[82] The crowdsourced encyclopedia holds a key position in the digital-textual landscape, and thereby plays a consequential role in shared social knowledge. As Musk acknowledged via his request for an edit, Wikipedia's account of you matters, and its entries therefore serve as sites of pointed rhetorical negotiation.[83] For that reason, Wikipedia entries are productive sites for close textual analysis (an ap-proach described in a previous chapter), and careful consideration of the particulars of textual presentation.

Wikipedia's editing guidelines state, "all encyclopedic content on Wikipedia must be written from a neutral point of view (NPOV), which means representing fairly, propor-tionately, and, as far as possible, without editorial bias, all the significant views that have been published by reliable sources on a topic."[84] And the editing process includes various guidelines in an effort to ensure just that, including the "conflict-of-interest" rules, which constrain how people may influence their own Wikipedia pages, hence Musk's request that someone else make the desired edit.[85] But as rhetoric teaches us, neutrality is elusive, even at the level of the individual word. As Kenneth Burke remarked, "even if any given termi-nology is a *reflection* of reality, by its very nature as a terminology it must be a *selection* of reality; and to this extent it must function also as a *deflection* of reality."[86] We might apply that quite directly to Wikipedia—any entry functions not only as reflection but also selec-tion and deflection. In this sense, Wikipedia entries do not merely convey social knowledge, they also participate in constituting it.

For example, even when they satisfy the "neutral point of view" criterion, word choices may nonetheless endorse certain perspectives, sometimes very subtly. If Musk is described as an investor, does it cast him and his initiatives in a risky light, potentially undermining his busi-ness reputation in some way? The order in which information appears is also significant. The same detail early in an entry may influence how one reads the rest of that entry, as compared to its appearance toward the end. As of the present moment, the second sentence of Kim Kardashian's Wikipedia entry notes that she was launched to fame, in part, via a sex tape she had created with her then-boyfriend Ray J.[87] Ray J's entry, however, does not reference that tape until all the way down in the seventh paragraph.[88] Does that ordering shape, subtly, the picture the Wikipedia entry paints of each one? Moreover, does the reader even make it to the seventh paragraph? Consider how many first lines of Wikipedia entries you have read versus how many entries you have read all the way to the end.

The very day Musk made his public request, someone obliged and removed the offending word; in fact, that day saw a flurry of activity on his entry. A critic can peruse the history of those edits because Wikipedia makes the full editing history of each entry publicly accessible. Wikipedia entries also include a readily viewable talk page, in which people discuss and debate what appears therein. On Musk's talk page, someone wrote, "I don't see why, what he wants 'his' wikipedia article to say carries any weight here?"[89] In analyzing a Wikipedia entry like Musk's, we can attend not only to what appears in an entry but, via the affordances of the digital, to its edit history and talk page, which serve as archives of rhetorical negotiation.[90] The history of edits to a page tells a story about the debates that occur around a particular topic. And this includes not just a page like Musk's but Wikipedia pages about issues like climate change, racism, matters related to public health, etc. In these entries, Wikipedia too reflects and shapes social knowledge about the highly consequential.

EXTENDED EXAMPLE 3: HASHTAGS AND ATTENTION

Disney's 2015 Share Your Ears campaign invited people to post photos of themselves on social media wearing either Mickey Mouse ears or some creative variation of thus, together with the hashtag #ShareYourEars. The campaign was billed as a fundraiser for Make-A-Wish America, and for every post, Disney made a $5 donation to the organization (up to a certain amount). It was also a powerful enactment of hashtag-driven viral brand marketing. According to Disney's own figures, people shared over 1.77 million such photos via the hashtag, with these then displayed over 420 million times across Twitter, Facebook, and Instagram feeds.[91] One way to take this campaign as a site for rhetorical analysis is to center attention as the organizing framework.

Hashtags first arose on Twitter as means to categorize messages. At once simple and powerful, they link otherwise distributed messages into a thread, thereby facilitating discursive exchange around a subject, as organized in and through the hashtag—and searchable by means of thus.[92] It took little time for them to take hold across social media platforms and become a prominent, potent discursive lever of the digital age. In both positioning a message in relation to an ongoing conversation as well as serving as an impetus for such conversation, hashtags can be instrumental in the scrabble for attentional traction. As Jennifer Reinwald argues, "hashtags . . . function as a rhetorical technique for attention creation."[93] And rhetorical criticism of hashtags, and the discursive exchanges they organize, can be oriented to them as such.

To analyze Disney's #ShareYourEars campaign via the lens of attention, you might first select some examples of the social media posts generated in response to it, representative and/or notable iterations. You might then consider them in terms of features that tend to underlie attention-garnering content, such as those detailed by Barbara Warnick and David Heineman's account of virality.[94] For example, pictures of puppies or celebrities bedecked in odd, fanciful ears offer some novelty, as do those featuring creative renditions of ears, such a those made out of fruit or flowers. Similarly, seeing someone look silly, especially in aid of a good cause, evokes certain feel-good emotions, particularly in the context of a campaign to benefit sick children. That is, the photos evince pathos.

The #ShareYourEars campaign is also characterized by another key feature of the attentional landscape of the contemporary digital era: interactivity. The #ShareYourEars campaign asks not merely that you pass along a message, spreading it via a click or share, but that you become involved as content creator, generating your own iteration of it. The campaign's invitation to expression—the impetus to and platform for personal expression that it provides—is part of its appeal. It engages attention via participation. A number of other notably viral hashtag campaigns do likewise; think, for example, of the #ALSIceBucketChallenge, which invited people to post videos of themselves dumping buckets of ice over their heads.[95]

Though I have chosen an advertising example here, activism is an important arena in which hashtags do significant rhetorical work, particularly via their capacity to corral attention, and for which attention therefore offers a productive analytic lens. Though I do not examine advocacy in this example, hashtags are instrumental in contemporary social movements and a number of rhetorical studies address such modes of activism, as enacted via hashtags such as #BlackLivesMatter, #SayHerName, and #YesAllWomen, among others.[96] These are all amenable to analysis that takes attention as organizing concern.

EXTENDED EXAMPLE 4: ONLINE GAMES AND PROCEDURAL RHETORIC

A Job for Me is a Public Broadcasting Service (PBS) kids' game, one of its suite of Sesame Street games, available for free via the channel's website.[97] The game features the popular *Sesame Street* television program characters Elmo and Abby, who, at the game's outset, walk to a virtual street featuring an array of buildings and storefronts. These house different businesses: a veterinary clinic, an architecture firm, etc. . . . . Elmo asks, "what job should we learn about first?" From there the player clicks on a building to select an occupation and learn more about it. While one might analyze *A Job for Me* via a number of different rhetorical perspectives, when it comes to games, procedural rhetoric offers an illuminating analytic framework.

Analyzing *A Job for Me*, or any game, as procedural rhetoric involves attending to structure, the way in which the game operates via rule-governed processes.[98] That is to say that one focuses on the rules or processes that govern action within the game. One can then consider how those rules and processes reinforce (and/or undercut) certain positions. In this case, *A Job for Me* arguably reinforces individual preference as a primary consideration in deciding on a career path. Via process, it makes the case that a job is something that is for me, as opposed to something that needs to be done.

A Job for Me is structured as a landscape which one navigates by clicking arrows to move to the right or left to traverse the series of buildings on the street, and then clicking on a building to enter into it. Once inside, one finds other places to click to get information, complete tasks, or just hear a remark (e.g., if you click on a cat, you hear "cute kitty!"). To understand how the process of navigating the game generates an argument about the primacy of individual preference, compare it to a cartoon a child might watch on TV. A cartoon could certainly convey the same general information about different types of jobs, but the experience of watching it would be quite different. In *A Job For Me*, navigating the content via a self-directed array of clickable options reinforces the primacy of your preference-driven choice-making and the view that contemplating careers is fundamentally about exploration on the basis of your interests. You interact with the items in the landscape based on what catches your fancy; if you do not have any interest in one, you can skip it. Via process, this game says that careers are a matter of choice, specifically your choice, which you make based on your own interests.

In contrast, and to further illustrate the point, the game does not present exploring career options as a process that involves identifying jobs that need to be done. We can imagine an alternative game, embedding alternative processes, that might reinforce this message. Elmo or Abby sees a pothole, which brings the child playing the game to a screen with information about careers that involve filling in potholes (city planner, construction worker, and so on). The game would be different in content, possibly, but the process would also differ, embedding need via process to direct the player to particular jobs that need to be done.

Importantly, the process of playing *A Job For Me* is open-ended and stress-free. There is no timer and no time limit, nor is there a limit to how many times you can return to hear any given message. You can stay as long as you want at a job, go back and forth between jobs at will, and return to jobs you have already explored as many times as you want. Compare that to something like Nintendo's *Overcooked*, which seeks to simulate the stressful experience of working in a restaurant kitchen, the main gameplay of which involves juggling and balancing kitchen tasks under sometimes impossible conditions of time pressure. One might make a very different argument about that game's procedural rhetoric.

PERSONAL REFLECTIONS

I decided to write about four different examples, each focusing on a different text, in order to illustrate a range of possibilities for the analysis of digital discourse. Any of the critical essays here could be elaborated on to produce a more focused piece, one that introduces a central thesis that it explores at length in order to make a sustained argument. In my classes,

I have found students are often interested in writing on digital topics, but are uncertain about how to get started and/or about what makes for a valid text to study. Rhetoric is often associated with serious, formal sorts of discourse, such as presidential speeches, campaign addresses, and the like; the study of such texts has formed the solid backbone of the tradition of rhetorical criticism and, for that reason, examples of these are frequently examined in classes and textbooks. But rhetorical theories are productively employed to criticize texts of all kinds, even those that seem frivolous and unacademic. As the chapter on "Criticism of Popular Culture and Social Media" makes especially clear, "entertaining" and "worthy of analysis" are not mutually exclusive.

For many of you, the sorts of public discourse you encounter every day in online, networked digital contexts feels more salient to your lived experience than what happens on Capitol Hill, in a Congressional session, as broadcast on C-SPAN. I hope the essays here give you some ideas about how you might proceed to harness the tools of rhetorical theory in order to enact analysis of these sorts of texts. Performing rhetorical criticism often involves focusing on something we take for granted, something that seems simple or obvious even—the tweet, the Wikipedia page, the hashtag, the game—and unpacking its persuasive dimensions, revealing how those underlying persuasive dimensions are actually far more complex and interesting than we might initially think. The familiar, "simple" text can generate a complex, insightful analysis.

POTENTIALS AND PITFALLS

Between the time that I write this sentence and the time that this book is in your hands, new technologies or new, unanticipated uses of existing technologies will have emerged, while those mentioned in this chapter may already be passé, outmoded, or even rendered obsolete by the next new thing. It is certainly true that every site for rhetorical criticism changes over time. Traditional, historically oriented work can shift dramatically, as a never-before-seen document is uncovered in an archive, or a new way of looking at old texts emerges, reshaping an area of inquiry. Yet there is something more in flux, more rapidly changing about digital rhetoric. And while that can at times feel unnerving, as digital texts and contexts can change even during the very process of writing about them, this is also just as much a potential as it is a pitfall. When it comes to rhetorical criticism of digital texts, one can always be assured of finding fresh sites for analysis.

CRITICISM OF DIGITAL RHETORIC TOP PICKS

Bogost, Ian. *Persuasive Games: The Expressive Power of Videogames.* Cambridge, MA: MIT Press, 2007. This book introduces the notion of procedural rhetoric to capture how video games persuade via structure and process. In it, Bogost focuses on games created in educational, political, and advertising contexts, which work to shape opinion—via structure and process—beyond those contexts.

Davis, Matthew, Stephen J. McElroy, and Rory Lee. "Ways of Knowing and Doing in Digital Rhetoric: A Primer" [video]. *Enculturation.* http://enculturation.net/ways-of-knowing-and -doing-in-digital-rhetoric. As befits a chapter on digital rhetoric, one of the top picks is a website-hosted video. In 2015, Indiana University held a Digital Rhetoric Symposium, where scholars met to discuss the emerging field of study. One result of the symposium is this video, which features interviews with several participants as they explore the question, "What is digital rhetoric?"

Demo, Anne Teresa. "Hacking Agency: Apps, Autism, and Neurodiversity." *Quarterly Journal of Speech* 103, no. 3 (2017): 277–300. This essay explores agency in digital spaces, with an emphasis on human-technological relationships. It analyzes two autism apps, demonstrating how the apps exert agency in conjunction with human actors.

Johnson, Jessica Marie, and Mark Anthony Neal, eds. "Black Code [Special Issue]." *Black Scholar* 47, no. 3 (2017). http://www.theblackscholar.org/now-available-black-code/. This guest-edited special issue of the *Black Scholar* focuses on black contributions to digital culture. It includes articles on social media rhetorics and hashtag activism.

Kennerly, Michele, and Damien Smith Pfister, eds. *Ancient Rhetorics and Digital Networks.* Tuscaloosa: University of Alabama Press, 2018. This collection offers a compendium of essays, each of which takes one or more classical rhetorical concepts and applies it/them to digital contexts.

Ott, Brian L., and Greg Dickinson. *The Twitter Presidency: Donald J. Trump and the Politics of White Rage.* New York: Routledge, 2019. Among other things, this in-depth study of Trump's use of Twitter considers how Twitter, as a platform, lends itself to Trump's distinctive rhetorical style.

Pfister, Damien Smith. *Networked Media, Networked Rhetorics: Attention and Deliberation in the Early Blogosphere.* University Park: Pennsylvania State University Press, 2014. This book traverses the landscape of the early days of blogs via a set of case studies, each of which illustrates a particular dimension of networked public deliberation. In doing so, it centers the roles played by both attention and emotion.

Warnick, Barbara. "Rhetorical Criticism of Public Discourse on the Internet: Theoretical Implications." *Rhetoric Society Quarterly* 28, no. 4 (1998): 73–84. Barbara Warnick was among the first rhetoric scholars to analyze online public discourse. Now over twenty years old, this article's rationale for turning our attention to digital rhetoric remains as true today as it was then, even if the opening lines about rhetoric scholars not having paid much attention to the internet no longer apply.

DISCUSSION QUESTIONS

1. Consider a commencement speech, such as that by US Navy Admiral William H. McRaven.[99] How does an audience's experience of watching it on YouTube differ from the experience of those who were in attendance at University of Texas at Austin's 2014 Commencement?

2. What strategies do you employ in your daily life so as to avoid being fooled by misinformation? Do you try to cut off circulation paths by which it might find its way to you (e.g., blocking certain social media accounts from your feed)? Or do you rely on your ability to evaluate the content you encounter? What makes you trust an online text? What leads you to distrust and dismiss one? Do you think studying rhetoric makes you better at these judgment calls?

3. As we observed in this chapter, digital rhetoric is a rapidly changing area of inquiry. Given the time that has inevitably passed between when I wrote this chapter and when you are now reading it, are there any updates you might make to it?

ACTIVITIES

1. Alone or in small groups, brainstorm a list of ideas or concepts from this chapter that might offer insight into how and why particular content goes viral. Then identify a video that went viral over the last couple of months and write up a short explanation of why you think it did so. Finally, imagine yourself in the role of content creator. If you wanted to create a video today that would go viral tomorrow, what sort of video would you create and why? How would you try to set the process in motion (i.e., how would you get that video into circulation)?

2. Alone or in small groups, choose a social media platform and describe the sort of posts you find there in terms of genre. That is, what are the characteristic features of posts on that platform? Are there any discernible subgenres? If so, describe those. Then craft two posts, (1) one that adheres to genre norms and (2) one that deviates from them in some way. You could use a social media post generator (e.g., zeoob.com) to do so.

3. Alone or in small groups, find a biographical Wikipedia entry focused on a public figure—it could be a politician, athlete, or celebrity, for example. Then imagine yourself as that person's biggest fan. How might you edit the entry to make that person sound better than they already do? You can think about this in terms of larger-scale changes, such as content you might add, or in terms of more subtle changes, such as reworking sentences or even changing single words to highlight positive attributes and/or downplay negative ones. If you were to make these changes to the entry, would you be shaping social knowledge in a meaningful way? Why or why not?

NOTES

1. Benjamin Peters, "Digital," in *Digital Keywords: A Vocabulary of Information Society and Culture,* ed. Benjamin Peters (Princeton University Press, 2016), 93–108.

2. A psychologist working on the human-environment relationship first introduced the concept of affordances to characterize how something's features or properties shape how we can engage with it. It has since become commonplace in digital studies. See James J. Gibson, "The Theory of Affordances," in *Perceiving, Acting, and Knowing,* ed. Robert Shaw and John Bransford (Hillsdale, NJ: Lawrence Erlbaum, 1977), 67–82.

3. Damien Smith Pfister, *Networked Media, Networked Rhetorics: Attention and Deliberation in the Early Blogosphere* (University Park: Penn State University Press, 2014), 9.

4. Douglas Eyman, *Digital Rhetoric: Theory, Method, Practice* (Ann Arbor: University of Michigan Press, 2015), 61.

5. See, for instance, Craig R. Smith, *Rhetoric and Human Consciousness: A History,* 4th ed. (Prospect Heights, IL: Waveland Press, 2013), and Jim A. Kuypers and Andrew King, eds., *Twentieth-Century Roots of Rhetorical Studies* (Westport, CT: Praeger, 2001).

6. Lloyd F. Bitzer, "Rhetoric and Public Knowledge," in *Rhetoric, Philosophy, and Literature: An Exploration,* ed. Don M. Burks (West Lafayette, IN: Purdue University Press, 1978), 67–94.

7. On the public sphere, see Jürgen Habermas, *The Structural Transformation of the Public Sphere: An Inquiry into a Category of Bourgeois Society,* trans. by Thomas Burger (Cambridge, MA: MIT Press, 1989).

8. Axel Bruns and Joanne Jacobs, "Introduction," in *Uses of Blogs,* ed. Axel Bruns and Joanne Jacobs (New York: Peter Lang, 2006), 5.

9. See, for example, Joseph Zompetti, "Rhetorical Incivility in the Twittersphere: A Comparative Thematic Analysis of Clinton and Trump's Tweets During and After the 2016 Presidential Election," *Journal of Contemporary Rhetoric* 9 (2019): 29–54.

10. Matthew D. Barton, "The Future of Rational-Critical Debate in Online Public Spheres," *Computers and Composition* 22, no. 2 (2005): 177–190.

11. Leisa Reichelt, a user design researcher and blogger, introduced the term "ambient intimacy" to refer to the closeness we feel to others when so regularly exposed to their daily lives via social media, "Ambient Intimacy," disambiguity, March 1, 2007, http://www.disambiguity.com/ambient-intimacy/. For both discussion and application of the concept, see Pfister, *Networked Media, Networked Rhetorics*, 89–133.

12. See, for example, Laurie E. Gries, *Still Life with Rhetoric: A New Materialist Approach for Visual Rhetorics* (Logan: Utah State University Press, 2015).

13. Sarah Manavis, "These Women are Using Tinder to Build their Instagram Followings," *GQ*, August 10, 2019, https://www.gq-magazine.co.uk/lifestyle/article/why-do-people-on-tinder-list-their-instagram.

14. On flow, see Joshua Reeves, "Temptation and Its Discontents: Digital Rhetoric, Flow, and the Possible," *Rhetoric Review* 32, no. 3 (2013): 314–330. Reeves draws on Raymond Williams's concept of "flow" to theorize how the Web channels audiences from one online experience/text to another.

15. See Nathan R. Johnson, "Information Infrastructure as Rhetoric: Tools for Analysis," *Poroi* 8, no. 1 (2012); and *Architects of Memory: Information and Rhetoric in a Networked Archival Age* (Tuscaloosa: University of Alabama Press, 2020). See also, Casey Boyle, James J. Brown, Jr., and Steph Ceraso, "The Digital: Rhetoric Behind and Beyond the Screen," *Rhetoric Society Quarterly* 48, no. 3 (2018): 251–259; James J. Brown Jr., *Ethical Programs: Hospitality and the Rhetorics of Software* (Ann Arbor: University of Michigan Press, 2015).

16. S. Scott Graham, Sang-Yeon Kim, Danielle M. DeVasto, and William Keith, "Statistical Genre Analysis: Toward Big Data Methodologies in Technical Communication," *Technical Communication Quarterly* 24, no. 1 (2015): 70–104. See also, David Hoffman and Don Waisanen, "At the Digital Frontier of Rhetoric Studies: An Overview of Tools and Methods for Computer-Aided Textual Analysis," in *Rhetoric and the Digital Humanities*, ed. Jim Ridolfo and William Hart-Davidson (Chicago: University of Chicago Press, 2014), 169–183; Michelle G. Gibbons and David W. Seitz, "Toward a Digital Methodology for Ideographic Criticism: A Case Study of 'Equality,'" in *Theorizing Digital Rhetoric*, ed. Aaron Hess and Amber Davisson (New York: Routledge, 2018), 169–183.

17. "Emergence of Advertising in America: 1850–1920," Duke University Libraries, Repository Collections and Archives, accessed November 23, 2020, https://repository.duke.edu/dc/eaa.

18. See Charles E. Morris III, "The Archival Turn in Rhetorical Studies; Or, The Archive's Rhetorical (Re)turn," *Rhetoric & Public Affairs* 9, no. 1 (2006): 113–115; see also Jessica Enoch and Pamela VanHaitsma, "Archival Literacy: Reading the Rhetoric of Digital Archives in the Undergraduate Classroom," *College Composition and Communication* 67, no. 2 (2015): 216–242; Jessica Enoch and David Gold, "Seizing the Methodological Moment: The Digital Humanities and Historiography in Rhetoric and Composition," *College English* 76, no. 2 (2013): 105–114; Jenny Rice and Jeff Rice, "Pop-Up Archives," in *Rhetoric and the Digital Humanities*, ed. Jim Ridolfo and William Hart-Davidson (Chicago: University of Chicago Press, 2014), 245–254.

19. Trump Twitter Archive V2, accessed November 23, 2020, https://www.thetrumparchive.com/.

20. See, for example, Brian L. Ott and Greg Dickinson. *The Twitter Presidency: Donald J. Trump and the Politics of White Rage* (New York: Routledge, 2019).

21. See, for example, Jennifer L. Borda and Bailey Marshall, "Creating a Space to #SayHerName: Rhetorical Stratification in the Networked Sphere," *Quarterly Journal of Speech* 106, no. 2 (2020): 133–155.

22. See, for example, Anne Teresa Demo, "Hacking Agency: Apps, Autism, and Neurodiversity," *Quarterly Journal of Speech* 103, no. 3 (2017): 277–300.

23. See, for example, Pfister, *Networked Media, Networked Rhetorics*.

24. See, for example, Eric S. Jenkins, "The Modes of Visual Rhetoric: Circulating Memes as Expressions," *Quarterly Journal of Speech* 100, no. 4 (2014): 442–466.

25. See, for example, Amber Davisson, "'I'm In!': Hillary Clinton's 2008 Democratic Primary Campaign on YouTube," *Journal of Visual Literacy* 28, no. 1 (2009): 70–91.

26. Elizabeth M. Losh, "Hacking Aristotle: What is Digital Rhetoric?," in *Virtualpolitik: An Electronic History of Government Media-Making in a Time of War, Scandal, Disaster, Miscommunication, and Mistakes* (Cambridge: MIT Press, 2009), 47–95.

27. See, for example, Ian Bogost, *Persuasive Games: The Expressive Power of Videogames* (Cambridge, MA: The MIT Press, 2007).

28. See Dexter Thomas, "Why Everyone's Saying 'Black Girls are Magic,'" *Los Angeles Times*, September 9, 2015, https://www.latimes.com/nation/nationnow/la-na-nn-everyones-saying-black-girls-are -magic-20150909-htmlstory.html.

29. Ott and Dickinson, *The Twitter Presidency*; see Katherine Haenschen, Michael Horning, and Jim A. Kuypers, "Donald J. Trump's Use of Twitter in the 2016 Campaign," in *The 2016 American Presidential Campaign and the News: Implications for the American Democracy and the Republic*, ed. Jim A. Kuypers (Lanham, MD: Lexington Books, 2018), 55–76.

30. James Gleick, "What Defines a Meme?," *Smithsonian Magazine*, May 2011, http://www.smithsonianmag.com/arts-culture/what-defines-a-meme-1904778/?c=y&page=4.

31. Jenkins, "The Modes of Visual Rhetoric," 443.

32. E.g., Jeffrey T. Grabill and Stacey Pigg, "Messy Rhetoric: Identity Performance as Rhetorical Agency in Online Public Forums," *Rhetoric Society Quarterly* 42, no. 2 (2012): 99–119.

33. See Gibbons and Seitz, "Toward a Digital Methodology."

34. See, for example, Michele Kennerly and Damien Smith Pfister, eds. *Ancient Rhetorics & Digital Networks* (Tuscaloosa: University of Alabama Press, 2018); Kathleen E. Welch, *Electric Rhetoric: Classical Rhetoric, Oralism, and a New Literacy* (Cambridge: MIT Press, 1999); Collin Gifford Brooke, *Lingua Fracta: Toward a Rhetoric of New Media* (New Jersey: Hampton Press, 2009).

35. James P. Zappen, "Digital Rhetoric: Toward an Integrated Theory," *Technical Communication Quarterly* 14, no. 3 (2005): 319.

36. Losh, "Hacking Aristotle," 54.

37. See Carolyn R. Miller and Dawn Shepherd, "Questions for Genre Theory from the Blogosphere," in *Genres in the Internet: Issues in the Theory of Genre*, ed. Janet Giltrow and Dieter Stein (Philadelphia: John Benjamins, 2009): 263–290; Carolyn R. Miller, "Genre in Ancient and Networked Media," in *Ancient Rhetorics & Digital Networks*, Michele Kennerly and Damien Smith Pfister, eds. (Tuscaloosa: University of Alabama Press, 2018), 176–204.

38. Losh, "Hacking Aristotle," 48.

39. Alan Liu, "Theses on the Epistemology of the Digital: Advice for the Cambridge Center for Digital Knowledge," August 14, 2014, https://liu.english.ucsb.edu/theses-on-the-epistemology-of-the -digital-page/.

40. James A. Herrick, *The History and Theory of Rhetoric: An Introduction*, 5th edition (New York: Routledge, 2013), 19.

41. Thomas B. Farrell, "Knowledge, Consensus, and Rhetorical Theory," *Quarterly Journal of Speech* 62, no. 1 (1976): 1–14.

42. See Abe Aamidor, "Fact or Fiction: Defining Fake News During the 2016 U.S. Presidential Election," in *The 2016 American Presidential Campaign and the News: Implications for American Democracy and the Republic*, Jim A. Kuypers, ed. (Lanham, MD: Lexington Books, 2018), 11–30.

43. See Samuel C. Woolley, "Automating Power: Social Bot Interference in Global Politics," *First Monday* 21, no. 4 (2016), https://firstmonday.org/ojs/index.php/fm/article/view/6161.

44. Eli Pariser, *The Filter Bubble: How the New Personalized Web is Changing What We Read and How We Think* (New York: Penguin, 2012).

45. Safiya Umoja Noble, *Algorithms of Oppression: How Search Engines Reinforce Racism* (New York: New York University Press, 2018); André Brock Jr., *Distributed Blackness: African American Cybercultures* (New York: New York University Press, 2020). See also, Michelle G. Gibbons, "Persona 4.0," *Quarterly Journal of Speech*, 7, no. 1 (2021): 49–72.

46. Jessica Marie Johnson and Mark Anthony Neal, "Introduction: Wild Seed in the Machine," *Black Scholar* 47, no. 3 (2017): 1; Tara L. Conley, "Decoding Black Feminist Hashtags as Becoming," *Black Scholar* 47, no. 3 (2017): 22–32.

47. Aaron Hess, "Introduction," in *Theorizing Digital Rhetoric*, ed. Aaron Hess and Amber Davisson (New York: Routledge, 2018), 4.

48. Richard A. Lanham, *The Electronic Word: Democracy, Technology, and the Arts* (Chicago: University of Chicago Press, 1993).

49. Richard A. Lanham, *The Economics of Attention: Style and Substance in the Age of Information* (Chicago: University of Chicago Press, 2006).

50. The matter of unwanted attention also deserves note here. See Jiyeon Kang, "Call for Civil Inattention: 'RaceFail '09'and Counterpublics on the Internet," *Quarterly Journal of Speech* 105, no. 2 (2019): 133–155.

51. Barbara Warnick and David S. Heineman, *Rhetoric Online: The Politics of New Media* (New York: Peter Lang, 2012).

52. Simon Usborne, "The Expert Whose Children Gatecrashed His TV Interview: 'I Thought I'd Blown It in Front of the Whole World,'" *Guardian*, accessed November 27, 2020, https://www.the guardian.com/media/2017/dec/20/robert-kelly-south-korea-bbc-kids-gatecrash-viral-storm.

53. Malcolm Gladwell, "The Stickiness Factor," in *The Tipping Point: How Little Things Can Make a Big Difference* (New York: Little, Brown, and Co., 2000), 89–132.

54. As quoted in Gladwell, "The Stickiness Factor," 95.

55. Henry Jenkins, "What Wikipedia Can Teach Us about the New Media Literacies (Part One)," henryjenkins.org, June 25, 2007, http://henryjenkins.org/blog/2007/06/what_wikipedia_can_teach_us_ab.html. See also, Henry Jenkins, Sam Ford, and Joshua Green, *Spreadable Media: Creating Value and Meaning in a Networked Culture* (New York: New York University Press, 2013).

56. Laurie E. Gries, "Iconographic Tracking: A Digital Research Method for Visual Rhetoric and Circulation Studies," *Computers and Composition* 30 (2013): 335.

57. See Natalia Mielczarek, "The 'Pepper Spraying Cop' Icon and Its Internet Memes: Social Justice and Public Shaming Through Rhetorical Transformation in Digital Culture," *Visual Communication Quarterly* 25, no. 2 (2018): 67–81.

58. Mielczarek, "The 'Pepper Spraying Cop' Icon." See also Natalia Mielczarek, "The Situation Room Icon and Its Internet Memes: Subversion of the Osama Bin Laden Raid and Fragmentation of Iconicity in Remix Culture," *First Monday* 25, no. 6 (2020) https://doi.org/10.5210/fm.v25i6.10531.

59. Jim Ridolfo and Dànielle Nicole DeVoss, "Composing for Recomposition: Rhetorical Velocity and Delivery," *Kairos: A Journal of Rhetoric, Technology, and Pedagogy* 13, no. 2 (2009), http://kairos.technorhetoric.net/13.2/topoi/ridolfo_devoss/velocity.html.

60. Gries, "Iconographic Tracking," 333.

61. Laurie E. Gries, *Still Life with Rhetoric*. As Lester Olson observes, recirculations always constitute repurposings that remake a text's meaning, "Pictorial Representations of British America Resisting Rape: Rhetorical Re-Circulation of a Print Series Portraying the Boston Port Bill of 1774," *Rhetoric & Public Affairs* 12, no. 1 (2009): 1–36. See also Mary E. Stuckey, "On Rhetorical Circulation," *Rhetoric & Public Affairs* 15, no. 4 (2012): 609–612; Jenny Edbauer, "Unframing Models of Public Distribution: From Rhetorical Situation to Rhetorical Ecologies," *Rhetoric Society Quarterly* 35, no. 4 (2005): 5–24.

62. Jenkins, Ford, and Green, *Spreadable Media*, 3.

63. Jenkins, Ford, and Green, *Spreadable Media*, 7.

64. Michael Calvin McGee, "Text, Context, and the Fragmentation of Contemporary Culture," *Western Journal of Speech Communication* 54 (1990): 274–289.

65. Megan Foley, "Sound Bites: Rethinking the Circulation of Speech from Fragment to Fetish," *Rhetoric & Public Affairs* 15, no. 4 (2012): 614.

66. Foley, "Sound Bites," 620.

67. Karlyn Kohrs Campbell, "Agency: Promiscuous and Protean," *Communication and Critical/Cultural Studies* 2, no. 1 (2005): 3.

68. See Cheryl Geisler, "How Ought We To Understand the Concept of Rhetorical Agency? Report from the ARS," *Rhetoric Society Quarterly* 34, no. 3 (2004): 9–17.

69. Gina Neff, Tim Jordan, and Joshua McVeigh-Schultz, "Affordances, Technical Agency, and the Politics of Technologies of Cultural Production," *Culture Digitally*, January 23, 2012, http://culturedigitally.org/2012/01/affordances-technical-agency-and-the-politics-of-technologies-of-cultural-production-2/.

70. Anne Teresa Demo, "Hacking Agency," 277.

71. Jane Bennett, *Vibrant Matter: A Political Ecology of Things* (Durham, NC: Duke University Press, 2010), 23; see also, Dustin Edwards and Heather Lang, "Entanglements That Matter: A New Materialist Trace of #YesAllWomen," in *Circulation, Writing and Rhetoric*, ed. Laurie Gries and Collin Gifford Brooke (Logan: Utah State University Press, 2018), 118–134. Nathaniel Rivers, "Tracing the Missing Masses: Vibrancy, Symmetry, and Public Rhetoric Pedagogy," *enculturation*, March 17, 2014, http://enculturation.net/missingmasses.

72. Ian Bogost, *Persuasive Games*, 28–29.

73. Justine Sacco (@JustineSacco), "Going to Africa. Hope I don't get AIDS. Just kidding. I'm white!," Twitter, December 20, 2013, 10:19 a.m., https://www.theguardian.com/world/2013/dec/22/pr-exec-fired-racist-tweet-aids-africa-apology. Following the backlash, she deleted her account, and someone else assumed her handle

74. As quoted in Jon Ronson, "How One Stupid Tweet Blew Up Justine Sacco's Life," *New York Times Magazine*, February 12, 2015, https://www.nytimes.com/2015/02/15/magazine/how-one-stupid-tweet-ruined-justine-saccos-life.html. For a comprehensive account of the incident, see Jon Ronson, *So You've Been Publicly Shamed* (New York: Riverhead Books, 2015).

75. Some also take issue with how Sacco was later sympathetically figured as an emblem of the problem of online shaming. See Patrick Blanchfield, "Twitter's Outrage Machine Should Be Stopped. But Justine Sacco is the Wrong Poster Child," *Washington Post*, February 24, 2015, https://www.washingtonpost.com/posteverything/wp/2015/02/24/twitters-rage-mob-should-be-stopped-but-justine-sacco-is-the-wrong-poster-child/?arc404=true.

76. See Ronson, *So You've Been Publicly Shamed*.

77. For an account of online public shaming as epideictic discourse, see Jodie Nicotra, "Disgust, Distributed: Virtual Public Shaming as Epideictic Assemblage," *enculturation*, July 6, 2016, http://enculturation.net/disgust-distributed.

78. See Aristotle, *Art of Rhetoric*, trans. J. H. Freese (Cambridge, MA: Harvard University Press, 2000); for an overview, see also James Jasinski, "Epideictic Discourse," in *Sourcebook on Rhetoric: Key Concepts in Contemporary Rhetorical Studies* (Thousand Oaks, CA: Sage, 2001), 209–215.

79. Nicotra, "Disgust, Distributed."

80. Elon Musk (@elonmusk), "Just looked at my wiki for 1st time in years. It's insane! Btw, can someone please delete 'investor'. I do basically zero investing." Twitter, December 22, 2019, 11:24 a.m. PT, https://twitter.com/elonmusk/status/1208830673995198465.

81. "Forbes' 35th Annual World's Billionaires List: Facts and Figures 2021," *Forbes*, https://www.forbes.com/sites/kerryadolan/2021/04/06/forbes-35th-annual-worlds-billionaires-list-facts-and-figures-2021/?sh=1c6d1a0f5e58.

82. Monica Anderson, Paul Hitlin, and Michelle Atkinson, "Wikipedia at 15: Millions of Readers in Scores of Languages," Pew Research Center, January 14, 2016, https://www.pewresearch.org/fact-tank/2016/01/14/wikipedia-at-15/; "Total Page Views," Wikimedia Statistics, accessed October 30, 2020, https://stats.wikimedia.org/#/all-projects/reading/total-page-views/normal|table|2019-01-27~2020-10-24|~total|monthly.

83. See also, Gary Trock, "Mark Wahlberg Accused of Editing Wikipedia After Hate Crimes Resurface," *Blast*, June 7, 2020, https://theblast.com/132854/mark-wahlberg-accused-of-editing-wikipedia-after-hate-crimes-res.

84. "Wikipedia: Neutral Point of View," Wikipedia, accessed November 28, 2020, https://en.wikipedia.org/wiki/Wikipedia:Neutral_point_of_view.

85. "Wikipedia: Conflict of Interest," Wikipedia, accessed November 28, 2020, https://en.wikipedia.org/wiki/Wikipedia:Conflict_of_interest.

86. Kenneth Burke, *Language as Symbolic Action: Essays on Life, Literature, and Method* (Berkeley: University of California Press, 1966), 45.

87. "Kim Kardashian," Wikipedia, accessed November 28, 2020, https://en.wikipedia.org/wiki/Kim_Kardashian.

88. "Ray J," Wikipedia, accessed November 28, 2020, https://en.wikipedia.org/wiki/Ray_J.

89. "Talk: Elon Musk," Wikipedia, accessed August 17, 2020, https://en.wikipedia.org/wiki/Talk:Elon_Musk.

90. See Damien Smith Pfister, "Networked Expertise in the Era of Many-To-Many Communication: On Wikipedia and Invention," *Social Epistemology* 25, no. 3 (2011): 228.

91. "#ShareYourEars," Disney, accessed November 25, 2020, https://dccr.disney.com/share-your-ears.html. The time frame to which these figures apply is unclear. It appears they reflect only the first few months of the campaign, but there is room for other interpretations. No matter the time frame, the numbers are impressive.

92. Julia Turner, "#InPraiseOfTheHashtag," *New York Times Magazine*, November 2, 2012, https://www.nytimes.com/2012/11/04/magazine/in-praise-of-the-hashtag.html.

93. Jennifer Reinwald, "Hashtags and Attention Through the Tetrad: The Rhetorical Circulation of #ALSIceBucketChallenge," in *Theorizing Digital Rhetoric*, ed. Aaron Hess and Amber Davisson (New York: Routledge, 2018), 185. See also Caroline Dadas, "Hashtag Activism: The Promise and Risk of 'Attention,'" in *Social Writing/Social Media: Publics, Presentations, and Pedagogies*, ed. Douglas M. Walls and Stephanie Vie (Fort Collins, CO: WAC Clearinghouse: Perspectives on Writing, 2017), 17–36.

94. Warnick and Heineman, *Rhetoric Online*, 62–74.

95. For a discussion of that particular campaign via the lens of attention, see Reinwald, "Hashtags and Attention."

96. See Catherine L. Langford and Montené Speight, "#BlackLivesMatter: Epistemic Positioning, Challenges, and Possibilities," *Journal of Contemporary Rhetoric* 5, no. 3/4 (2015): 78–89; Borda and Marshall, "Creating a Space"; Dadas, "Hashtag Activism."

97. As of the time of writing, the game is available here, https://pbskids.org/sesame/games/a-job-for-me/.

98. Bogost, *Persuasive Games*.

99. William H. McRaven, "University of Texas at Austin 2014 Commencement Address—Admiral William H. McRaven," May 19, 2014, https://www.youtube.com/watch?v=pxBQLFLei70&ab_channel=TexasExes

17

Critical Rhetoric

An Orientation Toward Criticism

Raymie E. McKerrow

Rhetorical criticism has had a long and distinguished history within the communication discipline. Although my purpose here is not to chronicle that history, it is important to recognize that our current endeavors have been made possible by working from our extension or alteration of earlier approaches. Critical approaches outlined in detail in other chapters of this text were based on earlier work, just as future approaches will be built upon, or emerge as counters to, current scholarly perspectives on what constitutes a useful approach.[1] The perspective labeled **critical rhetoric** emerged similarly—it was an outgrowth of key developments in critical inquiry in the 1970s–1980s as critics sought new ways to answer questions about specific discursive events. We had moved through a period in which a "public address" approach dominated scholarly inquiry in focusing on "great speakers" and their speeches.

As protests abounded during the tumultuous years of the civil rights movement and the Vietnam War, in particular, scholars began to critique older approaches as insufficient in analyzing protest discourse. As one example, Herbert Simons's now-classic essay on social movement rhetoric offered new tools for the critic; his work stimulated others to provide additional critical tools.[2] As early as 1972, Philip Wander and Steven Jenkins challenged the then-conventional approach to criticism in an essay titled "Rhetoric, Society, and the Critical Response."[3] At the time they were writing, the critic stood apart from the discourse and analyzed it in a purported objective fashion—his or her own political stance and what was thought about the values of the discourse being examined were considered off limits. Their conclusion with respect to making clear one's own political stance and addressing values implicit or explicit in a discursive act is worth repeating here: "The purpose of writing criticism is to share a world of meaning with other human beings. . . . The critic offers, along with a particular judgment, and way of judging, a definition of being. . . . [T]he critic is but one human being trying to communicate with other human beings. Criticism, at its best, is informed talk about matters of importance."[4]

A decade later, Wander followed up with an essay, "The Ideological Turn in Modern Criticism,"[5] that captured the conversation that was occurring at that time. This essay went beyond the "critical response" to articulate what the aim of such criticism might be: to engage readers with judgments about what thought and/or action might follow from the critical appraisal of a given event. In essence, the critic goes beyond a description of "what happened" to "what should have happened" and/or "what should happen now." This was a dramatic "turn" toward a new engagement with events in the world and the critic's role as an "ideological critic." In its broadest sense (and there are many definitions of the term), **ideology** captures the worldview of a person, group, community, and/or society at a given moment in time. As I write, Donald Trump has been impeached by the House, and the Senate is determining how it will respond once the House sends the articles of impeachment forward. The division between Democrats, largely supporting impeachment, and Republicans, largely against the action taken by the House, proceeds on the basis of two different, seemingly incommensurable orientations toward events. As another example, the oft-used phrase "political correctness," more than likely expressed in a disparaging tone, gives a name to a difference in ideological **frames**[6] between those who see language as potentially demeaning or denigrating of the dignity of others, and those who see such concerns as trivial nonsense.[7] An important point for us to remember is that the critic gives voice to his or her own ideological commitments in the act of evaluating the discourse of others. A "conservative leaning" critic may well come to different conclusions than another like-minded critic, and could agree on occasion with a "liberal leaning" critic. Thus, ideological stances are not tidy, discreet positions that preclude differences in judgment or the possibility of agreement across differences; nonetheless, the move in this direction among critics was a precursor to the articulation of what has become known as the "critical rhetoric project." That project takes its cue from Wander's conclusion: "Criticism takes an ideological stance when it recognizes the existence of powerful vested interests benefiting from and consistently urging politics and technology that threaten life on this planet . . . and commends rhetorical analyses not only of the actions implied but also of the interests represented."[8] This does not mean that all critical actions are equal or even successful. As I have written on an earlier occasion: "If it does what it intends to do—in creating a sense of how something works, or fails in some respect to achieve its goals—it may still be judged wanting. There is no guarantee set in advance of a critical act that it will produce something of value to those it addresses."[9]

STARTING POINTS: CRITICAL RHETORIC

What is meant by "critical rhetoric," and what does it mean to use it as a way to understand or analyze rhetorical practice? What's the point of criticism if judgment is not reached in some sense—so that we know what we think about an event? How should one frame critical rhetorical practice? Is it best conceived as a formalized *method* of rhetorical analysis? Is it the only way, or just another way, to critically appraise discursive events?

In what follows, I respond to the questions introduced above in underscoring the thesis that critical rhetoric is best viewed as a fluid and flexible **orientation**, not a formal, rule-governed method. It has never been intended to serve—either primarily or secondarily—as a conventional rhetorical perspective. I take my cue from Kenneth Burke: "Orientation is thus a bundle of judgments as to how things were, how they are, and how they may be." He goes on to note that "orientation is a reading from 'what is' to 'what may be.'"[10] How you see the world conditions how you respond to events within it.

Thus, the adoption of an orientation—in all that the term embodies—is the best way to ensure that critical rhetoric is applied to the fullest of its emancipatory potential. Conceived in this way, a critical orientation is a practice that "encourages a creativity unencumbered by specific or privileged methodological considerations."[11] It may employ more specific "analytic perspectives" which, as Jim A. Kuypers notes in chapter 3, function as frames "a critic uses to help guide the criticism of a rhetoric artifact." These perspectives are, within a critical rhetoric orientation, always in the service of an overarching orientation toward how discourse operates in a fragmented and destabilized social world. Adopting a critical stance toward the world is precisely the orientation that animates the critical rhetoric project. As Kent Ono suggests, "taking a critical stance means addressing issues of power; taking such a perspective helps broaden the focus of critical scholarship and brings together varying critical traditions."[12] In terms of emancipation from forces that dominate action, this approach examines possibilities for altering relations of power to enable a different, and hopefully more favorable, set of relations to come into existence.

Before taking up these matters in greater detail, it is important to revisit the putative "starting point" for the critical rhetoric project. From a traditional perspective, the starting point for criticism focuses on an active *agent* who seeks to effect change in his or her environment through suasive speech, symbolic expression, or other stylized means of broadcasting an idea, creating an event, or taking a public stand. Examples abound: annual "Take Back the Night" marches, environmental protests against "fracking," and the #MeToo movement are contemporary illustrations of citizens taking action. Each of the persons involved in these kinds of protests is, of course, identifiable as a sentient actor and may certainly be evaluated rhetorically for the words or deeds he or she has said or done at a particular time and place. Criticism that begins with the focus on the agent is a worthwhile endeavor, but it is not the only approach that might be useful in answering specific questions. Thus, while acknowledging the value of an agent-centered approach, I wish to stress that there exist other means of achieving answers to questions one might have about events. Such means are sometimes grounded upon conceptions of public space, power relations, and the nature of public speech and action that are not as accessible to analysis from an agent-centered approach. Contrary to John M. Murphy's claim that this orientation deprivileges other approaches, the intent of the original critical rhetoric article in 1989 (perhaps not as clearly achieved as I might wish) was to suggest that some questions may be better answered via approaches that work from a different position or utilize different approaches.[13] Not all criticism is created equal; some critical attempts will work better than others. Those engaged in a critical rhetoric perspective are not immune to this assessment. Nevertheless, as I have argued before,

> There is no single approach or perspective that stands above all others as the preferred means of enacting a critical perspective on any artifact. That said, it is equally the case that some approaches are better suited to analyze specific artifacts or events. The critical principle that underlies a value judgment on which approach is most likely to be helpful is first, what is the question being asked, and second, what is the best approach to use in answering that question. Some questions demand quantitative answers, while others are better suited to qualitative approaches.[14]

The starting point for the critical rhetoric project is not the active agent seeking change, though as noted above, I do not deny the efficacy or reality of **agency** as an ever-present persuasive force in human affairs. But I do, however, choose to begin elsewhere. In what may be the most oft-cited phrase in the original essay, "a critical rhetoric seeks to unmask or demystify the discourse of power. The aim is to understand the integration of power/knowledge in society—what possibilities for change the integration invites or inhibits and what intervention strategies might be considered appropriate to effect social change."[15] What this expression means in the act of critiquing discourse is the focus of the remainder of this chapter.

DIFFERENTIATING CRITIQUES OF DOMINATION AND FREEDOM

Consistent with Wander's injunction, there are two forms of critical analysis that form a common basis for a critical practice. As suggested above, both interrogate the existence of power relations between individuals, between individuals and agencies that have some influence or control over their lives, between groups (including those that are seen as belonging together and those that may be marginalized or excluded from participation), or even between nation-states. The first has been earmarked as a **critique of domination**. This critique has an emancipatory aim, what I have elsewhere noted as a "freedom from"[16] that which controls the beliefs or actions of others. In this context, power is seen as oppressive—as an example, consider the reason for the existence of "Hollaback" organizations within social communities. Women, tired of hearing leering, sexually suggestive comments from thoughtless males have taken to sharing their experiences online—"hollering back," as it were, in rejecting the, in their terms, sophomoric immaturity of grown men. In so doing, they assist in creating a sense of solidarity among those who no longer wish to be treated as an object. A critic examining the "Hollaback" movement would focus on the language and actions of both perpetrators and those who are on the receiving end of such unwanted attention. The power difference between those harassing women and the women themselves is a focus of the critique—how might one respond in a way that challenges the perceived right to annoy another?

The key problem with a sole focus on liberation or emancipation from oppression is "what happens next." The focus can be so tightly drawn that all one sees in front of them is the oppression and the possible means to remove its influence. Once "free," where does one go next? What change in life is presented in the absence of what has thus far been a controlling factor in choices made or not made?

The second critical practice can be seen as the "flip side" of the domination critique, as the **critique of freedom** focuses attention on "freedom to" be other than what one is at the present moment. In this context, the focus also shifts from a view of power as solely oppressive (putting someone under one's control) to a sense of power that is potentially productive. It is "a positive force which creates social relations and sustains them through the appropriation of a discourse that 'models' the relations through its expression."[17] A cautionary note is needed here: I am not suggesting that one critical practice follows the other in every case. Rather, what I want to suggest is that these two practices have a logic that can tie them together, but they also may operate independently of each other. As an example of a sole focus on "freedom" in practice, what are the possibilities in your own life for becoming other than you are at this moment in time? What are the openings for change that a productive use of present power relations between siblings, friends, or partners (one or all) might create? At this point, it may be useful to unpack "power relations" a bit more: consider a personal relation with a significant other. Who makes what kind of decisions? Who is "in charge" or are both sharing equally in deciding where to go, what to spend money on, etc? When might one defer to another's judgment? When might roles switch? Then, assume change of one kind or another in your personal relationship does occur—what then? Are you satisfied, are you comfortable with your new relationship? Are you finished? The key assumption that I am making here is this: one is never "perfected." One may always be on the move toward perfection but never quite reach it. Something is always open to criticism and the possibility of change. This is the essence of what has been termed **continual critique**. In this instance, "new social relations which emerge from a reaction to critique are themselves simply new forms of power and hence subject to renewed skepticism."[18] You may not make a change as a result of the critique, but your changes are always open to future reconsideration. Assume for the moment that a new world order has arrived, and the feminists are in charge (review that chapter and pick your type of feminism here—there is more than one). Is the world a perfect place as a result of the new relations of power that exist, the new values that determine what actions are now appropriate? It may be better for some, worse for others. The point of circling back and reexamining the new social relations is precisely to determine what the possible new future might be beyond what is now present.

In promoting an analytic perspective that underscores this commitment to continual critique, it might be useful to take up Kenneth Burke's injunction that "the symbolic act is the *dancing of an attitude*";[19] conceiving of discourse in this sense is another way to understand how one operates from within a critical perspective. Following Burke, a critic understands that words matter. It is not true that "sticks and stones may break my bones, but words will never harm me." Attitudes toward the world, and the acceptance or rejection of the power relations that exist within it at a given moment in time, are either explicit or implicit in the language used to reflect the world. With this much in mind, we would stress that what the individual agent can or cannot do assumes a much different flavor when the question of how power relations intersect with the possibilities for "who can talk to whom with what impact" is raised. In particular, within the critical rhetoric project, the rhetorical emphasis does not hinge on an agent's ability to perform certain rhetorical acts. Rather, the emphasis is on those seen or unseen relational properties within which the agent—as agent—is contained and with which he or she must contend in the social world.

To use Kuypers's language, we might say that the critical rhetoric project frames the rhetorical analysis from a different starting point than traditional approaches to criticism.[20] This is not at all to dismiss other modes of analysis or other starting points. To argue, for example, that an agent-centered point of departure is *the* premier analytic frame for all analyses of public action is as wrongheaded as arguing that the same distinction in fact belongs to critical rhetoric. Both assertions are or would be fatuous, indemonstrable, and unhelpful. As I have noted elsewhere, what prompts the adoption of a particular perspective is not the critical frame itself but *the questions one seeks to answer* (and this is just as true under more traditional formulations as it is for the critical orientation advanced here).[21] The chosen rhetorical mode is informed by the phenomenon, not the reverse. For this reason, critical rhetoric is (or should be) as open to embrace or dismissal as any other frame of inquiry. To be more precise here, it is not the case that critical rhetoric subsumes all other forms or approaches to criticism that engage power relations. It is not "the be-all and end-all" of critical perspectives. To claim that critics whose intent is to critique colonial domination are enacting a "critical rhetoric" is to diminish their entire cultural history and reason for enacting a critical assessment. To do so is a cultural misappropriation of their experience.

ENACTING A CRITICAL STANCE

The foregoing sets the scene as a prelude to actually employing a critical stance. How one enacts critical rhetoric has been a major question. Three considerations are critical here: (1) What is the "object" of study? (2) What should one look for/at in executing a critique? and (3) What role do persons, as communicators, play with respect to enacting this critical stance?

Critic as Inventor

With respect to the "object" of study, critical rhetoric reverses the phrase "public address" and instead focuses attention on *"that symbolism which addresses publics."*[22] If conducted as designed, the reversal assumes the critic is not looking solely at a speaker-speech scenario but is rather seeking to "invent" the object of critique out of the varying ways in which symbols influence people. This may be a speaker/speech situation, but it is not predicated on that context alone. Moreover, going beyond that "public address" to consider how the discourse operates within a broader context is also an option for the critic. The **critic as inventor** does not conceive of invention as making things up out of nothing but rather as discerning, within the vast and complex world of signs and symbols, what influences might be present in determining how one's own orientation is formed or altered. As an example, think back to when you were entering your teen years—what were the symbols that informed your sense of who you were and how you were supposed to look and act at that time? What would you examine now if you were looking to answer this question? Would teen magazines be one resource? Would television shows from that era be another resource? How do these resources influence the actions you took at the time to improve or change yourself? The choices you make in answering the question will differ from those others will make in answering the same question for themselves—that is not a problem, as the key is not to arrive at a single uniform answer but to construct one that makes sense not only to you but to others whom you inform regarding your findings.

Principles of Praxis

With respect to what the critic looks for, if this were a "method," a formal perspective, it would be fairly easy to establish guidelines for its correct use. In conducting Burkean criticism, for example, one will normally consider the pentad (see the chapter on Burke in this volume by Ryan Eric McGeough and Andrew King). If one is critiquing inaugural addresses, the methods outlined by William Benoit in this volume would be useful. An orientation lacks this precision with respect to identifying specific "tools" to utilize in engaging in criticism. However, all is not lost, as the **principles of praxis** introduced in the original critical rhetoric essay provide a direction—they serve not as guidelines for criticism but as ways of conceiving of the rhetorical act and as potential indices to consider when beginning to critique. These are presented below with a very brief explanation of the intent behind the principle:[23]

1. "*Ideologiekritic* [ideological criticism] is in fact not a method, but a practice."[24] The intent here is not to suggest that method is unimportant but rather to remind the critic that a slavish devotion to method may constrain the imagination. For instance, Burke never referenced the pentad explicitly in his classic essay on Hitler, nor do journalists outline their articles with subheadings indicating "who, what, when, and where." Instead, these function as possibilities to consider in examining any situation. In the same way, ideological criticism is an open-ended approach to understanding how people's worldviews condition their beliefs and actions.

2. The discourse of power is material. Quoting Göran Therborn is instructive here (though I would read "men" as an artifact of the times): "ideology operates as discourse. . . . [It] is the medium through which men make their history as conscious actors."[25] In making

history, we (all of us) recognize that words matter—they reflect who's in power and what that power might do for us or against us.

3. Rhetoric constitutes *doxastic* rather than *epistemic* knowledge. In this context, **doxastic** refers to the role of opinion in forming what we know about the world. **Epistemic** refers to that knowledge which is certain—which does not change as time changes. For the most part, we argue about those things that are not self-evident, that are not certain or epistemically grounded. Rhetoric operates in the realm of contingent knowledge—that which could easily be otherwise than what it is currently perceived to be.

4. *Naming* is the central symbolic act of a *nominalist* rhetoric. This principle draws on the assumption that language assists in constituting who we are—how we see ourselves. To give someone a name is to say something specific about how you see them—as "arrogant," "foolish," "studly," or . . . the list goes on in conveying an attitude that may be appropriately or inappropriately applied. **Nominalism** (the philosophical position a nominalist takes) in this sense suggests that when you hear a general term such as "dog," you automatically relate it to a specific dog you are familiar with—the general term has no explicit existence. "Criminal," as a designation of a person, has existence only in application to specific individuals who may or may not deserve that label.

5. *Influence* is not *causality*. Why did you do that? If you've ever been asked this question, you know the person is looking for the cause of your action. Influences on your behavior are not as precise—they may or may not lead to specific actions, as they may be ignored. The presence of a particular symbol may or may not influence you to see the world in a certain way or be important in considering how you should act.

6. *Absence* is as important as *presence* in understanding and evaluating symbolic action. This principle suggests that we need to examine the "not said" or the "not present" as well as what is said and seen in evaluating a situation. It is said that history is written by the victors—which likely explains why, for years, "Custer's Last Stand" was represented only as a "white man's" memorial. Only recently has a memorial to the Native Americans who died there been constructed. Unfortunately, their presence is still "absent" in the artifacts available to purchase.

7. Fragments contain the potential for *polysemic* rather than *monosemic* interpretation. If *mono-* represents singularity, it is pretty clear that *polysemic* suggests that there is more than one reading possible in critiquing any event. Your goal as a critic is not to "get it right" in terms of the one and only meaning an event might have. Rather, it is to provide a defensible interpretation—one that seems reasonable on its face, even while others may see something else in the event.

8. Criticism is a *performance*. You are performing your sense of who you are as a critic; you are implicated in the choices made in the act of criticizing and accept an obligation to argue on behalf of the claims you advance (a position already made by Kuypers in chapter 3 on what criticism entails). The latter commitment is what Wander means in suggesting that critique has taken an "ideological turn."

Agent as Effect

The third question, the role of the person in enacting change, is more complex. On the one hand, critical rhetoric does not deny the possibility of a person taking action to change a situation. The sense in which a person's saying or doing something is perceived as a cause is not precluded from critical rhetoric's scope. Far from it, for change would be almost impossible to consider if one were blinded to either person or agency—seen as the person's ability to act or influence an event. As I have noted, "the subject, as citizen and social actor, is capable of acting. . . . While not wholly formed through discourse, it is through that discourse that the subject gives expression"[26] to its being-in-the-world. As a speaking subject, a person expresses judgment in the form of critique—sharing or formulating a position on the world as it exists, leading to a world that it might yet become. What is implicit is that in and through its expression, the becoming world is once again subject to reflexive judgment as to its well-suitedness in the lives of those it engages. Hence, the work in this formulation is to seek to remain within a more traditional focus on the speaking subject as the source that effects all change.

On the other hand, critical rhetoric *does* pursue a reframing of the basis for that action, and it understands action's meaning(s)—in a sphere of social action—very differently. Instead of focusing on the person as the cause of an action, the emphasis shifts to their role as "an effect" of the event and/or language that has preceded their action. In other words, the critic focuses on what conditions produced the action taken—what were the constraints that limited the range of responses that were possible in this setting? The purpose is to consider the broader *rhetorical* possibilities for freedom (or limitation) of action that might exist in a given discursive context—either through its denial or resistance, or through its refashioning into an unfamiliar form—*prior* to essaying a formal evaluation of that action itself. Thus, the focus of a critical rhetoric is on unpacking and outlining the conditions that have created the present situation and from that analysis determining what the potential avenues for change are that might be further explored.

THE CONTEXT FOR CRITIQUE

Within the context of both a critique of domination and a critique of freedom, in considering the need for continual critique, the critic must insistently acknowledge that rhetorical power lies in whatever social activities ground the discursive act under investigation.[27] The power to do and say things in or for a community, for example, presumes that power is both a discrete possession that speakers control and one that they distribute as they choose. Once again, this does not suggest that the power to act is an illusion; but once again, the starting point for critical rhetoric is not with the agent as *rhetor*. It lies with a careful study of the social or communal situation out of which the rhetor acts.

The question here is not one of protecting a preferred version of the needs (or the good) of the community but rather one of being open to the possibility of any and all avenues toward *freedom*, for two reasons. First, a "critical rhetoric" is by definition one that seeks to liberate—whether from oppression (domination) or from a complacent acceptance of life as it is currently lived (freedom). In this latter sense, "a [critical rhetor's] critique of freedom . . . has as its aim a reflexivity that grounds its actions in a constant reflection on the contingency of human relations and can best be styled as a 'freedom to' move toward new relations with others."[28] Second, to begin with the presumption that the rhetor knows best, particularly in the absence of even partial knowledge of those formation(s) which may inform, restrain, or enable other options, is shortsighted. What are needed are opportunities for a critical rhetor's engagement with the community that permit the broadest array of choices for action—but with the clear and minimal understanding that whatever action is proposed or undertaken may well make for social or communal relations that are not as good or efficient or desirable as one might have hoped, or which are simply wrong for that society at that time. Commitment to change, even when selfless and well intended, cannot be enacted in a single-minded way.

CRITICAL ESSAY

As already suggested, there are a variety of approaches one might take in exercising a critical orientation in the sense outlined in this chapter. A focus on power can take multiple forms. For that reason, I wish to illustrate by examples how several scholars have utilized this orientation, as well as ways in which some have extended it in new directions, as a way to suggest possible avenues for critical inquiry.

USING AND/OR EXTENDING A CRITICAL ORIENTATION

Using CR

Jessica Benham's analysis of gender issues in television focuses on the *Doctor Who* show.[29] She works from both critiques of domination and freedom in illustrating the portrayal of the Doctor's female companions. This is an excellent method-driven study as it examines specific shows where a new female companion is introduced. Her study discusses five themes that implicate the role of power in both oppressive and productive senses: "violation of expected roles, lack of sexualization, destruction of the masculine power equation, development of romantic tensions, and lack of relationships between female companions."[30] A key attribute of a critical orientation is the way in which a researcher's background may influence the analysis. As noted earlier, the critic's role as a performer is an acknowledged facet of the critical act. Benham notes her fan status with respect to the show, as well as her roles as both a woman and a feminist, as her personal history impacts her interpretation of the way women are represented. In framing her study, she provides a brief account of the primary features of a critical orientation and notes specific accounts that critiqued the 1989 essay on critical rhetoric. Her conclusion provides her own recommendations for extending and improving the critical process. This essay serves as a "primer" with respect to how to integrate a systematic approach with a critical orientation toward the object of study.

Thomas Discenna's analysis of the graduate student unionization movement focuses on a "grade strike" in the 1970s at Yale University.[31] This study centers attention on power differentials, as graduate students were considered by Yale's administration to be "interns," not "employees." This distinction addresses the importance of how something is named and the reactions that follow from such decisions. In particular, graduate students were threatened with potential dismissal by their graduate programs if they participated in a "grade strike." Unlike employees, they had no recourse with respect to formal appeals if that action were taken. Discenna's analysis of the "rhetoric of academic professionalism" begins with a summary of unionization efforts by both faculty and graduate students. Are faculty "laborers" in the traditional sense of that term, or are they "professionals" and hence engaged in individual pursuits of the life of the mind, not that of workers seeking to better their working condition through collective action? Yale administrators at the time took advantage of this tension in claiming that graduate students were "apprentices" whose role was that of becoming professionals through their education and roles as "teaching assistants." Given this label, the prospect of a union was not an acceptable means for students to engage in as they sought to have a voice in improving their working conditions. The analysis is an adept illustration of how domination works to keep a group of people in a subordinate position. Discenna's conclusion recognizes that unionization remains "mired in a view of academic work as a life of the mind separate from the more prosaic field of labor."[32] This, plus the growing use of "contingent faculty" (part-time adjuncts), makes it more difficult for graduate students in particular to locate points of entry that would imply a freedom to influence their own future. The future for unionization is not bright, but Discenna notes that we must seek to alter the forced dichotomy between academic and work life in order to protect the rights we have to pursue our interests and be treated well at the same time.[33]

Jonathan Rossing merges critical, rhetorical scholarship with critical race theory (CRT) in an analysis of comedic discourse.[34] He argues that "the origins, aims and strategies of critical rhetoric and CRT present opportunities for reciprocal engagement."[35] After supporting this with a cogent examination of the similarities and the advantages that can be gained in merging these orientations, Rossing focuses attention on Stephen Colbert's use of a "satiric mock-editorial" in addressing the debate over Sonia Sotomayor's Supreme Court nomination. The analysis shows how both function "to address racial oppression and simultaneously work toward positive social transformation."[36] Comedic discourse provides an opportunity to take positions on sensitive topics while submitting values to critique. Rossing provides a detailed account of how Colbert's discourse interrogates white privilege in relation to choosing a Su-preme Court justice. As an example, Colbert's satirical statement is worth noting: "Take the *Dred Scott* case. Those justices' life experiences—being white men in pre–Civil War America, some of whom owned slaves—in *no way* influenced their decision that black people were property."[37] Rossing concludes by returning to his initial premise: comedic discourse is a rich vein to be mined by rhetorical scholars to "advance critiques of racialized culture and gener-ate opportunities to promote social transformation."[38]

As a final illustration, Kristen Hoerl's analysis of news coverage of Obama's inauguration focuses on the media's positive attention given to Martin Luther King Jr.'s legacy in noting that we had just elected the first African American president. The media also crafted a "postracial version" that implied an end to a racialized America.[39] In extending "critical rhetoric's en-gagement with the concepts of remembrance and forgetfulness in public discourse," Hoerl argues that "this myth precludes public memory of radical black dissent that has condemned institutional racism in the United States."[40] We thus forget our history in constructing a mythic portrayal of a race-free society, what Hoerl references as "selective amnesia." She concludes that "a critical rhetoric attendant to the discursive processes by which public amnesia is constructed may help to enrich our resources for envisioning social change and the means of attaining social justice."[41] Her study advances the case for a critical orientation to discourse that creates, through amnesia, an "absence" that must be noted.

Extending CR

Several scholars have worked from the original formulation in creating innovative exten-sions. For example, Brian Ott and Carl Burgchardt employ a critical rhetoric orientation as a starting point in engaging ideas that culminate in a divergence from that orientation, arguing that it does not possess "the dialogic dimension essential to critical pedagogy."[42] What they are saying, in effect, is that the critical rhetoric orientation does not demand attention to talk-ing together (dialogue) in a way that acknowledges the power differences between teachers and students (critical pedagogy is implied here). At the same time, they note the positive values of a critique of freedom and go on to suggest that "at a minimum, this means acknowl-edging one's own ideological commitments and positionality as they are mediated by socially contingent networks of power" in order to "foster agentive citizenship and promote political alternatives."[43] This is an excellent way of expressing what is intended in terms of a critique of freedom—permanent criticism is not a recipe for inaction but rather a recognition that power relations are open to change across time. That action requires due diligence with respect to how current power relations either foster or inhibit the possibilities inherent in improving our lives. They illustrate what they mean by a "critical-rhetorical pedagogy" and the importance of dialogic criticism through an analysis of the film *Schindler's List*. Their analysis underscores the value of using film as a teaching tool, especially in engendering dialogue that is instructive. In the process, they evince a very positive view of student accountability in engaging a productive (in the sense of power relations) conversation that enables them to develop critical awareness of themselves and their world. They conclude in noting that critical-rhetorical pedagogy "conceives of criticism as a dialogic encounter with(in) a much wider (and always unfolding) constellation of discourses involving the text, critical commentary on the text, and classroom conversation surrounding the text."[44]

Art Herbig and Aaron Hess articulate a promising new direction in addressing what they term convergent critical rhetoric—an analysis that integrates rhetoric, ethnography, and documentary film production elements into a cohesive framework.[45] The analysis builds on prior work that brings rhetorical analysis and ethnographic methods into conversation. In the past, these have seemed to be separate approaches, but "blending the tools of the rhetorician with the skills of an ethnographer can lead to insights that neither can produce alone."[46] Adding media production tools expands the potential for the critic, especially in directing attention to the way documentary film uses language. In preparation for the analysis, they attended the Rally to Restore Sanity and taped interviews with other attendees—they reference the YouTube video they created in supporting the claims advanced. A key advance in this study is the fact that the authors "productively participate in the discourses we also seek to critique."[47] This takes a critical orientation at face value in blurring the lines between critic as observer and critic as participant.

More recently, I coedited a set of essays with Art Herbig that appear in the *International Journal of Communication*.[48] Brandon M. Daniels and Kendall R. Phillips provide a historical review that, beginning with the original 1989 essay, chronicles the evolution of critical rhetoric's changes over the past thirty years. They treat, respectively, work by Dana Cloud; John Sloop and Kent Ono; as well as Michael Middleton et al.'s work on "participatory critical rhetoric."

The remaining essays extend critical rhetoric in ways that invite consideration for future developments. Tony Adams focuses attention on "forgiveness" in response to how others have treated us as individuals. While he does not provide a clear solution as to how one should best respond, he does force attention on the possibilities that are open to consideration. Art Herbig, Andrew Hermann, Alix Watson, Adam Tyma, and joan miller add a new "principle of praxis" to the original eight described above—#9: criticism is collaborative. Using their own collaborative work, featured on their "ProfsDoPop" website, they argue that criticism is not always a solitary venture. Collaborating with others enriches the overall critical product that is created.

Aaron Hess, Samantha Senda-Cook, Michael Middleton, and Danielle Endres extend their earlier work on "participatory critical rhetoric." They take a broad view of how one might "participate" as a critic, including observation and actual involvement in the event being assessed. Larry Frey and Joshua Hanan take critical rhetoric into the world of "social activism." They critique critical rhetoric for not privileging "activism" as a key component, and provide an analysis that offers a way to overcome this missing requirement. Dana Cloud also moves into new territory in focusing attention on Gramsci's orientation to freedom and domination. In the process, she offers this as an alternative to a reliance on critical rhetoric as the primary orientation toward criticism.

Jennifer Dunn incorporates an analysis of domination and freedom in her argument that Donald Trump is a "reality TV" president. In particular, she notes that Trump's use of tweeting as a key communication tool creates a new freedom for how future presidents might convey their ideas. Danielle Stern and Katherine Denker provide an incisive analysis of the need to create classroom space that privileges both instructor and student vulnerabilities. The space provides an atmosphere wherein sensitive issues can be discussed without judging individuals for the experiences they share.

Taken together, these essays suggest that, as an orientation, critical rhetoric remains a viable and useful perspective in analyzing communicative messages, regardless of how they are presented (as words, pictures, memes, tweets, or any other of a long list of possibilities).

Conclusion

This essay has sought to underscore critical rhetoric's practice as an *orientation* and to further the explanatory power of an inventional, critical modality in its engagement of discursive and artifactual fragments in the social world. How one carries the impetus to utilize its perspective forward remains open. As the above exemplars have done, you may also do: consider placing yourself inside an orientation that asks questions about the nature of language as it reveals particular formations between and among people, and interrogates the productive capability of power in inhibiting or fostering social action. Opening one's attitude toward events by considering the context whereby the event has come into being will go a long way toward realizing the potential of this critical perspective. Just as Burke eschewed using critical markers (e.g., elements of the pentad) in advancing critical judgment, we would remind readers that critical rhetoric functions as an intellectual backdrop to the critical act—it enjoins asking questions related to how the context forms discourse rather than how discourse effects publics. While recognizing the power accorded the speaker in traditional analyses of public oratory, it yet suggests that there is more to the story. By asking questions of speakers, seen as products of the discourse that produced them, we hope to understand how the discourse came to be in this rather than another time and what possibilities for freedom it hinders or makes available. Intervention as a means of remedying social ills demands no less from us than understanding how we come to be in this time and place, with these sets of attitudes toward events, ourselves, and others. Critical rhetoric is but one starting point in the path toward social action.

PERSONAL REFLECTIONS

Exercising one's voice is about choices, whether responding to another person who has asked a question or writing a scholarly essay. There are, of course, differences in the nature of each response, but the fact remains that one could choose several different ways to "style" one's commentary. My choice in this situation was to highlight the facets of the original critical rhetoric article—the twin "critiques" of domination and freedom and the principles grounding a revised approach toward rhetorical events. Instead of providing a "critical essay" that emulates a method, I elected to illustrate the varying ways in which a critical orientation might be employed, both in terms of remaining largely within the scope of the original critical rhetoric essay's suggestions for criticism as well as exploring ways in which the orientation has been extended in new directions. These exemplars illustrate how critical reflection might work in actual practice. In making this choice, the primary difficulty is in accurately reflecting how each example works from a critical orientation. Whether I have been successful in this goal is left to the reader's judgment.

POTENTIALS AND PITFALLS

In writing theoretical essays, one hopes to have an influence on the work of other scholars. With respect to what has become known as the "critical rhetoric project," it appears that the initial ideas have had a heuristic impact. As noted above, and as the following "critical bibliography" confirms, the "project" remains a viable approach to critical inquiry. These have taken form in ways that adhere fairly closely to the original theory, as extensions and improvements in responding to shortcomings or critical weaknesses, and as oppositional views in order to illustrate the fundamental flaws in the approach.

If you begin with the recognition that traditional rhetoric has a history of emphasizing the "great man speaking well," then **decentering** the role of the speaker as the origin of thought, words, and action raises significant questions. What becomes of the object of criticism if the focus is not on the person speaking?

Especially in this latter context, the following issues become relevant: (1) When you add to this purported "removal" of the active speaker/rhetor a commitment to a recursive or continual critique, a question about the possibility of criticism itself competes for attention. If critique is never ending, what can we say about any specific instance of communication as to its value in achieving specific goals? (2) If you then suggest that the nature of critique does not rest in "method" but rather exists as an "orientation" toward an object, the negative reaction becomes even more strident. How can you possibly know what it is you have, or can argue, if you cannot rest your argument on the mantle of objective, methodical assessment of an object or event?

What follows is an attempt to address two of the primary "pitfalls" that have concerned critics of the "project." First, consider the existence of a *subject*. I attempted to deal with this "flaw" in assessing the possibility of a subject (or speaker) within a critical rhetoric perspective:

> If the subject is decentered . . . can there be a role for the speaker as agent of social change? I answer this question in the affirmative. Resituating the subject does not necessitate the destruction of the speaker. . . . By giving voice to critique, the subject renews self."[49]

What is implied in this response to the issue is that the speaker, though decentered, is not "dead" to the issues involved. At the same time, it also means that we are already immersed in a set of social practices and rituals that are not of our own making—and that we speak from within a conversation that has already prefigured for us the possibilities of expression as well as the range of interpretations that might be most likely. This does not mean everything is "fixed" and determined ahead of time—but it does mean that the discursive formation is not open ended and infinite with respect to who can say what to whom with what effect. You can yell "Fire!" in a crowded room but, in so doing, you already know the possible impact of giving voice to that expression—if there were no fire, nor a possibility of one, what would happen to you as a consequence of people's believing you and acting on that belief? Kuypers does an eloquent job of considering this issue, arguing in part that the role of critical rhetoric "diminishes" the speaker's contribution.[50] While I would not use that label, it is the case that critical rhetoric changes the landscape within which speakers act and react. In aiming for the retention of what is termed "prudence" or "practical wisdom," which in turn actively engages ethical conduct or action, Kuypers argues that a critical rhetoric perspective may fail to contain prudence or "prudent action." Ethics is not automatically removed when adopting a critical rhetoric perspective. Rather, the "scene" (to use a term from Burke's pentadic orientation toward criticism) shifts from the speaker to the context in which the speaker acts. Prudence, as reflective of moral conduct or right action, is still possible within the rhetorical moment. The critical concern is not in "not accounting for the agent as the causative force" but rather lies in "accounting for ethical action or its absence in the rhetorical context." Reminding us of the importance of ethical considerations is a valuable contribution to the project; hence, Kuypers's points are well taken—and accommodated within a slight shift from a focus on the speaker as active agent to the speaker as part of a larger context in which rhetorical action is taken.

My second pitfall involves *the possibility of criticism.* We might start with the observation that criticism and critique are different objects. Criticism is the shallower, narrower term, with a focus on "making things better." Critique, on the other hand, goes deeper and broader—its focus, while on "making things better," is also on the assumptions that ground the very object of critique. As I noted at an earlier time, the propaganda critics of the early twentieth century certainly were focused on improving democracy.[51] But they did not go beyond that to actively suggest that the very assumptions on which democracy was premised were themselves subject to revision. When invoking "critique" as the operative term, we are suggesting that not only do we want to improve our lot, we want to subject the foundations underlying our social relations to scrutiny. Critique does not mean "everything we find is wrong"—that is, it is not inherently fault-finding. We may decide, after examination, that for now at least, specific social practices are fine the way they are. That isn't always likely, but it is at least a logical possibility—and one we need to retain in order not to fall into an irreversible litany of "this is wrong. . . . this is wrong," ad infinitum. Cloud argues, among other things, that the critical rhetoric project may well rob us of the possibility of critique.[52] If we can never finish, how do we say anything is ever "wrong" or in need of correction? Consider the possibility that rhetoric is a moral and material force: it acts on us at every moment of our lives. If that were not the case, we would not be able to affirm such phrases as "a child who lives with criticism learns to criticize." Living in a social relationship bounded by the continual expression of one's flaws may well have an impact on how one sees oneself. Kent Ono and John Sloop's articulation of a "telos" (purpose/goal) for a "sustained critical rhetoric" adds immeasurably to the power of the theoretical stance to make a difference.[53] What is suggested is simply this: we act with purpose within discrete historical moments, and we do judge the social worth of our actions at that moment as hopefully positive. What the critical rhetoric orientation suggests is not that we can't decide anything in the moment, but that once decided, once acted on, as we move on we can't just rest on our laurels. We can't just brush the dust off our hands, say the job is done, and assume all is now right with the world. It may be for then, and for always, but we owe it to ourselves to ask: what changes in power relations does this action portend, and how do those changes affect others? Does the correction of one inequity produce another down the road—one that also should be remedied? What the orientation commits us to is not indecision in the moment but the realization that action is never final. There is no *fini* to the play of human life.

CRITICAL RHETORIC TOP PICKS

The following lists are not exhaustive but reflect work done in advancing the "critical rhetoric project" in both theoretical and critical terms.

McKerrow, Raymie E. "Critical Rhetoric: Theory and Praxis." *Communication Monographs* 56 (1989): 91–111.
———. "Critical Rhetoric in a Postmodern World." *Quarterly Journal of Speech* 77 (1991): 75–78.

———. "Critical Rhetoric and Propaganda Studies." In *Communication Yearbook*, vol. 14, edited by J. Anderson, 249–255. Newbury Park, CA: Sage, 1991.

———. "Critical Rhetoric and the Possibility of the Subject." In *The Critical Turn: Rhetoric and Philosophy in Postmodern Discourse*, edited by I. Angus and L. Langsdorf, 51–67. Carbondale, IL: Southern Illinois Univ. Press, 1993.

———. "Corporeality and Cultural Rhetoric: A Site for Rhetoric's Future." *Southern Communication Journal* 63 (1998): 315–328.

———. "Space and Time in a Postmodern Polity." *Western Journal of Communication* 63 (1999): 271–290.

———. "Critical Rhetoric." In *Encyclopedia of Rhetoric*, edited by T. Sloane, 619–622. New York: Oxford University Press, 2001.

———. "Critical Rhetoric." In *Encyclopedia of Communication Theory*, vol. 1, edited by S. Littlejohn and K. Foss, 234–237. Thousand Oaks, CA: Sage, 2009.

Primarily Theoretical Works Related to Critical Rhetoric

Charland, Maurice. "Finding a Horizon and Telos: The Challenge to Critical Rhetoric." *Quarterly Journal of Speech* 77 (1991): 71–74. While finding much to commend in the perspective, it raises concerns about the potential for "continual critique" to turn into an infinite process, with no end in sight. McKerrow's response to these two pieces is "Critical Rhetoric in a Postmodern World" cited above.

Cloud, Dana L. "The Materiality of Discourse as Oxymoron: A Challenge to Critical Rhetoric." *Western Journal of Communication* 58 (1994): 141–163. This essay chronicles the shift toward a discussion of discourse as material. In particular, McGee and McKerrow's work is critiqued for its alleged shortcomings in advancing ideological criticism. Cloud proposes an alternative perspective in remedying the problems inherent within McGee's and McKerrow's formulations.

Gaonkar, Dilip P. "Performing with Fragments: Reflections on Critical Rhetoric." In *Argument and the Postmodern Challenge*, edited by R. E. McKerrow, 149–155. Annandale, VA: Speech Communication Association, 1993. This essay critiques the alleged absence of reason that follows from assuming a critical rhetoric stance.

Hariman, Robert. "Critical Rhetoric and Postmodern Theory." *Quarterly Journal of Speech* 77 (1991): 67–70. This essay, along with Charland's (see above), is an invited response to the critical rhetoric essay. The essay notes the problematic status of the rhetor as active agent affecting a specific audience if one adopts the orientation provided by a critical rhetoric perspective.

Kuypers, Jim A. "Doxa and a Critical Rhetoric: Accounting for the Rhetorical Agent through Prudence." *Communication Quarterly* 44 (1996): 452–462. As the title suggests, this analysis provides a "correction" to the absence of a central agent enacting change by recasting the sense of doxa and its corollary, "prudence" or "practical wisdom" (e.g., doing the right thing). The changes place responsibility for ethical action within an understanding of the community's will to action.

Murphy, John M. "Critical Rhetoric as Political Discourse." *Argumentation and Advocacy* 32 (1995): 1–15. This essay interrogates McKerrow's penchant for creating dichotomies (in this case—disassociations between opposites, as in permanence/change or domination/freedom) and critiques the absence of an active subject seeking change through the power of the word.

Ono, Kent A., and John M. Sloop. "Commitment to 'Telos'—A Sustained Critical Rhetoric." *Communication Monographs* 59 (1992): 48–60. This essay is sympathetic to the project, and responds directly to the criticism that continual critique makes it impossible to ever "take a stand" for some specific change, as one is always in the mode of critic rather than acting to create change.

Owen, A. Susan, and Peter Ehrenhaus. "Animating a Critical Rhetoric: On the Feeding Habits of American Empire." *Western Journal of Communication* 57, no. 2 (1993): 169–177. DOI: 10.1080/10570319309374440. In a trenchant critique of what they style as "American Empire," they offer clear charge for critical rhetoric: "The practice of critical rhetoric must become as public, as accessible, and as attractive to the broader community as are those cultural forms of empire which seduce us all." (p. 175).

DISCUSSION QUESTIONS

1. The text notes that "the critic goes beyond a description of 'what happened' to 'what should have happened' and/or 'what should happen now'" and that "there is no guarantee set in advance of a critical act that it will produce something of value to those it addresses." Given these two statements, engage others in a small group discussion about what it means to be a critic who goes beyond mere description.

2. The text suggests that "issues of power" are involved in taking a critical stance. Engage others in a small group discussion of how power differences operate in your experience; when do you see power as oppressive—as in some way limiting your ability to act as you might desire.

3. Given the "'principle' that *Naming* is the central symbolic act of a *nominalist* rhetoric," work in small groups to answer this question: How does "naming" operate to both improve or limit the possibility of discussion?

ACTIVITIES

1. Write a short essay (1,000–1,200 words) in which you provide examples that would be possible subjects for a "critique of domination" (e.g., examples which would lead to critique as an emancipatory aim) and a "critique of freedom" (e.g., examples which would emphasize ways "to be" other than one already is).

2. Write a short essay (1,000–1,200 words) in which you engage the following statement in the text: "The **critic as inventor** does not conceive of invention as making things up out of nothing but rather as discerning, within the vast and complex world of signs and symbols, what influences might be present in determining how one's own orientation is formed or altered." Choose a topic area (e.g., what it means to be a feminist) and then describe the influences that one might pull together in understanding how one describes a particular kind of feminist (e.g., what influences would a ten- to thirteen-year-old experience in coming to a belief in feminism?).

3. The text distinguishes between "criticism" and "critique." Write a short essay in which you describe how these terms differ—with specific examples of what one might do in engaging in each term.

NOTES

1. The development of this essay is no different, as it is based on prior versions coauthored with Jeffrey St. John, published in 2005 and 2009 under the title "Critical Rhetoric: The Context for Continual Critique."

2. Herbert Simons, "Requirements, Problems, and Strategies: A Theory of Persuasion for Social Movements," *Quarterly Journal of Speech* 56 (1970): 1–11.

3. Philip Wander and Steven Jenkins, "Rhetoric, Society, and the Critical Response," *Quarterly Journal of Speech* 58 (1972): 441–450.

4. Wander and Jenkins, "Rhetoric, Society, and the Critical Response," 450.

5. Philip Wander, "The Ideological Turn in Modern Criticism," *Central States Speech Journal* 34 (1983): 1–18.

6. See Jim A. Kuypers, "Framing Analysis," in *Rhetorical Criticism: Perspectives in Action*, ed. Jim A. Kuypers (Lanham, MD: Lexington Books, 2009), 181–204.

7. For a rhetorical critique of political correctness see, Richard Bello, "A Burkeian Analysis of the "Political Correctness" Confrontation in Higher Education," *Southern Communication Journal* 61, no. 3 (1996): 243–252.

8. Wander, "The Ideological Turn," 18.

9. Raymie E. McKerrow, "Criticism Is as Criticism Does," *Western Journal of Communication* 77 (2013): 549.

10. Kenneth Burke, *Permanence and Change*, 3rd ed. (Berkeley: University of California Press, 1984): 14–15.

11. Raymie E. McKerrow, "Critical Rhetoric," in *Encyclopedia of Rhetoric*, ed. Thomas O. Sloane (New York City: Oxford University Press, 2001), 620.

12. Kent A. Ono, "Critical: A Finer Edge," *Communication and Critical/Cultural Studies* 8 (2011): 93.

13. John M. Murphy, "Critical Rhetoric as Political Discourse," *Argumentation and Advocacy* 32 (1995): 1–15.

14. McKerrow, "Criticism Is as Criticism Does," 547.

15. Raymie E. McKerrow, "Critical Rhetoric: Theory and Praxis," *Communication Monographs* 56 (1989): 91.

16. Raymie E. McKerrow, "Critical Rhetoric and Propaganda Studies," in *Communication Yearbook*, vol. 14, ed. J. Anderson, 249–255 (Newbury Park, CA: Sage, 1991).

17. McKerrow, "Critical Rhetoric: Theory and Praxis," 99.

18. Ibid., 96.

19. Kenneth Burke, *The Philosophy of Literary Form* (Berkeley: University of California Press, 1941/1973): 9, emphasis his.

20. Kuypers, "Framing Analysis."

21. McKerrow, "Criticism Is as Criticism Does."

22. McKerrow, "Critical Rhetoric: Theory and Praxis," 101.

23. The principles are derived from McKerrow, "Critical Rhetoric: Theory and Praxis," 102–108.

24. Michael Calvin McGee, "Another Philippic: Notes on the Ideological Turn in Criticism," *Central States Speech Journal* 35 (1984): 49.

25. Göran Therborn, *The Ideology of Power and the Power of Ideology* (London: NLB, 1980): 15, 3.

26. Raymie E. McKerrow, "Critical Rhetoric and the Possibility of the Subject," in *The Critical Turn: Rhetoric and Philosophy in Postmodern Discourse*, ed. I. Angus and L. Langsdorf (Carbondale, IL: Southern Illinois University Press, 1993), 64.

27. McKerrow, "Critical Rhetoric: Theory and Praxis," 98.

28. McKerrow, "Critical Rhetoric," *Encyclopedia of Rhetoric*, 619.

29. Jessica L. Benham, "Saving the Mad Man in a Box: A Critical Analysis of the Role of Female Companions in *Doctor Who*" (paper presented at the National Communication Association convention, Las Vegas, November 2015).

30. Ibid., 2.

31. Thomas A. Discenna, "The Rhetoric of Graduate Employee Unionization: Critical Rhetoric and the Yale Grade Strike," *Communication Quarterly* 58 (2010): 19–35.

32. Ibid., 32.

33. Ibid.

34. Jonathan P. Rossing, "Critical Intersections and Comic Possibilities: Extending Racialized Critical Rhetorical Scholarship," *Communication Law Review* 10, no. 1 (2010): 10–27.

35. Ibid., 11.

36. Ibid.

37. Ibid., 18.

38. Ibid., 22.

39. Kristen Hoerl, "Selective Amnesia and Racial Transcendence in News Coverage of President Obama's Inauguration," *Quarterly Journal of Speech* 98 (2012): 178–202.

40. Ibid., 179.

41. Ibid., 197.

42. Brian L. Ott and Carl R. Burgchardt, "On Critical-Rhetorical Pedagogy: Dialoging with *Schindler's List*," *Western Journal of Communication* 77 (2013): 16.

43. Ibid.

44. Ibid., 28.

45. Art Herbig and Aaron Hess, "Convergent Critical Rhetoric at the 'Rally to Restore Sanity': Exploring the Intersection of Rhetoric, Ethnography, and Documentary Production," *Communication Studies* 63 (2012): 269–289.

46. Ibid., 270.

47. Ibid., 284.

48. See: Raymie E. McKerrow and Art Herbig, "Critical Rhetoric Special Section: Introduction"; Danielle M. Stern and Katherine J. Denker, "Privileged Vulnerability: Embodied Pedagogy as Critical Rhetorical Praxis"; Tony E. Adams, "Critical Rhetoric, Relationality, and Temporality: A Case for Forgiveness"; Brandon M. Daniels and Kendall R. Phillips, "Between Critical and Rhetoric: McKerrow's Contribution to Contemporary Critical Practice"; Aaron Hess, Samantha Senda-Cook, Michael K. Middleton, and Danielle Endres, "(Participatory) Critical Rhetoric: Critiqued and Reconsidered"; Jennifer C. Dunn, "Critical Rhetoric in the Age of the (First) Reality TV President: A Critique of Freedom and Domination"; Lawrence R. Frey and Joshua S. Hanan, "Toward Social Justice Activism Critical Rhetoric Scholarship"; Art Herbig, Andrew F. Herrmann, Alix R. Watson , Adam W. Tyma, and joan miller, "Critical Rhetoric and Collaboration: Missing Principle #9 and ProfsDoPop.com"; and Dana L. Cloud, "The Critique of Domination and the Critique of Freedom: A Gramscian Perspective—Commentary," *International Journal of Communication* 14 (2020): 799–936.

49. McKerrow, "Critical Rhetoric and the Possibility of the Subject," 64.

50. Jim A. Kuypers, "Doxa and a Critical Rhetoric: Accounting for the Rhetorical Agent through Prudence," *Communication Quarterly* 44 (1994): 452–462.

51. McKerrow, "Critical Rhetoric and Propaganda Studies."

52. Cloud, "The Materiality of Discourse."

53. Kent A. Ono and John M. Sloop, "Commitment to Telos—A Sustained Critical Rhetoric," *Communication Monographs* 59 (1992): 48–60.

Appendix A

Writing Criticism: Getting Started

Writing your first piece of rhetorical criticism—not a summary of something but rather the creation of new knowledge and the sharing of new ideas—can be a daunting task. There is no template or rubric for this type of paper, which makes answering the question, "How do I begin?" all the more important. Although there is no standard formula, there are some key elements to keep in mind as you write: theory and rhetorical artifacts, the actual analysis, writing the paper, and judging your product.

STEP 1: RHETORICAL ARTIFACT OR RHETORICAL THEORY?

Unless you are blessed with a Eureka! moment as discussed in chapter 3, your first step in writing a piece of rhetorical criticism is determining whether you should begin with a rhetorical perspective or a rhetorical artifact. At first this decision will be challenging, but the more time you spend learning about rhetoric and criticism, the easier this step becomes. Your professor might assign one or the other starting point, or leave it up to you. If the latter, this choice should be made based on your personal interests. There are several points to keep in mind depending on whether you begin with theory or artifact.

For example, let us say that as you progressed through this book, two rhetorical theories really stood out: metaphor and Burke's notion of identification. As you think on this, you decide that you are particularly interested in how metaphors work in society and in our persuasive communication, so you decide metaphor is the theory you are going to use to write your critical paper. So far, so good. Now comes the decision about artifact. Unfortunately, you can't pick just anything, plug it into metaphor theory, and end up with a good piece of criticism. To ensure a good match with the theory, the artifact you decide on will need to have major elements of metaphor working in it. The range of potential artifacts can be broad depending on your professsor's assignment—so, a speech, a debate, advertisements, social media campaigns such as NASA's #GlobalSelfie in honor of Earth Day, a popular cartoon show such as *SpongeBob SquarePants* or *Star Wars: The Clone Wars*, and many others. To keep from feeling overwhelmed by the choices available, ask your professor for examples of acceptable artifacts. Also keep in mind that whatever artifact you decide on must contain elements of the theoretical perspective you are going to use. For example, if metaphor is your theory, make certain whatever artifact you decide on has significant elements of metaphor.

There are many ways you can move from a theory that you like to finding an appropriate rhetorical artifact. For example, in terms of metaphor, say you have an interest in America's relationship with its Central and South American neighbors. You also happen to be binge-watching *House of Cards* episodes and noticed one that included references to South America, but you decided they were too fleeting to be meaningful for analysis. Then, in the course of reading some news articles about this area, you find a reference to Ivanka Trump's 2018 speech at the third CEO Summit of the Americas where she "announced an initiative that will provide funding to help businesswomen in Latin America."[1] You are excited about this speech as a possible candidate for your criticism paper. You obtain a copy, but as you read through it you discover that there is no significant use of metaphor. Although there are certainly other ways of analyzing the speech, using metaphor theory is just not a good fit. Later that evening, while checking out YouTube videos, you come across Denzel Washington's 2011 University of Pennsylvania commencement speech.[2] You listen to it and love it. Something he says catches your ear and, as you review the speech with metaphor in mind, you discover that you think there is a significant use of metaphor: Washington's use of "fall forward." You now have an artifact that matches up with the rhetorical perspective you are using.

However, suppose that you are able to first choose an artifact and then decide how to analyze it. If this is the case, when you initially came across Ivanka Trump's speech mentioned above, you would simply say, "I like this speech; it's interesting. *This* is the speech I'm going to analyze." As you read the speech, you are looking for elements that suggest a particular theory that will be helpful in analyzing how it works. Because the speech doesn't really make use of metaphor, you naturally identify another theory that relates more directly to the content of the speech. While reading, you notice the sections about empowering women. You feel drawn to how Trump described those ideas and believe she was making an attempt to depict this new policy by "identifying" with young women in Latin America. So you decide that if examined through the Burkean lens of identification, an analysis of the speech could bear fruit. You have now matched up a perspective to the rhetorical artifact that initially caught your eye.

STEP 2: ANALYSIS

Before you actually begin to write your paper, you will want to perform the analysis of your rhetorical artifact. Time is necessary; lots of time. You simply cannot zoom through your artifact once and expect to produce insightful criticism, much less engage in any interpretation as discussed in chapter 3. So be certain to review your artifact extensively. I suggest reading (or watching) through several times just to become thoroughly familiar with it. Refrain from immediately taking notes or making an outline. Simply allow yourself to walk through and engage with it—you are taking a "first look." After this, then go through and begin the process of highlighting, taking notes, and otherwise analyzing the text numerous times. Remember, you will need to be able to describe this artifact in your paper and do so in a way that allows it to speak for itself. That initial reading without preconceptions is important. As an example, let's say you really enjoyed your university president's convocation address and decide to analyze it. You obtain a copy of it through university relations and watch it. Then you watch it again, taking notes. (If you really want to be able to deeply analyze the text, you might obtain or make a transcript of the speech as well.)

Next, review the key concepts of the theory you are using and read through (or watch) your artifact with those in mind. How did they play out in the artifact? Were some stronger than others, or were some missing? How is the artifact better explained when viewed through the lens of the theory? What insights are gained? Some critics bring these key concepts to the artifact when first reviewing it. This certainly works well for many critics. I prefer to engage the artifact first, to try to get a feel for it on its own terms, and then bring theory to bear.

At some point you ought to develop a research question or questions. Although these can be informal—that is, kept to yourself—many critics (and professors) prefer formal questions that can be shared in the essay. Research questions help guide you as you conduct your analysis. Depending on your purpose, you could have a narrowly tailored research question that seeks its answer from your particular artifact (e.g., as discussed above, What are the dominant metaphors in Washington's speech?), or it could be broader in that numerous artifacts or studies would be necessary for a complete answer, although your own study would certainly contribute to the answer. This latter focus is the more popular. For example, one could ask, "How does metaphor work to create audience unity in commencement speeches?" You would need more than just the one study of Washington's speech, but it would certainly produce information that would help answer this question.

I have always appreciated research questions: we critics are explorers, and research questions help guide us and keep us on track without being too controlling of our imaginations. There are no formal hypotheses in criticism as in the sciences. Remember, insight and appreciation are the twin goals of the art of criticism, although in more formal academic criticism, theory building is considered quite important by many scholars. With that in mind, consider asking yourself how your study sheds light on how the theory you used works; does it extend the theory or modify it in some way? Ask your professor about this issue and whether or not he or she wishes this in your paper. If theory building is an important part of what you are doing, then that ought to be reflected in your research question(s).

Remember, you are not concerned with finding one true interpretation of your artifact—the ultimate reality of your artifact. That is impossible. You are instead offering an interpretation to enrich us, to provide insight and foster appreciation, and perhaps to contribute to rhetorical theory. Your work, then, is a type of argument, asking others to agree with your way of viewing, your way of understanding the artifact. This necessitates that your essay be well reasoned. That is, your claims must be supported by actual evidence from the artifact, other sources, and your own reasoning about how the evidence supports your claims.

STEP 3: WRITING THE PAPER

Although there is not a standard organizational formula for writing a rhetorical criticism paper, there are certain elements that ought to be included, and these are found within the common organizational pattern of introduction, body, and conclusion.

An introduction provides an overview of the subject on which you are writing, providing brief exposure to the main elements that will be in the body of your paper. Be certain to get straight to the point in your introduction. Although you may start by broadly contextualizing what you are doing, you want to quickly zero in on the specific analysis you are going to conduct. Do not forget to make a statement about the importance of what you are studying—not just why *you* find it important, but why *others* reading what you have written will find it

important as well. Not all such statements begin with, "This study is important because . . .";
however, they do imply why the study is worthy to read. Here are two examples:

1. We believe that our study of the Netflix original series *The Witcher* contributes to our
   understanding of the nuances of postfeminist narratives embedded in the show and their
   relationship to contemporary feminist themes operating in American society.

   This could also be reworded to read,

   This study is important because it contributes to our understanding of the nuances of
   postfeminist narratives embedded in the show and their relationship to contemporary
   feminist themes operating in American society.

2. "I argue actor-networks are not only rhetorical, as many ANT scholars claim, but that
   the entire network can and is often invoked in rhetorical practice as an inventional
   resource, an important insight that will help scholars further understand how scientific
   controversies are engaged in contemporary contexts."[3]

It is important that you include some variation of a topic statement (some say thesis statement), which is really a sentence or two about the general subject of your rhetorical criticism
paper. Usually it shares the general *argument* you are advancing or the *understanding* you are
sharing. Importantly for a criticism paper, you are making some type of assertion with it, not
simply relaying the general area you are writing on. It has the crucial function of focusing your
readers' attention on the specific area where you will be taking them, letting them know what
it is that you seek to prove. The topic statement is usually followed by a transitional listing of
the main ideas or main points you will share in your paper: "The pages that follow are divided
into four sections: first, I will . . . ; second, I . . ."; and so on.

Here is an example of a topic statement (albeit extended) and listing of the forthcoming
main points from a published essay of criticism:

In the pages that follow, we use a form of cluster analysis as a means to discover the rhetorical
workings of the phrase Make America Great Again as Trump transitioned from candidate and pres-
ident-elect to president. Moreover, through this analysis we discovered that even as Make America
Great Again was technically used only once in [Trump's] inaugural speech, offering a break from
the campaign trail and its contentiousness, the terminological screen surrounding the phrase ran
strongly throughout the speech, thus offering ideational continuity with Trump's prior rhetorical
efforts. For our analysis we first provide a brief history of Trump's road to the White House that
includes a summary explanation about the Make America Great Again phrase associated with
Trump and his campaign. We next provide a brief overview of terminological screens and cluster
analysis. We then examine Trump's inaugural address and offer insights into both the workings of
terminological screens and Trump's use of Make America Great Again.[4]

After reading this, one knows what the main arguments are going to be and how the essay will
be organized. It serves as an orienting gateway into the body of the essay.

The body of your essay will include both a description of the artifact and the theory you
use, followed by your analysis/interpretation. The description of your rhetorical artifact is
crucial to allowing your audience to follow you as you conduct your analysis, since not everyone will be familiar with your artifact. When describing the artifact, you should maintain a
detached sense of curiosity about it. As you point out the artifact's important elements, keep
in mind that your task at this point is not to judge it, or to express like or dislike, but to be

fair minded. Try to describe it in such a way that the major elements you are going to analyze are shared and so that the artifact's voice is heard, not your own.[5]

The description section also involves a review of relevant literature. Generally you will need to review literature that covers both the artifact you are examining and also the theory you are using to guide your analysis. Are there previous studies on your artifact? For instance, on Washington's commencement address, are there any studies of that, or of metaphors in commencement addresses? If not, don't worry; you are going to be creating new knowledge about something—how exciting! If so, what did they say, and how does that relate to what you are going to do in your essay? What, in particular, are the key elements of the theory you are using, and how do they relate to how you are using the theory in your analysis? What have others written about this theory that is relevant to what you are doing? You do not have to summarize every idea and every study, but you do need to define key terms and explain key ideas enough so that someone unfamiliar with the theory can follow along and know how they relate to what you are doing. In a sense, you are *positioning* your study in relation to what has previously been written about your artifact and the theory you are using. Where does what you are doing fit into what is already known?

There is a tendency among beginning critics to overquote other critics. Unless a particular critic makes an especially cogent point or contributes in a significant way to your understanding of a concept or the artifact you are analyzing, do not feel you have to quote every person who has written on your subject. It could be, though, that a particular critic raised an issue to which you are responding, or perhaps the critic leaves off where you are beginning and you wish to establish that you are extending this critic's work, or even that you are quoting a particular critic who agrees or disagrees with you on a particular point. What you want to avoid is a patchwork of quotes from other critics about your artifact or the theory you are using instead of presenting your ideas about how your analysis is going to work.

The conclusion to your rhetorical criticism paper should be brief and to the point. You will need a short summary of your major findings and then extend from there. Make certain that you relate how you made the case put forth in your topic statement. If you actually wrote out your research questions, make certain you answer them in your conclusion. Be certain to discuss how what you found relates to what others have said. This is where you highlight your essay's contributions to insight and appreciation, and also perhaps how it contributes to rhetorical theory. You want others reading the conclusion to have a sense of what it was that you did that adds to the conversation about your topic.

STEP 4: JUDGING YOUR PRODUCT

There is no such thing as good writing, only good rewriting.[6] Good criticism is like that. After following the steps above, you will have a draft, not a completed product of criticism ready to share with the world (or even with your professor). Set it aside for a while (good criticism takes time) and then come back to it with fresh eyes that will allow you to rework your essay in various ways. The more times you can repeat this, the better—until ultimately you feel it is complete. To successfully arrive at that point, keep in mind several questions as you move through the draft process:

- Do I have a strong topic statement?
- Have I provided a rationale for doing this study? Have I relayed the importance of what I have found?

- Have I provided clear statements of my claims that are then followed by actual examples?
- Is my essay well organized? If uncertain, let someone else read it with organization in mind.
- In my conclusion have I actually moved beyond summary and provided clearly the insights generated in my analysis?
- Have I reviewed the instructions provided by my professor?

What I have written here is only one way of writing a rhetorical criticism essay, although it is in keeping with what would be considered normal inclusions and concerns. Ultimately the best way to learn how to write good criticism is to read examples of published criticism, write your own criticism, and allow others to provide you with feedback.

NOTES

1. Ivanka Trump, "2X Americas Announcement in Lima, Peru—Ivanka Trump," YouTube, April 15, 2018, https://www.youtube.com/watch?v=8kh1KoCsPwE.

2. "Denzel Washington' Commencement Speech," YouTube, December 14, 2011, https://www.youtube.com/watch?v=QyDo5vFD2R8.

3. Richard D. Besel, "Opening the 'Black Box' of Climate Change Science: Actor-Network Theory and Rhetorical Practice in Scientific Controversies," *Southern Communication Journal* 76, no. 2 (2011): 122.

4. Jim A. Kuypers and Caitlin McDaniel, "The Inaugural Address of Donald J. Trump: Terministic Screens and the Reemergence Of 'Make America Great Again,'" *Kenneth Burke Journal* 14, no. 1 (2019), https://kbjournal.org/kuypers-mcdaniel-inaugural-address.

5. See note 9 in Jim A. Kuypers, "Must We All Be Political Activists?," *American Communication Journal* 4, no. 1 (2000), http://ac-journal.org/journal/vol4/iss1/special/kuypers.htm; and also Jim A. Kuypers, "Criticism, Politics, and Objectivity: Redivivus," *American Communication Journal* 5, no. 1 (2001).

6. I have seen this quote attributed to novelist Robert Graves, Samuel Clemens, Supreme Court Justices Oliver Wendell Holmes and Louis Brandeis, and my wonderful high school American literature teacher, Mrs. Gretch.

Appendix B

Additional Rhetorical Perspectives and Genres

Critics have a rich variety of perspectives and genres of criticism at their disposal, including but by no means limited to those discussed in more detail in the preceding chapters. Likewise, the following is not meant to be a comprehensive list of *every* perspective and genre available. Rather, it represents a sampling of areas not already covered in this text, as well as areas that represent my (the editor's) own interests and the interests of numerous critics with whom I regularly converse. Arranged alphabetically, each entry provides a brief overview and highlights one exemplary essay.

Apologia: This is a genre of discourse explored by critics rather than a perspective for engaging in criticism. *Apologia* is the term used to describe a variety of apology strategies. For example, B. L. Ware and Wil A. Linkugal list four basic apology strategies: denial, bolstering, differentiation, and transcendence.[1] One type of apologia is "image restoration." Bill Benoit suggests five strategies rhetors may employ when repairing their public images: denial, evading responsibility, reducing the event's offensiveness, taking corrective action, and mortification.[2] Given the prevalence of apologies in public life, there is a rich and long history of apologia examples and literature.

See: Noreen Wales Kruse, "Apologia in Team Sport," *Quarterly Journal of Speech* 67, no. 3 (1981): 270–283.

Cluster Analysis: Initially developed by Kenneth Burke, it is one way of determining the worldview of rhetors through the analysis of key terms within their discourse. Using this approach a critic identifies key terms in a rhetorical artifact. Key terms are determined by either their intensity (how strongly they are used) or their frequency (how often they appear) or a combination of both. Once these key terms are discovered, the critic then charts "clusters" or groupings of other terms surrounding the key terms; these subordinate terms help to provide the meaning for the key terms. Finally, the critic analyzes how the cluster of terms coordinate, or produce patterns, in order to discover what messages are being presented to those exposed to the rhetorical artifact.

See: Adriana Angel and Benjamin Bates, "Terministic Screens of Corruption: A Cluster Analysis of Colombian Radio Conversations," *KB Journal* 10, no. 1 (2014), http://kbjournal.org/angel_bates_terministic_screens_of_corruption.

Conceptually Oriented Criticism: A flexible orientation (as opposed to perspective) on criticism. The starting premise is that a text in which a critic is interested will itself suggest a "concept" or a "conceptual" question the critic can explore. A critic with this orientation is particularly interested in how the text interacts with its historical context and the central concept(s) within the text itself. There can emerge an evolving interaction between the critic, the text, the historical context, and the concept as the critique unfolds; this process can lead to insightful discoveries about the text's impact on human consciousness. The key idea here is that the "conceptual orientation examines the way that particular concepts that shape or inform symbolic activity are expressed in significant texts and using this exchange to explore shifts in human consciousness and standards of judgment."[3]

See: Stephanie Houston Grey, "Conceptually-Oriented Criticism," in *Rhetorical Criticism: Perspectives in Action*, ed. Jim A. Kuypers (Lanham, MD: Lexington Books, 2009), 341–362.

Fantasy-Theme Analysis: Initially developed by Ernest Bormann, it is a perspective that specifically examines how a group dramatizes an event and at how dramatization creates a special kind of myth that influences a group's thinking and behaviors. In this context, the word "fantasy" does not refer to make-believe. Instead, it is a technical term used to understand the social reality of the worldview shared by a rhetorical community. Fantasy-theme analysis allows critics to answer important questions such as, "How does communication function to divide individual from individual, group from group, and community from community? How does communication function to create a sense of community, integrating individuals and groups into large, cooperative units? How does communication function to interpret reality for symbol using beings?"[4]

See: Thomas J. St. Antoine and Matthew T. Althouse, "Fantasy-Theme Criticism," in *Rhetorical Criticism: Perspectives in Action*, 2nd ed., ed. Jim A. Kuypers (Lanham, MD: Rowman & Littlefield, 2016), 167–190.

Framing Analysis: Critics using framing analysis examine the process whereby communicators act—consciously or not—to construct a particular point of view that encourages the facts of a given situation to be viewed in a particular manner, with some facts made more or less noticeable (even ignored) than others.[5] Framing analysis can be used to better understand any rhetorical artifact, with critics examining a text to discover how some aspects of reality are highlighted over others, and also how frames act to define problems, diagnose causes, make moral judgments, and suggest remedies. Frames are central organizing ideas within a narrative account of an issue or event; they provide the interpretive cues for otherwise neutral facts.[6]

See: Michael C. Sounders and Kara N. Dillard, "Framing Connections: An Essay on Improving the Relationship between Rhetorical and Social Scientific Frame Studies, Including a Study of G. W. Bush's Framing of Immigration," *International Journal of Communication* 8 (2014): 1008–1028.

Judgmental Analysis: Seeks to examine the ideas expressed in discourse by asking what judgments a text is asking its audience (readers, viewers, listeners) to make. These are called judgmental appeals. Judgmental analysis is useful in exposing "the judgments audiences are asked to make by a speaker."[7] It allows critics to determine the standards of reason that a rhetor asks his or her audiences to use when judging the situation under discussion. In some senses this type of analysis allows critics to "chart" the rhetorical patterns of persuasive appeals made in a text.

See: Jim A. Kuypers, "From Science, Moral Poetics: Dr. James Dobson's Response to the Fetal Tissue Research Initiative," *Quarterly Journal of Speech* 86, no. 2 (2000): esp. 148–150, 163.

Movements (social, rhetorical): Critics in this area examine the discourse of rhetors who are part of a large, noninstitutionalized group or collective seeking to change, remove, or protect some aspect of the current economic, political, or social order. Such efforts at public advocacy, when popularly (grassroots) generated and of a sustained nature, are generally called social or rhetorical movements. Examples include the civil rights movement, the pro-life movement, the slow food movement, the men's rights movement, and the animal rights movement. Critics may be interested in individual speakers (movement leaders) or specific manifestos or single-event messages, although it is more typical to look at broad rhetorical strategies used in making a particular movement successful (or not), as well as in identifying the core, common rhetorical features of movements.

See: Eric C. Miller, "Phyllis Schlafly's 'Positive' Freedom: Liberty, Liberation, and the Equal Rights Amendment," *Rhetoric & Public Affairs* 18, no. 2 (2015): 277–300.

Mythic Criticism: Richard Slotkin defined myths as "stories drawn from a society's history that have acquired through persistent usage the power of symbolizing that society's ideology and of dramatizing its moral consciousness. . . . Myths are formulated as ways of explaining problems that arise in the course of historical experience."[8] Critics exploring myth often use rhetorical theory mixed with psychological and anthropological theory. Archetypal myths can provide patterns from which similar stories are made, and critics operating from a mythic perspective attempt to discover how myths operate rhetorically in everyday discourse.

See: Janice Hocker Rushing and Thomas S. Frentz, "The Mythic Perspective," in *Rhetorical Criticism: Perspectives in Action*, ed. Jim A. Kuypers (Lanham, MD: Lexington Books, 2009), 231–256.

Postcolonial Criticism: A critical perspective starting from the premise that third world and non-Western countries are influenced by Eurocentrism and Western cultural imperialism inherent in Western discourses. "Articulated mainly within the intersectional critical space of cultural studies, postcolonialism primarily challenges the colonizing and imperialistic tendencies manifest in discursive practices of 'first world' countries in their constructions and representations of the subjects of 'third world' countries and/or racially oppressed peoples of the world."[9] Critics using this perspective often ask questions such as, How do global media practices, especially those of the United States, act as a forceful cultural insertion into other cultures, fomenting a type of cultural imperialism, perpetuating racism and a type of neocolonialism? and How do the discursive practices of Western nations, "in their representations of the world and of themselves, legitimize the contemporary global power structures?"[10] Some current efforts in this area focus on "decolonization," or a kind of responsible corrective to the difficulties caused by colonization; this "reconstruction" seeks to find respectful and responsible solutions to problems perceived by the critic.

See: Jason Edward Black, "Rhetorical Circulation, Native Authenticity, and Neocolonial Decay: The Case of Chief Seattle's Controversial Elegy," *Rhetoric & Public Affairs* 15, no. 4 (2012): 635–646.

Public Memory: "A shared sense of the past, fashioned from the symbolic resources of community and subject to its particular history, hierarchies, and aspirations."[11] For critics it is in part the analysis of public sites created for remembrance. Critics working with public memory are concerned with the rhetorical process of how public memory is created, stored, and retrieved. They ask questions such as, How does public memory become "embedded in the available structures of lived experience"?[12] and How is public memory discursively constructed? They often begin with the assumption that "public memory lives as it is given expressive form; its analysis must therefore presume a theory of textuality and entail an appropriate mode of interpretation." Thus not only museums and memorials but also reenactments, ceremonies, and rituals can be analyzed for their role in public memory.

See: Nicole Maurantonio, "Material Rhetoric, Public Memory, and the Post-It Note," *Southern Communication Journal* 80, no. 2 (2015): 83–101.

Queer Rhetoric: A critical perspective tracing its main academic roots to the mid-1990s gay, lesbian, bisexual, and transgendered rights movement. Critics in this area look at how GLBT groups' activism shapes and interacts with public discourse, specifically asking what constitutes the various rhetorical modes of GLBT expression. Distinct from gay cultural studies, a queer rhetoric suggests that the GLBT rights movement "as it enters a new phase of consciousness [in the mid-1990s] could be accountable for having developed a specific rhetorical practice in the public sphere."[13] Contemporary practices have expanded on the earlier examples of queer rhetoric to embrace a larger concern of critiquing discourses of sexuality that establish norms (what is considered normal) for sexuality in the public sphere. Such critiques often offer counterdiscourses that actively seek to offer alternate views on sexuality. In short, "queer rhetorical practice focuses in particular on *sexual* normalization and the regimes of discursive control through which [human] bodies" are categorized as sexually normal or as Other.[14]

See: Charles E. Morris and John M. Sloop, "'What Lips These Have Kissed': Refiguring the Politics of Queer Public Kissing," *Communication and Critical/Cultural Studies* 3, no. 1 (2006): 1–26.

Rhetoric of Argument: Critics examining arguments certainly look at types of arguments and how they function in certain contexts: inductive or deductive, enthymemes, signs, parallel cases, analogies, and many others. These critics are interested in how people "justify their beliefs and values and [how they] influence the thought and action of others."[15] Beyond analysis of particular argument types, critics are also interested in "the rationality or reasonableness of claims put forward in discourse."[16] A wide range of artifacts can be analyzed, from specific instances of argument in a text to broad national or international issues discussed over a period of time, such as the degree to which human activity is responsible for climate change.

See: Eric C. Miller, "Fighting for Freedom: Liberal Argumentation in Culture War Rhetoric," *Journal of Communication & Religion* 37, no. 1 (2014): 102–125.

Rhetoric of Music: There are two broad aspects examined by critics in this area: the analysis of song lyrics and the analysis of music (without words) for its persuasive effects. Critics are interested in music and song because they "can create socially shared meanings in both the artistic and rhetorical sense."[17] In terms of song lyrics, "music functions both as an expression of the artist and as an invitation to the audience to identify with the themes, ideas, and emotions expressed. If rhetoric is conceptualized either as constructing or interpreting reality, music is a powerful part of that process."[18] Song lyrics may be analyzed from any number of rhetorical perspectives. Of particular interest to critics are songs designed to inspire attitude change. Yet one can analyze the music that carries the song lyrics, or even nonvocal music composition, for rhetorical dynamics as well. Music is, after all, a symbolic language, with a particular vocabulary and grammar. Musical notes, keys, harmony, and other elements have parallel structures to written and oral language and may be analyzed to determine the rhetorical aspects of a musical composition. The idea is that music can represent emotions and ideas and thus have effects similar to that of written and spoken language.

See: Caroline C. Koons, "The Rhetorical Legacy of 'The Battle Hymn of the Republic,'" *Southern Communication Journal* 80, no. 3 (2015): 211–229.

Rhetorical Reception Studies: Scholars in this area combine studies examining how audiences receive messages (reception analysis) with rhetorical analysis of the utterances that audiences encounter.[19] Instead of just moving conjecturally from textual traits to their assumed effect on audiences, rhetorical reception studies also move from the responses of audiences to the text itself, to establish the rhetorical traits that may have contributed to the response. The aim is to understand the interaction between rhetorical situations, characteristics of utterances, and what audiences actually pay attention to and how they negotiate their understanding of the rhetoric. Rhetorical reception studies acknowledge that audiences are complex, fragmented, and active, and that all utterances are polysemic.[20] Simultaneously, such studies adhere to the fact that utterances have rhetorical power to influence, and that audiences necessarily base part of their reactions on the form, content, and character of utterances. Rhetorical reception studies teach us about forms of rhetoric, forms of reception, and how these are connected.

See: Jens E. Kjeldsen, ed., *Rhetorical Audience Studies and Reception of Rhetoric: Exploring Audiences Empirically* (London: Palgrave Macmillan, 2018).

Rhetoric of Science (also known as rhetoric of inquiry): Critics in this area explore the interrelationships among reality, language, and the nature of knowledge, in particular questioning the idea of an absolute grounding for knowledge. There is a particular focus on analyzing the discourse of scholars and scientists when transmitting their "knowledge" to others. The idea is that both scholars and scientists write rhetorically (whether to a greater or lesser degree).[21] Thus critics in this area are critiquing both the reading and writing practices of scholars and scientists.

See: Celeste Condit, "Insufficient Fear of the 'Super-flu'? The World Health Organization's Global Decision-Making for Health," *Poroi: An Interdisciplinary Journal of Rhetorical Analysis & Invention* 10, no. 1 (2014): 1–31.

NOTES

1. B. L. Ware and Wil A. Linkugel, "They Spoke in Defense of Themselves: On the Generic Criticism of Apologia," *Quarterly Journal of Speech* 59, no. 3 (1973): 273–283.

2. William Benoit, *Accounts, Excuses, and Apologies: A Theory of Image Restoration Strategies* (New York: State University of New York Press, 1995).

3. Stephanie Houston Grey, "Conceptually-Oriented Criticism," in *Rhetorical Criticism: Perspectives in Action*, ed. Jim A. Kuypers (Lanham, MD: Lexington Books, 2009), 342–343.

4. Questions from Moya A. Ball, "Ernest G. Bormann: Roots, Revelations, and Results of Symbolic Convergence Theory," in *Twentieth-Century Roots of Rhetorical Studies*, ed. Jim A. Kuypers and Andrew King (Westport, CT: Praeger, 2001), 221.

5. Jim A. Kuypers, "Framing Analysis as a Rhetorical Process," *Doing News Framing Analysis*, ed. Paul D'Angelo and Jim A. Kuypers (New York: Routledge, 2010), 286–311.

6. For an example of this, see Joseph M. Valenzano, "Framing the War on Terror in Canadian Newspapers: Cascading Activation, Canadian Leaders, and Newspapers," *Southern Communication Journal* 74, no. 2 (2009): 174–190.

7. Roderick P. Hart, *Modern Rhetorical Criticism* (New York: HarperCollins, 1990), 102.

8. Robert Slotkin, *Gunfighter Nation: The Myth of the Frontier in Twentieth-Century America* (New York: Atheneum Books, 1992), 5–6.

9. Raka Shome, "Postcolonial Interventions in the Rhetorical Canon: An 'Other' View," *Communication Theory* 6, no. 1 (1996): 41.

10. Ibid., 42.

11. Stephen H. Browne, "Reading, Rhetoric, and the Texture of Public Memory," *Quarterly Journal of Speech* 81 (1995): 248.

12. Ibid., 248.

13. Philippe-Joseph Salazar, "Queer Rhetoric," in *Encyclopedia of Rhetoric*, ed. Thomas O. Sloane (New York: Oxford University Press, 2001), 649.

14. Jonathan Alexander and Jacqueline Rhodes, "Queer Rhetoric and the Pleasures of the Archive: Introduction," *Enculturation: A Journal of Rhetoric, Writing and Culture* (January 16, 2012), http://enculturation.net/files/QueerRhetoric/queerarchive/intro.html.

15. David Zarefsky, "Argumentation," in *Encyclopedia of Rhetoric*, ed. Thomas O. Sloane (New York: Oxford University Press, 2001), 33.

16. Zarefsky, "Argumentation."

17. Karyn Rybacki and Donald Rybacki, "The Rhetoric of Song," in *Communication Criticism: Approaches and Genres* (Belmont, CA: Wadsworth, 1991), 275.

18. Michael McGuire, "'Darkness on the Edge of Town': Bruce Springsteen's Rhetoric of Optimism and Despair," in *Rhetorical Dimensions in Media: A Critical Casebook*, ed. Martin J. Medhurst and Thomas W. Benson, 2nd ed. (Dubuque, IA: Kendall-Hunt, 1991), 305.

19. J. E. Kjeldsen, "Audience Analysis and Reception Studies of Rhetoric," in J. E. Kjeldsen, ed., *Rhetorical Audience Studies and Reception of Rhetoric: Exploring Audiences Empirically* (London/New York: Palgrave Macmillan, 2018), 1–42.

20. Jens E. Kjeldsen, "Studying Rhetorical Audiences: A Call for Qualitative Reception Studies in Argumentation and Rhetoric," *Informal Logic* 36, no. 2 (2016).

21. Alan G. Gross, *Starring the Text: The Place of Rhetoric in Science Studies* (Carbondale: Southern Illinois University Press, 2006); Nathan Crick, "When We Can't Wait on Truth: The Nature of Rhetoric in the Rhetoric of Science," *Poroi: An Interdisciplinary Journal of Rhetorical Analysis & Invention* 10, no. 2 (2014): 1–27.

Appendix C

Glossary of Terms

agency: refers to a person's ability to enact change in a specific situation.

allegory: a narrative in which characters and events correspond with persons, events, and issues outside the text to convey a secondary meaning beyond its surface meaning.

analysis: discovering what is in a rhetorical artifact and explaining how the rhetorical artifact works. Analysis provides a sketch of sorts, showing how the artifact is put together: what its parts are, how they go together, and what the whole looks like.

anaphora: a rhetorical figure of speech that involves the repetition of the same word or phrase at the beginning of each clause.

artistic proofs: arguments invented by the speaker as evidence or "proof" to believe him or her. (See *logos, pathos,* and *ethos.*)

assemblage: a collection of different parts or components. A rhetorical assemblage is a collective of entities that enact persuasion in concert.

attention economy: Richard Lanham's term for a social context in which attention has become a central commodity. It arises when content is so abundant that the limited bandwidths of human attentional capacity become the resource in high demand.

audience, rhetorical: within a rhetorical situation perspective, this is the collection of persons who are capable of modifying the situation's exigency.

characters: stories are driven by the conflict between the protagonist or hero and the antagonist or villain, who may be a person or some other obstacle that must be overcome.

circulation (textual): a text's movement though and among different spaces and contexts.

cisgender: someone whose outside appearance conforms to societal expectations about their sexed body.

close textual analysis: an approach to rhetorical criticism seeking to account for the ways in which texts produce meaning and activate convictions in public contexts.

constraints: within a rhetorical situation perspective, these are elements that can influence both what can and can't be said concerning the modification of the exigency. "They are made up of persons, events, objects, and relations which are parts of the situation because they have the power to constrain decision and action needed to modify the exigence. Standard sources of constraint include beliefs, attitudes, documents, facts, traditions, images, interests, motives and the like; and when the orator enters the situation, his discourse not

351

only harnesses constraints given by the situation but provides additional important constraints—for example his personal character, his logical proofs, and his style."[1]

content: textually produced meaning reduced to its propositional level. Content cannot be divorced from form.

context: the various circumstances that surround a particular situation, event, and so on, to which rhetors attend in shaping potentially persuasive messages. Variables may include, but are not limited to, the historical moment in which rhetor and audience find themselves, the dynamics of the sociocultural milieu in place, and the nature of the immediate setting (for instance, assumptions and preparation that precede a political speech at a campaign rally surely differ from those that guide planning for funeral remarks to note the passing of someone revered universally). It is the field of operation within which a text is placed, and with which it interacts to produce meaning, action, and effect. Context cannot be divorced from text.

continual critique: this phrase assumes that any particular change in human relations (or power differences between people) is not a sign that perfection has been reached; thus, they are open to reexamination. You may not make a change as a result of the critique, but any change in power relations is always open to future reconsideration.

critic as inventor: in this role the critic does not conceive of invention as making things up out of nothing but rather as discerning, within the vast and complex world of signs and symbols, what influences might be present in determining how one's own orientation is formed or altered.

critical act: the actual act of performing and sharing criticism. Consists of three parts: the conceptual stage, the communication stage, and the counter-communication stage.

critical rhetoric: references a way of approaching criticism that enables the critic to examine relations of power that either inhibit or foster new human relations.

criticism: "the systematic process of illuminating and evaluating products of human activity. [C]riticism presents and supports one possible interpretation and judgment. This interpretation, in turn, may become the basis for other interpretations and judgments."[2]

critique of domination: this critique has an emancipatory aim, a "freedom from" that which controls the beliefs or actions of others.

critique of freedom: focuses attention on "freedom to" be other than what one is at the present moment.

cultural feminists: believe that a women's innate nature, primarily shaped by the ability to give birth, is decidedly different from men's, and thus represent a "culture" that is inadequately reflected in today's society.

cultural studies: an interdisciplinary field concerned with the relationship between culture and power. It focuses on the ways that symbolic action reproduces, resists, and transforms existing power relations and conditions of inequality. This approach to criticism explains how mass media construct, affirm, and sometimes challenge social hierarchies based on categories of identity such as race, gender, class, sexual orientation, and nationality.

decentering: references a removal of the role of the speaker as the origin of thought, words, and action in order to focus attention on the context that brings discourse into existence.

deliberative discourse: is concerned with the future, and its auditors are asked to make judgments about future courses of action.

diachronic: in the context of ideographic criticism, the diachronic dimension explores a society's changing ideological commitments through time by tracing the changes in ideographic usage. In the United States, for example, over the past century <equality> has become an ever more important ideological commitment, and its prominence has come at the expense of other ideographs.

digital infrastructure: refers to physical and organizational systems (e.g., hardware and software) that underlie digital environs, such as the World Wide Web.

digital rhetoric: both rhetoric manifested via digital media and an area of inquiry concerned with rhetoric in digital formats and contexts.

discourse: refers to language in use, or more broadly, the interactive production of meaning.[3]

disposition: also known as organization; the arranging of the speech's (text's) materials in various structures to achieve a particular effect.

doxastic: refers to the role of opinion in forming what we know about the world.

dramatism: Kenneth Burke's theory of language and human action. Dramatism contains a number of Burke's central ideas, including the role of language to provide terministic screens, the role of identification in persuasion, the power of form to shape human perceptions and expectations, and the dramatistic pentad.

dual audience: criticism often teaches that a key variable for assessing a rhetorical experience is the extent to which a message is adapted to a "target audience." Complicating the task, though, are situations in which the speaker or writer must address a message to auditors with conflicting priorities. Political convention speakers, for example, are often challenged to excite or invigorate the immediate audience of delegates and political professionals, while simultaneously reaching, through the mass media, viewers whose politics differ from those at the convention.

enthymeme: generally understood as a syllogism that is missing a premise (truncated syllogism) which is supplied by the audience. The missing premise is understood as an unstated assumption, one created jointly by its author and the audience who provides the missing part of the argument. Its purpose is to persuade.

epideictic discourse: is set in the present and concerns speeches of praise or blame, with the values that hold the audience or society together. Its auditors are being asked to make judgments concerning how well the speaker accomplishes his or her goals.

epistemic: refers to that knowledge which is certain. Epistemology refers to the nature of knowledge.

epistrophe: a rhetorical figure of speech that has the repetition of the same phrase at the end of each clause.

ethos: an interpretation by the audience of qualities possessed by a speaker as the speaker delivers his or her message. Thus, by the way a speaker constructs and makes an argument, an audience will make judgments about his or her intelligence, character, and goodwill.

exigence: "an imperfection marked by urgency; it is a defect, an obstacle, something waiting to be done, a thing which is other than it should be."[4] To be rhetorical in nature an exigency must need discourse as part of its successful modification. In any rhetorical situation there will be at least one controlling exigency, and this will convey an organizing principle to the situation and also determine what audience should be addressed.

exordium: the introductory part of a speech. It reviews the purpose of the speech, and the type of cause being presented.

feminism: a pluralistic movement interested in altering the political and social landscape so that all people, regardless of their identity categories, can experience freedom and safety, complexity and subjectivity, and economic and political parity—experiences associated with being fully human.

forensic discourse: is concerned with past acts, and its auditors are asked to make judgments concerning what actually happened in the past.

form: linguistic resources that give conspicuous structure to otherwise abstract formulations, typically elements of style, voice, and genre. Form cannot be divorced from content. It can be a pattern that invites our participation; it arouses our desires and promises to fulfill them. We see the power of form when we know a pattern and expect it to be repeated.

generic antecedents: modes of expression established by traditional usage and that in turn may shape and give effect to any given instance of textual action.

generic application: a deductive approach to generic criticism that begins with a genre that has already been described; it applies the characteristics of that genre deductively to another instance of that genre in order to explain or evaluate it.

generic description: an inductive approach to generic criticism that begins by identifying the defining characteristics of the suspected genre, then looks for and carefully examines examples of discourse from that suspected genre for similarities, and then explains discovered similarities in order to identify the characteristics of the new genre.

generic hybrid: see *rhetorical hybrid.*

generic rhetorical criticism: involves looking for the observable, explicable, and predictable rhetorical commonalities that occur in groups of related discourses as well as in groups of people.

hegemony: the process by which the system of social hierarchies, structures, institutions, relations, customs, and values remain stable by generating the voluntary consent of its members.

homology: disparate sets of discourse that have a similar underlying structure that orders human experience. Looks more at the formal patterns across discursive elements rather than in content of ideas.

iconographic tracking: an approach within the field of visual rhetoric that tracks the circulation of images across time and media to trace their transfigurations, i.e., changes in meaning and functions. Those changes are a result of the public's use and reuse of images in different contexts.

identification: an extension of the traditional notion of persuasion, associated with Kenneth Burke, that takes into account unconscious persuasive effects. It is thus the often-unconscious processes by which we align ourselves with others and act based on similarities or shared interests. Identification occurs when you choose a path of action not simply based on weighing the pros and cons of that action, but because you perceive that action as aligning you with other people like you.

ideograph: term coined by Michael McGee to designate an ordinary-language term found in political discourse. It is a high-order abstraction representing commitment to a particular but equivocal and ill-defined normative goal. Examples of ideographs, which are usually placed inside angle brackets when discussed by critics, would include <property>, <liberty>, <democracy>, <freedom>, and <rule of law>.

ideological turn: Philip Wander has characterized the ideological turn in modern criticism as reflecting "the existence of crisis," acknowledging "the influence of established interests and the reality of alternative worldviews," and commending "rhetorical analyses, not only of the actions implied but also of the interests represented."[5]

ideology: any system of ideas that directs our collective social and political action. Can also be "a set of opinions or beliefs of a group or an individual. Very often ideology refers to a set of political beliefs or a set of ideas that characterize a particular culture. Capitalism, communism, socialism, and Marxism are ideologies."[6]

inartistic proofs: evidence not created by the speaker but existing in its own right: contracts, wills, and constitutions, for example.

interpellation: in cultural theory refers to the process by which ideological discourse constructs subject positions for individuals and groups from which they can make sense of their experience. That is, our own identities are the products of ideology. We internalize ideological discourses that offer us a certain image of our place in the world and then use that image to guide our beliefs and behaviors.

interpretation: determining what a rhetorical artifact means. It is the act of the critics trying "to account for and assign meaning to the rhetorical dimensions of a given phenomenon."[7] Such interpretations can focus on the external or internal dynamics of a rhetorical artifact. External interpretations focus on how the rhetorical artifact interacts with the situation that surrounds it, and internal interpretations focus on how different parts of the rhetorical artifact act together in forming a whole.

intersectionality: a theoretical framework that uses the intersections, or overlapping elements, of a person's different identities (race, gender, religion, appearance, sexuality, abilities/disabilities, etc.) as a way of exploring different modes of discrimination or marginalization against certain groups.

intertextuality: the generation of meaning by the patterns and confluences across texts, where all meanings draw on other meanings.

invention: one of the five classical cannons. It involves the discovery and the creation of the appropriate materials and arguments for the discourse.

kinesics: broadly speaking this is the study of various body movements. Specific to rhetorical studies, it is concerned with using the body to convey meanings and emotions.

liberal feminist: believes the oppression of women exists in the systematic failure to include them in dominant structures and cultural production; asks how women are excluded from systems of representation.

logos: one of the three artistic proofs, a logic based on reason. This is not a scientific logic but rather a rhetorical logic, one based upon probability. Involves both inductive and deductive argument structures.

male centeredness: the notion that our cultural attention is mainly focused on males.

male domination: refers to the fact that men have populated most positions of authority in major societies throughout history.

male identification: the notion that our cultural values reside mainly in maleness and masculinity.

materialist feminists: believe that human beings are symbol-using, and thus our understandings of ourselves are largely socially constructed, not biologically driven. A materialist feminist is interested in analyzing social conditions—such as the influence of ethnicity, sexual orientation, and class—that work together to define women and men as categories and seemingly erase the possibility of other categories being established, such as intersex and transgender.

metaphor: a figure of speech often used to make new ideas "come alive," often by comparing unlike things to a known thing. For example, "teenage drinking is dynamite in the hands of babies." Such an expression conveys the potential harm of underage drinking more powerfully than the literal, "teenage drinking is dangerous." Although marked historically as a topos of rhetorical style, metaphor's utility as an inventional resource, particularly in constructing arguments, is increasingly apparent.

motive: in Burkean theory, the underlying worldview and philosophy of the speaker and the worldview the speaker wants us to adopt. By using the pentad to explore how a speaker explains an action (Should the act be understood as a result of the "scene"? Was it for a higher "purpose"?), we can better understand the worldview/philosophy of the speaker. Burke argues that when explaining an action, the choice to emphasize a particular element of the pentad corresponds with a particular philosophical orientation: scene corresponds with determinism, agent with idealism, agency with pragmatism, purpose with mysticism, and act with realism.

narrative: a form of rhetoric drawing on the power of stories to help people understand the world and persuade others.

narrative fidelity: the degree to which the story rings true in relation to the experience of the audience.

narrative form: the combination of characters, plot, setting, and theme.

narrative function: the work done by stories in rhetoric. That work includes providing the audience with a worldview and persuading them to accept a new viewpoint.

narrative paradigm: the theory developed by Walter Fisher that all forms of communication can be understand as forms of narrative.

narrative probability: the dimensions of a narrative that make it coherent.

nominalism: suggests that when you hear a general term such as *dog*, you automatically relate it to a specific dog you are familiar with—the general term has no explicit existence.

orientation: the way in which you approach the world—your attitude toward what things are good or not may be one example.

paralepsis: a rhetorical stylistic device used to bring up a subject while the speaker or writer denies actually bringing it up. Particularly used to make a subtle ad hominem attack on one's opponent.

paralinguistic features: aspects of vocal communication that move beyond the basic verbal message consisting of proper grammar or argument structure. For instance, varying volume, rate of speaking, or tone.

paratexts: the variety of materials including advertisements, movie trailers, and interviews with actors that comment on or refer to a primary text such as a movie, television program, or recording.

participatory media: those texts that invite active audience engagement, to include generating and disseminating content. This is in contrast to media that invite more passive forms of consumption.

pathos: one of the three artistic proofs, it is an appeal to the emotions of audience members through the construction of arguments that are designed to induce specific emotional states. Once audiences are in the emotional state, they become more easily moved to a particular action.

pentad: the goal of pentadic analysis is not to simply name each of the five parts but rather to identify the relationships between them and determine which term dominates the others. Consists of five terms. Act: the pentadic term for the action. It answers the question, what happened? Texts that emphasize act demonstrate a philosophy of realism. Scene: the pentadic term for the context in which an action occurred. It answers the question, what was the situation/context? Texts that emphasize scene demonstrate a philosophy of determinism. Agent: the pentadic term for the person who acts. It answers the question, what kind of person performed the act? Texts that emphasize agent demonstrate a philosophy of idealism. Agency: the pentadic term for the means by which the act was accomplished. It answers the question, what technology, method, or technique was used? Texts that empha-size agency demonstrate a philosophy of pragmatism. Purpose: the pentadic term for why an act is performed. It answers the question, to what end or with what purpose did someone act? Texts that emphasize purpose demonstrate a philosophy of mysticism.

peroration: the final part of the speech (the conclusion). This section would be used to re-mind the audience of the main ideas contained in the speech and in persuasive efforts to rouse the emotions of the audience to help induce them to action.

plot: the action in the story.

power: actual advocates try to influence the course of events in a manner that promotes their interests. Some advocates have more resources (money, access, technology, networks of influential friends) than others. Some advocates press a case on behalf of established institu-tions and traditional ways of doing things, while others work for groups with little social or economic standing and who find their interests at odds with the status quo. These dispari-ties in power make a huge difference in the ability to influence audiences.

power/knowledge: the position that all knowledge is implicated in questions of social power, which is productive and circulates through all levels of society.

pragma-dialectic: an approach to understanding discourse that analyzes arguments by focus-ing on the process of making the argument as well as on the critical evaluation of the claims advanced. The approach considers both verbal (oral and written) and nonverbal elements of an argument, and stresses a practical understanding of images interpreted using the context of the other speech acts that surround them.

principles of praxis: serve not as guidelines for criticism but as ways of conceiving of the rhetorical act and as potential indices to consider when beginning to critique.

procedural rhetoric: a concept introduced by Ian Bogost to capture the way in which pro-cesses can enact persuasion.

public knowledge: the knowledge held in general by a community of persons who "share conceptions, principles, interests, and values and who are significantly interdependent. This community may be characterized further by institutions such as offices, schools, laws, tribunals; by a duration sufficient to the development of these institutions; by a commit-ment to the well-being of members; and by a power of authorization through which some truths and values are accredited."[8]

public sphere: refers to a space in which people come together to deliberate about matters of shared public interest. Introduced by Jürgen Habermas, the concept has generated a considerable body of scholarship, to include the introduction of specific iterations, such as the blogosphere, which refers to the web of interconnected blogs as a site for collective public deliberation.

rhetor: another term for communicator.

rhetoric: the strategic use of communication, oral or written, to achieve specifiable goals.

rhetorical artifacts: specific acts of rhetoric that critics single out to analyze.

rhetorical criticism: the analysis and evaluation of rhetorical acts.

rhetorical hybrid: sometimes termed a generic hybrid, discourse that entails traits of multiple classes or categories of speech. Political convention keynote addresses, for instance, may be termed epideictic because the dominant issues are praise and blame. Since speakers employ praise or blame to promote their own party, however, their messages are often equally de-liberative or political, as well as ceremonial.

rhetorical perspective: a theoretical orientation a critic uses to help guide criticism of a rhe-torical artifact.

rhetorical situation: a theoretical construct advanced by Lloyd Bitzer. It is "a complex of persons, events, objects, and relations presenting an actual or potential exigence which can be completely or partially removed if discourse introduced into the situation can so constrain human decision or action as to bring about the significant modification of the exigence."[9]

rhetorical velocity: crafting a text with its future trajectory in mind, attentive to how it might be reused and repurposed.

rhetorician: in the time of Cicero, an orator-statesman who would use rhetoric as a means of serving the people. Today we use the term to denote one who studies or who uses rhetoric.

scientism: a belief system that promotes science, or the scientific method, as the best way for society to determine its normative values and policy actions.

setting: literally the place where the story occurs, but more broadly the place where similar stories often occur.

signification: the process by which meaning is constructed through the relationship among signs that prompt the reader, viewer, or listener to think of something other than itself.

simile: often referred to as a metaphor that uses "like" or "as," a simile serves much the same function as its sister trope. Thus, extending the example of a metaphor, a simile might be cast as "lowering the drinking age to eighteen is *like* giving a stick of dynamite to a baby."

social knowledge: the shared body of ideas, opinions, and information within a given community. It encompasses both the overtly acknowledged and that which is unspoken and taken-for-granted.

social order: refers to a system of social hierarchies, structures, institutions, relations, customs, values, and practices that correspond to specific ideological assumptions.

spreadability (textual): a text's capacity for dissemination, as determined by both its content and technical features.

stickiness (textual): Malcolm Gladwell's term for the quality of a text that compels us to attend to and remember it.

style: the use of the right language to make the materials of exposition and argument clear and convincing.

syllogism: a major form of logical argument that uses deductive reasoning to arrive at a conclusion. It is based on using two or more propositions that are asserted to be true. The classic form of this argument is composed of a major premise (a general statement), a minor premise (a specific statement), and conclusion. A classic example of this type of argument is all men are mortal (major premise), Socrates is a man (minor premise), and thus we may validly conclude that Socrates is mortal (conclusion).

symbolic action: a phrase describing how language operates rhetorically, with particular stress on textual performance, function, and effect.

synchronic: in the context of ideographic criticism, the synchronic dimension explores the tension among ideographs at a particular time. During the struggle for civil rights, for example, the two sides clashed over the tension between the rights of <private property> and the commitment to <equality>.

telos: in terms of rhetoric, the idea that all rhetorical communication is directed toward some end state or goal.

tenor: one of two parts of a metaphor. It is the focus of the metaphor, the object, concept, or issue that is presumed to be not fully or correctly understood by the audience, according to the rhetor's point of view. In other words, the tenor is the understanding or "thing" that the rhetor is trying to help the audience understand specifically. It is linked with the vehicle or "frame" to provide this understanding.

terministic screens: the capacity of language (terminology) to encourage us to understand the world in some ways while filtering (screening) other interpretations out. The specific language we use to describe an object or event draws our attention toward some aspects of the event and thus away from other aspects.

text: a provisionally bounded field of discursive action. Text cannot be divorced from context. Generally speaking, a text is a discrete rhetorical artifact that can be analyzed: the text of a speech, the text of a radio broadcast, the text of a debate, the text of a war memorial, and so on.

theme: the message of the story.

topics (topoi or topos): categories used in a type of systematic brainstorming using pre-defined categories.

traditional perspective on criticism: criticism guided by the theory of rhetoric handed down from antiquity, usually including theories of Aristotle, Plato, Isocrates, Cicero, and Quintilian.

trope: the use of a word or phrase for a literary or artistic effect—a figure of speech. They can also be considered in terms of motifs in literature and public address, common or frequently used rhetorical devices or themes.

vehicle (frame): one of two parts of a metaphor. It is discontinuous with, or of a different class of experience from, the tenor or "focus." The vehicle typically is a more familiar or understood object, concept, or issue that will be used to help form the audience's understanding of the tenor. When the two terms, the tenor (or focus) and the vehicle (or frame), are together, audiences are invited to see the comparison between the two and realign their thinking on the subject of the metaphor.

virality: the phenomenon whereby a text circulates extremely widely in a very short amount of time.

visual archetype: a type of a visual symbol rooted in popular cultural narratives (e.g., fairy-tales, the Bible, Greek and Roman mythology) familiar to audiences.

visual argument: claims put forth by images to build propositions of a visual argument that induce the audience to embrace certain conclusions during the process of interpretation.

visual demonstrations: are images that convey messages that are best or most easily expressed visually. A chart or a pictorial instruction manual that lays out procedures step by step through reenactments captured in drawings or videos are some of the most common examples.

visual flag: images that draw the attention of the audience to the message that they attempt to convey, typically through a striking or arresting composition.

visual metaphor: a rhetorical device that makes figurative visual claims by portraying something or someone as something or someone else. Example: A politician drawn with a body of a snail is meant to comment on the person's slow actions.

visual rhetoric: an approach in visual communication that treats images as communicative devices that convey meanings and serve various functions to their viewers.

visual symbol: a rhetorical device in the form of an image that is used to stand in for something it represents within a culture. Example: A drawn Statue of Liberty symbolizes the United States of America.

white supremacist capitalist patriarchy: the theoretical notion that we not only live in a male-dominated, sexist society but a society that discriminates based on economic circumstances and race.

NOTES

1. Lloyd F. Bitzer, "The Rhetorical Situation," *Philosophy and Rhetoric* 1 (1968): 8.

2. James Andrews, Michael C. Leff, and Robert Terrill, "The Nature of Criticism: An Overview," in *Reading Rhetorical Texts: An Introduction to Criticism* (Boston: Houghton Mifflin, 1998), 6.

3. Robert T. Craig, "Communication," in *Encyclopedia of Rhetoric* (New York: Oxford University Press, 2001), 135.

4. Bitzer, "Rhetorical Situation," 7.

5. See Philip P. Wander, "The Ideological Turn in Modern Criticism," *Central States Speech Journal* 34 (1983): 1–18.

6. Vocabulary.com, s.v. "Ideology," http://www.vocabulary.com/dictionary/ideology. The *Oxford English Dictionary* defines *ideology* as "a systematic scheme of ideas, usually relating to politics, economics, or society and forming the basis of action or policy; a set of beliefs governing conduct."

7. Michael Leff, "Interpretation and the Art of the Rhetorical Critic," *Western Journal of Speech Communication* 44 (1980): 342.

8. Lloyd F. Bitzer, "Rhetoric and Public Knowledge," in *Rhetoric, Philosophy, and Literature: An Exploration*, ed. Don M. Burks (West Lafayette: Purdue University Press, 1978).

9. Bitzer, "The Rhetorical Situation," 6. According to Webster's dictionary online, http://www.merriam-webster.com, *exigence [exigency]* is "that which is required in a particular situation."

Appendix D

"On Objectivity and Politics in Criticism"

Edwin Black

In his invitation to participate in this colloquium, the editor wrote, "These are opinion pieces, so it is your thoughts on these matters our readers will be interested in."

It is my thoughts that readers will be interested in? What a luxury! Does it mean that I don't have to be "objective"? That I can write whatever I please, without restraint, without discipline, without discretion? Well, not quite. I still want to avoid appearing to be an ass. And so, out of concern for my reputation (subjective), I will try to present something that will make sense to an intelligent reader (objective). Which, in turn, suggests that the polarities of subjective and objective are not always antithetical. Sometimes they may be complementary.

I can certainly understand how the issue of objectivity in criticism arises. Scientific inquiries always seek to minimize the influence of the investigator by their methods of research and their requirement of replicability. This quest for objectivity has become, along with other attributes of scientific inquiry, an intellectual standard that some people apply indiscriminately. It's a mistake. Objectivity is not universally desirable.

No one, to my knowledge, has represented criticism as scientific. At most (or least?), it has been characterized as "prescientific"—a condescending representation that assumes, quite gratuitously, that human mental activity is a pyramidal hierarchy with something called "science" hovering halo-like above its apex and a grotesquely conceived "criticism" buried somewhere in its nether region. The conception itself is prescientific in the historic sense in which anything medieval can be called prescientific.

If we want to know about criticism, we look to people who have practiced it, who have engaged its problems and have somehow resolved some of them in tangible acts of criticism. And what accomplished critic has ever claimed that criticism should only be objective? Criticism is not supposed to be always objective. It is, of course, supposed to be always intelligent. More to the point, it is supposed to be always fair. Sometimes fairness requires objectivity, and sometimes it doesn't. Therefore, the relationship between objectivity and criticism is not constant; it is variable.

In my use of the term *criticism*, I cannot extricate it from its origin in the Greek term *krisis*, which translates into "judgment." The critic exercises judgment. In fact, in Greek the term for "judge" and the term for "critic" were the same term. Let's play with that ambiguity a bit.

We do not demand that a judge in a courtroom be uniformly "objective." We demand that the judge be fair. If the judge's being fair requires, at some phase of the judicial process, neutrality or detachment or distance—all qualities associated with objectivity—then those are what we expect. On the other hand, if the judge's being fair requires, at some other phase, empathy or compassion or introspection—all qualities associated with subjectivity—then those are what we expect. What is important is that the judge be whatever is required for being fair. Exactly the same obtains with the critic.

Sometimes, at some stages of the critical process, it is important to be as objective as it is possible to be. There are critical problems that require for their solution a puritanical self-control—a disciplined indifference to one's own proclivities and one's own local conditions. That is especially true of rhetorical criticism, which can be at its most valuable when it focuses on odious rhetors—bigots, demagogues, habitual liars—the understanding of whom may require critics to suspend their repugnance temporarily and, for a period, try to see the world with the cold neutrality of a sociopath. But such acts of objectivity are only intermittent, and never an end in themselves.

Of course, the analogy between the critic and the courtroom judge can be taken only so far. A critic's being fair in criticism is not wholly the same as a judge's being fair in a courtroom. Conventional procedures of law prescribe to a considerable extent the claims and counter-claims to which a judge is obliged to attend in order to be fair. Such a prescriptive order is not available to the critic. The critic's procedures are, when at their best, original; they grow ad hoc from the critic's engagement with the artifact. And because the critic has to generate not only a judgment of the artifact but also the procedure by which the judgment was reached—because, in short, the critic's responsibilities are legislative as well as judicial—the critic may have to be subjective more often than the judge in the court. That is because critics, unlike judges, cannot lay responsibility for their judgments on any code for which the critics themselves are not individually responsible.

The critic's subjectivity is also the consequence of the critic having no powers of enforcement. The critic cannot compel our compliance with the critic's judgment. The critic can only induce us, and therefore it is we, the readers of criticism, who demand the critic's compliance with certain of our expectations. We expect the critic to see things for us that we are unlikely to see for ourselves until the critic has called them to our attention. That means that we expect the critic to tell us things that we do not already know. Because the critic's perceptions are supposed to be valuable and uncommon (otherwise, why would we bother to read about them?), there is much in critical activity that ought to be subjective in the sense of being individual, novel, unconforming, sometimes even shocking.

So, far from encouraging critics to be objective all the time, I hold rather that a critic can be excessively objective. Indeed, excessive objectivity is a failure that occurs with unfortunate frequency in criticism.

Impersonal criticism is, by definition, objective. Objectivity, therefore, is manifested in more than just a passive facticity. Objectivity inheres in the substitution of any a priori method for the critic's own perceptions and judgments. It follows, then, that the application in criticism of a political or ideological program that is not the critic's own invention is an exercise in objectivity. And such exercises frequently display the deformities common to excessive objectivity in criticism, which are predictability and pedantry and wearisome uniformity. That is why excessively objective criticism—criticism that is without personality—is so repressive to write and so deadly to read.

Political judgments are certainly relevant to criticism, and political presuppositions are probably unavoidable in criticism. But politicized criticism—criticism that is in the service of an ideology—is another matter. The problem has been that so much of politicized criticism is heavy-handed and closed to discovery. The impetus of politicized criticism is to exploit its subject for the ratification of itself.

In 1844, Karl Marx said, "The essential sentiment of criticism is indignation; its essential activity is denunciation." Marx's view is reflected in much of the dyspeptic criticism written by his acolytes, even those who are many levels removed from the master: the echoes of echoes of echoes. A critical agenda that confines itself to indignant denunciation seems to me awfully constricted. Criticism has richer possibilities.

Good criticism is always a surprise. It is a surprise in the sense that you can't anticipate what a good critic will have to say about a given artifact.

I don't think that the expression of conventional opinions constitutes interesting criticism. By "conventional opinions" I mean to refer not just to the views of the Rotarian in Peoria; I mean to refer also to the pieties of any coterie whatever. The inventory of opinions that defines a political movement—no matter whether progressive or regressive, rational or psychotic, popular or insular—must become, at least to the adherents of that movement, conventional. It must in order to function as the ideological adhesion for a collective identity. Even anarchists have an orthodoxy.

Although it seems impossible for any of us to live a civic life without subscribing to some body of received doctrine, that doctrine, even if the critic conceives it vividly and believes it ardently, is not the stuff of enlightening criticism. Whatever its merits may be, it is derivative, and it intercedes between the critic and the object of criticism by effecting trite observations and stock responses in the critic.

T. S. Eliot wrote that "the readers of the *Boston Evening Transcript* sway in the wind, like a field of ripe corn." They're not the only ones. We all have episodes of marching in the parade or dancing in the chorus. It is gratifying sometimes to move in synchrony with others. But we just shouldn't try to be professional critics while we're in the ripe corn mode.

It seems to me reasonable to demand of any writer: surprise me. If the writer can't deliver, the writer can be dismissed, no matter whether what is written is critical or political or fictional or anything else. Note that the demand is not "please me"; nor is it "comfort me." It is not a demand for conformity to any sort of bias in the reader. It is simply a demand that a writer have something to say. And repeating the pieties of an ideology is not having something to say. I think it was Truman Capote who once said of a fellow novelist's work, "That isn't writing; that's typing." The same can be said of echoic ideologues.

So that these remarks are at least the semblance of an argument instead of being simple dogma, let me try to be clear about their premise. They are predicated on a proposition having to do with the relationship between criticism and its reader. The proposition is that although criticism is generically epideictic, since it engages in praise and blame, it is not functionally epideictic. That is, I am assuming that you do not read criticism solely in order to have your own opinions confirmed but that you read criticism in order to be brought to see something that you hadn't noticed on your own. If, on the other hand, it is personal confirmation that you want—if you want to be reassured and to have your intellectual passions licensed—you don't then sit down and read criticism. You seek an epideictic occasion—some sort of rally or ceremony where co-believers can celebrate their articles of faith. Really good criticism is too singular to be confirmatory.

We don't want to read criticism that tells us nothing that we didn't already know. We don't want to read criticism that reiterates yet again what we have heard before.

Certainly there is nothing wrong with a critic's having political convictions. It is unavoidable. Only an idiot is without political convictions—in rare cases, maybe a holy idiot, but an idiot all the same. The very term *idiot* is from the Greek word for "nonpolitical person." We don't want to read rhetorical criticism written by an idiot, which really means that we don't want to read rhetorical criticism that has no political dimension to it. It may be possible to write apolitical but still luminous criticism of pure music or of nonrepresentational painting, but it is hard to imagine apolitical rhetorical criticism that isn't desiccated. So, yes, rhetorical criticism is likely to have a political dimension, and it ought to.

The inhibiting complication is that although the critic's political convictions may merit respect, they are not necessarily going to be any more interesting or intelligent or original than the general run of political convictions. Just being a critic doesn't qualify one to have anything to say about politics that has not already been said—and maybe better said—many times. So, I think that unless the critic has something fresh and knowledgeable to say, the critic should just shut up about politics. If the critic does that, then the political convictions of the critic will be presuppositional. That is, the critic will observe, judge, and argue from some political convictions rather than to them. The critic's politics will be implicit rather than explicit. Even so, the contours of the critic's political convictions will be clear enough from the criticism.

In the end, there are no formulas, no prescriptions, for criticism. The methods of rhetorical criticism need to be objective to the extent that, in any given critique, they could be explicated and warranted. But it is important that critical techniques also be subjective to the extent that they are not mechanistic, not autonomous, not disengaged from the critics who use them. The best critics have so thoroughly assimilated their methods that those methods have become their characteristic modes of perception.

The only instrument of good criticism is the critic. It is not any external perspective or procedure or ideology but only the convictions, values, and learning of the critic, only the observational and interpretive powers of the critic. That is why criticism, notwithstanding its obligation to be objective at crucial moments, is yet deeply subjective. The method of rhetorical criticism is the critic.

Index

abortion, 72, 156, 214, 226, 281

act/action, 14, 208, 259, 334, 336: collective action, 167, 329, 335; course of action, 12–13, 15–16; genre, acts in, 56–57, 58–59; government action, 16, 46, 54, 216; in the "Hollaback" movement, 324; moral action, 245–46;, 265 rhetorical action, 23–24, 25, 45, 50; speech acts, 183, 213, 254–55; visual argument in action, 266, 268. *See also* critical act; symbolic action

act-act ratio, 163, 165–66

Acton Institute, 236, 237–38

Adams, Tony, 331

advertising, 129, 167, 173, 211, 218, 282, 339; advertisements as rhetorical symbols, 11; Burke, understanding of, 156–57, 159; Disney #ShareYourEars campaign, 311, 320n91; as the dominant source of individual identity, 210; feminist critique of, 182, 183; *Hunger Games* advertising tie-ins, 289–90; Nike ad campaign, 220, 223, 284; rapid audience response, hoping for, 160; scholarly studies of, 71, 72, 245, 252, 301; stickiness, ads aiming for, 306

advocates, 38, 58, 208, 223, 224; audiences, ability to influence, 209, 215; feminist advocates, 178, 179, 198; power and influence of, 287, 357

Afghanistan, 46–47

African Americans, 55, 105, 222, 280; civil rights for, 199, 261, 262; discrimination against, 180–81, 192; Obama, political candidacy of, 100, 101, 330

agency, 169, 213, 246, 304, 307, 308, 314; agentive citizenship, 159, 330; audience, free agency of, 74; in bureaucratic speeches, 166–67, 170; coercive agency, 212; of ideographs, 214; in pentadic analysis, 173; in public shaming incidents, 309

agency-act ratio, 58, 164–65, 172

agent, 39, 158, 161, 163, 305, 333; active and forceful agents, 9, 171, 172, 334, 335; agent-centered approach, 323, 325; defining, 162, 351; as effect, 327–28; public-relations agents, 72, 76; scene and purpose, at intersection of, 58–59; stressing the agent, 167–68

agent-act ratio, 58, 163, 164, 172

agrarian concerns, 159, 168

Alien film franchise, 150

allegory, 103, 151, 285; defining, 284, 351; in *Animal Farm*, 150; in *Hunger Games*, 287–88, 291

Allen, Mike, 30

Al-Qaeda, 59

#ALSIceBucketChallenge, 311

Althouse, Matthew T., 346

American Anti-Slavery Society, 84

American Dream, 151–52, 168, 210, 254

American exceptionalism, 101, 235, 239–40, 283

analogy, 57, 113, 212, 362

analysis: framing analysis, 346; generic analysis, 54, 64; ideographic analysis, 215–17, 225; judgmental analysis, 235, 245–46; narrative analysis, 140, 141–45, 149–51, 293. *See also* close textual analysis

anaphora, 88, 351

59; propaganda conveyed via, 279; rhetoric, as a form of, 11, 285, 294; televangelism, 245; television audience, 72, 101, 283, 292; television criticism, 235, 238–40
"Telling America's Story" (Lewis), 140, 151
telos (end state), 72, 334, 336, 358
tenor, 112–14, 115, 116, 118, 119, 121, 127, 129, 358
terministic screens, 155, 156, 236–38, 359
terrorism, 134, 165, 209; 9/11 terror attacks, 46, 137, 143, 150; Bush speech against, 59; Iranian-sponsored terrorism, 34, 35
Texas rock houses, 240–42
text. *See* close textual analysis
The Last Supper imagery, 200, 260–66
theme, 147, 150, 233, 295, 342, 356, 359; fantasy-theme analysis, 346; in *Hunger Games,* 287, 288, 290; in narrative analysis, 141, 143, 145–46; narrative theme, 134, 135–36, 140
Therborn, Göran, 326
"third world" countries, 347
Thonssen, Lester, 90
Three Mile Island nuclear disaster, 137
Tiananmen Square massacre, 243, 244
TikTok (social media platform), 302, 304
timing, importance of, 80
To Kill a Mockingbird (Lee), 137
tolerance, 210, 214, 262
Tompkins, Joe, 286, 290
topoi (topics), 77, 253, 254, 359
totalitarianism, 82
"tough love" narrative, 140
traditional criticism, 71–82, 89, 90–91, 323, 359
Traister, Rebecca, 201
transgender identity, 180, 183, 294
treason, 215, 223
Treichler, Paula, 177
tropes, 104, 112, 116, 185, 196, 245, 359; in close textual analysis, 96; as digital rhetoric, 302; "Karen" trope, 201; odor, use as a trope, 121, 126; in restaurant reviews, 120; of "upper" and "lower," 122; virality and, 306–7. *See also* hashtag activism; memes
Trudeau, Justin, 259
Trump, Donald, 40, 90, 101, 194, 259, 277, 322; Baghdad drone attack speech, 34–35; COVID-19 pandemic, responses to, 73–74, 117; rhetoric of, 7, 151–52, 167–68; Twitter use, 117, 301, 303, 314, 331
Trump, Ivanka, 270; CEO Summit of the Americas speech, 340, 344n1; at

Osaka G20 Summit, 259–60, 262, 266; #unwantedivanka and the Last Supper, 263–66; #unwantedivanka and the March on Washington, 259–63
truth, 7, 9, 15, 36, 88, 171, 208; community truths, validating, 46; credibility as backing truth, 137, 142; in the dramatist pentad, 160; ideological truths, 38, 209, 213, 279, 351; political handling of, 47, 78–79; political truths, 167; power and promulgation of truth, 213; provisional truth, 170; reality, corresponding with, 161; standpoint, truth as a product of, 210–11, 224; whole truth, not revealing, 75
Tuck, Eve, 128
Tumblr (social media platform), 18, 289
Turnbull, Nick, 50
twentieth century, 155, 178, 212, 262, 334; discursive fragmentation in, 307; influential speeches of, 47–48; language and rhetoric studies in, 10, 16, 96, 99, 138
Twitch (social media platform), 304
Twitter, 18, 45, 47, 277, 300; trolling as part of, 282, 308–9; Trump, use of, 117, 301, 303, 314, 331; tweets, 63, 65, 281, 300, 304, 313, 332. *See also* hashtag activism
Tyma, Adam, 331
tyranny: *Hunger Games* as portraying, 287, 288; of Mickee Faust character, 189, 191, 194, 196; political and governmental tyranny, 84, 85, 87, 88, 146, 167; <tyranny> ideograph, 214
Tyson, Neil deGrasse, 281

Uncle Tom's Cabin (Stowe), 136
University of Texas, 190, 314
University of Wisconsin, 105, 106
upward-mobility, 9, 126
utilitarian conception of rhetoric, 15, 71, 220

Valenzano, Joseph M., III, 60, 235, 238–40
values, 13, 138, 161, 164, 208, 239, 262; American values, 146, 148, 210, 268, 279, 283; architecture as revealing, 242; basic values, tapping into, 137, 142, 143, 149; comedic discourse, critique of values in, 330; common values in ceremonial addresses, 74; counterculture values, 280; of the critic, 29, 364; of feminism, 325; ideograph analysis of, 214, 217, 225, 226; justifying of values and beliefs, 348; male identification, cultural

About the Contributors

William Benoit is professor of communication studies at the University of Alabama, Birmingham. He has published over 300 journal articles and book chapters and is the author or editor of twenty books. The American Communication Association has presented him with both the Outstanding Teacher at a Doctoral Institution Award and the Gerald M. Phillips Mentoring Award. He has served as the editor for the *Journal of Communication* and *Communication Studies*. His primary interests are rhetorical theory and criticism and political communication.

Edwin Black (d. 2007) was professor of communication arts at the University of Wisconsin–Madison. He was the author of the seminal book *Rhetorical Criticism: A Study in Method* and a host of landmark essays of criticism. He twice received the Speech Communication Association Golden Anniversary Award.

Emma Frances Bloomfield is assistant professor of communication studies at the University of Nevada, Las Vegas. Her research explores environmental communication and scientific controversies, particularly around issues of climate change, human origins, and the body. Her book, *Communication Strategies for Engaging Climate Skeptics*, was published in Routledge's Advances in Climate Change Research series in the summer of 2019. She has published in a variety of journals including *Rhetoric Society Quarterly*, *Environmental Communication*, *Communication Studies*, and *Argumentation and Advocacy*.

Adam Blood is instructor and director of speech and debate at the University of West Florida. His research specializes in loyalty discourse, demagoguery, and the rhetoric of the sacred. He received his doctorate in communication with an emphasis on rhetoric and public culture from the University of Nebraska at Lincoln and his master's and bachelor's degrees from the University of Central Missouri. He teaches courses on public speaking, rhetorical criticism, propaganda and persuasion, and communication and Christianity.

Stephen Howard Browne is professor of rhetorical studies at The Pennsylvania State University. He teaches courses in rhetorical theory, rhetorical criticism, and social protest rhetoric. He is the author of *Jefferson's Call for Nationhood, Angelina Grimke: Rhetoric, Identity, and the Radi-*

cal Imagination, and *Edmund Burke and the Discourse of Virtue*. His book on Angelina Grimke received the National Communication Association's Diamond Anniversary Book Award, and he has received the Karl R. Wallace Award from the Speech Communication Association.

Michael Lane Bruner is professor of rhetoric at the University of Nevada, Las Vegas. He is the author of many scholarly and creative books, the most recent of which include *Rhetorical Unconsciousness and Political Psychoanalysis* and *Why Must You Say These Things Out Loud?* as well as dozens of scholarly essays and book chapters on language, power, and subjectivity. His creative writing has appeared in such venues as *Evergreen Review* and *The Outlaw Bible of American Poetry*, and he currently teaches argumentation and advocacy to doctoral students in public policy in the Greenspun College of Urban Affairs.

Mary Evelyn Collins is retired professor of speech communication at Lamar University. Her research interests include folk speech and cowboy humor, child and family advocacy, rhetorical depiction and culture type as a critical tool in rhetorical analysis, and the intersection of cultural tradition and popular culture forms. She is a past president of the Southern States Communication Association. In retirement she is turning her hand to writing short works of fiction and doing charity work.

Zoe C. Farquhar is a PhD student in rhetoric and public culture and a graduate teaching assistant at the University of Nebraska–Lincoln. She teaches courses in communication theory and professional communication, and has published in *Communication Teacher*. Her research explores mediated representations of whiteness and white privilege in popular culture. She earned her master's degree from West Chester University of Pennsylvania.

Kathleen Farrell is retired professor in the Department of Communication, St. Louis University. She taught and researched instances of contemporary and historical public argument, argument theory, and argument pedagogy. She has published in numerous scholarly journals, edited volumes, and proceedings. She is the author of *Literary Integrity and Political Action*.

Michelle G. Gibbons is assistant professor of communication at the University of New Hampshire, where she regularly teaches courses in rhetorical theory and criticism and digital rhetoric. Her research includes studies of digital phenomena, such as search engine optimization, and medical technologies, including fMRI and X-rays. She also investigates the rhetorical deployment of commonsense psychological precepts in public culture. Her work has been published in *Rhetoric Society Quarterly*, *Quarterly Journal of Speech*, *Technical Communication Quarterly*, *Philosophy of Science*, *Journalism History*, and *Argumentation and Advocacy*, among other places.

Mark Glantz is associate professor of communication and media studies at St. Norbert College. He teaches courses in political communication, communication technology and social change, television criticism, and crisis communication. He is coauthor of *Presidential Campaigns in the Age of Social Media: Clinton and Trump* and he has published in journals such as *Journal of Radio and Audio Media*, *Journal of Communication Inquiry*, and *Environmental Communication*.

Forbes I. Hill (d. 2008) was emeritus professor, Queens College of the City University of New York. He published in the field of history of rhetoric and public address. Among others, he is the author of "Aristotle's Rhetorical Theory" in James J. Murphy and Richard Katula's volume, *A Synoptic History of Classical Rhetoric*.

Kristen Hoerl is associate professor of communication studies at the University of Nebraska–Lincoln. Her teaching and research explores the role of popular culture in the process of social change. Her book, *The Bad Sixties: Hollywood Memories of the Counterculture, Antiwar and Black Power Movements*, won the 2018 Best Book Award from the American Studies Division of the National Communication Association. Her articles appear in a variety of journals including the *Quarterly Journal of Speech*; *Critical Studies in Media Communication*; *Communication and Critical/Cultural Studies*; *Communication, Culture, and Critique*; the *Western Journal of Communication*; and *Argumentation and Advocacy*. She also edited *Women's Studies in Communication* from 2017–2019.

John W. Jordan is associate professor of communication at the University of Wisconsin–Milwaukee. His research and teaching focus on rhetorical theory and criticism, mass media representations, intersections between technology and public rhetoric, and medical decision making regarding body alterations. He has published numerous pieces in *Quarterly Journal of Speech*, *Critical Studies in Media Communication*, *Rhetoric and Public Affairs*, *Southern Communication Journal*, *Journal of Popular Film and Television*, *Women's Studies in Communication*, *Argumentation and Advocacy*, and others. Several of his essays have been republished in edited volumes and handbooks, and he is a frequent guest/commentator in various media.

Andrew King is professor emeritus at Louisiana State University. He divides his time between Baton Rouge and the Catskills, where he is engaged in launching The Renaissance Farm, a modern Chautauqua for artists and writers. He is the author of *Postmodern Political Communication* and *Power and Communication* and coeditor of *Twentieth-Century Roots of Rhetorical Studies*. He is a former editor of the *Quarterly Journal of Speech and the Southern Communication Journal*, and is a recipient of the American Communication Association's Outstanding Teacher at a Doctoral Institution Award. His academic interests lie in the areas of communication and power, and medieval and Renaissance rhetorical theory. He is a past president of the Kenneth Burke Society.

Jim A. Kuypers is professor of communication at Virginia Tech. He is the author or editor of fourteen books, including *Purpose, Practice, and Pedagogy in Rhetorical Criticism* (winner of the Everett Lee Hunt Award for Outstanding Scholarship) and *Partisan Journalism: A History of Media Bias in the United States* (a 2014 *Choice* Outstanding Academic Title), and numerous journal articles. He is the recipient of the American Communication Association's Outstanding Contribution to Communication Scholarship Award, the Southern States Communication Association's Early Career Research Award, and Dartmouth College's Distinguished Lecturer Award. His research interests include political communication, metacriticism, and the moral-poetic use of language.

Ronald Lee is professor emeritus of communication studies at the University of Nebraska–Lincoln. He teaches and writes about contemporary rhetoric and political culture. His work has appeared in the *Quarterly Journal of Speech*, *Political Communication*, the *Western Journal of Communication*, *Communication Studies*, the *Southern Communication Journal*, *Argumentation and Advocacy*, and *Technical Communication Quarterly*. He is the coauthor (with Rachel

Friedman) of the recently published book *The Style and Rhetoric of Elizabeth Dole: Public Persona and Political Discourse.*

Ryan Erik McGeough is associate professor of communication at the University of Northern Iowa. He has published in the areas of pedagogy, visual argument, new media technology, and public deliberation.

Raymie E. McKerrow is emeritus professor in the School of Communication Studies at Ohio University. He has published in the areas of modern rhetoric, argumentation theory, and critical/cultural approaches to contemporary rhetoric. He is past president of the Eastern Communication Association and the National Communication Association, and he received the Douglas W. Ehninger Distinguished Rhetorical Scholar Award and the Charles H. Woolbert Research Award from the National Communication Association.

Natalia Mielczarek is assistant professor in the School of Communication at Virginia Tech. Her research interests include visual rhetoric, iconicity of news images, internet memes, and transfigurations of images in remix culture. Her work has been published in journals such as *Visual Communication*, *Visual Communication Quarterly*, *First Monday*, and *Journalism and Mass Communication Quarterly*. She has also contributed chapters to edited collections on news coverage of the 2016 US presidential elections, journalism, sport and religion, and visual propaganda. She is a former newspaper journalist.

Donna Marie Nudd is professor of communication in the School of Communication at Florida State University and executive director of the Mickee Faust Academy for the *Really* Dramatic Arts. Her major areas of interest include andragogy, queer studies, gender studies, performance studies, and disability studies. Her essays have appeared in *Text and Performance Quarterly*, *Bronte Society Transactions*, *Communication Education*, and *Liminalities*. Nudd and her lifelong collaborator, Terry Galloway, are corecipients of the National Communication Association's Irene Coger Award for Lifetime Achievement in Performance.

Robert C. Rowland is professor of communication at the University of Kansas. His many publications include *Shared Land/Conflicting Identity: Trajectories of Israeli and Palestinian Symbol Use* (with David Frank), which won the inaugural Kohrs-Campbell Book Award; *The Rhetoric of Donald Trump: Nationalist Populism and American Democracy*; and more than eighty essays on rhetorical criticism, argumentation, and narrative. He received the Douglas W. Ehninger Distinguished Rhetorical Scholar Award from the National Communication Association in 2011. Rowland's research interests include critical methodologies, public argument, argumentation theory, and political communication.

Joseph M. Valenzano III is professor of communication and department chair at the University of Dayton. He teaches courses in rhetorical theory and criticism, religious communication, persuasion, and instructional communication. His scholarship focuses on the intersection of religion, politics, and the mass media in American culture. He is coauthor of *Television, Religion, and Supernatural* and has also published articles in *Communication Monographs*, *Communication Education*, the *Journal of Media and Religion*, and the *Southern Communication Journal*. Valenzano is the editor of the *Basic Communication Course Annual*.

Kristina Schriver Whalen is dean for the School of Fine, Applied, and Communication Arts at City College of San Francisco. Her work has been published in *Text and Performance Quarterly* and *Women's Studies and Communication*, among others. Her research explores the intersection of feminist argument and performative protest and equity issues in higher education.

Marilyn J. Young is the Wayne C. Minnick Professor of Communication, *Emerita*, at Florida State University. She has published numerous articles and book chapters and authored two books, *Flights of Fancy, Flight of Doom: KAL 007 and Soviet-American Rhetoric* and *Coaching Debate*. With David Marples, she edited *Nuclear Energy and Security in the Former Soviet Union*. Her research interests are in argumentation, rhetorical theory and criticism, and political (particularly international) rhetoric, especially the development of political language and argument in newly emerging democracies. Along with coauthors Michael K. Leuner and David Cratis Williams, she is currently working on a two-volume series examining the development of democratic rhetoric in Russia.